Critique of Dialectical Reason

VOLUME II

Critique of Dialectical Reason

VOLUME II *(Unfinished)*

The Intelligibility of History

◆

JEAN-PAUL SARTRE

Edited by
Arlette Elkaïm-Sartre

Translated by
Quintin Hoare

VERSO
London · New York

First published as *Critique de la raison dialectique*, tome II,
by Editions Gallimard
This edition published by Verso 1991
© Gallimard 1985
Translation © Verso 1991
All rights reserved

Verso
UK: 6 Meard Street, London W1V 3HR
USA: 29 West 35th Street, New York, NY 10001-2291

Verso is the imprint of New Left Books

British Library Cataloguing in Publication Data

Sartre, Jean-Paul *1905–1980*
Critique of dialectical reason.
Vol. 2 (unfinished) The intelligibility of history
1. Marxism. Dialectical materialism, history
I. Title   II. Elkaim-Sartre, Arlette   III. Hoare, Quintin
IV. Critique de la raison dialectique. *English*
335.4112
ISBN 0–86091–311–2

US Library of Congress Cataloging-in-Publication Data

Sartre, Jean Paul, 1905–
[Critique de la raison dialectique, English]
Critique of dialectical reason / Jean-Paul Sartre.
p.   cm.
Translation of: Critique de la raison dialectique.
Contents: – v. 2. The intelligibility of history (unfinished)
/ edited by Arlette Elkaïm-Sartre : translated by Quintin Hoare.
Includes bibliographical references and index.
ISBN 0–86091–311–2 (v. 2)
1. History–Philosophy.   2. Existentialism.   3. Dialectical
materialism.   I. Elkaïm-Sartre, Arlette.   II. Title.
B2430.S33C713   1990
142'.78–dc20

Typeset in Times by Ponting–Green Publishing Services, London
Printed in Great Britain by Biddles Ltd

Contents

Editor's Preface

DOES HISTORY HAVE A MEANING? That was the question to which Sartre intended to find an answer by the end of this second volume of his *Critique*, drafted in 1958 but never finished. The plan he had in mind at the outset can be reconstructed, thanks to clues present in the existing text. It comprised at least two major sections, one dealing with synchronic totalization, the other with diachronic totalization. The former was to be developed through two main examples, moving from the more integrated to the less integrated ensemble: (1) Russian society after the Revolution (directorial society); (2) the bourgeois democracies (non-directorial societies, which he also calls 'disunited'). But only the first of these examples is fully covered in the body of the text. As for the contents of the projected second section, it is hard to work out what they would have been. As with the example of bourgeois societies, all we have is an outline in later notebooks (1961–2), the substance of which is included here in the Appendix. However, a number of comments anticipating its thrust – taken together with these notebooks – suggest that he meant to interrogate History in a still broader fashion: on p.77, for example, he speaks of studying wars between nations, on p.118 of world history, and on p.300 of comparative history. This would no doubt have obliged him to restructure his work, as we can verify by reading (in the Appendix) his drafts for a reordering of this kind. I have endeavoured to indicate this in a number of editorial notes. However, since the present edition is not a critical one I have refrained from pronouncing on any theoretical problems possibly connected with the author's hesitations on this point.

Such as it is, the text represents the direct continuation of the first volume announced on the latter's last pages and in the Introduction serving both volumes: namely, the progressive movement of critical investigation. It takes the form of a final draft – one last reading might simply have removed a few stylistic flaws. In fact a rereading did take place, probably in 1962, when the author began taking notes again with a view to continuing his work. But his aim then was to refresh his memory of the whole and refine certain ideas, rather than to achieve a final form: he added a dozen or so notes, but made few corrections.

The mass of historical, sociological and scientific works the author would have been obliged to read (and perhaps of specific studies he would have been induced to write) in order to complete his undertaking – see, for example, his notes on the history of Venice; he was also reflecting upon Chinese history, feudal France, the history of colonialism, and societies 'without history' – was too immense for a single individual. This is what he often said to explain his abandonment of the work. It must also be recalled that *The Family Idiot*, the third volume of which appeared only in 1972, had been held up until the completion of *Words* in 1963 and required further research.

The point of departure for this second volume is the following. Since *History is born and develops in the permanent framework of a field of tension engendered by scarcity*, reflecting upon its intelligibility involves first answering the preliminary question: are struggles intelligible? Here again, the procedure moves from the simple to the complex: individual combat, struggle of sub-groups within an organized group, struggles in whole societies. The initial plan underlying the work enables us to identify certain major divisions and their subordinate parts. I have attempted to translate these into titles and sub-titles, in the hope that this will make the book more manageable and perhaps easier to read. Since none of these can be attributed to the author, no purpose would be served by placing them in brackets: indicating the fact here should be sufficient. At the end of the volume, the reader will find a glossary of the main notions/tools used in the work as a whole. Asterisked footnotes to the text are the author's own, while my editorial notes are numbered.

Arlette Elkaïm-Sartre

BOOK III
THE INTELLIGIBILITY
OF HISTORY

I

IS STRUGGLE
INTELLIGIBLE?

1

Conflict, Moment of a Totalization or Irreducible Rift?

The Three Factors of Dialectical Intelligibility

DIALECTICAL intelligibility – whether we are dealing with constituent Reason or constituted Reason – is defined through totalization. This is simply praxis achieving unity on the basis of specific circumstances, and in relation to a goal to be attained. Contradictions, via the praxis of the practical organism, are defined as moments of this praxis. They spring from the fact that the labour brought to bear upon the practical field is an irreversible temporalization. Thus any transformation accomplished in the field by action, or in action through synthetic unification of the field, must appear as a partial development of that totalization in progress we might term the practical interaction between the subject and the field in view of a future objective to be attained, a future product to be realized. And the intelligibility of this partial development lies in its very contradiction: as a local determination of the field, for example, it is endowed with limits and its negative particularity; as a moment of action, it is the action in its entirety at this moment of its temporalization. In fact, its synchronic particularity refers back (with or without a gap, this will have to be seen) to a diachronic particularization of praxis: this is a totalized totalization only at the ambiguous instant when it is suppressed by being resumed in its total product. But at present (this functional present is defined not as an instant, but as a partial operation: hence, as a temporalization in progress) praxis is contained in its entirety, with its past and its future objective, in the preparatory task that it is accomplishing: in other words, in the totalization of the field and the 'promotion' of a sector or zone of that totalized unity. To that extent, therefore, the 'privileged' sector – i.e. that which is worked, highlighted as a means to be constructed and as a form against a synthetic background – is the field as a *whole*, viewed as the very meaning of its practical unification of the

3

moment, while at the same time it discards into the indistinctness of a background all that is not presently emphasized by work.

But this discarded ensemble is *also* the field. Thus the emphasized sector, in its manner of being the totalization of the field, is negated by the less distinct or previously worked zones: its mere highlighting constitutes them dialectically as the totality of the field that encircles it and from which it is differentiated by a kind of retraction that isolates it. In fact, temporally, the ensemble already worked or not yet worked represents against it the diachronic totalization of praxis, in so far as it already has a future and a past. This ensemble tends to negate the singularized form and reabsorb it into itself, just as this will anyway be retotalized with everything once the object is entirely manufactured. And when I say that it *tends* to negate it, I am referring not to some kind of Gestaltist magic, but on the contrary to the simple effective force of praxis as such. It is the living totalization which engenders and sustains tensions in the field it organizes. And it is through action itself that sector A, for example, stands opposed: (1) to other specified sectors (B, C, D, etc.), via the mediation of the totalized field; (2) to the totality in fusion of sectors BCD, as a background seeking to reabsorb the form it sustains; (3) to the synthesis of praxis and the field, in so far as it also appears as a particularized reality and one that is posited for itself as such; (4) to itself (since it is posited at once as the present meaning of the totalization and as a particular, limited being: in other words, a singular totality); (5) to the actual development of praxis, which must negate it and break its limits in order to transcend it. But contradictions are at the same time relations to the totalizing movement, and ultimately express only the *intelligible* relations of the part to the whole and between the parts themselves, in so far as they are *realized* in a singular temporalization. This general intelligibility is in fact concretized, in our example, as *comprehensibility*. This means that the ensemble of these shifting oppositions can be decoded in the light of the projected aim and the transcended circumstances. In short, there is contradiction at each moment of action, since the latter requires at once totalization and particularization (of a sector, a state, a detail, etc.); and it is as the original structure of praxis that the contradiction is intelligible and establishes the latter's intelligibility.

Unity of Struggle as an Event

But if it is true that totalization, particularization and contradiction are the three factors of dialectical intelligibility, how could we conceive of a struggle between individuals or between groups being dialectically intelligible? Of course, neither Hegelian idealism nor 'external' dia-lectical dogmatism bothers about the problem. For both of these, persons and collectivities oppose one another as the partial moments of a total-ization that produces and transcends them. But since we have renounced any a priori to situate us in History, nothing can exempt us from critical investigation: how could we assert, prior to any examination, that struggle, as a binary praxis of antagonistic reciprocity, is assimilable to a particular kind of contradiction – in other words, that it is a specific moment of a totalization? For the difficulties which arise, as soon as any attempt is made to effect this assimilation without critical precautions, are evident. If contradiction is action itself as a progression through splits and as a negation of these splits in the unity of their transcendence, how can we speak of contradiction when we are confronted by *two* actions: in other words, by two autonomous and contradictory totalizations? To be sure, we have noted that antagonistic reciprocity is a bond of immanence between epicentres, since each adversary totalizes and transcends the totalizing action of the other.[1] This indissolubility has sometimes been taken for a unity: thus two wrestlers rolling on the floor of the ring sometimes appear, from a distance, like a single animal with eight limbs, grappling with some unknown danger. But this is because weariness or distance causes us to lose sight of reality: actually there is, if you like, a single movement of those two bodies – but this movement is the result of *two* conflicting enterprises. It belongs to two practical systems at the same time, but for this very reason in its concrete reality it escapes each of them (at least in part). If the plurality of epicentres is a real condition of *two* opposed intelligibilities (inasmuch as there is a comprehensive intelligibility in each system and based on each praxis), how could there be *one* dialectical intelligibility of the ongoing process?

There are, in fact, two ways of watching a boxing match, and two alone. The inexpert spectator will choose a favourite and adopt *his point of view*; in other words, he will consider him as the *subject* of the fight, the other being merely a dangerous object. This is tantamount to making the duel into a hazardous but solitary activity and to totalizing the struggle *with* just one of the contestants. Enthusiasts or experts, for their part, are capable of passing successively and very rapidly from one system to the other. They appreciate the blows and parries, but – even should they succeed in changing system instantaneously – do not totalize the two opposed totalizations. To be sure, they do give *to* the fight a real unity: as they leave they say 'It was a good fight ... etc.'. But this unity is imposed *from outside* upon an *event*. In fact, in so far as boxing is a

---

1. *Critique of Dialectical Reason*, vol.1, London 1976, pp.735 ff.

sport, a job (related to other jobs – manager, trainers, seconds, referees, etc.) and a spectacle which corresponds to certain requirements of a certain society – in so far as, within the framework of a certain economy, you can organize a bout and reckon on it drawing numerous spectators – this bout itself, as an objective to be attained (with all the operations you may imagine, from the signature of the contract to the renting of the hall and the publicity), becomes *an object*. And it is likewise as a particular object – as an event that interests or thrills and will actually take place in a real and limited time; as a certain opportunity to see this or that boxer in action, etc. – that the spectators will go to see the fight. In particular, they will make it *the aim* of sometimes difficult undertakings (booking seats for a championship bout, etc.), and in some cases *the means* to bring off other undertakings (betting on one of the contestants, earning money by managing a team of boxers, etc.). An object for individuals, groups and collectives – defined as a totality by language, the press and the organs of information; then later designated (in the past) as a unity in its past-being by memory ('It was the day of *the* Carpentier–Dempsey *fight*) – the bout, in itself, appears as one of those mathematical symbols which designate an ensemble of operations to be carried out, and figure as such in the series of algebraic equivalences without the mathematician's ever actually troubling to carry out the indicated operations. It is an object to be constituted, utilized, contemplated, designated. In other words, it figures as such in the activities of others. But no one is concerned to know whether this reality – the noetic and unified correspondent of individual and collective praxis – is *in itself*, as an internal operation to be carried out by two individuals in a state of antagonistic reciprocity, a real unity or an irreducible duality. *For me*, their bout is the spectacle that will fill my evening and necessarily have an outcome. For each of them, it is *his* bout, his – perhaps sole – chance to win a title, his attempt to defeat the other and his personal risk of being beaten. From a certain point of view, it can be maintained that there is not really any problem. Nothing, in fact, prevents a practical ensemble – depending on the angle of vision and the activities to which it is related – from presenting itself as a more or less determined unity, duality or multiplicity. It is the present action which decides whether the objective determination of my practical field is the valley, the meadow or the blade of grass. Only we shall not consider the problem in this relatively simple light. We shall concern ourselves – albeit, of course, admitting that *the* fight may exist differently for the backers or for the boxers – with knowing whether *as a struggle*, as an objective act of reciprocal and negative totalization, it possesses the conditions for dialectical intelligibility.

Inadequacy of Analytical Study

That it is *rational* is clear. To take an example of the same kind but one which involves opposed armed groups, the officer studying the art of war can reconstruct all the operations of the battles of Leipzig or Waterloo, or better still of the French Campaign. What does he do? He reconstitutes the material ensemble (situation of the armies, from their relation to their bases to the morale of their soldiers; geographical configuration of the battlefield; totalized ensemble of circumstances). This means that he totalizes successively the practical field of two contrasting viewpoints. On the basis of this, he considers each manoeuvre as a concerted effort to achieve full use of the given circumstances and means in order to obtain the destruction of the adversary. He thus grasps each one through *comprehension*. But on the basis of this historical hypothesis (in the absence of any evidence to the contrary, we consider that the general staffs are made up not of traitors or cowards or incompetents, but of officers investing all their professional consciousness and all their patriotism in the present undertaking), he reviews all *possible* manoeuvres in the situation under consideration, in order to determine whether the one carried out in reality was indeed *the best possible one*, as it should (and claims to) be. These *possibles* have never had any real existence, but they have been highlighted in most cases by a hundred years of discussion in military academies. Each of them is the source of another battle, with perhaps another outcome. And each of them must be studied at once from the viewpoint of the modification it entailed in the group under consideration and from the viewpoint of the adversary's possible responses. Among the latter, a distinction will be made, moreover, between more and less likely reactions. It is then necessary to move back to the *other* epicentre's point of view and to envisage its possibles *comprehensively*. On this basis, we may note that the real battle becomes a particular case of a complex ensemble of n^x possibilities strictly linked to one another. For the officer, in fact, the problem is not historical but *practical*: he thus envisages for a given situation the ensemble of possible manoeuvres (among which the real manoeuvre figures), and for each of these manoeuvres the possible ensemble of ripostes with all the consequences which the latter and the former entail for each of the armies. His advantage over the combatants derives from the fact that he knows the outcome of at least one real ensemble of possibles, and from the fact that the documents available to historians give him a far more precise and accurate knowledge of each army than that which the enemy general staff possessed. The lack of information, the material difficulties, the specific interests and the interplay of passions which actually confronted the armies in their historical singularity are factors that he envisages abstractly, but that remain extraneous to him. The temporal necessity of moving immediately to parry the attempt by one of the enemies to turn the left flank of the other no longer exists for him, nor that of finding the parry in the midst of ignorance and error (in other words, on the basis of uncertainty, partially mistaken assessments, etc.). A certain schematization – inevitable and, what is more, desirable at a certain juncture in the practical training, on condition that a return is made subsequently to the true contingencies and ambiguities of the concrete – is enough to transform the comprehensive study of the battle into a formal theory, into a quasi-mathematical calculus of possibles. The reality of the conflict fades – ultimately we find a calculus of probabilities. We know, moreover, how fighter planes have machine-guns designed to fire in the direction of an enemy plane's probable position at a given instant and to correct their aim automatically if it is mistaken. We are back at the example of the chess game.[2] We should not, however, imagine that we have remained within dialectical rationality. In the first place, it is not unity which has replaced the duality of the real combat: it is a multiplicity of relations among possibles. It is enough to introduce a few definitions, then it will be possible to put the ensemble of these relations into a mathematical form. There is no longer either attack or riposte, but linking of a variable to a function, or a function to a variable, or of several functions among themselves. We have avoided the scandal of irreducible antagonism, only to lapse into conditionings in exteriority. In other words, we are confronted once more by analytic Reason.

But in addition, even in this positivist treatment of the question (anyway indispensable from the *practical* point of view), the dyad remains in an abstract form. In the natural sciences, it is at least theoretically possible to choose the independent variable. But in the analytical study of an antagonistic reciprocity, the reconstitution of the ensemble of *possible* reciprocal determinations requires one to transport oneself at each instant from one group of variables to the other. If the ensemble x, y, z – Army No. 1 – is envisaged as a group of independent variables at instant t, and if the variations studied entail the consequences α, β, γ in Army No. 2, we can evaluate the backlash only by considering the group x^1, y^1, z^1 at instant t^1 – in other words, Army No. 2 as affected by the other army's action – as the ensemble of independent variables whose variations will entail specific consequences in Army No. 1. Of course, the new values of these variables, and perhaps their relationship

---

2. *Critique*, vol.1, pp.812 ff.

to the different functions, *already* include the modifications α, β, γ which have been the decisive factors in these internal changes. It remains true, however, that the results obtained will be falsified if any attempt is made to reduce this twofold system of relations to a single one. We are certainly a long way from what might be called the irreducible singularity of epicentres. In simple terms, the object studied – albeit a pure multiplicity of exteriority – is such that the backlash effects of the variations upon the variables must be envisaged *on the basis of* the variables which these variations have first modified, and taking these modified variables as independent variables.

Above all, this positivist schema is an instrument of practice. It is orientated towards future struggles which will be more complex since they will comprise within themselves, in the guise of automatic solutions, the questions raised in past struggles. But it has definitively abandoned all the characteristics which make up the historical reality and temporal individuality of a particular conflict. This reality and this individuality, in the guise of negative determinations, come to the combatants from a triple *scarcity*: scarcity of time, scarcity of means, scarcity of knowledge. They are *grounded* upon a more *fundamental* scarcity, which conditions and *grounds* the conflict – right back to its deepest source – in the opposing interests, in the violence which brings the combatants into confrontation (this scarcity, variable in nature, concerns the material conditions of their existence). A real combatant is a violent, passionate man, sometimes desperate, sometimes ready to meet death, who risks all to destroy his adversary but manoeuvres in a time measured out to him by the rhythm of the other's attacks (and by a hundred other factors of every kind); who has at his disposal, for example, men and arms in limited numbers (which rules out certain operations for him); and who struggles in a variable but always profound ignorance (ignorance of the enemy's real intentions, the real relation of forces, the real position of the adversary's and his own reinforcements, etc.) which obliges him to take risks, to decide what is most likely without having the necessary elements for calculating this, and to invent manoeuvres which take several eventualities into account (if the enemy is disposed in a certain manner, the operation will take place in such and such a way; if it is discovered in the course of action that he is disposed otherwise, the operation is designed to be capable of instantaneous modification, etc.). It is this blind and passionate inventor – who gambles in uncertainty while attempting to limit the risks, and all of whose actions are conditioned by external and interiorized scarcity – it is this man whom we call a fighter. Positively, his reality as agent derives from the synthetic transcendence of these negative determinations. One *decides* because one is ignorant; were one to know, the *act of will* would be redundant: the thing would be done automatically. From this point of view, it must be added that his fighting activity – as an effort to transcend ignorance – is itself defined by the antagonistic separation of the two adversaries: in so far as the *other*, being (more or less) ignorant of my action, provokes my ignorance of his own, I make myself into praxis thanks to him through the transcendence of *this* induced and interiorized ignorance. And each of our antagonistic acts, if it is to be dialectically comprehensible, must be able to be understood *in its inadequacy, in its imperfection and in its mistakes*, on the basis of the negative determinations which it preserves as it transcends them.

The historical problem is not just to know if operation x was the best possible in the given historical circumstances, but also to know why it did not correspond – and could not correspond – to the practical and totalizing schema which summarizes it in the lessons at the War Academy. In fact, the historicity of an action consists in the fact that it is *never* assimilable without further ado to the best possible solution, since the best possible solution can be found only if you possess all the elements of the solution, all the time required to assemble them into a synthesis which transcends them, and all the calm and objectivity necessary for self-criticism. Science is a necessary moment of action, but action is necessarily transcended ignorance since it determines itself as the far side of knowledge. Or, if you prefer, knowing is a practical illumination of knowledge by the ignorance that envelops it, in the movement which transcends both of them towards a future goal.

If, then, the dialectical intelligibility of the struggle must be able to exist, it is at the actual level of the concrete, when the adversaries, dominated by their twofold reciprocal action, know and do not know what they are doing. *From the standpoint* of each combatant, the difference between knowledge and ignorance, between their being-a-subject and their being-an-object, between the project and the execution, etc., is much less noticeable: the action carries everything along, rationalizes everything. Most of the time a boxer knows what he is doing (in so far as what he does is the ongoing realization of his project, and not in so far as his act is an event which develops also in the autonomy of the objective milieu); but he has trouble totalizing what his adversary is doing, he is too busy thwarting the latter's tactics to be able to reconstitute his strategy (it is his manager and seconds who carry out this totalization on his behalf and communicate it to him between rounds). If he is not too clearly dominated, he often even believes himself the subject of the fight and scarcely feels the blows: he is amazed to learn that he has been defeated on points. This attitude is limited, but contains its own intelligibility: it is the objective and comprehensible development of *one* action, on the basis of *one* epicentre, in so far as the agent is really the *subject* of the fight (since – even dominated – he adapts to the other's tactics and in this way always foils the latter's attempts, limits his own losses, avoids the worst, etc.). But if *the* bout must be dialectically intelligible – in other words, if it must reveal itself as a *unity* – its intelligibility must be that of a very particular praxis-process, since the process is defined here as the deterioration of one praxis by the other.

The Labour–Conflict Relation, Constitutive of Human History

These comments allow us to formulate the two essential problems.

The first is this: as common individuals, individuals or sub-groups – if common praxis accentuates their role – can be the real actualizations within a group of a developing contradiction. We have already shown this,[3] and shall soon have occasion to stress it further. But, in order to be able to assimilate a fight to a contradiction and its protagonists to the terms of the developing contradiction, it would have to be possible to view them as the transitory determinations of a larger and deeper group, one of whose current contradictions was actualized by their conflict. Conversely, the group would have to retotalize and transcend their pitiless struggle in the direction of a new synthetic reunification of its practical field and an internal reorganization of its structures. We shall have to determine whether this condition can be fulfilled, whether it is fulfilled sometimes or always, and – in the event of its being fulfilled – what relation it implies between the antagonistic couple and the society which maintains and surrounds the latter. It will also be necessary to rediscover in the singularity of each struggle, on the basis of the group in which it is engendered, the three features of dialectical intelligibility: totalization, particularization and contradiction.

The other problem is that of the objective process. The struggle determines events, creates objects, and these are its products. Furthermore, in so far as it is itself an event, it must be seen as its own product. But all these products are ambiguous: insufficiently developed, in any direction whatsoever; undetermined by overdetermination; non-human, because too human. But these non-comprehensible objects (or objects which appear such) are in fact the factors and conditions of their subsequent history; they mortgage the future and infect the struggle unleashed by them with their own opacity – their ill-posed questions, ill-resolved problems and ill-performed liquidation. They are objects of every kind, and this is no place to attempt a classification. These residues

---

3. *Critique*, vol.1, pp.524 ff.

of struggle may in fact be anything, since struggles take place on all levels at once: the strange battle of Valmy, and the no less strange Prussian retreat, as much as some undertaking – like the National Workshops in 1848 – sabotaged by a class enemy who has not been able to prevent it entirely. Confronted by these objects positivist Reason is quite at its ease, since it aims to reduce the complex to the less complex and if possible to its basic elements. It will successively study the initial project, the riposte, the riposte to the riposte; it will be satisfied if it can 'explain' each of the characteristics of the object under study by reducing it to the action of one of the groups or to the reaction of the enemy groups. At the present moment of our dialectical investigation, however, we encounter these products of History as instances of *aporia*; for, at the same time as appearing in the guise of results of a common enterprise, they simultaneously demonstrate that this enterprise has never existed, other than as the non-human reverse side of two opposed actions each of which aims to destroy the other. In the dialectical perspective, we encounter these objects as human productions endowed with a future (the National Workshops are defined on the basis of a social need of the moment and as the enterprise which can satisfy that need). Thus, in themselves, they appear as totalizations in progress. If we look more closely, however, we perceive precisely – even before knowing the circumstances of their creation – that this visible future is already (has always been) put out of play, reduced to a mere mystifying clue or secretly deviated. Yet the object is not a trap either – in other words, a human and thoroughly comprehensible construction. For, despite the partial alterations and cancellations, something remains of the original project and the enterprise retains a confused efficacy leading to unforeseeable results.

But herein lies the problem: if History is totalizing, there is totalization of struggle as such (it does not much matter, from the formal point of view we are adopting, whether this struggle is an individual fight, a war or a social conflict). And if this totality is dialectically comprehensible, it must be possible through investigation to grasp the individuals or groups in struggle as *de facto* collaborating in a common task. And since the task is perpetually given, in the guise of a residue of struggle – be it even the devastation of a battlefield, inasmuch as the two adversaries can be seen as having jointly burned and ravaged the fields and woods – it must be possible to grasp it as the objectification of a work group, formed itself by the two antagonistic groups. But it is quite obvious that the joint devastation has not been the object of a concerted praxis, and that only topological unity, for example, can give the battle-field the aspect of a systematically razed whole. As for the National Workshops and social objects born of a struggle, you could go so far as to maintain that these are historical realities only in so far as they do not conform to any of the projects that have realized them in reciprocal antagonism. They have a kind of genuinely historical existence in so far as, albeit made by men, they escape them (even if, like the Convention, they are themselves groupings) without thereby falling back to the level of unworked matter; in other words, in so far as they deviate from all the paths people may wish to assign to them, in order to take an unforeseen path of their own accord and produce results impossible to conjecture; in so far, finally, as overdetermination and indetermination are manifested in them as the production of these non-human objects through a surplus of human labour, and their non-signification is in fact oversignification through interpenetration of antagonistic meanings. It is not a matter here of alienation (although, considering the facts in a less schematic light, alienation is found underlying struggle itself, as transcended and conserved). Nor is it either inanimate materiality as exteriority or seriality which robs each adversary of his act. It is each of them who robs the other of his act. It is in the reciprocity of the groups already constituted against seriality and alienation that precisely this new and living *process*, which is born of man yet escapes him, is forged.

These problems are of capital importance. It was enough to formulate them for us to step across a new threshold of critical investigation. We have, in effect, just encountered History. Of course, it presents itself in its most abstract form. But the present difficulties are, as we shall see, of a historical nature; on the basis of these, it will perhaps be possible later to formulate the problem of History's intelligibility. The example of the fight shows us, in effect, that an infinite number of social objects – and of the most varied kinds – contain as their inner structure the twofold negation of themselves and of each component by the other. There is thus at least – i.e. before any conception of historical factors and motive forces – one certain aporia in every social ensemble: apparent unities and partial syntheses cover splits of every kind and every size. Society, from afar, seems to stand unaided; from close to, it is riddled with holes. Unless the holes themselves are, in some way, the appearance – and the totalization is the unity. On the other hand, however, we already know that conflicts and social struggles as much as individual battles are *all* conditioned by scarcity: negation of man by the Earth being interiorized as a negation of man by man. Thus do we begin to understand the importance of those first experiences – which are, in any case, so common that they have been reduced for everyone to the level of mere determinations of language. At the time of studying the intelligibility of struggles, it is as well to recall that at all events struggles are never and nowhere accidents of human history. They precisely represent the manner in which men live scarcity in their perpetual movement to transcend it.

Or, if you prefer, struggle is scarcity as a relationship of men with one another. We thereby signal a fundamental bond between man and himself, through the interiorization of man's relation to the non-human object. The practical and technical relation of man to the Universe as a field of scarcity is transformed in and through work; and these transformations are necessarily interiorized (alienation) as objective transformations of interhuman relations, in so far as they express scarcity. As long as abundance – as man's new relation to the Universe – has not replaced scarcity, the displacements of scarcity (scarcity of the product becoming scarcity of the tool or scarcity of man, etc.) are interiorized and transcended as displacements of human struggles. Although it is classes which through their opposition create struggle, it is the permanent existence of these struggles which creates classes at a certain level of the technical development of production. The incest taboo, as Lévi-Strauss has shown us, presents itself as a conflict refused by a mediated reciprocity (though it remains always possible); or, if you prefer, as perhaps the simplest cultural attempt to correct chance by a redistribution of certain goods. In these classless and sometimes historyless societies, conflicts – sometimes avoided by rigorous systems of mediations/compensations – remain present as a special tension in the group in question. For example, American sociologists have clearly shown how, in certain groups, the elders' monopolization of women – by making the young bear the full weight of scarcity – determines a latent conflict between the generations. The institutions prevent this conflict from occurring as a reality, as a visible splitting of society into antagonistic generations. But it is expressed by a malaise of the entire society, which appears in the relationship of young men to old, of young men to women, of old men to women or women to old men, and between young men.

But at the same time as we grasp the twofold *labour–conflict* relation as constitutive of human history, we must recognize that our history is a singular case among all possible histories, and that history is a particular relation and a particular case of the systems of possible relations within practical multiplicities. Reciprocity, for example – in so far as it is able a priori to be negative or positive – is a valid relation for all practical ensembles. But it is not demonstrable a priori that the whole practical ensemble must secrete a history, nor even that all possible histories must be conditioned by scarcity. The preceding considerations are of interest only in so far as they claim to be limitative: they are useful to us simply to mark the boundaries of our knowledge and our assertions. *For us*, the problem of the intelligibility of the transformations under way within riven societies is fundamental. For a theory of practical ensembles claiming to be universal, however, the developments envisaged present themselves with all the contingent richness of a *singularity*. If one wished to make struggle into a universal structure of *all* histories, it would be necessary to prove that the only original relation between practical organisms and the outside world which nourishes and maintains them must be scarcity. All we can say is that this demonstration is not possible today. However it may be, study of the intelligibility of antagonistic reciprocities (and, as a consequence, of human history) remains within the formal framework of our critical investigation. A priori, this negative possible presents as much interest as its opposite. At this level, we can at once grasp the link between this intelligibility and that of the historical process. In the framework of scarcity, constitutive relations are fundamentally antagonistic. If one considers their temporal development, they manifest themselves in the form of the event constituted by struggle. But the latter – even if, from a certain viewpoint, it must be possible to consider it as a unity – engenders products which will become the material circumstances that other generations thrown into other conflicts will have to transcend. What is more, in so far as it outflanks each of its adversaries, it engenders itself as its own process. We see this rigorously human event, being produced beyond every praxis as indetermination and overdetermination of its products and itself by practical surcharges, *simultaneously* – all through and from every angle – referring back to praxis (we can and must interpret the material circum- stances which condition it, or which it engenders, only through the transcendence that preserves them and that they orientate) and *at the same time* outflanking its adversaries and *through them* becoming some- thing other than what each of them projects. As must now be clear, this is the very definition of the *historical process*, in so far as it is an ongoing temporalization of *human* history.

Formal Contradiction in Marxist Theory

The solution of the problem – if one exists – while remaining theoretical must have specific repercussions: it is within its framework that dialectical materialism will have to find the principle of its intelligibility. For if we consider the Marxist interpretation carefully, it must be acknowledged that it relates simultaneously to two terms that seem opposed, without troubling to establish their compatibility: while presenting the class struggle to us as the motor of History, it simultaneously reveals to us the dialectical development of the historical process. Thus our formal contra- diction recurs in the concrete examination of Marxist theory and we perceive, in fact, that Marx did not avoid it. In other words, if the class struggle is to be intelligible to the historian's dialectical reason, one must be able to totalize classes in struggle – and this comes down to discovering the synthetic unity of a society riven through and through. There can be no doubt that Marx was aware of the problem: certain formulae we have cited present the capitalist process as the development of an antisocial force *in society*.[4] On the other hand, he always refused – and quite rightly – to give any reality to the verbal entity people call society: he saw it as just one form of alienation among others. The problem thus remains open: since the dialectical contradiction is immanent – in other words, since it is a rift maintained and produced by the unity it rends – is there a unity of the different classes which sustains and produces their irreducible conflicts? We shall examine this question in the paragraphs that follow. But it is necessary to recall that our examination applies to these historical conflicts only as an *example* enabling us to elucidate the problem we have just formulated. In other words, Marxists have concerned themselves with the *material* success of their hypotheses. They have verified them by applying them to the data of historical investigation and seen their value as deriving from the number of facts they enable us to regroup and illumine, as well as from the possibilities they disclose to praxis. But the formal problem of intelligibility has struck them as otiose, or at any rate premature. Later on, we shall see the historicity of the dialectical investigation of History. It was legitimate for it to impose itself through its content and develop through practice. But it is precisely when the machine seems jammed that it is appropriate to unravel the formal difficulties hitherto neglected.[5] Marxism is strictly true if History is totalization. It is no longer true if human history is decomposed into a plurality of individual histories; or if, at any rate, within the relation of immanence which characterizes the fight the negation of each opponent by the other is on principle *detotalizing*. Of course, it is neither our project here – nor a concrete possibility for us – to demonstrate the plenary truth of dialectical materialism (we shall doubtless attempt this elsewhere, in a book devoted to anthropology: in other words, to the concrete as such).[6] Our aim is solely to establish if, in a practical ensemble riven by antagonisms (whether there are multiple conflicts or these are reduced to a single one), the very rifts are totalizing and entailed by the totalizing movement of the whole. But if we actually establish this abstract principle, the materialist dialectic – as movement of History and historical knowledge – needs only to be proved by the facts it illumines, or, if you prefer, to discover itself as a fact and through other facts.

---

4. *The Problem of Method*, London 1963, pp.85, 158.
5. *Critique*, vol.1, Introduction (especially pp.40 ff.); also p.801 n.
6. This project was never carried out. See Sartre's interview on anthropology for *Cahiers de philosophie* (1966), in *Situations IX*, Paris 1972.

Relations between the Individual Conflict and the Fundamental Conflicts of the Social Ensemble

Incarnation and Singularization

I F TOTALIZATION is really an ongoing process, it operates everywhere. This means both that there is a dialectical meaning of the practical ensemble – whether it is planetary, or has to become even interplanetary – and that each individual event totalizes in itself this ensemble in the infinite richness of its individuality. From this point of view, at an initial stage of the critical inquiry one might ask oneself whether each individual struggle is not, in itself, the totalization of all struggles: in critical terms, whether the comprehension of a conflict – for example, the boxing match we were discussing – does not necessarily refer back to the totalizing comprehension of the fundamental conflicts (scarcity) characterizing the social ensemble that corresponds to it. At this level of knowledge, we are not yet posing the problem of the totalizing unity at the heart of the negation of reciprocity: that question remains unanswered. At a subsequent stage, however, the answer will be facilitated if a struggle – as any old event in History – appears to us, in the very irreducibility of its protagonists and the rift between them, as a totalization of the ensemble of contemporary irreducibilities and rifts: in other words, as though each of them were interpreted as the *present* signification (here and now) of all the others, precisely in so far as the movement of knowledge – in order to reveal its own meaning – must go in search of all the other conflicts in which it is totalized. We encounter here, as a condition of intelligibility, the reciprocity (of partial events in relation to one another and of each event in relation to the totalization of all totalizations) that characterizes synthetic unification.

Let us consider, for example, the boxing match that is currently taking place before our eyes. It matters little whether such and such a title is at stake, or whether it is just any old fight between professionals or even between amateurs. For from the very outset we understand that the deep truth of every individual fight is competition for titles. Of course, most boxers know their abilities and limit their ambitions. If they do not know themselves, their manager will inform them; and, ultimately, it is he who chooses to 'push' one of his protégés or decides that another is not yet ready to make his debut. But this is not where the problem lies. What counts is the fact that there exists a competitive hierarchy – recognized by all (even if the value of the 'holder' of such and such a title is contested), which can even legitimately be seen as an objective structure of national and international societies – and that every fight takes place at the very heart of this hierarchy: indeed, derives its meaning from it. For informed spectators, it is not just a question of seeing two men trading punches, or even of seeing 'good boxing'; it is a question of being present at an individual episode of an ascent, and at a moment which may begin or accelerate a decline. Ascent and decline have any meaning, of course, only if they are to be understood in terms of the entire hierarchy. At a certain level, no doubt – for example with some bouts added to the evening's programme as fillers – the spectator has no illusions. Neither of the two men now fighting will go very far. Neither will rise very high, neither will fall very low. These mediocre but solid boxers who know their job will continue indefinitely to fight supporting bouts on evenings when others are playing the star roles. But *even this* qualifies them in terms of the hierarchical ensemble: they represent the first rungs – tough and almost inert – of the ceaseless to-and-fro movement which makes up the world of boxing. And this necessary totalization of their bout, on the basis of all the immediately preceding and immediately following bouts (those already announced by the press), finds its concrete and retotalizing signification in the very place this bout occupies on the programme. The evening is hierarchical – a twofold hierarchy: build-up to the big fight after the interval, wind-down towards a final bout – and this hierarchy is lived in *tension* by the spectator, whose attention grows (in principle, of course) from one fight to the next. Through his very anticipation of this hierarchy (the boxers will be more and more skilful) and through his more or less impatient expectation – sometimes, too, through the lateness of half the spectators, who arrive in the course of the evening, and through the objective aspect of a half-empty hall – the initial bout on the programme is synthetically united with the rest as the first moment of an ongoing process. And, precisely because of this, it is an integral part of the temporalizing totalization. In other words, it *signifies* the whole evening as it is about to unfold. This does not, of course, mean that it can announce the reality (in any case often hard to forecast) of the bouts that are to follow; simply that, in this operation which is the organization of an evening of boxing, it has its totalizing relation as a part to the whole by virtue of the fact (impossible to ignore) that it is *the beginning*. Thus the diachronic synthesis (living hierarchy that gradually becomes established) is *at one and the same time* a real product of the synchronic synthesis (the organizers have chosen the bouts on the basis of the *hexis* and reputation of the fighters) and the retotalizing temporalization of the synchronic hierarchy. The *beginning* of the evening is the temporal equivalent of the *first rungs* of the ladder. Spectators, organizers, boxers live this hierarchy in its unfolding and, if the bout lends itself to this, the event appears under dual control. At the same time as this ephemeral reality – the first bout – vanishes, determining (with its very disappearance) and confirming its immutable place in the spatio-temporal hierarchy, the two opponents move up, move down: in short, find themselves after the fight on a different rung. (Sometimes they move up together – a drawn fight, they have fought well – or down together; usually they move in opposite directions.) The winner, for example, we saw mounting the ladder, even though he simultaneously remained on the first rung. This contradiction is still perfectly intelligible – it simply discloses a rather more distant future. The spectators' applause and the judgement of the experts will ensure that next time he is given a higher billing.

Conversely, what would a contest for the title be, if the two boxers were not already at the top of the ladder? If they were not known? If their previous fights had not remained in people's memories? If their superiority was not *really established* by the number of opponents defeated and reduced to vegetating in obscurity (the earliest of all, moreover, often having sunk back into anonymity)? These two men very much (seemingly) at their ease, who climb into the ring amid the applause in their brightly coloured robes, are in themselves 'common individuals': they contain within them the opponents they have already defeated and, via this mediation, the entire universe of boxing. In another way, you can say that the hierarchy supports them: that they are its illuminated peaks. And yet again, what is testified to by the evening itself and the moment of their appearance is the following. The preceding bouts have taken place, they have come to an end, they have dissolved into the total process. Their engulfment in the past realizes the objective temporalization of the champions' hierarchical superiority, at the same time as it refers back, through its deepest signification, to a real and elapsed temporalization: that which is identified with the professional lives of the two contestants (at least in the immediately preceding years) and which, amid countless vicissitudes, has caused them to realize the synchronic hierarchy themselves in a diachronic movement, by passing from rung to rung, thanks to the fights they have won – in other words, *at one and the same time* by meeting increasingly skilful boxers and by

having an increasingly prominent billing on programmes. Thus the movement of the evening replicates the movement of their lives; and the
preceding bouts reproduce the history of their own fights, the return to
oblivion of almost all those they have defeated.

If it is established that the fight, whatever it may be, is the present
retotalization of all fights; if it is clear that it can be decoded only *by
them*; if it has a meaning only in so far as it is put back in the *real*
perspectives of contemporary boxing (number of boxers, value of each of
them, national or international importance of boxing, passion or dis-
affection of the spectators, etc.) – then it will easily be understood that
boxing in its entirety is present at every instant of the fight as a sport and
as a technique, with all the human qualities and all the material conditioning (training, physical condition, etc.) that it demands. This must be
understood as meaning that the spectators have come to see – and the
promoters have taken steps (successful or otherwise) to give them –
some *good boxing*. And this means a fighting practice (on the part of
each of the contenders) which transcends a learned technique, even while
realizing it wholly at every instant. The movement itself will be *invention*:
choice of hitting with one's left an opponent who has dropped his guard,
perhaps as a ruse; risks incurred unwittingly, etc. But all this cannot even
be attempted without an ensemble of technical acquisitions – speed,
punch, legwork, etc. – and, at a still deeper level, without the habit of
putting all the weight of one's body into every punch without losing
one's balance. Boxing consists in this, as *hexis*, as *technique* and as each
individual's ever novel invention. One must not, of course, be fobbed off
with mere words: there are *specific* boxers, trainers and managers; and
the progressive improvement of such and such a boxer's ability to punch
or 'duck' is an individual event in an individual life. But – and we shall
have to return to this – these individuals, linked in groups, through
thousands of encounters and in all the world's locations, have gradually
perfected techniques. These techniques have been unified by professionals
who have become instructors or trainers. The synthetic ensemble first
became the unity of tricks of the trade, teaching methods, diets, etc.,
before being theorized subsequently (more or less) via the mediation of
languages. And this practical and theoretical unification was necessitated
by the very fact of the fight: in other words, by the obligation for each of
the antagonists to fight the other with his own technique. Here, we meet
again what we were mentioning earlier: the synthetic unity of the national
and international organizations which agree to formulate the body of
rules to be observed and to realize – as the unification of a practice and a
theory – what is often called *the art of boxing*. The social object thus
created possesses an objective reality as a *constituted product*. But from
this angle it has only an abstract being, as an ensemble of possible

meanings and practices. At the same time, however, it is *whole* – as realized and transcended power – at every instant, at every moment of training, at every twist and turn of a fight. At once outside and inside: determination of the body, *hexis*, technical expertise – in short, slow production of a social man, the boxer; and, at the same time, omnipresent ensemble of theoretico-practical meanings to which everyone refers simultaneously (from the manager to the spectator, by way of the boxers, the trainers, the seconds, etc.) and which is at once the *transcended*, since each punch is understood and foreseen on the basis of that ensemble, and *transcendence*, since it envelops the present bout and effects the concrete totalization of all contemporary bouts. The boxer transcends boxing, and boxing envelops the boxer since it itself requires that transcendence. It is entirely contained in that punch; but conversely that punch neither is, nor can be, anything other than a requirement of boxing. From this point of view, it is necessary to point out at once that the rift represented, at the bottom of this immense pit, by the fierce antagonism of the two opponents can really occur (whatever it may finally be in its fundamental intelligibility or unintelligibility) only through the totalizing unification of a technique perfected by united organisms. To go still further, their very encounter can take place only on the basis of an agreement (which does not mean that this agreement is always respected): to accept the rules, to contend *in the same art*.

Thus each fight is all of boxing. It may be present totally and positively, as when the boxers are champions and devote all their ferocity to defeating one another. Or else the totalization is effected negatively: the spectators gauge the inadequacy of the fighters because, in their operations, *they do not even realize* – far less transcend – that theoretical and practical experience we have termed the art of boxing. But this does not mean that boxing, as an art, as the 'noble sport', does not have a *present reality*, in the hall and in the ring. Quite the reverse: it is what determines the limits and capacities of the two opponents; it is what defines their future place in the hierarchy – their career – through the exigencies and protests of the hall, as registered by the promoters and managers. You may even feel its bulky presence, precisely in so far as it dominates the fighters without their being able to transcend it; in so far as it possesses them through the ensemble of the rules, rituals and aims to which they submit, without their interiorizing it by their retotalization of the practical field. This bout in which the two beginners are embroiled, each a victim at once of his own blunders and the other's, has a reality all the more striking in that such domination of the labourers by their labour, by producing their future before the eyes of all (they will vegetate at the foot of the ladder or abandon the profession), causes it to be seen and touched as a signification and as a destiny. For it is a signification, in so far as it can be manifested through determinations of language ('They're useless', 'They're clapped out', etc.); but it is a destiny, in so far as this present domination of the boxers by boxing is directly grasped as presence of their future misfortune.

Thus the boxing match appears *to all* as a single event – which elapses irreversibly and pits singular individuals against one another – and as *all of boxing*, present and implicated in this same event. In every fight boxing is *incarnated*, realized, and elapses as it is realized. In every fight it is there, fixed and totalizing, as the milieu that produces *in itself*, like a widening crack, *the* fight between these two singular persons. No one can understand the enthusiasm of the spectators – and very often of the boxers themselves – if he does not recognize this twofold dimension of the match, as well as the twofold presence of boxing. This scrap would be devoid of interest if it did not *totalize*, in its concrete temporalization, this fixed and abstract world which retotalizes it. But this totalization would remain schematic and formal (which is the case when a boxer and his sparring partner give a 'demonstration' without landing blows) if it were not incarnated in the singularity of an 'uncertain contest': i.e. one of inexhaustible exuberance and, at the same time, at least partial unpredictability.

However, we cannot deny that, for most spectators, things do not go further. Every fight retotalizes boxing and all other fights. Boxing (as the objective hierarchy and 'ranking' of boxers) in turn retotalizes every fight that elapses. But it does not strike them as necessary to wonder whether these organized rifts in the social fabric are, in themselves, a totalization of all rifts in that same 'society'. Or, in other words, whether the social ensemble is incarnated with the multiplicity of its conflicts in such a singular temporalization of negative reciprocity. At least it is not necessary for the *aficionados*: but perhaps this is because they are *themselves* the fight in progress. On the contrary, in certain milieux hostile to violent sports, nothing is more commonplace than to present boxing as a product of 'human aggression' and as one of the factors liable to increase this innate aggressiveness. Without lingering over this idealist and naturalist notion of aggression, it is worth noting that the violence of boxers is linked to ongoing conflicts in two different ways: that is, directly and via a series of mediations.

Immediate Totalization: Incarnation

In a direct sense, the fight is a public incarnation of *every* conflict. It relates, without any intermediary, to the interhuman tension produced by the interiorization of scarcity. It is this type of relation that we must first describe. What do we see? Men gathered to watch a particular duel with eager interest. But we already know that this duel is the present incarnation of a certain kind of regulated violence called boxing. Now the ensemble of rules and technical imperatives constituting this 'art' derives its origin from a systematic and continuous perfecting of the most direct and naked violence: that of unarmed men making themselves into their own weapons of combat. All social groups known to us today are armed – however rudimentary their technique may be. But in each the possibility remains, for individuals pitted against one another by anger, to return to a mode of combat which seems the *original struggle*, although this cannot be proved actually to be the first confrontation between individuals located in a field of scarcity. What is certain is that, in every brawl, the deep source is always scarcity. It would take too long to explain here the causal sequence through which the *challenge*, for instance, is the translation of human violence as interiorized scarcity. But it will easily be understood how violence, at first practical and self-interested, may be posited for itself as disinterested virtue, before an audience of violent men. In fact the disinterest is a mirage: the fighters wish to assert themselves, earn esteem and glory, obtain a material advantage. It remains the case that the fight in itself is 'gratuitous'. Victory does not directly give the winner wealth or the loser's woman. It is necessary to introduce a complex social world of judges, referees and spectators. There is *reward* rather than *conquest*. In certain cases (in a bout where the titleholder is defeated by the challenger) the loser has the consolation of earning much more money than the winner. By cutting every link with immediate interests, by imposing the mediation of the entire group, by making the 'purse' into a kind of bonus for merit, and victory (except in the event of a knockout) into a pondered decision by competent witnesses, violence loses its extreme urgency. It sheds the significations, forming an integral part of it, that blur it and refer back to motives. Whatever the pugnacity and anger of our fighting cocks may be, they are rarely separated by hatred. The passionate will to win, the fury, spring from the function – in other words, from the violence *to be exerted* – rather than the violence springing from the anger: just the opposite of what happens in a brawl. At the same time, the ensemble of precautions taken (gloves, gumshield, box, prohibition against dangerous blows) and the professional technique of the combatants contribute to reducing the disordered aspect normally presented by street fights. For on the streets, two angry individuals who hurl themselves at one another are of equal strength and respect no rules or technique. They may be paralysed by their mutual ignorance, roll on the ground, kill one another or barely hurt each other, as chance will have it. It is not so much naked violence that emerges as a kind of grotesque calamity marking man's limits. So everything conspires to blur that first image of *conflict*. Besides, it is not a spectacle but a fever. The onlookers may either separate the combatants or else all pitch into one another.

The moment when conflict – naked, freed from all visible constraint, strongly delineated by knowledge, rules and skills – is presented by itself as a spectacle corresponds, in all communities, to a valorizing acquisition of awareness. Not only does the individual grasp himself in his actions as threatened by the violence of counter-men, and as having to respond by a counter-violence; he also gives a *value* to defensive violence (and even to offensive violence, in so far as he does not reject the possibility of preventive aggression). In the Manichaeism of scarcity, violence is in the service of Good – it is Good itself. The individual – and the group does just the same – assimilates his human dignity to the counter-violence which maintains it. He dignifies the latter with the name of *strength*. The upright man must be strong; strength is the proof of his right.[7] The reason is simple: if he is defeated, he is subjected to the other's right, the Manichaeism is reversed, the defeated man must be wrong. Thus that which was merely a material conditioning, piercing the individual and opposing him to the Other, becomes a *hexis* that exercise must develop and that must be able to change into praxis as soon as the situation requires it. This is why – whatever the weapons, whose origin is social – the individual who assumes violence first asserts his strength at the level of his weaponless nakedness. We shall see that there are a hundred, a thousand different ways to realize oneself as strong (in other words, as Good making itself terrible); and that these depend upon the inherent structures of the group – hence, ultimately, upon the ensemble of material circumstances and of techniques. And there is no question but that, in communities where the ruling class is a military aristocracy, the noble cannot be distinguished from his weapons; he refuses the nakedness of the fundamental combat precisely in so far as this combat *qualifies* commoners, those who do not have the technique and sovereign use of the sword. But this is not what counts here. The essential thing is that, by assuming violence in the guise of manly strength, the individual (just like the group) posits it for himself as his duty (to become stronger every day) and his privileged means. He necessarily makes it into *an object* and, precisely in so far as his Manichaeism detaches it from the particular or collective interests it has to defend, a disinterested *virtue*. The fight as actual reciprocal violence is *posited for itself*, in warlike societies, precisely in so far as violence – a means in the service of Good

---

7. On the ethics of force and on these three types of violence, see *Cahiers pour une morale* (written in 1947), Paris 1983, pp.194 ff., 216 ff.

– has to become aware of itself as being ultimately the negative realization of Good itself (through destruction of Evil) and eventually posits itself as an end. It would be wrong to think that the fight which takes place *in public*, and with no other end than to exist publicly as an absolute event, is charged with *representing* violence. For it to represent violence, in fact, the latter would have to be *imaginary*. But it really exists and may be fatal, depending on the mode of combat. It would be wrong even to say that the combatants *present* violence: they are too busy fighting, especially if the struggle is hard and risks becoming fatal. What is involved is not in any sense play-acting, but rather a *perfect realization*.* In contrast to the uncertain encounters of war, the tournament was an opportunity for knights to realize violence in its regulated purity, in the form of a 'laboratory experiment'. You risked your life to take another's, but the field was cleared of all those foot-soldiers always ready to hamstring the horses, of all those archers – and even those other nobles – whose intervention cloaked or hindered the true unfolding of the single combat. The society that posits its violence as an object must, on pain of lapsing into idealism, realize it as a material object – in other words, as a public and free event. The violent 'game' *incarnates* the type of violence characterizing the society in question: but this characteristic (to which we shall return), which refers back to practical *mediations*, must not prevent us from seeing that the public combat is an embodiment, in front of everyone, of the fundamental violence.

For the spectators have an ambiguous attitude. To listen to them, they go to see 'fine sport', 'good boxing'; they go to appreciate human qualities – courage, skill, intelligence, etc. And that is true. But these forms of technical and moral appreciation would not even have any meaning, if they were not provoked by the reality of a dangerous struggle. It is one thing to be moved by the imaginary representation of courage in the theatre; [quite another] [8] to discover courage gradually, within an event which is actually taking place and whose reality strikes you first. And, precisely, it is no game of chess: the spectator sees men bleed, suffer, sometimes fall; he sees their faces swell beneath the blows until they burst. Precisely because the event is not imaginary, moreover, the spectator does not have the means to remain passive. The strength of the imaginary derives from the unbridgeable distance which separates me from it – in the theatre – and reduces me to impotence. But the spectator of that purified brawl is an actor, because it is really taking place in front

---

* In the same sense in which people speak of a 'perfect crime'.

8. The manuscript has 'or' here.

of him. He encourages the boxers or finds fault with them, he shouts, he thinks he is making the event as it takes place. His violence is wholly present and he strives to communicate it to the combatants, in order to hasten the course of the fight. That violence, moreover, is not satisfied with objectively helping the efforts of each antagonist. It would not be violence without favouring, without preferring, without opting to be partisan. The spectator *chooses* his point of view: he acclaims the fighter who is his compatriot or whose career he has followed; or else he makes his decisions, in the course of the bout, for specific reasons. For example, he chose the boxer from Marseilles because he led for the first two rounds; subsequently, he will persist in seeing him as the winner, refuse to see the blows taken by his favourite and encourage him – not just vocally, but by a kind of passionate, vain effort to endow him with his own will. Ultimately he identifies with him, he fights through him. He is himself the incarnation of violence, sometimes to the point of hitting his neighbour: a free-for-all in the hall is always possible, as a normal and foreseen result of the bout.

At this level, it is indeed the fundamental violence that is incarnated. Even if he has some empirical knowledge of boxing, the spectator cannot appreciate the blows without giving them, down there in the ring, through the fists of his favourites. He cannot maintain his enthusiastic partisanship without sharing the fighter's anger. As I have said, anger – in the 'combative' boxer – is aroused by the first punch, sometimes even as soon as he climbs into the ring. This anger is expressed by the sudden, 'mean' nature of his attack, and this visible expression is grasped in so far as it arouses the same anger in the spectator. This, however, does not spring from danger or the will to win. It is not a struggle against fear. It is the incarnation of a pre-existing violence which derives originally from the very situation of this witness, and persists in him – except in the moments when it can exteriorize itself – as malaise, nervous tension, sometimes even unhappy passivity. In this sense, the violence of the crowd – which sustains the boxers, which suffuses and inspires them, and which they incarnate in their bout – is that engendered within each of its members by social constraints; by the oppression they have under-gone; by the alienation they have experienced; by serial impotence; by exploitation; by surplus labour; and, just as much, by 'inner' or personal conflicts which merely translate those latent conflicts into the domain of the individual. The two boxers gather within themselves, and re-exteriorize by the punches they swap, the ensemble of tensions and open or masked struggles that characterize the regime under which we live – and have made us violent even in the least of our desires, even in the gentlest of our caresses. But at the same time, this violence is approved in them. Through them, that which is moroseness, malaise, hatred not daring to avow itself, etc., becomes courage, effectiveness, Manichaean virtue of strength. The audience *produces the boxers*: not – as everyone tries to do – by the encouragements and criticisms it bestows upon them, but materially and in a very real sense because it finances the vast operation you may call world boxing. Thus the feeling each spectator has that he himself is the living strength of the fight, and that he inspires his favourite with this strength, is not mistaken. It translates a practical truth into individual attitudes, and those attitudes (enthusiasm, screams, whistles, etc.) contain the implicit understanding of that truth: if these witnesses allow themselves to shout, to rage, to revile, *it is because they have paid*. But, conversely, the boxers incarnate in a real and dated conflict the fundamental violence and the right to violence. This incarnation transforms the whole hall, for the crowd *takes part* in it and its violence is embodied in the boxers. The fight is everywhere, omnipresent war wheels about. The crowd is a collective which finds simultaneously, down there in the ring, its unity as a group and its innumerable rifts. A spontaneous and shifting dichotomy transforms each neighbour into his neighbour's adversary or (if they are backing the same fighter) into brethren-in-arms.

Precisely in so far as, in a synthetic unification, the part is a total-ization of the whole (or of the overall totalization), *incarnation* is an individual form of totalization. Its content is the totalized ensemble, or the ensemble in the process of being totalized. And by this we do not mean that it is the symbol or expression of the latter, but that it realizes itself in a very real and practical sense *as totality producing itself here and now*. Every boxing match incarnates the whole of boxing as an incarnation of all fundamental violence. And one must be careful not to confuse the different procedures of comprehension. For I do not say just that the fight *refers* to the contemporary ensemble of boxers, their hierarchy, their rankings and the secrets of their art. Nor that this ensemble *refers* to the contemporary forms of violence, as abstract and transcending significations to which the present event must be related. On the contrary, I say that the fight encloses the fundamental violence within itself, as its real substance and as its practical efficacy. It is directly here and everywhere in the hall. It is the very stuff of the movement of temporalization as production of the fight by the spectators and as unification (and reciprocal confrontation) of the spectators by the fight. And the reason for this incarnation is not mysterious, since it is the diffuse violence of each spectator retotalizing itself, on the basis of organizations and groups that have set themselves up to furnish it with opportunities to retotalize itself. And when we insist on the presence 'in person' and in its entirety of the fundamental violence, this must not be taken to mean that it does not exist *elsewhere*; it is simply that we find this violence is always *entire* wherever it exists. Positivist Reason would obviously confine itself to signalling a host of conflicts provoked by different factors, reducible at best to a common denominator. Just because of this, it would debar itself from understanding how a particular fight relates both to violence and, on the other hand, also to the vast network of organizations and federations constituting the world of boxing. An act of violence is always all of violence, because it is a re-exteriorization of interiorized scarcity. But this scarcity is never an abstract principle, or one external to the social ensemble. At every instant, it is a synthetic relation of all men to non-human materiality and of all men among themselves through this materiality, inasmuch as the ensemble of techniques, relations of production and historical circum-stances gives this relation its determination and its unity. Thus the interiorization is that of the *particular* contemporary scarcity as an objective reality; and the violence of each individual exists only as the swirling violence of all, since scarcity is defined through its relation to the number and needs of the men who today constitute the social ensemble under consideration. The oneness of this violence does not realize the unification of individuals and groups, since on the contrary it pits them against one another. In each violent action, however, all violence exists as unification – in and through this deed – of all the oppositions which pit all men against each other and have provoked it. It is enough to see how much oppression, alienation and misery the act of a drunken father who beats a child gathers within itself, in order to understand that all the social violence of our system has made itself into that man and his present rage.

But we have spoken of incarnation: by this we mean to say that totalization is *individuated*. That fundamental violence explodes here and now, but with all the features of a here and a now: in other words, with the opaque richness of the concrete and its negative determinations. It is a boxer from the Nord and one from Marseilles who are up against one another in front of these Parisians, each of whom has come to watch the fight as a result of the development of his history, which is strictly personal to him. With its incidents and its accidents, the bout defines itself as a singularity and, through its singularity, a *dated* evening, filled with unique events, hence irreducibly individual, *even* if it is strikingly commonplace ('Nothing very much happened.' 'The bouts were pretty ordinary.'). This fight is all violence and, at the same time, it is *other*, it can exist only as its particular determination. Is it to be understood that the fight bears the same relation to *the* fundamental violence as the individual has to the concept? No: this relation – which might exist at the level of analytic Reason – in fact requires three conditions to be fulfilled in order to establish itself. Even if, in the course of our investigation, the concept is discovered in the individuated object and as an essential structure of the latter, it still in fact remains transcendent to it, as an abstract and already given rule, which survives even if the contingent and empirical limits of the reality under consideration are caused to vanish. Then the relation – and this comes back to the foregoing condition – is not created by action (it is the object which can be created, not the relation to the concept or the concept itself); it is an ontological and logical relation, which can yield itself only to contemplative reason.* Lastly, the empirical features of the object fall outside the concept and manifest themselves in relation to it as mere accidents; this defines the concept as an ensemble of abstract determinations – of the type $y = f(x)$ or s *implies* q – that can have no material reality other than as a determination of language (or a transcendence of such a determination as a signifying unity). This obviously implies that the ensemble of determinations, within the concept, is bound by relations of exteriority. It is a matter of features or characteristics which present themselves in experience simultaneously or according to an invariable order of succession, as is apparent when you consider the concept of swan (transformed by the discovery of black swans in Australia) or that of karyokinesis.

We can better show the meaning of *incarnation* if we contrast it to exemplification of the concept, as well as to the conceptualization of experience. This incarnation, in fact, is never contemplative: it is praxis or praxis-process. An act of violence never has *witnesses*. Of course, the police – or tomorrow the historian – will seek the testimony of individuals who have been present at the action without taking part in it. But these individuals do not exist. And this is even the reason why testimony – whatever its source may be – is, on principle, suspect. The so-called witness is a participant: he intervenes to stop a brawl or else lets it run its course – out of cowardice, sadism or respect for tradition. The proof

---

* I do not mean by this that the practical stance should be quietism. The concept, or the relation of the object to the concept, manifests itself in the course of a scientific investigation, for instance, which implies an interrogation, a project of finding the answer, a construction of experimental mechanisms with the help of instruments, etc. This is what occurs, for example, when the chemist seeks to determine whether a given body belongs to a given category, and is defined by a given collection of properties. There can even be a decision at the actual level of the ontologico-logical relationship, as when the scientist (in the case of certain salts, e.g. tartrate and para-tartrate) decides to forge two classes in order to satisfy the principles of his science, whereas experimental discovery reveals only one. No matter. Through activities, grasping the concept through its object remains the goal of a project of contemplation, because the relations between that object and that concept – even if they are *decided* – are *given*, *established*: it is not the object that *realizes* practically its concept, nor the concept that *is realized practically* in the object. This inertia constitutes the scientist himself as a de-situated investigator. We rediscover the 'pure being-alongside ... ' that Heidegger defines as a scientific attitude.

is that most legislative systems have laws providing for sanctions against persons guilty of 'non-assistance'. In a building where certain tenants beat their children, sometimes to death, the other tenants are necessarily thrown into a situation which imperatively demands a choice: either to inform (but what reluctance is felt by many of those unfortunates – victims of society as a whole, who sympathize *on principle* with one of their own battering his children, not inasmuch as he is a childbeater but inasmuch as he is a victim – what reluctance to hand over a comrade to the cops!) or else to make themselves accomplices. In either case, they decide – together or separately – on the event. If they allow themselves to be hushed by a too-weighty silence and the victim dies (as has been known to happen), they are themselves the executioners. For the very notion of complicity, sidetracked by analytic Reason, supposes the immanence of the relationship and not its exteriority. The accomplice realizes the act in its entirety by his own practice, and no one can say a priori if he is more or less guilty than the individual whose hands accomplished the crime – that depends on his situation within the group or collective.

Hence, no witnesses to violence, only participants. Non-violence, even and especially when it is erected into a watchword, is the choice of a complicity. Generally the non-violent person makes himself the accomplice of the oppressor: in other words, of the institutionalized, normalized violence that selects its victims.* The brawl is a *common event*. Some produce it with their rage, which is the sudden exteriorization of a violence constantly suffered and interiorized. Others with their fear, which springs from an anticipation of future violence, based on the living memory of past violence. Action and knowledge are fused in this event, as we have always signalled. And that means, in particular, that the reality produced is *lived* (in other words acted, felt, known in the indissolubility of projects) as dialectical development and as irreversible temporalization, but not *contemplated*. The wisdom of praxis is defined by the latter and confines itself to illuminating the latter's progress, without any separation. It is not a matter here of *comparing* acts with one another, in order to derive a common concept: it is parties, organizations, the press, the government, that can reintegrate *this* particular case into statistics and draw conclusions about delinquent or battered childhood. The participants are actually *living an absolute*. And the real absurdity would be to introduce, at the level of the act, some relativism or other. Does anyone imagine you could die or sell your soul for *the relative*? The fear which makes a man cowardly despite himself – does anyone imagine this could be anything but a fear of the absolute? And murder? Here, we

---

* Though subversive advocates of non-violence do exist.

find again what I said in *Being and Nothingness*: relativism is a historical attitude that can be based only on the absolute character of daily, immediate life.[9] In other words, the relative is unintelligible if, before being relative to other relatives, it is not first relative to the absolute. But this absolute must be understood: we are not thereby referred back to some kind of theological dogmatism or idealism. The absolute is *above all* the difference separating life from death – in my own case and, for me, in every other case. It is the gap between existence and Nothingness. It is neither *life* that is an absolute for a start, nor death: but death, inasmuch as it comes to threaten fundamentally what lives; or life, in so far as it is stripped from the real by the death that threatens it, and in so far as it can hurl itself of its own accord to shatter intentionally upon the reef of death. Thereby, it is the ensemble of individuals and things that threaten life; it is the ensemble of those for whom you agree to give it up or risk it; it is the climate of violence which, in the form of conflicts or fraternity-terror, defines life as risk of death and mortal fate, death as the non-transcendable and threatening term of every life. Every violence-event is produced, lived, refused, accepted as *the absolute*: first, because it actualizes in the present the diffused and confused ensemble of the *multiple violences* that have made me fundamentally violent; then, because it arises absolutely and in the immediate as a struggle for life (and for the Other's death), revealing for all the participants that the life of each can be based on the death of another (or others). Thus, by conflict, life reveals itself in its precious uniqueness, in its irreversibility, in its fragility, and in its fierce assertion of itself, through the alternative: kill or be killed. It matters little that the conflict is not in itself a mortal struggle: death is there, in the blood that flows, as the completion that will not be completed, as the future truth that will not be attained and, finally, as the deep and fundamental truth. Death, clean and bare as a bone, is present in the boxing match. Not just because a badly or too well placed blow can kill. Nor even because cases of blindness, madness – lower forms of physical liquidation – are very common in former boxers. But quite simply because the act of punching is an act that gives death (something implicitly acknowledged by the existence of gloves and protective gear); because the knockout – always risked, always awaited by the crowd – is a public realization of death. *Symbolic* realization? No – the man collapses and dies, it is the end of the battle. Whether he revives in the dressing-room or not, the spectator has followed through a fight to its bitter end: in other words, to the ambiguous moment when its plenitude and its disappearance are produced by one another and simultaneously.

---

9. *Being and Nothingness*, London 1956, pp.521ff.; also *Cahiers pour une morale*, p.437.

But this present death is neither death in itself nor the concept of death: it really is that which threatens a given individual (the child dazed by his father's blows, the boxer, etc.). No one among the neighbours or in the audience wanders off into abstract considerations upon death *as such*. Each participant simply – by tolerating a child's agony or by egging on the boxers – *involves himself* as a murderer or as a batterer (as is proved clearly enough by the shouts repeated so often during a fight: 'Kill him! Kill him!' or 'Go after him! Finish him off!'), precisely because he perpetually sees himself as battered or as physically liquidated (by forced overwork, by a poverty artificially maintained through a social choice, by the ever possible violence of the 'forces of order' or, if he makes common cause with oppression, by the violent actions of a revolutionary movement). Down there he kills, he is killed, in each antagonist, and then his choice ends by making him a killer via his favourite and a victim via the other: at his own peril, since a reversal of the situation is always possible. And in so far as the conflict being settled in the ring is *sustained* by each person with the whole audience and against his neighbours, that which is produced *down there*, *here* and everywhere in the hall is – through those individual lives – the concrete totality of life, of death, of the human relationship of life and death. No conceptual or merely verbal signification: what makes these lives into the incarnation of life is quite simply the passionate seriousness of praxis for all the participants; their present inability to tear themselves away from the fight, which *for the moment* they put above all else, albeit knowing that they have concerns of a quite other importance. It is as though, altogether, there had never been any *outside*; as though beyond the closed doors nothing existed, neither city shrouded in darkness nor countryside around the city; as though the whole of humankind had never been anything but that handful of men producing that struggle to the death as the incarnation of their destiny; and as though, on the contrary, two billion men remained outside, lost in serial dispersion and impotence, but totalized and fused in this unique and capital struggle whose stake was nothing less than the fate of humanity.* From this latter angle, the totality of non-spectators is totalized by the fight itself in so far as they themselves become participants, directly through the boxers and indirectly through the mediation of the spectators. And the real basis for this totalization is the fact that commentators are already recapitulating

---

* In fact, the boxing match is a *blank Manichaeism*: everyone knows that Good will triumph over Evil. If the favourite knuckles under in the last rounds, the spectators will abandon him and be incarnated in the other. The case is more complex when local patriotism is involved: but defeat, in spite of everything, remains recuperable.

the fight for radio listeners *while it is taking place*: the fact that tomorrow's press will disseminate the results everywhere. Every non-spectator is like a paler and paler reproduction of the sole living and practical reality: each spectator as a producer and support of the fight. So each spectator gathers and fuses within himself these shadows; he totalizes and compresses the maximum amount of practice and experience – a maximum that will be decompressed into pale abstract knowledge and at once lose its ontological status.

But, for this very reason, there can be no ontological or logical difference between totalization and incarnation, except that – precisely because it is concrete and real – totalization operates only through the limitations it imposes. In other words, every *internal* totalization (enveloped by the overall totalization*) is effected as praxis-process of incarnation; or, conversely, every practical and concrete reality has no positive content other than the totalized ensemble of all ongoing totalizations. This content makes its materiality, governs its temporalization and constitutes itself through it. Present *without distance*, since it is made by the participants and not contemplated by witnesses, it refers to no transcendent signification and there are never grounds – in the moment of productive praxis – for referring to alien concepts or rules: the event produces its own rule. If this rule is the art of boxing, boxers and spectators reproduce and realize this art through real combat, transcending it by every invention and every tactical move. But this incarnated totalization, common handiwork of the participants, is never *named* or *thought* during the operation: neither as totalization (at the expense of the limitations that incarnate it) nor as incarnation (in other words as a simple, particular event). If you want to imagine participants taking these extreme positions, they must be prescribed extreme situations. It does indeed sometimes happen that a foreigner, taken by a friend to a sporting event of a violent kind, sees in it, if it is strictly local, only totalization (or at least the *national* aspect of totalization). For many North Americans, it is all of Mexico (or all of Spain) that is revealed – without words or concepts, through an unease – in the first corridas they are shown. I recall for my own part having perceived – rightly or wrongly, it is of little consequence – heaven knows what Cuban savagery in the cockfights of Havana. Those cocks epitomized men. Conversely, after the fights, the blind violence of those *humanized* creatures became a grid, a synthetic schema through which – despite myself – I decoded

---

* We do not even know yet if the totalization-of-envelopment can exist. We shall see further on that it is the foundation of any intelligibility of History, and we shall perceive that it is – albeit in a different way – *incarnated likewise*.

everything I saw. A kind of formless tragedy, floating between my eyes and the city, caused me to *discover* the poverty, although the direct link between it and fights between animals was not apparent to me at all.[10] In fact, even for the foreigner, totalization does not refer to any *idea*. The Cubans' national sport referred me to *that* beggar. And the reverse was also true: illuminated by my recent experience, the beggar in turn incarnated Cuba and its cockfights. If, on the contrary, you seek to reduce the fight to its nature as a strictly individualized event – pitting this individual, whose career you know, with that other one, and with the concrete perspectives that are going to open up for them – you have to take the practical viewpoint of the promoters and managers. In that case, it will be indispensable to note that reduction to the singular is effected by the intermediary of a new totalization. If the promoters do not waste their time decoding the fight as fundamental violence, it is because these lords of the 'Noble Art' – as common individuals of their organizations, or all-powerful sovereigns (and thereby still common), engaged in less brutal but equally violent competitions with other sovereigns – make themselves the spokesmen of *boxing* itself. It is totalized by their judgements, and this enveloping totalization reduces the present fight to just a little local event within the total world of boxing. It is really a matter of confirming forecasts, reclassifying boxers, and determining each one's value and ranking as settled in the course of the event. Boxing is expressed through the promoter's assessments, just as capitalism is through the acts and words of the capitalist. And, as we shall see in a moment, in bourgeois democracies capitalism itself is expressed through boxing.

It can doubtless be conceded that most spectators oscillate around a middling position. But (unless they fulfil the required conditions) none really reaches either of the extreme positions. In fact, it is not even a matter of saying that boxing and fundamental violence are present *through* the contest. This contest *is*, indissolubly, the singular conflict between a young boxer from Martinique and a Parisian boxer, boxing itself produced in common by all the participants, and human violence exploding publicly.

Mediated Totalization: Singularization

It follows from this that the relationship between the singular features and the incarnated total can no longer be defined as that between contingencies and the concept or essence. We have in fact seen that, in

---

10. Memories of a trip to Cuba in 1949.

relation to the abstract universal, every specification is a contingency. Analytic Reason will explain this contingency by external factors, but has forever barred itself from seeing it as a determination engendered by the universal itself, referring us back ultimately – this is the paradoxical unintelligibility at the heart of positivist intelligibility – to 'encounters between series'. In order to understand fully the reality of incarnation, we must ask ourselves whether chance has the same meaning for dialectical Reason; whether it does not appear as having a function of its own and thereby an intelligibility. We shall return to this.[11] Attending first to what is most urgent, however, we shall simply ponder upon the relations between the singularities of the fight and the concrete universals that it totalizes. For that, we must abandon the description of immediate totalization, which has furnished us with the essential, and approach the problem of mediated totalization.

This new totalization is effected by the same participants, but although produced by each of their gestures and through the project of totalizing human violence, it is not produced as a practical self-awareness. It is the being itself of all those men that is totalized: it appears in the object itself and is the rule of incarnation, but this rule does not constitute the object of a knowledge; it is the structure itself of the lived and, as such, is defined as the objective and (for them) *implicit* determination of the practical field. Only an observer rigorously situated in relation to the multiplicity of participants, but outside this, will be able to discern the ensemble of mediations through which these boxers, this boxing, these organizers and these spectators have reciprocally produced one another. Our aim cannot be to outline here a historical and dialectical interpretation of boxing. We shall limit ourselves to indicating what kind of research should make it possible to ascertain the true limits of the process of incarnation.

Boxing made its appearance in the East only recently. It is an induced process there, one that develops in the totalizing framework of competition in all domains with the capitalist West. It was born in our bourgeois societies and must first be studied in this guise. If it is true, moreover, that such societies are divided into classes, some exploiting and oppressing the others, bourgeois boxing must be studied on the basis of the real structures of the exploitative system. At this level, we shall observe that boxing is an economic enterprise, and that its entrepreneurs recruit its workers among the exploited only to subject them to another kind of exploitation. Most boxers, in fact, are of working-class origin, though

---

11. See note 97 on p.334 below; also *L'Idiot de la famille*, vol.3, Paris 1972, p.434, n.2.

sometimes they are very poor petty bourgeois and in rare cases peasants. These young men, formed by the violence to which they have been subjected, are well fitted to subject others to violence. What they will incarnate in their fights is the same violence* that the ruling class exerts against the labouring classes. We thus see that the fundamental violence is singularized: it appears, in its historical form, as *the violence of our society*. But it must be added that this violence, when it is reassumed *in common* by revolutionary parties and trade unions, is entirely absorbed in social praxis and becomes the *common* source of class actions. This means that individual violence is exerted without manifesting itself through the actions of the group: the individual – outside common praxis – is as if relieved of all *personal* rage. He has become violent at the level of organized communities, as a *common individual*. By socializing his anger and returning it to him as a deposit for which he is answerable to his class, the workers' organizations release him and allow him, moreover, to choose – as a practical free organism – all forms of positive reciprocity *vis-à-vis* his setting. The future boxer is *already selected* by the material circumstances of his own life: if he agrees to become a pro, it is because he wants to struggle free from his class; and the reason why he wants to struggle free from his class is that his family situation, the events of his childhood, have not allowed him to integrate himself into it. On the other hand, however, since birth he has suffered the violence of oppression and exploitation, which has been interiorized in him as in his comrades. But his personal history, by isolating him from other workers, alienates him from this violence, whose basic character – so long as the combat group has not been formed – is that one can never define it either as wholly passive and suffered or as wholly active. This stifling violence, which crushes the individual and at every instant risks exploding in uncontrolled brutalities, becomes at once the consequence and the source of his non-integration: he turns it back against his own people. In the same way, his fury is directed at once against the rich who exploit him and against the workers who claim to provide him with the model of what he must be – and in whom, precisely, he hates the image of what he will be. This violence, for want of being socialized, becomes self-aware and posits itself for itself: more or less vaguely, it sets its own norms. Of course,

---

* No doubt most of the time it is one poor man hitting another poor man: one of the exploited hitting another of the exploited. But these expressions of violence are precisely most common in the practical ensemble as a whole. Thus Fanon points out that the colonized man – when he has not reached the revolutionary stage – hits the colonized man. Induced violence, which in him is violence against man (because he has been made sub-human), finds an outlet only by attacking his *fellow* (i.e. his brother).

there is the possibility of some kind of fascism in this passionate morality of strength and defiance. It is at this level that common ground can actually be found between paramilitary organizations of the Right and the isolated victims of bourgeois oppression. In the case of a particular isolated individual, the violence with which the oppressive order has imbued every oppressed individual may be siphoned off by the oppressors and turned via him against his class of origin. Where there is no such enrolment, isolated explosions of violence (scuffles, brawls, perhaps criminal misdemeanours) still represent a transcending of the original situation (membership of the oppressed and exploited class; non-integration into this class) and, as it were, an obscure desire forcibly to struggle free from the class whence he sprang. When, in the boxing-halls he frequents, the instructors pick him out for his *aggressiveness*, they will really only be recognizing as a necessary virtue of boxing what is basically the *individual* violence of a desire to escape from his condition. It goes without saying that such aggression is effective in the ring only if the individual possesses exceptional physical skills. But it would be wrong to think in terms of a chance conjunction: had he been weak, the lad would have found other outlets for his violence. More sly and adaptable but more resentful, perhaps, he would have pursued the same ends by roundabout means. Furthermore, part of the strength, agility and speed required by the 'noble sport' have to be developed gradually by training and the first bouts. In this sense, boxing produces its man.

This *contractual moment* – one party's considered project of making his violence into a commodity in order to leave his class; the other's project of purchasing that violence and making it into the source of his profits, *as if it were the labour-power of a worker* – is the decisive instant of incarnation. By inventing the idea of having himself treated as a commodity, in order to transcend the status of his class all of whose members are commodities – by alienating his violence, selling it, in order to preserve it and henceforth be defined socially by it alone – the young man reinvents boxing, as the transcendence towards the universal that will preserve his particularities and as the chosen transposition of his original alienation. But it is precisely *with his transcended particularities* that the fans and organizers will adopt him. Boxing is not a clash of faceless strengths, it is men who fight one another, i.e. concrete individuals divided by their interests but *different* in their reality – by virtue of their physiques, their characters and their pasts. In other words, if boxing does not pit mass-produced robots against one another and 'the best man' has to win in this human duel, the sport – via the mediation of the organizers and participants – *requires* it to be a man who triumphs over another man by virtue of his human qualities, i.e. by virtue of his intrinsic particularities and the use he can make of them. Not just – if it is a question of physique – through his qualities (size, reach, musculature, etc.), but through the use he can make of these *and of his weaknesses*. Not just through learned technique and 'natural' skill, but through an ensemble of tactics (aggressiveness and caution, courage and tenacity, etc.) which derive from the 'psychosomatic' particularities – the individual history – of the winner. Both from his childhood and adolescence and, at the same time, from his career as a boxer. In the tactic of a rather ponderous Scandinavian boxer – forever dropping his guard, with the aim of inducing his opponent to leave himself open as he throws a punch and then getting in a stunning jab – a whole past is reflected. The idea is to 'go for a big punch', at the risk of taking rather than giving one. This presupposes that the boxer has considerable physical resilience and confidence that, therefore, the other's punches will barely shake him. Also, of course, inexhaustible courage and the strength of an ox – though he is not very mobile or dexterous, but rather slow in his movements and manoeuvres. At the same time, his plan of attack is quite specific: to make himself a victim in order to win more easily. There is a certain passivity at the heart of this practice, which seems to come from a misery endured, a long patience accompanied by a passive – but thereby all the stronger – rage. This tactic effectively contains within it at once a terrible past, the harsh travail of men, and the best technical use of the fighter's psychosomatic ensemble viewed as an instrument of destruction. This use is partly devised by the boxer, partly encouraged by his manager. Produced by circumstances, it produces its man. The very features of the boxer, what is most individual about him, are disfigured by such a style of boxing. Taking punches in order to return them with interest, he has a broken nose, puffy eyebrows, cauliflower ears, etc.: in short, a mean look – involuntary mimicry – that scares the beginner but, to an experienced opponent or well-informed spectator, reveals from the outset his intentions and the narrow limits of his efficacy. What is more, his destiny is written there, his sad destiny as a boxer and a man. As a boxer, he will never climb to the higher rungs of the hierarchy; he crushes beginners, but is always beaten on points by clever fighters who, when he drops his guard, hit him with all their strength while taking care not to let themselves be hit. As a man, the quantity of blows received makes him exceptionally prone to detachment of the retina, shattered nerves, or madness. But boxing *needs* this ignorance, these imperfections, this dauntless courage, this fearsome efficacy that risks being transformed into inefficacy. It needs it because the fighter must be an individual, with the synthetic ensemble that his practice reveals and that, in every movement, unites somatic structures and history (the history resuming the somatic structures), positive and negative qualities, tactics, the past and the future disclosed as destiny.* In other words, there are no *contingencies* here; there cannot be any, since they are *required* as contingencies and transcended by a technique. Between these two middleweights, the difference of height, reach and musculature is considerable: one is tall, with an impressive arm extension but a *relatively* underdeveloped musculature; the other is of medium height, with a shorter reach than the former, but he is very muscular. From the start, we know that these bodily structures are transcended and preserved by tactics that they impose and that are continually reinvented. We know that the former relies on his speed and legwork, seeking to score points with his left while keeping as far away as possible from his opponent; and that the latter, his head tucked down between his shoulders, blocking punches with his gloves, walking rather than dancing, moves forward all the time, tries to get under his opponent's guard and work away at his body in the clinches. Everything is inscribed in advance on these bodies and these faces. For neither one of them is any other tactic possible, but each vicissitude of the bout requires the reinvention of all experience in a feint, a sidestep, a lightning blow, an accurate judgement of distances and risks. Moreover, this reinvention functions precisely as the synthetic actualization of each individual history – the bravery, coolheadedness, skill, etc., that will probably decide the final outcome – and is the very life of each fighter as a style of practice. At this level, the *contingent* differences between the opponents (one is fair, the other dark; one pleasant-looking, the other unattractive) – i.e. those that are not really relevant to the art of boxing – are themselves required because they directly *signify* the reality of the individuals as such. Actually, it is rarely possible to establish a dialectical relationship between such psychosomatic data and a boxer's characteristic style (in particular, the 'nice' looks of one or 'unattractive' looks of another often very accurately express transformations that have nothing to do with moral qualities: the former is nice-looking because his height and speed have sheltered him from blows and thus allowed him to keep his face unmarked, while the latter is unattractive because he bears traces on his face of the violence of others). But though it is true that this golden-haired champion does not owe his victory to the fact that he is

---

* The intelligent, quick boxer, by contrast, never initially appears limited by a destiny: his future is open, with various possibilities. And it is precisely the interest of boxing to pit that open future against a closed future. Nothing proves a priori that victory will go to the more skilful. Perhaps he is too frail – physically inferior to the other. It will then be enough for him to let himself be caught once in the trap of 'dropping his guard'; even if the first five rounds are his, he risks being destroyed by a single blow – by brute strength. The contrast between the risk of being destroyed by a single right-hander and that of losing the fight on points is precisely what makes a boxing match.

blond, it is his blondness and striking head that concretize his victory for the participants and those who will see his photograph in the papers tomorrow. These features, offering themselves up immediately to intuition, incarnate praxis – or individual and effective transcendence of an individuality – as atemporal *hexis*: present, that is to say, at every stage of temporalization. From this point of view, it is *also* the requirement of boxing that life should be incarnated in the face as condensed history and destiny, and that it should be transcended in practice by the expression (smile, look of intelligence, more or less feigned nastiness, etc.). For the time being, the face thus incarnates the ongoing temporalization, which it condenses – down to the very movement of 'negation towards ... ' – through its physiognomy and the latter's fleeting (hence, atemporal: the face in the photo becomes a *frequentative*) changes.

At this level, we have thus encountered the necessity of contingency and the dialectical intelligibility of chance circumstances. Far from having to be eliminated as accidents of no consequence or meaning, produced by the encounter of independent series, they are required by boxing itself in so far as they will be enveloped, unified and transcended by a human practice that they singularize and that, as a praxis and like every praxis, is in itself the far side of every singularity. Every manoeuvre is a rigorous determination of this body as a function of this history, and so on. But, at the same time, it is *one* skilful feint, *one* skilful sidestep, one skilful *piece of* boxing. Incarnation is precisely that: the concrete universal constantly producing itself as the animation and temporalization of individual contingency. Hence, *one* punch, like *one* dance, is indissolubly singular and universal. In this sense, the fortuitous character of a bout holds for all the fortuities of all bouts: it is a necessary structure of conflict. But the necessity of this structure is produced and grasped by the participants in the very individuality of the bout and as its character of an absolute event. In this singularity, all boxing and all violence are singularized and the lived singular reveals their singularity.

If, in fact, we now return to the contractual moment which makes a young worker into a trainee boxer, we shall soon discover that *boxing* – as a quasi-institutional ensemble of international organizations and as a unity of events (matches) governing one another – is itself a singularity. Or, if you like, the moment of the abstract universal, an often indispensable mediation in the development of an investigation or concrete study, must dissolve in the final movement of totalization. At the moment of conceptualization, in fact, for want of possessing the necessary knowledge, we stumble over *possibles* – i.e. *here* over an indetermination of learning – and are compelled to grasp the reality under study as a particularization of possibles. This is the standpoint imposed upon us by the narrow limits of our knowledge, when we attempt to construct a theory of practical multiplicities. Perpetually encountering unverifiable possibles obliges us to conceptualize the dialectical investigation. A little further on, we shall see the dialectic dissolve this conceptual formalism. At the point we have reached, what counts provisionally is to observe – when the knowledge concerning a real process is sufficient – that from the totalizing standpoint the possible is a structure of the real. This relativity of the possible to Being – which we shall study in itself somewhat further on[12] – makes the abstract universal into a secondary structure of concrete totalization. Even when the positivist historian studies an individual or a singular grouping, he conceives them both as exemplifications of *possible man*, i.e. of the concept (individual man, man in society). Now History as a dialectical movement (whether it is a question of praxis or of comprehension) knows nothing other than *the human adventure*. For History, there have been (and could be) no men other than those who have existed and defined themselves by the possibles they engendered. Possibles, in fact, are practical determinations of the social field. They are defined as objective margins of choice and depend on the singular totality in the course of totalization as well as on each historical agent. Thus the enormous singularity that is temporalized by each of us as the history of humanity can never be anything other than an incarnation deciding concretely between the possibilities it engenders within it. It may be that other worlds exist, but insuperable distances separate them from ours for ever; at all events, today we are totally ignorant about the practical organisms inhabiting them. From this point of view, whether we are dealing with an eternal pluralism – i.e. an eternal impossibility of totalizing – or simply with a present limitation of our praxis and its science, *our* adventure still appears as a particular case. *In the human adventure*, however, the particular case does not exist as such, and all reality internal to that adventure must be conceived *with its possibles* as a plenary incarnation of the ongoing totalization.

The outstanding success of a few champions should not hide from us the fact that, in a certain sense, the great majority of boxers are in a situation hardly superior to that of workers and often more precarious. Moreover, their years are numbered. They have ten or twelve years to succeed and then, if they have not 'made their name', caught by the 'age limit' they relapse back into the proletariat or vegetate on the margins of bourgeois society. They are not, of course, producers of consumer goods, of commodities. But they are exploited: in the form of destructive

---

12. Sartre was not to make an exhaustive study of possibles in the present work. However, see p.412 in the Appendix below, and footnote 97 on p.334. Also *L'Idiot de la famille*, vol. 2, Paris 1971, p.1815, n.2.

violence, it is indeed their labour-power that they are selling. The number of professionals multiplies with the development of bourgeois society and the increased share of income it can devote to entertainment. The immense and rapid development of sports in the twentieth century is directly conditioned by the second industrial revolution, whatever new values may also be expressed in them. The growth in productive strength – particularly notable with the appearance of semi-automatic machines – creates jobs for fragmented or pauperized elements of the working class: they graduate to being *servants* of the bourgeois class. Such will be the boxer's job. And if this labourer [*travailleur*] is not a worker [*ouvrier*], it does not follow that he should be treated as an *unproductive* labourer, since he produces capital. For the boxer gives more labour than he receives in the form of wages. He is taken on by an entrepreneur, who gets him to box in order to 'make money'. By exchanging his labour-power for capital, he reproduces money as capital. Promoters, hall-owners, etc., live off the boxers. Training is a kind of visible caricature of employment, for they are treated like some machine to be constructed and then maintained; and everything is calculated as a function of this aim: to give – and retain for – them the greatest destructive efficacy, taking account of their possibilities. To get at the truth of their condition from both sides at once, moreover, you could also speak of licking a fighting animal into shape: training is a human equivalent of stock-rearing. It results in alienation of the individual from his own body, conceived as pure destructive power: all his activities, all his needs, are subordinated to the instrumentalization of his physical person. What may be deceptive, here, is the fact that the requirements of fighting imply that the boxer should be kept 'in shape': in other words, should be got into top psychosomatic condition. If it is true, however, that his body may be the envy of every amateur sportsman from the bourgeoisie – not to speak, of course, of workers stunted by their work – it is also true that the goal of this treatment is fighting and, if bouts are too frequent, they will have the effect of destroying him physically within a few years. It would doubtless be possible to avoid such destruction by a calculated reduction in the number of annual bouts for each boxer, depending upon his particular characteristics. That is doubtless the way things are done in the people's democracies. It is also what happens in the West with many amateurs – workers or petty bourgeois who do not wish to 'turn pro'. But when it is a matter of professional fights, two factors combine to accentuate overwork and overexploitation. On the one hand, owners of 'stables', promoters of every kind, etc., have their sights on the surplus-value produced. They determine the number of bouts per season and per boxer on the basis of demand – in other words, of the fighter's popularity and the drawing-power of his name – and also on the basis of possible matches (i.e. combinations that will excite curiosity). On the other hand, however, the boxers themselves, when they have not achieved any real renown, are their own victims. Only too often the promoter will over-exploit a 'hope' and tend to neglect the old lags who are no longer a draw. So it is necessary to thrust yourself forward constantly – seeking one new fight after another and climbing back into the ring just a week after taking terrible 'punishment', though still not properly recovered from the blows received – or else starve and eventually quit the game.

The alienation is total. The growing lad used to locate his value and his freedom in his individual violence. He refused to believe that he was accountable for it to his comrades or to his class. In the name of that ethic of strength and domination – and in order to escape the common fate of the oppressed, in whom he discovers and detests his own wretchedness as a victim – he sells his strength, his agility and his courage. He sells even that rage which makes him so combative. At once, *it is no longer his*, it is taken from him. The assertion of his sovereignty becomes his livelihood. Obedience replaces anarchistic pride, lordly will shrivels before harsh discipline. The exercise of violence – directed, channelled, orientated in the direction of maximum profit for the promoters – is no longer the easy demonstration of a brutal superiority. It is instead a painful and dangerous labour that is faced in anguish and often pits the boxer against a better-armed opponent: he learns the limits of his power through the sufferings inflicted on him. This conjuring away of violence is a constitutive element of the young man's new personality. That aggression he used to possess is *really* removed from him, confiscated and returned to him on the day of the bout. Except in the ring, most boxers are courteous and gentle. Violence, in becoming their daily bread, is separated from their living reality: it is *serious*, like an instrument that must not be over-used, and at once loses its character of a wild and liberating passion.

Yet he regains it when he climbs into the ring (since those who do not regain it are eliminated in advance). But now it is public and socialized; its meaning has entirely altered. As long as he remained in the working class, it was a lonely individual's blind, explosive reaction to exploitation. Once he is a servant of the bourgeois class, his fight in the ring incarnates his fight for life in the bourgeois system of competition. To tell the truth, it is not a matter of free competition, as described by the economists of the last century. There are trusts and semi-monopolies – decisions are taken at the level of the promoters. It should also be added that the rules of the game are more or less bent by such scheming. But such features are common to all sectors of the bourgeois economy; and if competition does not relate directly to the customers, at least every boxer relies on the favour of the crowd to influence his employers. The employers, for their part, are directly in contact with the customers: it is up to them to know and cater for their tastes; but via the customers' mediation, the living commodities hope to assert themselves *vis-à-vis* the employer.

We grasp the order of metamorphoses: particular circumstances have determined that an individual, as a loner, has felt the common violence suffered by his class and exteriorized it into universal and anarchistic aggression. Precisely by doing so he became – if his physical abilities allowed it – the unintegrated element who could produce individual violence: the very one boxing picks out and pits against other loners. His violence being, in and of itself, an ever fruitless spasm to struggle free from poverty and his milieu, he accepts that it should precisely be the instrument for his promotion into the other class. In fact, the promotion does not really take place (except for a tiny minority). He sells his violence, remains one of the exploited, and on the boxing market finds the same competitive antagonisms that pit workers against one another on the labour market. But with workers, years of trade-union experience and social conflict have at least ended by reducing these antagonisms and developing a class solidarity. The boxer, by contrast, a lone exploited individual who from childhood has been unable to solidarize with the workers, experiences all the harshness of competition. What is more, he produces this competition, undergoes it, and lives it, in and through each of his fights. Wishing to knock out his opponent, it is not just against the latter that he struggles but also against his more favoured stable companions – and more generally against all the boxers in his weight division – to prove he is worth more than them, by waging a more brilliant battle against the foe. Thus the violence which, in every fight, takes hold of him and hurls him against an enemy brother, was in its origin the same violence that moves from the oppressors to the oppressed, then back from the latter to the former, and makes it possible to call the opposition between classes a struggle. For this very reason, it already incarnated – in the specific form this takes in industrial societies – the interiorization of scarcity. By purchasing it, however, the bourgeoisie recuperates and transforms it. Alienated, the aggression of the oppressed individual is changed into a competitive antagonism: commodities clash as if they were men and each seeks to force up its price by destroying or forcing down the other. This inversion of the struggle should be noted: competition, in a period of liberalism, results in lower prices. Fights, in one sense, do not escape the general rule. If there are too many of them – if there are too many boxers – boxing risks a momentary depreciation. But in this incarnation of economic competition within a closed field, the one who best asserts himself will sell himself more dearly in the next fight. For, in the case of boxers, worked matter does not serve as a mediation between men: it is men themselves who are worked matter *as men.*

Impossibility of a Conceptualization of the Fight

These few observations allow us to understand the extent to which, and why, boxing is a singular reality, a totalizable process but one impossible to conceptualize. For, on the one hand, it brings out the virtues that moments of violence reveal: courage, coolheadedness, tenacity, etc. On the other hand, however, these virtues, very real in the ring, are objectively commodities: the spectator pays to enjoy human courage. People are taking part in the public alienation of free actions. In this ambiguous event – the bout – the participants thus produce and grasp the reality of their own alienation: in other words, of the whole man down to the root of his freedom and the reality of emancipatory violence. But the latter sets itself against alienation only to alienate itself still further. Shut in on itself, the event constitutes for the spectators at once a participation in fundamental violence and a localization – a distantiation – of that violence which, by being channelled and contained in an individual contest, manifests itself as an external event, finite and dated. The event that is temporalized encapsulates for everyone the individual embodiment of each of the adversaries: the singularization within him of the violence of the oppressed and, thereby, his alienation. But this temporalization *incarnates* an ever true aspect of oppressive and exploitative systems: alienation of the violence of the oppressed. So long as the order of the oppressors is kept operative by the police, the army and economic circumstances acting in their favour, the violence of the oppressed – produced within them by *repression* [*compression*] but reduced to impotence by that repression itself – knows no outlets, no decompressive explosions, other than individual and mostly hidden acts, ranging from sabotage to theft, which self-destruct if they are discovered. In effect, the violence within them is manifested and discredited simultaneously and the workers, imbued despite themselves with bourgeois ideology and values, judge these fruitless revolts with the same severity as do the bourgeois. Of course, however, the epoch which engenders boxing is punctuated by gigantic struggles and the proletariats have become aware of their class violence. But it still remains true that at moments of downturn – when the old order is re-established against them; when they are locked into the 'price–wage' circle of hell and their action on wages, even when victorious, is at once annulled by the action of the bourgeois upon prices – violence grasps itself as impotence, which is simultaneously true and false: true, if we limit ourselves to registering a quite provisional moment of the struggle; false, if we mean thereby to unmask what has often been termed 'the impotence of the common people'. And, of course, bourgeois propaganda will seek to show the latter in the former. In so far as it succeeds and, in moments of discouragement immediately after a lost battle, the workers allow themselves to be mystified, violence – suddenly judged *from the viewpoint of order* and 'democratic' laws – is de-realized by becoming disqualified. Its reality, if you prefer, is its *local* power of destruction; its *de*-reality is its global inability to make itself an instrument of liberation. This disqualifying de-realization is merely a mystification, but it has *all the social reality* of a mystification. Well, it is that very mystification that is incarnated by the fight: violence that dominates two individuals, pits them against one another, and ends by becoming – for and through the participants – the real, riven being that seeks to rediscover its unity by amputation and liquidation of one of its halves. The resulting phenomenon is that this particular conflict will find its solution *in boxing*, but that *boxing is not a solution* (precisely in so far, for example, as the winner will have demonstrated, at the same time as his superiority to the other, his real inability to rise to the higher rungs). The violence of the participants is simultaneously unleashed and de-realized. It becomes a show, without ceasing to be lived in its explosive power. The event produced by all is quite real: real the punches, the wounds, the injuries perhaps, which will bring these boxers to a certain physical diminution, even to a certain infirmity; real are the tactics of each, real the sufferings endured, real the courage and doggedness of each. But the ensemble of prohibitions which reduce the contest to a convention between representatives of the ruling class, by incarnating total violence in this deliberately mutilated violence, refer this absolute, useless adventure of two men back to all the participants as the incarnation of their radical powerlessness – i.e. the alienation of their sole emancipatory power. Of course, this aspect of boxing is not concerted; it is by no means a matter of some kind of propaganda. But when propaganda exists elsewhere, we shall see that everything incarnates it.

It is still true that the contest excites the participants. But it refers popular audiences back to the reality workers' associations have already transcended: the antagonism pitting sellers of labour-power against one another on the competitive market. This competition is merely a projection (on the labour market) or, if you prefer, only an incarnation of the competitive regime capitalism itself engenders as the condition of its development. Inasmuch as their interests pit them against one another, the workers are in a very real sense men of capitalism and its products. They constitute themselves as 'the sentence it pronounces upon itself' only when they produce against it apparatuses of struggle and organs of union. Well, it is not enough to describe what the popular audience watches – that competition between two peers – as the image or symbol of competition within the same class, since it is simultaneously a very real episode of this (the boxers, as we have seen, relying on the bout to improve their situation) and its present incarnation. Through this contest, the 'world' of boxing is in fact totalized as a multiplicity of contests which, in each weight, pit each against all and each against the other, and can find a solution only in violence. These boxers, all rivals, all possible adversaries, all produced by boxing in such a way that they find their own life only in the destruction of the other's,* reproduce in themselves and by their actions the social structure of the system that has produced them. Through them, competition – as a fundamental relation between the individuals of the dominant class; as a relation imposed on the individuals of the dominated class, and rejected by their will to unite against exploitation – is produced in all its nakedness as the concrete event that a popular audience approves and supports (an audience, in other words, most of whose members condemn the competitive system and combat it by union). And it is boxing's ambiguity to be, in a certain sense, made by its public. When a championship is involved, the bourgeois public stirs itself. Without any unease or contradiction, it finds in the contest unfolding before its eyes the daily reality of its struggles and its ethical values – individualism, etc. For it is *in this form* that fundamental violence has interiorized itself and re-exteriorizes itself *within the bourgeois class* (without, of course, taking account of the fundamental fact of oppression and exploitation as relations of this class to the other classes). For the popular audience, the manifestation of naked violence constitutes itself contradictorily as a determination of the common violence of the oppressed and – through a *de-realization* – as a transfer of all back to the bourgeois field of the competitive market. The violence changes its nature as it is realized, and it changes them in their present reality. Accepted as a class revolt, it *wins acceptance* as an inter-individual conflict and, very precisely, as a competition between men-as-commodities *stimulated by the exploiting class*, which even provides it with its rules.

Thus the bout is a singular process, based on the singularities of the boxers, which takes place as a dialectical singularization of fundamental violence, through the simultaneous, contradictory incarnation of the different forms that present-day society imposes on the latter. This

---

* To be sure, boxing does not kill *on the spot*: but it damages. Above all, moreover, the winners help to *eliminate* the loser. His successive defeats will eventually refuse him any means of living in and through boxing. He will be expelled from his profession and have to die or find another.

incarnation is not simply a production of dialectically opposed specifications. Inasmuch as it is realized by the ensemble of participants, it is defined at the same time by its ambiguity. By this, I do not mean just that the actual participants give themselves the determinations of the collective or group and of their reciprocal antagonism, through temporalization of the produced event; but also, and above all, that their membership of different classes and milieux produces the same event with a multiplicity of incompatible meanings, but without these badly articulated incompatibilities achieving the definite form of contradictions. The synthetic unity of the event can thus under no circumstances be expressed by a concept. On the contrary, we see the necessity of its singularization, and that it bears within itself the foundation of its 'accidental' singularities. But this rapid description allows us to understand better the relationship between incarnation and the enveloping totalization. All our violences are there, supported by the fundamental violence from which they derive; everything takes place in the insupportable tension of scarcity. But the different projects that combine to produce the event (from those of the organizers to those of the audience, passing by way of the alienation of the boxers and their freedom) cross mediating fields which are themselves concrete universals and totalize them as they singularize them. This means that they preserve them as the singular quality of the movement that transcends them. Everything is given in the least punch: from the history of the one who delivers it to the material and collective circumstances of that history; from the general indictment of capitalist society to the singular determination of that indictment by the boxing promoters; from the fundamental violence of the oppressed to the singular and alienating objectification of that violence in and through each of the participants. And if everything were not present and transcended, the singular invention – the unique and concrete reality that is *this* punch, delivered on *this* day, in *this* hall, in front of *this* audience – would not even be possible. The incarnation as such is at once unrealizable, other than as a totalization of everything, and irreducible to the pure abstract unity of what it totalizes. Its concrete reality is, in fact, to be an orientated totalization. And this orientation is precisely the other aspect of its singularity. The project is singular by virtue of the quality that the transcended mediations give it; but these mediations are singularizing because it has singularized them by its very orientation. And since it is the conflict that we are for the moment studying, as an event temporalizing itself towards its suppression, we see that it is a process by overdetermination: in other words, by a multiplicity of antagonistic actions. For this reason, as a process, it appears as the product – overflowing any human intention – of all singular intentions: in other words, of all the contradictory singularizations of the totality.

Thus one can and should say, at the end of this critical investigation, that each struggle is a singularization of all *the circumstances* of the social ensemble in movement; and that, by this singularization, it incarnates the totalization-of-envelopment constituted by the historical process. I have said, and repeat, that we have not yet proved that this enveloping totalization exists. But for the moment it is enough to make the observation that every singular totalization is enveloping as a totalization as well as enveloped as a singularity. The fact is that, just as *this* fight envelops all fights – particularly those that are taking place everywhere on this same Saturday evening – so too each fight elsewhere envelops *this* fight in its objective reality. From this point of view, two dialectical procedures are possible on the basis of an identical social reality. On the one hand, a procedure of decompressive expansion which starts off from the object to arrive at *everything*, following the order of significations (for example, the banknote *refers* to all the economic, social and historical significations we know); in this case, thought may be termed *detotalizing* and the event loses out to the signified ensembles. On the other hand, a procedure of totalizing compression which, by contrast, grasps the centripetal movement of all the significations attracted and condensed in the event or in the object. If some Micromegas were to visit a boxing-hall, it would in effect be necessary to explain everything by relations transcending the external facts, objects and significations. The mere sight of individuals queuing in front of the ticket office and exchanging banknotes for entrance tickets could not be understood, without reference being made to the prevailing monetary system and ultimately to the whole present-day economy. In the same way, the powerful bulbs lighting the ring must necessarily refer our interplanetary traveller to the contemporary state of our industrial technology and physical sciences, etc., etc. But all these elementary and fundamental structures are directly gathered into the event itself, which is exchange – production of surplus-value – for the entrepreneurs and, at the same time, utilizes and thereby even unifies in its singularizing movement certain technical resources, grounded upon scientific knowledge. These determinations themselves, interiorized, suddenly help to singularize it; and grasping how they exercise a specific action within the incarnation is precisely a new dialectical procedure. The first procedure, which is unfortunately that to which Marxist 'analyses' too often limit themselves, effectively dissolves the event into the ensemble of mediations as *non-singularized* concrete totalities; the second – which alone is capable of grasping the dialectical intelligibility of an event – strives to discover within the event itself the interactions constituting the singularity of the process on the basis of singularization of the circumstances. It is actually *through the project* which condenses them that the mediating fields receive a new status of efficacy. These last remarks allow us to note another difference between the concept and the incarnation: in the former, the 'inner' determinations are united by bonds of exteriority; in the latter, at all levels, all the determinations are concrete and it is a bond of immanence that unites them.

Conclusion

Our first inquiry has allowed us to establish a minimal intelligibility. Even if struggle, as such, had to be revealed as refractory to any totalization, it remains true that every struggle – as a rift – is the incarnation of all others: in other words, at once of the fundamental scarcity and of the specific forms that contemporary society gives to this scarcity. However, if these conclusions allow one to oppose positivistic pluralism, and even if one can *understand* a particular struggle as an incarnation and singularization of the class struggle as it unfolds in contemporary societies, it still remains the case – so long as we do not push our investigation further – that the living rift constituted by conflict seems the insurmountable limit of the totalizing effort. In particular, what could be the historical unity of a society chopped up by class struggles? And the term 'chop up' may even seem inappropriate: for it refers to a unity anterior to the mutilations. But even if Engels was right, even if this unity did exist in the golden age of unrecorded History, it disintegrated so long ago that we should waste our time if we sought to relate the divisions of all History to that lost paradise of intelligible unities. It is within the actual struggle that synchronic totalization must be able to operate, if History is to be dialectically intelligible. And it is in the thick of the battle that we must now seek it.

Intelligibility of the Conflict within a Pledged Group

Indetermination and Contradiction

HOWEVER, we shall attempt to impose a certain order upon this new investigation: mediations are needed. It would be impossible to determine immediately whether class conflicts, in a given society, constitute or not the realization of a contradiction. For such a contradiction implies the existence of a totalization, of which each class would represent a specification excluding the other. Moreover, we do not yet have the knowledge and instruments available that would allow us to unmask this totalization: i.e., for example, to decide whether *national unities* exist; or whether the nation is just a collective, and the individuals are bound to it only via the mediation of worked matter (by the soil and subsoil, in so far as they are exploited; by the ensemble of geophysical and geopolitical conditions; by the heritage of previous generations, etc.). Before tackling the problem, it seems prudent to examine another, to which the solution seems easier. In the case of large historical ensembles, we do not know if the synthetic unity of the practical multiplicities exists. On the other hand, in innumerable particular cases it is possible for us to study a conflict within a real totalization. Frequently, in fact, violent antagonisms manifest themselves within organized or institutional groups and give rise to struggles whose intensity increases *pari passu* with the integration of the communities in which they take place. So our first question will be: should the sub-groups in struggle within an organized group be considered as simple agents of destruction, which sap the common unity and will eventually rend it apart; or as men taking responsibility for – and realizing, through their conflict – a contradiction of the group, as a dialectical moment of its temporalization?

The answer is clear. Of course, for a situated dialectic, contradiction is not an absolute which a priori produces its men. But conversely, men within the group – whether they are aware of it or not – can enter into struggle only by actualizing a contradiction in the process of development. Let us first note, in fact, that every internal conflict takes place between pledged individuals and against the synthetic background of fraternity-terror. Furthermore, each of the hostile sub-groups opposes the other *in the name of that unity* which it claims alone to represent. Each presents the other as a priori criminal because it breaks the common unity by its claims. At the same time, however, each opposes the other through the totalizing praxis of the organized group, in the name of this praxis and on the occasion of it: each sub-group claims to give a different orientation to the common action. In this sense, the conflict can never spring from differences (individual or collective) prior or external to the constitution of the group. At the outset, the milieu from which the individuals of any sub-group emanate matters little. The characteristic features and history of each matter little. The conflict pits against one another *common individuals* – transformed by the pledge, provided with offices and powers – who exist as such only through the group and for the praxis that it has assigned itself; and who are defined as *the same* on all points *except* in relation to the precise object of the dispute. Of course, all prior differences (origin, history, etc.) will immediately be *reactualized* by the conflict. What is more, differences of condition (origin, history, education, former milieu, etc.) often cause one individual or sub-group to understand better than others a particular aspect of the internal contradictions. That does not always happen: in the Convention, Montagnards and Girondins alike belonged mostly to the intellectual petty bourgeoisie. But when such factors do come into play, their action at the outset is merely of a detecting nature. For they are not *recognized* by the group, they are merely tolerated. In the integrated group, each person lives in cohabitation with his own memories, with his character: his official existence is conferred upon him by action through an office. In a party in movement, the opposition between sectarians and opportunists can *reveal* differences of character, it can base itself upon – and be reinforced by – these, but it cannot actually spring from them. The classification is carried out through the history *of common individuals within the group*: it is through their functions that they discover the need for relaxation or a tough line. Or, if you like, their functions require of them a certain activity, through which they see the objectives of the whole group. The vicissitudes of this activity lead them to call for an orientation of the common praxis that will allow them to perform their office with success. At the same time, the common objectives are refracted through the particular objectives that are assigned to them. But all this is still just a static determination: there are 'hardliners' and 'moderates', that is all. For this difference between common individuals to become an antagonism, it is precisely necessary for the circumstances of the common struggle to harden their attitudes, by demanding new and urgent options. In this sense, it can be said that the determinations of the common individual are a product of his group work; and that the practical evolution of the group obliges the common individual to make his option on the basis of the determinations the group has inscribed within him. And, of course, the common individual is only the inert limit of freedom: it is the practical organism that makes the option. But it makes it precisely on the basis of the determinations introduced into its sworn inertia.

Thus conflicts spring up on the basis of free options: in other words, of singular events – anxieties, outbursts of anger, quarrels and reconciliations. But such forms of behaviour are stimulated by the evolution of common practice, inasmuch as this evolution demands a perpetual re-working of internal organization and constantly provokes dissatisfactions, maladjustments, disqualifications and reclassifications. The contradiction is revealed and sustained by conflict, but the conflict could not fail to spring from the transformations of praxis. It is the relationship of forces between the total group and the external groups, the relations between the group and its practical field, that decide. Through its directing organs, the common praxis slows down or accelerates, regresses or is radicalized. It is necessary to initiate first one turn, then another, and each time the changes require a reclassification of the personnel. Common individuals are the products of an action furnished with a certain rhythm, which sought to attain certain objectives by specific means. If the rhythm, means and ends (at least, the proximate ends) are transformed, it is necessary for the men to break down themselves and liquidate their prior determinations; or for them to be liquidated (that may simply mean they will lose their position and rejoin the mass of militants); or for them to oppose, in the name of the prior determinations of praxis, those who represent its new orientation. And, of course, it is not just a question of a conflict between past and present, but everything is involved, necessarily. And it is not necessarily the 'men of the past' who harm the evolution and success of praxis, or the 'new men' who express the real exigencies. In fact, studying the real conflicts within a group shows the extreme complexity of the options and their ambiguity: how the more 'conservative' is, despite everything, innovatory and the more 'novel' imbued with routinism and outworn traditions. Precisely for that reason – and provided one does not imagine contradictions as sharp and precise as the Hegelian thesis and antithesis – it is clear that conflict is the sole real form a contradiction within a group-in-activity could take; and, conversely, that no conflict is even possible in an integrated community, if it is not the actualization by men of an objective contradiction.

But, it will be asked, in what latent form does this contradiction exist prior to its violent actualization?* We shall find the answer without difficulty, if only we consider a few very familiar examples. Here is a banal one: the dispute over competency. In an organized group, one organism wishes to deal with a matter while another claims jurisdiction over it. If the circumstance recurs often, the rivalry of the two sub-groups is transformed into open warfare. But why does it recur? Most of the time, we find at the origin of the dispute a real but relative indeter-mination of the respective competencies.

And where can this indetermination come from? No doubt it may have existed at the outset. But this is rarer than people think: men always do everything they can in a given situation. In fact, the development of common praxis has created this indetermination, by introducing un-foreseen changes into internal relations. For example, the two bodies clash because the progressive improvement of links, effected with quite other intentions, has eventually brought them into contact. At the outset, they actually had identical functions; but the difficulty of communication made both indispensable, since neither had the means to carry out its activity on the terrain on which the other was operating. In other cases, the evolution of the global situation is marked by the appearance of new events within the group. Inasmuch as they involve a certain originality, these events are relatively unforeseen: no particular organ is thus in charge of dealing with them. But inasmuch as they *also* involve old significations, several bodies – with *different* competencies this time – think they recognize matters here which come under their own juris-diction. Each organism, sensitive to certain aspects, wishes to take the matter over, whereas in reality none is qualified. The group will have to reorganize and create new offices, which will be defined on the basis of these new realities, or else it will proceed to a reconstitution of the old organisms. We shall return to this struggle, as such, and to its product.

In the meantime, these abstract examples suffice to show us the dialectic of contradiction. Clearly, it is not explicit before being assumed by praxis. For example, the basic form of the trouble in our chosen example is an indetermination. But if we look at it more closely, this indetermination (whether due to the multiplication of links or to a new and unforeseen situation) is an *objective reality*: objectively, for the situated observer or for the historian, there is an indeterminate – in other words, insufficiently determined – relationship between the offices and

---

* It goes without saying that contradictions develop and, before ending in conflict, represent the *inner tension* of the group: i.e. often (looking at things positively) a factor in its cohesion.

the event. And the indetermination does not move from the functions to the object – as would happen if competencies *at the outset* had not been sufficiently defined. It moves retroactively from object to functions, because it is the object as a new consequence of action that makes the functions obsolete and disqualifies them. But the object, as will already have been grasped, is the incarnation of praxis itself. Thus it is the whole action that calls into question its own attainments, i.e. the inner determinations with which it has endowed itself. This means, for example, that the historian, in order to bring the indetermination to light, will have only to compare the objective meaning of the event with the organizational or institutional definition of the functions. Yet this indetermination – although it is an objective feature of the group's internal relations, inasmuch as they are entirely under the sway of its action – remains, in this historical form, at the level of abstract significations. It has been realized *practically* only through the activities of sub-groups; it has been *brought to life* as hesitation; or, if you like, it has had practical reality only in and by its interiorization. In other words, although it might subsequently be elucidated as *structure*, it is concretely and at first manifested as behaviour. There is nothing surprising about this. Inasmuch as pledged inertia constitutes an ensemble of passive determinations characterizing the common individual in everyone, the relationship between the object and its determinations is objectively indefinite. We are in the domain of passive-being and syntheses of the inanimate. But inasmuch as this common individual must be sustained and continually re-created by the practical organism, this relationship of indetermination can be realized only in the form of a synthetic and living relationship, in the course of the functional praxis of individuals or sub-groups. And of course, to *realize* it is to transcend it, to make a *practice* out of what was a certain inertia, and to organize it in immanence as the structure of a project: hence, continually to *make it an internal relationship, in a relation of interiority with other interiorized relationships*. To transcend is not to liquidate a difficulty or resolve a problem, it is simply to constitute what has been transcended as a particular orientation of a praxis. In the example chosen, transcendence will consist in the fact that the sub-group, negating the indetermination and profiting from it, will seek to appropriate a certain series of matters, even though it is not sure they are within its competency. In this decision we must, of course, see a singularization of the common praxis: the sub-group, in the name of common interests, extends its competency to new events through the project of contributing as best it can to organized action. We do not yet grasp indetermination (to consider this alone) as a contradiction. Moreover, it would be enough for the other sub-group never to have been created, for this appropriation or amassing of functions, far from engendering disputes,

to be able to be seen as a positive initiative. Contradiction will not
appear even when the other sub-group takes the same initiative, but at
the precise moment when *the same matter* is claimed by each sub-group
against the other: i.e. inasmuch as the indetermination transcended by
both organisms becomes the very mediation which unites them in
antagonism. In other words, indetermination *is never* in itself a contradiction, for the simple reason that a contradiction exists only in so far as
its terms are determined. But when common praxis has created organs
(similar or different) which both claim the non-determined object, the
objective contradiction becomes the meaning of their conflict. And this
contradiction is nothing other than the impossibility, for two internal
structures of the group, to be temporalized together in this moment of the
global temporalization. However, it would be wrong to say that these
new objects reveal that impossibility. Actually, they determine objectively
and simultaneously the two [sub-]groups to realize it practically. And the
practical realization of an impossible coexistence precisely constitutes
the conflict. At this level, we can make some pertinent comments.

First of all, the origins of the conflict are free, contingent and anecdotal.
They are free because each sub-group has assumed and interiorized the
indetermination. It has made up its mind to it, without any doubt and
after deliberation. Without there even having been a ballot, the attitude
of those managing the office has won the votes of the majority of
collaborators, or vice versa. The sub-group's self-assertion is what is
termed – in an unfortunately too idealist manner – *esprit de corps*.
However, since each of the new events that are going to fuel the conflict
is in itself a singularizing incarnation of the total praxis and its consequences, the matter will always present itself in the form of contingent
facticity. It is a particular affair affecting individuals or communities and
– by virtue of this very fact – clear in its deep signification (indetermination), but complex and obscure as a singular event. For the actual
beginning of the conflict it initiates – in so far as, against the background
of fraternity-terror, each sub-group first wishes for a negotiated solution
– is *anecdotal*, because individual initiatives, quid pro quos and misunderstandings help to envenom a dispute people would like to stop. But
just as the singular event is the incarnation of that moment of praxis (of
the present relation of its means, objectives and movement to the evolution
of its practical field and enemy activities), so too the misunderstandings
and 'personality' clashes will disappear in a flash if they do not *in
themselves* have a function of totalizing incarnation: in other words, if
through them coexistence of the sub-groups does not reveal its impossibility. When some Girondins, well before the great struggles of the
Convention, reproached Robespierre for having invoked Providence at
the Club des Jacobins, this was just an anecdote, an incident quickly

shelved. But in fact this 'affair' very precisely incarnated the fundamental conflict between a de-Christianized bourgeoisie, which despised
the people and its 'superstitions', and a group of petty bourgeois whose
policy was above all to make the Revolution for the people and,
consequently, to show consideration for popular beliefs. The entire
religious policy of Robespierre, the entire future conflict that was to pit
the atheist Jacobins against the religious masses, *were* in this sally that
had no aftermath. They were there because *they were realized in it*: the
action itself proclaimed its future contradictions in a totalization that
liquidated itself because it was at once inevitable and premature.

Thus the conflict *makes* the contradiction. It is *men* who decide that
their coexistence is impossible; and they decide it *in singular circumstances*, which are sometimes accentuated by singular features. For as
long as the struggle lasts, it will always seem to other members of the
group, and even to opportunists in the sub-groups, that the very contingency of events and the qualified freedom of individuals express the
contingency of the conflict itself, so that it is always possible to put an
end to it. But, in reality, the illusion derives from the fact that decisions
are actually taken by free practical organisms, whether grouped or
isolated. These free acts of transcendence, however, are performed in so
far as each person is in the service of a non-transcendable pledged
inertia. And this very inertia, as material product of a free pledge, is
constituted as a destiny of impossible coexistence, inasmuch as freedom
itself places it in a relation of immanence with that other inertia constituted, for example, by the indetermination of powers. On the basis of
that, we grasp the dual character of the struggle: it freely realizes the
conflict but, to that very extent, it becomes a mediation between the two
contradictory terms of a non-transcendable inertia. Or, if you like, the
absolute necessity of that contradiction, as an objective, internal structure of the group, derives from a clash of inertias *constituted by the sub-
groups themselves in their free practical movement*. By virtue of this, the
common individual, through the action of the practical organism, receives
the new, common determinations that come to him from the group's
global action and its internal consequences. Projects are like fields of
force, whose practical tension connects and organizes inert data. And
these data, in the framework of temporalization, manifest themselves as
the unity of a new objective structure and as the irreversibility of praxis
– here, of the struggle. Or, if you like, this impossibility of turning back
is the expression of new circumstances, inasmuch as they constitute a
destiny through the non-transcendability of sworn inertia (as a practical
aspect of the common individual and as a formal rule of his future).

The Common Individual Realizes the
Practico-Inert as Pure Negative Praxis

These few observations necessarily take us back to counter-finalities and collectives as inner cancers of the group. For, if we follow closely the appearance of an internal conflict, we soon see that it is impossible for it to occur as an immediate result of the global praxis: mediation of the practico-inert is needed. Nevertheless, in an integrated group, at the tensest moment of its action, the practico-inert is not manifested as in a decompressed social ensemble without practical integration. In the latter, as we have seen, what occurs in front of everyone and through everyone is equivalence of the practical agent and the inert reactor, via the mediation of worked matter.[13] In the fully active group, however, counter-finalities are produced only inasmuch as they are recovered and revived by a practice. Or, if you like, they are grasped not as transformation and alienation of an action in the milieu of mediating exteriority, but as obscure and wholly immanent limits that freedom itself seems to give itself. It is through questions like: 'Why didn't they go further?', 'Why didn't they take it upon themselves to give that order?', 'Why didn't they *understand* such and such requirements of the situation?' and other similar inquiries that an objective limit of transcendence can be glimpsed. And this limit, which at first appears negatively although it is necessarily tied to the sworn limit, seems *suffered by freedom* precisely in so far as it is *produced by it*. In the framework of destiny, transcendence gives the transcended its own non-transcendability.

If we return to one of the chosen examples – that of two [sub-]groups in conflict as a result of the relative indetermination of their respective functions – we shall observe, in effect, that counter-finality is manifested only as *reverse* of the positive results. Let us consider, for example, the multiplication of links. It may be a matter of a technical improvement in the means of communication (whether a restricted, 'private' group grows wealthy and disposes of cars, planes and telecommunications; or whether a 'public' group builds roads and clears routes through the effective work of its members, etc.). In other cases, it will be a matter of rationalization of 'internal relations', 'contacts', etc. (The action of a strongly integrated party – one that has been constituted through the most rigorous centralization, which often implies that the base elements communicate only via the summit – can, by means of the transformations it imposes on itself to attain its goal, impose either provisionally or definitively a certain decentralization and, as a consequence of this, a

---

13. *Critique*, vol.1, pp.165 ff.

multiplication of direct contacts with the base. It may equally well happen that a more or less clandestine group undertakes to make an inventory of its sub-groups or its members, and that it sets up linking bodies to co-ordinate their activities.) Other conjunctures are possible too. A group may 'take advantage' of public works that improve the transport system, in order to serve the State, a particular class, society, etc. At any rate, however it may present itself, we are dealing with a definite type of praxis-process. It is praxis, moreover, that is first revealed in it. What appears objectively, in fact, is a common action of internal reorganization, i.e. a mixing of men accompanied by a more or less considerable labour that these men, or others linked to them, carry out upon inanimate objects. Moreover, this action is inseparable – for those in the groups who are its beneficiaries (as common individuals) – from its practical results. Through the bodies that are constituted and the contacts that are multiplied, the sub-groups – in one comprehensive view – grasp their leaders' concern and the progress of their integration (they are better informed: for example, the questions they ask and the reports they send up to the central organisms no longer remain unanswered, or else the answers arrive more swiftly, etc.). Besides, in this reorganizing activity they are never inert objects: praxis assumes and requires their participation; the new links and new means of transport are also their instruments when they themselves have to take the initiative in communicating; furthermore, they are furnished by the reorganization itself with new functions, or else their functions present novel features – which means that they interiorize the change and re-exteriorize it as a complex system of powers and obligations. Everything, in short, is action. The global praxis, by the leaders' decision (for example), engenders a global reorganization: this undertaking is diversified at the level of the local sub-groups; they become aware of it precisely in so far as they discover themselves in their new status as its products; and they accept responsibility for it, while transcending it towards more or less fresh objectives. From this point of view, the very discovery by [sub-]group A of a [sub-]group B which seems to exercise the same functions immediately presents itself – and within the framework of a global enrichment of powers and knowledge – as a positive gain. The multiplication of links is marked by a *detailed* new awareness of a group that each sub-group used to grasp globally and in a fairly rough-and-ready manner. The totality on the way to totalization arrives for each and through each at the moment of differentiation. And this objective differentiation is not an object of contemplation, but a practical process on the way to realization.

Yet counter-finality is already given. Before the two sub-groups were brought into contact, their respective utility could not be denied; *afterwards*, it becomes necessary for one of them to be reabsorbed, or for it to be liquidated, or for third parties to fuse them together. It may happen, moreover, that the fusion is decided at the level of the two organisms and by simple agreement: this means that the former exigencies of action have not determined in each of them a local particularism (perhaps then justified). But if this fusion by spontaneous agreement seems impossible to them – if their particular reality, under the influence of the development of the global praxis and their activities within their restricted practical field, has been posited for itself in its particularity – *then* counter-finality is undeniable. The function of each sub-group, as untranscendable (but always transcended in its concrete realization) and determined inertia, finds itself abruptly produced as supernumerary by the abrupt appearance of *the same* function *elsewhere* and *as other*. And this appearance is itself produced by the development of links, inasmuch as it is not just praxis but also *process*: e.g. inasmuch as it is *this* inanimate ensemble (the road, the railway, telephonic communications, or the new system as a real planning of links and as an objective structure of the total group) that is established through praxis, and that *in it* – at first invisibly – serves as a mediation between the two sub-groups. What has occurred, in fact, albeit the result of an action that we can assume here to be as conscious and long-sighted as possible, is already – as synthetic unity of the inert – a negative reversal of that action. *The road*, for example, appears at once as the result of a labour and as the prop of real actions (it is *true*, in this sense, that it is the material form of regulated displacements, and the inert means actualized as a means through concrete undertakings). But for this very reason, it is also an inert determination of the field of possibles for each common individual of the group: i.e. for those very ones who do not belong to the sub-groups under consideration (whether they are integrated into other organisms of the global group, or whether they constitute in the group itself a controlled, directed but non-organized multiplicity). Thus each of these common individuals *finds himself*, from a certain moment on, defined in himself – alongside all his other characteristics – by the inert material possibility of going from *such and such a place* (where sub-group A is to be found) to such and such another (residence of sub-group B). If, as our hypothesis has it, transport is swift and cheap, if the reasons to undertake these trips are multiple, the *'dis-utility'* of the movements becomes next to nil. In that case, *the road* (or *the railway*) – through all praxis and common actions as well as through a proliferation of 'private' activities – is constituted *by itself*, and for any member of the groups, as an inert indetermination of his relations with sub-groups A and B. This indetermination enters in the guise of a *possible* into the framework of the *passive-being* he has given himself by pledge. And in relation to the two sub-groups – perhaps also, moreover (depending on the case), for the individuals – this indetermination, which constitutes them as relatively indeterminate, can be nothing other than a revenge of the practico-inert and a new form of *exteriority* at the heart of the deepest interiority.

Nevertheless, this indetermination, as inert possibility of a non-transcendable fate, cannot *by itself* be considered as a contradiction. Through worked matter, the relations between the two sub-groups and their members (between the sub-groups via the mediation of the members, between the members via the mediation of the sub-groups) should instead be revealed as the foundation of an infinite (and circular) seriality. This is what happens, moreover, in looser, barely serialized groups, when one or other of two institutions is superfluous and they are maintained without conflict, by tradition – i.e. by the force of inertia represented by *the past*. There is no struggle, with items of business going indiscriminately here or there, or else each sub-group referring them to the other. Eventually, everything is engulfed in the circularity of impotence and each of the two organs becomes *other* and is no longer anything but *the other of the other*. By contrast, in a fully active group, fully alive – where *fraternity-terror* is the deep bond (even if it remains hidden) between all its members – suddenly bringing the two organisms into contact causes indetermination to appear as a *negative action*. In fact, this indetermination – which will appear later and to third parties as an objective structure – is itself produced in acts. For each non-organized member (or each member belonging to other organisms) the possibility of addressing themselves equally well to sub-group A or to sub-group B is realized *practically*. It does not constitute the object of a contemplative learning, but the individual will quite simply address himself to one or other according to his convenience; and one or other will welcome him and study his request, suggestion or complaint, viewing the matter as really belonging to his competency. But it is precisely the positive ensemble of these acts – X addresses himself to sub-group A, which takes the matter in hand – in short, it is the normal course of practice which, suddenly, appears to sub-group B as a threat to its very existence, i.e. to its function and its right to exercise it. We grasp here, in real life, the constitution of a praxis as a process: *since* the two [sub-] groups exist, the action of one is constituted in spite of itself as a violation of the rights of the other; and this constitution, *as a real relation to the other*, overflows the action itself and is not at first revealed to the agents. No more, moreover, than to the members of the injured sub-group. In the imperious movement of common action and in the perspective defined by this action – from the standpoint of its particular and its overall objectives and of its immediate and its long-term aims – the group, through all its common individuals, produces itself for itself *as pure activity* and discovers material circumstances only inasmuch as its action transcends or modifies them. In this assertion of praxis by itself, constituted Reason is grasped as constituent Reason; practice seeks to be practice and translucidity right through. The *negative by default* (lacks, impotence, local setbacks) then appears as plenary and destructive activity. A piece of clumsiness or even an accident for which nobody is responsible appears as sabotage or as an assassination attempt. At a certain level of emergency, in the climate of fraternity-terror, any opposition – as Merleau-Ponty has said – is treason.[14] And this is not, as is too often thought, due just to the historical circumstances that define the situation. These circumstances, on the contrary, acquire their effectiveness only within the framework of the following dialectical law: in a group in the midst of action, each common individual is objectively produced as radically active, and everything he produces is necessarily interpreted in terms of action. By this I do not at all mean that the *truth* of opposition is treason, quite the contrary: just that, in the movement of practice, treason is its lived reality. This is due to the fact that – as we have just seen – the inner counter-finalities engendered by praxis never manifest themselves and praxis, at whatever level, is produced as the co-ordination of local and particular actions; just as each of these never encounters the practico-inert, except in so far as other actions produce it in them and hide it. Thus the action of an organism is immediately revealed to the rival organism as *hostile praxis*: its goal is to strip the latter on behalf of the former. But at once the antagonism intensifies. Each sub-group, in effect, pursues the common aims of the group and, as a specific formation made up of common individuals, *incarnates* the entire group, as the part incarnates the whole. This means, in particular, that it produces for its own part and demands *unity*: i.e. maximum integration of the group, inasmuch as common action has to realize it in the name of the objective to be attained. It itself *is* that totalizing unity, in the sense – precisely – in which common action is the very substance of its action; and it demands it of all the other sub-groups, inasmuch as systems of mediations and compensations, weights and counterweights, have transformed – from the outset or little by little – their possible conflicts into a real equilibrium. In this sense these contained oppositions do not trouble any sub-group, in so far as each, by virtue of its functional and practical singularization, realizes in itself the totality – but in a specific form and through a particular action, i.e. a particular determination of the total action.

---

14. *Humanisme et terreur*, Paris 1947.

Unity as Meaning of the Antagonistic Relation

But when we grasp two [sub-]groups which live the common indetermination of their functions in the astringent milieu of totalizing unity and in
the practical perspective of that unity, each of them – as an incarnation
and as a particular production of the practical unity – is brought into
contact with *another* which claims to produce *the same unity*. And, to be
sure, the common praxis presents itself as being everywhere *the same*,
here and now. In an organized group, however, this means that each
specialized activity is integrated into the total unity, inasmuch as this
specialization is a necessary differentiation of the totalizing action. The
common individual and the sub-group, as common, *are the whole*; and
on this plane of the immediate, recognition of one by the other – of one
lot by the other lot – is spontaneous: 'You're me'. This is what occurs,
for example, when certain isolated members of the group recognize one
another in the thick of an indifferent or hostile crowd. In concrete and
organized action, however, mediation is necessary and only differentiation
of functions allows the group's fundamental unity to subsist in each
person as the relation of the part to the whole. From the moment that this
differentiation no longer exists* – as soon as two parts, otherwise distinct,
are objectively the same in their specific relationship to the whole in the
course of totalization, in a context where each of them 'duplicates' the
other (i.e. when no dual determination of that indetermination is possible) – the same objectively occurs as *the other*. It is in effect the same,
not inasmuch as it is integrated into the same unity, but inasmuch as it is
similar or even *identical*. The simultaneous existence of two sub-groups
finding themselves provided by History with *the same attributions*, when
just one of them should be enough to assume these, puts the practical
unity in danger by the introduction of a *dualism of identity*. The sub-
groups are really and numerically two: i.e. they *can be counted*, since
their relationship of immanence (objective co-operation in the same total
undertaking) is, at least partially, transformed into a relationship of
exteriority. *For resemblance and identity* are factors that are revealed to
positivist analysis. At the limit of the serial and the masses, we have
found the proliferation of *identical* particles as a factor and a product of
the reification of human relations. Thus indetermination is a danger of
internal rupture at the heart of totalization, even – and above all – if it

---

* It can, of course, put up with the numerical multiplicity of agents fulfilling the same
function, *if* the multiplicity is required by action. In that case, each individual is the same
as his colleagues in terms of his specific functions; but it is the sector in which he will
exercise them, for example, that will differentiate him.

appears as the historical product of that totalization itself. And this
identity immediately appears as a threat: the identical *is the Other*, in a
milieu *where there are no Others*. But it is a particularly hateful and
dangerous Other: each sub-group, inasmuch as it is identical to another,
discovers this other as its own reality become alien praxis. And the
practical existence of that other is a danger *not just for the identical and
opposed sub-group*, inasmuch as identity contests the uniqueness of its
relation to the totality in the course of totalization, *but also for the
totalization-of-envelopment* – i.e. for the whole group, its efficacy and its
aims.

Thus the 'moment' must be suppressed for the sake of the ensemble.
And in so far as a particular sub-group seeks the death of the other, it
really seeks it for the sake of the ensemble, although it is also impelled
to do so by a need, a passion or an interest of its own. In the political
struggles inside a party – which can be terrible and even bloody – it
would be fruitless to try to distinguish the ambition of certain milieux, of
certain factions or certain men, from their assessment of the party's
policy. The error of bourgeois psychologism has been to separate in
every case ambition from programme. It is true that the very conditions
of bourgeois parliamentarism produce men who justify such a separation:
their careerism is empty, they grasp at any programme (though within
the framework of the social principles that are based on bourgeois
relations of production). In periods when the pressure of History is
heightened and struggles intensify, the ambitious individual is not a
psychological and abstract type: he is, for example, a politician who
identifies himself with a certain programme and battles relentlessly for
the realization of that programme – on the assumption, however, that the
political directives in question will be realized *by him*. Success will thus
be his objectification. But this objectification will, at the same time, be
the new and totalizing orientation of the party's praxis. It would be
absurd to ascribe to Stalin the 'will to rule'. It would be wholly idealist
to see in him the mere incarnation of the historical process. The truth is
that the historical process is made by Stalin's iron will and that this will
is preferred only and solely to the (albeit considerable) extent that it
prefers to everything an objective programme, methods, a praxis, presuppositions, a way of posing and resolving concrete questions. To that
extent – and since certain material conditions realize Stalin's adaptation to his role as dictator – the historical process sustains and carries the
man who makes it. Thus opponents become traitors. Danger is discovered
and reinteriorized as hatred, at two levels of sacredness: first, inasmuch
as the bond between the part and the whole is *the function* of the sub-
group, i.e. a juridical power recognized by all common individuals;
secondly, inasmuch as this identity constitutes in itself an internal fracture

of totalization as a sacred aim of the common individual and his sworn faith. And this danger, as we have seen, does not appear – or at least not initially – as a counter-finality produced by the evolution of common action, but rather in its twofold *and sacred* form (the sacred is ambivalent) as the result of a negative activity. It is the sub-group that manifests itself as *other* – i.e. *as other than all the members of the group and all the sub-groups* – inasmuch as it is produced by a deliberate praxis *as other than some particular sub-group*. The question of fundamental treason is immediately posed: this usurpation of functions is necessarily a manoeuvre to break unity. And it is true *objectively* that the claim – of each of the two organisms – upon the (partial or total) competency of the other occurs through actions. In the same way, it is true that this claim is manifested as a rupture of unity, precisely inasmuch as it introduces into it a reciprocity of antagonism, i.e. a plurality of epicentres.

But it must also be seen – and this is perhaps the essential thing – that each of the epicentres enters into conflict with the other *in the name of unity*. For since it exposes the other's action for setting the destruction of that unity as its objective, it seeks to liquidate the enemy [sub-]group (or at least reduce it to impotence, subjugate it, i.e. reintegrate it into an organized hierarchy) in order to reconstitute that broken and threatened unity. In the chosen example, each of the two wishes to suppress the disastrous indetermination that makes every common individual into a member of two equivalent organisms, one of which is supernumerary. That indetermination, by itself, disintegrates every common individual. It creates in him a possibility of choice, which frees him from the unitary harshness of the organization and allows him, if need be, to use conflicts between the two rival organs to *play his own game* (as a free and practical individual) against the group. In other cases, it expresses itself merely by a hesitation that impairs behaviour; but this hesitation itself marks the objective dissolution of the common individual who, in the exercise of his functions, finds himself paralysed by his dual dependence. Thus all the moments of the conflict, all the tactics used by the two adversaries, are defined by a sole, identical objective – to re-establish the compromised unity – but each attempts to re-establish it to his own advantage. From this point of view, it matters little whether sub-group A or sub-group B was initially responsible. Or rather, the 'first wrongs', the 'first skirmishes', as anecdotal origin of the conflict, have an importance for comprehension of the group and its practical movement. The anecdote is in effect the incarnation, in its very contingency, of the global moment of praxis. But so far as the conflict itself is concerned, the true origin necessarily lies in each of the opposed sub-groups, since each by its mere practical existence assumes and transcends the practico-inert indetermination, organizes it in the formal non-transcendability of the framework of pledged inertia, and cannot avoid producing it *in the name of the group* as a demand for unity.

It is here that we can grasp the real bond between the conflict and the contradiction within the group. Each of the opposed sub-groups, in fact, is really produced as an incarnation of the group, and each truly does incarnate it. For the simple fact of their being placed in an antagonistic relationship, while limiting each to the surface as a relatively undetermined mode of the totalizing action, actualizes in depth its relation to the ongoing totalization: it is its deep reality and its reason, precisely in so far as it is its objectification in the internal milieu of the organized group. Within each sub-group, it is the group that is fighting to preserve or regain its unity. In truth, moreover, it is really the group that opposes itself. The two epicentres are, in fact, each the centre of this totalization 'whose centre is everywhere'. And, of course, it is not a question of idealizing the contradiction, or of resorting to a hyper-organism. These organs are the incarnation of the whole, inasmuch as they are produced as such, and it would be only metaphorically that one might say that the whole is produced in them. The totalization is incarnated in and through their particular activity and in their antagonistic practices. But if it is true that they produce it – and that, once again, it is men grouped in a partial organization who are the concrete origin of the whole conflict – it is also true that they are, as common and pledged individuals, determined in such a way, at the innermost core of their freedom and through it, that they necessarily produce their free claim. Ontologically, the pledge has produced the group in each and through each. Practically, in the evolution of common action, each sub-group defines itself as *the incarnation of the group by itself*: in fact, inasmuch as it is a question of an ensemble of common individuals exercising functions, the antagonism, the claim and the intimate grasping of the group-in-totalization come to each ensemble through the other, at the same time as each produces them actively against the other. Right is disclosed when it is contested. In this very conflict, through each sub-group, the group tends to reinforce its unity by violence, and 'fraternity-terror' is actualized. Unity, called into question, becomes the most immediate internal requirement. But this very tendency, because it occurs in a dissociation of epicentres, places the group's very existence – i.e. its unity – in the greatest danger. Yet there are not, there will not be *two* unities (unless there is a split, a schism – but in that case it is two whole groups that are re-formed as independent unities). Each sub-group, in fact, in its struggle against the other refers not just to the same objectives (at least to the same long-term objectives), the same praxis, the same traditions and the same common experience, *but also* to the same organisms, the same hierarchy, the same global ensemble of functions and the same personnel. Each struggles within the framework of the rules and practices governing internal transformations of the group. Each appeals to the same superiors (if there are any), the same inferiors, the same organs of sovereignty (as a centralized unification of the ensemble) and the same internal opinion (as a totalization of all common individuals). In this way, each accepts – and reinforces by this acceptance – *all incarnations except one*. Conversely – at least in a first moment of the conflict – the whole group, in all its forms and through all its incarnations, recognizes the being-in-the-group of each of the warring sub-groups. For the third party, as a common individual, the conflict is at first manifested as simple appearance. The reciprocal negation appears as objective nothingness: it is, for example, a misunderstanding – it will be enough to reflect, to explain. In this very way, the practice of each organ and of all the common individuals *unifies* the adversaries by differentiating them. Each of the two incarnates the totalization in its own way, and the ensemble of the two must be capable of being totalized (e.g. inasmuch as both are attached to hierarchical unity as a synthetic rule of organization).

Thus the conflict would not even be possible if unity did not rise up against itself. Far from the struggle, when it appears, being in itself a rupture of unity, it is unity that makes it possible. Not only does this unity represent the intimate bond between each side and the group, it also constitutes *the meaning* of the antagonistic relation itself. And the violence of the duality is just the unremitting effort to restore unity. The practical attitude of all, moreover, first constitutes the struggle of unity against itself as a calm synthetic becoming, whose negative aspect is merely a superficial appearance. In fact, this indetermination that is realized by conflict is actually a unitary achievement of the group itself. It can be defined in the objective, as the permanent readaptation of institutions (or organs) lagging behind the development of praxis. And it is actually a difficulty that – even if it must remain local – characterizes *the whole group*, as a moment of its development and as an exigency of the totalizing activity towards itself. Nothing prevents one calling this contrast (between new tasks and partly outdated institutions) a contra-diction, since it precisely presents itself as a synthetic and internal determination that only the synthetic unity of a praxis can produce in itself. For what it is, in short, is a repercussion of worked materiality, inasmuch as the latter inscribes its determinations in the framework of pledged inertia. But for it *really* to involve a contradiction in the dialectical sense of the term, rather than just an inert adversity to be transformed, it would have to become *motive power* – and this is what happens when the practical organs realize it in conflict.

The contradiction, as we can see, is ontologically ambiguous in each of its terms: in each, it is objective as inertia and real as praxis. Or, if you like, it is a praxis that produces contradiction while thinking to suppress it, but in practice manifests itself only as conflict (accidental conflict – apparently and at first – or struggle of Good against Evil). In fact, on the basis of the practico-inert determinations being resumed as antagonism through pledged passivity, the entire unity of the group is called into question by the struggle of its incarnations. It is this *practical* calling into question, moreover, that produces the living intelligibility of the contradictory: it is unity that engenders the duality of the epicentres; it is unity that – in them and in all – is produced as the absolute exigency of transcending the duality; it is unity, finally, that is incarnated in each epicentre as liquidatory violence. But if the contradiction appears as a complex reality, one of whose faces is the praxis of struggle and the other the inert exigency of the moment, this – as you will have understood – is because the group's unity is never, in fact, anything other than its permanent practice of reunification. In this perpetual movement, whose motor is the common action, the least hysteresis, the least difference of phase, the most insignificant lack of adaptation, are necessarily produced as practical impulsions. On that basis, the divergence of the solutions proposed – which reflects the diversity of incarnations – produces itself as a contested unification. When the organs of mediation are effective and the choice of a solution is relatively simple (when certain choices are easily eliminated or one is revealed as being obviously the only valid choice) the contradiction remains masked and implicit, because the conflict has not manifested itself. So unification, in such circumstances, seems to have liquidated the divergences without calling itself into question: it is thus, if you like to use the metaphor, the practical substance that produces and liquidates momentary oppositions. In reality, however, we must understand that it has implicitly involved itself, just as much as in the case of conflicts – but the situation has allowed a crisis to be avoided. Conversely, moreover, conflicts are intelligible in an organized group because they are produced as a moment of reunification: the one in which material difficulties are of such seriousness they can be resolved only by the liquidation of certain [sub-]groups incarnating their different aspects. In cases where the third party's mediation is possible, in fact, this mediation can succeed only as a real synthesis of the opposed 'viewpoints'. In other words the mediated sub-groups, by their situation inside the group, produce themselves as a totalization of the problem but, at the same time, as its singularization. Or, if you prefer, they actualize the problem in the perspective of a singular solution and in that very way accentuate their singularity. The antagonism is then perfectly intelligible, because it expresses the impossibility for this concrete problem to realize all its exigencies through a single incarnation, i.e. according to a single practical perspective.

Thus the problem is realized by antagonisms as a multiplicity of perspectives and imperatives – not through the magic of some dogmatic idealism, but quite simply because it has its origin in inert materiality as a mediation between several [sub-]groups and, consequently, must be produced by the action of these [sub-]groups as a multiplicity of antagonisms, before being bent back into a synthesis that transcends and conserves everything. In this case, the present antagonisms are comprehensible in the perspective of a concrete solution that suppresses them as it organizes them: i.e. in the movement of present and past unity being transcended towards a future unity. Solution – as invention – reconciliation and comprehension are one and the same thing: the partial appears as such through the totalization that it provokes, and that is projected through it. The antagonism then appears for what it is. In a certain way *it is nothing*, since totalization makes it disappear in aid of a tighter organization. In another way, it is the only means of realizing the unfurling of perspectives: for each one, it is a way of being produced in the practical movement of a group that posits itself for itself through it. But to posit itself, here, is to determine itself, i.e. to negate. Thus the incarnation of a perspective is at once, for the ongoing unity, the greatest risk of being riven (i.e. the source of the worst violence) and, simultaneously, what will reveal itself as pure nothingness (reciprocal negation) from the viewpoint of the realized mediation. The *meaning* of the conflict disappears then, since the compartmentalizations are broken in aid of the unified synthesis: people no longer understand – literally – why they were fighting. This means that, from the standpoint of future plenitude, totalization will appear never to have been brought into play other than by unthinkable limits, by absolute positions that were merely unfulfilment. Later, the historian reconstituting the truth will understand that these absolute positions were not the mere, empty negativity that revealed itself as their reality after mediation, but the necessity – in a totally practical totalization – that everything, including the negations themselves, should realize itself *through praxis*, i.e. here through struggle. It is never the actual difference that posits itself for itself in its negative determinations. It is the sub-group that posits it by positing itself – and this very act of positing is indistinguishable from the first blows it strikes at its adversary. Thus mediation seems simply to negate an inconsistent negation, to explode limits. In fact, this Hegelian conception could have a meaning only if the dialectic were a transcendent reality, a suprahuman development. To mediate is not just to fuse the multiple aspects of the problem into a synthetic unity – i.e. find the solution to it. It is *to have this solution accepted* by two [sub-]groups which, assuming responsibility for the differences, have eventually produced themselves in their originality by these very differences, inasmuch as they manoeuvre to suppress contrary perspectives. Contradiction is born in this way: it is necessary for thesis and antithesis, in fact, to be the twofold practical perspective that two ensembles adopt towards one another; the *substance* of contradiction is practical reciprocity, i.e. the invention of destructive tactics which *in each* are the actualization of the contradictory. This is why the limits separating one partial aspect from another are *simultaneously* inconsistent negations, from the viewpoint of the mediation already accomplished, and the sole *human reality* of the contradictory: i.e. its practical existence, by men and for them. From the point of view of the new unity, in fact, it seems that the divergences (as inert givens of the problem) have engendered the conflict. But in fact, as we have seen, the divergence is immediately practical and it is actually conflict which determines it as contradiction, by communicating all human violence to it. Similarly, mediation – in the more or less protracted struggle to which it has just put an end – sees only a muddled series of manoeuvres and counter-manoeuvres, whose sole result was to 'harden positions' and make conciliation more difficult by the day. But we now know that the most insignificant moments of the battle – so far as both adversaries are concerned – are an incarnation of the entire struggle and a practical actualization, *in this very present*, of the contradiction in its development.

No matter. It is significant that past struggles should present themselves as a superficial disturbance of the unity of unification: i.e. that unity should appear the substance, and disunity the contingency that can occur only *supported* by the substance. For there have never been two unities, just two ways of realizing the same unification – each positing itself as the exclusion of the other. Everything thus takes place – through the real unwinding of particular actions, produced by individuals and the [sub-]groups constituted by them – as though unity itself were unfolding its own difficulties and sharpening them into contradictions, the better to specify them and finally break their limits. For what must not be forgotten is that unity is practical: it is perpetually maintained and tightened by – and for – global action. If we had to accept it (other than metaphorically) as a substantial reality, it would be impossible to understand it splitting and opposing itself. But if it is, in fact, the common project in each person – here and everywhere in the group – then we understand that this project is precisely *the same* in the sub-groups obliged by the total development of praxis to produce themselves as adversaries; and that it constitutes the motive and signification of the conflict.

These considerations authorize no idealist optimism. Nothing proves that mediation must always take place. Quite the contrary, it presents itself as a particular case of praxis; and we have envisaged it only the better to show the movement of totalization at the very heart of the conflict. But it often happens that one of the sub-groups liquidates the other. It goes without saying that everything depends on the circumstances and the structures. If the conflict occurs on one of the lower echelons of a very strongly hierarchized group, mediation is all the more likely in that it is often a recognized function of certain organs of the upper echelons. Which does not mean that this mediation is necessarily a synthetic transcendence of the opposing perspectives. The arbiter may be prejudiced in favour of one of the adversaries. His concern for unity may induce him to do violence to both sides, without taking account of the partial truth which each represents. He may – inasmuch as his work has produced him and provided him with certain instruments of action and thought – not be capable of *comprehending* the problem; may at once invent a false (i.e. incomplete) transcendence. For he has to worry less about the singular details of the conflict than about the objective exigency that is manifested through him, as an exigency of the totalizing action itself at this stage of development. For example, he has to grasp, as fundamental unity of the struggle, the practical obligation to adapt these organs to the new tasks that praxis throws up. When mediation is imperfect, the objective problem of internal reorganization subsists in its original form or in another: the struggle continues between the [sub-] groups that started it, or else it is displaced and shifts to another sector, or again it widens and involves the entire group. All this in no way prevents the practical development from remaining intelligible. The comprehension of action obviously implies that of its failure: the latter, in other words, presents itself as a comprehensible limit of comprehension, in so far as this is defined as the project revealing itself on the basis of its objectives and through action; there is a signification of every failure and each one incarnates, in the group, the very difficulties of totalization.

In the same way, if mediation does not occur and the two sub-groups remain confronting each other alone – either for lack of mediatory organisms or because, ultimately, the struggle through them pits one part of the group against all the rest – intelligibility does not therefore disappear. At first, in fact, absence of mediation is a real factor only if mediation is possible but refused. If the structures of the group do not include this possibility, the movement of comprehension must – disregarding a non-being of exteriority – comprehend the real movement that engenders a non-mediated conflict. This means that the objective exigency will be grasped, via the adversaries' actions, as demanding *this* struggle in a group defined by *these* structures. And as *these* structures and *this* exigency are produced at different moments of the totalizing praxis, the comprehension of this struggle is identified with that of the global praxis as an ongoing temporalization. On the other hand, in this struggle which for want of arbitration risks becoming a struggle to the death, it would be tempting to believe that we shall find nothing resembling the intelligibility of mediation as a praxis of dialectical reunification by invention of the solution to the problems. But that is only partially correct. To be sure, it may happen – in specific circumstances – that the conflict ends in a schism. The break-up of a group obviously cannot pass for a positive solution of its contradictions: on the contrary, it manifests the non-transcendability of the positions taken up. But we must first understand that *every* unification, by the movement that dissociates it within the group, really places itself in danger. The opposition between sub-groups is actually the only way in which the group can actualize the practico-inert risks of break-up determined at every moment by action. In other words, that opposition is reunification itself, inasmuch as circumstances oblige it to split within the totalization. In that case, it is easy to understand that the schism is determined at once by the problem itself (inasmuch as this does not include a solution in the circumstances in which it is proposed), by the impossibility – recognized in practice – of liquidating either one of the adversaries, and by what we shall call the fragility of the group.

This fragility has come to it through action. It has been slowly determined by the internal action of counter-finalities. It ends up *qualifying* (by brakings, sudden starts, reversals, losses of speed, etc.) the praxis that maintains and aggravates it while transcending it. The slowness and insecurity of communications between Rome and Byzantium, the geo-political and social necessity for those two religious centres to live two separate historical destinies, the very clear-cut differences that pitted Eastern against Western Christians – all these were factors of break-up within Christianity. But these factors themselves had been at least partially engendered by the Church's praxis: the construction of Byzantium was a religious act, which until the schism never ceased to intensify its counter-finalities; evangelization of the East and Barbarian conversions accentuated the heterogeneity of the 'milieux' and – through a quite normal backlash – the new faithful transformed the faith. But if one seeks to understand how the praxis of the Church Militant progressively defined itself, starting from its origins, by transcendence and utilization of situations that it was producing, one will gradually see fragility being engendered as an objective structure, changing into fissure, being resolved as break-up: all that, of course, in particular acts and through them. At once, schism appeared *as a solution*. That which, for a third party, took place as a break-up was produced by each religious community as an *amputation*. Each recovered its unity purified by the expulsion of the other. Each defined itself as perpetuating the unity of the original Church. And, indeed, each lived and realized this dissociation as a reunification. From the standpoint of each group, the praxis was not fundamentally different from the *exclusion* through which a community recovers its integrity by expelling unassimilable elements. But the difference is apparent to a third party, because this time the exclusion was reciprocal.* Henceforward, the problem of intelligibility is transformed: it is no longer a question of showing that duality in unity is intelligible, since there are precisely *two* distinct unities. It is still necessary to understand the process that transformed the split unity into two separate wholes: i.e. the final passage from struggle to separation. But in so far as praxis actualized inert objectivity, the intelligibility of the rupture remains whole. The twofold decision – as the final moment of totalization – actualized this last *state* of internal objectivity. Between the sub-groups in conflict, the practico-inert had become the sole real mediation. In other words, it is never *the struggle* that directly produces the rift, as it remains a unificatory movement to the end. Quite the contrary: it is the meaninglessness of the struggle – and the impossibility of effectively pursuing it and winning – that are actualized and transcended by the rupture. So we find here the moment of the anti-dialectic – alienation of the fighters by the counter-finalities secreted by the fight – as failure of the antagonistic dialectic, and the transcendence of this negation by the rupture that actualizes it – i.e. causes it to pass into the world of human praxis as *'aufgehoben'*. The anti-dialectic as mediation by the practico-inert is incorporated by the dialectical movement of decision, which transforms this non-human mediation into two human refusals of any mediation.

Does the Victory of One Sub-Group over Another Always Have a Meaning?

On the other hand, when one [sub-]group gains victory by liquidating the other, one cannot avoid posing the question of transcendence. For it is above all a synthetic reunification of the split unity. And this victory – in the temporalization of the struggle within the group – places itself beyond the actual conflict, as its term and its solution. Indeed, the risk of break-up – for all that the conflict may re-emerge for other reasons and between other organs – is, so far as this specific event is concerned, *totally annihilated*. In this way the irreversibility of temporalization is highlighted: this *'afterwards'* is constituted as the diachronic totalization of all the synthetically linked *'befores'* that culminate in it (we shall

---

* In certain cases, the exclusion remains univocal but the excluded are subsequently regrouped to constitute a schismatic group.

come back to this point when we speak of diachronic totalization and its intelligibility[15]). For the victorious sub-group is itself produced by its victory as other than it was. Its importance within the group has grown steadily; its victory has determined new attitudes towards it (hostile or friendly, respectful or indignant, uniform or themselves contradictory, it matters little) on the part of all the other sub-groups and all the common individuals. In other words, its reality-for-the-other, the new obligations created by its new situation, the ensemble of communications that have been established (between it and everybody, between it and the total-ization), the internal currents, the tensions – everything in short, right up to the modifications introduced by the very fact of its victory into the structures of common action – everything designates it as the distinctive product of its victory. It has to interiorize it as a new inner tension – i.e. as a redistribution of forces in its internal force field – in order to re-exteriorize it as the practice that its new status demands. In short, in a certain manner it envelops within itself the sub-group it has just destroyed.

At first, in fact – in the event of destruction aimed at the organ without affecting the individuals – it may perhaps incorporate part of the members of the liquidated organization (sometimes even the majority). But above all it necessarily inherits – whether the liquidation concerned the sub-group as such, or was accompanied by an extermination – attributions of the vanished organism, and must fulfil the functions the latter used to fulfil.* So it will aggregate its own offices with those of the defeated body, and this aggregation cannot be maintained for a moment without a synthetic reworking of all offices in relation to one another. By this very means the victor acquires a growing complexity, since ultimately it is *given notice* – by the exigency of common praxis – to absorb and represent the dissolved community within a new unity. In certain countries, the Communist Party – or some other authoritarian and centralized left-wing party – has eliminated the formations of the Far Left (leftists), along with the democratic parties (social democracy, etc.) that used to constitute the right of the Left. All these parties used to govern together and, despite their differences, praxis united them. When a series of contradictions induced the strongest to liquidate the rest, remaining alone it found itself compelled to become at once its own right and its own left. Or, if you prefer, praxis itself generated within it a sectarian

---

* At least provisionally and until the group as a whole has shared out these attributions among various sub-groups, or created a new sub-group to fill them which no longer has to (or is deemed not to have to) oppose the old one.

15. See Preface above.

leftism, a right opportunism and a central and centralized mediation, whose function finally revealed itself in all its complexity. For it was necessary to *reconcile* the extremes; to exploit their divergences; to utilize one or other of them when praxis required a change of personnel, without ever allowing a success to benefit one wing at the expense of the other – in short, to discover the situation, the problems and the objective exigencies with the help of the practical knowledge of both – in order to realize all perspectives before uniting them in the same transcendence. This centralized, authoritarian party, refusing conflicts, interiorized the opposition while submitting it to the iron rules of unity. It interiorized it *in order to make use of it*, in so far as – by liquidating the other parties, more harmful than useful to praxis – it had to fill the void created by a controlled differentiation. One must not imagine a concerted operation. But, for example, when the right of the left existed, in every circumstance it used to adopt a position that became 'rightist' for the opportunists of the Communist Party. The latter would be reassured, despite themselves, because this position – restraining, or more flexible, or simply dictated by the interests of broader layers of the population – was actually adopted, and its actualization obliged the Communist Party to declare itself in relation to it. But at once this hesitant or timid position was being realized in and by a political group alien to the Party, and in relation to which they defined themselves negatively (as temporary allies, etc.). They had no need themselves to produce *that* particular political motion, since the right was taking care of it and the Communist Party would take it into account, in order to preserve the union of the popular parties. So they would not recognize it as *their* initiative – and, indeed, it was not *theirs*. Their opportunism, cut off from them and negated, would be developed in and through another sub-group – partly 'fellow-travelling', partly hostile. As for them, therefore, they could integrate themselves strongly into the Party – *their* party – and manifest, on the contrary, the common intransigence (or a common flexibility, inasmuch as this presented itself as provisionally necessary in order to keep allies). The void on the right – which they had contributed to producing in the undifferentiated unity of a battle or a *coup d'état* – abruptly *qualified them*. With nobody any longer putting forward opportunist motions, they became the opportunists they were. The adversary-ally had formerly incarnated their apprehensions about the rapid pace – for example – of collectivization in the countryside. Once he disappeared, that apprehension which had formerly been theirs *as other* became their own apprehension. Through them, the social-democratic party reappeared – in a form obviously more 'integrated' and without real contours distinguishing it from the rest – inside the Communist Party. Of course, such interiorization is at the same time a denaturing. It is in the name of the Party's aims that opportunism will be produced in particular attitudes and propositions (this simple fact must suffice to differentiate it: it is an attitude that has really been defined *for Communists, by them* and within the Party, in the perspective of common objectives). This production, though, has been effected through liquidation of the adversary and as interiorization of an absence. It may be argued (and this is true) that the circumstances of their personal history – and above all, as we have seen, their functions in the Party and their history as common individuals – had already determined them as opportunists. But it can equally well be argued that without the Communist Party victory this opportunism would not have had the opportunity to manifest itself in practice. Which means, in reality, that it *would not have been* – even as *hexis*. For each member of the Party would have remained subject to a certain pressure internal to the latter, and itself conditioned by the presence of the allied groups.

However, if it is certain that the victorious sub-group transcends itself by transcending the defeated one, whose tasks and functions it assumes in a new unity, the liquidation of one of the terms of the split unity by the other can be considered in itself as a transcendence only if, through it, the praxis of the whole group is transcended towards a moment of tighter integration, more advanced differentiation and greater effectiveness in relation to its main objectives. Everything comes back to wondering whether victory always has *a meaning*: i.e. if it always expresses a progress, from the standpoint of common action.* Perhaps one might be tempted to reply that this depends on situations and circumstances – and doubtless one would not be wholly wrong. Yet the problem of intelligibility must be envisaged in an a priori critical investigation, in this case as in all others. And that means, here, that it is necessary to determine the limits within which the varied possibilities resulting from victory must be kept, if they are to be intelligible.

There are two attitudes that must be rejected equally, because both rest upon dogmatic presuppositions: optimism and pessimism. Pessimism, in the case that concerns us, is less the assertion of Evil than a disorder which allows Evil to triumph more often than Good. Good must be understood as the steady progress of the undertaking; Evil as its regression and involution. From this point of view, victory – depending on fortuitous circumstances, on accidents – is in itself accidental. Not only is it not – in itself – the deep meaning of the struggle, but we may conceive too that it probably *has no* signification (other than that of the dated event

---

* I am here taking 'progress' in its simplest sense. I mean by the word: irreversible progression towards a fixed end, i.e. development of the act in progress.

which has made it possible). We must point out, however, that we are not yet considering the struggle in large ensembles presenting themselves (at least at first sight) as non-totalizable, but in the internal force field of the practical totalization called a group. It is already obvious that the intensity and violence of this struggle will be proportionate to the urgency of its tasks, the external dangers and its internal strength of integration. And the latter, in turn, expresses the determination of the common individuals and their pledge to carry the enterprise through. Victory, of course – as a final moment of temporalization – is singular: it appears as a unique and dated event manifesting its contingency rather than its necessity. But also, no one is crazy enough to expect it to appear with the abstract harshness, rigour and translucidity of a *logical consequence*. The human event is at once contingent and necessary. Its facticity – product of the fundamental facticity of historical agents – can be defined as the necessity of its contingency. But inasmuch as it is actualized as the incarnation of a group in action – i.e. of an ongoing totalization – it manifests the contingency of its necessity: that it is necessary for its necessity to take the form of contingency, precisely in so far as this necessity is produced as a real determination of the concrete. Everything is new in this victory, but it cannot be produced without incarnating – as an internal and local temporalization – a certain moment of the ongoing totalization. The victor incarnates the group, precisely in so far as the victory is a triumph of unity over dissociation. Conversely, victory can fall only to the sub-group that incarnates the true movement of praxis to reabsorb its inner duality. If we imagine a clash between patrols during a war, it is perfectly conceivable – and has often happened – that the weaker and less well-armed unit will defeat an adversary superior in every respect, thanks to an element of surprise for which it is not even responsible: the chance of their respective routes has simply meant that it saw the other patrol before being spotted by it. In this case, the outcome is non-signifying. But that is because it involves two micro-organisms which do not belong to the same ensemble, and whose clash can only be accidental. If the final victory of one army over another is envisaged, or of one group of nations over another, we shall see that the question is posed very differently.[16] But in any case, these two patrols are lost in the solitude of a no-man's-land. From this standpoint, moreover, chance takes on a signification again. Such skirmishes are dubious in themselves and fundamentally, since the patrols are linked only by inert or practico-inert mediations; if one of them is destroyed by 'the hazards of war', the necessity of that destruction is located at a lower level – it is the

---

16. These questions were never dealt with, since the work remained uncompleted.

objectification of a concerted project (the chosen route) and its alienation in the practico-inert, inasmuch as the nature of the terrain places one of the patrols at the mercy of the other.

On the other hand, when it is a matter of one sub-group struggling against another, the struggle is kept inside the group; and it is produced, of course, on the basis of counter-finalities and makes itself the free expression of practico-inert exigencies. But even were no organ of mediation to exist, even were no concerted mediation to be attempted or possible, it still precisely remains the case that struggle is itself a mediated activity. For it takes place in a human and practical milieu. All the other sub-groups, inasmuch as they totalize – each in its own way – the development of the conflict within the perspective of their own objectives and the objectives of the group; all the common individuals, inasmuch as each of them is the group itself here and now; the totalized ensemble of these individuals and these [sub-]groups; finally the group itself, inasmuch as it supports, encompasses and penetrates each enemy [sub-]group through the practical unity of the totalizing action: all these constituent and constituted dialectics form the moving field of the battle, the living density of the mediations. This simple oleograph – two military factions vying for command in a besieged city during the 'Italian wars' – is all that is needed to show from the outset to what extent internal struggle is a function of common action. In fact, it is through the vicissitudes of the defence – growing pressure from the enemy, problems of supply, abortive sorties, attacks repulsed – that the struggle of the two factions unfolds, as a series of internal determinations inscribed transversally within every military operation and every event: in short, as a lateral temporalization which often remains hidden from the historian by the overall temporalization, or appears as a simple singularization of that common temporalization – i.e. as a certain secondary quality of singularity. If, on the other hand, one considers it in itself, the whole common event is present in it at every instant – as its fundamental structure, its meaning, its 'curvature' and its intimate contexture – and is what decides on its tension. From this standpoint, the vicissitudes of the particular struggle are determined by the common event, via whose mediation a mistake on the part of the faction in power is produced as an objective superiority of the rival faction. For this very reason we encounter another mediation, since such superiority is objective only by virtue of the attitude of the soldiers defending the town and – to a variable extent – that of the civilians. All these men – in groups or masses – determine the superiority of the sub-group which has not gone wrong, inasmuch as they are themselves polarized by the struggle against the besieger. And the importance of that superiority, its objective force, depends upon the objective sericusness of the mistake (for the outcome of the common fight) and upon the urgency with which its real and possible consequences are lived by all – including the 'forces of order', i.e. the coercive bodies at the disposal of the faction in power. This practical attitude (which engenders a regroupment in the totalizing organization itself) is the product of a twofold movement of interiorization and re-exteriorization – for each [sub-]group or common individual – of the global event itself. If some attack has almost succeeded because a particular spot was left unprotected or caught off guard, the capture of the town – which suddenly became the immediate future, but was finally avoided (perhaps through an initiative of the opposing faction) – is. precisely what is transformed into internal tension. It is discovered as an immediately possible – though at the last moment rejected – destiny, but one which may impose itself from one instant to the next. The rejection of that destiny, for each individual, is identical to his rejection of death for himself and all his fellow-citizens. And the distrust, the anger at their leaders and the hope placed in the rival faction are budding actions – i.e. the practical inception of an internal reorganization. Via the mediation *of all*, the event determines the sub-groups in struggle, favouring one and handicapping the other.

This twofold determination is fundamental. In an organized group, in the absence of any arbitration and in cases where schism is impossible (the siege of the town, for example, would make it inconceivable: the threat of total extermination represented by the enemy is interiorized in the town as indissoluble unity until victory), the liquidatory sub-group imposes its unification on the other thanks to the support (tacit or effective) of the community – as a whole or in its majority. No bid for power is conceivable so long as the community as a whole backs the organisms that make it effective. Or else, if chance and the practico-inert *allow* one faction to destroy the other, it will be destroyed in its turn and the community will restore the old forms. Within the group, action in its present reality – as a particular synthesis of positive and negative results – controls the struggle of the particular organs through each individual. Conversely, each faction fights against the other by seeking to win allies. It is not necessarily a matter of gaining the support of the totality of common individuals (for example, of the rank-and-file soldiers or of the 'humbler classes' in the town). But the fight *for alliances* reveals the actual structure of the group (and its historical signification) through the options manifested in it. For, by these options, the hierarchy of powers re-produces itself in practice and confirms itself. In certain cases, it will be enough to ensure the support of other sub-groups directly above or below in the hierarchy. The totality of common individuals, grasped precisely outside of the organs that separate them and assemble them according to rules, may not count for anything. At other times, it alone decides. It is the ensemble of circumstances (present and past) which decides, in the light of the future as destiny and possibility. For us, in any case, one thing counts and one alone: alliances will be forged on the basis of various conditions that must be simultaneously given. First, a certain homogeneity between functions and projects: it must be possible to reconcile the *practical perspectives* of each organ as such. Secondly, a real agreement between *interests*. We saw earlier what an interest is.[17] In a sub-group, it is its objective being in the internal field, inasmuch as it escapes it and is threatened by other sub-groups and, at the very same time, constitutes itself as the objective possibility of increasing its action and incarnating the totalizing action more widely, more precisely and more effectively. So what we have here is the victory of one faction over another, manifesting itself as a general reorganization carried out in a common perspective by an ensemble of united organs, and in this sense being produced as the reappearance of the reunified unity in the victorious sub-group, inasmuch as it directs the battle. In this sense, the liquidation of the defeated sub-group follows hard upon its *dis-incarnation*. Regrouping themselves around the other, the organisms or common individuals strip the defeated sub-group – from without and from within – of its power likewise to incarnate the dissociated unity on the path to reunification. Before the last assaults, it is already no longer anything but a *body alien* to the group, which the community is obliged to digest or eliminate in order to achieve its reunification. The third condition is the emergency or – as we have seen – the exigencies of the ongoing action, its risks of ending in failure, etc. The bond that unites these conditions is naturally dialectical, and they all react upon one another in the synthetic unity of praxis. But the fundamental decision belongs to the common action; or rather, every other condition is like a threshold to be crossed, and the level of this threshold varies according to the common emergencies and common dangers.

From this standpoint, the victory by liquidation is dialectically intelligible. For it is produced as the reunification of the dissociated unity, through the regrouping of organs and individuals according to new common perspectives, and under the interiorized pressure of the emergencies and dangers characterizing the development of the total praxis.

To be sure, there are passive resistances related to the practico-inert. The impotence of certain organs, in institutionalized groups, corresponds to the strength and efficacy of the apparatuses of coercion controlled by the sovereign or the ruling sub-groups. Traditions can separate – and often brake – movements of reunification, etc. In all cases, however, it is

17. *Critique*, vol.1, p.197.

a question of thresholds to be crossed – which common dangers can lower. The organs of coercion, by interiorizing a partial defeat of the community, can be turned back against the power they support. Traditions can be dissolved within the ongoing unification. Sub-groups in fusion can be constituted, by the dissolution of sub-groups organized and separated by the limits of their powers. And so on. Thus victory is a transcendence by diffuse mediation of the entire group: via this mediation, one of the terms of the contradiction liquidates the other; but by this liquidation – and even in the event of its occurring as extermination – it absorbs it and itself becomes the synthesis that transcends at once the thesis and the antithesis.

It is also necessary for this transcendence of itself and the other to be *practical*: i.e. to be realized through concerted manoeuvres, operations and a tactic. It is not enough for the oppositional faction to benefit passively from the advantage gained by the ruling faction's mistakes – it must *exploit* it. We are returned here to free praxis, to invention, to singular incarnation. Perhaps the actual history of this faction, the disagreements that paralyse it, the milieu where it has recruited its members (and, for example, a certain idealist timidity, whose origin is to be sought in the material circumstances conditioning that milieu, or else a certain incompetence whose sources are similar), or simply the internal structure of the sub-group (the difficulty of liaison and the slowness of communications resulting from this, which in turn conditions the possibility of taking decisions) – perhaps all these factors, still others, or just one of them, are expressed by an ill-adapted practice, lagging behind events and perpetually ineffective, or even by *negative* results. But it must first be observed that the errors, failings and gaps of this praxis are precisely intelligible as negative determinations, in so far as this praxis is in fact *praxis-process*; hence in so far as the internal composition of the sub-group, and its objective relations with all the other organs, constitute an inert objectivity encountered as the immanent limit of its practical transcendence. For there really are transcendence, invention and illumination of the practical problem (by the sub-group, and by the common individuals who are its members). But what is always striking *after the event*, in common praxis, is that it always presents itself as a free transcendence transcending material circumstances but going *to a certain point and no further*.

From the situated viewpoint of the historian, in fact – even taking account of all that we do not know and the imperfections of our intellectual tools – it is often obvious that those responsible for an action 'could have' undertaken it on rather different grounds, taken account of risks that they neglected, calculated the objective results of the action performed, and above all – thanks to that and to the choice of more effective means – carried it through to its distant completion, instead of halting on the way. In the actual conception of a plan there is a negative determination, an imperceptible limit that *for us* is confused with invention itself. But invention is precisely only another name for the dialectical transcendence of a given [*d'un donné*]. And in so far as it is precisely *this* given that it transcends – i.e. the ensemble of social fields *in a perspective* that is actualized through the project – it remains qualified by the data [*les données*] that it synthesizes. In so far as the end is a synthesis of the means, action is the synthetic unity of the given ensemble (exigencies, risks, difficulties and available means), inasmuch as it transcends the latter towards that end. But transcendence is nothing but transformation into concrete practice: each *operation* is totalization and compression of all the given into a transcendent relationship of regulated transformation of the practical field. Thus the limits of transcendence are, on the one hand, the transcended data and, on the other, the transcendent structures of the practical field: you do not transcend any old thing towards any old thing, but precisely *this* towards *that*. Comprehension of the limits of action is always possible, since comprehension is nothing but praxis grasping itself on the basis of determined ends and limits that singularize it. In a room containing a damaged fan, to comprehend the action of the man who gets up to open the window despite the wind and rain means recalling – in the comprehensive project – the fact that the fan is out of order. Likewise, to comprehend a leader taking a certain decision, whereas the objective situation suggested another (and doubtless better) one, is to interiorize in the comprehensive project the fact that the absence of certain intellectual tools, or the presence of a certain *hexis* based on the initial pledge, must have restricted from within the range and wealth of options. It must also be remembered that there is no comprehension based on negations of exteriority: the absence of tools – a wholly external qualification – should simply prompt a reproduction of ideative and practical approaches on the basis of the tools actually used. But we can precisely grasp the signification of these – and of their 'availability' to the agent – on the basis of the latter's history, inasmuch as this is grasped through that of the group, as a singular incarnation.

Thus, to comprehend how the sub-group exploits the situation – and, for example, the advantages this offers it – is to comprehend an action in its two aspects: i.e. in what it has that is new and irreducible, and also in the determinations singularizing it. It must be added, moreover, that the determinations mark insuperable limits *for the moment*, but do not strictly decide the act. There are these frontiers, these 'habits', these means and these exigencies of the object. But – precisely in so far as action transcends its own limits and envelops them, only to find them again as enveloped limits of their own transcendence – the practical option remains unpredictable, inasmuch as it is positive singularity and concrete novelty. This unpredictability is an actual datum of comprehension, precisely in so far as the latter – far from presenting itself as a present intuition – constitutes itself as an undertaking that is temporalized right up to the last moment of the praxis to be comprehended. In short, the common individual or the sub-group freely adopt as their own – and as free determinations of themselves – the inert structures that condition them. And if one wishes to grasp the ultimate meaning of these, one will be referred back to the whole group and its history: i.e. simultaneously to its practical temporalization and to the counter-finalities this has secreted in it (as well as to any previous attempts to suppress these counter-finalities). It is *freely* that this faction leader has deluded himself about the possibilities of his 'band'. It is *freely* that he has neglected to exploit this or that advantage. But this mistaken assessment gathers into itself, incarnates and reproduces the sub-group as a whole, including even its fundamental relationship to the group that has produced it: this is what makes it comprehensible. In other words – and sticking to our example – it has really underestimated the advantage that the errors of the rival faction gave to its own faction. But in so far as this underestimation is a deep expression of the objective structures of the advantaged sub-group and its deep relationship with the group, it reveals the sub-group's destiny as it produces it: to be defeated, because it let the opportunity slip. But by letting it slip, the sub-group proclaimed itself defeated: it reproduced its original relationship with the group in the practical shape of hesitation, lack of self-confidence, respect for legality, timidity in the face of the sovereign faction, or quite simply incompetence. And thereby it revealed a certain truth of the struggle: namely, that the group which had produced it could be incarnated in it only as an incarnation defeated in advance; that the moment when the ensemble of common individuals turned away from the ruling faction, to place their hopes in the rival faction, could be only provisional. The ambiguity, the transitory difficulties, the complex problems that the oppositional faction had actualized in practice by its struggle designated it – from the outset, albeit invisibly – for defeat. It turned out, for example, that counter-finalities had decided a dissociation of unity that automatically pitted a solid organ, solidly supported and equipped with every tool, against a secondary sub-group, badly armed, whose internal unity itself was compromised by this abrupt promotion. The latter – not widely known – detached it from the other sub-groups and made it incapable of really attracting the trust of all or winning serious allies. Or else it found itself so situated, between the totalized ensemble of common individuals and the ruling faction, that its very situation debarred it from opposition: the rulers imposed themselves as an *incarnation* and any opponents, by revealing themselves as such, would have alarmed all their possible allies; the slightest declared resistance would have constituted them as *factionalists* – hence, would have turned the common individual away from them, in the name of the common praxis. The fact remains that later, in an uncertain battle, the group did turn for an instant towards them; but their 'fatal' hesitation was a re-exteriorization of the mistrust the group had shown towards them, which they had interiorized as lack of confidence, inferiority complex, defeatist behaviour, etc. Through them, the group's original mistrust contrasted with the current trust it displayed in them and disqualified it. In a certain way, however, through that underestimation the group reached a true estimation of its relationship with the sub-group: *it would not follow it into action.* First, because the attitude of the 'factionalists' was not capable of swaying it. Secondly, because the trust it currently displayed towards them was merely negative: only a fleeting mistrust had turned the group away from its real leaders. The first factor might appear like an outdated survival, exercising its braking power: the group had changed, but the sub-group had kept its old determinations. And it is true that there was a lag here. But the second factor refers us back to the current correspondence between the group and the sub-group. In positive terms, it may be said that through their hesitations the factionalists realize the visible incarnation of the group's actually unshaken trust in its leaders. There remains, however, a slight gap between the diachronic and the synchronic (we shall study this problem in its entirety below[18]), and it remains the case that this gap allows a phantom of indetermination to subsist. The group turns to the factionalists because of their attitude yesterday or the day before, but the factionalists, disconcerted by the indifference it displayed towards them then, are not there to meet it. And although there is a perfect correspondence between their hesitations and the entirely temporary character of the group's trust, it may be wondered whether another faction, of a different calibre, would not have taken advantage of this rallying to their cause and – on certain conditions – transformed the temporary into something definitive. In other words, the group has *diachronically* made other factionalists impossible; but – although it has hardly changed, or the change is still superficial – in the present and synchronically it does not reproduce this impossibility in its full rigour. I confine myself here to signalling the gap. It represents, if you like, *the opening of History.* In any case, it does not suppress intelligibility, since it is itself the product of a dialectical temporalization. Only, *the opening* is secreted as inert objectivity, or if

18. See Preface above.

you prefer (we shall come back to this) as dead-possibility.[19]

In short, it is the strongest, craftiest and best armed which wins. It crushes its adversary because it invents the best manoeuvres; because it is not fooled by the traps laid for it; because the losers fall regularly into the traps it prepares for them. But it is endowed with this strength and intelligence and skill via the mediation of the entire group: i.e. they express its mode of recruitment, its history, the evolution of its structures, and its fundamental relationship with all. And its victory is not a consequence of the past: required by the developments of common praxis – already inscribed in these developments, albeit invisible – it is an exigency of the future.

We have shown that the struggle is intelligible. Basically, the fact is that unity is dissociated within a vaster unity, i.e. that of the totalization-of-envelopment. The intelligibility of the struggle appears as soon as it is deciphered on the basis of this totalization, and in the perspective of the common praxis. The totalizing unity is the permanent mediation between the two terms of the dissociated unity: on the basis of it, the conflict appears as sole possible solution to an inert problem engendered by the counter-finalities of praxis. At this level, the rift takes on a new meaning: it is the practical and human reinteriorization of the separation in exteriority produced by the practico-inert. This separation or negation of exteriority is realized in molecular solitude as a pure and simple absence of relationship between the terms (or, which comes to the same thing, as a reification of relations: we have seen this in the practico-inert moment of investigation). Against it, the struggle is produced as a negation of immanence – i.e. as a synthetic relation to two epicentres – and this negation of immanence reassumes the separation of exteriority in the form of a twofold reverse attempt at reunification. Contradiction appears here as the *meaning* of the conflict, i.e. as the human movement that transcends the risk of non-relation towards the practical relation of the rift. Hatred, will to murder, refusal of reconciliation, are born as the human interiorization of inert materiality, when this materiality makes itself invisibly into mediation in the milieu of fraternity-terror. So the intelligibility of the struggle appears, when it is considered through its very transcendence, as the unfurling of the problem that mediation will refurl in the complex unity of a solution. And the complex signification of its episodes, of its sinuosities, of its reversals, is yielded up if one adopts the viewpoint of the group turning back, after reunification, to the history of this action in action and grasping itself as producing this dissociation within the unity of one totalization. In other words, the

---

19. See footnote 97 on p.334 below.

totalization-of-envelopment – i.e. the integration of all concrete individuals by praxis – has never ceased to be everywhere as its own cause
(we know now what these metaphorical terms mean here, so we use them
without fear of misunderstanding) and as its own mediation. Beneath the
rift of antagonistic dissociation, we find not the infinite void but unity
again, and human presence. The fissure between the enveloped incarnations
allows the plenitude of the unity of immanence to appear as a totalizing
and singular incarnation *of all incarnations taken together.*

But this investigation of intelligibility should not make us, therefore,
fall prey to optimism. It is true that victory comes to the victor via the
mediation of the whole group, and that it incarnates a moment of the
totalizing activity as praxis-process. But this does not mean that it
realizes a progress of the group towards its own objectives: a priori we
can decide nothing. The circumstances of the praxis and its material
conditions alone can tell us. For nothing proves that the liquidation of a
sub-group does not express an involution of praxis. Perhaps it disappears
not because it arouses mistrust, not because it is sacrificed in the name of
unity, but amid general indifference, because the members of the group
lose confidence in their common activity – unless an unforeseen and
considerable complication of the conditions of praxis (the appearance, *on
the outside*, of new enemies, new problems) creates a more or less
definitive, more or less deep, gap between the common means of the
group and the exigencies of the practical field surrounding it. Then the
conflict still springs – as in all other cases – from internal problems, but
the struggle is conditioned by the fact that the group is dominated by the
adversary, or overwhelmed by its own action. The choice it makes of one
or the other sub-group, and the features of its implicit mediation, then
express its bewilderment. The struggle and the victory remain perfectly
intelligible, but they are the intelligible product of this bewilderment and
will contribute to aggravating it. Perhaps, by this tacit choice, the group
has passed judgement upon itself.

Nothing proves, moreover, that each of the two organs in conflict
represents a lucid and valid perspective – a partial but precise option. It
is generally the contrary that occurs. The sub-groups, when a practico-
inert danger contrasts them as partial viewpoints, as a practical and
dissociated unity, are already products of the group's history and their
own history. The objective difficulties that they interiorize and re-
exteriorize in conflict are deflected from their true meaning by the very
structure of the sub-groups, whether the struggle *adds* adventitious
significations to them as it is realized or whether it takes place as an
impoverishment of the problem. Thus the real, deep conflict can be
expressed by abstract and scholastic oppositions: it can happen that
people fight over myths and absurd 'opinions', or over the articles of a

dogma. Naturally, this mythologization of the conflict's object cannot prevent it from being a deep reality, or from bringing us back through praxis to the level of need. Equally naturally, its scholastic and abstract character is itself intelligible, since it refers us both to the tools of knowledge and action produced by praxis itself and, equally, to the ensemble of contemporary structures and the historical conjuncture. Nevertheless, the intelligible fact that it expresses itself on an abstract terrain, through the clash of fetishized symbols, cannot be held as irrelevant to the nature and meaning of the conflict. To tell the truth, it *cannot* express itself otherwise. But this means that it can manifest itself only in an altered form; that it produces itself by producing the prison which encloses it; and that it partly loses its signification, in so far as this symbolic expression is posited for itself. As a result, every operation – in both [sub-]groups – remains intelligible on the basis of the deep movement that engenders it, but becomes bogged down and goes astray, leading the entire conflict rather further astray. People could kill one another over the sex of angels – and that reflected a deep malaise of Byzantine society. But it is precisely one of the meanings of that malaise that people could kill one another – at Byzantium and at that moment of its history – *over the sex of angels*: i.e. that a theologians' dispute had to be burdened with all the real divisions sapping the city and the Empire, or else contradictions be allowed to fester beneath that overstratified society. The polarization of practical forces by symbols must necessarily entail a partial loss of energies: in that case, the victory remains intelligible – but its meaning is as confused as that of the conflict.

It would actually be far too simple to consider, in the name of a transcendental dogmatism, that these mythological forms of struggle are epiphenomena: a mere ineffectual expression of the real transformations taking place. In fact, if we are to push materialism *to the end*, as we must, we shall recognize that these fetishes are things – determinations of matter, the synthetic unification of inert diversities – and that these things will act *as things* upon adversaries. In other words, struggle and victory are alienated in advance. But this alienation of every struggle (despite, as we shall see, the progressive growth of awareness) is the very character of what Marx calls pre-history. Even the revolutionary struggle produces its fetishes and is alienated in them. Even in the Communist Party, people struggle over the sex of angels. This does not at all mean that History has no meaning (this fundamental problem – which we shall tackle later[20] – cannot be dealt with on this superficial

---

20. See Preface above; also, in the Appendix below (pp.402–24), Sartre's notes on 'Progress'.

and abstract level of our historical investigation). It merely means that it is not a priori necessary, in a conflict between sub-groups within any group, for one of the two adversaries to represent progress – i.e. *a progress for the group towards its* common objectives – or for the victory really to represent 'a step forward'. Of course, it is always possible in religious disputes to consider that one viewpoint – even in the most abstract myth – represents the effort of certain sub-groups, emanating from certain milieux, to reconcile dogmas with practical and scientific Reason (however obscure this may still be). For the most part, moreover, the effort actually does unite the sub-groups drawn from the 'rising classes'. But the question is not so clear. In so far as each organ of the group takes part in the conflict, the struggle is obscured by the very fact of the alliances contracted: still intelligible in terms of the structures and circumstances, but often disconcerting and paralysing for the combatants, because the existence of fetishes – masking the real interests of the sub-groups and the group itself – gives an often monstrous character to the antagonistic groupings. Proust, for example, enjoyed showing the tight synthetic interconnection, but perfect heterogeneity, of the anti-Dreyfusards. And this interconnection can be *comprehended*. The fact that servants who were the slaves of a declining aristocracy – along with certain big bourgeois who had passed from a profound vulgarity to a false culture and from that to snobbery – should seize the opportunity to weld themselves to that very aristocracy goes without saying. But it is no less important that the internal exchanges, osmoses, etc., should be effected under the practical code of anti-Semitism and in relation to the fetishized Army. The Dreyfus Affair, as a contingent and necessary incarnation, occurred as the final battle waged by the radical bourgeoisie to drive the representatives of the landed aristocracy from the key posts it still held. But groupings were formed on the basis of Dreyfus's own case, the Honour of the Army, or pure Justice, and that is what gave the struggle its wavering aspect (which in fact reflected the actual ambiguity of French society). I shall not labour this example, which goes beyond the present framework of our investigation, since it refers to the problem of the struggles between groups within a society.[21]

Besides – assuming a clear awareness in the two sub-groups of the common objectives and real factors of the conflict – the liquidation of one sub-group by the other (even in the positive hypothesis of a group in the thick of action) a priori harbours the danger of *deviating* the common action. The opposition may have its function, obliging the leading bodies to transcend themselves and transcend it by making themselves mediators

---

21. See next chapter.

(through the devising of more complex plans). Once liquidated, we have seen how it reappears inside the victorious sub-group, albeit in another form. So long as it existed outside, the contradiction was clearly defined. From the moment it is interiorized, this contradiction becomes unclear and is really produced as ambiguity. Not (which would be of less importance) because the opposition has to be semi-clandestine or entirely clandestine, depending on the sub-group's degree of integration; but because the dissidents are tied to those in the majority by what you might call *adhesions*. A common history has first made them the *same*, as we have seen.[22] After the victory, they want to remain *the same* until the total praxis is completed. And if they oppose the majority, it is precisely within the perspective of, above all, preserving unity. Thus the opposition in the victorious sub-group remains without reality, in so far as the dissidents refuse to be an opposition or have a 'fractional activity': i.e. in so far as they are in full agreement with the majority about sacrificing their own conception of praxis to the unity of the sub-group. This is expressed in various ways. In particular, if they dare to propose a modification of the plan worked out under the majority's control, this modification must be nullified if it is not adopted by a majority. Which, in fact, means that it will eventually be rejected unanimously. But in this way practical reason is subordinated to the inert structures of the sub-group. The proposition is in fact never rejected *only* because it is unrealizable, but also – and sometimes primarily – because by being enacted it would modify the internal structures. Besides, those in the majority evaluate it through the structures that have produced them, with their intellectual tools. Thus the contradiction never surfaces, since it is refused by everybody at once: by the majority in the name of the plan of action, and by the minority inasmuch as it above all refuses to be a minority. Such perpetually stifled oppositions and contradictions never-theless express objective and internal difficulties within the sub-group. Open conflict and transcendence via mediation [represent] the only *human* way of assuming them – i.e. of channelling them to the practical, in order to reveal and resolve them. To realize a totalizing unity against them immediately (without the mediation of conflict) means to contain them for the moment but, in the overall temporalization, to aggravate them. By refusing to assume them, the sub-group pursues its action according to the principles and means – and as a function of the ends – that it has set itself. However, since such difficulties express within it certain exigencies of the group's totalizing action, and consequently certain internal variations of the whole community, the sub-group's

22. *Critique*, vol.1, pp.372 ff.

activity *deviates* because it seeks to remain the same. The deviation comes to it *from outside*: i.e. from the external transformations of the practical field that the group seeks to modify, inasmuch as these are interiorized by all the common individuals and, through them, re-exteriorized – even if they do not act *together* – as a profound modification of the sub-group's situation, or rather of *its reality*. (We shall see further on, in relation to social conflicts, the group of Soviet leaders transformed in its very reality – i.e. in its relations with the ensemble of Soviet citizens – just by the counter-finalities of its praxis.) It changes because it remains the same, it strives to remain the same in order not to break unity. Yet if the sub-group as such is a directing body, it plays the role of organizing and co-ordinating partial activities in order to integrate them into the overall praxis. So it decides the latter, within the narrow limits imposed by circumstances and the situation. The *deviation* of the sub-group's particular practice is necessarily repeated, though to a lesser degree, in the group's praxis. But this deviation remains sufficient, in certain specific circumstances, to lead the common praxis to *other* objectives or to failure. A dialectic is actually established between the transformation of praxis under pressure from the transcendent, the deformation of the internal deviation by this transformation, and the action of the transformed deviation upon the praxis in transformation.

Conclusion

These observations allow us to reject pessimism and optimism alike. The conflict is intelligible *on the basis of the totalizing praxis*, because it is the practical assumption of the inert oppositions that action's counter-finalities produce. And it is in this sense that the dissociation of unity is a certain moment of a reunificatory enterprise, even though this dissociation is constituted not magically and ideally by unity being dissociated, but by the unificatory project of the two practical unities, autonomous as organisms and initially undifferentiated inasmuch as both – by pledge – are the same common individual (prior to any subsequent functional differentiations). In this sense, unity is the conflict's *matrix* and *destiny* (at least for the historian who studies it in the past); and the solution as a practical reunification contains within it, in the guise of inert and re-organized structures, *all* the oppositions previously reproduced and humanized in the binary movement that has engendered the reciprocity of antagonism. Furthermore, totalizing comprehension of the struggle implies that it is grasped as a *mediated* opposition, even if the organs of mediation are lacking, inasmuch as it cannot exist or develop in one direction or another without the continuous mediation of *all* the common individuals. It is in this realistic and practical sense that we must understand how unity produces and maintains its own rifts. But although comprehension is always a priori possible, provided only that we have the necessary information at our disposal, this dialectical rationality of internal conflicts in no way prejudges their development or their outcome. Deviations, errors and failures, far from eluding comprehension, form an integral part of it. It is even possible, in certain cases, to comprehend why a conflict unwisely embarked upon, on the basis of insurmountable difficulties, reflects the slow degradation of a community and ends by hastening its total destruction. By this, moreover, I do not mean just that the degradation and negative course of the conflict are the mere practico-inert obverse of what we have called praxis-process. I mean rather that in praxis *as such*, in the choice of means, in the determination of immediate and distant objectives, etc., this degradation produces itself as a qualification of its own transcendence. It is what will, in fact, manifest itself – through instances of defeatist behaviour, overestimation or under-estimation, etc. – as the deterioration of practical fields and instruments in the actual hands of those who use them. In this sense, even 'loss of contact' – as a real and objective separation of the central organs from the base – is an intelligible fact in the perspective of the totalizing temporalization. Not just because above all it is an interiorization of the total historical process by a definite group, *but also* because this interiorization is *practical*. The objective hiatus separating the base from the summit is never grasped in its inert reality as a breach of continuity: it is realized by acts and their results (orders not followed, passivity or hostility of the rank and file, cards not renewed, joining other groups, etc.). At the same time, it characterizes the actual behaviour of the warring sub-groups – their leaders oscillating between ineffective authoritarianism and a dangerous 'tailism', etc. The struggle itself languishes and becomes stratified, so to speak. Or, quite to the contrary, it takes on a character of bitter ferocity at the summit. In short, whatever their circumstances and evolution may be, the internal conflicts of a group are totally intelligible because, the group being totally practical, its practico-inert determinations never reveal themselves except as the material and abstract conditions of its praxis. In this sense they become factors of intelligibility, since we have to discover them in the midst of action in order to find the movement of the project that transcends them, by positing them in order to suppress them.

From this point of view, even chance is intelligible – by which I mean 'Cleopatra's nose', or 'the grain of sand in Cromwell's urethra' – since it is circumstances and dangers reproduced as organized conflicts that in each sub-group, and via the mediation of all the rest, decide the exact importance of the individual action. The 'grain of sand' was important only because Cromwell's regime could not survive Cromwell, which was due precisely to the fact that it was not supported by the society that had engendered it. In short, it was brought down by its own contradictions, which were the practico-inert resistance of the base assumed by the practical transcendence. It obviously remains the case that Cromwell could have died five years later. As I have already said, I am far from sharing Plekhanov's fine indifference and declaring, like him, that the outcome would have been just the same. That is anti-historical and inhuman dogmatism: the fortune of the *particular* men who would have died under Cromwell during those five extra years just does not interest Plekhanov. But that is not what we shall say. To be sure, *at a certain level of abstraction* the outcome would have been the same. At the level of concrete totalization, it would have been at once the same (inasmuch as it contains within itself the abstract structures of inertia) and different (for the concrete men who would have lived it). For us, however, the important issue lies elsewhere. It is that we should be able to define dialectically, on the basis of a practical comprehension of the undertakings and conflicts – as well as the structures – of the group and sub-groups, the necessary margin of indetermination in which chance (i.e. a series alien to the ensembles considered) may operate. In a durable, aware group, supported by its base and strongly integrated, this margin is reduced to the minimum: it is as close to zero as possible. Sicknesses and deaths do not thereby disappear – but they lose all historical efficacy. A system of replacement is already created, and the urgency of the situation forces the successors to continue the policy of those who have left the scene. We shall see later that the diachronic synthesis is cross-hatched by deaths and births, i.e. by *generations* (a discontinuity in continuity).[23] But the problem does not exist at the level of the directing organs of a strongly integrated group, where the dead man will be replaced by a contemporary – often one of his closest collaborators – who has shared his experience and assisted him in his activity, so that the disappearance of individuals does not succeed even in inflecting a policy or creating a discontinuity. When it does, however, succeed in doing so, this is because the role of the individual is already greater and, by virtue of that, the deeper unity of the group more precarious. It is even possible, on the basis of circumstances and the common action, to determine the limits within which change can occur. If Stalin's death marked the end of Stalinism, that was because in a very real sense Stalinism survived only

---

23. Sartre tackles this question on p.312 below. See also *L'Idiot de la famille*, vol.3, pp.436 ff.

through Stalin, and because – for reasons I have set out elsewhere[24] – he incarnated organic unity in the eyes of the Soviet ruling group and realized it by terror. Curiously, but very *intelligently*, that individual realized in himself and through his acts the sacrifice of every individual – by himself and by everybody – to the unity of the leadership. But the end of Stalinism – apart from the fact that it represented a slow and difficult transformation, which at least initially assumed the maintenance of certain practices and certain principles – was, unlike the death of Cromwell, not the end of the regime. His age made it possible at any moment: the date was a chance one, but the intelligibility of that chance was due to the fact that Soviet society, still masked by the centralized bureaucracy, was *already de-Stalinized*; or, if you prefer, to the fact that Stalin had ceased to be useful (or perhaps ceased to be more useful than harmful), yet the praxis of those last thirty-five years had integrated the leading group so that it could not transform itself in Stalin's lifetime. And Stalin, a product of his own praxis, was producing their past in the form of a continued praxis, a future already invisibly contested. Even that was no accident: this gap – this failure of the leader to adapt to the situation his praxis had produced – was intelligible only at the conclusion of a long and painful reign. It was then and then alone that *praxis* and *hexis* were strictly equivalent, and every new invention was only the re-exteriorization of the interiorized common past. But, precisely, this old age of the leader placed him at death's door. Thus indetermination as a historical factor was contained within the narrowest limits; or rather, it formed part of intelligibility. For, in the ruling circles, one element of the conflicts in progress was precisely the expectation of Stalin's death – i.e. the predictability of the event, but relative unpredictability of its date. The fundamental character of the internal struggles, however, was conditioned by Stalin's old age, since it was that old age which created the objective contradiction between the policy of the leaders and the new Soviet realities. Thus, step by step, we could show how in every case it is the actual history of the group, in its dialectical intelligibility, that defines the role it leaves to chance and, at the same time, determines the *function* it assigns to the latter: i.e. the *objective* which chance is charged with realizing. If chance is indeed given a task, this is because the balance of forces and the complexity of the struggle do not allow praxis to accomplish everything by itself. But however surprising the outcome may appear to contemporaries, chance – as an intervention of the practico-inert at the heart of the dialectic – merely executes the verdict delivered by praxis itself. Even if it were to decide the annihilation of one

24. In *The Spectre of Stalin*, London 1969.

sub-group and the triumph of another, that would simply mean that, for specific reasons, the whole group must have decided to leave things in the hands of chance – divesting itself in the latter's favour of its own mediating powers.

4

The Unresolved Struggle as Anti-Labour

T HERE remains our second question.[25] Within the group the warring sub-groups – via a kind of negative collaboration – accomplish by their very antagonism a common *anti-labour*. For if we use the term labour – a quite superficial and practical definition – for a material operation aiming to produce a certain object as a determination of the practical field and with a view to a certain end, we must call the dual antagonistic activity *anti-labour*, since each sub-group is striving to destroy or deviate the object produced by the other. But this anti-labour is productive: the struggle, as a reciprocity of labours that destroy one another, objectifies itself in an ensemble of products which, henceforth, occupy the internal field of the common group and contribute to inflecting its action. Actually this dual attempt at destruction is never entirely successful: it never achieves a reciprocal nullification of the realities produced. And even were it to achieve this, the labour of destruction presupposes an expenditure of energy, an accumulation of means and a transformation of the practical field: in short, the constitution – whether by degradation or disintegration – of new realities inside the group. When, for example, the leading body is riven by violent conflicts, i.e. when it divides into sub-groups clashing fundamentally over the common praxis, it often happens – in the period that precedes the liquidation of one side by the other – that every project (economic plan, law, temporary and directly applicable measure or, if we are dealing with a party, action programme), as soon as it is put forward by one faction, finds itself rejected by another, while a third – simultaneously judge and participant – tries to make itself the mediator, in order to impose itself on the former two. The outcome of

---

25. See, on pp.11–13 above, Sartre's outline of the two problems he considers essential for the intelligibility of History.

these various stances is: an initial project of sub-group A, a counter-project of sub-group B, a conciliatory project of sub-group C. This last will in turn be modified by each of the two former contestants, both because each will seek to win it over and also because neither will wish to leave it the merit of its arbitration. The product of this shifting struggle will in one way or another bear the mark of the three sub-groups, but it will no longer correspond to the intentions of any one of them. Each of its determinations will in some way be the negation of a certain proposition, perhaps incorrect or dangerous, but rationally conceived, clear and equipped with a signification. What is more, there will have been other propositions in the course of the bargaining that were the negations of those negations, and so on. We do indeed have the image of a collaboration, but *in reverse*. As for the object, these negations determine it in its concrete reality, but they prevent it from being related to any human intention, any global project. Moreover, the antagonisms present have managed to achieve the nullification of certain initial dispositions, with the result that the object is qualified *also* by a partial indetermination. An indetermination and also an overdetermination, as we saw earlier. Whether it is a decree, an administrative measure or a law, its application still has to be ensured. At this new juncture – in the name of those same conflicts – the executive fouls up. This is at least a permanent possibility, frequently realized. At this level, realization makes the object produced into a monstrous and deformed reflection of a project that had itself preserved only a confused signification: the cycle of inhumanity is completed. Let us recall – the example is distant but one of the clearest – how the project of establishing National Workshops conceived by Louis Blanc, already rendered unrecognizable by amendments introduced in the Assembly, was into the bargain systematically sabotaged by Marie and his collaborators. Is it enough, then, to study the conflicts inside an organized group for the deformity, the semi-effectiveness, the total ineffectiveness and the counter-effectiveness of the products of *anti-labour* to find a new signification, and for the opacity of these confused works to recover a dialectical intelligibility? We need only press ahead with our critical investigation in order to perceive that the answer is affirmative.

There is, to be sure, no question but that the product thus disfigured belongs to nobody, and cannot be interpreted as the objectification of a project. But that is not the issue. It is simply necessary to know whether – as in the abstract hypothesis of two non-totalizable [sub-]groups – we must enumerate the changes it has undergone and relate them to more or less independent, more or less irreducible factors: i.e. to layers of signification that cannot be fused in a synthesis. Or whether, on the contrary, on the basis of the totalization-of-envelopment, the monstrous product can itself be grasped as the dialectical totalization of the two antagonistic tactics *in their irreducibility*. For in the produced object, which – precisely inasmuch as it is no longer directly assimilable to a human project – constitutes a real determination of the practico-inert, this irreducibility is objectified and alienated into a multiplicity of interpenetration. For we have already noted that the synthetic unity of the inanimate itself produces an interpenetration of meanings, through the reciprocal action of synthesis and passivity. Thus the successive deformations of the initial plan – having been acts of war, each of which conditioned the other and aimed to destroy it – in the passive synthesis constituting the final object assume the status of a quality sustained by objective inertia. As such, each extends through the other, or rather a unique quality of the object (a particular feature of its deformity) fuses them together. The whole struggle has objectified and alienated itself in its product. And undoubtedly, this can justifiably be envisaged as a practico-inert reality. So we might say that, as such, it escapes intelligibility. But in an integrated group that is only partially true. For the product, whatever its worth and whatever its deformities, is *utilized*. If it is a law or decree, these are applied. In short, they become bad means for a free praxis, just as in the constituent dialectic the instrument integrates itself into the praxis of the free organism and becomes a structure of the act. Of course, the results may be negative. The creation of the National Workshops – after the mutilations and transformations undergone by the initial plan – had as its direct consequence the insurrection of June 1848. On the one hand, however, certain leading circles *were expecting* this revolt of the poor and did not fear to provoke it; on the other, we have just seen that the intelligibility of History is in no way linked – at least at this level of our critical investigation – to the problem of its ultimate aims. So what needs to be pointed out is that the *product* – in so far as it is *at one and the same time* an inert result of *anti-labour* and a means integrated into a new action – presents itself as a reinteriorized objectification of the conflict and, consequently, as a negative (through worked matter) yet practical (through its reintegration into praxis) unity of the duality. Or, if you prefer, the product of anti-labour is neither more nor less signifying, in relation to the reciprocity of antagonism, than is the tool – a product of common labour – in relation to the reciprocity of mutual aid. Intelligibility, to be sure, falls to a lower level; but this is not due to the conflict as such. The decrease of level would be exactly the same if we attempted to grasp a united group through the instruments it forges with the agreement of all its members. It is just that we grasp the practico-inert as a product whose utilization *is in progress*, and that we endeavour to comprehend it in the twofold movement whereby the group produces it and, precisely by doing so, makes itself its product. A passive synthesis revitalized by action, it is transcended inertia that constitutes within it the fundamental support and secret limit of its intelligibility. We shall return to this point when we have to show how the two dialectics and the anti-dialectic separating them are totalized in the synchronic totalization.[26]

Precisely because it is a passive and revitalized synthesis,* however – in other words, because it functions *despite* its defects of construction; because it lives *despite* the malformations that make it unviable (and, naturally, also *because of them*) – this product is maintained and preserved in its being by the totalizing praxis, i.e. from another viewpoint by all the common individuals, at least until it explodes and perhaps causes the group itself to explode. And through this inert perseverance in its being, it reveals another type of mediation of the group between the sub-groups in conflict. In other words, the group – by maintaining it in its internal field – manifests a real adaptation of the product of anti-labour to the common situation, inasmuch as it is actualized by all organs and all common individuals. There is *a practical meaning* of anti-labour that dialectical Reason can discover and positivism will not discover.

I shall take just one example, a contemporary one: the emergence in the USSR of the ideological monstrosity of 'socialism in one country'. Critical investigation will show us: (1) that this slogan was a product of the conflicts rending the leading bodies; (2) that *beyond and through these conflicts*, it represented certain contradictions and transformations of Soviet society as a whole; (3) that inasmuch as it survived, it created other verbal formulae that supplemented and corrected it – in other words, enriched knowledge and practice by transcending the monstrosity and transforming it into truth. We have no intention, of course, of going into the extraordinarily complex history of the conflicts that divided the Soviet leaders after Lenin's death, let alone of embarking on a dialectical interpretation of those conflicts. We are simply taking an example, which we shall consider not *for its own sake* but for its pedagogic value.

1.   Trotsky had no more illusions than Stalin about the situation of the USSR in those difficult years. He had once believed that the Revolution would break out in Germany and other bourgeois democracies, and that this internationalization of the working-class victory would modify the co-ordinates of the Russian problem in the short term. But events had

_____

* For our purposes, it matters little *when* and *by whom*. It is of no importance whether a particular law functions *after* the liquidation of one of the [sub-]groups and even after the disappearance of the two adversaries. What counts is that it gives information about them – even if they are destroyed and forgotten – inasmuch as a praxis preserves its actuality; inasmuch as it is a *function* and creates duties; inasmuch as it regulates the communication of goods, men or verbal determinations.

26. See below, pp.272 ff.

disabused him. He was as conscious as Stalin of the temporary ebb of the European workers' movements. For both of them, the USSR stood *in mortal peril*. Alone and encircled by formidable and hostile powers, it needed to increase its industrial and military potential – albeit at the cost of the most extreme sacrifices – or resign itself to disappearing. At most, it could be added that the circumstances defining their former activity had made the *émigré* Trotsky more aware of the importance of the foreign revolutionary movements, while Stalin – who had practically never left Russia – was more ignorant about Europe and more mistrustful. But Stalin did not claim that a *Communist* order could be achieved in the USSR, without simultaneously being installed on a universal scale. So the two leaders and the fractions they represented could seemingly agree on a minimum programme, as required by the actual situation: to embark at once on building the new society, without for the time being relying on any outside help; and to sustain the revolutionary ardour of the masses by indicating the direction in which that construction should proceed – in short, by showing them *a future*. It was necessary to tell the Russian people, simultaneously: 'We *must* hold out' and 'We *can* construct' and 'It is by constructing that we shall hold out'. But those very simple exigencies did not imply that building this powerful Russia – on the twin basis of industry and armaments – should go beyond the stage of what we might term a pre-socialism. The working class would appropriate the instruments of labour, and industrialization would be accompanied by a progressive installation of the structures and cadres which, once the international situation had changed – i.e. once revolutions occurred elsewhere in the world – would allow the establishment of a truly socialist society. There was another point, too, on which it was *possible* for Stalin and Trotsky to agree: poverty cannot be socialized. Despite the threat from abroad, it was necessary to embark on the difficult stage of pre-socialist accumulation. And Trotsky, of course, was the first to insist on the need to carry the process of collectivization and industrialization through to the end.

The two men discovered the same pressing needs and the same objective exigencies. For both, the praxis of Revolution in the USSR had to be both defensive and constructive. Reliance on one's own resources, moreover, would last as long as the circumstances that made it necessary. The conflicts actually developed in other spheres. The two men represented two contradictory aspects of the struggle that the revolutionaries had waged in the past against Tsarism. Trotsky, a remarkable man of action when circumstances required it, was nevertheless first and foremost a theoretician, an intellectual. In action he remained an intellectual, which meant the action had to be *radical*. Such a structure of practice is perfectly valid provided it is adapted to circumstances, which is what allowed him to organize the Army and win the war. Behind that lay emigration. The exiled revolutionaries, without actually losing contact with the Russian masses, for a time had closer links with the working-class parties of the West. The internationalism of the revolutionary movement was the real stuff of their experience. And Marxism, as a theory and as a practice, appeared to them *in its universality*. Universalism and radicalism: these, if you like, were the way in which Trotsky interiorized his encirclement by the West – and his exile itself, which tended to make him, like all *émigrés*, an abstract universal. The theory of permanent revolution was simply the articulation of these interiorized characteristics by determinations of Marxist language, and as a matter of fact the theory actually came from Marx. The only thing that came from Trotsky – but this was *everything* – was the imperative urgency those theses assumed under his pen. In a single dialectical movement, the Revolution had to be perpetually intensified by transcending its own objectives (radicalization) and progressively extended to the entire universe (universalization). And that meant – before 1917 – that the proletarian Revolution would take place in Europe, in a highly industrialized country. We all know how astonished those 'Westernized' figures were, when circumstances led them to take power in an underdeveloped country. It will be recalled how they hesitated and envisaged creating transitional forms, until events obliged them to press ahead.

Stalin, by contrast, always represented an intermediary between the *émigré* leaders and the Russian masses. His task was to adapt directives to the concrete situation and the real men who would do the work. He was on the side of those men. He knew the Russian masses and, before 1914, did not hide the somewhat contemptuous mistrust he felt for the *émigré* circles, with few exceptions. The history of his conflicts with them after 1905 illuminates what we might call his practical particularism. The important thing for him was to carry out instructions *with the means at hand*. He knew those means – and reckoned that the *émigrés* did not know them. For him, Marxism was a guide to tactics, rather like Clausewitz's *On War*. He had neither the culture nor the leisure required to appreciate its theoretical dimension. Though he admired Lenin, Stalin was shocked when he wrote *Materialism and Empirio-criticism* and thought it a waste of time. In that sense, the universality of Marxism – although, of course, he *spoke* about it – constantly eluded him. It was actually incarnated *by him*, in a praxis always singularized by the circumstances in which it was produced (Tsarism; rapid industrialization, but immense lag behind the West; foreign capital; proletariat still weak and immature, albeit growing in numbers; bourgeoisie practically non-existent, or made up of 'compradors'; overwhelming numerical superiority of the peasant class; political power of the landlords). These circumstances, moreover, had a dual aspect: on the one hand, they necessitated a constant adaptation of precepts forged in the struggle of proletarians against capitalists in the Western democracies; on the other hand, for a person fighting day in and day out and exploiting them for his activity, they revealed – contrary to the expectations of the *émigrés* and contrary to *the letter* of Marxism – that agricultural Russia was ripe for a workers' Revolution.

So the two men were divided far more by the practical schemata through which they grasped any situation than by abstract principles or even a programme. Through both of them alike, praxis was constituted as a voluntarism. But Stalin, having spent twenty years as a party militant, was an iron-fisted opportunist. Not that he did not have well-defined objectives – but those objectives were already incarnated. The essential thing was to save what had been achieved, and that could be done only by building a defensive apparatus. What he wanted to preserve at any price was not principles, or the movement of radicalization: it was the incarnations – or, if you like, the Revolution itself inasmuch as it was incarnated in *that particular* country, regime, or internal and external situation. He would compromise on everything, in order to preserve that fundamental basis. In order to save the nation that was building socialism, he would abandon the principle of nationalities. Collectivization? He would push ahead with it when circumstances required, in order to ensure that the towns were supplied. Industrialization? After initially braking it, once he had understood it was necessary he would try to pursue it at such a rapid rate that the targets of the first plans would not be met; and he did not hesitate to extract extra labour from the workers, whether directly by raising their norms or indirectly by Stakhanovism and the re-establishment of piecework. What he hated about Trotsky was not so much the measures he proposed as the overall praxis in whose name he proposed them. If, when Trotsky began to advocate them, he was initially hostile to stepping up industrial production or moving towards collectivization, this was because he understood their proponent's global project. This sought to industrialize and collectivize with a view to an ever more intensive radicalization of revolutionary praxis – at least, it was in this form that Stalin grasped Trotsky's *intention*. So what he feared was a Revolution heading for defeat, through attempting to remain an abstract dialectic of the universal at the very moment when its incarnation had singularized it. Obviously this view was never expressed in such terms or in any other verbal formulation. Stalin simply saw an absolute difference between practical arrangements or operations advocated by Trotsky and *the same things* implemented later by himself. In the former case they were alarming, inasmuch as through them The Revolution tended to look upon the concrete situation of the USSR as a means of realizing itself. In the latter case, though they led to identical measures, they were reassuring, because they sprang *solely* from concrete exigencies. As advocated by Trotsky and the Left, collectivization was a leap in the dark – a practical assertion that no form of defence existed apart from all-out attack. Stalin too was hard and aggressive. He was well able to go over to the offensive when necessary. But such a priori determinations of praxis, the direction of temporalization or future schemata of action alarmed him, because he grasped the situation in terms of what was to be preserved, consolidated and developed, rather than what was to be created.

This difference was to recur, of course, on every level of practice. It was precisely what prevented analytic Reason from understanding anything about the struggle – in which the two adversaries successively, and sometimes simultaneously, adopted more or less similar positions, while each nevertheless presented his own as the opposite of the other's. Initially, however, Stalin – in the guise of a 'centrist' and mediator – exploited the conflict between Right and Left rather than seeking to involve himself in it. The Right, too, struck him as abstract in its lack of trust and instinctive opportunism. It wanted a breathing-space, and only gradual progress towards real socialism. In short, with this simple idea that the revolutionary seizure of power should be followed by an *evolution*, it was reproducing the desire that most of the Bolsheviks had displayed before the seizure of power: to periodize this outrageous Revolution that was taking place in an underdeveloped country. Stalin was no more the man of post-revolutionary evolution than he was the man of permanent revolution. He would not radicalize revolutionary praxis as such, because circumstances were against it. For example, he would not hesitate greatly to widen the salary-range, in order to stimulate production through competition. On the other hand, however, he would radicalize the constructive effort required of everyone.

From the moment when these two praxes clashed – that of Trotsky, and that of Stalin supported by the Right – monstrosities made their appearance. And these monstrosities had a quite specific character, proper to this very struggle. Each faction proposed the same response to the same objective exigency. But since this similarity of short-term aims hid a radical divergence over longer-term objectives and over the very meaning of revolutionary praxis, each faction was induced to intensify the immediate differences over concrete projects and reproduce – there and then, through a tangible incarnation – the deeper differences over practical orientations. Thus, in its designation of the immediate objective and the means of achieving it, the majority – hardened by the minority's provocation, which they had themselves provoked – introduced the following hypothesis: rejection of motives and distant aims that might lead *others* to join them. The effectiveness of this manoeuvre was based on the absolute necessity of preserving the unity of the leading bodies, despite the conflicts under way. Or, if you like, of transforming the majority into unanimity. In that way, the minority would wear itself out, forever suppressing itself after every debate. Or else it would frankly declare itself to be an oppositional faction and – amid the besetting dangers – thereby acknowledge itself as splittist and 'anti-party'. As Merleau-Ponty has put it, opposition would be defined as treason.

Waged at every level and over every objective, this struggle interests us here only inasmuch as it produced the slogan 'Socialism in one country'. This formula was a monstrosity inasmuch as it said *more* than was necessary. In other words, it falsified the precise exigencies of the situation by giving them a synthetic unity whose motivations were contemporary, but which claimed to be based on distant objectives and the total praxis in its future temporalization. It was a *manner* of speaking: 'Let us rely only on ourselves'. But that very manner contained a verbal formulation presenting itself as a theoretical evaluation of the possibilities of socialism, though it was in fact a manoeuvre to put the minority on the spot. For them, adopting it meant a priori renouncing the idea of a practical interdependence of the international proletariats. At a yet deeper level, moreover, it meant recognizing that *everything* – and first and foremost the working-class movements of Western Europe – had to be subordinated to the constructive defence of the USSR, which obviously meant in turn that the Soviet Communist Party had to exert a real dictatorship over the Communist Parties of Europe and through them mobilize the proletariats to defend the USSR, even if in a national context their revolutionary interests did not coincide with the imperatives and exigencies of that *defensive* tactic. In other words, it meant deciding that the revolutionary offensive of a European proletariat within a national context – and possibly the revolutionary seizure of power – were not necessarily the best ways of defending the Revolution. It meant admitting that the socialist Revolution was universal and international only when it remained ideal – i.e. before its incarnation. And that once it was incarnated, it was present as a whole in the single country that had made it and was continuing it, through the specific tasks that its own structures and History imposed upon it. But, precisely, recognizing this meant rejecting *en bloc* Westernism, universalism, and the postulate that the proletariats in the great industrialized countries had taken their emancipation further than the young proletariat in the USSR and – by taking power – would dispose of an economic and technological power that should make them the true animators of the international Revolution. It meant renouncing internationalism and 'Permanent Revolution'. Therein lay the trap. Trotsky, like Stalin, recognized the exigencies of the situation – about these objective exigencies there could be no disagreement. But by presenting them in the form of a dogma, the majority obliged Trotsky either to disown his practical principles, or to refuse the practical content of the dogma (even though he accepted it as a response to the temporary exigencies of the situation). Against universalist radicalism, Stalin infelicitously defined what might be termed a particularist radicalism. And, of course, that monstrous object did not remain at the level of a verbal formulation. Inasmuch as it was to define a propaganda, a permanent character of praxis, and a certain future, it could be termed an *institution*. And this was indeed the root of the institutionalization of the Russian Revolution: for maintaining *also* meant consolidating, and in the social sphere consolidating meant stratifying. We shall return to this. But in this new *object* we can already see the implicit coexistence of Stalinism and Trotskyism. The real relationship between the USSR and the Western proletariats in a more or less distant future could have been left *undetermined* (precisely because, for the Soviet leaders, it was the object of a real ignorance). But its dogmatic determination incarnated Trotsky's revolutionary internationalism as a *rejected position*. And no positivist Reason can *comprehend* that presence of Trotsky at the heart of a determination that disowned him, since presence and interior negation – in their indissoluble synthesis – represented the singular incarnation of a multidimensional conflict, i.e. its totalization in the object *by the two adversaries*.

2.   But the conflict itself was a totalization – through the adversaries – of a contradiction in the Party's common praxis. This contradiction in turn interiorized a real but less compressed, more diffuse, clash that was produced and lived by Soviet society itself, through the ongoing transformation of its outworn institutions. Despite the integration achieved by the regime, it goes without saying that Soviet society could *in no way* be seen as an institutional group: it was riven by struggles, by its practicoinert divisions, etc. Besides, we have not yet even begun to investigate social unity. If it exists, this must obviously be different from the unity of groups. But whatever form may be taken by the struggles, the various conflicts, the serialities or the group relations in a given society, what interests us here is the totalizing interiorization of this diversity by the Party and its leadership: i.e. by the sovereign group.

(a) Any positivist history that sought to explain the Stalinist slogan by the internal weakness and isolation of the USSR around 1925–30, and regarded these as *passively suffered*, would miss the crucial point. Of course, everyone did suffer poverty, they all did suffer isolation; but *at the same time* these conditions were *products* of revolutionary praxis. What is more, inasmuch as they were produced and preserved with a view to being transcended, they represented a moment of that praxis itself. Poverty, shortage of technicians and cadres, encirclement: these were mortal dangers for the Revolution, and at the same time *they were* *the Revolution itself* coming into being in a particular situation. The Allies would have helped a bourgeois democracy that endeavoured to carry on the war: as bourgeois, they would have been favourable to the overthrow of Tsarism. The treaty of Brest-Litovsk and the Bolshevik seizure of power were acts that in themselves entailed civil war, economic blockade and encirclement: not just *passively suffered* as a condition, but *produced* by a praxis whose objectives were long-term ones. Russia's poverty in 1924, the absence of cadres, the encirclement: these were the Revolution itself on the march. In taking power Lenin knew what he was doing; the Bolshevik Party knew likewise: their praxis was constituted by having to pass through that needle's eye in order to go beyond it. What the Soviet revolutionaries were perhaps less prone to mention – though they certainly accepted its results – was that the Russian Revolution itself, as praxis, was partly responsible for the defeats and divisions of the Western proletariat: because of the abortive attempts it stimulated more or less everywhere (Hungary, Germany, above all China); because of the debilitating conflict that sprang up everywhere between social democracy (which simultaneously betrayed the working class and represented the interests of an 'elite' of petty-bourgeois and craft workers) and the new Party identifying with the USSR; and, finally, because of the violent reactions of a frightened bourgeoisie and the transformation of certain bourgeois democracies into fascist states. In other words, the Revolution, incarnated in the centre of the world as a long-term praxis defined by definite material circumstances, could not itself develop without engendering – by its actual course, albeit in contradiction with its leaders' project – the impotence of foreign proletariats. In this sense, it can be said that its incarnation was in direct contradiction with its universalization. And this situation – as a practical consequence of the seizure of power – in turn conditioned the USSR's relations with foreign proletariats. The contradiction here derived from the fact that the proletarian Revolution in the USSR, instead of being a factor in the liberation and emancipation of Europe's working-class masses – as it *should have been* – was achieved at the cost of plunging them into relative impotence.*

---

* There are many other factors (technical transformations, etc.) that can account for this impotence. But the key thing is that these factors were always *regrouped* in relation to the Russian Revolution. The evolution of industrialization and Malthusianism in France are *sufficient* determinations to explain the divisions of our working class. But the violence of internal conflicts is precisely due to the fact that these divisions of a technical and craft origin intersect with *political* disputes, whose deep signification is *always* differing attitudes towards the USSR. Naturally, we are here envisaging the USSR in the first phase of the Revolution. The subsequent and crucially important achievements that it has made since then, directly or indirectly (defeat of Nazism, triumph of communism in China, emergence of the Third World), do not have to be taken into consideration, because – although they were present in embryo in the period in question – they did not yet appear explicitly.

Once interiorized, this contradiction was manifested as a conflict, and this conflict was precisely the one we have just been outlining. On the one hand, in fact, even if it had no expectations of them, the revolutionary government was obliged in practice to help foreign proletariats as much as it could. On the other hand, the relative weakness of those proletariats, the strength of the bourgeois regimes, threats of war and the economic blockade constrained the Soviets to the most extreme prudence. Perhaps helping one proletariat in its revolutionary fight would indeed have encouraged all the others to act. But since they were paralysed even by their divisions, the only foreseeable result might well have been a regroupment of the capitalist powers and war – a war that the USSR could not have won in the existing situation, and that would in any case have made socialist construction far harder, whatever the outcome of the fighting. This difficulty was never to be resolved, because – given the balance of forces between the USSR and the bourgeois democracies – it was *in reality* insoluble. Stalin himself, despite innumerable acts of treachery, did still help the Chinese, Spanish, etc. to the extent he believed *possible* without provoking armed intervention by the West; while Trotsky himself, in exile, entrusted the proletariats of the entire world with the task of defending the USSR in the event of its coming under attack, because – despite everything – the foundations of socialism did exist there.

From this point of view, 'socialism in one country' was the product of revolutionary praxis reflecting upon its effects and the contradictions it had engendered. Synthetically, and approaching the dogma via the Bolshevik Party's interiorization of these contradictory results, it can be grasped in its intelligibility as an attempt to lift the mortgage of inter-nationalism, while retaining the USSR's ability to give assistance to foreign revolutionary parties in accordance with its means and the risks involved. What was consciously broken was any relation of reciprocity: if the USSR could build socialism on its own, it did not really *need* foreign help; and if it still *had to* intervene – when it could – to aid revolutionaries in danger in the capitalist nations, this was its *mission*, its *'generosity'*. In short, the leaders had a free hand. The slogan *theorized* the practical necessity. The Trotskyist Left, had it been in power, would not have adopted it; but if you discount personal factors (less significant in this case than in many others), its policy towards the European and Asiatic Communist Parties would doubtless not have been perceptibly different. And at all events that praxis would have had to produce its own theoretical justification: in other words, in terms of our earlier discussion, its own *idea of itself*. This idea, of course, would not have been expressed by the slogan 'socialism in one country'. But it would have contained the same contradiction, albeit as it were in reverse. Radicalization and universalization would at first have been affirmed, but these would then have imposed their own limits in the light of the situation. No doubt it can be said that such an 'ideation' of praxis would have been more in line with reality, more *true*. But that is only because we have hypothetically suppressed the other term of the conflict. Without the radical Left, Stalin would undoubtedly also have given an inter-pretation of the totalizing praxis more in line with the truth. Conversely, if we visualize a majority led by Trotsky in conflict with a Stalinist minority, the situation would have obliged Trotsky to formulate his praxis *provocatively*, in order to compel Stalin and his allies either to capitulate or to proclaim their treason.

(b) This conflict pitted *men* against one another: i.e. practical beings, irreducible to ideas or even to a *common* activity (hyper-organism). But they had first made themselves into *common individuals*, so that their singular individuality as free practical organisms was, as we know, perpetual transcendence of the inert exigencies of their pledge at the same time as the realization of these in every concrete circumstance. When we go more deeply into the circumstances that pitted them against one another as common individuals – i.e. as members of an integrated Party in which they occupied functions defined by the group as a whole in the course of past struggles – then the fundamental situation that sustained and produced those conflicts takes on a *historical* density – as a diachronic totalization of the past by the present. For the isolation of the USSR after the Revolution was not simply what we have just seen it to be: the result – both sought and suffered – of a *revolutionary praxis* (sought, inasmuch as there was Revolution and negation of the bourgeois order *within the foreign nations themselves*; suffered, inasmuch as the repercussions of that negation placed the Revolution in danger). In short, it could not be reduced simply to the isolation of the first socialist country within an ensemble of capitalist powers. Had England been the first to make the Revolution, as Marx sometimes envisaged, it would have produced – thanks to its insularity, as well as to the development of its industrial technology (and to many other factors, of course) – an *other* socialist isolation; it would have been encircled *otherwise*. Soviet isolation was first and foremost that of a monstrosity: an underdeveloped country passing without transition from the feudal order to socialist forms of production and ownership. This at once refers us back to the past, to Tsarism, to the economic structure of the country before 1914, and to foreign investments (the existence of such investments explains, in fact, the particular ferocity of certain economic and financial groups against the Soviets).

But these relations with the outside world were really rooted above all in the economic and social history of Russia as a whole, seen in the context of its geopolitical situation (inasmuch as that situation conditioned historical transformations and was conditioned by them). We should not be worried about introducing a diachronic perspective here, even though we have yet to subject it to critical investigation. For what is involved here is not matching it to synchronies, but simply showing how – in a manner that remains to be determined – it constitutes their depth. In fact, what counts is the fact that Russia's relationship with Western Europe was lived by the Russian people through a history that produced the Tsarist Empire as a gigantic mediation between Asia and Europe, and as a perpetually contested synthesis of European and Asiatic populations. Sometimes this changing relationship would pass from negative to positive and vice versa. Sometimes it would present itself as a variable combination of two contradictory attitudes (inasmuch as it was produced in Russia and by the Russian people): on the one hand, fascination with foreign technology, political systems and culture (always more advanced than in the Russian Empire) and, as a consequence, the sustained effort by the ruling classes and the intellectuals to assimilate Europe's contributions; *on the other hand*, however, a mistrust and particularism that were based on the radical differences between the systems, their respective relations of production, and their 'superstructures' (including, especially, their different religions).

In this perspective, the conflict we have taken as an example assumes its singular historical depth: a universalist ideology and practice, born in the most industrialized countries of Europe and imported by circles of revolutionary intellectuals towards the end of the nineteenth century, in a country that its economic and geopolitical structure seems to designate, in the name of Marxism itself, as a *particularity* – i.e. as a nation so 'backward' that Marxist practice (mobilization of the working-class masses, etc.) does not seem to be able to develop there, at least not without profound modifications. For Tsarism, perched on top of a bourgeoisie that was beginning its development, maintained itself by police methods which enforced clandestinity (at first sight, the *opposite* of mass action). The Marxist experience, by contrast, involves open struggle (even if repression temporarily obliges organizations to reconstitute themselves clandestinely). It is the actual experience of the proletariat, as engendered and developed by industrialization, in the context of democracies forming and evolving under the pressure of that same industrialization. Acclimatizing Marxism was thus bound to mean *particularizing* it, since it would be asked to guide revolutionary praxis in a feudal country where the proletariat represented practically nothing, while the rural masses constituted virtually the totality of the population. Before 1917, however, Russian Marxism was still universalist and abstract, since it was a doctrine and a strategy for working-class militants, intellectuals and *émigrés*. After the Revolution, it became the basis of the culture of the masses. Its systematic implantation in the Russian *people* was conditioned at once by education, inasmuch as this was defined by the rulers' praxis, and by the constant growth of working-class concentrations – i.e. the draining off of peasants into the factories. These workers – still so uncouth, so hastily manufactured and so close to the peasantry – transformed Marxism as they were being imbued with it. *It was incarnated* by becoming a popular and national culture, when in Europe it was still just the theoretico-practical movement of History. To speak in Hegelian terms (whose idealism is too flagrant to be a problem), it was *the objective spirit of a people*. It became a dogma precisely inasmuch as it allowed those mystified peasants to liquidate all dogmas; it was vulgarized as it knocked the rough edges off them; it was alienated in them as it emancipated them; it was ossified as they transcended and reinvented it in every systematic decoding of their experience. At the same time as it was incarnated, its intimate character – which was 'the becoming-world of philosophy' – contributed to giving it, in the eyes of all, a new preponderance *as reality lived and perpetually produced by the Soviet masses*. In the name of its own principles, the universalist Marxism of the West was subordinated to a particularist Marxism: a product distilled by the Russian people and by the Revolution entering upon its constructive phase. This was the prime inversion. The incarnated and thus singularized universality became the truth of the abstract universal. It was for the USSR to comprehend the revolutionary movements of the West, since they stood on this side of the seizure of power while the Russian Revolution had passed beyond it. The vast historical transformation of that society produced within it the transformation of Marxism, inasmuch as it caused it to become the ideology of that transformation – i.e. inasmuch as praxis conferred its new features upon it. The universal, subordinated to the singularity and contained within it, directed and transformed in conformity with the transformations of that singular history: on the theoretical and cultural level, this was already the objective reality of the slogan 'socialism in one country'. And, at that level, the conflict was clearly designated. By being incarnated in an underdeveloped country as its culture, the theoretico-practical ensemble that was Marxism dissociated its unity as a universalist dialectic into two particular universalities. The universality of the *several* revolutionary movements of the West became abstract, and saw itself refused the right to interpret dialectically Soviet history as a *non-privileged* historical process; its singularity lay in being an *abstraction* trailing behind the historical and concrete development of incarnated Marxism *in the USSR* – receiving its knowledge from the latter instead of illuminating it through research. The universality *of Russian Marxism*, on the other hand, was to alienate itself in the history of the USSR, precisely inasmuch as it objectified itself in it. In this sense, the slogan 'socialism in one country' was at once the definition of that alienated Marxism, the object of History rather than its knowledge, and simultaneously its first theoretico-practical product – the first determination of that uncouth culture. No doubt things would have been different if a sequence of revolutions, diversifying the incarnations of Marxism, had allowed it to rediscover via new contradictions a living and concrete universality.

Thus the historical and revolutionary isolation of the USSR, the ebbing of the revolutionary movements, the capitalist encirclement, the singularization of Marxism by the Russian masses, and the emancipation of Marxism through alienated Marxism: all these were particular determinations each of which expressed all the others. It is at this level that we find, readopted in the form of practical attitudes, the fundamental determination of Soviet man: the nationalism suffered and proclaimed through socialism; the particularism interiorized as an incarnation of the universal; the national pride ('this people is the guide of all peoples'), combined with a lucid awareness of technological backwardness (universality was already present, albeit in a wholly modified form, in the way in which Lenin already insisted strongly on the need to learn from experts in the USA). From this standpoint, moreover, the liquidation of the 'leftist' opposition was to have the effect not of suppressing the contradiction that produced *those* men, but of defining Stalinism ever more clearly inasmuch as it reproduced the contradiction *within itself*. In the same way, Trotsky in exile rediscovered via Trotskyism the abstract universalism of Marxism. He disincarnated it, as a theoretico-practical schema, and interpreted the social evolution of the USSR in the light of universal Marxism. But he did not eliminate the contradiction entirely and his attitude towards the USSR reflected, through its oscillations and hesitations, the fact that – despite everything – Trotskyism could grasp Soviet society in the course of its construction only as a deviation operating *on the basis of a real incarnation*. (Even if the Bureaucracy was to strip them of their rights, the foundations of socialism had been laid; Trotsky gave one of his works the significant title 'The Revolution *Betrayed*'.) In that sense, the conflict between the Third and Fourth Internationals found its origins in the tension that, before World War I, pitted the *émigré* intellectuals against the militants working in Russia. Born of this tension, the subsequent struggle incorporated it – transforming and radicalizing it, and endowing it with its full meaning. Inasmuch as Stalin and the Stalinist bureaucracy made themselves into the instruments of that particularization of the universal in the USSR, Soviet man – who was the product of a particularist praxis and of Marxist influence among the masses – *recognized himself in his leaders*.

All the European revolutionaries, by contrast, who wished to adopt the Russian Revolution as a capital moment of History, a universal transformation, while simultaneously retaining for the European proletariats their absolute autonomy within the framework of an International of the old (universalist) type, recognized their practical exigencies in the activity pursued by Trotsky. Trotskyism, in short, to a certain extent represented revolutionary Europe striving to release itself from the Soviet grip. Indeed, the *actual* Trotskyists – the activists constituting the rank and file – were 'Westerners'.

But the contradiction was not thereby transcended – *nor could it be* – because the entire practice of the Fourth International was in fact determined by a conflict that pitted two leading factions of the Soviet Revolution against one another: first within the USSR, then on both sides of the frontier, and always *about* the Revolution as an incarnation. From this viewpoint, the slogan 'socialism in one country' defined Soviet man as he was produced, and as he produced himself, theoretically and practically between the wars. And the overdetermination of that *object* – the traces that both adversaries left upon it – became a pure determination. That is to say, seen from the standpoint of the whole group (the Party and its allied sub-parties in the USSR), the oversignifying gap between the exigencies of praxis and the dogma that defined the practical solution became a simple signification of the way in which that country – still traditionalist and peopled by illiterates – absorbed and assimilated, all at the same time, a transformation of its secular traditions, a traditional withdrawal into its shell, and the acquisition of new traditions via the slow absorption of an internationalist and universalist ideology illuminating, for peasants sucked in by industry, the passage from rural labour to factory labour. The slogan was deformed because, at the level of the leaders' conflict, it represented the product of contrasting activities. From the viewpoint of the Party – i.e. of the ensemble of objective givens (interiorized, as it were, by a systematic retotalization) – the deformity was *in itself* a practical and *comprehensible* signification. In its uncouth, misguided crudity, it signalled the reincarnation of Marxism through men whose wild voluntarism and youthful barbarism it expressed by the very deviations it received and transmitted. This monstrosity, unintelligible as a verbal idea or theoretico-practical principle, was comprehensible as a totalizing act which, at that precise moment of action, kept together and united the theoretical and the practical, the universal and the singular, the traditionalist depths of a still alienated history and the movement of cultural emancipation, the negative movement of retreat and the positive movement of hope. Its singularity as an ideological deviation was a totalized totalization, since it expressed and simultaneously reinforced revolutionary praxis in the historical singularity of its incarnation – i.e. in the particularity of its objective tasks, inside the community under construction and outside in the practical field. Thus the theory of gold as a commodity is comprehensible, inasmuch as it is the idea of a certain monetary practice at the time of the exploitation of the Peruvian mines. This should not be taken to mean that the idea is true, or self-evident, or – in the case that concerns us – in conformity with the principles of Marxism. Or even that it is 'valid' in the long term, i.e. effective without too many counter-finalities. The historian will simply comprehend it in a single totalizing act, because he will see it not as a scientific assertion but as praxis itself deviating and going astray, only to find its way again through its own contradictions, i.e. through conflicts between common individuals. Inasmuch as the *factors* are diverse, within a totalization in progress, we must know that each one of them is a particular expression of that totalization. So comprehension will consist in grasping each factor as a perspective – at once objective and singular – upon the developing whole, and in totalizing these perspectives by the totalization that each of them singularizes, which is also an enveloping though singular synthesis of all these singularizations.

Thereafter, of course, complementary consideration must also be given to the slogan (or any other, similar product) in its development as a *process*. It was hardened by its duration (by its past; by the stratifications that it helped to produce and that sustained it). It borrowed its ossified permanence from the inertia of language and the pledged passivity of common individuals. As such it exercised powers, developed its counter-finalities, helped to create the practico-inert of constructive activity – in the Party and in the new society. But this new problem of the relationship between the dialectic and the anti-dialectic is not yet within our competency, though our investigation will soon lead us to it. What we have striven to show is that, within a group, the meaninglessness of any given product of secret conflicts appears at the level where the product has been constituted not by one act (or by an ensemble of solidary activities organized around a common aim) but by *at least two* actions, each of which tends to cancel the other, or at least to turn it into a means for destroying the other agent. And this is the level, of course, at which practices are produced in their concrete reality as groups of people themselves determining their activities on the basis of a situation. But these people have been produced as *common individuals* inside the group as a whole. Their disputes – like the anti-labours which culminate in the product under consideration – confront each other through their fundamental unity (for instance, as leaders of the Bolshevik Party propelled, after the seizure of power, into the urgent task of preserving what had been won by building the future society). As such, they are likewise supported by all common individuals (at the various levels of hierarchical organization), inasmuch as these constitute *the group*. If, moreover, in the first period of struggle such support is given simultaneously to both adversaries, this is because each individual is common by virtue of his pledge to maintain the unity of the totalizing group. It is also because the conflict expresses, in the form of a real and public contradiction, the implicit and non-thematized contradiction that pits each individual against himself in his movement to interiorize the objective difficulties of common praxis.

From this point of view, through its common activity the group supports the monstrosities generated by anti-labour. It decides irrevocably whether they are viable or stillborn. And when it supports one of these monstrosities – i.e. when it adopts it and realizes it in detail through its praxis – this praxis is in itself tantamount to *comprehension*. Each common individual and each sub-group supports and nourishes the monstrosity, inasmuch as it presents itself as an intelligible and practical transcendence of their contradictions. This certainly does not mean that such transcendence is the true synthesis of, and solution to, the objective difficulties. Yet the monstrosity is comprehensible through and by virtue of the interiorized contradictions of everyone, as the re-exteriorization of these in an undertaking. For the contradiction is implicit and enveloped in everyone. It occurs as a determination of comprehension (among other aspects), i.e. as an invisible limit on freedom and an immediate familiarity with the object produced. In the case that concerns us, the limit was due to the necessary vulgarization and particularization of Marxism, as the first phase of a culture. The particularization and vulgarization of the universal were the contradiction itself, but enveloped, since it at the same time expressed everyone's level of culture: i.e. their implicit familiarity, never *seen* or mediated, with themselves. But in this negative framework, incapable at first of grasping the absurdity of the slogan 'socialism in one country', they *recognized* its positive aspect. For if it was true that the situation, taken in the abstract, did not necessarily involve that dogma, and if it was abstractly possible to base propaganda on more modest reasons for acting and hoping, everything changes once we look at the concrete people who made the new Marxism and, in the name of the very ideas Marxist education had produced in them, proclaimed an absolute certainty. For them, in fact, the negative moment had been transcended. Pursuing the Revolution meant building a new order. As Trotsky was later to express it: 'The masses needed to breathe.' This meant that their simplistic culture prevented them from believing in the *positive* value of a systematically pursued liquidation of every last trace of the old order. In their eyes, that order had *already* disappeared. So it was not *the situation* that required this object, but the actual men who lived it. But since they made it as they lived it, we might more accurately say that the abstract exigencies of the situation became clear and were imbued with (often contradictory) significations by becoming concrete exigencies through living men. This *product* became intelligible in terms of the totalizing group, *inasmuch as* it was acknowledged and supported by common individuals, i.e. inasmuch as they re-produced it as a response to their own exigencies. And this was just what the sub-group whose manoeuvre came off was counting on. It hoped to be *borne along* in its operation by the participation of all.

There is still, of course, the case where the conflict is adopted as its own by the entire group, and where every common individual belongs to one camp or the other. In such circumstances, the intelligibility of products tends to disappear. But this is because a split is imminent. In fact, in the event of one sub-group restoring unity by liquidating the other, the group – as we have seen – has to be a permanent mediator. This precisely assumes that the essential integrity of the practical community is preserved – and it is this integrity which renders the products of anti-labour intelligible. In effect, they become the chosen instruments for an operation by the group upon itself.

3. Finally, it should be pointed out – although such considerations take us to the threshold of diachronic totalization – that if the monstrosity survived, it was to be reorganized by common praxis and lose its immediate unintelligibility by being integrated into a new intelligibility. Praxis re-established its practical truth by correcting its own deviations, and the origin of this correction lay in the deviations themselves. But the irreversibility of temporalization made it impossible to turn back the clock. So the correction had to function by way of an enriching tran-scendence, which preserved the deviation at the same time as endowing it with truth through a sometimes very complex system of additions, developments, compensations and transmutations.

The slogan 'socialism in one country' actually involved a certain indetermination from the outset, since the word 'socialism' was fairly ambiguous. In Marxist writing, the words 'socialism' and 'communism' are, in fact, often used interchangeably to denote a single social order: the society that the proletariat has the task of realizing in the future. In this case, the word refers as much to the withering away and disappearance of the State as to the elimination of classes, and the ownership by all workers of their instruments of labour. On the other hand, however, inasmuch as social democracy too identifies with this key word but claims it will reach the socialist society at the end of a long reformist evolution, the term 'socialism' undergoes a slight alteration in that it can serve to denote the reformist illusion of social democracy. In this case, the term 'communism' will have the advantage over it of exactness: it will denote the order in question precisely in so far as this can be realized only through Revolution.

Thus the word 'socialism', as employed in the slogan we are considering, was distinguished from the word 'communism' by a slight indetermination. This *semantic* distinction was soon to be made sharper, becoming a difference in the structure of the objects designated and in the moments of temporalization. In other words, 'socialism' gradually took on a new accepted meaning: it was *what comes before* the communist order or, if you like, the transition between capitalism and communism.* This transitional order, despite everything, was *beyond the revolutionary seizure of power*. It was characterized by a necessary and fundamental transformation of the relations of production: society as a whole appropriated the means of producing. Yet the State continued to exist. It was the body by whose agency the proletariat exercised its dictatorship. That meant, of course, that classes were not liquidated – far from it. In particular, hidden in the depths of the new society, the representatives of the oppressor classes united and constituted counter-revolutionary forces. Later Stalin was not to shrink even from adding that class conflicts intensify as socialist achievements grow in number and importance. Such a system – harassed by enemies without and within; characterized by a strengthened State apparatus, at the very moment when transformations of ownership were initiating the progressive withering away of that apparatus – was necessarily riven by contradictions. Indeed, official Marxists gradually began to raise the question of 'the contradictions of socialism'. Taking on these new meanings under the pressure of circumstances, the term 'socialism' changed its signification. It came to denote more narrowly (but still inadequately) the singular order that was progressively established in the USSR, and that presented itself as transitional. Did this, therefore, simply involve moving backwards and changing the content of the concept 'socialism', until it *meant* merely what we earlier termed the 'pre-socialist order'? No. The term 'pre-socialism', by its very make-up, involves a serious error of assessment. For, in a sense, there is only one pre-socialist order and that is capitalism itself – quite simply because it comes *before*. But when the proletarian Revolution is made, socialism is *already there*. For what characterizes it fundamentally is *neither* abundance, *nor* the total elimination of classes, *nor* working-class sovereignty – even though these features are *indispensable*, at least as distant aims of the essential transformation. It is the elimination of

---

* Similar distinctions may be found in a number of authors, even before 1914. But they then had only a logical and philosophical value. *Terms* were distinguished in the name of theories. The novelty appeared when, in the name of a dogma ('socialism in one country'), the distinction between 'socialism' and 'communism' took on a practical and popular value: when it served to denote stages in the evolution of Soviet society.

exploitation and oppression, or – in positive terms – the collective appropriation of the means of production.

But this appropriation – whatever the distress of a country ravaged by war, whatever the dilapidation of its industrial installations may be – was accomplished as soon as the Soviets took power. It was never called into question, whatever meaning people might seek to assign to the emergence of a bureaucratic layer reserving a considerable share of surplus-value for itself. And the only real danger it ran could be identified with those imposed on Soviet society as a whole by capitalist blockade and encircle-ment and the efforts of the enemy within. In fact, *it really was* a socialist order that was established in the USSR. However, that order was charac-terized by the practical necessity (a necessity of freedom) of either disappearing or becoming what it was through a gigantic and bloody effort. That collective appropriation of ruins beneath the foreign threat had to be changed progressively, through the labour of all, into a common ownership of the most powerful means of production. And if it was necessary to build socialism in one country, this was precisely because socialism appeared in its most abstract and impoverished form in a country whose isolation it adopted and accentuated. Thus the formula, which was false, became true provided socialism was made into a *praxis-process*, building an order on the basis of machines and a fundamental socialization of the land, in emergency conditions and through the perpetual sacrifice of *everything* to the most rapid intensification of production rates. Doubtless its basic contradiction lay in being simul-taneously a swift victory, swiftly institutionalized, and an undertaking stretching over several generations. But the emergency conditions – with the practical consequences these entailed (commandism, authoritarian planning, idealist voluntarism, strengthening of the State apparatus, bureaucracy, terror, etc.) – necessarily entered into the definition of that order-undertaking, since they were what brought it about as a conse-quence of the terror it inspired in the bourgeois democracies. So what was left as a distant objective – as the non-incarnated other side of the daily struggles and of the whole undertaking – was the communist order itself. This is what still defined itself, abstractly, as internationalization of the Revolution, disappearance of the State, abundance, liberty. *Social-ism*, in this theoretical synthesis, was essentially *homogeneous* with communism, in so far as the radical transformation of econqmic and social structures was carried out in the very first years of the Revolution. It was quite simply the mediation between the abstract moment of *socialization* and the concrete moment of *common enjoyment*. This meant that in certain historical circumstances it could be a synonym of *Hell*.

Thus the Stalinist formula – at first false, then more and more true – eventually decayed and lapsed into an honorific role when the situation no longer justified it: i.e. when the Chinese Revolution and the appearance of the people's democracies in Central Europe abolished 'socialist isolation' and required another praxis on the part of the Soviet government. Meanwhile, of course, the counter-finalities of that transcended praxis had transformed the USSR: stratifications, practico-inert structures. That singular incarnation was progressively singularized in the process of institutionalization. The adaptation of such a highly specific reality to the new exigencies was to be long, arduous and obstructed. The fact remains that what was essential had been preserved. The transformations might be violent, but they would no longer have the character of a revolution. In this way, the monstrous slogan acquired its practical truth, because it had truly been the *idea* of that monstrous, inevitable transformation: of that *deviant* praxis, whose singular deviation was none the less the reality (hence the truth) of the incarnation transcending itself in an undertaking that it conditioned from the outset, and that remained *qualified by it*. Through the twin totalization – synchronic and diachronic – historical Reason thus grasps the product of anti-labour as also – both in the particular moment and throughout the temporalization – the intelligible outcome of the common unity and the totalization-of-envelopment.

5

Are Social Struggles Intelligible? (A Historical Study of Soviet Society)[27]

The Three Phases of Historialization

THE FOREGOING example has only a limited scope, since struggle appears in it only as the avatar of an already integrated group. What we have basically shown is that if synthetic unity already exists, as both effect and condition of a common praxis, internal conflict – as the practical assumption of the counter-finalities secreted by action – in its movement of antagonistic reciprocity as in its objective products is only an incarnation and a historialization of the global totalization, inasmuch as this must *also* totalize its disassimilated and waste products. And we have clearly noted that totalization is not an ideal and transcendent movement, but operates through the discrete activities of individuals on the basis of the common pledge. But although it frequently occurs in concrete experience and at all levels of practice – in short, although it belongs *to the proper domain of History*, as a condition and consequence of the global evolution of the society where it occurs – this privileged case in which unity precedes and engenders internal discord can obviously present itself only as a specification of the historical process. And since the ensembles whose structures and temporalization the historian has to study always present themselves – at least at first sight – as deprived of true unity, the intelligibility of social struggles seems very hard to defend.* And how about our regressive investigation? What has it taught us about 'societies' in the strictly historical sense of the term?

---

* I am speaking here only of *national* ensembles, because critical investigation has to pass through national histories before tackling the problem of so-called 'world' or 'universal' history.

27. See Preface above, and plans for the projected work in the Appendix below.

Nothing yet, except that they seem to be characterized simultaneously by a unity of immanence and by a multiplicity of exteriority, whether we are dealing with a Flemish city in the fifteenth century or with 'France' between 1789 and 1794. For there is a relationship between the city or nation and the ensemble of towns or nations that surround it; and this interiorized relationship manifests itself inasmuch as it is grasped by the multiplicity in question as its objective practical unity. But it will be pointed out, of course, that series extend and ramify throughout the entire society. So this interiorization – unless it is carried out by a specific group – will be metamorphosed in the milieu of recurrence into a serial bond of alterity. In the same way, the institutional ensemble manifests as such – and in the constituted bodies that are charged with applying the law – a certain sovereign integration of the social plurality. As we have already noted, however, the sovereign's power rests on the impotence of series.[28] It is *as an Other* that the practico-inert individual is the servant of the laws and lets himself be manipulated by forms of other-direction.[29] What have we seen, in fact? Groups that are heterogeneous (in terms both of their origin, structures, objective and speed of temporalization and of the nature, extent, intensity and importance of their actions) and sometimes condition one another more or less directly, sometimes oppose one another, and sometimes ignore one another, but are all themselves drawn from series and seem poised to lapse back into seriality. Apart from that, the mediation of worked matter always and everywhere – between individuals and even between groups (when these are not directly deter-mined in mutual solidarity or reciprocal opposition) – creates the passive unity of the practico-inert, through *alteration* and *reification* of the immediate bonds of reciprocity between men. In certain cases, as we have seen – and particularly when classes enter into struggle via the mediation of organized groups – the unity of the group is reflected in the inert depths of the collective as a possibility of unity for each individual (as a possibility of transforming his *Other-being* into *common individuality*).[30] Were the whole class to liquidate its seriality, however, it would still be the case that exploitation, oppression and the struggle against oppression are conditioned by the practico-inert rift. In the organized group, the latter only ever appears through a praxis that has already taken it over. In 'societies', however, the practico-inert is an objective reality that manifests itself independently, in and through the alienation of every praxis. It is individual practice that seems taken over and absorbed by inanimate matter.

---

28. *Critique*, vol.1, pp.601 ff.
29. *Critique*, vol.1, pp.253 ff.
30. *Critique*, vol.1, pp.678 ff.

Thus class conflict too appears as a transcendence and taking over of counter-finalities by each class and against the other. In reality, however, combat groups, parties and unions, far from emanating *from unity*, strive to realize the unity of one class as a practico-inert seriality against the other. Similarly, the basic (albeit most abstract and distant) aim of every class organization – to suppress the other class or (which comes to the same thing) subjugate it definitively and constitute it as a slave demanding its enslavement – is not, as in the organized group, imposed by the practical necessity of re-establishing unity of action. On the contrary, it is in order to realize [this aim] that unity of action is established in each class; and it is the actual rift of the practico-inert that produces it, as the sole conceivable means to create a society governing its materiality, in which man is the permanent mediation between men. Here, in short, two antagonistic unities *are invented*, in opposition both to one another and to a seriality of impotence produced by a practico-inert process. Or within the group, if you prefer, conflict was a moment of the constituted dialectic. But how should we conceive the *dialectical* intelligibility of that negative reciprocity which is installed on the basis of an anti-dialectical break separating the constituent dialectic and the constituted dialectic? Is History not perhaps, at the level of large ensembles, an ambiguous interpenetration of unity and plurality, dialectic and anti-dialectic, meaning and meaninglessness? Are there not, according to the circumstances and ensemble in question, *several* totalizations – with no relation between them other than coexistence or some other relationship of exteriority? Is it not up to the historian alone, in his historical investigation, to determine the directions in which a single praxis-process sees itself resumed and retotalized at different levels, and to demarcate the signifying constellations to which a single event gives rise in the most disparate milieux? If we were to accept this thesis, we should be returning by a detour to historical neo-positivism. For many modern historians admit, more or less implicitly, what might be termed *dialectical sequences* within a history that remains pluralistic and analytical.

Before deciding, however, we must recall that men make History in so far as it makes them. In the present instance, this means that the practico-inert is engendered by the counter-finalities of praxis precisely in so far as serialities of impotence, by producing the impossibility of living, give rise to the totalizing unity that transcends them. Thus the movement of historialization has three phases. In a first phase, a common praxis transforms society by a totalizing action whose counter-finalities trans-form the results obtained into practico-inert ones. In a second phase, the antisocial forces of the practico-inert impose a negative unity of self-destruction upon society, by usurping the unifying power of the praxis that has produced them. In a third phase, the detotalized unity is retotalized in the common effort to rediscover the goal by stripping it of counter-finalities. This is what we must study more closely. Before embarking on the example of bourgeois democracies[31] – the most complex and most specious – let us return to the Russian Revolution, but this time to consider it through the history of Soviet society in all its diversity.

Unification by the Future

The goal of the proletarian Revolution was to allow the construction of a society in which the worker would have permanent and integral control over the process of production. From this point of view, common ownership of the instruments of labour could be considered *the only possible means* of achieving such control. But however necessary this radical change in the relations of production might be, *it represented only a means*. It was the basic immediate goal, in the sense that the revolutionaries could achieve it in the first years following the seizure of power. But the history of the USSR is there to show that nothing had yet been achieved: genuine control over their labour on the part of the workers also required them to have a direct grip on the economic process, which presupposed a certain prior accumulation of production goods. In this sense, the joint decision by the Party and the sovereign organs to step up as far as possible the drive to industrialize and collectivize did not aim just to preserve the foundations, through perpetual transformation and enrichment of the economic means. It presented itself as the only route leading to man's control over production – whose meaning clearly had to be the suppression of anti-human mediations (by worked matter) and liquidation of the practico-inert as a field of human alienation. This had to mean also that practical freedom implied that the workers should have a common relation to their work such that they would have the ability to suppress its counter-finalities, or at least prevent these from ever being able – by aggregating into an inert heap – to reconstitute the anti-dialectical rift within the new dialectical relation-ship uniting the practical organism to the common individual. In any case, *it was this* that was involved, as much in this fundamental form as in other incarnations at other levels of praxis. For example, it was *this* that was meant by the progressive withering away of the State, which – through progressive liquidation of the defeated classes and the retreat of penury – would gradually become a useless factor of alienation, an

---

31. See Preface above and, in the Appendix below, Sartre's notes on 'Totalization in Non-Dictatorial Societies'.

absurd and harmful intermediary between the producer and production. This sovereign praxis (and by sovereign I mean at present the CPSU, as it developed and changed between the Revolution and 1954) was totalizing for a specific society, and through it for all societies, in that it attempted to give the ensemble of disparate collectives and groups called Russia the means that would forge its human unity, on the basis of a given historical situation. If you prefer, there was a real and present unification of that multiplicity *by the future*. And the future here was neither a simple eventuality nor a dream, nor even the hope of an individual or group. It was the distant, absolute goal (posited *simultaneously* as the inevitable term of 'pre-history' and as an immediate and fundamental exigency of present needs, as well as of sufferings and conflicts), abstract, not *conceivable* but rigorous, on the basis of which the practical hierarchy of objectives assigned by the sovereign to the ruled collectivity was ordered. And each producer – whatever his attitude, i.e. whatever the nature of his work and his degree of emancipation – grasped this future (a common direction of the finally shaken heavy ensemble) through the very materiality of the productive effort (adversity-coefficient of the object under construction, grasped through hardship and exhaustion; increased exhaustion and hardship, as a function of the destitution following the years of civil war). If he agreed with this praxis (we shall speak in a moment about opponents, groups and classes which rejected it – or rejected it *in this form* without rejecting the ultimate objective), national unity would first appear to him as a future synthesis manifesting itself inexorably through a kind of convergence of all individual destinies. Millions of motives were embarked upon trajectories inflected towards one another. In each generation the motives exploded, expelling new motives, and this change of motives was accompanied by a closer convergence of movements.

At this level, if the individual was not integrated into the sovereign (albeit approving his praxis), the action imposed upon him – or simply the work that provided him with the means of reproducing his life – took place simultaneously as *free assent in practice* of a Soviet citizen and as the inexorable objective orientation of his destiny through his daily life. From this point of view, the convergence – i.e. the sovereign praxis grasped as irresistible force of the historical process – was *the same* in every worker: there was a single continuous drawing closer of all destinies in relation to each individual one. Through the temporally regressive hierarchy of objectives, the future goal designated the past as 'national' precisely because it was in itself the exigency of a suppression of nationalities. Through this internationalism – a *future* unity of peoples – the Soviet citizen discovered that *his* country was *designated* (by History itself) to draw all nations into the convergence of a single destiny. At the time of nationalism, this people was discovered as *the* nation that would save all others from their national solitudes: as *the chosen people*, in short, whose sufferings and heroism had to be commensurate with its responsibilities. This destiny could appear only in the perspective of a *national personality* (the very one which would one day disappear in world unity, but which – at the moment of construction – was on the contrary described in itself by the epic of the Revolution): i.e. a historical past inscribed in the materiality of present circumstances. Future history of the USSR and past history of Russia were illuminated by a reciprocity of lights. But if the unity of past history was disclosed as the living depth of an ambiguous multiplicity, this was because the inert unity of the social past (as a passive synthesis of worked materiality) was *reanimated* and *reconstituted* in the indefinite of its former moments, as producing and undergoing in its depths the unitary exigency of its future destiny and the actions capable of preparing – obscurely and indirectly – the Revolution. The abstract and mystical unity of Tsarist mythology (*the* Russian people), lit by the singularity of the national destiny, became a kind of dim awareness (devoid, however, of active awareness) that the Russians have always had of their extraordinary task. In this, properly speaking, there was neither mystification nor 'fetishization'. It was more a matter of the necessary interaction between two popular cultures (one folkloric, but partially alienated by the religious and social ideology of the old regime; the other materialist, but imbuing the people on the basis of sovereign decisions and with the inflexibility of praxis), of which the new was singularized by the old inasmuch as it rationalized it. At the juncture we are considering, in fact, for the peasant too hastily transformed into a worker by industrialization, *receiving* a Marxist education – and thanks to it interpreting the historical singularity of the Revolution in terms of the economic and social circumstances that had made Russia into *that* particular country, torn by *those* particular contradictions – came to much the same thing as seeing his country in the guise of the chosen nation (even if he had more or less liquidated his religious beliefs and given up 'practising'). But the education itself, inasmuch as it was *received*, was produced in everyone as praxis of the sovereign, as a unification undergone and assumed by a *taught* culture. It was already, in short, a synthesis of all into one: an effort to make each practical organism, through the interiorization of an ensemble of theoretico-practical schemata and determinations, into a common individual.

So it would seem, a priori, that the sovereign praxis forged unity at the same level as the serial dispersions and against them. This, moreover, is what the official propaganda proclaimed, at home and abroad. The electoral system was designed, in fact, for majorities to be so great and minorities so tiny that in practice the latter tended to be nullified and the former to become tantamount to *unanimity*. The aim here was not just to show that the population supported the government's policies – a big majority would have been enough for that. It was actually a matter of retaining the electoral system, while replacing the massifying dispersion of bourgeois votes (the electoral body is necessarily a *collective* in capitalist democracies) by a praxis-process of reunification. The result of the vote, in the USSR, was to reflect everyone's vote back to them as the action of a common individual in a group, or more precisely still as the unanimous act upon which any even minimally durable grouping rests: as a pledge (for wherever unanimity comes from, it can emanate only from a collective; it can be produced only if every voter aims to achieve agreement with all the others, even at the cost of considerable sacrifices). It mattered little, for the moment, that this unanimity was more or less a façade, or even that the sovereign was counting on serial impotence to realize it in reality. What counted was the determination to find the unity of an entire society, by integrating it into an irreversible praxis. The universalist culture of a bourgeois democracy gives everyone – at least at first sight – timeless orders. Through culture and propaganda, the sovereign group in the USSR gave everyone concrete, dated tasks: i.e. tasks that were determined – in relation to a more or less short-term objective, and within the perspective of the final aim – as the partial activities whose integration would cause the total praxis to progress and whose absence would risk provoking its regression. In this way, every practice had to be integrated into the totalizing temporalization with a positive or negative sign. And this determination in positivity or negativity was itself *temporalizing*, since it marked the functionality or counter-functionality of practice in relation to the orientated development of the totalizing praxis.

From the Government of Men over Things to Bureaucracy: Praxis and Praxis-Process

Thus the sovereign praxis did indeed aim to produce unity. But it was its very movement which, *via the attempted totalization*, was to constitute the practico-inert field by developing its counter-finalities. For when Stalin died, the appropriation of land and machines remained collective. On the other hand, control of production had passed entirely into the hands of the ruling bureaucracy. We find ourselves in the presence of a new historical fact: the radical separation of *appropriation* and rule. The whole French Revolution and all of the bourgeois nineteenth century were characterized by the identification of ruler and owner. This identification was even justified theoretically: it was explained that the owner was personally *interested* in a wise administration of the public weal; and that, ultimately, he alone could take command of national affairs, since his particular prosperity was a function of the general security and prosperity. It is striking that socialist doctrines – and Marxism itself – had only to preserve this fundamental relationship: *in theory*, the community of workers is the owner of the means of production; for that very reason, this community must command and control the process of production. And this relationship is based on a twofold interest. On the one hand, it is the organized community which alone can decide upon a truly *common* management – it is its own end. On the other hand, the new ownership system, by suppressing the mediation of the practico-inert (for example, by refusing the regulatory or pseudo-regulatory 'mechanisms' of the market and other collectives), in the shorter or longer run allows the united producers to construct a self-aware economy, which contains within it and dominates the inertial forces it uses, without ever allowing them to be posited for themselves as inhuman mediations between men. Thus unity of production and management must characterize the socialist order: socialist man is human because he governs things; every other order is inhuman, to the (variable) extent that things govern man.

Now the fact is that, as soon as the Revolution took place, the Bolshevik Party was driven by the dangers pressing in on it to reduce to a minimum the government of men by things. It was not enough with a stroke of the pen to wipe out small and medium individual ownership. The *interest* of the Revolution was to *realize* common ownership in all sectors – including the rural sectors – and to replace small farms by large ones everywhere: first of all, because *necessarily* – for example in the kolkhozes – common ownership of land and machinery enlarged the enterprise; secondly (we are dealing with a circular conditioning), because productivity is theoretically* higher in large enterprises than on small farms. So, from the outset, there was an apparent match between features imposed on the leaders' praxis by the situation and the fundamental aim of the socialist revolution. Even before the movement of industrialization achieved its full tempo it was necessary, on pain of death, to reduce the effects of the practico-inert to a minimum. In short, it was necessary – as one sociologist has recently remarked** – to transform an economy *in itself* into an economy *in itself and for itself*.

----

* I say 'theoretically', because the principle is true only in the abstract. An ensemble of historical circumstances, particularly the attitude of the rural classes, may distort its application. In Rakosi's Hungary, the productivity of the kolkhozes was on average lower – all due allowance being made – than that of the surviving private holdings. The reason, of course, was the passive resistance of the peasants. We shall come back to this.

** [Note missing in manuscript. The sociologist is Raymond Aron: see, in particular, *Eighteen Lectures on Industrial Society*, London 1967.]

But it was precisely through interiorization and transcendence of the practico-inert sector that the ruling praxis, in the course of its development, was to secrete in Soviet society – i.e. in the practical field where it was exercised – new practico-inert concretions and new rifts. For it should be noted that if the Stalinist system was characterized by unity (in a permanent relationship of circular conditioning) of these two features – ownership of the instruments of labour *by all*; rule of a relative narrow group *over all* – the original connection between those two features is not even conceivable other than as the result of a unifying praxis, even though it appears at the same time as an *inert characterization* of the regime or, if you like, a *process*. The historian, sociologist or economist grasps the unity of these significations, each of which has a meaning only through the other. At the same time, however, he discovers that this unity is merely a passive synthesis, borrowing its synthetic power from praxis itself and inscribing it in inert matter. The *system*, as a process, was produced as it produced.

For, at the outset, the leadership found itself confronted by two major difficulties. First, it had to modify entirely the demographic aspect of the country, precisely inasmuch as it attempted to provide it with industrial plant. It had to create its cadres from scratch and increase the size of the working class considerably. It might have asked for help from a proletariat already emancipated by social struggles, had the Revolution taken place in an advanced capitalist country. But it could not expect any from those workers, many of whom were still illiterate and remained peasants even in the factory. In a certain way, it can be maintained that Russia forged its working class *after* the October Revolution. Those rustics transformed into townspeople were to emancipate themselves only progressively, and slowly, in the course of the terrible effort demanded of them – which could not in itself be considered revolutionary.* The idea of workers' self-management, workers' councils, etc. – entirely acceptable in 1958 – had no meaning in 1930, when the Soviet worker was painfully freeing himself from the peasant gangue and homogeneous working-class concentrations were still an empty dream. This emergent class – still uncertain, and whose most advanced elements had either disappeared in the upheavals of the civil war or found themselves exhausted by ten years of fierce struggle – could not counterbalance the strength of the Party by exerting a constant pressure on the ruling strata. In the same way, the lack of cadres, the time that had to be put into *making* a technician, and the incompetence of the first hastily formed engineers, all required of managers that they should assume every

---

* Let us say that it is useful to the Revolution: that is all.

function in turn. Their authority could not initially be limited by their competency; on the contrary, the scope of their competency was determined by their authority. This meant, in effect, that the leader produced his sovereignty as omnipotence, despite himself and in the absence of resistance *shown by men*; but at the same time he speedily had to accumulate responsibilities and practical knowledge, in order to overcome the resistance of things as quickly as possible. Through this relationship with the led, the main features of the leadership were gradually produced. First, a reversal of Marxism in practice took the form of the political asserting its predominance over the economic. For, on the one hand, the lack of technicians obliged the politicians to take technical decisions – hence, to take them *as politicians*. On the other hand, planning – which was simply revolutionary praxis itself, inasmuch as it continued the Revolution by other means – had both immediate and long-term aims of a political nature. The point was to save the regime. But this regime was incarnated in a certain society that had to be defended. So the point was actually to provide a specific country, the USSR, with a certain industrial and military potential, which was determined in the light of internal possibilities but also of relations with external powers. More generally, it can be said that the distribution of resources (between consumption and investment) and of investments between the various sectors did not become established as a simple economic fact (in the way that things occur or seem to occur in a bourgeois democracy). Instead, they were the object of a genuine decision, which took account synthetically of the needs of the population (i.e. the minimum level beneath which disturbances would threaten, or passive resistance, or a real diminution of labour-power); of armament needs (inasmuch as such needs are directly linked to the armaments of foreign powers, and to the international conjuncture); of the obligation to develop capital equipment (in connection with the economic blockade, later with the possibilities for external trade, later still with the exigencies of a policy of expansion and aid to underdeveloped countries): in short, of directing the Revolution (maintaining, consolidating and deepening it, and extending it to the whole world).

The *voluntarism* of the Stalinist period produced itself on the basis of these practical exigencies. On the one hand, in fact, the 'directory-of-all-work' that established itself in the leading strata of the Party learned to demand everything of itself – i.e. to replace all the missing or defaulting technicians during the transition period. On the other hand, the passivity of masses in mid mutation placed the leaders in a situation where they were demanding everything of these masses, without giving them the least responsibility in exchange. Finally, subordination of the economic to the political was in practice tantamount to subordinating 'is' to

'ought'. The absolute necessity of cutting corners (combined development) and leaping over a fifty-year lag to catch up the West deprived
planning of all flexibility. There was no attempt (because they had
neither the means nor the right to make it) to allow the different
economic sectors to determine their possibilities and needs themselves,
in a reciprocal and at the very least provisional independence – albeit
with a view to gathering the estimates together subsequently at the top.
Centralization, necessary at the time of the clandestine struggle, retained
its necessity in the period of construction. Possibilities were defined *on
the basis of exigencies*, rather than the other way round. You must, so
you can.

But the very development of industry, precisely inasmuch as it was in
line with the plan – i.e. with the common praxis – reacted upon the
ruling strata to stratify them and multiply the organs of rule. In fact, the
characteristic common to all large industrial enterprises – whether
capitalist or of a soviet type – at that precise moment of technology and
production was the fact that they required a considerable development of
the functions of control, administration, co-ordination and rationalization
(preparation of tasks, simplification of services, etc.). In one way or
another, moreover, as Lukács explained, every industrial complex of any
size, if it is to develop or even maintain itself, requires specialists to
resort to a kind of *economic combinatory*. His mistake was to limit the
use of that combinatory to capitalist enterprises. In fact, it was literally
indispensable to Soviet planning, even though it was not always applied
to the same problems. First borrowed from the private enterprises of the
capitalist world, it developed independently. Planning implied an algebra
of organization and a calculated determination of all possibilities, on the
basis of a calculation of the international conjuncture and its repercussions on the national situation. And organization, of course, as a structure
of pledged inertia, is identical with the calculation that is its practical
knowledge – its deciphering – and that furnishes the guidelines for its
constitution. We know this type of *objective thought*: economic calculation is to organizational groups in industrial societies what abstract
knowledge of kinship relations is in certain 'archaic' societies. Based on
the possibility of establishing or revealing rules – i.e. inert systems of
relations themselves based on pledged inertia – its guidelines are basically
the *minimum* of synthesized passivity (on the basis of the already existing
organizational ensembles) that praxis must transcend towards the practical
situation, in order to adapt itself to it by a new creation (of a new
organization). The organizational schema is thus worked matter. It is the
inert, abstract ensemble of the general possibilities for organizing pledged
inertia – and thus in itself *that inertia*, but transported to the level of
abstraction at which (for the calculator) it will be the express condition

of transcendence of the status quo. In short, the organizational schema represents the inertial determination that the organizer has himself produced by his praxis, and to serve that praxis – which represents the framework indispensable for any transcendence but, for that very reason, strictly limits the possibilities for inventing replies to every situation. The leadership is produced in the very inertia that will gradually define it in the process of determining relations between the led. In other words, it interiorizes their pledged or serial inertia (we shall return to this), in order to be able to re-exteriorize it – transcended and negated by the invention of new groupings operating on the basis of that seriality.

What illustrated most tellingly this petrifying backlash of praxis upon itself, I think, was when the leaders confronted the question of wage differentials. The principle of the Bolsheviks in 1917 and even after that was, as far as possible in that first period, to equalize incomes (i.e. the shares of the national income allocated to each individual). But, as we have seen, the proletarian Revolution, *because it was incarnated*, presented itself with singular exigencies deriving from the singular situation in which it developed – whose singularity necessarily contradicted the Bolsheviks' principles. It was not true that these could be preserved and the Revolution be saved. But it was not true either that the integrity of the revolutionary development could be saved if they were thrown overboard. It was necessary to choose between disintegration and *deviation* of the Revolution. Deviation also means detour: Stalin was the man of that detour. 'Hold on! Produce! ... Later generations will go back to principles.' And this was right, except that he did not see how in this very way he was producing generations which contained within them – as the inert materiality of the circumstances to be transcended – the deviation that had produced them and that they interiorized (just as the development of culture and raising of living standards was making it possible for universal principles to reassert themselves and come into conflict with particularism – but that is another topic). The leadership put its intransigence into preserving, at any cost, a reality (rather than a principle): collective ownership of the means of production, inasmuch as this had been realized in *that* moment of History and in *that* particular country. The only way of safeguarding that reality, moreover, was to increase pitilessly, day by day, the rate of production. So what empty scruple would prevent them from introducing wide wage differentials, once they were convinced that high wages were the best incentive to produce?

Here again, we may observe that the practical field they organized proposed to them – and often imposed upon them – the chosen solution. *Today*, the Soviet leaders like to speak of *interesting the masses in production*, and the decentralizing measures taken by Khrushchev, among others, have this aim. But this is because the present standard of living, technical improvements and mass culture make decentralization possible and necessary. In fact, formulated in these discreet and almost aristocratic terms, the question being posed is that of total control over production. Ever since the masses became aware of the situation and themselves, there has existed only one way – sufficient and necessary – to 'interest' them in producing, which is to give them control over management. After World War I, however, the lack of education and indifference of that working class in full crisis of growth, together with the poverty of the workers, made it quite impossible to awaken a *common* interest in increasing the rate of production. In the period following the Revolution, the politicized, emancipated worker already found a new contradiction within himself: inasmuch as he *wanted* socialism, he could accept intensifying his production for the common good and restricting his consumption; but inasmuch as socialism was *also*, indeed in his eyes *first and foremost*, the end of overwork and underconsumption, his individual needs came into contradiction with his praxis as a common individual. At once, he no longer identified so closely with revolutionary construction as he had done with the social movement (as a negation of the bourgeois order) before the Revolution. Before the Revolution, his personal demand was the common demand (once competitive antagonisms had been overcome by trade-union ties); and the common demand had the triple effect of maintaining mass agitation, contributing to working-class emancipation, and – if the bosses yielded – shaking the system. After-wards, since the common activity was a planned construction, the social-ist individual was relegated to the level of the contingent. His real exigencies were presented to him as always capable of being reduced, precisely in the name of the common objective. But since the common objective was such that the means of attaining it were the object of economic calculations which specialists or specialized bureaucrats alone could carry out, it was *not even he as a common individual* or the unified ensemble of his comrades who determined the norms, the yield and the distribution of investments. His fate came to him via the sovereign, in the form of a strict determination of objectivity. His tasks were fixed for him, on the basis of statistical data establishing the exigencies of plant to be produced, armaments and consumption, and it was through simplified résumés of these calculated data that they were communicated to him.

This implied a reification of the citizen's relations with the sovereign. The former was defined through the latter's calculations as a mere unit of production and consumption. Between the two of them, there was the mediation of the *Plan*: an ambiguous reality which was *both* the volun-tarist political project of a certain ruling milieu and *at the same time* – at least as it presented itself through the instructions imposed on *this* factory or *that* combine – the simple, rigorous determination of the conditions to be fulfilled by each and every one in order to save the USSR (the foundations of socialism). The most emancipated workers were thus stripped of their rights to control and leadership, not by a deliberate operation on the part of the leading organs but by the growing disproportion between the requirements of the economic combinatory and their relative ignorance of these problems.* Their obedience to the sovereign was *reified* (as much as in capitalist systems, but in a qualitatively different way), inasmuch as it was lived as submission to physical laws. Through planning, in fact, the full rigour of economic laws that liberalism was so fond of evoking was rediscovered – the sole difference being that this rigour was perceived *through a system*, whereas the liberals grasped it in pure exteriority. The organizers of the Plan and the producers who realized it could be compared to the crew of an aeroplane struggling against a storm and grasping the 'facts of nature' in practice, inasmuch as they had already been filtered and reassembled by the inert synthesis of the system, whereas the *Homo oeconomicus* of liberalism was, so to speak, outside – submitted to natural forces without mediation, both he and the works he erected outside himself. In any case, a first inert constraint created a kind of void between managers and producers, which determined the former to assume the functions that the latter could not exercise.

We have still spoken only of the conscious core of the emergent working class. But let us not forget that non-agricultural jobs (tertiary and secondary) went in four years (1928–32) from ten to twenty million (out of a population of 151 million persons), and from twenty to forty-five million between 1932 and 1955. Since 'services' were less developed (we shall see why) than in the bourgeois democracies, most of the newly 'urbanized' joined the workers of the 'secondary' sector. For the period that interests us ('28–'32), the doubling of the working class had the result of paralysing it. The newcomers – torn from agriculture; illiterate, or barely knowing how to read and write; brutally changing their rhythm of work and way of life; lost – were unable to conceive or understand the common interest of workers, until a long and difficult adaptation had made them aware of their new condition. When the leaders are reproached, moreover, with having deprived them of their rights, I am tempted to ask: 'Supposing that these rights had been acknowledged, how and with what intellectual tools and in the name of what unity would they have exercised them?' It is obvious, moreover, that their demands – if they had been able to get a hearing – would have

---

* [Note missing in manuscript.]

been of a negative kind. Those new workers *cost a lot* (especially in heavy industry), so the wage *had to be low*; and they were exhausted by the effort asked of them. So they would have demanded less work and higher wages. It goes without saying that such demands could not but express the reality of their needs, so they were perfectly justified. But it also goes without saying that since they did not present themselves in the context of general control over production – hence in connection with *positive* adjustments to the Plan – they were determined *for the leaders* as possible fetters on industrialization. So planning took account of minimum needs in order to avoid demands and the possibility of a working-class resistance that would find its unity in struggle: hence, as objective and negative elements that it should be possible to contain *by a minimum expenditure*. The barest rationally calculated satisfaction of needs, combined with propaganda and coercion, sufficed to prevent a negative unity of those workers still not very aware of their class or their rights.

Yet education aimed to transform those social atoms into *common individuals*. But it endowed them with their common reality inasmuch as they had to contribute to maintaining and transcending the norms of the Plan. This positive synthesis presupposed that massifying forces would continue their massification from below, and of these forces the most important was the monstrous growth of the secondary sector.

So, for some, propaganda and education could inculcate the duty of producing. But *the interest in producing* could not *be realized*, at the level of the masses, as an objective condition of their work. They were still too backward to be able to demand control over the process of production, while the government was too poor – and the Plan required investments that were too great in the capital-goods and armaments industries – for it to be able even to envisage raising the real standard of living in proportion to the progress achieved in industrialization. More-over, a rise of that kind could not occur of its own accord, in a system resorting to commandism in order to close a half-century gap and rush through the stage of accumulation. Opening up wide wage differentials was a *means born of poverty*. The same with productivity bonuses, Stakhanovism, emulation. The aim was clear: (1) To give *anyone* the chance to improve his own living standard, seeing that it was impossible to raise *everybody's*. By this method competitive and antagonistic prac-tices were reintroduced, not at the level of the capitalist market (which no longer existed) but in the actual factory, at the level of production. Everyone *could* be better paid, if he imposed upon himself a harder effort; but in the end only *some* would benefit from the bonuses and increases. (2) The presence in a factory of a core of activists contributed in itself to raising norms. Thereby, it introduced a negative interest for the other workers: they would work more *so that their wage would not go down*. In short, that whole mandarinate of heroes of labour, Stakhanovites, activists and Stalin prizewinners; that refusal to level wages at the base; that working-class *chin* [rank] (where wage differences were further accentuated by the opportunity, for the elite, to enjoy special advantages – e.g. an apartment, etc.); all that emulation they tried to stimulate by competitions between factories or by honorific distinctions (inclusion on the roster of merit, etc.) – all that was constituted by the leaders' praxis, in an effort to verticalize the voluntarism of production (by means of an elite that would 'raise' or 'drag along' the base), for want of having the means to stimulate a profound movement in the masses by 'interesting' them in producing. The leadership's praxis had to confront a fundamental option. Since it was impossible to obtain increased productivity by mere coercion, it was necessary to choose *stimuli* and *incentives*. But the necessities of industrialization prevented them from telling the masses they would improve their lot inasmuch as they increased the rate of production. So all that was left was a choice between principles (the egalitarianism of 1917) and the only *possible* stimulus (which was not a sly return to capitalist competition, but integration of a managed competition between workers – and on the terrain of work – into the system).

The practical aim which made it necessary to choose the second term of the alternative was thus *certainly not* to introduce a stratified hierarchy into the world of work. It was a matter rather of setting off a to-and-fro movement between base and elite, and compensating for the present misery by opening up a field of living possibilities *for everyone*. But whatever the objective might be, it *had* to be realized in practice through a stratification. The constant growth of the secondary sector in fact necessitated the creation of an ever more extensive system of bonuses, distinctions and privileged positions – without there being any chance of those already occupied becoming free again (it was young men who occupied them, they were not going to reach retirement age for a long time). The effect of this 'creaming' of the masses was to produce a voluntarist elite in the image of the ruling groups. For its members, *it was true* that they would improve their lot by participating in industrialization with all their strength: the common interest and the individual interest coincided. But only individuals – inasmuch as they constituted themselves as such *against the masses* (denying that they were part of them; becoming if not bosses, at least objectively pacemakers) – could achieve this fusion. For this very reason we find in them – inasmuch as they interiorized the sovereign's voluntarism and re-exteriorized it in their own work – a very singular synthesis, proper to the 'Soviet elites', between individualism (ambition, personal interest, pride) and total dedication to the common cause, i.e. to socialism. But in so far as it was the leaders who had determined for them the possibility of emerging from the masses, they were hand in glove with the sovereign. And in so far as the leaders' praxis had stimulated the elite in the voluntarist perspective of building socialism, they conceived the construction of the socialist society only through that sovereign praxis. For those two reasons, their discipline was military. They temporalized the practical enterprise represented by their life in the totalizing milieu of the globalizing temporalization. They assimilated their progressive elevation in the hierarchy to the progressive realization of socialism in one country. Thus the leadership recruited its own auxiliaries and created them in the perspective of its planning activity, as voluntarist products of its sovereignty and as the depositaries of its inflexible will. The Plan created the man of the Plan. But the Plan was a praxis of men.

Conversely, however, the ensemble of ruling and administrative organs suffered the backlash of its praxis: it qualified itself and determined itself by its wage policy. In that hierarchical society that it created by widening wage differentials and multiplying honours, the ruling group found itself objectively modified by the hierarchical structures – as determinations of the social field into which it was integrated. It was designated no longer just as a revolutionary ensemble, which drew its sovereignty from its praxis, but as an institutionalized sovereign, whose power was objectified and determined by the place the directors occupied at the apex of the hierarchy. For how could you conceivably create a hierarchy, without thereby defining yourself as the man (or men) of the top rung? How could you distribute honours, if you did not enjoy the highest honorific distinctions? How could you decide the top of the ladder and the bottom rungs, without ultimately creating all the intermediary rungs? How could you define wage increases as a recompense, without attributing to yourself the highest wages? It is pointless in fact to imagine that a group of poor revolutionaries, without privileges, refusing all distinctions – as Lenin was – could, to serve the needs of praxis, engender a society of dignitaries in which merit was ceremoniously recompensed. Yet the greater the dangers that were run by the regime and the more arduous the effort required, the more blatant the ceremonial had to be. Thus praxis developed its counter-finality: via the intermediary of the voluntarists whom it distinguished and raised above the common rut, it transformed its agents into *dignitaries*. Social stratification became at once the obligatory means of realizing economic growth by planning in *that* underdeveloped country and – as a consequence entailed by praxis but not willed by it – the practico-inert and anti-socialist result of the search for *incentives*, in a situation which did not allow interesting the masses in production.

In this first stage of our investigation, what interests us primarily is to find the factors which conditioned the appearance in the USSR of a practico-inert, and of fissures between the social milieux. We have, in fact, just seen the birth of those layers of social inertia termed *strata*; and it must above all be appreciated that this stratification occurred as *the process of praxis*. For the separation between managing functions and the right of appropriation assuredly represented a structure of negative inertia. An impassable internal limit on the relationship between the masses and the administrators. In short, a reification. But planning, in itself, at once constituted that proletariat – formed out of heterogeneous layers and constantly growing – as a collective. The internal structure of that enormous mass in perpetual disequilibrium was the practico-inert result of a *practical process*. For the Plan anticipated the creation of new factories or enlargement of the old ones, so it was directly concerned to create *working-class jobs* for certain members of the peasant population. That meant ensuring that these new jobs would find occupants, and committing the necessary expenditure to ensure that every occupant would have the right tools and to *make* a skilled worker out of an agricultural labourer. Eventually, the leaders would themselves define the rural zones that could support an exodus. Perhaps they would even sovereignly fix the contribution of each province, according to its human resources and the relationship between its population and its production (itself judged from the standpoint of the requirements of the Plan). Of course, these decisions could be taken by different bodies at the top, and this possibility was itself an expression of managerial *inert-being*, to which we shall return. No matter. Even if certain aspects of the task were defined by various sub-groups, unity remained intact, because the central body had defined the general line, the objectives and the global exigencies of the future undertaking (Gosplan). The activities of the sub-groups had the aim of ensuring the *specification* of praxis. They operated on the twin fundamental basis of synthetic unity of the Plan (which, in an already global and concrete – though less detailed – form, required final adjustments) and sovereign power. Those two bases were one and the same: the central managing group created subaltern positions *for* the Plan and *by* it; so praxis, while being objectified in the current Plan, was *still and always praxis* when it created organs of its own for itself (albeit on the basis of an already received and inert hierarchical structure). It was *at the level* of the demographic upheaval which it had produced in its entirety, and above all of the social consequences of the latter, that it found itself *undergoing* – as a material, inert circumstance to be transcended and altered – *its own results*. How did this come about?

The reason was clearly the following. History has two principles. One is human activity, simultaneously all and nothing, which without the inertia of things would at once evaporate like a volatile spirit. The other is inert matter, within the agents themselves and outside them, which supports and deviates the whole practical edifice at the same time as having stimulated its construction (inasmuch as it was already a synthetic and passive deviation of the previous praxis). Thus every action of the group upon inanimate matter (by which I mean a collective as much as a lump of coal) has as its necessary consequence the interiorization, within the group itself and in a form defined by its previous structures, of the very inertia in which its praxis is objectified. And *through the internal transformation of the group* interiorized inertia will deviate praxis at its source and be re-exteriorized as deviated praxis. The fact is all the more intelligible in that the group, as the practical free organism, re-exteriorizes its inertia to act upon the inertia outside via the mediation of a directed inertia. At the level of interaction, moreover, you necessarily find in the case of individual work the unity in exteriority of the physico-chemical world, but in the case of common work the unity in exteriority of the physico-chemical world and the human world (inasmuch as this is strewn with worked objects which make mediations between men). In 1928, the illiteracy of the peasants represented a serious danger for the Party's agrarian policy. But on this terrain (where we shall meet it again), it was a negative material *given* for the leaders that they inherited without having produced it, that they discovered as a passive resistance to praxis, and that was characterized at once by its universality and its dispersion. Furthermore, that inertia *was merely a lack*. But what was involved here was not an *external* negation, as when Marx explains the emigration of the Ancient Greeks by their ignorance of the practical applications of the natural sciences, but an *internal* negation: i.e. one that was discovered and constituted – by the action which revealed it, came up against it and grasped it within itself – as the absence of a means, the presence of a risk and the urgency of inventing a recompense.

Apart from this *negative* element, *positive* and *practical* features were discovered. The peasant from a given region, who practised a given culture in a specific context, was characterized by a *way of life* – a mixture of abilities and inertia, or rather an ensemble of abilities based on the inertia these had gradually produced (e.g. the capacity to work in conditions that would be almost unendurable for townspeople; but, conversely, determination of a rhythm as a practical schema and inert limit of temporalization). It was the ruling praxis that deprived those very features – as organic resistance to a new qualification of their work, and as an inanimate brake on their adaptation to working-class life – of their *practical* aspect, viewing them instead only in terms of their inertia. In reality, the peasant's *abilities* were useless to him in the factory, since they were exclusively a means of carrying out his work as a farmer. So what was left was the determinations on which they were based –

particularly the rhythm of work, which by now was only the difficulty or non-possibility of adapting to production norms. Lastly, it must be added that the peasant, at the beginning of his 'urbanization', remained above all a peasant. Lost in the 'landscape' of the working-class suburbs, he worked to live and could not at first feel his solidarity with that universe. That sense of being lost (which, of course, tended to diminish in the case of a particular individual, but remained constant in the working-class masses as a whole, or even increased along with the tempo of urbanization) was a *suffered* relationship between the new worker and his new milieu. Or rather, it was the negative relation resulting from their being *brought into contact*: through being brought into contact in this way (in accordance with the Plan), the material milieu as a medium for inert syntheses became a mediation between men (habitat, factories, machines, etc.).

These inert determinations were the basic relationships upon which all others were established. And it is easy to see that they were *produced by praxis*. Braking action and resistance of the organic rhythm, disorientation, etc., became negative realities in the milieu of the working-class concentrations; and the latter were not inert groupings around the towns, but demographic currents determined and controlled by the leadership.* Among the elements of those inert determinations, moreover, certain elements in other milieux (in the rural areas) could be alive and play an active role in production. The essential thing was that sovereign action produced a new milieu (the working-class concentrations) in full evolution, within which it maintained a singular curvature-tension; and that, through this tension and this inner curvature, the previous determinations were modified by one another and constituted inert concretions and braking or deviating mechanisms. In short, a practico-inert field. And this field drew its unity from the totalizing praxis: that alone allows us to call it a system, a process, or simply a mechanism. But it drew *its being* from the inertias reassembled and fused together by that practical synthesis. In other words, for the Russian working class of the thirties it became a source of permanent atomization or serialization, so that this class – imbued with an ideology simplified and modified for propaganda purposes – could find its unity only outside itself, via the mediation of the sovereign. Above all, moreover, that transcendent and superficial unity in fact represented only the unity of the sacrifices that were demanded of its members, whereas the true relations with the leadership

---

* The latter, in fact, did not confine itself to increasing urbanization. It also controlled and limited it in the case of each specific town, taking all factors into account (for example, *simultaneously* the needs of industry and the housing shortage). It was forbidden to reside in Moscow if one was not required to live there *by a specific function or job*.

remained provisionally reified. Mystifying mirage of transcendent unity; reified relations with the leaders; internal structures of atomization and seriality; perpetual intermingling as a result of new arrivals: that was the *reality* of the working class during its crisis of growth. That was what a priori made it inconceivable that it should seize the levers of command and exercise dictatorship on its own. That was why the leaders were constituted *by it*, as exercising that dictatorship *in its place* – precisely in so far as, by its mode of recruitment, they constituted it as incapable for the time being of controlling production. So there was a reciprocity of conditioning in inertia, at the very heart of the total action and the practical field that this had determined. It was the workers who made the leaders, in so far as the leaders made the working-class concentrations.

To go still further, however, it is necessary to understand that the features inscribed in that working class – which did not find any assistance even in its trade unions – reflected a still deeper given, which was no more or less than the very circumstance revolutionary activity sought to transcend. (1) From the outset, the 'underdevelopment' of the USSR was necessarily transferred on to the demographic terrain, by an extraordinary numerical disproportion between the non-agricultural and the rural workers: in the domain of customs, culture and revolutionary consciousness, this led to radical differences. (2) The state of emergency and all the dangers necessitated an unprecedented acceleration of the process of urbanization: the working class which had made the Revolution was, you might say, invaded and dismembered by barbarians. Thus praxis integrated the countryside with the town, tending thereby to produce a new balance in which the masses freshly emerging from the hinterland would become partially urbanized, whereas the urban masses – invaded – would lose their autonomy and their unity. That gap between the rural immigrants and the oldest workers was simply an incarnation and reflection of the gap to be filled between the current situation of industry and the situation it was supposed to achieve by the end of the Plan. Moreover, even assuming – since this was the aim of praxis – that the gap between those two moments of production would be filled five years later, it still remained the case that it had been interiorized by the working-class masses, inasmuch as they had received within themselves more alien elements than they could absorb. Everything has its price. To act means to interiorize a contradiction through the very ensemble of the acts that suppress it externally. The industrialization of that agricultural country was – through the urbanization of the peasants – the ruralization of the working class, and the provisional lowering of its political and cultural level in favour of its growth. This was also signalled by the fact that production increased much faster than productivity.

Thus the provisional features of the working class were the metamorphosis into present and reified human relations of a synthetic relationship between the economic situation in the USSR as a practico-inert reality in 1928 and its future situation (in 1933 or subsequently) as an objective defining the sovereign praxis. The fact that *this* class provisionally had to present *these* features was, without a doubt, *inevitable*. By this we mean that, *in the framework of that praxis and on the basis of the circumstances which engendered it*, urbanization *had to be accomplished* in that way and in no other. But that does not at all mean that we should present it as *'typical of (or a model for) industrial growth in socialist countries'* – as though industrial growth first existed as an economic process determining itself, and as though its determinations were modified in one way or another depending on whether it occurred in a socialist country or in a capitalist country. This non-situated and, therefore, even non-human viewpoint is that of economic sociology. But it can be said to rejoin the anti-human dogmatism of the transcendent dialectic. For, instead of showing necessity as an ensemble of objective practico-inert connections alienating praxis, it is presented to us as preceding and conditioning the latter. According to this hypothesis, the Soviet leaders were *in the service* of that transcendent growth: it was realized by them in so far as it constrained them to realize it whatever they might do. And, of course, the sociologists do not at all deny that there is a *history* of that growth, they simply confine themselves to observing that this history is not their department. That is enough to signal the *autonomy* of their economic and social model. But they forget that this model could not stand up, if it were not the inert objectification of a unity; and that this unity can precisely be nothing but sovereign activity transcending the present towards the future. In vain do they present it in its autonomous functioning, determining it through statistics: they will lose sight of its signification, if they do not agree to see in it the transformations of a practico-inert *by a history*. To suppress Soviet history; to forget that industrialization was accomplished practically under foreign bombardment (and interrupted by a devastating war); not to take account of the consequences it had externally (ebbing of the working-class movements, fascism, etc.), which also reacted upon it; to forget the evolution of the revolutionary parties, their contradictions, etc.: that amounts to considering an inert sum, without taking account of the orientated totalization which produces it by its operations, supports it and transcends it. And when Raymond Aron, for example, points out that there are other types of socialist growth (the countries of Central Europe, China), he forgets that those other types were possible – with their negative aspects, as with their positive aspects – only in so far as they were grafted on to the Soviet 'model': i.e. in so far as the industrialization of the USSR was necessary to produce them and sustain them; in so far as every one of the

measures taken by the leaders of the people's democracies – good or bad
– cannot be understood by itself and in its mere practical relationship
with the exigencies of the national economy, but must necessarily be
related to the political relationship of the country in question with the
USSR and to the history of Soviet socialization.*

As soon as the multiplication of industrial centres required improved
communications – to take just one example – a synthetic but inert
relationship was established between such and such a town which needed
a certain raw material and another which represented the nearest mining
centre. The relationship manifested as an inert exigency of town A
towards town B could be revealed by innumerable dangers: a drop in
productivity for want of materials, the risk of partial unemployment, an
overequipment of centre A in relation to its real possibilities (i.e. its
possibility of being 'supplied' by B). That exigency was a reality – at the
level of the town itself, and at the level of the USSR. But this reality
came from the towns being brought into contact through praxis. Town A
had been founded or considerably developed; its factories had been
equipped *with the prospect* of centre B transmitting ore to it in sufficient
quantities. In this way, the inert terrain lying between the two centres
was abruptly *synthetically unified*. It was *simultaneously* separation and
unification. The long and short of the matter was that it became an inert
mediation between two human activities (the mine, the factory), but
played that role *in the context of the Plan*. It was, in fact, *the Plan* – and
not the private interest of this or that capitalist – which endowed the
materiality of the terrain (with its irregularities, its relief, its hydrography)
with that mediating role and that possibility of developing unpredictable
counter-finalities. In particular, once factors of an entirely different kind
– but still integrated by praxis – allowed town A to intensify its
production considerably (*provided* it was more regularly supplied by B),
this was enough for the problem to take on a new urgency. Originally
established in A because a railway line linked A and B and the conditions (number of wagons, state of the rolling-stock and tracks, staff, etc.)
were assembled for a certain number of return trips to be made in a
certain space of time, the factory became a problem in itself within the
perspective of an accelerated growth that necessitated overlooking
nothing that might increase its output. The problem arose, in fact,
because the existing rail traffic between A and B became clearly
inadequate, while on the other hand the Plan reduced investment in
transport to a minimum. The latter stipulation was obviously not grat-

* A fair number of measures taken in central Europe were actually just the routine
application of measures that had succeeded in the USSR *before 1939*.

uitous. It arose from the situation itself (the possibility of supplying most factory centres from nearby or relatively close mining centres; an attempt to group the various stages of a product's manufacture – from mining to finishing – in vertical concentrations; the need to invest above all in heavy industry). The balance of the Plan required it. But the contradiction emerged here, through praxis itself, from the bringing of different inertias into relation with one another. By increasing the rate of production in heavy industry, and by organizing a system of bonuses and honours which wrested the worker away from the mass and allowed the manager access to more important positions, the sovereign gave town A the means – hence the duty – to increase its output. But that meant giving itself the obligation – *in the name of industrialization* – of reinvesting in transport, which it rejected *in order to achieve industrialization more successfully.*

Of course, it was not just a matter of two centres. There would have been no problem then. But what happened most frequently was that the same overall movement provoked the same exigencies in quite a number of different regions, which presupposed a choice – and perhaps a reworking of the Plan. In any case, this example shows us how praxis itself creates its own necessity, inasmuch as it synthetically unites inertias of exteriority. For it was praxis, through expansion of the factory, which created the scarcity of rail traffic – just as earlier, by the establishment of town A, it had created the terrain A ↔ B as a mediating exteriority. And finally it was praxis, through the already accomplished distribution of investments, which made that scarcity into a practical problem and – through the practico-inert ensemble – confronted the need to choose. But the choice itself, in so far as it would be objectified by labour in worked matter, would resolve the *particular* problem only to pose others. For the objects produced, as inert syntheses, would be realized through the social universe as permanent possibilities for mediations. However, at the same time as action created the type of synthetic necessity that was specifically human necessity, its singular historical character (it was a sovereign action, a 'commandism') led it to *retain within itself* the practico-inert that it engendered: either in the guise of exigencies to be met and problems to be resolved; or else in the guise of exigencies on the way to being satisfied (or already satisfied) and problems on the way to being solved (or already resolved), on the basis of which other practico-inert concretions would be determined (or were already in the process of being determined) in the practical field, with other exigencies and other solutions. Thus, through this simple example, we can grasp necessity – in the case of a sovereign and commandist praxis – as the temporary alienation of that praxis in its own practical field by the synthetic bringing into relation of different worked passivities. This means, if you like, that action is overwhelmed from within by the depth of the world and must at every moment resolve problems to which it gives birth, without having been aware of engendering them. The process (and from this viewpoint what economists call growth is a process) is the exteriority of praxis, inasmuch as it reveals itself at the heart of its interiority. All industrial societies are doubtless characterized today by *growth*.* But this growth (something true also, as we shall see, of bourgeois societies) is the exteriority of a praxis which – in given circumstances, with specific technologies – strives to overcome scarcity. The *unity* of the process is the projection into the inert of the synthetic unification of the totalizing praxis.

Thus, to return to our example (Soviet planning as praxis-process), the Russian population and the farmlands that fed it were totalized at every moment by the managers. For the immediate practical field of the latter (inasmuch as the temporalization of the most urgent undertaking and its spatializing extension determined one another reciprocally) was precisely the entire nation, with all its resources and all its problems, grasped through the accomplished Revolution, the objectives to be attained and the interiorization of the threats hanging over it as a result of capitalist encirclement. So it got its alienations and deviations from the inert concretions it produced in its practical field, rather than – as in the case of the individual – from outside. In particular, the leading group was *in* the practical field that its own action transformed, and was what was affected by the inert determinations its action produced in the field. So praxis was to be deviated by stratification of the group, and the group was stratified precisely in so far as the need to increase production was expressed in practice by a series of measures whose practico-inert result was working-class impotence and a hierarchy of wages. So the deviation of praxis was not directly the consequence of its development. But it independently became an institutionalized praxis, *recognizing itself* in the *chin* [rank] it had established despite itself when the leaders were transformed by the whole society and with it: when they ceased to be revolutionaries and became dignitaries of the Revolution. In other words, in a socialist society and during the period of commandism the practical agents are inside their own praxis and undergo the backlash of the changes it inaugurates, via the mediation of the practico-inert. Praxis, moreover, changes in turn only via the intermediary of transformations affecting the agents. Praxis makes society; society, within the framework of praxis, makes the leaders in its image; and the leaders change praxis, as a function of their new *hexis*. But this *precisely* means that the relationship between ruler and ruled presents itself as a reciprocity of

---

* [Note missing in manuscript.]

totalization. The rulers *make themselves* rulers of *those* particular ruled via the mediation of the practico-inert.

Industrial growth, to be sure, comprises a first phase termed that of accumulation, in which it is necessary to build the factories and manufacture the machines to manufacture machines. In that first period, investment goes primarily into heavy industry. It is characterized by a first demographic movement: growth of the secondary sector at the expense of the primary; a larger number of workers is necessary because there is a larger number of factories in absolute terms. In the second phase of growth, however, a new progress is realized by the increase of 'productivity'. The latter implies the appearance of another demographic current. To be sure, in so far as the numerical diminution of the rural population must be compensated for by intensifying the productivity of the agricultural labourers, the primary sector continues more or less to supply the new recruits for the secondary sector. But as the size of the farms or farming groups requires a permanent labour of control and organization, and as at the same time one of the essential factors of productivity is the co-ordination of efforts and preparation of tasks, the tertiary sector grows at the expense of the secondary. There is a circularity, since *productivity* requires *fewer* manual workers and *more* white-collar workers.

In the USSR, commandism, through a combined development, sought to carry on simultaneously the struggle to accumulate production goods and the struggle to increase productivity. For that reason, the strongest demographic current went from the primary to the secondary sector. There existed, moreover, an instinctive reluctance among the leaders to multiply unproductive jobs; at the same time, as we have mentioned, there were not enough cadres, despite an admirable effort to develop technical schooling. As a consequence of this twofold practical determination, the ensemble of political and administrative organs was constrained to assume the function of the higher tertiary sector. This was in line, moreover, with the other objective of praxis: to preserve the *political* character of planning. The technician determined what was, the politician determined what could be done, in the light of what had to be. But the very necessity of construction obliged them to demand surplus labour from the workers as well as from the peasants. The worker, according to Marx, receives a wage representing a lesser value than that which he has produced; the remainder, in a capitalist society, goes to the boss and is partly reinvested in the enterprise. This is what makes accumulation possible. In a period of socialist accumulation, however, could things be otherwise? How could plant be developed, if the value consumed by the producer were equal to that which he had produced? All the same, it was not a matter of exploitation. Through the Plan, it was the whole collectivity which decided – in the interest of all – to reinvest the difference between the value consumed and the value produced. But this collectivity was not mature enough to control its leaders, still less to manage itself. Was it not at the same time necessary to *create* that working class, which was to emancipate itself through work and culture? So the leaders were awkwardly situated: as a singular group determining *for everybody* the use to be made of what – if a bourgeois democracy were involved – might be called surplus-value. This highly singular situation was defined by their very action. It was necessary to take power, exercise it, decide sovereignly – or else give up the idea of defending the revolutionary achievement. On the other hand, however, they were constituted – by the very task they assumed – as the allies of the future community against the present masses. And by 'future community' I do not mean, of course, the far-off communist society, but simply these common individuals – marked by the same *hexis*, aware of their duties and their rights, transformed by culture, each of whom might be a specific example of what is called 'Soviet man' – fitted, as of now, by their capabilities and knowledge to support their leaders and, precisely by doing so, to control them. In short, I mean these young Russians of 1958, such as their leaders have very genuinely attempted to produce them and such as they have indeed produced them in reality. They make Terror pointless, and perhaps they will soon make it impossible. In 1930, however, the leaders derived their isolation from the masses they had forged, and re-exteriorized it in distrust and coercive measures. Here again, it is necessary to understand that first fissure – which sprang from action itself. Loss of contact with the masses was not mainly, or first, a consequence of the Terror: it was its source. For praxis was producing masses with whom the leading revolutionaries no longer had any possible contact. First, because their situation and their activity obliged them to take part of the value they produced from them (to *fix* even the scale of the exaction), in order to reutilize it arbitrarily (arbitrarily only in so far as, *for those masses*, their power was arbitrary and justified solely by the future outcome). Secondly, because their pre-revolutionary formation, their struggles, their Marxist culture, and their interiorized violence would have brought them far closer to any proletariat in a capitalist country than to those millions of lost peasants, many of whom had undergone the Revolution without making it, or else had been too young to take part in it, and who could not express the desperate violence that springs from misery other than against the very regime that was making them into workers. At the same time, however, the constructive movement they embarked on, with all its revolutionary violence, carried them ahead with respect to the still negative phase of the working-class movements abroad. For these isolated groups, the only possible justification of their authority was the *objective process*. The practical success of the October Revolution proved that the time had indeed come for the seizure of power. The leaders would be *qualified* – they would truly represent the interest of the working class – if they achieved industrialization: i.e. if praxis was a rigorous technique, based on precise measurements and calculations. Sovereignty was justified by absolute objectivity, and the manager was dissolved into his activity – i.e. into the strict determination of a plan that liquidated him and dissolved him into himself, as the mere detector of the objective.

But in proportion as the leading *individual* was obliterated, the leading *function* was affirmed and had to be respected by all. The hierarchical system was constituted in circularity. Without a doubt, the necessity of introducing emulation (as we saw earlier) did determine a hierarchy at the lower echelons; moreover, the latter did designate the leading circles as the upper ranks, still vague but *to be defined* and made specific (relationship: function ↔ wage ↔ rank). Conversely, however, that hier- archized power was itself undoubtedly the result of the leaders' author- itarianism, which merely expressed the need for voluntarism in a society where the base – stirred as it was by various movements – remained temporarily cut off from the summit. More deeply still, the stratifications of the summit expressed the reinteriorization by praxis of a political necessity. In order to preserve the predominance of the political (construc- tion of the socialist world) over the economic and the technical (in order to eliminate the risk of a government of experts, i.e. of a technocracy), it was necessary – in that society in the throes of development – that the leaders should not participate in the universal mobility of those classes in fusion. Their *action* had to be adapted at every moment to new circumstances, to be enriched, and on occasion to be disavowed without hesitation; but the extreme flexibility of that action necessarily depended on the personnel being maintained in their posts. The latter had to be the permanence that produced, controlled and directed change. If personnel changes had been too frequent, there would have been interference between these and the metamorphoses of growth transforming the country: the result would have been paralysis or instability – oscillations following no inner law. For this very reason, it was quite simply growth that inscribed itself upon the leaders as its own rule – as the permanence it required, in order constantly to adapt to its own problems and to world conjunctures – in the same way that their own revolutionary culture was limited, reinforced and illuminated by the lack of culture of the masses; and in the same way that, reciprocally, this culture alone – because it was revolutionary – defined the lack of culture of the masses *historically*, not as the mere absence of universal tools but as its temporary inability to understand the meaning of the Revolution in progress.

Thus a certain *political* activity, born in given circumstances and exerted by rulers recruited by the former praxis, determined within the practical field the ensemble of the ruled as integrated into an irreversible temporal movement – rather than (as in other societies) into a cyclical movement of repetition. Thanks to that, a nation was no longer a *being* but a *making*, an enterprise – and this enterprise aimed to construct politically the economic foundations of social life. On this basis, *praxis* designated the sovereign realizing it as a *political group assuming economic and technical functions*: i.e. one that limited and controlled the production of tertiary cadres, and absorbed into itself all those produced by the tertiary sector, by integrating all high functionaries into the Party. This distrust of the pure technician (combined with the fact that years were needed to produce him, since it was necessary first to produce his training), by obliging the members of the sovereign to concern them-selves with everything, defined their practical characteristics for them: a hasty, disorganized culture, acquired as new questions were posed; and voluntarism (the technician was a potential saboteur, inasmuch as he was the person who declared: 'You can do *that* and *no more*'). A sovereign whose practical field was the totality of national activities; who – embarked upon a gigantic undertaking – struggled against the scarcity of time as much as against that of tools or consumer goods; who combined the political and sovereign function with those of the tertiary sector (administration, co-ordination, organization); whose voluntarism itself – as an interiorization of the scarcity of time, and as the consequence of a void separating the masses from the managers – produced simul-taneously, at the cost of the most terrible effort, a permanent trans-formation of Soviet society and an ever more developed stratification of the leading circles, which consequently pitted the slowness, lack of initiative and monolithism of their administration against the mobility required of the ruled by the sovereign, their flexible movements and their adaptability (as masses stirred by provoked currents): do we not here recognize the Soviet *Bureaucracy*, as its functions of leadership without appropriation had made it, in the irreversible temporalization of an activity that mobilized the masses without being able – for the time being – to be controlled by them? And that *Bureaucracy* was the inert-being of the sovereign, its inanimate materiality (as we have seen, it was the rebirth of the collectivity within the sovereign). But there would have been no totalization if those practico-inert structures had derived from its praxis as mere *suffered* effects. In fact, there was a dialectical movement of interiorization and re-exteriorization. It is necessary to say at one and the same time that the sovereign *was bureaucratized by* activity and that it *bureaucratized itself for* activity.

Truth to tell, however, this latter viewpoint risks leading us astray. In reality, bureaucratization was under no circumstances the sovereign's aim, not even as a means of governing. But via the mediation of inert materiality, which – as we have seen – exists even in the best integrated groups, bureaucracy became the synthetic meaning in exteriority of all the measures the sovereign took in the practical temporalization. To cite just one example, it was via the mediation of the masses' inertia that the fierce will to save the Revolution became an idealist voluntarism on the sovereign's part, expressed by the proud consciousness of alone being that Revolution (as a practical temporalization). It was through that finality, everywhere present and everywhere deviated, that the being-in-exteriority of praxis – i.e. the bureaucratic status of the group – drew its inert unification from its objectives and acts, as temporalized interiority. And because it was constituted as a counter-finality through the orientated activity of the agents, it necessarily referred back to the aims of that activity as its foundation, its positive means and its permanent unity. So it makes no difference whether the historian settles the meaning of the activity and goes on from there to its counter-finalities, i.e. to the external apparatus it constituted for itself; or whether he begins by studying the transformations of the external apparatus and then goes back to the activity, as the principle they required precisely in so far as they had refracted and deviated it and, in this degraded form, it deter-mined their inert unity.

Ambiguity of the Latent Conflict

As for the latent conflict which, in the practical field, pitted the workers against the managers (we know there had been sabotage more or less everywhere, on several occasions – John Scott gave an eye-witness account of instances at Magnitogorsk – and the conflict could take other forms too, such as passive resistance, moonlighting, black-marketeering, etc.), we now understand that this was the readoption as activity – or as practical features more or less explicitly qualifying activity – of the practico-inert rift engendered by the common praxis. The latter produced the workers by the work it assigned to them; it produced the leaders by the workers' presence in the practical field. In so far as the class-being of the workers and the bureaucratic-being of the bosses were projections into the practico-inert of the synthesis in progress, and in so far as workers and leaders conditioned one another reciprocally in their being via the mediation of the passive exigencies of worked matter, the latent conflict – as passive resistance of the former and as authoritarianism of the latter – was an *assumption* of the set oppositions it was attempting more or less clearly to transform into a fight.

This latent conflict, however, was not comparable to those we considered earlier. The others (within the Bolshevik Party, for example) had occurred inside a group whose unity they expressed. Here, the unity still existed but it was no longer that of the common internal field. It was the unity of the leaders' activity and of the practical field. Praxis, by objectifying itself, constituted a practical field in which the managers and the managed were simultaneously integrated. In other words, in the politico-economic combinatory the calculators were elements of the calculation, which dissolved them into itself only to reproduce them in direct connection with the other elements it transformed in its field. In other words, the conflict no longer had the same meaning. The leaders would have liked to dissolve *certain* practico-inert structures, not because of their inertia but because – as such and in given circumstances – they could constitute a braking system that slowed down the activity undertaken. From this viewpoint, they could be induced to increase the construction of workers' housing in order to avoid a concentration of miseries. They could also, through propaganda, create the superficial illusion that the working class was a group and its members were common individuals. At the same time, however, they wanted to maintain the serialities of impotence, whose origin was the heterogeneity of the working-class concentrations, and which made any concerted activity practically impossible. What is more, by virtue of its inertia that mass became an apparatus you could operate like a lever, provided only that you knew how to use the passive forces of seriality. It was then integrated into the common praxis like a hammer in the hands of a carpenter; it was transcended and objectified in the results it inscribed in the practical field. However paradoxical it may seem, in fact, the leading group *totalized* the various series as series. The measures taken to accelerate production in a given sector, to transfer a certain amount of labour from one sector to another, and so on, enclosed within themselves and transcended the anticipation of serial reactions, and the procedures to neutralize these (or use them) on the basis of a practical knowledge of the structures of seriality. But could the sovereign be said to totalize the series, since this was defined as the fleeting or wheeling unity of detotalization? That depends on what you mean by 'totalize'. If you were to mean by it that the leader dissolved inertia in order to unite the *Others* in a pledged group, it goes without saying that any such attempt – dangerous to the regime – was a priori ruled out, except in its mystifying form (and another – very secondary – form that we shall examine in a moment). Indeed, this real totalization would have had the effect of changing an inert lever into a community forging its own sovereignty. But if we consider the words used by the leaders – the masses, public opinion, the people, the workers, etc. – we at once observe that they were chosen *because of* their ambiguous signification. In so far as these words were material and inert realities, whose meaning created the synthetic unity, they seemed to relate to totalized objects. But the action that used and transcended them disclosed at the same time that they referred to scatterings mediated by inanimate matter. Yet that ambiguity was revealing. The series was totalized by the sovereign in the same way in which a mathematician totalizes arithmetical recurrences by the notion of transfinite number. These numbers are a practical transcendence in the sense that they are defined, basically, by the ensemble of operations they enable one to perform. As transcendence preserves the transcended, moreover, the practical modality of the operations on transfinite numbers is determined by the real structures of the series. Via the mass media, the government addressed itself to series explicitly targeted as such, and its activity aimed to obtain a global result through the transformation of seriality into other-direction. So totalization appeared only at the origin and at the end of the process: at its origin, since the movement propagated was the object of a synthetic project relating it to the totality of the practical field; at its end, since in the event of a success the series would be objectified in a totalizable outcome. For example, a given collective (the workers who work in the blast furnaces), if handled capably, would produce ten million tons of pig-iron by the end of the five-year plan. And those *millions of tons* represented in one sense a scattering of exteriority that corresponded exactly to the serial scattering. But in another (and the most important), they were totalized by the practical transcendence that was already transforming them into machines via the mediation of another working-class collective.

In this sense the totalization of the series in its product was carried out *against itself*, since it had been objectified in that product *as a series* and the ensemble of worked matter reflected its alienation to it. So what was involved was actually an operation directed by the sovereign against the masses; and one that consequently maintained them in the separation of alterity, the better to make use of them. But this objective character of the activity (whose origin was accumulation) was not accompanied by a premeditated attempt at oppression. Similarly (and it is to these groups, selected from the collectives by the sovereign, that I was referring earlier), activists and other propagandists created soon-to-be-fragmented nuclei of unity around their persons, just long enough for these local and positive regroupings to thwart the spontaneous formation of negative groups. Moreover, the pyramid of organs constituting the Soviet hierarchy also had the effect of removing the cream from the masses, depriving them of their most active elements; and of preventing insurrectional regroupment by creating fields of possibilities – and a future *external* to the working class – for the 'elites'. Assuming the need to make the latter carry out surplus labour, and adapting their praxis to the instability and impotence of that giant collective in mid growth, the leaders were *obliged in practice* – i.e. by the synthetic coherence of their project, and by the efficacy achieved within this project by the passive syntheses it retotalized by transcending them – to re-exteriorize the original contradiction of the post-revolutionary period as a latent but constantly present oppression. In this they were – at least partly – responsible for the conflict, inasmuch as they sought reunification of the field. In the historical circumstances of Russian industrialization, the *meaning* of their praxis (which does not mean its truth or its justification) was to destroy those workers as free practical organisms and as common individuals, in order to be able to create man out of their destruction. Of course, that is what they are *reproached with*. And our intention here is not to defend them. That they sinned all the time and everywhere is obvious – just as it is obvious at every moment of every historical process, for all rulers and sometimes all the ruled. It will be necessary later on to ascertain what a sin is, and our historical investigation will doubtless lead us to pose this question from a formal point of view.[32] But in any event, *here* the sin *may* have lain (assuming that we already know what a sin is) in the harshness of the oppression, or in the concrete use of the organs of coercion. Oppression was itself the basic characteristic of a praxis whose aim was to realize the phase of accumulation along with the phase of productivity. Lenin's slogan about 'Soviets plus electrification' has often been quoted, and people have sought to derive an argument from it against the *principle* of Stalinist oppression. It should have been realized, they say, that those two conditions are dialectically linked and the powers of the soviets should have been increased *pari passu* with electrification. But that would have been possible only if the working class had remained more or less homogeneous: only if the labour begun by the fathers had been continued by workers' sons. People forget that rapid industrialization exploded the structures of the working class, drowning the old workers in a tide of newcomers. Emancipation was indeed to be *real*, as a long-term process. However, although workers aware of their condition and the future to be defended did increase as an absolute quantity, their proportion – within that amorphous mass suffering from overexpansion – remained more or less identical. It is only since Stalin's death that the radical transformation of that class and the high level of its culture have been revealed.

So the leaders' praxis was *qualified* as oppressive, by virtue of the

---

32. This comment gives a hint that the whole investigation of the *Critique* is a long detour in order to tackle once more the problem of ethics in history, raised in 1947 in *Cahiers pour une morale*.

necessities it engendered within it in the internal milieu of its totalization. It is also necessary to understand the ambiguity of that oppression. For if it was genuinely necessary to obtain 'at all costs' (Stalin's watchword in 1928) an almost unendurable tension of the working-class forces, and if for that purpose it became necessary in practice to maintain the seriality of impotence, it must also be recognized that the sovereign's mistrust sprang from the internal imbalances of a working class that it was itself in the process of forging. Moreover, at the same time as it was maintaining recurrence by practices often involving police repression, it was striving to lay the foundations for a true socialist community, through a considerable effort to raise the cultural level of all. It thereby encountered again – both before the latent conflict and beyond it – the common unity of the ruled, inasmuch as they themselves directly became the goal of its praxis and no longer just its means. Thus the ambiguity of the latent conflict pitting the Bureaucracy against the workers was encountered again in the implicit contradiction of bureaucratic praxis. Or, if you like, the possibility of conflict within the practical field was given, with all its ambiguity, in the contradiction that was temporalized within the totalizing praxis.

Conversely, if we consider the other term of the conflict – the working-class masses – we shall find that same ambiguity. Considering first only the nucleus that made the October Revolution, it has to be recognized that the contradiction emerged within it on the morrow of victory. For at the moment of insurrection it was the masses which led 'the apparatus'; and the organized movement was profoundly transformed, in so far as the masses transformed themselves into organized groups. Without a doubt, the sovereign reality of the permanent group – the Party – was grasped deep in the heart of seriality as a possible unity of serial individuals through suppression of the series. I demonstrated this earlier.[33] There can also be no doubt that this schematic existence of its own totalized unity was lived from within, and under the pressure of revolutionary circumstances, as a factor of a totalization in progress. Yet this totalization, when it took place under emergency conditions, aimed to submerge the Party or render it useless. The Party controlled and guided only if it could adapt: i.e. transcend its own limits under the revolutionary impetus. The Bolsheviks took charge of the spontaneous organizations when they became aware of the real limits their praxis had received, and when they reinteriorized those limits by transcending them: in other words, when they renounced all 'stages' in favour of taking power alone and organizing the socialist revolution.

I have shown elsewhere why the masses are necessarily radical in the

---

33. *Critique*, vol.1, pp.414 ff.

movement of dissolution of serialities.[34] *Reality*, at the level of serial impotence, is the impossibility of living. The common awakening to power through liquidation of alterity and destruction of the practico-inert is accompanied by a metamorphosis of *reality*: the latter, a practical field of common power, becomes the manifest impossibility of any impossibility of living. Precisely in so far as they can want nothing without exploding the system, the masses, as soon as they unite to demand *something*, are led by their very unification to demand *everything*. And *everything*, in Party terms, is the seizure of power and the construction of a new regime. But in so far as the Party takes control, avoids the reefs of dual power (soviets and government apparatus) and retains leadership of the movement, it involves itself in a transformed praxis that is going in turn to be determined not just by its conscious aims but by its limits, and that will define the Party itself in its new singularity.

Right from the seizure of power, in fact – i.e. from the decision to radicalize its goal – it is defined by its contradiction with the movement to liquidate series. And this contradiction is due precisely to the fact that it too totalizes the popular demands, but as a Party. For these demands, inasmuch as they are the very movement of the united and revolutionary masses, are atemporal. It would be inaccurate to say that the groups in formation demand everything *at once*. But it would be an even more serious mistake to think that their demand takes the form of a long-term constructive project. In reality, there is an immediate and contradictory relationship between the objective – which is plenary humanization of the sub-human through satisfaction of his needs – and the practical constitution of the popular groups, which is that selfsame plenary humanization but through the violent passage from impotence to common praxis. In the climate of fraternity-terror, indeed, *man is born* as a pledged member of a sovereign group. But this man can be really and entirely humanized only by satisfying his needs – by suppressing his misery. However, not only are the material conditions for satisfying them not given, but in addition the distinctive feature of revolutionary situations is that – in a climate of violence, and political and social tension – a lost war or economic crisis has deprived the country of a considerable part of its resources. So when the impossibility of living is no longer just the necessity of dying your life, day after day, under the domination of an oppressive and exploitative class – when it means instead a real risk of famine or immediate death – under the pressure of such threats the masses group together and organize to make that impossibility impossible whatever the circumstances. And the very

---

34. *Critique*, vol.1, pp.405–7.

momentum of their regroupment radicalizes their praxis to the point of making them demand everything. The atemporal character of this demand is due to the fact that the worker freed from the practico-inert asserts himself as a man confronting death, whereas he is a man only in order to die: no system, no policy and no government can at present give him the means to *live as a man*. So Everything is simultaneously given and refused; immediate and out of reach; lived and realized in revolutionary praxis, vainly demanded by hunger and misery.

But this contradiction is reversed. The leaders, by adopting the radical demands, necessarily commit themselves to a long-term praxis. In them, the Revolution-as-apocalypse becomes a temporal undertaking. 'Everything' – as an immediate objective of the masses – becomes the final objective of an organized activity. And the immediate objective must be to restore *an* order. A new order, assuredly, but one which – since the inherited misery is that of the *ancien régime*, sometimes temporarily made worse – resembles the vanished order in that it is the coercive organization of penury, and reality once again becomes the impossibility of living. So it is impossible for the revolutionary groups not to produce themselves as in conflict with the leaders they have given themselves. The latter have to incarnate the impossibility of any immediate amelioration – i.e. reassume the negative powers against which the oppressed classes rose up. But that necessity of vegetating in misery at the very moment of victory – it is still popular praxis that creates it, in so far as it goes to the *political* extreme (overthrowing the regime, taking power) in order to realize the *economic* extreme. It is popular praxis which in the practical synthesis – by *bringing those factors into contact* – constitutes that revolutionary paradox and that permanent contradiction between the radicalism of the here and now and the radicalism of the long-term undertaking. It is popular praxis which produces leaders and pits them against the masses in the process of fusion, just as it groups the masses by dissolving series and pits them against the leaders emanating from them.

On the other hand, the workers cannot enter into total conflict with the leaders, in so far as they produce *in themselves* the contradiction that pits them against the Party. At the same time they *are* the temporal undertaking, inasmuch as this gives itself its own knowledge and engenders and discloses its own temporalization. In other words, they are the men simultaneously of the immediate need and the long-term objective – while as class individuals they are the mediation between the two. In other words, those producers are aware that there is an identity between the ultimate aim of the undertaking and the most immediate goal of the need, at the moment when reality is impossibility of living.

The possibility of translating a single objective into two languages and envisaging it turn and turn about in two systems – the instant and the temporalization – was clearly shown by the enthusiasm of the Russian proletariat when the first *pyatiletka* was decided in October 1928. The crying needs of the undernourished (beyond a certain threshold, of course, short of which such activity ceases to be possible) were developed and temporalized into a *practical tension*. It was then a question of the satisfaction of *all the needs of everybody* being the deep meaning of that total mobilization. The individual's need would not be assuaged, but it became the vectorial tension of his effort and was transposed into practical radicalism – i.e. into voluntarism. In this practical form (one of whose aspects was to be the Terror), it partly (and *temporarily*) lost its physiological urgency. In the perspective of socialist construction, undernourishment – which had previously been unbearable – would be borne for a time. In the context of this voluntarism of conscious workers, the unity of masses and leaders was realized. But obviously the organism would itself fix definitively the threshold that could not be crossed (exhaustion, sickness, or constant hunger, etc.). By this relapse into the immediate (into the physiological necessity of immediate satisfaction) the opposition of the masses to the leaders was resuscitated *in unity*. That means there was a whole dialectical movement here. The rank and file *recognized* their leaders because they readopted their project. They *objectified* their hunger by interiorizing the leaders' voluntarism. Tension – which was realized by transcendence and preservation of the need, in and through the undertaking – thus became an objective reality within them, at once *the same* and *other* and (in certain circumstances that it would take too long to enumerate) *possible alienation*. But precisely because they recognized the sovereign's powers through *the unity of the undertaking*, they demanded of him – and often against him – the means to pursue it. Need itself was objectified. It was lived as suffering and danger, and at the same time defined as that which had to be assuaged if the rate of production was to be increased. On this point, moreover, they found a common language with the leadership, which likewise reckoned that consumption could not be lowered beyond certain limits without compromising productivity. The source of opposition was neither in the language nor in the intentions: it lay *simultaneously* in the determination of the standard of living below which it was no longer possible to produce and, even if agreement was achieved on that point, in the slowness of organization, the difficulties of supply and the errors of bureaucracy – in short, everything that constituted the sovereign as inferior *in fact* to its function. The deep difference was there. In a system of capitalist exploitation, penury, discomfort and misery are *recognized* as the normal and constant products of the society. In the system of socialist construction, however, they were attributed to the faults of groups or of men, or to the particular necessities of the moment. In so far as the opposition of the emancipated proletariat would be able to manifest itself explicitly and find its organization and its expression, it would require a change – perhaps radical – of the leading personnel and a reworking of the Plan; but it would not go back *either* on the revolutionary basis of the regime *or* on the necessity of pursuing the undertaking initiated. The practico-inert that the workers wanted to suppress was not so much the sclerosis of the leading layers and the serialities in the labouring class. It was rather the ensemble of secondary counter-finalities (delays, waste, lack of co-ordination, lethargy or careerism of local functionaries), which were by and large consequences of the bureaucratic system – hence, of praxis-process itself – but which in the immediate, specific instance always presented themselves as remediable. On this point too, moreover, the frictions presupposed a certain unity, since the distinctive feature of *that* bureaucracy (not, as has been claimed, of *every* bureaucracy*) was to prosecute bureaucrats bureaucratically – i.e. to attribute mistakes to men rather than to the system that produced them. It is well known that in the socialist democracies under Stalinism, men were sometimes changed spectacularly in order to change things – and sometimes in order not to change them.

To be sure, the unity of the leaders and the rank and file was not that of members of a group. At the level of the nucleus of revolutionary workers, however, it must be noted that interiorization by both leaders and rank and file of the original contradiction of socialism – hence, the adoption of the same inner conflict by the leaders and the rank and file – would have made it possible to avoid *oppression* in the true sense of the term. For, in so far as rejection of the impossibility of living became *voluntarism* by being temporalized, it was possible to imagine a centralized, tough, authoritarian praxis, but one supported (and thereby controlled) by the rank and file themselves. Reciprocally, the leaders would have taken more care to search out and suppress abuses, if these adjustments had been demanded in the name of the common voluntarism by a working class of which they had been sure. At this level, the latent conflict would thus have manifested itself within the unity of the constructive praxis, by intelligible products and not by misshapen

---

* The bureaucracy, as inertia of the sovereign, does not rise up against itself in the historical groupings that live through a period of stability. On the contrary, it expresses that stability (which may be a slow movement of involution, for example) and the latter reflects it: everything is all right (at least *for* the bureaucrat, who finds his justification in the course of things). The Stalinist bureaucracy is in perpetual contradiction because it combines two incompatible features: it is a *voluntarist bureaucracy*. In it, there are *simultaneously* combined the fiercest activism with inertia. Or rather, the latter is the means of the former. Thus, perpetually, bureaucratic activism denounces the bureaucrats.

monsters. Working-class pressure would in fact have tended to suppress bureaucratic excesses and to limit hierarchy. In such a case – anyway abstract, since it signals the beginning of industrialization – the struggle as a latent contradiction in the leading groups *and* in the masses (i.e. in individuals suffering their impotence) can be said to be *in itself a factor of unity*: it does not suppress the authoritarian commandism or the planning carried out by the guiding centre, but it makes oppression useless; perhaps (as idealists who have not understood the fact of industrial growth have wished) it makes it possible to increase the powers of the soviets in direct proportion to the progress of electrification.

We know, however, that this nucleus was shortly to explode under the pressure of immigrants, and that the leaders would have to handle a volatile, uneducated, disunited mass liable to change from one day to the next. Most of these workers were not revolutionaries. Before the seizure of power they had been peasants, and even if they had 'set the red cock loose' on big farms or in châteaux, such acts of violence had expressed an uneducated revolt: though they might lead to the appropriation of seigneurial estates, they at all events could not spontaneously transform themselves into a voluntarism of industrial production. Similarly, those new workers would clearly long remain urbanized peasants, and their class consciousness could not be formed for long years to come. And what could it be, anyway, in those early stages? What would its *practical* content be, since the seizure of power was an accomplished fact; since the exploiting class was defeated; since those peasants, driven from their villages by misery or brutally transported, saw work in industry *despite everything* as a curse – especially if you think of the prodigious effort that was asked of them – rather than as a duty or an honour. But without yet understanding what the Revolution was, they were not unaware that if they revolted they would be counter-revolutionaries. That regime which was proletarianizing them was the same one which had driven out the landlords. The leaders' mistrust of those yokels, most of whom were still under the sway of the Orthodox Church, was interiorized in each one of the newcomers as mistrust of the rest. In that socialist country achieving full employment, this mistrust – which engendered oppression – played the role of competitive antagonisms in the capitalist world: it serialized. Everyone became once again the *Other* for his neighbour: not the *Other* who could be taken on in his place, but the *Other* who could denounce him or whose imprudence could provoke an arrest. In that immense collective, insurrectional unity was not even imaginable. Radical powerlessness was lived as resignation, or in extreme cases transformed into passive resistance. In other words, powerlessness to rise up was re-exteriorized as powerlessness to produce, while sometimes individual violence was expressed by an act of sabotage.

So the conflict existed, but it had no name. Oppression was not exploitation, there was no class struggle, and anyway the working class existed *in itself* but not *for itself*. On the other hand, the newcomers, whatever their attitude towards the regime, were simultaneously serialized in relation to one another – by their origin and histories and by the leaders' operations – and unified by the sovereign praxis (precisely in so far as this treated them as inert serial unities), inasmuch as they were integrated into the practical field it delimited: i.e. into the country, as an ensemble of material givens (shortages and resources), accumulated goods and men. This integration in no way prejudged their real relations with any particular practico-inert ensemble or group. It merely meant that everything always came to them via the mediation of the sovereign, i.e. via sovereign determinations of the practical field. If it was a matter of founding a city around blast furnaces or steelworks, *the bureaucracy* took care of transporting them to the site; *it* distributed makeshift equipment to them (tents at Magnitogorsk); *it* had already decided to build flats; *it* would achieve that with numerous delays for which it alone was responsible. It was the leadership which took care of supplies, or set tasks and norms. If need be it would have a double track built, to replace the single track upon which the freight trains initially travelled – the ones that transported the coal or the steel. As the worker became educated, as he assimilated his craft experience and his culture grew, he discovered himself more clearly within a system unified and constituted by two centres of production, 2,000 kilometres apart. One of these, situated in the Urals (Magnitogorsk), was constituted around iron deposits (extractive industries, steelworks), while the other (Kuzbas) had been founded in the vicinity of coal mines – the latter sending fuel to the former, the former sending back to Kuznetsk surplus iron extracted from the Urals. On the basis of this, the worker grasped his own practical field as a tiny determination within the sovereign field. His work was *foreseen*. The practico-inert exigencies of his machines (we spoke of this earlier[35]) directly expressed the invisible synthetic exigency of the sovereign. Those machines were foreseen by the Plan, constructed in conformity with it, and their expectation (they awaited *their* worker) was a passivization of the sovereign's expectation. They made themselves the conducting milieu of that unitary praxis that came to seek the worker out, right to the foot of that *Magnetic Mountain* where he had been transported in anticipation of the needs of production. His life, i.e. his food and the satisfaction of all his other needs, depended upon the way in which he would fulfil his prescribed task (which had designated him in

---

35. *Critique*, vol.1, pp.185 ff.

advance); and that prescription was a mere specification of the overall plan. But even his zeal could not ensure that he would manage to surpass – or merely attain – the norms determined by the sovereign. Even that depended on the rate of extraction of coal at Kuzbas, and on the transport. In practice, moreover, that universal dependence did not establish any solidarity between him and other workers in other sectors of production. What he needed was intensive work by the Kuzbas miners, by the railwaymen, by the train drivers and – inasmuch as he was personally designated to have a flat – by the building workers. In fact, that solidarity in reverse led everyone to demand the most intensive effort from everyone else, so that he would be able to reproduce his life by pushing his own effort to the maximum. It was with the leadership that the worker felt some solidarity. In order to be able to accomplish the task it had prescribed for him, he expected of others *exactly what the leadership expected* of them: the maximum – the *'optimum variant'*.

Leadership was a mediation between men by things, since it stirred the practico-inert by transfinite operations. It was also a mediation between things by men, since the worker in the Magnitogorsk steelworks depended on the Kuzbas mines and the frequency of transport and *at the same time* on the miners themselves. Since in both cases, moreover, the dependence turned into a dependence *vis-à-vis* the sovereign, that manipulated inertia through its very seriality revealed the sovereign unity of the manipulating praxis.

But if series were in practice totalized, the serial individual nevertheless remained the man whose freedom – in and through his radical alienation – realized his serial-being through an other-direction that revealed itself as a fascination with totality and an infinite movement propagated under the sovereign's influence. This meant that the serial individual was determined inasmuch as he existed *as Other* for the sovereign itself: i.e. for a *praxis-knowledge* that presented him with his particular practical field as *already totalized* by the leadership and with his serial-being as expressly aimed at. In that sense, the practical totalization he carried out at every moment (when he conducted himself in any way as a serial being) was a totalization of the already totalized. (In the same way, the practical field of children is the totalization of a field already explored by their parents, where the objects it discloses are already seen, already named, and have an already settled usage.) In that sense, if the propaganda had succeeded he grasped the sovereign's totalization as the depth of his own totalization. His practical field was the country, as it was for the Politburo and its expert assistants, and if he had been able to develop his knowledge and functions infinitely, he would merely have rediscovered the total depth of his own field. In a certain way, the sovereign totalization was his powerlessness and ignorance: he was determined by it in his negative particularity. In another way, however, it was his possible knowledge and his own participation in the praxis of all. For individuals, the sovereign was the mediation between their ignorance as particularity and their total knowledge as possible totalization of the country by each and every person. On the other hand, the totalization of series, though purely operational, was manifested to every serial individual as a recuperation of the infinite flight by the sovereign's totalizing praxis. Thus serial-being was lived as organic-being. As we have seen, this is the very nature of other-directed activity.[36] Following the above description, however, it remains the case that the leading group's totalization was retotalized by the individual precisely in so far as this retotalization was already foreseen and provoked in the leadership's totalizing praxis.

Although there was a reciprocity of reflection here, however, the leading group remained *the Other* inasmuch as the individual was himself maintained and conditioned by others and in the milieu of alterity. From this standpoint, the two totalizations presented themselves simultaneously as the same and as *other*: or, if you like, the individual lived the totalization of his practical field as being deciphered and explained *elsewhere*, in those radically other beings whose sovereignty was lived as group power through serial powerlessness. At that level, alterity appeared as a *sacred* characteristic: totalization of the individual practical field remained a synthesis at the surface of a synthesis-in-depth whose type of being was the sacred. Obviously, this characteristic would have dis-appeared in the event of revolt and insurrectional dissolution of all series. We are really accounting here for a particular alienation: inasmuch as an individual's daily activity totalized him, the country remained profane; inasmuch as that obscure totalization was carried out in the full clarity of a sovereign totalization that escaped it, the country became sacred.

But we have also noted the complementary praxis. Activists provoked ephemeral dissolutions of seriality at strategic points that the government had carefully determined and that figured as synthetic objectives in its totalizing praxis. In such regroupments, as we have seen, fraternity-terror reappeared with the sovereignty of each person, as a common individual readopting the decision of the Party or Politburo. At that level, the individual reabsorbed the sacred inasmuch as he dissolved seriality and deepened his practical field. There was homogeneity between his own totalization and the sovereign's. What is more, the movement of his own totalization (inasmuch as he had the importance of some decision – for society as a whole and for himself as a member of it – explained to

36. *Critique*, vol.1, p.655.

him) made it into a kind of moment of the sovereign totalization: a kind of stage on the infinite route that would make it possible to realize this in its entirety. A dialectic was established between those two contradictory relationships of the individual totalization to the common totalization (alterity and the sacred, on the one hand; radical homogeneity, on the other) through a new attempt at totalization by the individual (or in local groups). The new transformations resulting from this are, for now, of little concern to us. The example was simply designed to indicate: first, that the sovereign totalization integrated non-totalizables in practice; secondly, that it determined itself as a function of the singular totalizations which retotalized it, and did so in such a way that the retotalization was in conformity with the chosen objectives. And reciprocally that, in a society thus integrated, each person was as a Soviet citizen *at the very least*, through other-direction, an intermediary between the serial Other and the common individual – since he totalized his practical field within a global totalization that he revealed and transformed by each of his activities, and since he acted in any case as an agent already foreseen and guided by the totalization in progress.

Yet each singular totalization, as a transcendence of the sovereign totalization towards a particular goal (work, wage, living standard, etc.), appeared in turn as a totalization of the totalization – i.e. as an ultimate totalization. Thus the Leadership's totalization, embracing individuals and groups, found its concrete reality only in the diversity of the concrete totalizations that retotalized it, each from the standpoint of a local praxis. In this sense, however, it can be said that the sovereign totalization was simply a praxis whose objective was to be realized by the foreseen, accomplished unity of its retotalizations (be they serial, or common, or singular). The heterogeneity of the series and groups did not count, since the sovereign took account of this – or rather relied upon it – in order to realize its own objectives. As soon as that heterogeneity entered into the practical reckoning, it became a necessary moment of totalization: the means of orientating and limiting (etc.) retotalizations, of opposing or fostering them in the direction of the project. Everything went on as though each individual lived under the pressure – and in the light – of a sovereign totalization, in which he figured as a totalized element; and as though the sovereign totalization had grasped itself as a project of passion and incarnation, since it caused itself to be retotalized by everyone as a non-transcendable totality.

By this, I do not mean to refer back to any kind of pre-established harmony or social optimism. It is simply a matter of showing that, in a society characterized by the presence of a sovereign, historical significa-tion – whatever it may be and from wherever it may emanate – requires to be comprehended in the twofold movement of retotalized totalization and totalization of the directed retotalizations. After that, dreadful disputes may arise, and clan struggles, police oppression and class conflicts may grow worse. All we mean is that these very struggles can take place only within the framework of a retotalized totalization. It is at this level that contradictions explode, at this level that groups form to oppose the sovereign, precisely because it is at this level *also* that the sovereign praxis has previously been able *to succeed*, i.e. achieve its objectives through directed retotalizations. The positivist historian has distorted History and made comprehension impossible, whenever he has shown the organized forces' project determining 'the masses', or 'public opinion', or any category of individuals or groupings, in the same way that a physical factor can condition the variations of a 'natural process'. He has suppressed any possibility of totalization, by suppressing one of the essential moments of historical praxis and remaining blind to the following obvious fact: inasmuch as History studies *the action of action upon action*, the milieu in which any given praxis may create any other in accordance with strict predictions is necessarily that of retotalization. From this standpoint, conflict and the stages of every struggle are comprehensible: these reciprocal retotalizations of each opposing praxis by the other, when they are themselves retotalized, likewise constitute a contradictory milieu where each action creates the other as its practical nullification.

So the conflict with the sovereign took place within the practical field, and in the produced and revealed unity of that field. The latter was originally just the moving synthesis of the environment by an action in progress. But the contradiction was due here to the fact that in that unified environment, as particular determinations of the field, there were men – i.e. *several* sovereigns (inasmuch as each had his practical field). This would still be only a partial explanation if those men had been enemies of the sovereign: i.e. had negated the practical field embracing them and had had to be negated by it. But the reality of oppressive commandism was more complex. By virtue of the oppression that kept them in seriality – and *by that very means* extracted the maximum effort from them – the leadership was against them. They interiorized within them their status as *means* – i.e. as reified individuals, as transcended transcendence – whose sole freedom seemed to be to yield themselves up wholly to the sovereign praxis, and to flee reification in the alien voluntarism that imbued them. On the other hand, however, those *means* of praxis were also its ends. As forced labour (or rather, forced consent to the mode and to the norms of labour) proceeded and the first results of action made themselves known, *Soviet man* was created. His *pride* sprang from his first achievements (*although* – and above all *because* – most of them, e.g. the gigantic Magnitogorsk steelworks, were not destined directly to raise his standard of living). His *toughness* was just interiorized oppression (he was tough on himself *and* disciplined, quick to denounce as slackness the relaxation of his neighbour, who – through the inverted solidarity established by the sovereign – risked slowing down the rate of production for everyone). His *passivity* (entirely temporary) *vis-à-vis* the managers was not just the interiorization of his impotence, but also a fundamental conviction – acquired gradually through culture – that transformation of the leading personnel was in itself less important than industrial growth; and that, assuming the system was to be saved, the individual and collective tasks, the effort to be contributed and the standard of living would be more or less the same at the same *moment* of socialist construction. I am not saying that this 'Soviet man' – the first *really* to define the present in terms of the future (and on the basis of the past) and his individual future in terms of the socialist future – had been created cheaply. Perhaps in many cases he had even appeared only with the second generation, i.e. with the sons of the pre-war immigrants. It remains the case that this type of man would never have been produced in a bourgeois democracy. For oppression makes no difference to the fact of common ownership of resources and the instruments of labour; and the oppression that causes people to work for the benefit of bosses is *one thing*, while that which causes fathers to work for the benefit of their sons, the latter for the benefit of grandsons, etc., in the perspective of a growing liberation, is *another thing*.

Thus, little by little, the newcomers or their children adopted the viewpoint of the revolutionary workers, apart from the fact that they had the sense of a constant – and constantly reformist – evolution, within a State that they were retaining (along with the pious myth that it would wither away of its own accord) because that State had emerged from a *revolution that they had not made*. This singular mixture of conservatism and progressivism was the interiorization of the totality within each individual. It expressed the very meaning of praxis: to progress in order to maintain (the essential conquests); and to maintain in order to progress (stratifications born of hierarchization, as a means of inciting to produce). At the same time, it realized the true relation of the urbanized peasant or his son to the Revolution, as an insurrectionary seizure of power followed by a radical change in the relations of production. Precisely, *it was not he who had made it*, but the education given him by the sovereign born of it, as well as the need to save the meaning of his own life – together with the objective reality of the new regime – all ensured that this *received* (or suffered, if you prefer) order was nevertheless *adopted* and could not conceivably be called into question. Or, if you prefer, education and propaganda had eventually determined in each individual a zone of almost pledged inertia that was precisely the Revolution itself, inasmuch as by every concrete action he transcended it in its original abstraction and in its past-being; inasmuch as it was the distant aim of his undertaking and his life – his *non-transcendable* destiny; in short, inasmuch as he *realized* what others had established as an absolute but abstract beginning. From the moment when he was himself involved and with a single movement grasped his practical field as a singular determination of the sovereign field – and his own life as an undertaking in progress, a limited singularization of the sovereign temporalization – his opposition to the sovereign was waged in the name of the sovereign itself. There were no flats, for example, not – as in a bourgeois democracy – because it was in nobody's interest to build any, but because the sovereign and planned decision to stagger their construction over months or years *had not been realized.* Yet the conflict remained latent, in the *Stalinist* period, since voluntarism was an optimistic decision: *everything* was *always* going well. The demands of the masses can be interpreted as a first control exercised over the sovereign *in the name of its own projects and the praxis that was realizing them.* But since optimism was always the source and the result of Terror,* the conflict remained at the level of a passive resistance at the very heart of the masses' voluntarism. And that resistance – as an inertia provoked (by bad working conditions, etc.) and maintained (as an anonymous manifestation) – was merely the interiorization within the unity of the practical field of that other inertia: bureaucratic sclerosis, turned back *against itself* by the very people it affected as their negation by the sovereign. Through the intermediary of these increasingly conscious men, Stalinist praxis accumulated in its practical field transformations that negated it; and this negation was turned back against it through the new generations of workers. Conversely, however, that negative project – precisely inasmuch as it was contradicted by hierarchized stratifications – was explicitly contained in the sovereign praxis as one of its long-term objectives. First, because that praxis had taken over the theory of withering away of the State, even though present circumstances seemed to it to require the latter's reinforcement. Secondly, because the very effort demanded of the workers in a period of accumulation (along with all the practical features emanating from this – voluntarism, authoritarianism, centralization, terror) was expressly given as *temporary.* Finally, because when the emergency diminished (because the USSR had caught up), although the State would still subsist, the appearance of technical cadres and the human and professional culture of the workers would combine to make the bureaucratic government and the stratified

---

* Inasmuch as it occurs as a fundamental feature of praxis (decision *on its possibilities*), at moments when pessimistic forecasts seem the most likely. Its savage character derives from the fact that it bears within it pessimism and despair as *negated* threats.

hierarchy less and less effective, and would oblige the ruling personnel to disappear or adapt the forms of government to the circumstances.

Thus the contradiction of Stalinist commandism was that its aim was *to make itself useless*, through the transformation to which it subjected both the ruled and the country's industrial and military potential. This contradiction, moreover, was just an expression of the fundamental contradiction of socialist construction in the period following the seizure of power. On the other hand, bureaucracy obviously asserted itself at the same time, and in so far as it was hierarchized Stalinist commandism tended to favour certain social layers. But this was because praxis, by determining the field of the practico-inert, had – via the intermediary of the whole practical field – produced Soviet bureaucrats in such a way that they assimilated the common interest and the private interest. For we know that these two interests were in contradiction in the working masses during the phase of pre-revolutionary construction. But we also know that the appearance of working-class hierarchy had tended to create a system of recompenses such that *for some of the workers* the contradiction had been removed: to work the best and the fastest was to be the best paid and most honoured. Precisely in so far as stratification had frozen the hierarchy, the latter tended to maintain itself *for itself and against the masses*, and at the same time *for the greater efficacy of the common praxis* – such as that efficacy might appear to bureaucratized agents. But the latter, in the very act that consolidated their power (*and by it*), limited its duration: they had become aware of this (at least the more cultivated ones – which does not mean the highest in rank), since all the ideology they had been taught explained how their power was 'for a limited time' and almost of an 'interim' kind. They could build the USSR but not construct a class: their very action prevented them from doing so, despite the privileges it conferred on them. Their bureaucracy consecrated the separation between management functions and mode of appropriation in a certain phase of industrial growth (whether planned or not, as we shall see). At the same time, however, it showed by its effects on the ruled the provisional character of this dissociation in a socialist system. So it can be said that emancipation of the Soviet worker – though different from the emancipation of Western workers – pronounced sentence upon the Bureaucracy. It must be added, however, that it did so *simultaneously* upon that bureaucracy and through it – and as a practical consequence that the latter had already accepted (at least in principle).*

----

* This does not at all mean that elimination of the Bureaucracy must necessarily be accomplished through some quiet progress. Circumstances alone can determine the speed and violence of that elimination. All that can be said is that the ensemble of the process – more or less complete agreement, or a series of difficult adaptations or bloody disturbances – should be seen in the context of a *reformist* praxis.

The more this wheeling, omnipresent contradiction – *the* contradiction of planned growth – helped to construct the unity of the men it had produced, i.e. of the rulers and the ruled, the more strongly and clearly did it manifest itself.

In this sense – not just at the beginning for the revolutionary nucleus, but gradually for all individuals and all groups through the partial reinforcement and partial dissolution of serialities – it was the totalization in progress that clarified the conflict, by tightening the intelligible unity. Let us simply recall that this totalization did not dissolve the collectives, nor was it the unification of a multiplicity into a group. It was actually that of every sovereignty defining its practical field in a fundamentally univocal relationship. The practical field was engendered by praxis and transformed perpetually by it. If it was right to speak of a transformation of the agents (and of praxis) by the field, this transformation did not break the univocal nature of the fundamental relation. The reaction was in fact produced by bringing disparate elements into contact within the field. It was activity, through its temporal profile and its qualification (objectives, tension, etc.), which realized that 'bringing into contact', as a synthetic immanence of exteriority. And it was *through* this synthesis that exigencies appeared against a background of interiorization of the exterior (e.g. inasmuch as quantity – millions of tons of steel or pig-iron – was interiorized as a scarcity, a possibility, an impossibility, a means, or a short-term aim, in the determination by praxis of its new goals*). If these exigencies transformed the agents and through them deviated praxis, they did not thereby testify to a reciprocity. For they were simply praxis itself, refracted by the material. So man was produced via the intermediary of his product, without this operation necessarily pre-supposing a fetishization of the latter. It is in terms of this non-reciprocity that the relations between the ruled and the sovereign must be considered. Inasmuch as the ruled were inert, manipulated serialities, their relationship with the rulers was univocal. Series are matter worked by transfinite operations; and the exigencies they manifest as such are the inert exigencies of every passive synthesis, inasmuch as it refers praxis back to its agents – but overturned, passivized and producing its own counter-finalities. In the case that concerns us, it was indeed the fundamental contradiction of socialism that was turned back against its builders, in the form of passive imperatives. And it was these imperatives that would transform the sovereign, through its very attempt to adapt its practice to them. In the same way, the individual worker – as a free

---

* It is synthetic unity into which it is integrated, rather than some kind of dialectic of Nature which here endows quantity with a practical *quality*.

transcendence through work (or through sabotage, etc.) of the situation that had produced him – could not thereby establish even a relationship of reciprocity with the sovereign. Yet he was free, he acted, he submitted or resisted freely (i.e. by assuming his impotence or his possibilities). No matter. We know that he was seen, foreseen, produced and provided with a destiny by the sovereign, and that his own practical field had itself been defined as a specification of the total field. The sovereign praxis imbued the individual and organized him along with the disparate ensemble of the practico-inert. If he objectified himself as a free practice, the sovereign was the Other by which the entire world became *other* (i.e. alienated to an invisible presence). If he really wanted to be united with the total field and assume the imperatives of production as his own, then he became the sovereign as Other. This circular and non-reciprocal unity suffices for intelligibility as a dialectical totalization: every object in the field was a totalization of all the others and their contradictions; but non-reciprocity preserved a hierarchy within the totalization.

The Open Conflict, Progress towards Unity

Nevertheless, in the practical field we have been considering, we have not encountered a real autonomy of the practico-inert (as a source of conflicts between groups or classes): i.e. a genuine resistance of the provisional result of activity to that activity itself (inasmuch as it was incarnated simultaneously in the sovereign and in the ruled). In the example considered, however, such autonomy did exist: it was what led to the veritable civil war that pitted the sovereign and the working class against the peasants.

From as early as 1923, Trotsky and his friends had wanted to put an end to the NEP. They had been the first to insist on the vital necessity of planning, which alone would enable the USSR to catch up industrially. But even at the purely theoretical level of this still abstract project, the practical unity of their proposal had created new synthetic and inert connections within the field. The development of already existing industrial centres, and the creation of new centres, had no sooner been merely *conceived* than they had presented themselves as *exigencies*. Here we grasp the most typical example of an internal synthetic connection: the mere multiplication of machines entailed the necessity of multiplying the operators. Not because the machine in itself, as a fragment of inert matter, presented that exigency; but because, as *social* and worked matter, it was the inert support of a passivized human design (that of the managers, the engineers and the builders) which constituted its unity. And when it had been living and concrete, this design had consisted precisely in determining the number of operators as accurately and economically as possible, on the basis of the object created and its functioning. Through these multiple exigencies – which grew, moreover, in proportion to the number and nature of the machines – abstract men would be designated as *operators required* in the perspective of industrialization. It must also be noted that – quite independently of the system – characteristics and circumstances vary from one country to another. The USA, a country of immigration, experienced an influx of foreign workers during its period of accumulation. Russia, encircled and poverty-stricken, lived off its own resources: this circumstance reflected the hostility provoked by its historical transformations. So the new machines could demand operators only from among the Soviet population itself, meaning that every increase *demanded* in the world of workers was *necessarily* accompanied by a diminution in the number of agricultural labourers. The heterogeneity of these factors will be noted: machines; the blockade and military encirclement, as a foreign riposte to the October Revolution; the underdeveloped character of the country, which implied that industry's reserves had to be sought in uneducated rural masses formed by centuries of feudalism. If the ensemble of such disparate facts constituted a first necessity, this was because the practical synthesis of the *project* established connections of immanence between them. Through such connections, moreover, new basic relationships were disclosed. These basic relationships were in themselves of a mathematical and logistic type, meaning that (taken in isolation) they were the province of analytic Reason. There were x workers and $2x$ jobs to be filled: this quantitative relationship became a practical necessity *for the peasants* only in a praxis that had the aim not just of filling all the jobs, but actually of multiplying them. In the same way, the strictly negative relationship: 'there was no foreign immigration' became a negation in interiority (i.e. concerned every Russian peasant in the innermost depths of his individual person) precisely in so far as praxis decided to take men where they were. We thus arrive at the very origin of the practico-inert – the interiorizing integration of relations of pure exteriority – and this origin reveals to us the fundamental contradiction of human history.[37] But we shall return to this. Let us merely note that Trotsky's project implied a potential unification of peasants and workers, in the sense that *the latter* were to be multiplied thanks to a selection made from among the former. At once, as we have seen, the new workers – and through them the ensemble of the working-class masses – temporarily took on characteristics, a *hexis*, of peasants. But precisely in so far as they did so,

---

37. See Appendix, p.450, 'Is History Essential to Man?'.

the peasants 'were workerized' (if only in their reactions of negative violence), inasmuch as for each of them the possibility of working in a factory could not be excluded a priori. This project of Trotsky's implied simultaneously a kind of osmosis and a progressive careful blending of populations.

But the *necessities*, as internal relations of exteriority, multiplied. I do not know whether Trotsky had foreseen the extraordinary movement of urbanization which *quadrupled* the non-agricultural labourers in less than thirty years. At all events, he could not have been unaware that the demographic transformation would be profound. Whether he had envisaged that the sovereign praxis would raise the number of workers from ten to thirty or from ten to forty-five million, he had not been unaware that he would be able to reduce the number of *rural producers* only by raising their *productivity*. Among the new workers, furthermore, many were assigned to heavy industry. This meant that the buying power of the working-class masses was reduced: the urban centres could not exchange slow consumption goods for foodstuffs, since the light industrial sector was deliberately maintained in a state of underdevelopment. This meant precisely that the towns did not have the wherewithal *to buy* the peasant crops (or, at least, the fraction of those crops that they needed). For the Left minority, there was only one solution: collectivization. Here again, it can be observed how the second layer of what will later be the practico-inert is constituted through action. For it was the proposal to invest above all in heavy industry (a proposal justified by circumstances *of another order*: encirclement, etc.) which abruptly introduced a *lacuna* – i.e. an inert breach of continuity – into the exchange flows between town and countryside. To tell the truth, these flows had already grown scarce. The black market, the restoration of medium property, etc. – all these factors, together with other, disparate ones such as deterioration of the means of transport – helped to bring the problem of supply to the fore, right from the regime's very first years. Yet if (an absurd and purely *economic* hypothesis) consumer-good industries and transport had been developed, exchanges would have increased swiftly. The regime would not have resisted, but would have collapsed under the impact of other forces (such as the foreign armies). The fundamental option in favour of heavy industry was expressed by the inert negation of exchanges: there was *something* on one side and nothing on the other.

Trotsky had seen only one solution to that twofold contradiction: to increase productivity. For the inert negation was going to be transformed into an *exigency*: the breakdown of exchanges risked destroying the towns – *i.e. the whole regime*. We see the contradiction arise that was to pit country people against town-dwellers. The former, scarcely out of the feudal era, still – in spite of themselves – held the fate of the latter in their hands. When we say 'in spite of themselves', we do not mean to give the impression that despite everything they were favourable to the new regime; but simply that they were indifferent to it, and that their activities in themselves aimed neither to preserve nor to destroy it. The historian Lefebvre has shown admirably how between 1789 and 1797 the French peasantry made its own Revolution, independent of the urban Revolution and not perceived by the bourgeois – or at least not understood: this was one of the reasons for Thermidor. It would have been the same after 1917 in the USSR, if the sovereign had not embraced the totality of the country in its praxis. Trotsky envisaged two main measures. Not being able to provide consumer goods, industry would supply machinery to the countryside – i.e. it would speed up the mechanization of agriculture: right from the first Plan, it was necessary to envisage building tractors. But this mechanization, accompanied by education of the rural population, could be accomplished only in and through collectivization: tractors, admirably suited to the great Russian plain, lost all utility in a system of small individual ownership; on the other hand, the productivity of a few large collective and mechanized enterprises would easily demonstrate to the individualistic small proprietor the technical and economic superiority of the kolkhoz over exploitation of the land by small plots. This operation would have a fourfold advantage: it would brake the development of the kulaks, which was threatening the regime; it would increase production; it would make it possible firmly to establish State control, always more capable of supervising large establishments than the plethora of individual enterprises; and it would allow the State to increase the share of the harvest which it had to exact by decree. These four practical advantages were complemented by two further ones of a less direct kind, in the shape of mechanization and collectivization: these contributed to bringing agricultural labour closer to urban labour, by making the peasant into a driver of machines; and they smoothly accomplished the unification of the socialist system of ownership. Within the project, you can see the moments at which sovereign praxis utilized the practico-inert in formation, and those at which it was constituted as a human relation between the sovereign and the citizens. The increase in productivity due to mechanization was a quantitative relationship, which could be established by a comparison *in exteriority*: in a given region, the average production of the small peasants was *so much*; in the same region, for the same crop, that of the large enterprises was *so much*. And this latter average merely laid bare the results of a machine – i.e. of a physico-chemical system whose inert unity derived from human labour and the objectives pursued. But we at once see that the machine itself was quite incapable of multiplying the yield, and that it was *the man of that machine* who could raise (or not) agricultural productivity (per hectare or per worker, according to the case), depending on whether he had understood the machine's use, appreciated its advantages and accepted its constraints. Hence the mechanization of agriculture became simultaneously the inert exigency of a system in danger of not surviving famine, and the synthetic enterprise of educators seeking to convince men by establishing human relations with them.

Trotsky's project was rejected. Its radicalism – on the morrow of the NEP – alarmed Stalin and the Bukharinist Right. But above all, it took no account of an essential factor: *scarcity of time*. Even had a start been made in 1924 on developing the industries necessary for mechanization of agriculture, it would not have been possible to outstrip the peasant movement itself: this was proceeding towards consolidation of small property and capitalist concentration (of which the kulaks were the first agents), and in 1928 it suddenly confronted Stalin with the *fait accompli* of the 'grain strike' – i.e. a mortal threat to the towns. Considering things from the standpoint that concerns us, this movement – though strictly conditioned in itself – occurred as the result of a *real indeterminacy* of relations between the sovereign and the agricultural masses.

It is no part of our plan, in fact, to study the process whereby, in underdeveloped countries, the dismemberment of feudal property is followed by a concentration of holdings, which may lead to the constitution of a rural bourgeoisie. What is certain is that this process can develop to the full only if the peasant world remains *relatively autonomous* within the nation: i.e. only if the State does not intervene in a system of exchanges, sales (by the poor peasant) and purchases (by the rich peasant) that culminates in a capitalist restructuring of landed property – or, of course, if it *favours* such a regrouping. The autonomy of the process in the USSR testified to the relative impotence of the sovereign. Once power had been seized, to be sure, the rural population as a whole belonged to the practical field. But the existence of a unified practical field must never be confused with total exploitation and total control of this field. Everyone – to borrow the example from the constituent dialectic – can see how much indetermination or ignorance *his own field* envelops. Such ill-known or unknown sectors, moreover, obviously correspond to an inadequate development of praxis: to the absence of techniques and instruments that would allow zones of independence and darkness to be illuminated and conditioned. The formal unity of praxis is not compromised, since – when all is said and done – this geography of the non-determined purely and simply reflects back to it its powers, its knowledge and its organization: in short, its present level of development. What may be in danger, however, is the *concrete success* of the action.

The 'grain strike' of 1928 was an incarnation of the main features – and instruments – of praxis up to that date. In the first place, the

Bolshevik desire to make the Revolution through the working class and in the urban centres (i.e. a decision in sharp contrast with the one Mao Tse-tung was to take a few years later, although that contrast itself should be interpreted in terms of the deep differences separating the two countries: in particular, the Russian revolutionary movement was inseparable from the rapid development of industry between 1900 and 1914). In the second place – as a consequence of that practical determination – an imperfect knowledge of the peasant class and inability to predict its reactions after distribution of the land. In the third place, the inert break we have signalled in the movement of exchanges, whose origin lay in the need to industrialize as fast as possible. In the fourth place, the inadequacy of the activist cadre, in relation to the vastness of the country and the number of peasants (which merely incarnated, in another form, the disproportion between the revolutionary class – i.e. the working-class masses – and the *guided* class, which then represented almost the entire population). Finally, the slowness and inadequacy of transport – a sector always sacrificed by Soviet planners – hence the scarcity and difficulty of communications. Basically, we encounter here in the form of lacks – i.e. inert negations – the very limits praxis gave itself, at the moment when it determined itself *positively* in relation to its means and its objectives. Moreover, we know that these limits themselves originated in the material circumstances that praxis transcended, negated and preserved within itself as its specification.

On this basis, we see a practico-inert zone of *separation* produce and consolidate itself, as a negation of all praxis at the heart of the practical field. The capitalist regrouping of land holdings was, in fact, a *serial* process: it marked the impotent isolation of the poor peasants. It was this isolation that produced kulaks when circumstances favoured them; and every concentration was the starting-point for fresh concentrations, in so far as the enrichment of the rich gradually determined the impoverishment of the poor. But this serial movement – as a mediation of men by the land – manifested itself only as an automatism escaping human control. And this negative determination constituted it immanently, originating as it did from the fact that the movement occurred within a practical field subjugated in its totality to the sovereign's control. In other words, this new recurrence – grasped in the practical field as a negation of the sovereign – was for the sovereign, precisely by virtue of this, his own inner negation. But this negation could take place only within the unity of praxis and the practical field, as a non-reciprocal reconditioning of praxis by the content of its field. At the same time, moreover – and because every praxis is a *practical* seizure of its objects – the negation manifested itself as a specification against the background of the total field; and the total field designated it as an object positing itself for itself, and having to be dissolved into the totality. Or, if you like, the entire field manifested itself as the inert exigency that this foreign concretion should be dissolved. This retotalization by the exigency manifested itself, for example, as a problem of supplying the towns – and, via that problem, as an immediate calling into question of the construction of socialism through industrialization. You can see the order of condition-ings and their circularity. (1) *It was the sovereign praxis that conditioned the appearance of the practico-inert as a counter-finality.* For in the event of a bourgeois revolution, the development of heavy industry would have had neither the same extent nor the same urgency nor the same unity of management. Market mechanisms (and foreign invest-ments) would have intervened to regulate exchanges. A light industry would undoubtedly have been constituted, to respond to the demand of the agricultural labourers. A certain harmonization would have taken place between industrial capitalism and the concentration of landed property. The peasants would have sold their harvest to the town, since in a bourgeois society selling would have been their specific interest. At the same time, the intensification of exchanges would have intensified the concentration of holdings and the expropriation of the poor. (2) It was *the practico-inert* which put praxis in danger of shattering, by the negative influence it exerted upon its principal means (the labour-power of the workers). For the recurrent movement of concentration developed simultaneously as a result of the distribution of land, and as the conse-quence of a deficiency on the part of the authorities. The latter reflected two pre-existing features of that underdeveloped country at once: the poverty of transport, and the numerical disproportion between the urban and rural populations. Moreover, precisely in so far as the sovereign sought to suppress that poverty by increasing industrial production, and to diminish that disproportion by pushing ahead with urbanization, it increased its own deficiency – since it had to mobilize its positive forces for the enterprise of industrialization. But this deficiency – inasmuch as it was lived and suffered; was transformed into a problem; engendered a new awareness; and was to be re-exteriorized as *solutions* (good or bad, it matters little) – *in its practico-inert consequence* became the *inner vice* of the action and *its intrinsic risk* of failing radically. It was thus integrated into unity, as the fleeting disunity that placed unity in danger. What is more, inasmuch as sovereign praxis encountered the threats of famine as *one* concrete and universal risk in all the towns, counter-finality robbed the action of its unity and was integrated into it as the unity of its negation. The mere fact that the serial event was then called a 'grain strike' – which implied an agreement, organized groups, a class consciousness, etc. – shows the extent to which the leaders had a synthetic revelation of the danger – and through it of its determining conditions – inasmuch as it appeared to them through the refractive and teleological medium of their own action.

But, in fact, *there was no* grain strike. There was a complex process (a regrouping of land holdings, the emergence of a new social order in the countryside, a new dependence of the poor *vis-à-vis* the rich on the basis of a transformation of the property system – i.e. of the passage from feudalism to the bourgeoisie – and through this contradiction a mistrust of the regime's tax collectors: it was not only, or mainly, the old traditions of the *ancien régime* that expressed themselves through this mistrust, which primarily reflected the incompatibility of the order being built in the countryside – i.e. the concentration of holdings as a collective – with the order being built in the towns, i.e. socialism) which was basically nothing but the decay of a sovereign activity left neglected for want of the means to pursue it. However, it was not wrong to speak of a 'strike'. That was not wrong from the standpoint of the sovereign and the towns, and in so far as the urban ensembles saw supply – from the standpoint of socialist construction – as a necessary means *not just to live, but to win the battles they were waging*. It was not wrong for the sole reason that, in the milieu of action, everything is always action (positive or negative), and the more urgent praxis is, the more the resistance of the inert – inasmuch as it necessarily manifests itself through men – appears as *sabotage*. Thus it was that when the engineers came to explain to Rakosi, after a few months' work, that the subsoil of Budapest was not suitable for the construction of a metro, he had them thrown into prison: through them, it was the subsoil he was imprisoning. Voluntarist optimism is necessarily Terror: it *has to* underestimate the adversity-coefficient of things. Hence, in the name of its confidence in man's power, it ignores the resistance of inertia, counter-finality, or the slowness of osmosis and impregnation (inasmuch as they increase the scarcity of time): it knows only treason. In this sense *too* – i.e. in its inner temporalization – action is Manichaean, as Malraux said. In the truth of the sovereign action, which was of a practical texture, the complex process that turned the peasant class upside down was thus *already* a unitary praxis of counter-revolutionary groups, from the moment its consequences endangered socialism. From this viewpoint, such a stance was the beginning of a practical *reunification* of the peasantry through coercion. A certain dimension of black humour may be detected in this last observation. But the humour was within praxis itself. Let us recall that the group-in-fusion is born when the collective interiorizes an external threat of extermination as a radically negative totalization. Praxis had to explode or dissolve within itself the practico-inert it had produced: in a first moment it gave it the negative unity of a group, and was to seek itself to produce *another unity* in the rural classes.

Collectivization, as we have seen, allowed control to be increased. It was to be the starting-point for a sovereign operation that raised the share of agrarian produce requisitioned by the State from 17 per cent to 35 per cent, while it also had the immediate political aim of suppressing the kulaks and transforming the capitalist concentration already under way into a socialist concentration. But *the scarcity of time* – i.e. the urgency of the danger in 1928 – was grasped in practice as an obligation to collectivize *under compulsion*: i.e. without mechanization and without preliminary education. The result of these acts of coercion is well known – two types of unification. On the one hand, transformation of the rural masses into communities grouped on large farms and strictly controlled (first by the 'forces of order', then by the establishment of the MTS[38]); on the other hand, beneath that superficial integration into the system, the emergence of peasant units (usually strictly local) of resistance, sometimes co-ordinated by authentic counter-revolutionaries. In a word, the sovereign's brutal intervention transformed the practico-inert – i.e. the resistance of things, and of men as mediated by things – into human groups that united against its praxis. The scarcity of time, combined with the scarcity of resources, transformed the contradiction into a conflict.

But this very conflict, as a contradiction adopted by the protagonists, although even more dangerous for the global praxis nevertheless represented a higher degree of integration. In the first place, it contributed to reducing the heterogeneity of the working-class masses. They supported the sovereign with a common enthusiasm, inasmuch as a common danger threatened them. Urbanization was carried on through the influx of labour from rural areas, yet unity was achieved in the towns against the countryside. (It matters little that people used to repeat piously at the time that the regime's only enemies were the kulaks: everyone knew that any peasant was a potential kulak; and they knew too that any enemy of the regime, if he was a peasant, would be treated as a kulak.) In the second place, the rural collective was broken. The situation, everywhere identical, provoked identical reactions *in the new groups*: in that identity, however, the conditions for an organized resistance were partially given. The results are well known. The peasants destroyed crops and stock with their own hands, and in the years 1932–3 famine raged. If the regime did not founder in this venture, it was *first and foremost* because the unity of workers and peasants (which had allowed the October Revolution) had become impossible. In 1917, the interests of these two classes had coincided. In 1930, they were opposed. The workers, generally in agreement with socialization of the means of production, did not agree

---

38. Machine and Tractor Stations, established in 1929 and abolished in 1958.

with a peasant resistance that was defined for them as a rejection of socialism. That disagreement, moreover, was signalled in practice by the fact that the workers' interest required massive and immediate requisitions. If they were to carry out surplus labour on behalf of the national community, the rural labourers would have to agree to feed them *by surplus labour*. The sovereign's voluntarist and coercive policy thus incarnated their own exigencies – they recognized it as *emanating from them*. The other reason the regime was saved was the impossibility *for the peasants* to pursue their practical unification through an organization branching out all across the country with common objectives and slogans. As a result, the dispersion *of groups* (replacing that of individuals) retotalized, as a negative condition of the peasant defeat, an ensemble of givens already totalized – but otherwise – by the sovereign praxis. The vastness of the country, the diversity of its languages and nationalities, and the lack of communications (shortage of transport), affected the rebels as much as the sovereign. More even, since the latter had access to certain means (telecommunications, etc.) that were not available to the former. The fact that the Revolution was above all *urban* (a fact that then seemed natural, but *today* singularizes the *Russian* Revolution – China's Revolution was *rural*) marked the limits of Russia's underdevelopment. Before 1914, an industry had existed and had been developing rapidly, creating sizeable working-class concentrations and thus determining an immense difference between the technological, cultural, political, etc. level of the townspeople and that of the peasants. The latter refused to go back to the *ancien régime* they hated (so that the Tsarist counter-revolutionaries, although they had an ideology and sometimes a certain experience at their disposal, could not really attempt to organize them), but they did not have the tools that would have allowed them to counter socialism with an action programme based on bourgeois liberalism.

So the main aspects of what has misleadingly been called the 'peasant war' – sporadic and 'suicidal' acts of destruction, then passive resistance – accurately expressed the 'town–countryside' relationship through revolutionary praxis. The peasants did *what they could* against the regime. They had to lose, because they *could do no more*: i.e. precisely in so far as the reason for their defeat (impossibility of uniting in a broad organization or of becoming clearly aware of a common objective, lack of education, illiteracy, technical shortcomings and lack of weapons) was quite simply the underdevelopment that had conditioned and produced the October Revolution, and that the revolutionary sovereign transcended and preserved in itself in so far as its main aim was to suppress it. The leaders, with the inadequate means available to an underdeveloped country, struggled to break the resistance of men who were the very incarnation of that underdevelopment. When they tried to suppress Russian poverty, they saw rising up against them the men produced by that poverty: through these men, poverty and past oppression became human to fight against them. Conversely, it was the scarcity of time that was incarnated in the atrocious brutality with which they repressed every attempt at rebellion, inasmuch as this scarcity itself depended on two factors: the twin emergencies of the external threat and the internal danger. But both these emergencies were conditioned by underdevelopment: it was necessary to industrialize fast, because the gap between the USSR and the capitalist powers was too great; *there was no time* to develop consumer-good industries; it was necessary to collectivize *by force*, because tractors were lacking; *there was no time* to educate the peasants.

Conversely, that brutality was to unify the sovereign action's *style*. The Bureaucracy assumed its dictatorship on behalf of the proletariat, and could maintain it only by latent oppression of the working class and open oppression of the peasant class.* It was *through* the struggle against the peasants that the dictatorship was to be radicalized, everywhere and in all sectors, as Terror. It was on the basis of that Terror – which necessitated a consolidated power – that the improvised hierarchy was gradually to become ossified. On this basis, finally, Terror (we have seen by what mechanism in a previous chapter[39]) as a sovereign praxis was interiorized and became a wheeling extermination inside the sovereign organs. The internal Terror, as a praxis of radical and if need be violent integration, reproduced the movement of the external Terror, as a radical unification – if need be by violence – of practico-inert diversities. And that interiorization was here again comprehensible. The sovereign could make itself into the strict and inflexible unity of its practical field only if it was *in itself* pure unifying power: i.e. synthetic praxis *without any passivity*. As, in fact, passivity was always present – as a multiplicity of common individuals – the sovereign was always involved in *reducing* the inertia that gnawed at it. It reduced *itself* both *in order to* unify the practical field, and because the diversity of the practical field actualized the sovereign multiplicity precisely in so far as praxis realized the unification of the field. It was *in order to* apply draconian measures that the leaders had to 'act as one'; but it was *on the occasion of* the conception and application of these measures that they rediscovered themselves (or *could* rediscover themselves, that was enough) as several. Unification of the practical field by pure sovereign power of synthesis, and reunification of praxis diversified by the very object it had dissolved in the totalization in progress,

---

* The reverse is also true, of course.

39. *Critique*, vol.1, pp.591 ff.

constituted dialectical moments of the temporalization.

To this extent, it can be said that the conflict was a progress towards unity: it substituted a class struggle for an inert impossibility of exchanges. Moreover, the classes in question did not really struggle against one another: the working class was in full growth, without any stability, suffused by series and by series of series; the peasant class was characterized by its own dispersion. In reality, the conflict appeared through the mediation of the sovereign. It was the latter that gave the inert relationship its aspect of a synthetic necessity, by making supply of the towns by the countryside into an emergency (i.e. by transforming – on the basis of its own objectives – the constant difficulties of exchange into a vital question). The sovereign – a mediator between the classes – established a reciprocity as first moment of the conflict, where there had been only a break. In order to avoid the peasant class making itself into the destiny of the working class, it was to use its coercive apparatus in the latter's name in order to make it into the destiny of the former.

But the conflict – however bloody it may have been – was not *liquidatory* in its actual aim. It was a question of controlling and increasing agricultural production and of permitting State organs to levy the maximum percentages, but *on no account* of suppressing the peasant class in the way the bourgeoisie was suppressed as a class. In fact, industry made it possible to begin the motorization and mechanization of agriculture; so gradually working-class production, inasmuch as it was utilizable by the peasants, was to justify the 'leadership' of the urban workers. In so far as that mechanization – which is far from having reached completion – is still being carried on today, we can see its goal and its limits. Beneath the unity of coercion, it seeks to introduce a *drawing together of men* – not by allowing them to discuss their respective points of view, but by producing them in such a way that the peasant, as a specialist in agricultural machinery, differs less and less from the worker, as a specialist in urban machinery. So it is necessary to bear in mind the totalizing but singular character of sovereign praxis in the field. Even as it brought the field's antagonisms to fruition (in order to transform into conflict the practico-inert that was in danger of rending it apart; and in order to make itself, simultaneously, into the two adversaries, the synthetic unity of each of them, and the coercive force that in itself determined the orientation and outcome of the struggle), it introduced despite everything into the peasant class, redefined by the oppression exerted upon it, not just a Marxist culture – which, if reduced to itself alone, would not even have been assimilated – but, by slow impregnation, the means of production that were to produce both increased productivity and the man of that increase, the man of the kolkhoz, propelled by his own tools into the productivity battle and defined, like the worker, by the struggle he was engaged in. The coercive apparatus would be able to slacken its grip, if not in the lifetime of *that* generation, at least when the new one had taken over from it – for those young kolkhoz inmates had known collectivization from childhood, they had seen the appearance of machines and the generalization of their use. So there would be *homogeneity* of the classes, a permanent possibility of interpenetration, and ultimately – with the industrialization of agriculture – the difference between town and countryside would tend in practice towards zero.

Naturally, these implications of that praxis are admissible only provided that certain precise reservations are formulated. In the first place, the industrialization of agriculture cannot be considered as a specific result of planned growth. In the countries of advanced capitalism, it is sometimes carried out at a far faster tempo. To be sure, productivity always increases more slowly in the primary sector. It nevertheless remains the case that in the USA 6,900,000 farmers today feed 165,000,000 people, whereas in the USSR 50,000,000 rural labourers are necessary *today* to feed 215,000,000 inhabitants. In fact, the improvement of productivity in the Soviet primary sector is far from corresponding to the very real increase in the number of agricultural machines. In 1958 as in 1928 – albeit with far less urgency – the problem of agricultural productivity remains in the forefront of the government's concerns.

But these reservations are explicable in so far as they allow the sovereign praxis to be interpreted in its exteriority: i.e. make it possible to determine the qualifications that it received from the counter-finalities engendered by its practical field – or, if you like, from its reflection upon itself through the inert materiality it had synthesized. Coercion, at the same time as it prevented in advance any positive action on the part of the oppressed, or perhaps even any intention of grouping in order to act, maintained those upon which it was exercised in a state of permanent resistance. Since this resistance, moreover, was inseparable from impotence (since constraint, under the seeming unity of the production group, maintained seriality), it was characterized as passive resistance. Nothing was *done* against the regime – something was simply *not done*, certain instructions were not carried out. The appearance of tractors did not regroup farmers, whose relation to the machines – which had come from the town and required additional work and a retraining of workers – was ambiguous. They were mistrusted and also – *rented out* as they were by the State Tractor Station – seen as a new means of control and pressure. Yet it could not be denied that they increased productivity. For such an increase to condition a raising of production levels, however, the rural population would indeed have had to welcome them with enthusiasm – i.e. would have had to have accepted entirely the socialist system and State requisitions. So the two orientations of the sovereign praxis (forced collectivization and gradual provision of the means to win acceptance for collectivization) tended – through its results – to conflict with one another.

The new generation on the kolkhozes, however, no longer calls into question mechanization or collective ownership of the land: the system itself has ceased to be an issue. Yet although it has been produced by motorization, Marxist education, etc., it still bears the mark left upon it by the impotent rages and misfortunes of the previous generation. At the present stage – despite the measures taken by Khrushchev, and in particular the dissolution of the MTS (hence, decentralization) – it demonstrates, if not a nationally based separatism, at least a kind of particularism. Only recently, *Pravda* was repeating some strange statements made by kolkhoz chairmen, aimed at nothing less than securing the autonomy of kolkhoz soviets, from top to bottom. We might say that these statements – if, as their publication in *Pravda* suggests, they reflect a general tendency – denote a kind of *class consciousness* among the peasants. These men – technicians, educated in Marxism, many of whom have studied in the towns – as the leaders foresaw in 1930 are 'Soviet men': tireless workers, courageous, voluntarist and convinced of the need to increase food production. *At the same time*, however, they have interiorized the Terror their families suffered, in the very distance they maintain with respect to their fellows in the towns. Uneducated, their fathers rejected compulsory extra labour and the new system of ownership. Educated, the sons will agree to increase production; they will defend collectivization itself; and they will support the Soviet system. But in them you can discern the consciousness, as a singularization of Soviet pride, of having reached maturity and of rejecting – within the socialist system and the better to defend it – the tutelage of the workers.

This attitude on the part of the kolkhoz workers – which must engender new changes in the sovereign praxis – is thus an objectification of Stalinist praxis. But this objectification – unlike that which occurs when, for example, the isolated worker or restricted group see *outside exteriority* robbing them of their work or its objective results – is realized as *inside exteriority*. That means that this *hexis* of the peasants – which can itself become action – incarnates and encapsulates within itself thirty years of the sovereign praxis, and at the same time pronounces sentence upon it. In short, the conclusion is a retroactive totalization. So the ambivalence of the rural population's attitude presents itself as *the privileged signification* of the sovereign's contradictions (inasmuch as these were expressed in its former action). We say *privileged* and not *definitive*, since nothing allows one to predict that the development of industrialization in the towns and in the countryside will not eventually realize the unity of Soviet men. In that case, and from the standpoint of that new result, the praxis of the leaders between 1928 and 1950 would receive new qualifications. But this further development forms part of what, following so many others, we have called diachronic totalization. It is through new circumstances, unforeseeable problems and an original praxis that such qualifications will come to the former praxis – and it will receive them passively, since it will not have produced them. The privileged signification is the inner conclusion of the praxis, inasmuch as it is the provisional limit of the practical temporalization, and refers *solely* to the relations of immanence (positive or negative) that have really been established in the practical field – and in the sovereign's interiority – in the course of praxis itself. In that sense, the present *hexis* of the peasant class totalizes retrospectively both the positive successes and the negative limits of the Stalinist Terror, in so far as it signals the ambiguity of Soviet society as a whole at the same time as the possibility, under certain conditions, of accomplishing new advances. Within groups formed by constraint, the effort of coercive unification has allowed large farms that could use tractors to be set up and maintained; and under pressure from the State apparatus, these groups have acquired their practical unity through the progress of industrialization, which has allowed motorized appliances to be produced. But this oppression – even if it has negatively allowed famine and the collapse of the system to be avoided – has, thanks to the resistance engendered by it, rendered itself incapable of achieving total integration of the peasant class into the 'classless society', and thereby of basing the increased level of agricultural production upon increased productivity. And what determines the inner, privileged signification here is, of course, the double changeover (change of generations, change of leaders). It nevertheless remains the case that the class conflict – inasmuch as it sought, and made it possible (despite all particularisms), to transform Russian peasants into Soviet men – must be intelligible even in its outcome, as a means of unification determined by the sovereign praxis and in return qualifying it by its counter-finalities. Its shadowy face – the half-failure – retrospectively retotalizes the inner exteriority of action, inasmuch as that half-failure has produced both a situation and men who transcend it by living it. The immanent negations contained by the privileged signification give way retrospectively to the synthesis of parasitic counter-finalities, born in and through the sovereign unity: in short, *the process is totalized*. The positive structures allow the objective meaning of the undertaking that has been condensed *there and today* – i.e. its own movement, *past* and *in the past*, of totalization – to be rediscovered. And, of course, these two directions of the retrospective study are wholly inseparable, as they are also in the action of the young kolkhoz workers, who retotalize them by transcending them.

Thus, within a sovereign praxis, the transformation of the practico-inert into a mediated class struggle represented a dialectical progress towards integration. The sovereign sought to liquidate the practico-inert concretions that it had itself produced while secreting its counter-finalities. But as the practico-inert – a mediation of the inert between men – expressed its passive resistance through the men mediated, the Terror was the sovereign's effort to liquidate the inert concretion by acting on the men it produced (and ultimately by actual liquidation of those individuals). The sovereign's victory, albeit Pyrrhic, illuminates the true meaning of the struggle – for the balance of forces was in its favour from the outset. By this, however, we obviously do not mean the mere numerical relation, for the latter would have operated against the working-class masses and leading bodies. The notion in question actually expresses a complex, dialectical relation – in each of the protagonists – between dynamic density (or men as mediated by the means of communication), the possibilities for organization and reorganization, emergencies, the enthusiasm that such emergencies conditioned in everyone singly and collectively, and the concrete means of mobilizing all forces by a programme of demands and action in which the graded objectives of praxis found their unity in the most distant objective. If the sovereign won, it was because these conditions were realized for it but not for the oppressed. Indeed, despite the grave dangers of 1931–2, the unity of the practical field was never compromised by the conflicts in progress. For the peasant masses, there was nothing to choose between lacking the material means to unite and not having the theoretical tools that would have permitted them to become conscious and formulate a programme. The technical and cultural underdevelopment of the rural masses was expressed – in their practical demands – by the impossibility of constructing their unity around a programme. Literally, the peasants did not want collectivization (especially in the brutal form that the sovereign gave it), but they were not conscious of what they did want because they could not want anything. The *true* kulaks, obviously, struggled to keep their property. But the poor peasant could defend *neither* land that he did not possess, *nor* the principle of bourgeois property (which he did not know), *nor* – especially – that continuous slippage which stripped him of his wretched patch of land and added it to the rich man's estate. Peasant resistance was defeated because it was *without principles*. But it was without principles because, in spite of traditions, local interests, con-straints and mistrust, the rural population could nowhere find any funda-mental reasons to be in opposition. Peasant resistance was *transcended* from the outset by the sovereign praxis, because the former was *outmoded* and the latter *progressive*. I do not give these words an absolute significa-tion. I call 'progressive' activities which, within a totalizing praxis and for a given social field, allow the projected totalization to be advanced, or at all events realized. I call 'outmoded' those which, without really being

able to produce the disintegration of the global praxis, express in practice
the impediments of a practico-inert whose origin is to be sought (in part,
at least) in the material circumstances that gave rise to the praxis itself. To
the extent (always incomplete, except when it is a matter of abstract
examples) to which the totalizing ensemble – praxis, practico-inert and
practical field – can be considered as an isolated system, the fate of this
resistance, however fierce it may be, is decided in advance. It has a chance
of winning – provisionally, at that – only if it benefits at the right moment
from outside assistance. In this sense – although it has been invented by
everyone, lived, and realized by free (and sometimes heroic) undertakings
– it is contained in the system of brakings and accelerations that praxis
itself engenders, be it only to reabsorb them, on the basis of the material
circumstances that have given rise to it and the objectives it has set itself.

From this standpoint, praxis does indeed appear like an enormous
'feedback' machine, whose unity is the determination of circularity (i.e.
the transformation of the cycle of repetitions into spirals). Nevertheless,
this aspect of action is precisely its inside exteriority. When the sovereign
organized its constraints and began collectivization, it simultaneously
knew and *did not know* its opponents' destiny. In so far as it was aware
of the *outmoded* aspect of their resistance, it foresaw their final defeat.
But in so far as the sovereign did not know an ensemble of factors, some
of which were internal to its action and engendered by it, others of which
(provoked by that praxis or not) were *external* dangers – in so far, too, as
the very nature of the practical prevented the sovereign from knowing
the signification and efficacy of its victory itself, as an object realizing
the totalized objectification of the act and creating in that very way, and
for others, an unforeseeable *afterwards* – the sovereign was deciding in
the dark. Its project, beneath the abstract and mendacious objectivity of
economic calculation, recovered the *hazardous* aspect that characterizes
every human undertaking: it is necessary to take risks and to invent. But
not to gamble, as people say, since gambling presupposes alternatives all
of whose terms are defined. Here, the final result, even if it was abstractly
foreseen (victory), was in practice unforeseeable: hence, undetermined
for those men inasmuch as they possessed *those intellectual tools*. The
best – transcending their own tools, but without inventing others, merely
discovering their limits – were to be able to *sense the outcome negatively*.
We thus discover the human features of praxis, as a lived aspect of
praxis-process and as the motor of the process itself. It goes without
saying, moreover, that this ignorance – i.e. the precise margin of
indetermination of the future – was itself an acceptance by the agent of
the material circumstances: of those very circumstances that defined and
limited his adversary's resistance. For the situated historian, it is thus not
an *obscurity* (as for the agent) but a translucid intelligibility.

Conclusion

We have just shown that in a society whose sovereign is a dictator, practico-inert rifts, conflicts and disharmonies – far from breaking the unity of praxis-process – are at once the consequences of that unification and the means it chooses in order to tighten up still further. Thus the historian *must be able* to comprehend dialectically – in the very unity of a sovereign praxis with the process that constantly overflows it and that it constantly reintegrates into itself – the vast historical upheaval which, between 1917 and 1958, has produced Soviet society as we see it. These conclusions are not in themselves either optimistic or pessimistic. We do not claim that the struggle was not atrocious, or that (innumerable) individual disasters do not irremediably damn certain practices (we shall return to the individual failure at the heart of a common praxis[40]). At the level of dialectical investigation we have reached, we do not even have the right to say that it was impossible to proceed otherwise (nor, more-over, the opposite right: we simply do not yet know anything about the possibles[41]). We have simply discovered that the sovereign praxis, what-ever it was, always presented itself in the form of a totalization. And in its very nature of praxis-process, we have established – it is our only optimism – that it was intelligible as a *constituted dialectic*. Before going on to the examination of a non-dictatorial society, however, a number of points ought to be clarified.[42]

---

40. See pp. 313–14 below.

41. See footnote 97 on p.334 below.

42. If we follow the order of the work as Sartre conceived it in his last plan (see Appendix, p.446 below), it seems that the interrogation of synchronic totalization (intelligibility of struggles) in non-directorial societies (which in this plan he calls 'disunited societies') would have found its place here. Then he would have gone on to the diachronic ('but precisely it is History'), hence, to History; and then to the problems of the totalization-of-envelopment, which are considered below but only in regard to directorial societies. It is an open question whether this plan would have survived. For, in the case of disunited societies, we do not find the unity to be restored of pledged groups or the 'unification by the future' of directorial societies, which through struggles make the totalizing project intelligible; instead, it is worked matter that unites these disunited societies, by the agency of men (see Appendix below, pp.433 ff.). We observe from the plan, moreover, that class struggles would have been studied again in the part dealing with the totalization-of-envelopment.

It should also be pointed out that in the notes published in the Appendix (which we have arranged in the most likely chronological order), Sartre first concerned himself with the diachronic (historical event, progress, etc.) – which led him to confront the fundamental problem of the meaning of History – before returning to his plan: totalization in non-directorial societies, and the totalization-of-envelopment, which he sometimes calls a 'system'.

II

THE TOTALIZATION-OF-ENVELOPMENT IN A DIRECTORIAL SOCIETY: RELATIONS BETWEEN THE DIALECTIC AND THE ANTI-DIALECTIC

Singularity and Incarnation
of the Sovereign Praxis

WHAT actually is what we have called the *totality*[43]-*of-envelopment*? What type of objective reality does this synthesis possess? By what expedient, in what perspective and to what observers (or what agents) does it reveal itself? Assuming that there exists a formation of this kind in the bourgeois democracies, we may surmise that it will be difficult to grasp and fix it, if we have not first studied it in the obviously less complex structures that define it at the level of directorial societies.[44] So it will be enough to go back over our example and look *in it* for this totalization.

We already know, in fact, that in Soviet society every local praxis, every singular destiny, is an incarnation of the totalizing praxis and of the overall process. In practical terms that means the following: as soon as a system arises – at the heart of that society in movement, whatever its scale and complexity may be – this system collects within it all the features of the praxis-process grasped in its totality. The practico-inert itself, as we have seen, inasmuch as it is produced by the counter-finalities of praxis as a local determination of the practical field, turns back to the sovereign *as an inert synthesis* (generally as an exigency or a danger) the very action through which a practical field exists: i.e. the spatializing temporalization of the fundamental project. However, it must be noted that every incarnation, being a singularization of the praxis-process, realizes within it that praxis-process in its integrality

---

43. Or rather 'totalization'. See end of this paragraph, and pp. 49, 85–6 and 117 above; also pp. 228 and 278–9 below.

44. The terms 'directorial' or 'dictatorial' society are used almost indiscriminately, since the sovereign may be a restricted group or an individual. The essential thing most of the time in Sartre's chosen example is the concentration of powers, as he stresses in a later passage (see his footnote on p.273 below).

(without there necessarily being any awareness of this realization). This is what we pointed out in relation to the example of boxing, when we stressed that the present incarnation is not a particular concrete case of which the totalizing praxis-process is the abstract concept.[45] That means very concretely that the totalization-of-envelopment, *if it exists*, must not be a mere rule – or even a synthetic schema – ensuring the temporalization of particular events from outside. It can be realized as a singular incarnation – at a given moment, and in a given fact (or a given action) – only if it is itself, in itself, singularity and incarnation. This, moreover, is what constitutes its *historicity*; and it is in the name of this historicity that we discover *the* Russian Revolution as a unique adventure and *the* Stalin regime as a quite singular phase of its development. It remains to be ascertained whether these expressions do not hide a fetishism of History, and whether the demystified historian does not have to stick to positivist nominalism.

Now the practical reality of the totalization-of-envelopment is proved by the dialectical investigation itself. For we have pointed out that every incarnation is tied in two ways to the historical ensemble: on the one hand, in fact, it realizes in itself the latter's condensation; on the other hand, it refers back in a decompressive blossoming to the ensemble of practical significations which determine it in its belonging to the social and historical field.[46] This particular boxing match takes place in a climate of international tension (for example, on the day of the Anschluss): the small number of spectators is the incarnation *here* and *at this moment* of the anxiety of the French. However, at the same time as this is lived here – by the organizers in the form of poor takings, and by each spectator through the rather dismal look of a hall normally full to bursting – it necessarily refers back to distant events, which preserve a relative autonomy even as they determine it *in interiority*, and to the hierarchy of the incarnations producing it in sectors of the same size or larger dimensions. The spectator, back home, will say: 'There was nobody at the fight.' And his wife will answer: 'The cinemas are empty too. What can you expect, people are staying at home.' And if the tension continues, luxury stores and entertainments will experience a crisis that is already taking shape and can be foreseen through the fiasco of the sporting event. This crisis refers back to the deeper structures of the French economy and, on the other hand, to the praxis of the government (foreign policy, etc.).

It matters little here whether serial elements or groups are involved:

45. See pp.28–30 above.
46. See p.49 above.

what counts is the simultaneous twofold reference to the interiority of the singularization and to the totality that envelops it. We still do not know for the moment if, in a bourgeois society, this totality is attainable. The significations refer to one another, to be sure, but everything may vanish into the serial or into the void. But for anyone who, through his actions, realizes in the USSR an event of any kind – an individual one – in the practical field, this event is in immanent relation with the whole in exteriority and in interiority. That means it is defined in relation to the sovereign praxis and as a singular determination of the unified practical field. No doubt, the extreme diversity of individual destinies can be pointed out: a stone's throw away from the steelworks – on the Siberian plain, and in the Urals – the 'shaman casts his spells'. It is easy to imagine the disorder of the universe in formation that is Magnitogorsk, with its Soviet workers (displaced populations), its labourers recruited on the spot (Siberian peasants), its foreign volunteers (of great technical and professional value) and its squads of prisoners sentenced to forced labour (mostly 'common criminals'). But even this disparate nature is not a pluralism. Everyone is determined by everyone else and, through the interiorization of his relations with everyone (through the sovereign praxis), realizes a singular incarnation of Soviet society at *this* moment of its construction. The presence of foreign volunteers and the *survival of shamans* demonstrate how far behind the society still is – the gap between the existing structure of Siberian groups and that of Magnitogorsk, as a Soviet town under construction. In the same way, therefore, *they all* incarnate the sovereign praxis, either inasmuch as it builds in conformity with the Plan it has decided upon, or inasmuch as it restrains itself by developing its counter-finalities. And *they all* refer back to that totalizing praxis, inasmuch as it polarizes all the significations of the field and no one or nothing is defined except on the basis of it and as an event of its interiority. And what everyone refers to is indeed a singularity of envelopment, rather than some dogmatic, de-situated rule. It is upon the basis of the local administrators' decree – itself provoked by a hierarchized series of decisions taking us back to the central organ and to the sovereign decision, inasmuch as this is the transcendence of a new aspect of the practical field – it is upon the basis of *this decree*, then, that the exhaustion or discontent or incomprehension of *some particular* peasant, urbanized too fast, will be expressed objectively by an act of sabotage. In other words, *this* specific act of sabotage refers back to *those* specific, dated consequences (unique in the temporalization under way as in the spatializing rearrangement that underpins it) of *a particular* (and equally unique) administrative measure motivated, as we have just seen, by *a particular* reconditioning of praxis by its field and by the transcendence – as a singular invention of the sovereign – of this reconditioning.

Of course, what may strike you here is the frequentative or even universal nature of the decree, at any level whatsoever of explanation of it. It generally presents itself – except at the moment of choice of present individuals by an equally present individual – as a judgement of a hypothetical and normative type: 'all *x*s must be *y*s', i.e. 'if *m* is *x*, *m* must be *y*'. But when the decree turns this face of universality towards those subject to it – which may deceive them – it is the indetermination of knowledge that confers this abstract generality upon it. In particular circumstances, this indetermination might be rediscovered as a lacuna within concrete totalities. For example, an order from Army Headquarters stipulates that *the Seventieth* division will be transferred to such and such a district and quartered in such and such a town. Headquarters knows the division's officers, but does not know the other ranks except as units. It knows that the division is 'at full strength'. It has further information at its disposal allowing it to determine the *morale* of this military unit (i.e. a complex relation that we do not have to determine here), which means that it decides to position it here or there depending on the circumstances. What is involved here is *a singular reality*, conceived as such by Headquarters (it has *a history*, in terms of which it is evaluated as the means for a new local praxis). But this reality is that of an institutional framework filled by men. Being incarnated by these men and in this practical field, the institutional framework has become an individuated reality. However, if this unity prevents Headquarters from transforming its indetermination of ignorance into universality, we can still see the strict identity between its fundamental ignorance *here* and *in the event of universalization*. It is pointless to stipulate in the order: 'If any soldier belongs to the Seventieth, he will be transferred with it, etc.' That is pointless since the whole is institutionally defined. But it is just a matter of originally identical formulations transformed by the synthetic ensemble that integrates them. Conversely, there exist numerous universalist commands in the Army. Yet it knows exactly the number of men, sub-groups and groups which make it up – the difference here comes from the circumstances. For example, the command may be addressed via the hierarchy *and directly* to the individuals themselves: e.g. concerning behaviour to be observed in town, on leave, etc. In that case, it is addressed currently to 6,752,309 men* (and *perhaps* – depending on its nature – to the 'rookies' who will replace those demobbed, whose number is likewise determined). But the totalization vanishes under the universalization, inasmuch as the order has to be accomplished by individuals as such (inasmuch as *everyone*, for example,

---

* I am, of course, picking a number at random.

has to shine *his* shoes or sow the buttons back on *his* jacket). And although the goal being aimed at is an overall effect – on the civilian population, for example – or a serial or synthetic one (the presence of a military division each of whose individual members is 'impeccable' will help to increase the confidence of the urban workers, inasmuch as it is *likewise* incarnated presence of the sovereign and the discipline observed allows them – under certain conditions – to gauge the regime's strength),* it is this very population that will be serialized or united by its objective movement to synthesize into *one* common reality each soldier's individual attitude: his casualness or the care he devotes to his turn-out, the behaviour he maintains towards his commanders, towards civilians, etc. The soldier is the target of his superior officers' order, as the individual means of provoking – through the mediation of the population surrounding him – a synthetic tightening of unity whose very movement implies unification of the soldiers by the group (or series) constituting their human milieu. But this order from the superior officer is aimed at the soldier inasmuch, precisely, as he remains unknown in his individual reality – except by the junior officers who have to deal with restricted groups. Thus these strictly individuated soldiers are aimed at as universals, inasmuch as their *given* individuality is simultaneously pointless and ignored here *and* inasmuch as their behaviour as common individuals has to be *the same* everywhere as a practical transcendence of that given.

In a more general way, a decision by the sovereign can in exteriority have the appearance of *universality*. A law duly passed by the competent assemblies as proposed by the executive may suppress or limit the right to strike for *all* public employees. We come back – even in the grounds for it, if there are any – to the formula '$y = f(x)$'. If x is a public employee (i.e. fulfils certain abstract conditions, enjoys specific advantages in return for performing certain services), he cannot be a striker. But this universality is in fact a historical and singular determination. Neither the sovereign nor the constituted bodies obedient to it are really thinking about strikes *in general* or servants of the State *in general*. From their point of view, the law is a response to certain social disturbances

---

* If we assume that the workers are supporters of the regime, what is involved here is a *synthetic unification of the townspeople*: confidence gathers them together. I am simplifying crudely, of course. Conversely, the deployment of disciplined military units, united to the point of automatism (or the mimed *representation* of automatism), helps – through the very unity this manifests – to increase serial impotence among the discontented, e.g. among the peasants. In a people's war – i.e. when the national liberation army is poor in men and in arms, but sustained, fed and hidden by the ensemble of the rural population – the struggle itself is a unification of the peasants: they unite inasmuch as they protect the army's unity. For this unity to survive, however, an iron discipline must be established in the military groups.

or to a strike that has just taken place. It shows, at this precise moment, the given (and singular) relationship between the various forces. (Can the 'forces of order' implement a general requisition order in the event of a strike? What reaction may this action provoke in the various social strata? And so on.) Moreover, it singularizes and realizes on a specific point the conception of the State that the sovereign formulates: i.e. in the last resort its political praxis; and this in turn reflects in depth the historical conjuncture (i.e. once again the relationship of forces, but envisaged in the light of the economic and social 'whole' and the direction of socio-economic changes), which is – at its own level – equally singular. Thus the decree or law has this dual character of determined indetermination, into which we shall go more deeply when we tackle the problem of the concrete universal.[47]

These examples show, in any case, that the sovereign itself – depending on the circumstances and the practical exigencies – can treat the *ruled* as members of more or less integrated *units*, or address them in their (individual or serial) indetermination through the mediation of the purely inert result in which their efforts are objectified. It can decide, in the event of war, that 'the civilian population of such and such a district will be evacuated'; or, on the contrary, decree in a plan conceived in peace-time that 'the number of tons of pig-iron produced in x years will be such and such'. At all events, it is not unaware that it is imposing a task upon a specified ensemble (or one whose very growth is specified). In the latter case, universality comes to men through inert matter, i.e. through all the identical tons of pig-iron they have to produce and through which – as *their* future objectification – the sovereign grasps them as *undetermined means*. But whether the order is aimed at a group or a category, it is actually a matter of producing a unique and definite outcome in particular circumstances. Grasped in exteriority, i.e. in the instant or – which comes to the same thing – outside temporalization, the millions of tons of pig-iron are exteriority unified by a passive synthesis: if the

47. It will be tackled only indirectly here, in the pages that follow. See also pp.40 ff. above. On this subject, see *L'Idiot de la famille*, vol.3, p.431, n.2: 'Hence, in every totalization in progress, it is always necessary to envisage, in their dialectical relations, the direct relationship between the general totalization and the singular totalization (a totalization of the singular by the concrete generality) – i.e. between the whole and the part – and the one between the macrocosmic totalization and the microcosmic totalization, *through the mediation* of the conjuncture: i.e. of the *concrete universal* produced by the latter, retotalized by every part, and determining the individual singularity at once by the conjunctural event (a totalized incarnation of the totalization) and by the general aspect of the world (i.e. by the real relationship between all the parts, not inasmuch as they directly express the whole, but inasmuch as they distinguish themselves from it by their movement to retotalize it – to re-exteriorize it inasmuch as it has caused itself to be interiorized by them) ... ' See also 'L'Ecrivain et sa langue', in *Situations IX*, pp.62 ff.

synthesis itself disappears, the physico-chemical ensemble is left. But if they are considered within the practical totalization, they encounter the unity of the means at the heart of the living end. They exist, in fact, as means necessary for certain practical realizations (i.e. the quantity of pig-iron produced will be precisely what heavy industry   and certain sectors of light industry – can and must absorb in *the same moment* of the temporalization); and, at the same time, they are intersected *as ends* (i.e. as intermediate objectives) by another unity (or rather by the same, but at another stage of circularity) which synthesizes them in the form of *passive exigencies* (*those* tons – as means of production demanded, for example, by *such and such* a region in the course of industrialization – require *those* means of transport as the specific ensemble that will allow them to fulfil their functions). In the other example chosen – 'evacuation of the civilian population' – the local military authorities and the soldiers who obey them are subordinated as synthetic ensembles to the task that must be accomplished through them. *The* civilian population, as object of the action and as its end, becomes the transcendent unity of their plurality (of their series, perhaps); and it is the preservation of this unity (during the evacuation) that will realize – as a constant signification of their acts and as a final outcome (if it is achieved) of their activity – the genuine and synthetic objectification of the practical multiplicity that they were at the outset. From this point of view, down to the lowest level (or almost), it is the job to be done which determines the agent – in the guise of an objective exigency reactualized by the officer – so he is determined only by an abstract relation, one that appears accidental. It is often 'a chance' if one regiment rather than another finds itself in a particular sector at the moment when the enemy, on the basis of plans devised independently of these non-signifying facts, launches operations which necessitate a certain number of ripostes and parries (and, for example, create the *urgency* of an evacuation of civilians under imminent threat of bombardment). Thus the attack (or the information which causes it to be anticipated), the task, the terrain and the lie of the land, etc., determine an objective exigency that is deciphered in the object and becomes the sole practical determination of agents otherwise totally undetermined.

But the fact is that the agent is actually only an inertly defined instrument: the genuine concrete is those women and those children in blazing houses. The relative indetermination of the agent comes from the plenary and concrete determination of the situation and of the civilians who risk death – each one of whom specifies the death he risks, moreover, by his age, his sex, his state of health, and his situation in the spatializing force field that encloses him.

Yet the soldiers of the regiment are not *any old soldiers*, precisely in so far as it is ultimately the free practical organism which executes the tasks adopted by the common individual. This observation starts off anew the circularity of incarnation, since – in its concrete and objective truth – the task that determines the soldier in his abstract being *becomes again*, by being executed, a concrete relation between concrete individuals and between groups. It is with his whole person, his whole history, all his means, that *one particular* soldier will manage to save *one particular* old man (or *one particular* defence sub-group, *one particular* popular ensemble); with the fatigue itself of the preceding march (the very one that led him, on orders, to this sector), which itself is *no longer* a chance but the precise (and, as a rule, strict) result of his biological temporalization in the framework of a campaign or a war. By the *final invention*, the soldier and the civilian he snatches from his blazing house constitute, in *positive* reciprocity and thanks to mediating third parties (officers, other soldiers, other civilians, wider and deeper exigencies at the level of social defence), a concrete and strict unity, whose synthetic totalization is the *behaviour invented by both* (by each other and together). And it is very precisely these reciprocal and common actions, necessarily individualized by the free transcendence of circumstances, which are *in reality* aimed at by the order decreeing the evacuation of a particular population. In the order given by the general, the indetermination of the soldier springs from ignorance of the strict circumstances that will necessarily occur in an absolute concretion, but *at the same time* from the empirically obvious fact that application of the decreed measures could not be achieved, even for a moment, except as a unique and strictly individual determination of men by *these* contractions of space-time, of the paths traced in space-time by *these* men. Universality – through the necessary ignorance of the commanders – is only an economy of means. But it does not refer to any species or genus. This *abstract* determination is swallowed up and dissolved by the true practical temporalization of the agents.

The lower aspect of the order may, through urgency and need to achieve a saving of time, take the form of an abstract indetermination and, thereby, seem to indicate *a genus*. However, we know that the same order, as an invention of the leaders (at whatever level they may be), is a singular production: i.e. a concrete – and *unique* – response given by an original and incomparable group to difficulties strictly *dated* and conditioned by historical circumstances (i.e. by circumstances that will *never* be found again *as they are*). The planning bodies, for example, will suddenly be obliged to introduce an important adjustment in the plan currently being implemented. But we know already that the organs of praxis have been singularized by it, and that they will invent by transcending their own intellectual tools (i.e. here by using them). We know too (to remain in the interiority of the field) that these difficulties reflect counter-finalities and the practico-inert that these produce, inasmuch as the same activity which produces *its own* men secretes *its own* viruses, on the basis of the particular circumstances that give rise to it. At the level of discovery of the problem and invention of its solution by *the men of that problem and of that solution*,* we again find incarnation as circularity (it will be transcended and 'overtaken' by the decision), and this incarnation produces its own knowledge: it is revealed as scarcity of *this* time, in *this* irreversible temporalization, at *this* moment of the temporalization. Thus the decision – whether it is an individual sovereign's or a group's – is produced by and for the person or persons who take it, *as an individuality*. In this perspective, it matters very little that the data of the problem should be statistics and that it should be elaborated by the economic combinatory of which we have spoken. The synthetic truth that is revealed through these figures is the very specific threat (for example, in those months in the summer of 1928) that a *historical* resistance of the peasant class *in this lived present* would place the towns on the brink of famine, and socialism on the brink of ruin. And the brusque decision urgently to take up Trotsky's plan again and embark, all out and without preparation, on collectivization of the land and forced industrialization, was precisely *historical* and singular in a twofold manner. First, in fact, a praxis took shape through innumerable difficulties as the sole response *possible* (i.e. considered as such by the sovereign) to the danger that threatened; and this praxis, unaware of itself in many sectors, was to begin the grandiose, terrible and irreversible temporalization that in History was to take the name of *Stalinism*. On the other hand, however, the historical moment of that decision was also that of the sudden left turn which cast the 'Rightists' into impotent opposition. Trotsky was still in the USSR, but he remained under house arrest. Thus, via this new circumstance and the decision that transcended it to negate it, it was the total victory of Stalin the *individual* over all his adversaries that was realized.

The dialectical meaning of this victory is clear. Stalin had relied on the Right to exclude Trotsky from the government because he was hostile by *nature* (i.e. by the interiorization of his praxis as a militant) to principles, to radicalism, to the Permanent Revolution. It was not the

---

* We are not implying by this any pre-established harmony: they are the men of that problem, because it is in them as their limit as well as outside them as their product. So this reciprocal incarnation may very well have as its result (in specific conditions) inability to find a viable solution; or the inevitable deviation of any new awareness, by the intellectual tools that produce the practical conceptions, and that interiorized praxis has produced in everyone.

content of the Trotskyist projects that repelled him, it was *above all* the intrinsic nature of the praxis expressed in them. In fact, he *did not understand* his Left opponents and, without being strictly speaking opportunistic, the only decisions that inspired him with confidence were those *demanded* by circumstances. When the 'grain strike' required energetic measures, it did not seem to him that the circumstances proved Trotsky right: for him, it was a matter of embarking on a concrete undertaking *the need for which was vouched for by the urgency of the danger.* Nothing to do, according to him, with any intellectual *apriorism*: the idea was the thing itself. But precisely because he wanted to discover the practical idea in the materiality of current exigencies, he detached himself from the Right, which likewise struck him as purely theoreticist, since its project (socialism at a snail's pace) was the product of general considerations regarding underdeveloped countries and the Revolution inasmuch as it had occurred in the largest of all – in Russia. Their caution was *precisely* what the danger of 1928 condemned: their caution, inasmuch as it was *theoretical inertia* – i.e. a practical instrument limiting adaptation to reality* – *rather than* Stalin's decision to be guided (within the perspective of building socialism) by material imperatives and construct his praxis *upon these*. In short, it was *the drama of 1928* that liquidated Zinoviev and Kamenev. But it liquidated them *through Stalin*: not inasmuch as Stalin was to be the instrument of the situation – of History – as Marxists too often think: but, on the contrary, inasmuch as Stalin made himself the man of the situation by the reply he gave to the exigencies of the moment. In other words, the day when the first Plan was decided, a

---

* For, in opposing any overhasty socialization, the Bolshevik Right referred to the following principle of Marx and Engels: in order to make the transition to communism, you must have reached a very high level of production. (The idea was present in Marx as early as 1844, in 'Economics and Politics' – which the Bolsheviks did not know – but it cropped up again in Engels's 'Anti-Dühring'.) This principle, obvious in itself, was nevertheless susceptible of different applications: for it could just as well lead to Kamenev's cautious slowness as to the Trotskyist determination to do everything possible to press ahead. In so far as the 'Right' used it to justify its opposition, it was congealed into a *partial truth* (i.e. a truth from which the rightist opposition claimed to emanate as its only possible consequence); at once, inasmuch as it prevented the dissidents from conceiving of other possibilities, it became a non-transcendable inertia – i.e. an inert determination of sworn passivity. And it would certainly be absurd to imagine that the practical attitude of the rightists *derived* from the principle. On the contrary, it was that attitude which had decided upon the latter's *limited*, negative utilization. Moreover, it is necessary, of course, to go back to the history of the revolutionary movement, inasmuch as it was incarnated *also* in these men, in order to discover and comprehend their practical determinations. But the circularity remained genuine, in this case as in others: the option-pledge, constituted through a *limited* and *a priori* assertion of the principle, was precisely what conferred upon it its inert rigour and its non-transcendable negative action. On this basis, the principle as an objective impossibility of adapting transformed the option into a destiny.

specific and individualized praxis replaced a hesitation and greater or lesser oscillations (these too given rise to, in their singularity, by the fact that the leaders were simultaneously Lenin's successors and the heirs of the NEP). But this praxis functioned by a recasting of the leading group (and – in a circular manner – occurred as a recasting of that group), which replaced collective leadership by the sovereignty of a single individual.

2

Incarnation of the Sovereign in an Individual

Contingency and Appropriateness of the Incarnation

I T IS NO part of my intentions to explain here the origin of that dictatorship of an individual, any more than to give the signification of the cult of personality: I have attempted that elsewhere.[48] What matters here is something quite different. Every contemporary reader takes for granted, in fact, that it is the movement of society and the recastings of the field by common praxis which decide the individual's power and role in the various social sectors. This determination of individual power, and of the efficacy of an action undertaken by a single person (or on the initiative of *one* leader), is not necessarily the *same* (proportionately speaking) for a given society, in a given period, in the different branches of human activity. If, within the directive organisms, the sovereign is *an individual* (a *common* individual), this is because the type of integration demanded by their praxis and their objectives can be realized and guaranteed only by abandonment, in favour of a single individual, of the powers specific to each. This abandonment, of course, is followed by the reverse gesture of the *gift*: to each, the sovereign gives back all or a part of his former powers, but as a gratuitous gift emanating from his free sovereignty. Certain imbalances, insoluble conflicts, or invasion of the group by the practico-inert, lead to this transformation. But this does not mean that the sovereign's power is anything other than *common*, or that his sovereignty is not a condensation of the sovereign powers of the group. It is simply that its strength and efficacy derive from the fact that, with his backing, the ensemble of the directorial group or groups has assigned itself new structures which – lapsing into inertia

---

48. In *The Spectre of Stalin.*

– ground his free mediatory activity upon the impotence of the common individuals, and upon the necessity of overcoming these passive resistances by the dual means of an ever more extensive integration and a multiplication of mediated relations. The sovereign, in a sense, is sustained by the serialization of the sub-groups exercising power – inasmuch as, in given circumstances, he is *the only one through whom this serialization can be dissolved and the groups reconstituted*. And, in fact, he unremittingly pursues this dissolution of series and these regroupments, by his totalizing praxis and for it. But dissolution and regroupments alike always remain provisional, and are limited to making a specific action possible. As soon as the sovereign withdraws, in fact, collectives reappear. And this is also the means of realizing his praxis sovereignly, through the wheeling impotence of his collaborators.

What matters, in any event, is the following. As a common individual, Stalin was not a mere *person*. He was a human pyramid, deriving his practical sovereignty from all the inert structures and from all the support of every leading sub-group (and every individual). So he was everywhere, at all levels and every point of the pyramid, since his totalizing praxis was transcendence and preservation of all structures, or – if you like – since his praxis was the synthetic temporalization of that entire inert structuration. But conversely, inasmuch as he was not just a man called Stalin but *the sovereign*, he was *retotalized* in himself by all the complex determinations of the pyramid. He was produced by everyone as interiorizing in the synthetic unity of an individual the strata, the hierarchy, the zones of cleavage, the serial configurations, etc., which were precisely the passive means of his action and the inert directions of the regroupments he carried out. In other words, as soon as Stalin had taken personal power, he was incarnated in the pyramid of ruling bodies and that pyramid was incarnated in him. This common individual, as a sovereign, was *in addition* a collective individual. However, this reciprocity of incarnation still remains abstract, since it does not take account of the historical reality of Stalin, a militant formed on the basis of his milieu and his childhood by the circumstances of his past struggle. The sovereign, that collective and common individual, was *incarnated* in an individual unique in the world whose *hexis* (as mere interiorization of the conditionings he had transcended) was as original as his physiognomy or his physiological constitution. This means that, as happens with every incarnation, Stalin was *more* and *something other than* that sovereign as common-collective we have just described. Or rather, that in his concrete existence he was the *facticity* of that sovereign praxis and that pyramid. Let us first understand by this that the *facticity* of the incarnation was exclusive of any reciprocity. It came to that vast stratified bureaucracy through the man who headed it. From this standpoint, Stalin was everywhere: not just on all the walls as peerless face of the Soviet adventure, but as a structure of interiorized inertia in everyone. In everyone, he was the living (and deceptive) image of pledged passivity, and also the concrete unity of all wills occurring in individuals as a strictly individual but *other* will (i.e. as a concrete imperative). But this time there was no totalizing surge that could flow back from the subgroups over the sovereign, since it was *his past, his body, his face*, that realized the supreme incarnation; or – if you like – since those particular features had been constituted in him by his former praxis, i.e. *before* he exercised his sovereignty and in a different society. Hence, this facticity indeed seems an irreducible. It is not even certain, moreover, at this stage of our investigation, that the different traits which make it up are not irreducibles with respect to one another.*

But the first observation to be made is that sovereignty realizes the socialization of the individual exercising it. This means, in the first place, that there cannot be a private Stalin who might – at least abstractly – be separated from the public Stalin. His facticity as a historical person is intimately integrated with his praxis, becoming its *qualification. Hexis*, as interiorized past (with its habits and instruments, etc.), is indissolubly tied to the *common individual*, to the point where every sovereign practice – far from being a free transcendence by the practical organism of pledged inertia – is a unitary transcendence of the common individual as a singular individual and vice versa. In other words, specific functions in groups, inasmuch as they existed before the arrival of the person currently exercising them and inasmuch as they will subsist after his departure for other posts or his death, relate to *the common individual* and constitute him – with a certain indetermination – as a singularized individual. And during the entire time that he fulfils his function the singularized individual, although ultimately realizing each task as a concrete determination of the temporalization, remains separated from his function by this very slight gap – this imperceptible yet fundamental void – which is constituted by the presence of an inert pledged (hence untranscendable) determination at the heart of praxis, which transcends it as a movement only to find it again in all the objectives pursued. *On the contrary*, Stalin sovereignly constituted the type and the organs of his power: in short, the singular reality of that power. And although the operation had taken place through processes of subsidence, collapse, stratification, regroupment, etc., in the bureaucratic pyramid, it nevertheless remained the synthetic unity (i.e. the use there) of those sub-

---

* Inasmuch, of course, as they all refer to diachronic structures and our investigation has not yet led us to the basic question: is there a *diachronic* totalization?

sidences, etc. But the concrete synthetic unity of the social transformations which gave rise to Stalin's personal power was necessarily
incarnated by the sovereign's person – his historical and bodily person –
inasmuch as *that power* was precisely a singular and chance event, *not
yet an institution* (this description would be worthless if it were a matter
of a dauphin receiving the throne as his inheritance after his father's
death* It was established *by* Stalin and disappeared with him. Although
Khrushchev holds a plurality of offices, his vast power is in no way
similar to Stalin's power. And even should he exercise a *personal power*
(an unlikely eventuality), he would exercise it in a society whose ossified
structures (on certain points) and whose propensities *facilitate* the seizure
of power by an individual, whereas Stalin *was establishing* the sovereignty
of an individual within a praxis that seemed to exclude any personal
dictatorship. Thus, not only was it practically impossible – at least in
certain cases – to determine whether the *way* in which a decision had
been applied (its bloody brutality, etc.) represented the practical reaction
of the leading ensemble to the urgency of the dangers or Stalin's *own
way* (inasmuch as it re-exteriorized the interiorization of a past practice),
but the same distinction was equally impossible to establish in each
leader (or administrator, from the highest to the most humble). For
everyone held his powers from Stalin and, by virtue of that very fact,
was buffeted about by Stalin's voluntarism. At the same time, everyone
was formed by his own praxis and his possibilities for acting within a
society structured in a specific way. But this praxis and its possibilities –
inasmuch as they were constantly interiorized, in the inert, as a past
transcended and preserved – had constituted him in fact as a more or less
distant and indirect emanation of Stalin. It was Stalin, to whom he
imposed obedience; Stalin, who through him was sacred; and Stalin
alone, who everywhere set in motion – and particularly there, through
him – the systems of balance and social compensation through which his
activity was carried on. I have shown elsewhere how, in the ascending
relation (*from the secondary leader to Stalin*), the local official was
cancelled as an individual in Stalin himself, grasped not as a person but
as the biological reality of maximum social integration.[49] Conversely, he
was Stalin in person in his relations with his subordinates. This meant

---

* Although every reign has its *colour* deriving from the king, there remains – despite
everything and up to the end (just remember the future Louis XVI's emotion at the death of
Louis XV: his anguish in the face of power) – a gap between person and sovereign, in the
very sense we have just defined in relation to other offices. The sovereign-individual is
sacred for himself; he knows *in himself* the ambivalence of the sacred.

49. *The Spectre of Stalin*; and also *Critique*, vol.1, p.655.

that his praxis of its own accord reproduced *the singular quality intrinsic to Stalin*: at once because it was the constant exigency of the Soviet adventure (scarcity of time), and because Stalin possessed it. In the indistinctness of the individual sphere, the power (as a function), the voluntarism (as speed of temporalization) and the savage will of Stalin were one and the same thing. Hence, within the framework of his common individuality, [the local official] received as untranscendable exigencies certain *absolutely concrete* determinations, which qualified him as the extended creation of whom Stalin was the creator, and as the incarnation – *here* and *now*, before *those* people – of that sovereign individual. Alienation here corresponded to absolute concretion: Stalin was incarnated in the local leader *as an Other*. It remained the case, however, that it would nowhere be possible to differentiate that inert – though singularized – alterity of pledged inertia, even in the case of a decision taken at the local level. Stalin gave the Revolution his own past as a common past.

At once, the singular and concrete nature of the leading praxis is apparent to us. That real incarnation of an abstract Revolution had to be singularized in such a way – by producing, on the basis of previous circumstances, its own means of struggle – that it would be obliged to push integration to the limit and be incarnated in its turn in a person. But we are not going to ponder here – at the risk of disappointing – over what would have happened if Stalin had died in Siberia, if Trotsky had been supported by the majority, etc. Would *another* Stalin have been found? Would Trotsky eventually have taken on the role of personal sovereign? Would he have been led to take practically identical decisions? Would he have been able to attempt another policy? Would the Russian Revolution ultimately have failed? etc. We are not yet considering the problem of possibles.[50] Moreover, Stalin's *practical* role, and his real importance in socialization, the conduct of military operations, etc., still seem ill defined. Sometimes, for example, he is portrayed in his office following the German advance on a globe and demonstrating a cantankerous incompetence (restraining or blocking the initiative of his military commanders); sometimes, on the contrary, knowing everything, deciding everything, organizing everything. The historian will assign him his true place later on. The key thing is that this socialist society – i.e., among other things, this society which envisages people through the social milieu that produces them, and reduces to a minimum the *historical* importance of individuals – should be obliged, by the nature of its undertaking, to determine at all levels its practical currents and its own

50. See footnote 97 on p.334 below.

reorganizations *through the mediation* of an individual. If you like, the most important thing is not to know whether Stalin was competent or not, when it was a matter of conducting a war. It is to realize that the group of military leaders, even if ultimately taking the decisions, found itself constitutionally obliged to take them *through Stalin*: i.e. to provoke a synthetic retotalization in him of the plan of attack they had already drawn up. And this retotalization could be only – hypothetically – an *incarnation* of the original plan: it had to contain more and less than the latter; it had to express the limits and the style of life that characterized Stalin.

This observation is valid, of course, for all the other sovereign decisions, from the Plan down to its detailed applications. In this sense, we can understand what that need to be incarnated in one man meant, for the unity of praxis and the practical field. Inasmuch as it *was* that man, the totalizing temporalization had to take on features which did not spring from its inner conditionings. Incarnation was required, so that the unity of the practical organism should be conferred upon the activity of the organized groups. But with this unification through the concrete individual, other aspects intrinsic to the practical organism found themselves conferred upon praxis and singularized it despite itself. First, those deriving from the human condition (ensemble of determinations-limits characterizing human organisms in a certain period) and [above all] the possibility of growing old and dying. The sclerosis of society would be incarnated in the ageing of Stalin; and the latter would maintain it *beyond* the time when new contradictions, without him, could have exploded it. Furthermore, the end of one phase of the Revolution would coincide with the sovereign's death. Our investigation has shown, in fact, that Stalinism outlived itself, masking the new structures of the society produced; and that the end of Stalinism can well and truly be identified with Stalin's death. Hence, incarnation was introducing (at least between the first and second phases of the Soviet experience) that discontinuity or rupture which comes diachronically to men from deaths and births, but which – for a given moment of temporalization – is not necessarily the mode of development of praxis. In the system in movement of the sovereign practice and its organs, that death of Stalin was the inner limit of the first phase, inasmuch as it already posed the problem of successors and constituted for all Soviet citizens (*even the opposition*) a death at the heart of their life. There would be an *afterwards*, unknown to everybody, which would be constituted on the basis of objective circumstances, to be sure, but *following a rupture that made it unforeseeable*. Thus the original phase of praxis had to be incarnated in the temporalization-towards-death of human life. A dialectic was established between, on the one hand, the finitude of a life and its terminal disappearance and, on the other, the march towards its term of the praxis of accumulation. Death, as radical negation of an organism, overtook victory, as a positive success of the first moment of industrialization.

But that is not all. As I have shown elsewhere, the essential nature of facticity is for each individual *the necessity of his contingency*.[51] This should be taken to mean that each of them *is not in a position to found his own existence*; that it eludes him, in so far as he ek-sists it; that it is characterized finally by a singular involvement in the world, which a priori excludes any *aerial view*. There is an individual only through *this* finitude; only through the singularity of *this* viewpoint. And all the subsequent transcendences, far from suppressing the original facticities, preserve these in themselves as the very exigency that qualifies action and pre-sketches the content of changes. So it is not a matter of knowing whether historically and practically *an other* could have played Stalin's role, or whether Stalin could have played his own differently: that is a question we shall discuss later on. But what is given in each person is merely *their contingency*, which means – precisely in so far as Stalin is not his own foundation and his facticity constitutes him as a *certain* individual among others, who does not derive from himself the reasons for his differences (in relation *to others*) and his originality (in the sense in which every determination is a negation) – that the total praxis of a society in the course of industrialization is imbued, down to its deepest layers, with this contingency. Far from presenting itself – as the engineers of the Plan would like – as the necessary response to questions posed by the necessary development of objectivity, the praxis appears – in the very rigour of its temporalization – as perfectly incapable of founding its own existence: i.e. as deciding actions to be taken and resolving problems on the basis of a past that eludes it, and through individual limitations which prevent it from grasping the field of options as a whole.

Now, as we have already shown, there can be no doubt but that praxis – even the praxis of an organized ensemble of groups and sub-groups – presents itself as a conservative transcendence of a facticity. What gives rise to it, in fact, and what limits while determining it, are former circumstances, inasmuch as they reveal themselves through needs and the original project seeks to change them. In this way, an ensemble of practical tools are constituted, among other things, which oblige agents to comprehend the evolution under way *through* the inert subsistence of the circumstances this evolution has to change. Yet this undeniable nature of every praxis – its contingency as an *heir* – finds itself considerably reinforced (beyond what praxis in general can require) when an individual

---

51. In *Being and Nothingness*, pp.79 ff.

incarnates this contingency by his own: when the ignorance and blindness intrinsic to every undertaking that casts itself towards an insufficiently determined future are identified with the ignorance, the blindness, the intellectual limits and the obstinacies of *one* particular individual. There can be no doubt but that this reinforcement can and must have positive results (at least in the 'ascending' period of action). It was the Russian Revolution's fortune that its voluntarism should be incarnated in the will of the 'Man of Steel'. But *by the same token*, certain negative features found themselves exaggerated by singularization of the sovereign. Stalin being *less cultured* than Trotsky, the sovereign as a whole would reproduce his shortcomings. The bureaucrat – tired out and, as circumstances permitted, hastily acquiring knowledge that was always new and always inadequate – would be characterized, *inasmuch as he was Stalin himself*, by a universal incompetence. Marxism ossified into a hardened dogmatism. We know, of course, that this was a practical necessity and that culture had to be vulgarized in order to raise the level of the masses rapidly. Peasants in the process of urbanization had made Marxism crude, but their sons – beneficiaries of this absolutely new inheritance: popular culture – would find again, in an expanded form, the exigencies of revolutionaries under Tsarism. *On the other hand*, however, that dogmatic crudeness was precisely a feature of Stalin the militant: a man of action for whom principles had to remain unshakeable, since it was impossible to act and at the same time call them into question. Likewise typical of Stalin was the constant invention of new principles, which were added to the others without contradicting them (or without it being permitted to make the contradictions explicit), and whose sole function was to furnish a theoretical justification for an opportunistic decision. Empiricism and pedantry: this mixture was not *rejected*, of course, by circumstances, but its actual source was Stalin himself. And when everything had been said to explain the appearance of the slogan 'Socialism in one country', there still remained that elusive residue that was the Stalinist incarnation: after all, *it was Stalin* who had invented it.

These comments lead further. If it were possible (though despite appearances this possibility is rarely given) for the historian to make a precise inventory *of what circumstances demanded*, and if on this basis he could construct – if only as an abstract schema – the programme that could have been realized by taking account only of the objective exigencies, then in the case of the sovereign-individual it might be possible to explain by contingency – by the finitude of *this* man – the gap between this minimum programme and the one that was actually implemented. Thus it is that, for many non-Stalinist Marxists, industrialization and collectivization necessitated an unbelievable intensity of national effort in the USSR, so could not develop without *constraint*. Peasant resistance too struck them as inevitable, and the immediate creation (from 1928 on) of large agricultural farms as the only way of ensuring food supplies. They simply wondered *whether it was not possible* to avoid the propaganda lies, the purges, the police oppression in working-class centres, and the terrible repression of peasant revolts. In so far as most concluded that these 'excesses' were in fact inevitable, it can be said that they acquitted the first phase of socialism – as a process of accelerated growth – and blamed Stalin alone (or, which comes to the same thing, his entourage and his advisers). For my part, I am not trying here to determine *what could have been avoided*. All that matters to me is the fact that (in a way which in spite of everything is fairly vague, and for good reason: the real history of the Plans and their implementation is still more or less inaccessible to us) the singularization of sovereignty leads to posing the problem of a deformation of praxis by the sovereign. He 'did' both more and less than necessary. In the absence of accurate documents, it is hard or even impossible to determine *the moment at which* the slippage began, which perhaps made inevitable *in those circumstances* the great purges of the last pre-war years. But precisely in so far as the exigency of those purges and the 'Moscow Trials' was not contained in the totalizing objectivity of industrial growth in an underdeveloped country, the origin of the slippage *must* be imputed to Stalin, for the simple reason that he was at once the sovereign totalization and the singularity of an individual. In this way, it seems that we are reintroducing a kind of positivist analysis at the heart of the dialectical movement: with more flexibility, more foresight, more respect for human lives, *one* would have been able to obtain the same result (collectivization, for example) without shedding a drop of blood; but Stalin – more inflexible, because more narrow-minded and less imaginative – took to an extreme the tendency of Russian constructivism, which was to subordinate man to the construction of machines (i.e. subordinate men to worked materiality); by *his* decision, production pronounced sentence upon men and condemned them to death if that was more *convenient*. Do we not find again here two series of independent factors, and thereby that irrational at the heart of positive Reason: chance?

Let us temporarily leave chance aside.[52] Let us just examine the two series of factors and attempt to determine if they are really independent.

Let us concede – which seems most likely by far – that the exigencies of the process did not entirely justify Stalin's procedures. If praxis (like truth for Hegel) *became*, that meant that the results obtained by Stalinist

---

52. See footnote 97 on p.334; also 'Is History Essential to Man?' in Appendix below, p.450.

coercion – even if *quantitatively* they were indeed those that industrialization as a whole required; even if the number of tons of pig-iron
produced in 1934 was exactly what the experts could foresee and demand*
– were *different* from the realizations that the praxis-process of safeguarding socialism demanded. We have seen, in fact, that they were not
mere quantities, but were determined at the heart of totalization by their
relations *of interiority* with all the other parts, in all the other sectors.
From this viewpoint – and for socialization as the liberation of man – ten
million tons of pig-iron obtained by threats and bloody measures of
coercion (executions, concentration camps, etc.) were *on no account*
comparable to ten million tons of pig-iron obtained in the same perspective
and by an authoritarian government, but without coercive measures. This
transformation of the result by the use of violence had to have its
repercussions in the immediate and distant future. The internally linked
ensemble of these transformations and their consequences, moreover,
could in the long run constitute a deviation of praxis. We have already
seen praxis deviated by its own results (for example, when the hierarchization of wages led to the stratification of social layers). But at least
that was only an internal reaction of the global action to its counter-
finalities. In so far as the purges and trials have to be blamed on Stalin,
however, the deviation resulting from them must be attributed to factors
that were personal, and for that very reason *extraneous* to the revolutionary totalization.

However, let us have a closer look. *What came* from praxis itself was
the fact that, through its temporalization, it had engendered circumstances such that the organs of sovereignty had no other means of
subsisting and acting than to resign their powers into the hands of *one*
individual. What was involved here was indeed a fundamental inner
characterization of *that* praxis – something which was all the clearer, in
that it had arisen in total contradiction with the conception of the Party
(centralized democracy with a collective leadership) and as *the only
outcome*. But *from the moment* when praxis demanded the facticity of the
individual sovereign, it contained within it – as an immediate counter-
finality – the need to bear the mark of an individuality. It is strictly
speaking conceivable, in fact, that a project produced by an office – each
detail of which has been fixed by *all* the collaborators, after discussion,
and above all after a systematic elimination by everyone of the personal
factor of each individual – should be able to present itself as a strictly
objective response to the objective exigencies of praxis and its field. But
this is because the unity of the common individuals has been accomplished

---

* Actually, we know that this was not the case.

over the negation of every concrete person. Thus an attempt has been
made to realize pure and anonymous action, which is determined or
qualified only in accordance with its object.* The truth is that, in so far
as this attempt has been successful, it has been confined to producing a
practical abstraction. It will be necessary to resort to mediated incarnations
in order to objectify it in the field. This matters little, however. If this
anonymity – this suppression of men, in favour of a calculated system –
can appear at a certain stage of the programme's construction, it is all the
clearer that the personal factor *cannot* be eliminated if the sovereign is
one person. Such elimination presupposes a wheeling reciprocity; a
certain distance between everybody and everybody else: in short, *plurality*
and – in a certain way – an integration that is not yet too 'extensive'. But
when the system as a whole demands a personal sovereign in the name of
maximum integration, and so that he can be – at the apex of the pyramid
– the living suppression of every multiplicity; and when the constructive
effort of the USSR implies that this society – which has driven out every
organicist ideology – finds its unity in the biological indissolubility of an
individual; then it is not even conceivable that this individual could be,
in himself and in his praxis, eliminated as an idiosyncrasy in favour of
an abstract objectivity. To be sure, he does not *know* himself in his
particularism: Stalin *did not know* Stalin and was concerned only with
the objective circumstances. But it is precisely when he does not know
himself that the individual – whether or not he is sovereign – is summed
up in his particularity. In a leading body, it is precisely in so far as
everyone knows each other's *hexis* that this can be eliminated. Well, on
the basis of this, everything takes on another meaning. To those who say
that *an other* would have had greater abilities, broader views, more
extensive knowledge, etc., we shall reply – without entering into a
discussion of possibles[53] – that this other, supposing he had existed,
would have been precisely *an other*: i.e. he would not have opposed
Stalin like pure objectivity opposing idiosyncrasy, but like *one singularity*

---

* We saw earlier, and shall see again later, that *even so* one does not escape the
singularization of praxis *as common praxis*. For it is not what objectivity demands, but
what *these* given men determine, on the basis of exigencies which they have grasped
through *their intellectual tools*. It remains the case, of course, that the object itself
corresponds, in its very texture, to the structures of the contemporary agents. But this does
not imply that you can avoid a certain *inequality* between the exigency (of the object, for
these given men in *this* given historical context) and the response (of this collegial group,
which has sought to eliminate any personal equation, but has merely suppressed singular
differentiations while preserving the common singularity of structures and pledged
inertias).

53. See footnote 97 on p.334 below.

opposing another singularity. When Stalin's policy is attacked, Stalinists often reply: 'Perhaps, but if Trotsky had been in power, we should be honouring the memory of the late Russian Revolution like that of the Paris Commune.' I do not know if that is true or false. Above all, moreover, we shall be seeing how much importance should be attached to 'ifs'. But the argument does have a merit (albeit one not realized by those who use it). This is the fact that it precisely contrasts the 'particularity' Trotsky with the 'particularity' Stalin. 'Yes, Trotsky was more intelligent, more cultured and, moreover, an excellent organizer; but who knows whether the radicalism he expressed, and which formed part of his idiosyncrasy ... ?' So we should be wrong to claim that the system required *a man*, as an indeterminate bearer of *praxis*, rather than Stalin. In fact (and even in this form we shall see that it is only half true), if the system requires a man, the latter will in any case be a strict synthesis of specific determinations (transcended in his idiosyncratic temporalization). The individual required by the system will be determined, and will determine praxis by his very determination. All that can be said, in such a case, is that his determination is certain, but – in relation to the exigency of praxis – indeterminate. As a consequence, the idiosyncratic determination of the totalizing praxis – and of the system through it – is *inevitable*, although at the outset it remains indeterminate. The first phase of socialization will bear the mark of a man – Trotsky or Stalin or some other – which means that this vast common undertaking cannot give itself a sovereign-individual without itself becoming, through certain of his faults and excesses, that individual in person. What is involved is a case of *overdetermination of History*: praxis is obliged to receive more and less than it has asked for; it demands to be integrated through the mediation of an individual, but is abruptly individualized. For the absolute model of integration is the classic example of idiosyncrasy, and these two characteristics condition one another reciprocally.

If the process of planned growth could be directed by an angel, moreover, praxis would doubtless have the maximum of unity combined with the maximum of objectivity. The angel would never be blind, or pigheaded, or brutal: in every case, he would do what ought to be done. For this very reason, however, angels are not individuals. They are abstract models of virtue and wisdom. In a situation, the genuine individual – ignorant, anxious, fallible, disconcerted by the sudden urgency of danger – will react (depending on his history) at first too softly, then, on the point of being overwhelmed, too brutally. Those jolts, those accelerations, those brakings, those hairpin bends, those acts of violence which characterized Stalinism – they were not all required by the objectives and exigencies of socialization. Yet they were inevitable, inasmuch as that socialization demanded, in its first phase, to be directed by an individual.

We have reduced the role of chance without eliminating it. We have signalled that the necessities of integration made that chance, whatever it might be, *necessary*. The fact remains that the content of the chance does not seem determined by exigency. However, let us return once again to the circumstances that tipped the balance in favour of Stalin.

For it should be recalled – *first and foremost* – that the sovereign totalization, even when the sovereign is a group, is *in itself* already singularized. Not only does it relate to particular objectives, but it also relates to them in a particular way. We have seen that one of the aspects of political conflicts within the Bolshevik Party reflected a certain singular situation defining the party's historical action. By virtue of this singularity, praxis escaped itself and was overwhelmed: if it had been able to recover and adopt it, in fact, it would have become a feature of the final objective rather than a quality of the action. Precisely in so far as this singularity was a determination of the practical without being a practical determination, praxis as a whole closed up and became a process.

For if we take the leading group in its objective reality – inasmuch as the observer or historian situates himself outside it and its sovereignty – it strikes us as a practical community formed by exfoliation from seriality, by dissolution within it of the alterity of impotence. The Bolshevik Party was constituted through a whole history that included becoming aware (for every member) of the Russian situation, militant activity in Russia, the 1905 Revolution, conflicts among exiles, tension between the revolutionary emigration and the militants who stayed in Russia, the War, the fall of Tsarism and the October Revolution. That means, first of all, that this practical group defined itself by transcendence of its serial-being. And this being had defined itself in alienation as a determination of the practico-inert field. This field itself was constituted at once as class-being and national-being. This should be taken to mean that the class-being of the proletariat as a series was particularized by the synthetic ensemble of the economic, social and political development that was contained and determined by the historical frontiers. And we do not mean just the circumstances so often mentioned: numerical weakness of the bourgeoisie and proletariat; persistence of a feudal State and a landed aristocracy; rapid industrialization, but inadequate and dependent upon foreign capital; contradiction in the peasantry between a traditionalist conservatism and a genuinely revolutionary violence; specific features of a working class in mid formation and without real homogeneity, etc. We are alluding also to characteristics of a geographical and ethnic nature (situation of Russia as a Eurasian nation, national minorities, etc.), as well as to historical and cultural determinations that depended on these (economic, political and cultural relations with other countries) and the specifically Russian contradictions that were the result ('European' tendency to universalization; particularist tendency to withdrawal into itself). These characteristics cannot for a moment be envisaged as separate factors: they existed, in fact, only in so far as they were transcended by collective or individual activities which preserved them by transcending them (that of the Baku worker seeking to unite with other workers who did not speak his language; that of the bourgeois employer who depended on European capital and remained isolated, cut off from the great economic currents of the West by the political and social predominance of the big feudal landlords; that of the revolutionary intellectuals, hesitating between a movement 'towards the people' – springing from Christianity or anarchism but specifically Russian – and a Marxist doctrine borrowed from abroad, etc.). Each of these activities was in its singularity the expression of all the others and their practical compre-hension. Free praxis, in fact, was only a totalizing transcendence of all the conditions we have enumerated; and these conditions themselves were only the ensemble of all free practices, inasmuch as they were mediated by worked matter and inasmuch as they were alienated in the practico-inert by being objectified in it. Thus every totalizing activity was a practico-inert element of a detotalized series – at once in the outpouring of its free totalizing project towards an objective goal and in its necessary alienation.

From this standpoint, the revolutionary movement – as a pledged, then organized, group – was simply the transcendence of *this* alienation and *this* necessity in the common tension of Fraternity-Terror. As such, it preserved *all* its characteristics. That means, in the first place, that the worker or intellectual who entered the movement did not thereby lose the totalized structures which caused him to realize his serial-being through the totalizing project that attempted to transcend it. So everyone, although changing by virtue of the oath sworn into a common individual, remained a singular and alienated totalization of all the other totalizations. The new awareness – which was a common praxis – was not the *de-situated* contemplation of class-being or the historical ensemble. The process was revealed by the individuals it had produced or, if you like, who had produced themselves by producing it: i.e. it was itself the limit and specific quality of its revelation, inasmuch as it had marked in an indelible way the practical organisms it had produced. In order to make this reflexive reversal more easily comprehensible, we shall express it in terms of pure knowledge and say that every militant deciphered the practico-inert process through and by the principles and presuppositions, the schemata and the traditions, that this process had produced in him, so that totalization was circular. Depending on the viewpoint, it is just as possible to see reflection as *retotalizing* the conditions totalized by the unreflecting project, as it is to see the synthetic totality of the transcended conditions as totalizing – in this very transcendence – the deciphering carried out by reflection.

From this standpoint, it was not just Stalin but – before his victory – all the members of the sovereign who were singular. It was the sovereign itself whose praxis was doubly singular: on the basis of the common stock of former circumstances, and as a singularized product of their conflicts and shifting alliances. Now, in this ensemble of organisms, it may *on the one hand* be considered that every common individual was *appropriated* to the exigencies of the ruled, because he had lived an identical past with them, and *on the other hand* that certain individuals or groups were more specifically close to the masses, because they had lived that common past in a certain specific way which caused them to comprehend better the situation and the demands of the ruled. From this point of view, we have already seen that Stalin defeated Trotsky *precisely in so far as* the proletarian Revolution, *by being born Russian*, was nationalized and, observing the ebb of the revolutionary movements outside, undertook a movement of withdrawal into itself – partly the product and partly the source of Soviet mistrust of the European prole- tariats. In other words, when the Revolution *was incarnated* in the USSR, it automatically effected a weakening of the internationalist emigration in favour of the national militants. Thus, from the moment of Lenin's death, there was an obvious adaptation of Stalin, the Georgian militant, and of the revolutionary incarnation. We have seen, moreover, that the country – even in its working-class elite – was hostile to theory, to universalism (an *intellectual* form of internationalism) and to radical- ism, and prepared to commit itself to a cautious, pragmatic construction of its new order. Nothing astonishing in the fact that the ruled found Stalin here, since he had lived the same past as they and in the same way. His singularity – as a retotalization of his practical thought by his past actions – met their own, and that of the socialization under way. And it was indeed as a representative of Russian particularism – believing in *dogmas* and mistrusting *theories*, imbued with the singularity of the problem of socialization in Russia (i.e. with the fundamental singularity of Russian events), convinced that no Western conception could find a field of application in that complex country, assured *both* of the techno- logical and cultural inferiority of the Russians compared with other Europeans *and at the same time* of their *human* superiority (energy, courage, endurance, etc.) – it was indeed as a patient militant, slow- witted, tenacious, seeking to discover the Russian truth progessively, that he had found the necessary alliances in the Party and even in the factories to get rid of the Right and Left theorists who opposed one another in the name of the same universality. From that moment on, it can be said that the revolutionary incarnation had chosen the singular over the universal and the national over the international. And Stalin, before being the singular chosen, appeared as the incarnation of the common choice of the singular.

To be sure, it is not because it was choosing itself in its singularity that the praxis of socialization made the choice of a singular sovereign. We know that Stalin's authority came from the emergency, and from the need for coercion in an incipient socialist order that was interiorized in the leading organisms in the form of an ever stricter exigency of integration. The Terror chose itself through Stalin. But even Stalin's place was marked by the combination of these two movements. The Terror was born of the emergency, the latter of the encirclement and blockade – hence, of *forced* singularity. On the other hand, the national singularization – as distrust of foreign countries and intellectuals – contained within itself, as withdrawal into itself, the elements of a social attitude: suspicion. Suspicion, as a serial rule, at once demanded its opposite, the man who was above all suspicion: he alone would be allowed to escape the round of suspects. Of course, suspicion could arise with maximum intensity only if the singularization of experience found itself facing an objective emergency requiring Terror. That vague distrust of foreign lands and all that recalled them was transformed, in *the contraction of the milieu* that was the inner structure of Terror, into *vigilance against traitors*. And that distrust – in the contraction-terror – was certainly not devoid of objective foundation: foreign countries were still to be feared, so long as the gap had not been closed between their potential for war and industrial production and that of the USSR. And as the very meaning of planning was *precisely* (in its urgency) to close that gap as soon as possible, at every moment of his own productive activity each person encountered the united bourgeois democracies, as *external* sources of the internal coercion that was imposed upon him. Furthermore, the counter-revolutionaries were or had been hand in glove with the foreigners, as the civil war had proved; faced with the growing dangers, moreover, everybody thought that the country was teeming with spies. But that mistrust, as an inner consequence of singularization, was precisely one of Stalin's typical attitudes: i.e. a sediment of his history. And without going into his life in detail, it is well enough known that this mistrust was produced and maintained in the articulation of Georgian particularism and Russian national unity; theory (conceived as a negative dogmatism from which there was no deviating) and praxis; the emigration that gave him orders and the militants left in Russia who obeyed him.

It is here that we touch on the fundamental nature of the sovereign incarnation. The common praxis demanded to be channelled into an individual praxis, and thereby to submit its inner necessities to the synthetic unity of a contingent facticity (*in fact, faced with the difficulties*

*of integration, the constituted dialectic sought to dissolve itself in the
constituent dialectic, to return to the womb that had produced it).* This
meant that it submitted itself to a sovereign-individual whose *qualities*
(*hexis*) overflowed action and were *something other* than what it demanded
(both more and less), which obliged the common praxis – i.e. the
sovereign group – simultaneously to adopt deviations whose origin was *a
single person* and to consider this phase of temporalization as limited *by
death* (by the death *of a single person*): i.e. to accept the risks of
disintegration in the future (and in a changed situation) in order to avoid
them in the present. But if it is true that by being incarnated in this way
praxis gave itself a deep structure of *contingency*, it is not true that any
old individual – as contingent – was fit to become its sovereign (and I am
speaking, of course, only of the *few* persons who could garner Lenin's
heritage). Totalizing action, in fact, also has its contingent singularity
(which, as we shall see, appears mainly to diachronic totalization),
which, for *its* part, is in no way exclusive of its dialectical intelligibility.
The study of Europe in 1914 might show that the feudal structures of
Russia could not resist a world war, and that the balance of forces –
within a historical situation – designated her *alone* to make the proletarian
Revolution. Diachronic totalization might show, subsequently, the strict
bond between proletarian revolutions and the underdevelopment of the
countries that make them (and which, paradoxically, are the least prepared, *it seems*, to make them). Yet it would still remain the case that
revolutionary praxis and the total movement of society inspired by it
were the *unique* (which will remain unique, because it happened *first in
time*) and singular incarnation (the other planned constructions will
occur in other circumstances, and *first of all* they will occur *after this
one*, which at once means they will take Russian methods for a strict
model and strive to benefit from the Soviet experience in order to avoid
errors); and that these features of uniqueness and singularity, far from
being mere inert qualities disclosing themselves to the contemplation of
historians, reveal themselves on the contrary by their historical efficacy.
Unique, the Russian Revolution could be crushed: the policy of the
bourgeois democracies was guided by this characterization, and that
same policy interiorized as mistrust was to sustain the Terror. Earliest in
time, the October Revolution would give the USSR an uncontested
leadership over the socialist world, etc. We have seen, furthermore, that
this historical uniqueness necessarily had to be lived and realized as a
national particularism. Thus *contingency* – i.e. the individual qualities of
sovereign praxis – was circumscribed and determined. The Russian
Revolution rejected Trotsky because Trotsky was the international Revolution. An undertaking which launched itself into the unknown, and could
refuse neither backward steps (as was seen with the NEP) nor compromises

(as was seen with the principle of nationalities) if it saw these as a practical necessity, it needed the rigidity of dogmas all the more in that it did not apply them. It kept them inviolable precisely in so far as it departed from them, so as to be able to return to them after such temporary detours. Hence, it demanded a sovereign who would be a dogmatic opportunist. Which meant, basically, that this sovereign had to have a keen awareness of the originality of the Russian experience; and that he had both to keep Marxism out of range – as the distant, universalist signification of that experience – and at the same time subordinate it to the latter, within praxis, as a practical and changing illumination of events (i.e. one susceptible of being transformed at any moment by them). It demanded – though I shall not insist on this – a militant known by the militants, knowing them and forged by militancy (he alone could *integrate* the Party). He was required too by the job he would perform (i.e. by the additional labour he would impose on the workers and peasants, with all the well-known consequences) as inflexible, coolheaded and unimaginative. Finally, the very fact that the experience was *singular* demanded that he should adapt action *to singular circumstances*, without any reference (other than formal) to principles, and that the mistrust engendered by isolation – result and source of national singularization – should be lived in practice by him as his own singularization. In so far as praxis demanded integration, it demanded also that its common orienta- tions should become, under the constraint of biological unity, *qualities* indissolubly linked to the sovereign's personal action. And in so far as these qualities came to the sovereign person as a retotalization of his current praxis by his revolutionary past (i.e. by the *common* past of the Revolution), the exigencies of totalization did not relate to a contingent exteriority – a happy chance that had supposedly provided the sovereign individual with these qualities – but, quite the contrary, to a certain way of having transcended and preserved the common past, whose particularity appeared in the light of the current praxis as the *developed truth* of the former practice and experience. Thus, not only did praxis require individuality inasmuch as this was forged by praxis (hence, inasmuch as its *hexis* was the sediment of praxis), and so require itself retrospectively; but it was also current action that gave *its meaning and its truth* to the practical experience of the individual it selected.

The Personal Equation: Necessity of Deviation

Can we say, then, that Stalin was required, even in what was most singular about him, even in the determinations that came to him from his milieu, from his childhood, from the *private* features of his adventure (for example, attendance at the Seminary, etc.)? Was *that Georgian former seminarist* really necessary? There will be a temptation to answer yes, if one of the themes developed in *The Problem of Method* is recalled.[54] I showed there, in fact, that the child, through his family situation, realizes the singularization of generalities (milieu and – via the milieu – class, nationality, etc.). This is what allowed us to view psychoanalysis as one of the mediations necessary within the Marxist interpretation. So some may perhaps seek to find in Stalin's rough childhood, inasmuch as it was interiorized as harshness, a factor of his future adaptation to revolutionary praxis. And that is perfectly correct. Nevertheless, a relative autonomy of mediated sectors must be considered here, within the living totality. This does not mean that each is not in the other, but it does at all events imply their practical irreducibility: i.e. the impossibility of dissolving them into a monism of homogeneity. In other words, Stalin's harshness and inflexibility, inasmuch as they had their source in his earliest childhood, were indeed the results (the preservative transcendences) of the social contradictions which, taken in their full dimensions, were certainly among the fundamental factors of the Russian Revolution. More accurately, the child – through that rough childhood and through the violence of his revolt – incarnated and singularized the practical totalization constituting that moment of Russia's history. However, in so far as that childhood tended to structure all his behaviour without discrimination – *inasmuch* as it occurred *as a childhood* and *with the specific features of that age* – this mediation between the individual and his social basis was also a separation that posited itself for itself, unless the aim of the historian (or merely the friend or enemy) is to comprehend the individual through his biography. For in the latter case, since the aim remains singularization of the social, we shall end up meeting all mediations in each one, *inasmuch as we are seeking there only the synthetic foundation of idiosyncrasy*. I have shown in *The Problem of Method* how the various mediations, through a practical and singular transcendence, are organized into a plurality of irreducible dimensions each one of which contains all the others and refers back to all the others.[55] But if our aim, as in the case of totalization of praxis by the sovereign-individual, is to show on the contrary *the socialization of the singular*, it is only the person's revolutionary past that is called into question, inasmuch as it *makes* the quality of his current praxis (for example, the fact that Stalin was active in Russia, inasmuch as he was thereby predisposed to understand better and favour the current of

---

54. See *The Problem of Method*, pp.57 ff.
55. Ibid.

national isolationism). For it is that past alone to which the exigency of common action refers. In other words, there is no irreducible *given*, in the sense that every separation is also a mediation and every mediation is itself mediated (autonomy does not imply an unintelligible pluralism).* In a previously specified perspective of study, however, the totalizing dialectic encounters irreducibles (varying in accordance with its object), simply because these sectors are produced by mediations that do not refer to the synchronic totalization in progress (even if, as we shall see, they may be recuperated by diachronic totalization).[56] From this point of view, in relation to the praxis that began in 1928 there are idiosyncratic and *relatively opaque givens*, although from another point of view they can regain their intelligibility. In reality, it is not a matter of the passage *from one order of facts to another*. Childhood is a social fact and the incarnation of the process under way, just as the action of the adult sovereign is. Rather, these are contradictions inherent in any irreversible temporalization which – as we shall see shortly – oblige the historian to vary his viewpoints, and to totalize the same social and practical evolution in different ways according to the incarnations under consideration. From the viewpoint of the dialectical biography of Stalin, nothing can be understood if you do not go back to that childhood and that milieu. But if the situation in 1928 in fact required the sovereign's inflexibility, this requirement left undetermined the question of the individual origins of that inflexibility. And since the latter could become the *hexis* of the person required on the basis of an infinity of conceivable childhoods, everything happened as though – its genesis being unimportant – it were presenting itself as *a given character trait*. For that very reason, moreover, it would also and necessarily present itself as *not being exactly the inflexibility required*. If engendered by the praxis demanding it, it might perhaps have been so. But in so far as it came, despite everything, from elsewhere (i.e. from that same praxis, but inasmuch as a certain relation of anteriority – varying according to circumstances – made it *other than itself*), its practical objective could not originally be the difficult construction of a new society; and the very situation that required it implied that it was not *fitted for its task*, but merely more or less unfitted. Which, of course, presupposed that the sovereign-individual would progressively adapt himself to praxis, in so far as praxis adapted itself to his pre-fabricated idiosyncrasy. From one compromise to another, the balance

---

* Unlike positivism, which enumerates character traits without there being any possibility of moving from one to another: 'He was an anti-Semite; he liked tennis; he had artistic tastes.'

56. See Preface.

would finally be achieved by a transformation of the man and a deviation of the undertaking.

But it is here, precisely, that the spurious rationality of Plekhanov must be rejected, since in fact he simply referred back to a positivist irrational. He sought to eliminate from praxis – even when the sovereign was an individual – any personal equation, *at least at the level of History*: i.e. once trivial detail was discounted.

Now there are two ways of attempting such an elimination: his own and another, even more extravagant. Both formally conceivable, but in practice absurd. It could be argued in fact – though no one, I think, has done so – that if all the possible variations of inflexibility, in quality and in quantity, had been produced in the USSR and had produced their men (one for each) by placing them in a position to take power, common praxis, through a 'struggle for life' that would have pitted all these inflexibles against one another, would itself have chosen the individual variety that exactly suited it. In other words, it would be a question here of an infinite series, in which the characteristic required (and the man, its bearer) would necessarily be contained as *one of the possibles*. Teleological adaptation – since it is assumed to be lacking – is replaced by a rational selection. This Darwinism of the sovereign-person is in itself so absurd that it has never been imagined, other than here precisely as an element in a *reductio ad absurdum*. But should Plekhanov's Lamarckism be seen as any less idiotic? He imagines Napoleon being killed at Toulon,[57] and Augereau or Moreau replacing him.[58] It had to be one of them, since the bourgeoisie demanded a personal sovereign. Now this is to assume not merely – and we have criticized him on this point – that the consequences of such a change of dictator are historically insignificant, *but also* that – essentially – Augereau or Moreau would have adapted to the exigencies of the Thermidorian bourgeoisie without deviating them; that they would have been able to fill the post they had taken; that they would not at once have been overthrown by other generals; that they would have ended the wars or carried them through victoriously – in any case, that they would not have lost them thanks to a series of ill-judged battles, and above all to the Army's mistrust. It is no use here replying that *the* Thermidorian bourgeoisie *had to* support the dictator (who alone would give it the regime it required), and that *the Army* as such *had to* win the battles (given its structure, its interests and the new function it

---

57. In 1793, when the city was taken from the royalists, Bonaparte was only a captain of artillery.

58. At the time already outstanding generals. We may recall that Moreau, who supported the 18 Brumaire, was Bonaparte's rival.

exercised in the nation). For the dictator was precisely required when the common forces *needed his mediation* to carry on their action. That means this mediation was not symbolic but *practical*: in other words, the sovereign-individual had to achieve the integration of the national forces or disappear, ruining the nation. And this, of course, was due to the very circumstances that had structured the social powers of the directing groups and the society – ruled *in such a way* that praxis would be either paralysed or centralized in the hands of a single person. So Plekhanov's error is manifest. Because he did not understand that society turns itself into an individual in the person of the dictator, and that in these conditions the latter's practical role is vital, he imagined that anybody would serve the purpose provided he was present at the right moment. So that ultimately his Lamarckism (the function creates the man who exercises it) converged with the Darwinism we have rejected: the historical process is neither incarnated nor individualized; as a general and abstract movement, it may pick up a man at one moment and assign him a sovereign function; but this man will be produced by his function, hence adapted to it; and if a few contingent *qualities* overflow his action (one being more combative, another more peaceful), at all events the process under way will by itself correct his temporary deviations. That means that the process – conceived as universal – universalizes the action of specific individuals.

Meaning of Deviation: Man Is Not Made for Man

But if we admit that the circumstance – i.e. the moving structure of society in action – decides the individual's powers; if we hold to be a strict consequence of that experiential truth the fact that these powers can be immense and consequently demand *abilities*; if, on the other hand, we are convinced by the ensemble of our dialectical studies that the adaptation of the man to his function – when it is a question of adults, and when it is the *function* that produces the *functionary* – is a difficult process (because of the interiorized past) and often very slow (because of the resistance of that structured past); if we observe – as we have just done – that this adaptation, if it takes place, deviates the function precisely in so far as it transforms the individual; and if, finally, against Plekhanov's universalization (i.e. decompression and detotalization), we pit the concrete and incarnated totalization: then we must recognize *simultaneously* that nothing can limit a priori the agent's role in a given historical ensemble, and that – when the ensemble requires of the sovereign-individual a genuine *ability* – human history is no longer defined merely by the scarcity of products, tools, etc., but *also*, suddenly, *by the scarcity of men.* This means that if it is inflexibility which is required, not only will *all* varieties of inflexibles not be found, but perhaps there will be just one – or sometimes *none at all*. In any event, the men who will be in a position to exercise power will *certainly* represent a number of practical possibilities infinitely small in relation to the totalized series of possibles of that kind. And every realized possibility – if it were to be replaced in the total series – would be separated by an infinity of possibles from the other realized possibles. At these *moments* of socialization of the individual and individualization of society, the candidates for sovereignty are *rare*. None serves the purpose fully. And the one who comes closest to the model required, even if he takes power, dragged down by scarcity of time will begin his operation before he has been able to adapt himself to the exigencies of praxis. It is a strict necessity that History, when it is determined by scarcity of men, should be totalized by a sovereign whose relative unfitness for his functions incarnates and singularizes that iron law of scarcity. As we have seen, scarcity – a dialectical fact, the interiorization of a practical relation between the man and the field – affects all sectors, all levels and all realities, depending on what circumstances demand. And *every time* it signifies that *the world is not made for man*.* Under the rubric 'scarcity of means', it is possible to classify the scarcity of *instruments* (worked matter) that is one of the factors in the constitution of classes (by exploitation) and – in the present case, *after* the overthrow of the landowner and bourgeois regime – that determines the necessity of the construction of machines to make machines and tools. But this scarcity of means *in turn affects* and defines man, if man is to be a means (in the

---

* It is an experience marked just as much by *superabundance* of men. For, in the functional, primary relationship of scarcity (it would be possible to find as many examples, albeit more complex, in secondary and tertiary scarcity, etc.), it may happen that the government takes men as independent variables: in a besieged medieval city, as in a modern nation at a time of economic recession, the experts will conclude that there are *useless mouths*. In other words, their surplus character (in relation to resources), far from being compensated for by their practical utilized, becomes a dangerously powerful brake for any common praxis attempting to correct the imperfections of the field or to destroy counter-finalities, at the (necessary) price of a terrible, savage effort (fighting without eating more than once a day, if we go back to the example of the people under siege). The liberatory or regulatory action designates its own waste-products. It is always possible to cast these out of the city (in the capitalist period, this means allowing the price index to rise and poverty gradually to liquidate the surplus). But *even these practices*, in their blithe casualness, are not always effective (or provoke rebellion and the regime's overthrow).

Scarcity and superabundance of men are often linked, moreover. Too many candidates for a post, but none fulfils the required conditions. Depending on the case, the post will not be 'filled' or it will be filled badly; and it will be necessary to envisage transferring the 'unlucky candidates' to other sectors, and perhaps to *reskill* them in work – which presupposes a social expenditure.

sense in which the sovereign serves praxis and is a mediator between groups). If it is true that there are not enough men – or not the right men – for a specific undertaking, we sense through this scarcity the incarnation of the following historical truth: man, as a product of the world, is not made for man.*

This experience constitutes the supplementary signification which, at moments when the conduct of national affairs is entrusted to a *person* or a specific aristocracy (*the* Venetian Senate and *the* Councils emanating from it), characterizes History itself. The men History makes are never entirely those needed to make History, be they even as unrivalled as Stalin or Napoleon. Of course, the complex nature of the military dictatorship (supported by the bourgeois and the Army) *proposed* the war; of course, it rendered war easier to make than peace; of course, Napoleon ended up wishing (but too late) to call a halt to the bloodshed; and, of course, the weight of the past – reinteriorized *in the enemy camp* by tense and shifting relations among the allies (conflicts that war alone could resolve) and by a stratification of internal structures (militarized nations and economies: arming and feeding the troops, realizing blockade economies, etc.), and retranscended in a project to carry the war through to the end – almost from the outset left little chance for negotiations (what happened with all the various meetings and treaties is well known). There can be no doubt, however, that peace was *required* – in the shorter or longer term – by the bourgeoisie which had supported the *coup d'état*, and that it would have been easy to get the officers to *accept* it (while as for the men, they were worn out and peace was the only thing they wanted). *The man of peace* (that Robespierre would doubtless have been, just as he had been the man of war against the suspected pacifists of 1794) was *in any event* not Napoleon. Since the bloodletting of the Terror, he had been absent. And the most remarkable war leader of modern times waged war to the bitter end with a people who wanted peace, while at the same time endowing the latter with institutions at once republican** (universalist) and dictatorial (centralization); at once peaceful (the Code has survived him, and has survived a century in which our wars – for once – have taken up less time than the periods of peace) and military (the idea being to standardize men by standardizing culture and education, etc., and – as under the Roman emperors – to return the individual to *his property* as his juridical and inalienable

---

* [Note missing in manuscript.]
** I.e. bourgeois. The Code was bourgeois, since it realized the wish of the Constituent Assembly: it was a casuistry of private property. It was military, because it reduced the person to his property, which – provided *property* was scrupulously respected – allowed practical rights (freedom) of the person to be reduced to zero.

particularity, while stripping him of his practical reality or channelling his actions to the government's advantage: Civil Code, etc.).

So far as Stalin is concerned, we have seen which circumstances required – at the outset – the incarnation to be *a withdrawal into themselves*. And we have seen how universal Reason – as an abstraction of the dialectic – was on Trotsky's side, but not that concrete Reason which reveals itself as it is formulated. To take just these few examples, however, such a withdrawal *did not demand* pushing cultural isolationism to absurd lengths. Similarly, the difference in living standards between the Western worker and the Soviet worker was so great at the outset that the situation *proposed* the 'iron curtain': but it *did not demand* that endless lies should be told about the condition of European workers. Especially since a few years later the Russian people – brought into contact with capitalist nations by the armies of occupation – was by and large (and contrary to Stalin's apprehensions) not at all tempted by the regimes it discovered. In other words, the official veil of lies and omissions could have been lifted progressively, especially after the 1945 contact. It was Stalin himself who maintained it: who systematically developed Soviet society's particularist mistrust (the objective reasons for which we know), and transformed it into acute spy-mania around 1950. His ever-present fear of a possible influence of European culture was, in a sense, only the development and new orientation of his rejection (between 1924 and 1928) of universalism. We know that this was to give rise to the radical negation of cosmopolitanism (merely a *cruder* form of universalism) in favour of national cultures. Yet the USSR was not embarrassed – and *with good reason* – about importing foreign technology; and the situation would have required her to be able to import and transform into her own substance foreign cultural values too. Its extraordinary industrial growth – for which Stalin, as sovereign and incarnation of Russian society, was primarily responsible – led the country in around 1950 to *require* a policy of expansion, while the leader and the organs of his power continued, in their mistrust, to pursue a policy of withdrawal. And it was Stalin again, through his hatred of all internationalism (as a *universal* link between socialist nations and revolutionary parties), who forged a *political* anti-Semitism at the very time when economic evolution was tending to make racial anti-Semitism disappear. It is likely that the insignificance of these facts would have amused Plekhanov. Construction was proceeding at full tilt, the building of socialism was continuing – *that was what would have counted in his eyes*. But he would simply have been unaware of the slowness with which societies in growth dissolve their residues, as the very striking example of American Puritanism proves: that atheist religion which has not yet managed to dissolve itself into pure atheism, and remains – like a pledged inertia – at the very heart of all the numerous contemporary conversions to Catholicism.* In other words, he would have been unaware of the 'diachronic', or would have got rid of it by simply mentioning the resistance of superseded significations, as if such resistance were not a capital factor of History. We shall return to this.[59] For the moment, let us note that Stalin dead is still interiorized in the majority of Soviet groups and individuals, and that practice still re-exteriorizes him as hysteresis of the responses adopted in relation to problems. He still represents *inert individuality* in certain cases of collective practice (and it matters little, as can easily be divined, whether the present agents hated him in his lifetime or not: the absence of an organization gives individual opposition the status merely of a 'subjective' mood; because of this, Stalin's enemy – in spite of himself and, above all, without knowing it – is Stalinized).

Excesses and failings – if the sovereign-individual manages to hold on and attain part of the objectives set – obviously go in the direction of the exigencies of social praxis. Stalin's *relative* lack of education was a *negative* element. But it protected him from universalism: from that universalism which the Revolution rejected, even while formally invoking it ('Workers of the world, unite!'). Conversely, his crudity and opportunistic dogmatism were useful to a working class that needed to *believe* – to be sustained by dogmas defining a hope. But inasmuch as they manifested a lagging behind of the individual in relation to the determined exigencies of action, they deviated the latter precisely in so far as they made it easier. In that sense, as I have said, the psychoanalytic interpretation of Stalin as an incarnation of Stalinism remains inopportune. First, because biographically important factors (and ones that, from the

---

* It is not true, as Max Weber believed, that Protestantism was *at the origin* of capitalism. But the opposite is not true either. In reality, they reflected their exigencies to one another at the outset and developed by virtue of one another. But it was capitalism which represented the *relatively* independent variable – to such a point that the progressive secularization of economic sectors 'ought' to have had as its logical conclusion the definitive liquidation of religion (by its withering away). From this standpoint, Protestantism – which in other respects, at the moment when it made its appearance, represented a revolutionary advance towards atheism – *braked* the advances of irreligion, by preserving the pure, universalistic, egalitarian Reason and the system of values that sprang from the synthesis of the individual with universality as a *sacred abstraction*. So, as has been repeated ad nauseam, the movement towards the future is realized as an evolution or, when *urgent*, as a revolutionary upheaval; but as a past, outworn signification, whose inert materiality nevertheless still carries weight, it remains one of the most effective brakes on future action.

59. This subject, linked to diachronic totalization, was not in fact dealt with in the present work (see Preface). However, see 'The Historical Event' in the Appendix, pp.397 ff. below.

individual's viewpoint, incarnate both what he has been made and his current praxis) – like, for example, his relations with women and his sexual life – are practically without influence on the practical total-ization, or from the standpoint of the social task have only an anecdotal importance.* Secondly, because the historical problem is not formulated as analysts like to imagine. *Even if* it were to be established that Robespierre suffered from an inferiority complex, it was not that complex which made the Terror. It was the necessities of the practical field and the exigencies of a praxis seeking to save the revolutionary gains, at a moment when the country was threatened with invasion and ravaged by civil war and when terrible struggles were raging among the Republicans themselves, even within the Convention. It was the exigency of the towns (food supplies) and the resistance of the countryside to requisitions. It was the ambiguous conflict (which later would decidedly be a class struggle) that pitted the sans-culottes against the Jacobins. It was the necessity for a petty-bourgeois government to keep the rich at arm's length and, at the same time, to channel and direct towards its own ends a Terror of popular origin which – despite a few temporary lulls – had not stopped growing since the taking of the Bastille. *Certain* men (Robespierre and others) had to invent governmental Terror (as a praxis transcending and utilizing these contradictions for the safety of the Republic) – inasmuch as it had to be organized and consequently *inten-tional* – as a practical exteriorization of the objective dangers they had interiorized. In so far as a complex would have sent some of them back (i.e. *would have had the strength* to send them back) to their private particularity in the very course of the work they were developing, these men would thereby have ceased to be *common individuals* and would have fallen outside collective action (as happened to Sade, who was president of the *Société des Piques* before relapsing into non-communication).

Thus, any interpretation of praxis-process *as a global ensemble* that

---

* I am thinking, in particular, of the suicide of his second wife, which was a *result* of private and public factors (to wit, Stalin's conjugal life and the dreadful wave of repression that was just beginning). But this *result* was not, in its turn, an *origin*. Perhaps it affected *in* Stalin that reality atrophied by action: the *private* individual. Perhaps the 'incident' (which, taken in itself, was a singularizing incarnation of the succession of suicides that decimated the Bolsheviks between 1928 and 1935) partly provoked the one and only *malaise* of which Stalin gave a glimpse throughout his entire praxis as a sovereign, and which led him to propose his resignation to the Politburo. At all events, the episode was settled at that very same meeting – since it could not be otherwise. For going into reverse would have meant the regime's downfall. Perhaps they might have avoided launching themselves so violently into repression. Once they had begun, however, they had to continue; which meant that, on the contrary, integration was tightened round the leader who had taken responsibility for this policy. After a short silence, Molotov begged Stalin to retain his functions.

did not limit itself to comprehending it *on the basis of itself* (i.e. on the basis of the factors we have described) would immediately take us back to subjective idealism. *Conversely*, however, the dogmatic attitude of Plekhanov tends towards objective idealism: pushing it to its ultimate implications would lead, in fact, to the idea that every praxis is always everything it can be – and everything it must be – and that it always finds all the men needed to direct it (or the men chosen always adapt themselves to their functions, and in the shortest possible time). In fact, if it is admitted that real History is at the level of social struggles (rather than, as he believes, at that of the practico-inert), the importance of the sovereign-individual (or of the restricted group that exercises sovereignty) – i.e. the scarcity of men – manifests itself *in the differential*: i.e. in the gap separating the objective exigencies from the realization. And in the world of scarcity this gap ultimately means only *the deviation of praxis by its incarnation*. We shall see later that this deviation manifests itself *also* when sovereignty is not incarnated in an individual.[60] But let us for the moment stick to our investigation. In the case of a sovereign-individual, deviation into partial success – i.e. the differential – is a strictly intelligible meaning of certain practical totalizations. Historically, as we have seen, and through the concrete exigencies they determined, these constituted themselves in certain circumstances as demanding *such and such a sovereign*. Thus the individualization of power is in itself comprehensible. Nevertheless, from this first standpoint, inasmuch as it is required by one moment of a praxis conditioned by a whole past, it limits itself to illuminating *the facticity* of praxis and illuminating itself through the latter: every praxis is an inheritance, every agent an heir. As conditioned by former circumstances and the ensemble of the field's materiality, the necessity of withdrawal into self and the necessity of oppression (one consequence of which might be Terror) manifested themselves as the *facticity of the Russian Revolution* through the facticity of Stalin, its product. On the other hand, however, the incarnation here manifested – through the *differential* it caused to appear in the results – a radical condition of that praxis: the fact that the action of men is conditioned by their own scarcity. There is a poverty of historical praxis inasmuch as it is itself a struggle against poverty, and this poverty – as an inner dialectic of scarcity – always reveals itself in the result, which will be at worst a terminal failure and at best a deviation. And it matters little that praxis, in its former developments,

---

60. Doubtless an allusion to the State in bourgeois democracies (see Preface). See also Sartre's footnote on p. 273 below.

might be partly responsible for this poverty (as can be seen when a government's mistakes and unpopularity deprive it of its means of defence). For if it is true that every praxis, by interiorizing its poverty, takes responsibility for it, it is also true that it can do nothing but *give it form*, never create it.

In that sense, Stalin and the Stalinist deviation (i.e. the deviation *to the limited extent* that it can be attributed to Stalin) expressed – in all dialectical intelligibility – the interiorized need for Soviet praxis *not to be just* the planned industrialization of *that* country, in *that* period, after *that* revolution, and under the threat of *that* encirclement, but to be also the reincarnation, in individual contingency, of its own incarnation. Suddenly, however, Stalin – as an individualization of the social: i.e. of praxis as poverty – incarnated the dialectical intelligibility of all the inner poverties of the practical field, from the shortage of machines to the peasants' lack of education. But an incarnation is not a symbol. He did not limit himself to tranquilly reflecting those shortages. If he incarnated them, he also synthetically added the shortage of men, through his own inadequacies – inasmuch as these would produce deviations. Similarly, the genuinely Stalinist deviations (the differential), considered in their outcome, were *something other* than the global deviation that constituted the Russian Revolution as the proletarian Revolution incarnate. Yet they incarnated it, inasmuch as they were its radicalization. Incarnated and singularized, the working-class Revolution deviated to the point of demanding the sovereignty of a single person. And this sovereign, born of a deviation, pushed it to the bitter end and revealed in the very contingency of his policy, i.e. of his own facticity, that praxis – as an incarnation deviated by its own counter-finalities, by its heritage and by the ensemble of the practico-inert – had to lead to the ultimate concrete individualization, by virtue of the very contingency of the unforeseeable and differential deviations which it had necessarily given itself without knowing it, through the idiosyncratic mediation of the required sovereign.

But let us be clearly understood: the individual and chance character of praxis can under no circumstances signify that it develops according to no laws. Contingency appears only through strict exigencies. Through all its deviations and all its sidetracks, we shall see later on that the *historical process* continues on its path. Only this path is not defined a priori by the transcendental dialectic. It is realized and determined by praxis, i.e. through corrections, rectifications and minor alterations; by agreed detours – and even sometimes by calculated regressions – across the generational rift, which alone creates the necessary perspective for new sovereigns: the tiny distance that allows them, in the name of common objectives, to assess the slippages and drift of the former praxis. We shall return to these problems concerning diachronic totalization.[61] Far from submitting History to contingency – to chance – I have sought to show how History *integrated* chances and contingency as the manifest signs and necessary consequences of its own facticity. There are too many men. The majority remain undernourished. But there are not enough men to make a rigorous history on a daily basis. This does not mean, however, that it is impossible to find rigour, by taking broader and more abstract views. Or that all of praxis, including its deviations, is not intelligible dialectically. History is not rigorous – in so far as restricted ensembles are being considered – because dialectical and totalizing reasons (not chance circumstances) oblige it always to be realized as a *chance* incarnation in relation to the objectives that are the source of praxis. It is not rigorous, because it always proceeds via mistakes and corrections; because it is *in no way* a universal schematism, but a unique adventure unfolding on the basis of pre-historic circumstances which – in themselves and in relation to all objectives and all practices – constitute a weighty and ill-known inheritance of fundamental deviations. In a word, Stalinism saved socialization by deviating socialism. Its successors remain, who have received from it the means to correct that deviation.

---

61. See p.238 below, and Preface.

3

The Totalization-of-Envelopment, an Incarnation of Incarnations

WORKING-CLASS revolution was incarnated in the October Revolution. Stalin was the incarnation of that incarnation. Should one understand that he was in himself the totalization-of-envelopment? Of course not: but we had to understand the meaning of Stalinism, in order to understand the problem better. We see from this example that totalization is a singularizing incarnation, since it presents itself – in the case under consideration – as the individualization of society in dialectical connection with the socialization of the sovereign-individual. Yet we already know that the totalization-of-envelopment can be neither a being (transcendental dogmatism), nor an existent (hyper-organicism), nor a rule imposing itself on the singular adventure (universalism of exteriority). So it is appropriate to ask oneself what kind of objective (and individual) reality it does possess. This question would risk remaining insoluble, if we had not already established that totalization does not mean totality. In other words, it actually belongs to the category of objects for which we have reserved the name of praxis-process. A pure and constituent praxis (for example, the work of an isolated individual, taken – by abstraction – *outside* the social conditions of its execution: Sunday odd jobs, for instance) is separable from the practical agent only abstractly, unless it is considered as the synthetic unity of the transformations passively endured by the object. In reality, it is the living and univocal relationship (with a halo of quasi-reciprocity) between the practical organism and worked matter, via the mediation of its field and tools. It is not possible to distinguish man's act, for it is abstract to distinguish the work from the material: the concrete reality is *a-man-shaping-matter-by-his-labour*. As Marx showed clearly, it is the social system of exploitation which, in specific circumstances, turns the worker's labour back against him as a hostile force. From this viewpoint, the structure of constituent totalization is quite different from that of constituted totalization. It is not labour that totalizes the agent, nor his objectification (i.e. his inscription in inertia). On the contrary, it is the agent who totalizes *himself, through* the limited transcendence that projects him towards certain objectives and through the concrete labour he carries out in the course of temporalization. Temporary unity returns from the future to the present and thereby determines the signification of the past, at the same time as the progressive movement of labouring temporalization incarnates and supports – through the difficulties of construction and the adversity-coefficient of matter – the short-term and long-term objectives as its future *raison d'être*, its unity, the meaning of its orientation, the approximate determination of the total temporalization and the deep signification of its effort. Yet we should see here simply the practical agent himself, inasmuch as his reality is simultaneously to be 'on deferment' and to totalize himself constantly by action. For each of us, it is one and the same thing to exist, to transcend oneself towards one's ends, to be totalized by this very transcendence, and to produce the demoniacal, inverted reflection of totalization and the foundation of History: the inert syntheses of worked matter. In short, from this viewpoint there are *individuals* and that is all.

Once it is a matter of groups, or ensembles comprising sovereign groups and series, praxis attains a relative independence which allows it to posit itself for itself and as an object in the face of every agent. It is for this reason that we have been able to signal a twofold movement: [the agent] incarnates the practical totalization, it transcends him and he refers the matter to the ensemble of objective structures constituting it. As we have seen, the reason is that – in each individual and for each individual – common praxis is wholly immanent, inasmuch as he is a common individual and differentiation of functions is given, as a superficial necessity that does not achieve either the absolute unity of sworn faith or that Fraternity-Terror which is the right and obligation to be everywhere *the same*, here and there. In other words, organic solidarity is only a redeployment of unity. On the other hand, however, in so far as the group is divided into sub-groups, and in so far as the action of some particular organ demands the collaboration of some other and the synchronization of these two tasks can be realized only by a third organ – itself controlled, like the others, by an organ of co-ordination or regulation, etc. – the action of each unity does not remain the mere objectification of a practical project. It becomes itself a passive object of control and co-ordination, adapted from outside to the needs of the ensemble. In this sense, the active sub-group (*inasmuch as it necessarily presents an inertia*: multiplicity of its members, physico-chemical mater-iality of the biological organisms, etc.) itself becomes worked matter (it is of little importance, moreover, whether it consents to this with enthusiasm or reluctantly). It is shifted, it is tightened up, it is increased, it is modified from outside by creating elsewhere another sub-group whose functions, by their mere coexistence in a practical field, alter its own, etc. Lastly – as all sociologists have already noted – its relative permanence and the relative instability of its membership (some only pass through it, others stay there, but retirement or death will cause them to sink outside it) contribute in reciprocal combination to give it a kind of constituted or pre-institutional inertia. But as every organ is defined by its function and it is the latter which is conditioned from outside (i.e. inside the group, outside the sub-group under consideration), it is ulti- mately the function itself which – in this form of predictable and modifiable objectivity – becomes a praxis-object.

Thus, precisely in so far as each person grasps himself objectively – and rightly – as *incarnating* the common praxis, he grasps himself also as a cog in an extremely complex machine, each element of which is at once passive and passively conditioned *by certain others* and – *for certain others* – an exigency or praxis positively of conditioning. At this level, the delays, the counter-orders and hitches, a whole braking of temporalization by spatial dispersion – or the difficulties of communi- cating, the lack of transport, the fatigue of long journeys, etc. – realize constituted praxis as a material and inert reality to be constantly sustained and corrected by human labour. We know – on this basis – that this first structure of passive objectivity will soon be enriched by the determina- tions of the practico-inert, through the counter-finalities of praxis. It is, in fact, within the practical process that determinations in exteriority lodge themselves, precisely because sub-groups – as mediated by direct- ing bodies – thanks to one another enter a state of passive exteriority (and no longer one of mere differentiation within a negative interiority). Through this ensemble, common praxis, by virtue of its very efficacy, is burdened and darkened by *its own exteriority*: i.e. precisely by the practico-inert that will inflect it, and that it will have to dissolve in order to recover its original orientation. Thus, through its necessary references to the other sub-groups (from which it demands such and such a contribu- tion, or which demand of it such and such a service via the appropriate mediations) and to the structures of the ensemble, the sub-group under consideration recovers a circular hierarchy of significations that is the projection, on the level of the practical community, of the very thing it incarnates in its specific action. Structures and significations support between them a bond of exteriorized interiority which tends – in the decompression and scattering of the inert – to transform itself constantly into a total exteriorization of interiority (i.e. into a disintegration of the group). But precisely because of this risk – and as the deep meaning of the risk itself – this interior exteriorization of praxis takes place against a background of immanence. And this immanence can be only the *living* unity of the common activity.

The contradiction thus manifests itself in the following way. The ensemble of passive syntheses form an action group only if they represent, in a certain manner, the *body* of praxis: the very inertia through which the solitary organism as much as the community act upon the inertia of the field. In other words, so long as every sub-group *really* contributes to the common action, praxis maintains its exteriority (i.e. its deterioration due to the wastes and toxins it secretes within itself in the course of its effort to realize its objectives) within the framework of its living interiority, i.e. of its dialectical temporalization: in the temporo-spatial field, the temporal synthesis integrates extension. But for every sub-group, and for every member of these sub-groups, this global unity of practical temporalization reveals itself as the beyond of interiority, and they can refer to it only via the mediation of the practico-inert exteriority that gnaws at the common field. In this sense, in the movement of work, i.e. of compression and incarnation, every sub-group rediscovers in itself – because it re-produces it – the unity of integration that is the total praxis and is *the same* in each. As soon as the delays, the lack of supplies, the slowness of communications, etc., steer it back into hierarchical channels, this praxis, without therefore being annihilated, passes behind the exteriority that it sustains, sometimes uses and transforms – and that risks ruining it. At this level, there can be an enveloping totalization only if it satisfies the two following conditions: to take account in itself of decompression in exteriority; *to incarnate*, in the very movement of that integration, compression and incarnation as a concrete realization of the common praxis within every sub-group. For in this way the totalization-of-envelopment will disclose its real difference from subordinate incarnations. It supports, by itself and in itself, the hierarchy of signifying structures and the inert movement of the process. So through this highly structured system it marks the place of every possible incarnation, and the ensemble of correspondences that makes of each – in its place and within its perspective – the incarnation of all. In other words, this structuration is precisely what is not found as an inert framework in secondary totalizations, because each of these transforms such relations of exteriority into immanent and synthetic conditions of praxis.* But it is precisely what allows them to exist, as a practical

---

* Any sub-group, inasmuch as it has *a number of* members, hierarchized or otherwise, and its function delimits a portion of the practical field, *likewise* supports – for each of the common individuals composing it – a system of interiorized exteriority. But these detailed structures do not necessarily, or even frequently, symbolize the framework of the totalizing system.

retotalization of an ordered system: in short, it is what produces this skeleton of inert (but governed and perpetually transformed *from outside*) relations, without which the possibility of any incarnation would not even be given. It must be added that it is precisely *the being* without which the totalization-of-envelopment would vanish, but which – in itself and without its power of practical unification – would be scattered in exteriority. Finally, we have seen by what mediations the real ensemble of this practico-inert gradually deviates the praxis that engenders and sustains it. We have shown, for example, how the first hierarchical determinations of the basic levels had ended by transforming the sovereign.

So the totalization-of-envelopment, inasmuch as it is implied and aimed at by all the partial totalizations, is praxis itself inasmuch as it engenders the corporeity that sustains and deviates it, and inasmuch as it attempts at every moment to dissolve its own exteriority into immanence. This latter point does not just presuppose that praxis is objectified, sustained and limited by its objectification in the inert, in the shape of process. It further implies that the incarnation of envelopment is realized at all levels of the practical process as a mediation and as a dissolution of the practico-inert (or as its utilization). As we reject any idealist interpretation, however, it goes without saying that this dissolving mediation is carried out by men. And since we have not left the example of Soviet society, this mediation was originally the achievement of the sovereign. By this, we should understand his *omnipresence* – a practical corollary of his *indissoluble unity as an individual*. For it was because he could be everywhere *wholly* that he *occupied* (by his image, by his speeches, by the propaganda in the mass media, etc.) all premises. He was both the task and the observer who checked the work. He was the boss, the eyes and the impalpable substance of the union – i.e. the USSR personified. He manifested himself at every point of that disparate ensemble, as the seamless unity of that undefined multiplicity. His millions of portraits were just *one* portrait: in every home, in every office, in every workshop, it realized the presence of all the rest, in the form of a synthetic milieu and an inexorable surveillance. Serialized by his presence in all terms of all series, he was a collective single-handedly; and that immediate, constant presence contributed, when necessary, to maintaining recurrence in the deceptive guise of unity. At the same time, however, wherever integration was realized to extremes, it was realized by him or in his presence. His voluntarism was produced in each person as an alterity of separation and as a will to union. He represented the identity of outside and inside. The cult of his personality was in fact addressed to the objectified interiorization of that enormous temporal and spatial event: the socialization of Russia (i.e. to Russia inasmuch as that 'fatherland' was socialized, and to socialism inasmuch as its appearance *in the USSR* added a new glory to the nation). So what was the totalization-of-envelopment during the Stalin phase of socialist construction? It was Stalin, if you like, but inasmuch as he was *made* and sustained by the praxis of all, as the sovereign uniqueness that was to integrate its structures and contain its exteriority. In other words, it was *first of all* Stalin, inasmuch as the sovereign praxis of the leaders (of whom he was one) proposed him and ultimately produced him as a non-transcendable model of unity, and with the illusory mandate to dissolve constituted praxis in the dialectical integration of its free constituent practice. And in the totalizing movement it was then Stalin as a socialized individual, i.e. one retotalized by the constructive movement of all (or, at the very least, all the directing organisms) in that very constituent praxis that through the common retotalization became the simple reactualization of constituted praxis: in other words, Stalin sovereignly determining the tasks of that society, inasmuch as it determined him itself and was interiorized in him by the sovereignty it allowed him to take; inasmuch as – in the ascending movement that produced and sustained him – it constituted *his depth*. And then, in a new moment of that temporalization, it was Stalin re-exteriorizing – with the deviations imposed by his idiosyncrasy – that interiorized depth: i.e. transcending towards *its* common solutions the common exigencies that retotalized him. At this moment of praxis, he sovereignly took hold of the national field and – by this very means – integrated the practico-inert ensemble into the unity of a praxis. We rediscover here the schema of enveloping totalization, as we have indicated it in the abstract. However, in so far as it was produced as common praxis maintaining its exteriority within the non-transcendable limits of an organic interiority, it was reactualized in every incarnation as a corporeal and visible presence of unity. What is more, it was this biological unity that everywhere presided over the incarnations (i.e. the singular totalizations) and gave them their meaning and their orientation. In fact, this new moment of totalization shows us Soviet society *assimilating* Stalin, being individualized by him, making his omnipresence into the proof that the agent's indissoluble unity was the *truth* of the apparent dispersion of men and things. But this meant that, with the help of the lower leadership bodies, this society riven by conflicts grasped itself at the same time – through each of its members (whether supporter or opponent) – as a national personality, whose thoroughgoing integration had been radicalized to become the idiosyncrasy of a single individual. For if the circular movement of totalization is grasped, there was a practical and dynamic unity of Stalin's retotalization by the leading groups and the socialist nation's retotalization by Stalin: i.e. of the deep assimilation of a fatherland as a semi-abstract entity with a person as a non-transcendable limit of the concrete.

But this singularization of a singular incarnation was a praxis of the sovereign, whose instruments were the mass media, ceremonies, activists, etc., and whose distant objective was the *self-domestication* of individuals. Stalin thought the withering away of the State would begin once it became useless: i.e. once it had been fully realized (which meant: once it had imbued all sectors and been interiorized in all individuals). When all individuals in a social ensemble were constituted as *common individuals* in relation to that ensemble, however vast it might be – when they had interiorized its constraints and censorships, to the point of transforming them into a 'second (or third) nature', i.e. into spontaneity – then the State as a separate (for all its extension) and specific reality would no longer have any *raison d'être*. Every individual, in his very reality, would be a fundamental relation to sovereignty as *other* and act spontaneously as *an Other than himself*. In this perspective, the cult of personality installed the sovereign State within every individual, as a censor and superego *in the concrete guise of an Other*: an Other completely individualized – with a face that photographers could make benevolent and likeable – who inhabited them all as if to mask from them the necessarily abstract character of duty. In this singularizing incarnation that was Russia on the march towards socialism, every worker's obligations were singularized by the face and voice of the one who imposed them. And this formidable sovereign strove to interiorize himself in every isolated or serialized molecule of the toiling masses, in order to become there the worker or peasant himself *as an Other* – i.e. as a sacred personality – so that the sovereign order could simultaneously be heard by everyone on the radio and be pronounced within every listener as his own sovereign decision, inasmuch as he himself was Stalin: i.e. the indissoluble organic incarnation of the socialist fatherland. By this common impregnation of all individuals by the sovereign, Soviet society – through Stalin's mediation – strove to bring the man of the masses closer to the common individual of groups. The cult of personality was the first known attempt to change into a pledged group a society in which, at the outset, the dissemination of farmers far outweighed (in terms of the number of scattered individuals) the working-class concentrations.

4

The Spiral: Circularity and Alteration

T HUS the totalization-of-envelopment was here the twofold movement – rising and falling – of groups escaping impotence (engendered
by the practico-inert) through the mediation of an individual sovereign,
who was socialized as an individual by becoming the idiosyncrasy of a
national society: i.e. the omnipresent incarnation – internal and external
– of a regime, a limitless task and a nation. In the same circular
perspective, moving back again from this individualized society to the
socialized individual, we shall see the new stratifications engendered by
his praxis transform the leading strata and, through it, change him as a
practical and sovereign support for common action: hence, deviate the
praxis that he pursued through society and society pursued through him.
We shall see the consequences of this deviation in the transformations of
the practical field and, by moving down again from the sovereign to
society – as well as by re-situating society in the modified field – we
shall find its consequences in the human relations of production as in
other sectors, only to return thence to the constituted sovereign and
discover in him the modifications produced by his new retotalization. If
we were to carry on this circular examination long enough, we should
eventually find a kind of hiatus between the sovereign, the real state of
society and the awareness it had of itself. Between 1948 and 1953,
Stalin's praxis became a monstrous caricature of itself. He could not
resolve the problems posed by the existence of new socialist States. The
man of retreat and solitude felt only mistrust when Russia emerged from
isolation: quarrel with Tito, absurd and criminal trials in the people's
democracies, resurgence of political anti-Semitism – nothing was lacking.
The same mistrust led him to condemn Mao for wanting to resume
hostilities. At home, the rise of new generations and the growing number
of technicians alarmed him: he returned to Terror and purges. The fact
was that he had grown old and become the pure product of his former

praxis. In that body and brain worn out by thirty years of furious work, the old formulae governing his stratagems – the themes that were organized in his actions – had become mortgages on the future: non-transcendable inertias. However, the society he had produced required a policy radically different from his own. So this time the individualization of the man was the result of his praxis (on the basis, it is true, of physiological ageing). This praxis, as we have seen, was by and large what the situation required (give or take a 'differential'). But inasmuch as it was no longer incarnated anywhere except in him – and inasmuch as it defined him by new limits, isolating him from the true social movement – it gave him the tragic idiosyncrasy of impotence and failure. Yet he was still the privileged mediation, in a society that still remained retotalized by his sovereign individuality. But Stalin became ossified in everyone as he became ossified in himself. For Soviet man he became the *negative* element separating him from others, from the practical field and from his own reality: he was the source of ignorance and unawareness. In this last period totalization remained circular, even if it had the result of revealing an explosive contradiction between the still very timid exigencies of a world forged by Stalin and the man Stalin as he forged himself in forging that world and by the world he forged. For it was within the very unity of interiority, and as the last moment of the circuit, that the contradiction had to explode.

Thus circularity alone can reveal the totalization-of-envelopment to us. And as the latter is a movement never completed, that circularity – in the perspective of temporalization – becomes a spiral. Of course, this can under no circumstances mean that only circular relations exist in the society under consideration: the relationships may be simply vertical, oblique or horizontal. Only it must not be forgotten that they are established through a movement of spatializing temporalization, which gives a certain curvature to every new fact. In other words, in a society of the type we have just been studying (and perhaps in other societies[62] – we shall come back to this shortly), whatever the structure of the relations considered may be, they necessarily participate in the type of contraction or refraction that constitutes the inner movement of the totalization-of-envelopment. Whatever, for example, the incarnation under consideration may be, the agent works in a practical field entirely conditioned by the sovereign-individual. Moreover, he is *imbued* with the propaganda of the mass media. Finally, none of his actions is quite immaterial to that society – so deeply integrated (amid the very conflicts

---

62. See, in the Appendix, the notes on 'Totalization in Non-Dictatorial Societies', pp.428 ff.

that rend it apart) by emergency – hence, to the sovereign himself or his local representatives. No more is needed for his friendships or even his loves – while remaining horizontal relations of reciprocity – to have a dimension of circularity. In other words, in one way or another every event – however 'private' it may be – must be considered as an incarnation. And each event, as an enveloped totalization, incarnates all the others via the mediation of the enveloping totalization.

Looking at this more closely, however, it is clear that the totalization-of-envelopment is not a praxis (i.e. the action of a free organism), nor even a *common* praxis (in the sense in which the action – constantly checked, co-ordinated and directed – of a sports team, for example, can be so called). There can be no doubt, to be sure, that we are not leaving the teleological sector: the action of the rulers has objectives, it never ceases to be corrected, the action of the ruled too sets its own goals. And it is certainly not the appearance of practico-inert concretions in the field of praxis that could change this. When the practico-inert appears as a danger, a negative inertia, a counter-finality at the heart of the practical field, the action sets itself the goal of eliminating it: that is all. Of course, we have noted that this action used to distil its counter-finalities unwittingly, and would then discover them through conflicts or inert negations of its objective. So already praxis has marginal results that did not enter into the calculations of the experts. No matter. Necessity appears, inasmuch as action mediates between separate elements of materiality. And the relationships thus established remain within the unity of a totalization, since they were produced by action and would not exist without its power of synthesis. In the same way, counter-finalities are destructive for the real and present men who struggle against them. Formally, however, they endanger the overall unity only in so far as they attack its content. For in themselves they are finalities in reverse, which could not exist outside a practical milieu and without borrowing their negative being from the positive ends that agents seek to achieve. However, as we have seen, the objectification of praxis – with the ensemble of counter-finalities accompanying it – has the result of changing the men who have undertaken it, and thereby of deviating it without the knowledge of its agents. Circularity appears here, since one is moving from men to their practical field through praxis, only to return from the practical field to men and to modified praxis.

Now, on this occasion, the result of this action of men upon themselves via the mediation of things is not just unforeseen, it escapes the very ones who are its victims; or else, if they discover it, it is through a faint unease and by means of intellectual tools that are themselves deviated. We are at the level at which praxis, as an immanent link between man and things, produces its own exteriority: it has an outer guise – a body. This is what will allow the circularity – precisely in so far as the ensemble of these unknown modifications is reduced to inert determinations, strata and structures. However, as we have seen, the agents maintain the unity of the action; they ensure the interiorization of the exterior. But that itself transforms them, and within the still preserved unity – without ever ceasing to act and, perhaps, succeed – the ensemble is imperceptibly transformed. After a few turns, these men have become other men intent on attaining other objectives by other means – yet they do not even know it. Of course, I am taking an extreme case. Distant objectives can – because of their very distance – remain more or less unchanged. But a swift *flash of awareness* – facilitated by certain circumstances: e.g. by a generational shift or a too blatant contradiction – may lead to a revision, and then the deviation can be more or less rapid. Everything depends on the context. *In its essence*, however, it remains the case that the spiral of envelopment manifests an alteration of praxis through inner and non-conscious reactions.

Yet this reality in movement cannot be called *practico-inert*. What characterizes the practico-inert, despite everything, is inertia. Here, from one end to the other, all is action. In our chosen example, all is activism and voluntarism. There is not a single one of the secondary and negative reactions which does not originate from praxis and its power of unity. Totalization *is temporalized* precisely in so far as totalized men are temporalized by action. Or, if you like, the totalization-of-envelopment, which closes upon agents and their metamorphoses, has as its real duration the dialectical temporalization of constituted praxis. For the same reasons, you could not speak of *alienation*. Alienation is the theft of the act by the outside: I act *here*, and the action of an other – or a group – *over there* modifies the meaning of my act from without. Here, nothing of the kind. The deterioration comes *from the inside*. The agent and the praxis were modified, to be sure, by the practico-inert – but in immanence: inasmuch as they were working inside the practical field. Finally, let us not forget that the practico-inert, through serial alterity, opens into indetermination and the universal (as undetermined). The totalization-of-envelopment, by contrast, is the incarnation of History's facticity by the facticity of an idiosyncratic (and wholly determined) contingency.

Indeed, the totalization-of-envelopment represents the moment of temporalization in which the agent – *despite* his success (if he succeeds) or perhaps *because* of it – loses himself in the act that produces him, derails him, and deviates *itself* through him. Thus it is *the act overflowing the man* that is totalized. It retains within it its wastes and disassimilation products, and if it is transformed by them this is because it has given them – in and through practical integration – the inner unity that allowed them to become effective. So although the deviations escape the agent (himself transformed from within), it is solely via the aspect of *practical unity* that we shall tackle the totalization-of-envelopment in our historical investigation. The proof is that – when it was a matter of judging the measures taken by Stalin, his foreign policy, some demonstration, or some statement made to the press – the action would appear to contemporaries in the bourgeois democracies as pure praxis, escaping determinations of facticity and internal breakdowns of structure or balance. Western Communists saw there only an objective and rigorous response to the specific and equally rigorous exigencies of the situation. Anti-Communists first discerned the 'manoeuvre' (propaganda for domestic or foreign consumption, etc.). At the same time, in order to be able to judge Stalin more harshly, they stripped all his praxis since 1928 of the 'pretexts' of efficacy and necessity. Since 'manoeuvres' are never required (at least in the specific form of their realization) – since it was possible to halt the 'grain strike', for instance, without that headlong collectivization that pushed the leaders on to the slippery slope of repression – it was patent that the *measure adopted*, the agrarian policy pursued, etc., reflected Stalin's character *alone* (or the evil nature of the Communists). Conversely, after having long declared the five-year plans ineffective for the simple reason that they did not believe in their success, when it became necessary to acknowledge the extraordinary growth of Soviet industry they hit upon another expedient. *Before* 1914 (and this is a fact) Russia's industrialization had been growing very rapidly. Without the pointless October Revolution, it would have carried on and the growth rate of production, under a capitalist system, would have been roughly equal in a given period to the socialist rate, while nobody would have resorted to coercion. The point is not to discuss this futile and baseless hypothesis, but to indicate its function in the propaganda war. If planning, and the bloody repression that accompanied it, led to nothing other than what a peaceful liberal and bourgeois industrialization would have sufficed to produce, socialist commandism was not even required by the objective to be attained. It was merely the systematic application of intellectual theories by a handful of tyrants tyrannized by the most tyrannical of all. Curiously, by stripping an action of its real efficacy, you simultaneously wipe out the weight of things and their adversity-coefficient: the action is no longer dominated by its own objectification – by the inert syntheses that it creates. Ineffective and inexpert when it was a matter of building a new economy, the Bolsheviks – within this perspective – had retained an absolute effectiveness when it was a matter of imprisoning or exterminating. The more gratuitous these crimes were, the freer they became. Imagining the difficulties of construction, one would at least be at liberty to ask oneself

– in the name of those very difficulties – whether measures of generalized repression were not going to compromise *immediately* (I am not even speaking of long-term deviations) the economic growth of the USSR. If at the outset, however, you consider such growth as assured under any system and whatever may be the perspectives, you are coming back to Plekhanov and turning his arguments against Marx. The Plekhanovist bourgeois makes the sovereign bodies *simultaneously* into pure epi-phenomena (in the domain of the economy) and *at the same time* into criminal and totally responsible (inexcusable) agents on the terrain of the repressive campaigns and the Terror. Ineffective as it was, that Terror came from them alone. Even without it, the development of the USSR was assured. It did not manage even to slow the latter down. In one domain, however, its efficacy remained complete: the sovereigns re-created and generalized the forced labour they were claiming to abolish, and they killed. These absolute acts – all the more free in that they were gratuitous – were characterized by their sole efficacy: destruction. And the latter was given, of course, as their objective. So the Bolsheviks – different in this from the industrial bourgeois – appear as fully responsible for the *negative* and *destructive* praxis imputed to them. The USSR appears through the mesh of their free activities, which surround it. And this Shirt of Nessus – transparent and corrosive, enveloping in a mesh of mortal activities that nation independently pursuing its industrial growth – is precisely the totality-of-envelopment, inasmuch as it is manifested to the anti-Communist as *freedom to do badly*. Its immediate character is to be a practical synthesis; and inasmuch as the anti-Communist discovers it – or thinks to discover it – in the sufferings *undergone* within the practical field by groups or individuals, he deciphers these *passions* (in the literal sense) as referring him back to the totalizing and concrete *action* that provokes them. Thus the common illusion is that *action* as a pure force is exercised upon its field in the manner of the Stoic 'cause', without *undergoing* the counter-shock of the changes it brings to it. It can be modified only by itself. And this control that it exercises upon itself – in order to adapt itself to circumstances – represents the highest degree of praxis, since it is a practical self-awareness and reflection of the act upon itself.*

But this illusion would not even be possible, if the investigation

---

* This structure of the act exists, and we have described it in relation to groups. It exists *also* for the Stalinist bureaucrat; it is even fetishized under the name of self-criticism (i.e. it is transformed into a synthetic determination of verbal matter and becomes a *thing*). But even were it to keep all its translucidity, *it* is still not what is in question. Though *interior* to the totalization-of-envelopment, as one of its practical structures, it is *covered* by the modifications *undergone* by praxis-process.

carried out by the anti-Communist abroad (or his adversary the Communist) did not reveal the USSR to him – in the international practical
field – as pure praxis without passivity. Even today, after Stalin's death,
the sovereign still reveals itself by acts (internal measures, like dissolving
the MTS; measures *vis-à-vis* the outside world, like the unilateral
suspension of atomic tests; practical achievements, like the launching of
earth satellites) which seem separated by obscure periods of gestation.
This means that the main feature of the totalization-of-envelopment (in
the case of dictatorship by a man or a party) is to produce itself above all
– in relation to situated witnesses – as the unity of a praxis that is
temporalized. Or, if you like, that the exteriority of praxis (its exterior-
being) is hidden within its very transparency. We have shown how
practical measures (recourse to bonuses and 'honours' to stimulate production), by transforming the leaders *from outside*, deviated their praxis
through the following distinction: a *chin* [rank] *had to* be re-established,
which would ultimately CREATE in every job an interest to be defended
for its occupant. Or, if you like, the functionary's interest is his own
alienated objectification in the material and honorific advantages of his
function. For most observers, the stratification and the appearance of
interests as a repercussion of praxis remained invisible. Communists saw
in the privileges of the Bureaucracy only the deserved recompense of the
bureaucrats' absolute dedication to socialization. Anti-Communists
argued as though the material interests existed *first* and the leading
circles – in the name of these interests or, as was usually claimed, *out of
self-interest* – had allocated to themselves the lion's share (had systematically diverted the major share of the national income into their own
pockets). The activist illusion is here carried *to its climax*. It presupposes
a perenniality of human nature (everyone pursuing their own interests),
and praxis becomes the instrument of individual selfishness or the
particularism of certain groups. In other words, the ambiguous position
of this Bureaucracy – which has *given itself interests on the basis of its
absolute dedication to the Cause*, and found itself 'interested' even
before understanding what was happening to it – all vanishes, in favour
of a rapacious and logical activity that inflexibly combines its means
with a view to attaining selfish ends, and unfailingly achieves its goal; it
is not the practico-inert – as being synthetically unified by praxis – that
has deviated the latter by the transformations it has caused men to
undergo, but from the outset – or at any rate from the moment the
objective possibility for this was given – it was the leaders who (without
changing themselves: they were *already* self-interested) deviated praxis
in favour of themselves, and deliberately sacrificed the revolutionary
ideal to their own interests.

In order to avoid falling either into this error or into transcendental dogmatism – which will explain the entire evolution of Stalinism by de-situated laws of exteriority – we shall say that the totalization-of-envelopment is *autonomous* praxis asserting itself as such, *inasmuch* as it produces, undergoes, harbours and conceals its own heteronomy as the passive and reactualized unity of its own by-products. In this sense, the totalization-of-envelopment reveals itself as a dialectical link between the intended result (with its foreseen consequences) and the unforeseeable consequences of that result, inasmuch as its incarnation in the totalization of the practical field has to condition from afar all the elements of that field, including the agents themselves. It alone allows – in the temporalized spiral – interpretation by one another of, on the one hand, the practical organization of sovereignty as a function of the emergency and, on the other (via a backlash), the appearance of a process of stratification borrowing its synthetic unity, its orientation and its counter-finality from action itself, and being produced at the heart of the latter as the actual waste-product of its temporalization. So we see forming – as the interior exteriority of a vast common undertaking, as a function of it, and in the guise of its projection into the inert – a vast *society-object*, which will be simultaneously an inert movement of industrial growth and, in its own structure, a social ensemble defined by the separation of ownership and sovereignty. But we should lose the guiding thread of this investigation if we did not see that it is the undertaking itself – in its calculated responses to the vital questions posed by the practical field – that produces *itself* and *instrumentalizes itself* as *this* society-object. More precisely still, if we do not understand that the signification of *this* society is that undertaking as praxis-process (as we attempted to show earlier), just as *this* society – which makes its necessity with action retaining the practico-inert within it – is the *destiny* of this undertaking.

Taken on its own, society would be a matter for sociology: you would link inert syntheses together – unities without unity – and sometimes growth would lead to stratification, sometimes stratification to growth, and sometimes they would lead to one another, depending on the sociologist. But the actual signification of a *unitary* phenomenon like an element of growth, or a determination of social morphology, must radically escape sociology, since this signification necessarily refers back to the very source of the inert unity – *which can only be action*. The sociologist in this case is like a man present at a game of bridge, who thinks he can construct an absolutely objective account by confining himself to describing the movement of the cards, their successive posi-tions, the dealing of the packs, their sudden reassembly and then their fresh division, without ever mentioning either the presence of the players (with their eyes which see, their hands which pick up) or the rules of the game (leaving to future sociologists – after a proliferation of monographic works on the shifting movements of playing-cards on so-called bridge tables – the task of reconstituting these rules by a bold, disputable and at all events disputed process of deduction, which, moreover, would establish them as a kind of natural law: i.e. in exteriority).

Conversely, however, if we were to consider praxis-process like the Stoic 'cause', we should fall into the error of Stalinism, which *never knew itself as it was* because it saw itself as a bodiless activity. That kind of idealism was not direct – it had come from the situation. Objectivity – i.e. for the leaders the practico-inert in the field – was their raw material; or, if you like, the object upon which their efficacy was exercised. But as a result it fell outside praxis, which was nothing other than the synthetic and practical bringing into contact (through modification of the elements of the field) of men, instruments and objects that until then had had no concrete contact. That bringing into contact itself (construction of a railway, for example) was defined – on the basis of objective resources and exigencies – as the *maximum* (*exactly* calculated) of what could be done within the overall perspective (itself governed by common objectives and the field as a whole). Praxis – as a *response discovered in objectivity*, and as an economic calculus of objective possibles – could thus be known as an object only in its objectification: i.e. in its result. And, to be sure, mistakes could be made. But these either had their origin in our nothingness (haste, lack of understanding, lightmindedness, indolence, etc.) or else they were bogus mistakes, hiding a counter-revolutionary act of sabotage. They could be eliminated by negation of the negation (coercion). But when a fully positive operation had been objectified in its result, the latter was nothing more and nothing less than the realization of the requisite exigency with the means available. Therein lay all the Stalinist optimism: the constructors escaped the consequences of the construction, the construction was in conformity with the objectives of the constructors. To be sure, the latter *made themselves* as they made things: but by making the right thing, they made themselves in the right way. And when Stalin declared that History was a science, he meant that Stalinist society had no history (in the sense in which, precisely, History is *also* destiny). The Stalinist made History, but History did not make him. He foresaw deeds and reactions on the basis of rigorous arguments, but he was outside the domain in which Marxism applied. He could be neither an object for a Marxist interpretation nor foreseeable as an object. He was a *subject of History*, and governed it as he liked. The crisis of Marxism came partly from that: a bound ensemble of socialist nations escaped History at the heart of History, since they claimed to make it without undergoing it; and since Marxism (theoretico-practical) was obliged to interpret theoretically the bourgeois democracies, and to justify practically (at the cost of what deformations!) the activities of the

Soviet leaders. In short, Stalinist praxis did not seek to assume its exteriority, and for that very reason *lapsed into blindness*: self-awareness was what it had to deny itself. So its attitude towards History, in the totalization-of-envelopment, became an integral part of its historic destiny: i.e. of the *being* that *the act* had given it.

The movement of circularity allows one, by contrast, to pass continuously from *being* (as sustained and produced by the act) to *the act* (as expressing its being by the very transcendence that preserves as it negates it). And it is precisely this perpetual passage – in the temporal spiral – from the being of the act to the act of being, from the practical signification of destiny to the destiny of praxis; it is the impossibility of considering for an instant the structured ensemble as a passive object, without at once rediscovering the group or groups as organizing themselves for and through the undertaking; it is the impossibility of totalizing the results of action, without being referred back by these very results to *their* results at the heart of the practical temporalization – sedimentations, deposits, concretions, strata, deviations; it is that perpetual necessity to climb to the apex of sovereignty, only to descend again to the base: it is all of these which constitute at once the mode of knowledge appropriate to the totalization-of-envelopment and the type of objective reality that defines it.

In a certain way, it realizes in practice the objectives of the agents (the leaders and the others); in another way, it transforms them into other men discovering other results, but believing they have attained their goals since they have transformed themselves at the same time as these. In short, men realize themselves by objectifying themselves, and this objectification *alters* them (of course, in the abstract hypothesis of a complete totalization, one not capped by other syntheses coming from elsewhere). But as the alteration comes precisely from the realization, and since the realization is altered in success, between signification and destiny a relation of deep intelligibility is revealed. This particular signification had to produce this destiny: the latter is already found in it as its future being, through its present relations with the practico-inert; and the destiny realized is the signification of this signification in the sense in which the objectified result represents – projected into the practico-inert – the limitation and deviation that this signification had to give itself, through the very praxis that realized it. One can clearly see, for example, the link between *this* society-object (Stalinist society) and *this* praxis of planned and accelerated growth in *this* underdeveloped society; and, equally well, the relation linking the past transcended and preserved in praxis to the objectification of the latter as an inert synthesis in Being: i.e. in materiality, or – which comes to the same thing – in the past. Between the becoming-past of the act and the becoming-act (or inert structure of the act) of the past, there is a reciprocity of perspectives; as there is between the sovereign-individual – pivot of praxis and the deviation undergone; of signification and destiny – and the bogus unity given by his common interiorization to inert and practical ensembles: i.e. to workers *undergoing* their condition and *producing* (by realizing the latter precisely through transcending it) their equipment and their means of subsistence.

From this standpoint, the totalization is really exhaustive. This should be taken to mean that it is not the abstract interplay of a formal signification and a very general destiny: it leaves no element of the practical field (men, things, praxis, practico-inert, series, groups, individuals) outside it, and this for the reason that it is produced *by all*. Planning, as a determination of the ruling praxis, will remain just a dream if all the workers – willingly or under constraint – do not contribute to realizing the Plan. Conversely, however, it is inasmuch as these men endure in serial impotence (or – for others who are activists – in enthusiasm) pressures that transform them, and social reorganizations that strip them of any power and re-create hierarchies, only to be victims in the end of a systematic enterprise of 'possession' by the sovereign-individual; it is in so far as peasant revolts and the repression of these create that new man, at once loyalist and separatist, represented by the kolkhoz worker: it is to *that* extent, in short, that this *society-object* (with its oppositionists, its supporters and its neutrals; with its hierarchy, its astonishing élan and its inertia; with its relations of production, its relationships between rulers and ruled, its 'infrastructure' and its 'super-structures'*) has a *reality*, a practical efficacy, an idiosyncrasy, a concrete wealth and a future. If we were to remain at the level of abstract structures and objectives, we should merely find ourselves back with sociology.

---

* I am using these terms provisionally. We shall see later on whether it is useful to keep them, or whether the perspective of circularity does not remove all signification from them.[63]

63. Sartre was not, in fact, to return to this problem in the present work. But it may be interesting in this connection to read his 1966 *Cahiers de Philosophie* interview on anthropology, in *Situations IX*.

5

The Three Factors of Unity

HOWEVER, let us not now lapse into hyper-organicism. No supra-human synthesis is being realized here. Every one of the men who, in their very movement, formed Russia as a socialization in progress remained a free practical organism, transcending the circumstances that had produced him, even if only to alienate himself in the practico-inert or to integrate himself into some group in the form of a common individual. Unity came simply from *three factors*.

1. The first is that the ruling praxis was real, material and coercive, based on a party and a police apparatus that gave it its true weight. Orders were not mere verbal determinations, gracefully interiorized by those who received them. And unity was not that of the 'kingdom of ends', or the unity which idealism terms a mutual agreement of minds: it consisted in an integration obtained *by a labour* – by the pretty disgusting labour that cops execute upon suspects (i.e. everybody) in a dictatorship (even a socialist one). But it really was a labour. Tracking down, arresting, dragging off to prison, beating – or just watching, following, searching – all this was energy expended. And the blows or the years of imprisonment, the life in the camps – those were real results, and there was *a labour* on the sufferer's part to reabsorb them as submission. In so far as this twofold labour aimed to reduce opposition, moreover, it operated within the broader framework of the labour of the regime's supporters, who sought to preserve its unity and (while producing in accordance with the dynamic unity of the Plan) exercised their control and censorship *really* – upon each other and each upon himself. Thus praxis was maintained by a labour of integration that was exercised constantly and was a material action by man upon man, provoking in the labourer an expenditure of energy and in the sufferer organic modifications. The unity of praxis was thus a material production of men at work (and taking themselves as an object of their work). It was not a spontaneous unity, but established. It was even that unity (anyway *in progress* and never completed) as an *ontological* reality of the common praxis constituting, if you like, the first appearance of the inert at the heart of totalization. And when I say 'first', I mean only to mention the fundamental and logical priority of the abstract framework within which passive syntheses were inscribed.

2. On the other hand, the creation by coercive force and by all forms of labour of a sovereign unity – i.e. an institutional and practical relationship between the sovereign and the practical field – transformed for everyone the milieu of his life into a spatio-temporal determination of the sacred field of the sovereign-Other; and simultaneously constituted the field of the individual and sub-group as virtually coinciding with the field of sovereignty (inasmuch as everyone was himself, and inasmuch as he was the Other – i.e. Stalin – a mystifying unity situated at the infinity of all serialities: but this dialectic cannot be developed here – it would take us too far). It is not a question here, of course, of 'subjective' determinations. Very really and very objectively – in the field of sovereign totalization and via the mediation of the sovereign (i.e. via administrative and police apparatuses or propaganda organs, etc.) – *nothing could be produced anywhere* without provoking *everywhere*, from far away and without any practical relation having existed prior to this influence, an *inner* modification of *all human facts* (from the organic and constituent praxis of *that person* to the practico-inert). The logical foundation of that possibility, of course, was the formal reciprocity that links anyone to anyone (as I established at the appropriate point). Every man is linked to every man, even if they are unknown to one another, by a reciprocal bond of immanence. But this fundamental bond is entirely undetermined – as much in its content as in its sign (positive or negative) or specific tension (*strength* of the bond of solidarity or antagonism). This indetermination of realities in constant readiness to be actualized (what at a first encounter, for example, is called a 'mutual liking' or a 'mutual antipathy') reveals through this new *knowledge* the relationship of two persons as having *always* existed.[64] By the judgement 'I don't like him', generally unmotivated, each aims at the other in his totalized past, and in his future conceived as repetition. And precisely in so doing, he is determined in the same way. 'From the day of his birth until the day of his death, this individual is made to be disliked (or liked) by that one' gives way to an even more rigorous and objective determination, beneath the unifying and sovereign action. This is fundamental in the field, inasmuch as it everywhere marks the objective paths of immanent relations. But the concrete unification of the field, through this infinity of

---

64. *Critique*, vol. 1, p.109.

infinities of paths, produces every singular modification as having to affect all the occupants of the field (men and things, men via the mediation of things, things via the mediation of men) through the actualization of certain of these paths.

In that sense, reciprocity is a relational milieu (like geometric space) in which the act, by its very movement, creates thoroughfares. To take things at the level of the most abstract significations, statistical data on *individuals'* standard of living do not have the same meaning at all if one tries to establish them (which is, as everyone knows, very hard – if not practically impossible – for want of a *real* term of comparison) for an ensemble made up of different peoples (the 'underdeveloped countries', Europe, or the entire population of the Globe) as they do in relation to the USSR. We shall see what they signify in the former case:[65] but it is immediately comprehensible – precisely because of the difficulty of finding the common denominator between men whose ways of living are extremely different – that quantitative relations should be established in exteriority, and on the basis of a certain character (apparent or profound, provisional or definitive: we shall have to ask ourselves this) of dispersion and detotalization. Whereas, in the case of the USSR, the quantitative appears against a background of unity and prepares the unity of a sovereign decision and its application. Each person's standard of living *conditions* the production of all. So each person is determined by all in the very perspective of the praxis of socialization. In that sense, the averages are true. Of course, they do not yield the concrete individual, and – depending on the information available to them – they sometimes do not take sufficient account of regional differences. What then? That means that other averages should be taken, nothing more. The standard of living at the regional level (even taking account of social categories) is no closer to the individual case: it gives a better account of structures, that is all. But that *typical living-standard* – which is nobody's – is in fact that of each individual and of everybody. Before knowing the averages calculated (which they will perhaps never know), all workers have realized for themselves a kind of average. Disadvantaged in relation to certain social strata – which they envy, and in relation to which they define their own purchasing power and the possibilities refused to them – they are privileged in relation to other milieux (albeit very slightly), on whom they are dependent (for production) and whose destitution alarms them. [The salary of the individual][66] – privileged and disadvantaged all

---

65. Sartre was not to return to the problems of totalization at the level of world history.

66. Sartre's manuscript had: 'Privileged and disadvantaged all at once, oppressed [...], the salary of the individual ... '

at once, oppressed by some and subordinate to others – marks the latter's objectivity at the heart of totalization: the synthetic ensemble of his powers and obligations, inasmuch as they are determined on the basis of Others. The relationship between his living-standard and that of the social categories immediately above and immediately below defines for him at once the real relation of his objective existence to that of Others (through the wage, the sovereign determines for each person the *qualification* of his labour: i.e. turns his professional ability in such and such a job into a quality-value) and his opportunities for maintaining his integration into the common praxis (directly, and above all through his relation to the less advantaged, since it is ultimately this relation that objectively decides his attitude towards them if they carry on passive resistance or rebel openly: for if the gap between their standard of living and his own is narrower than it is between his standard of living and that of the closest people with privileges over him – and, of course, in the absence of any other factor – then he can reveal himself objectively as 'one of them'; while in the opposite event, in solidarity with the closest people with privileges, he will be simultaneously against them and subordinate to them – and the more *against them*, the more answerable to them he is and the more his own wage, tied to his production, depends upon their labour). By this means, the wage of Others constantly enters *his own wage*, and can even – through the unrest provoked by its inadequacy – reduce the purchasing power of the individual under consideration without affecting his nominal wage. Thus the misery of a particular agricultural province is directly contained in his purchasing power (in his real wage) as a threat – as *the fragility* of his living-standard – while the privileges granted to others are also to be found in the immanent determination of that living-standard, as its *unjustifiability*. The demand (even implicit; even unknown to himself) that privileges should be reduced to a minimum is joined with this other demand: 'My suppliers [of raw materials or food products] must have enough to fill their bellies'; and to this third: 'My standard of living must be raised' (numerous inquiries have shown – in the West, it is true, but the fact is not dependent on the system – that everyone, whatever his material situation and the radicalism of his social and political attitudes, demands an increase in his real wage varying between 25 and 33 per cent; this constant and immediate claim can naturally be more unyielding or less so, depending on living conditions). And the unity of the three demands tends in itself to establish a kind of unified wage, which would bring some down to a slightly lower living-standard in order to raise the others to a higher level. The unity of this ideal wage is precisely the womb in whose unity statistical assessments of the real wage are produced.

Furthermore, the functionary himself – without giving up his privileges – sees wages (as a share of national income strictly defined by the Plan) as having to be fixed, taking account *both* of the 'voluntarist' hierarchy that has forged him and that he represents *and* of an adjustment of living-standards (by raising the lowest and freezing the highest; by an authoritarian lowering of all prices; etc.) such that nobody can be rendered incapable of working, by malnutrition or sickness. That propaganda poster the Poles saw on the walls one day (at which they had a good laugh, and which was indeed laughable as a sign of the elimination of men by objects) – 'Tuberculosis Holds Back Production' – manifests at once a thoroughgoing idealist aberration and, in spite of everything, the exigency of a certain equality of conditions (which does not mean it can be achieved), in the name precisely of production. *One privilege, at least*, should not be reserved for the ruling bureaucracy: to be exempt from tuberculosis. If the Tuberculosis campaign could be brought off, the miner would be made equal to the minister at least in this particular respect. Precisely, however, in this movement of internal reorganization of conditions (if not through wages, at least – as in the Polish example – through increased social services), the moment of statistics is indispensable; and it reveals the synthetic unity of the practico-inert, inasmuch as this is maintained, forged and to a variable degree liquidated by praxis. The unity of averages – in a people's democracy or the USSR – is the inner unity of exteriority, inasmuch as it is produced and reunited by praxis. If the dispersion of individual cases of illness can be grouped into *regions* and localized according to *job*, housing and social category, etc., that is because – already – the sovereign praxis has defined its own objectives. It already defines itself by the obligation to *improve conditions* in the regions (before even knowing these, though a pre-statistical knowledge actually allows it to determine them by and large); to devote a larger share of income *to building houses, clinics, etc.*; to struggle in the factories themselves *against the counter-finalities of certain jobs* and the occupational illnesses caused by them; lastly – to the extent that this is possible – to raise in one way or another the living-standard of those social categories where the scourge is most virulent. Thus statistics are merely exteriority itself (at least, in the case of the sovereign-individual) being revealed through the interiority of praxis as *itself* constituted by relations of interiority between men and things, or between men via its mediation. It discloses the practico-inert outcome at the heart of praxis as the outcome of a unitary practice, and as a product of disassimilation which reveals itself in the perspective of an already constituted undertaking that aims to dissolve it.

But synthetic inter-conditionings are not confined to big events that can be measured.* The appearance or disappearance of a group modifies the deep reality of any individual, even one situated outside this community. An intellectual work published in certain circumstances – albeit devoted to relatively non-current questions such as the history of the Tsars, or to giving an account of scientific experiments without any prospect of immediate practical application – sees its inner meaning transformed to the point of changing its author into a counter-revolutionary or an oppositionist (hence, a traitor), for the sole reason that circumstances have changed and he is changed by them. Some historical work exalting the 'spontaneous' resistance the Russian people put up against Napoleon during the Russian Campaign might be extolled in 1930: it helped to glorify the popular epic, attributing to the people the merit that Tsarist historians used to claim for the feudal armies; it was in line with the nationalist particularism of socialization; and in the event of war, it offered a model to the peasants. Fifteen years later, however, in another practical concretion, it received *from outside* another signification. Distrust of popular spontaneity was at its peak, the hierarchical system had become ossified and the cult of personality was being maintained by every means. The official version of the 1940 war was as follows: it had been won by the Russian Army under Stalin's leadership. The Russian Army was its soldiers, to be sure, but only inasmuch as they were led by their officers. Even if honour was accorded to the Resistance and the activity of partisans behind enemy lines, it went without saying that the heroic peasants waging that terrible struggle were inspired and led by the Party. Fadeyev was obliged to correct his work *The Young Guard*, because he had not taken sufficient account of the role played by the Party. What was at stake, in that moment of exacerbated Stalinism, was exactly this: any regroupment of the masses not carried out under the guidance of the established cadres, be it even to defend the regime, was seen as counter-revolutionary – or at all events dangerous. On that basis, the work – extolled fifteen years earlier – received a *subversive* content. And, let us be clear, it received it *objectively*. First, by virtue of the very hostility that its republication would arouse among the bureaucrats and in part of the working population (the part that had rallied totally to the regime and would see its obedience challenged). Secondly, because for other circles it would represent precisely an element of demystification and perhaps regroupment.

Let me be well understood. This description of the deviation of the

---

* I call tuberculosis an event and not a *state* of the society under consideration, in so far as the latter strives to reduce it and succeeds – albeit to a minimal extent – rather than enduring it as an inert burden.

meaning of a work through the deviation of common praxis is a simple description of the data yielded by dialectical investigation. *By no means* does it imply political and moral approval suppressing any *even retrospective* freedom of expression, in that – ultimately – the work was banned and its author forced to make self-criticism precisely in so far as it might contribute to a new awareness and a correction of the deviated action. But our problem is purely formal, and we must recognize that the signification of the work had really changed, for the simple reason that its relation to current reality had been modified through modifications to that reality itself. It was *the other term* that was transformed. But as the work – a past and (*in this strict sense*) inert determination of culture – did not change, the relation altered. If this work (like Soviet encyclopaedias, or official histories of the Bolshevik Party) could have been continually touched up, *by the mere fact* of its constantly checked adaptation to the synthetic milieu and its transformations it would have remained the same, in so far as it would have become other. This means that its living relation to the Soviet reader (as a relation of univocal immanence and quasi-reciprocity) would have remained constant, in proportion as it moved away from its *absolute meaning*: i.e. from the meaning that had been established at the moment of publication, through the dialectical interaction between the author's intentions and the exigencies of his audience. In so far, however, as it persevered in its cultural being, the readers condemned it, considering that they had been misled by sham appearances when they had approved it. For we have seen that at the same time as action deviates, it loses any chance of knowing its deviation. So it was not Soviet society that could assess its own drift in relation to its 1925 reality – or rather, it assessed that drift inasmuch as it appeared to be that of the book itself.

For the same reason, all condemnations are retrospective. Even if it is a recent act which is the object of the sanction, the grounds seek out past – hence, inert – acts that the practical drift, inasmuch as it is unconscious, has constituted as culpable. From this standpoint, I cannot refrain from citing the example of an incident that occurred in the USA, and that I came to know about (even though our inquiry is devoted solely to the USSR). For in the first place, we shall thus be able to glimpse that this type of *refringence* of the practical milieu is encountered in all societies, albeit in obviously differing forms. And secondly, the case was absolutely typical. It involved a public official who was seriously harassed in 1952 because he had shouted 'Long Live Russia' some ten years earlier, when Field-Marshal Paulus surrendered at Stalingrad. It was of no avail for him to point out to the investigators and his superiors that the USSR had then been an ally of the United States. The others, as may be imagined, had not forgotten this. They had merely not, *for their part*, shouted

'Long Live Russia' on that day – neither had anybody they had ever heard of. So the existence *in the past* of that differential (insignificant at the time when it appeared: people would have called it exuberance, or perhaps – without real anger – progressive sympathies) became, *through* the practical milieu of 1952, the proof that the individual in question had *long been an other*, an enclave within the nation.

As may easily be surmised, integration of the USSR by the praxis of socialization could only exaggerate that tendency of the past to make itself *the denouncer of the present*. Some person who had been arrested for his links with the opposition between 1927 and 1930, but soon released, would often be arrested ten years later *on the same grounds* – and this time executed. This is because, at the fluid moment when tendencies had been clashing and the rivals (all of them, and each for the other) had incarnated in a certain way the unity of communist praxis, the fault ascribed to the accused man had been venial: he had made a mistake, he had let himself be seduced by an unviable programme or specious propaganda, but how could that lapse ally him with counter-revolution, since the defeated leaders – the Right and Left oppositionists – were still Communists, who were seriously mistaken but not counter-revolutionaries? Ten years later, the exiled Trotsky was objectively and subjectively a traitor for the Soviets. The Right oppositionists had been executed or else, like Bukharin, they had admitted their crimes. Ever closer integration around the sovereign-individual; oppression of the workers; Terror rebounding even on the Bureaucracy; the threat of war – all these contributed to the radicalization of grievances. But if Trotsky *was* a traitor, if he had been preparing his criminal actions since the death of Lenin, his supposed former 'allies' had in reality been his *accomplices* and their so-called lightmindedness became *in fact* a *treason*. Of course, it will be said that this is not true. Even if Trotsky's treason were to be admitted, in line with the Stalinist propaganda, that would not necessarily imply the culpability of his allies in 1927. Mistakes can be made in good faith. By this very judgement, however, we are signalling that our degree of integration into praxis is *at the very least* much lower that that of the Soviet functionary or activist. Because of the emergency, he defines his acts by their practical outcome – they will be positive or negative – and deliberately confuses their global signification with their intention. In a sense, as we saw in *The Problem of Method*, this attitude is correct (more than ours, which remains idealist) on condition that the act is viewed in its multidimensional objectivity, or – if you like – at all the levels of its relations with the social ensemble and with groups and individuals.[67] But

---

67. *The Problem of Method*, p.98, n.1.

since the only practical aim was to construct, the Stalinist apparatus –
ossified round its privileges and identifying with construction – never
viewed the act other than in its relations with the sovereign (seen as a
mere faceless force). On this basis, that sovereign bureaucracy – which
sought to change men by acting upon the material conditions of their
lives – could not even conceive that the guilty might change, or adapt. It
endowed them with an *immutable-being*, because it grasped them on the
basis of its own ossification: i.e. its alienation from the interests it had
given itself. So what changed in the past of Soviet individuals was not
just the material fact (the alliance with the oppositionist becoming
complicity with the traitor) but – through bureaucratic changes – the way
of evaluating them (rejection of nuances: complicity became immutable,
the distant past always had more importance than the present or, if you
like, the immediate past). Whatever the individual's recent service record
might be, moreover, it would be interpreted on the basis of his old errors.
If he had been successful in the post to which he had been appointed
between two purges, this meant that he was seeking to evade the vigilance
of the apparatus. How should the still fluid ensemble of his present
undertakings weigh in the balance, as compared with the vast monolithic
block of the old error?

By being interiorized, this way of judging – of judging *oneself* – ended
up making Stalinist man into an extraordinary contradiction. He was
wholly thrown forward like a bridge towards the socialist future, and at
the same time he remained indefinitely what he was. His past, against all
experience, became his unalterable law. For everyone was modified,
even in his self-awareness, by a bureaucratic ossification that – inasmuch
as he *was not* a bureaucrat – was not produced directly within him, but –
inasmuch as he was linked to the Bureaucracy, at least by the immanent
relation of obedience – *determined him from afar*, whether he modified
himself to adapt to the modification of the other term and preserve the
inner relationship that united them (command-obedience) or did not
manage to modify himself and appeared in society itself as drifting
beneath the weight of his old actions: i.e. as suspect. In the former case,
the induced transformation was absolute, the identity relative to the
system in which he was situated. In the latter case, the transformation
was graspable only in and by the change in the system (and its
unawareness of changing), so it would be termed relative; on the other
hand, to assert that identity remained absolute it was necessary oneself to
be situated *outside* the system. In conclusion, therefore, it was merely a
matter of different reference points. If one views things in this way, it is
easily understandable that the members of the system in evolution should
reasonably be able to reverse the terms, treating as an absolute what we
term relative (and vice versa). It goes without saying, of course, that on

this basis a dialectic – at once singular and polarized by the orientated temporalization of everything – is established, in every group and every individual, between the absolute and the relative (whatever definition may be given of each of these); and this dialectic has to determine *from afar* certain transformations in other social categories.

I think it is worth recalling, to conclude this section, that action *from afar* – and via the mediation of the relation of immanence – must be distinguished radically from all forms of direct activity of men upon things or upon other men.[68] For it is a matter of a *supplementary outcome* of the sovereign praxis of integration, rather than ordinary practices (orders, obedience, constraints, indoctrination, explanations, distribution of tasks, division of labour as a function of the exigencies of material and equipment, professional activities, etc.). The totalization-of-envelopment – at least at the level at which we are considering it: i.e. on the supposition of maximum integration – produces itself as a unity of astringency in the milieu in which individuals live (i.e. in the practical field such as the sovereign has defined it, and such as it has defined the sovereign). And its dialectical law – perfectly intelligible, moreover, since it is quite simply the relationship between a totality in the process of being accomplished and its parts, and mutually between its parts via the intermediary of the totality – demands that every determination of the practical temporalization, wherever it may take place, be actualized as a determination in interiority by all the elements participating in this temporalization. It must be added, however, that certain types of internal activity – above all in struggle – can utilize this law to transform an individual or group without seeming to touch them. For example, a regroupment *elsewhere* of certain ensembles is enough to fill a restricted community with inefficacy: to make it, *despite itself*, slip to the Far Left or the Far Right. On other occasions, provoking the disappearance of the most left-wing group has been enough to oblige the adjacent group to take on its role, despite itself (this misadventure happened, as is well known, to Chaumette and Hébert after the arrest of Roux and Varlet).[69] But this – more or less pragmatic – use of the *rule of totalization* can *in any case* appear only in the polarized milieu, and following integration (although it can, subsequently, intensify the latter).

3. The *third factor* of totalizing unity is *incarnation*. By this I no longer mean the incarnation of the summit – i.e. the sovereign – but

---

68. *Critique*, vol. 1, pp.664–5.

69. The Hébertists, of course, having helped to eliminate the Enragés (Roux, Varlet), adopted their programme and were themselves condemned to death by the Revolutionary Tribunal in 1794.

simply, at all levels, the retotalization of the totalization-of-envelopment
by every event, every praxis and every particular *hexis*. I shall not come
back to this, since I have already spoken about it. I just want to note a
few of its features, inasmuch as it occurs in the polarized milieu of
spatializing-temporalization. In so far as the unity of the drama, for the
individual, implies the diversity of levels at which it is played, and in so
far as every aspect of behaviour can be considered *at once* as referring to
the organic totality (i.e. to the ensemble of significations of the *whole*
person) and as incarnating – in a particular milieu defined by its
astringency and its degree of explicitness, involution (or display), violence and radicalism, etc. – that same free totality of the practical
organism, to that extent the singular incarnations of the totality-of-
envelopment are rigorously grounded. I have shown elsewhere how the
intrusion of adults into the moral life of an adolescent can be felt
ethically as a condemnation *and* as an injustice, but lived *sexually* as a
rape.[70] Sexuality, here, radicalizes – simply because it has to grasp all
conflicts as a confrontation of bodies by desire. So in so far as this
intrusion *must* be felt *by the body in its materiality* (and precisely in so
far as adults have made impossible a *non-sexual incorporation* of the
condemnation: for example, by avoiding 'corporal' mistreatment) this
relationship of non-reciprocity will be lived *sexually*. Sex, if you like,
will be the form of incorporation. Suddenly the intrusion – a pure
practical signification: they have watched the child, caught him, forced
open his drawer to steal his secrets from him – takes place carnally as
penetration. The flesh realizes the metaphor by the only *passion* it
knows. And the child's ambivalence towards adults will become an
ambivalent structure of desire (horror of penetration by the other;
fascination by the role of rape victim). The whole event is thus incarnated.
It is *other*, and it is *total*. If the analyst intervenes, it will precisely be to
realize a Catharsis and explain – as a synthetically bonded ensemble of
transcendent significations – what sexual procedures realize fully, but
obscurely. This fleshing out of incorporation has effectively radicalized
the event. Having itself become the body, it will be resuscitated in desire
itself by the orientation it gives to this. And if by this very means the
adolescent slides towards homosexuality, he will live – as *incorporated*
by carnal procedures and their consequences (reactions of others) – this
relatively benign condemnation as a radical exclusion. It is not his free
practice that set itself exclusion as an objective, nor is it some outraged
unconscious. Sex and sexual life, however, being in themselves the
source of a radicalism and the domain of a mute violence, the *sexualized*

---

70. In *Saint Genet: Actor and Martyr*, New York 1963.

offence was realized with maximum violence and as irreparable.

This example allows us to understand that every individual procedure represents, from the standpoint that concerns us, the re-production of *the* social totalization-of-envelopment in the form of *an* enveloped totalization. Can it be denied, in fact, that – sticking to our chosen example – the praxis of socializing integration has to be interiorized in everyone as *incorporation*? No doubt this incorporation is complex for the very reason that symbols are replaced by real actions. It is effected just as well by the interiorization of assemblies (job skill), by fatigue, by affective procedures (that are nothing but lived praxis) and occupational illnesses, or by a certain way of reproducing within [oneself] the urgency and extreme speed of a constantly accelerated temporalization – as nervousness, instability or, on the other hand, voluntarist harshness – as it is by a strictly sexual procedure. Yet there is no doubt but that sexuality is affected. I have reported the case of those neo-proletarians – peasants recruited from the hinterland by the new factories of Le Mans and transformed into workers after six months' apprenticeship – who became electrical welders and paid for this overhasty transition from rural to industrial rhythms with the more or less total ruin of their sexual life: the percentage of impotence (there, as in Saint-Nazaire for the same job) is considerable from the age of twenty-eight on. The exploitation of the peasant – the violent action exerted upon his body, and upon the organic rhythms defining his behaviour – he lives radically, at the level of sex, as *castration*: in short, as an irreparable *deficit*. In others, however, less radical sexual procedures can be found, and our experts think they can detect traces here of that invisible and phantasmagorical reality they term the psychic – just because radical passivity is replaced by passive *procedures*: sexual indolence; scarcity and crude simplification of desire, which when it does arise becomes indifferent to its object; long periods of indifference; intermittent impotence, etc. In the former case, impotence was the direct, physiological result of adaptation disorders. But the procedures I have just enumerated are nothing different. Only, as the deficit is not so great, they are still lived in the form of a need-project (or rejection of the project, through temporary absence of the need); which means that the organism remains defined by a relation to the future, instead of the future on this singular score being simply blocked by a total, inert negation. In the case of impotence – as it is merely *suffered*, in the guise of an inert determination of the physiological – it can be said that incarnation is reduced to its simplest expression; or, if you like, that it is a matter of a negative (and for that very reason abstract) consequence rather than a singularized totalization. Of course, this impotence is lived in interiority as an incorporation of life's misery, exploitation and transplantation, and in turn *as a moral diminution* and injury to the living source of praxis. But these are already *incarnations* of the latter, in other practical sectors, whereas in itself it retains the indetermination that characterizes every deprivation. By contrast, however, in the case of the sexual procedures we have enumerated – in which the practical and the physiological remain basically undifferentiated – incarnation is whole, since there is a reassumption of the determinations suffered and the life imposed, but on the plane of sexuality. Without a doubt, sexual procedures in one way or another incarnated the accelerated urbanization in the USSR of peasants recruited by industry and, as a consequence, the extraordinary exodus of those who have since been called 'displaced persons': i.e. at once the exodus, the difficulties of acclimatization, and the reaction of the practical organism to those determinations undergone. Even if the latter *negates* them, in fact, he interiorizes them to re-exteriorize them. From this very standpoint, he radicalizes them. It is perhaps on this plane that he will express the rejection – the irreconcilable opposition – that he does not have the means to express elsewhere. Or else, quite to the contrary, a certain indifference to sexuality, riven by violent, brutal and simplified desires, may be realized in some people as the incarnation of *activism*: i.e. of a practice entirely devoted to work and social action. This *practice* becomes a pure *negative* presence in the organic milieu of sexuality. However, at the same time – precisely because this present '*négatité*' is not a pure and simple destruction – it is re-exteriorized in a twofold transcendence: one enveloping, the other enveloped.

(*a*) From the former standpoint, sexual indifference (since this is our example) is already preserved in the social and political praxis that transcends it. For at this level, celibacy – as freedom to produce (or, if it is a matter of ambition, as freedom to succeed by such productive activity) – may find itself implicitly *contained* in the very temporalization of praxis, as an immediate consequence of the scarcity of time. Circumstances will or will not be able to explain – *afterwards* – this provisional option. It should above all not be thought, moreover, that celibacy – as an implicit option – is a pure absence of any relation with marriage. The sexual bond is a real and constant determination of the reciprocal relations between men and women. It *exists* within the practice of celibacy, because this practice is an abstention *in relation to an institutionalized and socialized mediation* of the carnal relationship as a bond of fundamental reciprocity. (It is well known that this mediation, in every society, aims to transform the ambivalent reciprocity of the couple by creating *on its behalf* a sovereign mediation – God or the law – which transforms [the partners] into pledged or common individuals. In other words, the couple – institutionalized – via the mediation of a mandated third party constitutes itself as a unity of integration *for this third party*:

i.e. for the sovereign. And in relation to this *mediated and non-transcendable* unity, each partner is defined as the same common individual, *here* and *now*, as their partner. In fact, the non-transcendable unity of the couple is an alienation, precisely in so far as it hides reciprocity. The more this alienation reflects a social hierarchy – for example, the superiority of the male – the more reciprocity is driven back into subterranean relations of eroticism. By contrast, the more social circumstances highlight reciprocity, the more the synthetic institutionality of the couple is fragile and the more its *unity* is called into question.) In the same way, the celibacy of priests is not just an attitude towards their fundamental sexuality but a transcendence of that sexuality, whose value itself must come – in a sacrificial perspective – from the fact that it is preserved as it is transcended. In short, even in the case of the young activist set on celibacy (at least temporarily), the problem of sexual life is implicitly present through the very presence of the flesh (as a permanent possibility of *incorporation*): will he be chaste, or will he confine himself to brief encounters at the behest of his desires? The decision may be explicit only in the case of deliberate chastity. Depending on the various viewpoints (internal to Soviet society), the other option may appear a kind of blithe confidence in life, or a 'military leave', or – on the contrary – a persistence of the past, bourgeois customs, etc. And such viewpoints, of course, are not those of just any old individuals, reacting at the whim of a more or less innate 'character'. Rather, they define – in themselves, and on the plane of sexuality – the various milieux and groups, and the functions differentiating them. The practical weight of such options (many of which are already passivized, particularly in the upper echelons of the hierarchy) will partly decide the activist's individual choice. But this itself shows us, in cross-section, his real relations with the various strata of society. Depending on whether he is merely after an increased wage or wants to try and make a career, he will have contacts with different layers of the Bureaucracy. Conversely, however, his contacts – at least implicitly, and inasmuch as his origin or original behaviour have themselves determined these – by defining him through a position (an inert perch) and through a particularization of the field of possibilities, themselves take account of the *opening* of his ambition. It is within this circularity that he decides his praxis, and his praxis decides on his sincerity. Thus his sexual option – even though it remains implicit – nevertheless succeeds in *situating him in the social ensemble*: above all, if he is considered in his singularity and in his developments (chastity can be a *labour*, and in a sense the practice of sexual freedom can become one too). On the level of the total praxis that characterizes the individual and always mobilizes him as a whole whatever he may do (even, and above all, if he wishes to abstain) – at the

level even of the social, ethical options, or relations with institutions –
sex is present as a synthetic determination in interiority, and as the
relationship of reciprocal immanence of this man with any woman,
inasmuch as every woman – absent or present, and in one way or another
– determines *also* his praxis-body as a carnal body.

(*b*) But that particular totalization is the totalization of the practical
organism as a free constituent praxis. As such, it might be compared to
the totalization-of-envelopment (although one is the dialectic itself, as a
free constituent foundation of intelligibility, while the other is the dialectic-
as-constituted-reason). Moreover, the same sexual attitude can obviously
be encountered again in the form of an enveloped totality. Whatever, in
fact, his personal option may be, the fundamental existence of the sexes
as a bond of reciprocity (undetermined, of course, outside circumstances
and movement) disposes [the individual] in his carnal depth – and within
the framework of the historical conjuncture – to reactualize, by transcending, the relation of immanence that conditions him in his flesh by
means of *that* particular woman: i.e. to realize himself as sexual behaviour
at every 'opportunity', in every *encounter*, i.e. (outside of work) in a
permanent way – whether it is a matter of rejecting, renouncing, seducing
or brutalizing. *Desire* is at the bottom of these procedures: either as his
own desire, or as the desire of the other – troubling, alarming, repulsive,
etc. I have explained elsewhere how *the body makes itself flesh*.[71] But it
must be added also that *the flesh becomes act*, while retaining the opaque
passivity of fleshly thickening, to the very point of orientating practically
(towards the other's fleshly thickening) and revealing its own arousal.
That is what gives its deep meaning to the term (of ethical and religious
origin): '*the carnal act*'. The body-instrument becomes facticity, inasmuch as it is determined in interiority by the concrete encounter of a
particular *other* body (of the *other* sex) and – through this facticity
transcended towards the other – strives to wrest the other's body away
from instrumentality. The result, if the *carnal act* takes place, is that it is
the flesh being transcended – in its very solitude and in its contingency –
towards the solitude and contingency of the other. So its ambivalence is
understandable, since it is simultaneously action and passion. It is, in
fact, the carnal contingency of lived experience being transcended by
being turned into passivity, only to act through this very passivity upon
the *flesh* of the other. And its objective is itself carnal, for we are beneath
the level of corporeal instrumentality setting an abstract objective through
its procedures: i.e. outlining, within temporalization, a schematic future
that every new way of behaving will help to particularize. The object of

---

71. In *Being and Nothingness*, pp.387 ff.

desire is an immediately present concrete reality: the flesh of each person, in himself and in the other, inasmuch as it cannot be realized or even desired except through the movement of the instrument to become flesh in itself and in the other.

Now this relation, as a reciprocal action, is particularized in every case by a finite – albeit hard to enumerate – ensemble of factors. It matters little to us. What counts for us is the fact that in the case of the ambitious young man we have envisaged, the carnal relation – inasmuch as he is one of its terms, and we are viewing him (abstractly) apart from the other – has to *incarnate* in turn his totalizing option. To the extent, for example, that he has produced himself, through his actual labour, as *instrumental hexis* – i.e. to the extent that the ensemble of his procedures, inside and outside work, tend to maintain (*simultaneously* as an ensemble of motor habits, and a synthetic perception of the practical field and through it of his own body, *and at the same time* as a kind of pledged inertia) the practical reality of his body as that of an instrument for directing instruments (i.e. as inertia exteriorized and controlled by praxis) and as efficacy of inertia moulded upon inert materiality – *to that extent*, the threshold to be crossed (under the sway of need more than desire) in order to pass from instrumentality to the flesh will be higher. And even were this threshold to be crossed, the sexual behaviour risks remaining more instrumental than carnal. The offered passivity of the other appears like a living matter – *to be handled*; to be disposed in such and such a way; to be penetrated – yet carnal contingency is not experienced deeply as such, but remains the abstract prop of arousal.

Of course, this sexual behaviour may be of various kinds. What counts is that in the singular moment of the embrace or the caress it resumes – and, in a transcending movement to realize itself and attain its goal, *incarnates* – the boy's total behaviour. For if it were the mere inert outcome of his social activities, we would not be able to view it as a living incarnation: at most, it would refer to the decompressed ensemble of practices. But it is a matter of the real relations between him and some woman or other, in their particular development and in their singular temporalization. Moreover, everything is indeed singular, as the irreversible unfolding of an *affair* common to two individuals. From the outset, the woman's physical and moral personality is already a kind of *internal* factor in the singularity of *this* young man's present behaviour patterns – with respect to his comrades and himself. These relations – whether he rejects the woman or seduces her – are a free practical invention, in so far as the flesh is transcended towards the flesh and the circumstances of their union (or conflict) simultaneously require certain behavioural forms. But this very invention is the project that transcends and negates the former circumstances, thereby preserving them as its internal characteristic. In particular, it must be understood that the sexual relation of this individual to this woman *realizes* his practical relation of instrumentality with inert matter, as the actual limit of his arousal or as the particularity of his sexual life. In other words, his total praxis is realized *here*, in this instant, in and by these acts which preserve a kind of *private singularity* and – in this very way – fall outside the great historical undertaking in which he seeks to play his role. Not just in the strict realization of the 'carnal act', moreover, but actually in the bound ensemble of behavioural forms (against a background of explicit or hidden reciprocity of the sexes) which have prepared his union with this woman, and which – by virtue of that very preparation – have given it a certain ethico-practical structure. Indeed, if he has shown himself 'sly', 'boastful', 'cowardly', etc., or, on the contrary, 'frank', 'open', etc., these 'qualities and defects' – which for the woman who loves him merely represent his private character, and concern only his private relations with her – are *on the contrary* the actual realization of his objective relations with his work and his bosses: his possibilities of 'getting ahead' and wresting himself away from the masses, and as a function of this his opportunism (i.e. the *quality* of his total praxis and, *at the same time*, the signification of his social activities) or, on the contrary, his sectarianism, etc.

Still more fundamentally, moreover – as the sexual relationship is a relationship of contingency, arousal and flesh, but for that very reason is perhaps the deepest incarnation of the relation of reciprocity between 'human beings', at once as free organisms and as products of the society in which they live – it is not just the individual who pronounces sentence upon himself and his human reality through the relations he establishes: it is society that causes itself to be judged by this free incarnation. Not that 'worse' or 'better' relations cannot be found in other circumstances, and by considering other couples. But simply because the fundamental relation between the sexes is defined as a field of possibles *within* the objective limits set by the worst and best couples. These limits, as is well known, for a specific society and a specific moment are not so far away from one another. Every individual, in every couple, condenses the sexual and conjugal field by his very incarnation, inasmuch as he produces himself through the synthetic determination of the field and as the realization of one of its possibilities. It will already be clear, in fact, that this very field – as an integral part of the sovereign field – is interiorized by everyone, inasmuch as relations of production, institutions, totalizing praxis, education and traditions (reinforced or combated depending on the case) produce him as a sexually socialized individual, defining anew – through him – the fundamental relationship between the sexes and giving this a new and singular prominence, by virtue of the reciprocal significations and reflections established by each individual between the sexual institution and other institutions.

6

Objectivity and Idiosyncrasy (an Objective Drift: Stalinist Anti-Semitism)

S O THE enveloping totalization is incarnated by every singularity, and every singularity defines itself simultaneously as an incarnation and an enveloped totalization. Yet there is nothing irrational here: neither Gestaltism nor any of those ambiguous, vague forms that strive to re-establish a hyper-organicism, in one shape or another. These enveloped totalizations incarnate the totalization-of-envelopment for the sole reason that individuals as practical organisms are totalizing projects, and there is nothing else to totalize – in a society integrated by a sovereign-individual – except the totalization-of-envelopment itself. The latter totalizes them (by concerted and co-ordinated actions and by the exigencies of the practico-inert, as well as by the determination in interiority of each person by everybody and everything) inasmuch as it produces them. They retotalize it, inasmuch as it is through the practical transcendence of the interiorized factors that they make themselves its products. But this retotalization enriches it with the concrete ensemble of particular circumstances and goals. So the totalization-of-envelopment is found in every enveloped totalization as its signification: i.e. as its integration into everything. It should not be thought, however, that the signification of envelopment is to the enveloped incarnation as the abstract is to the concrete. In a praxis whose sovereign is an individual, the signification of envelopment is itself – as we have seen – individuated: i.e. the practical unity of action is also the indissoluble organic synthesis represented by a man; and for this reason the totalizing totalization *likewise* defines itself by contingency, by concrete facticity, by the limits and riches of the singular.

However, as we have also seen, although the sovereign praxis can be described as individualized (as praxis of *this* sovereign, obeyed by *these* men and not others) and thus discloses *the scarcity of men* as one of the counter-finalities of human history, it still remains the case that the praxis is defined – in this very singularity – as an objective response to the real exigencies of objectivity (on the basis of the already posited goals). Singularization is merely facticity as necessary contingency, and as incarnation of a common action whose objective laws emanate from the external circumstances, the aims and the counter-finalities secreted in the course of temporalization.* *Here* – in *this* historical conjuncture – the objective laws of the group's (or nation's) praxis must be incarnated *by the option of the sovereign-individual*, and as possessing the dual aspect described earlier: a fanning out of objective prescriptions concerning imperfectly determined individuals or groups; and the individual temporalization of one option, through transcendence and actualization of *this* particular practical organism. In this sense, *we shall encounter in the decree* at once the common individual – constituted by the sovereign forged by circumstances – and his specific differential, as a lag *in this perspective* between his incarnation of the revolutionary past (and, beyond that even, of some vanished Russia) and the actualization demanded by circumstances. It is remarkable, moreover, that this differential is grasped in the decree inasmuch as it offers itself as common objectivity and – falsely – as a universal law. If no oppositionist notices it, at least the historian will unearth it. But the key thing here is that idiosyncrasy, as a differential, appears through an insufficiency or exaggeration of the pseudo-universal content of the law. All things considered, the historian – with all the documents at his disposal – declares (and even this is questioned, though eventually accepted) that the objective situation did not require all those stipulations; or that it required still more; or, above all (this is the most common case), that it required more, fewer and something else (within the very limits where idiosyncrasy can play a part). Through these comparisons between objective, partially undetermined possibles and objective exigencies (of imperfectly determined categories of men; or of the practico-inert illuminated by the objectives to be achieved), it is paradoxical that one should be able to determine an *idiosyncrasy*. But the paradox disappears when you reflect that since the individual is socialized in so far as he has individuated his society, his idiosyncrasy is precisely *that objective lag* (and – considering the temporalization throughout its development – *that objective drift*), inasmuch as it is not produced as a parasitic development of the practico-inert inside the field, but on the contrary refers to a practical option: *its immediate foundation*. And this option – inasmuch as it involves synthetic operations, a final decision, and the formulation of a project through services and corrections contributed

---

* Leaving aside, hypothetically, transcendent actions by external groups, foreign nations, etc.

by the sovereign – is itself nothing other than the synthetic temporalization of that decree, inasmuch as the unity of the temporal development gives the latter its synthetic reality (through irreversible integration) and its borrowed power to transcend itself. The sovereign is simply the practical unity of the project, and this unity of living immanence characterizes itself in interiority by the lags and drifts which signal the objective content of the law or decree. This originally signifies simply that it is *this particular sovereign idiosyncrasy from which emanates THIS lag of the practical with respect to principles and objects*. It is possible, for example, to consider that the way in which Stalin conceived and utilized the notion of 'optimum variant' (borrowed by him from the first programmes of Trotsky and the Left before 1925) clearly reveals his characteristic 'brutality'. In the case of such a sovereign, however, what will *brutality* be if not precisely a voluntarism expressed in decisions by a gap between the exigencies of the objective or the real situation and the tasks (pointlessly multiplied, pointlessly arduous) sovereignly exacted by the *real* praxis (such as it *is*, not such as it ought to be)? Interiorization of this 'brutality' – for the oppositionist, or for the historian – consists in seeing it as the free future of sovereign decisions and as the destiny of citizens. Hence, this simply means that its *re-exteriorization* is foreseen, in measures to come (literally to come, for the oppositionist living under Stalin; not yet studied fully by the historian of planned growth in the USSR, so determining the future content destined to appear in his work).

The best example is perhaps Stalinist anti-Semitism. If Stalin had been obliged to answer for his actions before some revolutionary court, he would have denied fiercely *having been an anti-Semite* – and to a considerable extent he would have been sincere. For anti-Semitism, in its basic form as *racism* (*this* particular Jew is irredeemably lost by virtue of the existence within him of *his race*, which drives him to act badly: drives him into anti-national or antisocial activities), was obviously condemned by Marxist ideology (as, indeed, by mere democratic liberalism – as a mystification based upon positivist Reason). His attitude towards the Jewish problem, the increasingly anti-Semitic measures he took against Soviet citizens of Hebrew origin – that whole well-known ensemble – was objectively motivated in the sovereign's eyes by the *political* difficulties which integrating Jews into the nation of socialism caused. The links (real or imagined*) between Jews at home and in the

---

* It is true that, after the Tsarist pogroms, emigration had the effect of partly dispersing Russia's Jewish families – so that every Jew has, or may have, a cousin in the West. But it is also true that these people have long been separated; that they no longer have anything in common; and that they no longer communicate (partly also because of the Terror, which prevents *all* Soviet citizens from communicating freely with other countries).

capitalist nations – and later the emergence of a Jewish state under the particular control of American capitalism (via the mediation of Jews in the United States), the activities of the Zionist League, etc. – all this represented to the suspicious Stalin not just a *possibility* of nuclei forming, but the real presence of a nucleus of traitors within (some active, others potential, all in cahoots). The old nightmare of revolutionaries was reincarnated here, in an unexpected form: what the men of 1793 used to call 'the *émigré* within'. The notion of racism was thus (seemingly, at least) not applicable. It simply happened that historical circumstances, by multiplying their links with the capitalist foe, had constituted a specific ensemble of Soviet citizens – precisely the Jews – as a permanent danger to socialization. This first meant that any specificity had to be denied them (whereas the linguistic or folkloristic specificities of national minorities were developed). Yiddish, for example, if it were to become the organ of a Jewish culture (with novels and plays in Yiddish), would heighten the integration of that harmful grouping and – for that very reason – its self-awareness as a specificity. That culture and that language could have only one result. By uniting the Jews *against* other Soviet citizens (or at least by isolating them from the latter) they activated their links with other Jews – those who spoke Yiddish and had created a Yiddish culture in the countries hostile to socialization. Liquidation of the specific tools of their culture, however, was accompanied by a police surveillance that at once destroyed any possibility of integration. The contradiction was manifest: they were denied any cultural autonomy, because it prevented integration; but they were denied integration, because their historical past already designated them as traitors and they had to be kept under constant surveillance. On that basis, of course – within the sovereign field, where relations of immanence conditioned everything by everything from afar – the opportunities for repression and deportation multiplied *ad infinitum*. Indeed, by virtue of the very contradiction of Stalin's policy – and since the Jews had to be *de-Jewified* without it being possible for them to be *integrated* – the inescapable solution was extermination. Assimilation, through total physical liquidation of the assimilated, for the benefit of the assimilator!

In so far as this policy defined Stalin – above all the Stalin of his last years – as a virulent anti-Semite, it designated him precisely by the measures he had taken and by those he would take (or that death would prevent him from taking). From that standpoint, we shall recognize in his policy towards the Jews a *neo-anti-Semitism* of a political rather than ethnic origin, springing from the suspicion of the sovereign (and through him of the entire individuated society) towards any social ensemble that might regroup independently – outside the sovereign directives – in the name of a common historical past or certain similarities of situation; and at the same time from the particularism incarnated by Stalin himself, who rejected universality and outside the USSR saw only the rotten world of capitalism. (From the standpoint of that particularism, the link between a Moscow Jew and a Jew from Tel Aviv or London could only be corrupting – in the name of a false universalism, a Western bourgeois was seeking to corrupt a socialist worker – and universalism was repudiated in the degraded form of *cosmopolitanism*, etc.).

It forms no part of my purpose to study the Jewish problem in the USSR under Stalin. The example interests us here *from another viewpoint*: it raises the question of the idiosyncrasy of the deeper levels. Should the historian content himself with reproducing political anti-Semitism, in its reality and its significations, as an immediately graspable idiosyncrasy of the sovereign: i.e. as a pattern of behaviour provoked by false problems and false exigencies that only the sovereign and his team of secondary leaders could determine, inasmuch as they had themselves been produced by Terror, mistrust and anti-universalism (a backlash of praxis described above)? Or should he not ask himself whether that supposed 'neo-anti-Semitism' did not spring from the old anti-Semitic racism and derive its virulence from that?

The question is raised, to tell the truth, on two distinct levels – at first sight, at least. For if you look at the measures taken and their implementation as praxis – realizing itself through the vertical regroupment it produces by its very temporalization in the various social layers – there can be no doubt but that the sovereign practices were partly sustained by the young mistrust of encircled socialism. But it is even more obvious that these populations knew and shared the racist anti-Semitism of Tsarism, and had not been demystified (*even less so*, in that political anti-Semitism made demystification impossible: educators condemned racism in words, but – by virtue of its very resemblance to Tsarist persecution – the persecution of Jews by the sovereign obliged such education to remain a dead letter). In this sense, as you moved farther away from the top level (it is purely provisionally, moreover, that we are granting this level the benefit of the doubt), the driving force for the subaltern officials and the masses was still racism. This was enough to transform the sovereign practice, through the social layers it regrouped in the unity of a provisional temporalization. Perhaps neo-anti-Semitism, as a policy towards the Jews, was really applicable only in so far – precisely – as at the lower levels of society it quite simply dissolved into racism. If that is true, it must be said that Stalin exploited the racism of the masses (it matters little, from the standpoint we are adopting here, whether or not he meant to) and, thereby, the socialist sovereign accepted such racism and by its actions helped to reinforce it. Popular anti-Semitism, in the USSR as elsewhere, had actually had an economic

foundation: the peasants had been anti-Semitic when the merchants were
Jews. Socialization, from the outset, had contributed to dissolving this
foundation. What remained was the petrified web of traditions (outdated
significations, activity of the Church, etc.). These too would have
dissolved in their turn, if the sovereign had not revived them by replacing
the vanished foundation with a political basis. Conversely, those anti-
Semitized masses could henceforth – especially at moments of danger –
demand *out of racism* that the government should organize pogroms, or
sanction those which they carried out spontaneously. The campaign
against the Jews once more took on that diversionary aspect that it had
always had, under all governments. By reinforcing racism, political anti-
Semitism ended up dissolving into it.

Thus the Stalinist option revealed more clearly its *idiosyncrasy*. Rather
than renounce political segregation, the sovereign risked a resurgence of
racism. Anti-Jewish racism was thereby determined as less dangerous for
socialism than the free existence of Jewish communities or individuals
joined together by cultural bonds. Thereby, the sovereign was *called into
question*. To be sure, Stalin, under the pressure of circumstances, had
often compromised on principles (the less he had respected them, the
more dogmatically he would reassert them, albeit with an imperceptible
deviation); but here the gap was so big that it had perturbed his own
troops (or, at least, the more enlightened minority of the executive). For
Stalin not to recoil a priori from those police methods, which could have
no other effect than to reawaken the racism of the masses – and for the
rebirth of the old Tsarist anti-Semitism not to strike him, at all events, as
a regression on the part of the working classes and, as such, as a negative
result to be avoided at all costs – must Stalin not have been won over,
subtly and right from his harsh Georgian childhood, to the traditional
(rural or semi-rural) forms of anti-Semitic racism? In order *really* to
have believed in the Jewish danger, in the USSR of 1950 (even if Zionist
follies, spying affairs, etc., are taken into account), revolutionary and
particularist mistrust were insufficient. For it was necessary *already* (and
in all countries) to be racist – to consider that, *out of all the specific
groups* (national minorities, or closed societies within the larger one
particularized by their working or living conditions), the Jewish group
was dangerous by its nature – in order to attach any *real* importance to
the *potential* relations that Soviet Jews might (if the regime were
different) maintain with Western Jews. If the question is posed in this
light, it is immediately clear that the supposed political neo-anti-
Semitism in the USSR had always existed in bourgeois countries, as one
of the structures of anti-Semitic racism. For the bourgeois too, Jews are
countryless. It was the bourgeois who first condemned the universalism
of Reason – the very same that Stalin termed 'cosmopolitanism' –

baptizing it with the name 'Jewish International'. It was the bourgeois (which was why Marx called anti-Semitism the socialism of fools) who, confusing the international relations between capitalisms with the human relations between Jews belonging to different countries, first saw the Hebrew as an individual in the service of foreign interests, whose nay-saying universalism – parading as Reason – sought to dissolve the national particularity of what ought to be his *country*. And this 'conception' – formulated, as may well be imagined, in the less stupid anti-Semitic circles – seeks to preserve racism while claiming to transcend it. For those who advance such propositions usually add that, for their own part, they would have nothing against Jews if they would only leave the nation on which they are battening, and go off to populate some new country or settle in Israel; for it is not some internal virus, but History – the 'diaspora' – that has made them what they are. This latter point, though, was not accepted fully by Stalinist anti-Semitism: for it would have meant allowing Jews to opt between Tel Aviv and Moscow, whereas it would have been an intolerable absurdity for a Soviet citizen – even a Jew – to have been able to show that in certain cases it was possible to prefer a bourgeois democracy to the fatherland of socialism. So the USSR would keep its Jews, in order to exterminate them.

Hence, the sovereign did not limit himself – as we had initially said – to making use of the old racism, in order to maintain a policy of repression rooted in *politics*. In defining that policy (by actions) he actually reconstituted racist anti-Semitism in all its signification (and across all social layers). He merely reserved for himself and the ruling circles the option of concealing the baser currents, through elucidation of higher significations; and of disguising the racist movement in the historical interpretation. We need only re-identify circularity as a common law of the practical event and our investigation, in order to grasp the conditioning of the masses by the sovereign act (a political praxis claiming to be Marxist) and the totalizing reconditioning of the sovereign by the masses reinforced in their racism.

For the intelligibility of the totalization-of-envelopment, this is enough. Stalin and his collaborators were retotalized as racists by the masses. The act, via the mediation of the whole society, came back to them and determined them. You can see why *intention*, in this case, was irrelevant. If it had not been *racist* at the outset, the act had still objectively been the result of racism; above all, moreover, through the very operation of circularity, *the intention was to become racist subsequently*. You can grasp here – from real life – the extent to which the sovereign autonomy of praxis was not incompatible with its strict conditioning. It was not necessarily as an interiorization of popular reactions, and as a tran-scendence of these, that racism was re-exteriorized as an intentional signification (among others) of action. *Through the action from afar* that his sovereignty made possible, rather, the sovereign found himself *qualified* as having to undertake a political campaign against the Jews in a society whose masses revealed themselves in all their racism, and that he would himself integrate by racist slogans (or semi-racist ones, to leave the principle intact). This meant precisely that he *reinvented* grassroot racism, as a means for his political campaign and, perhaps, as a possible procedure for integration. Gradually determined* by the circumstances that gave rise to it, the objective it pursued, the means it created for itself, the retotalization of groups and series that it effected, and the intrinsic currents which this retotalization produced – and which in the form of exigencies retotalized the sovereign through his under-taking – this praxis became specified in the course of its spiral temporal-ization and ended up defining itself as a *free choice of a single possible.* For the choice did remain free, in the dialectical sense in which we understand it. It transcended the present towards an objective defined by negation of the former circumstances. And by virtue of having been chosen among others, *the most faraway* possible objective of that praxis was – and would remain – defined by the option (what is more, it could not even be said a priori that new circumstances, in the historical context, made it necessary to pursue its aim). But through the circular interactions we have pointed out (which were all *synthetic* and *integrative*) action found itself compelled to invent its sole current possible – and invent it freely. For it transcended *theoretical* resistances in order to choose racism as the sole possible way of making that policy popular. Choosing it, moreover, it turned itself into racism. Mental reservations or cynicism were merely verbal determinations. When they did exist, they showed the opposite of what the leaders sought to convey by them. They confirmed that anti-Semitism is racist through the desire evinced by a particular individual (at some informal gathering, or to himself) to take his distance – *as an isolated individual* – from the common praxis: i.e. from the common individual who was helping, in himself, to realize it.

These observations allow us to understand that the second question we were posing just now may remain unanswered, from the viewpoint of the synchronic totalization-of-envelopment. Since circularity shows us the transformation of neo-anti-Semitism into racism as at once free and inevitable, and since it allows us to grasp its intelligibility through the relations between totalities in progress and their parts, it matters little whether Stalin – through the backlash of his praxis – chose *one particular action* because the inner transformations of the field had dissolved all

---

* [Note missing in manuscript.]

possibles save *that one*, or whether (in addition to that free necessity of deviation) references to the sovereign's past have to be introduced as supplementary factors. In reality – as frequently if not always occurs in history, as we shall see – there was an overdetermination. Political anti-Semitism became racist anti-Semitism through an inexorable dialectic. After that, it is very possible – even probable – that Stalin carried to his grave the marks of a childhood racism that dared not speak its name. From that viewpoint, however, it is a biography that historical research will illuminate: Stalin's, of course, but not as a sovereign mediating between enveloped totalizations; rather, as a certain enveloped totalization incarnating the possession of every individual by the sovereign-person. Moreover, the incarnation can be studied only in the movement of the diachronic synthesis. But our historical investigation has not given us the tools for this new study. The fact remains that, in a certain way, Stalin – a *practising* and *unconscious* anti-Semite – appears as the synchronic and enveloped incarnation of praxis-process, inasmuch as it is made (in *this* case) without knowing itself and grasps the distance or the transformation of its objects as a negative movement deriving from them, whereas this practical knowledge is merely the false consciousness of its drift.

7

Dialectical Intelligibility, a Circular Synthesis of the Disorder of Order and the Order of Disorder

WITH THIS last example we have closed the circle, since we have seen the sovereign as an enveloped totalization of his sovereignty. So now we can gather together in a few pages the conclusions of our investigation of the totality-of-envelopment[72] (in the case of a society with a *personal* sovereign).

It is an objective and material reality, manifesting itself through *orientated transmutations of energy*. It would be quite impossible to escape idealism, if you forgot that everything – be it a battle or an execution – is always *human labour*. In every instance, reserves of energy (in the organism at work, and in the objects he works as well as in the tools that help him work) are *expended* in order to raise in specific proportions the energy potential of certain practical realities (or to destroy that of enemies or counter-finalities). Conversely, however, we would lapse into the most absurd *meaninglessness* if we did not define the ensemble of such transformations within the human perspective of a temporalization orientated towards a series of staggered objectives.

For if we took these movements merely in their strict physico-chemical reality, they would scatter beneath our eyes in molecular agitations. We should rediscover the laws of Nature, but we should have lost the specificity of human intelligibility. It must be added, moreover, that this observation is valid for *every practical multiplicity*. If the Universe is everywhere made up of force fields (fields of attraction, magnetic fields, meson fields, etc.), whatever the operation under consideration may be, it will have to be seen as the temporalization towards an objective of transmutations based on the principles simultaneously of conservation of energy and its dissipation. In the case of men, if the

---

72. See footnote 43 on p.187 above.

objective is positive it can be only a displacement of energy resources, carried out in one given sector at another's expense, in order to ward off an emergency: i.e. suppress a scarcity. On this basis, however, as we have seen, since the domination of matter (even relative, or *above all* relative) is paid for in human alienation (or alteration of human actions),[73] men at work – mediated by worked matter – constitute the layer of the practico-inert that defines the first structures of praxis and simultaneously ossifies them, realizing the equivalence of the agent and the acted instrument. We shall see whether, despite serialities and recurrence, bourgeois societies manifest themselves as totalizations-of-envelopment.[74] At the level of our investigation, however, this totalization is the vast physico-chemical and practico-inert process, inasmuch as all that inertia of exteriority is unified and interiorized in the practical field by a personal sovereign. It is he – assisted by the organs of leadership, co-ordination, administration, control and repression – who defines the common objective (inasmuch as historical circumstances, and the exigencies of the workers and the practico-inert, designate him to fulfil this role as the personage who will be *least ill suited* to his function). This tight, rigorous unity,* initially at least, does not so much define the tasks as produce an inner synthetic milieu where everything is a function of everything, and every reality – even a collective – determines the other realities from afar, in the very integration of the *temporalization towards* an objective gradually specified.

Nevertheless, although the temporalization is the essential determination here (as the metamorphosis of a society – with its rhythm, its speed, etc. – towards a goal), it must be pointed out that totalizations remain synchronic. For it goes without saying that synchronism does not apply just to the moment – to the momentary cross-section in a praxis under way – for the moment is just an abstraction. By synchronism, we mean the development of praxis-process inasmuch as it is defined by an ensemble of the following: former circumstances; objectives defined *in*

---

* A less striking example of authoritarian integration could have been taken by recalling in broad outline the history of patrician Venice. For what counts is not *above all* that *a single individual* should be in power; it is that the ensemble of true leaders (an individual or a very restricted oligarchy) should define the rigour of its internal integration by that of the integration it imposes upon society as a whole (and vice versa). Of course, very different – and perhaps incomparable – systems are involved. Nevertheless, for the purposes of our study, the borderline runs between historical societies defined by the *concentration* of powers and those defined by their *separation*.

73. *Critique*, vol.1, pp.184 ff.
74. See Preface, and the notes in the Appendix on 'Totalization in Non-Dictatorial Societies' (p.428), 'Totalization: [the History of] Venice' (pp.442 ff.), and 'Totalization-of-Envelopment' (pp.447 ff.).

terms of those circumstances (hence excluding all those that will be defined subsequently, on the basis of the realization – and transcendence – of the first); detailed resources, whose *scarcity* gives the action its present urgency; operations governing one another; and the permanency of certain operators (sovereigns). This was how the planned growth of Soviet industry – in a period of capitalist encirclement and after the ravages of war – constituted a 'first stage' of socialization, concluding with Stalin's death (i.e. its end was marked not by objective exigencies, but by the sovereign's facticity as its fatal contingency). Throughout the whole of this stage the totalization-of-envelopment remained synchronic, because it did not aim to integrate the restricted temporalization into vaster temporal ensembles, in which it would be necessary to take into consideration ruptures between generations, the passage of praxis *into the past* – inasmuch as it was taken over and transcended by the new personnel – and the emergence of new significations retrospectively determining the meaning of the elapsed stage in a univocal relation (the generational rupture does not allow the past to condition the present *in continuity*, i.e. synthetically and totally; the present, on the other hand, constitutes the meaning of the past without the latter having any recourse other than a distant future, where the discontinuity of men will allow the past to be judged *on appeal*; and it does so by the very fact of determining its own immediate past, sovereignly and without recourse). There was a unity of Stalinism that was temporal, one of whose main features was that the past – as an inner determination of the temporalization – adhered to the present without any gap and, by forming the inert determination of each and every person, itself produced the tools to evaluate it. So however crazily the machine might zigzag, the temporalization remained a synchronic totalization because there existed a circularity between past and present, and because that society – which made itself without knowing itself – never really disposed of the proper distance for determining its past.

This synchronic temporalization – a mere realization of an undertaking – does not always have the very clear limits that marked the first stage of Soviet socialization. The action may become lost in itself, bogged down in its own waste-products; or the drift may be such that it suddenly considers its past *as other* and defines itself in relation to that drift; or else either internal circumstances (scarcity of men or resources) or external ones (foreign intervention) may disintegrate it (i.e. conclude it with a failure), which can also be effected by the initially unnoticed development of inherited contradictions; or else, again, a more funda-mental but integrated, masked and totalized praxis – on the occasion of a sequence of given circumstances – may turn back upon the totality-of-envelopment and totalize it in its turn, transforming the meaning of the undertaking, its objectives and its means, without the agents having any feeling of a genuine break (it seems to them, rather, that the objectives manifest a disturbing and unexpected ambiguity – that they have become 'unrecognizable'; by keeping the same slogans, a skilful propaganda will persuade individuals that they are the only ones who have changed). In that case – as much *in itself* as for the situated historian – no precise moment (even approximate) can mark the date of a transformation that was continuous. What might be called here (in a very different sense from that which is usually understood) the reversal of praxis seems a *revolution*, however, more than an *evolution*; but this revolution may remain masked by the identity of certain enveloped totalities (which, however, no longer have the same meaning). In the case of the sovereign-individual, for example, it has been known to happen after a palace revolution that some individual, reduced to the most total impotence, is retained officially with his sovereign attributes to demonstrate the continuity of a politics. A thousand other cases could be cited. Dialectical intelligibility has nothing in common with the contemplation of an *order*; or, if you prefer, the positivist order is an outer skeleton supporting analytic Reason, while the dialectical order is simply intelligibility itself (i.e. the circular synthesis of the disorder of order and the order of disorder, in the temporalization of envelopment; disorder is actually an *other* order – here, at the heart of praxis, it is the practical order *as an other*).

For anything like the dialectical and synchronic intelligibility of a society in development (in the case of a sovereign-person) to be produced, it is necessary and sufficient for that development to be produced – to be realized – even for a brief moment, before disintegrating under external pressure or being rent by contradictions; and for this realization, as an orientated temporalization of a vast material upheaval, to be determined as a praxis generated through everything and (in immanence) in everyone, via the mediation of a plan established by the sovereign, which – for everyone, and for everyone's mutual relations – will be retotalized as a specific praxis, and retotalizing as a fate. For the situated historian, intelligibility is in the relation of the total objective to the ensemble of former circumstances, inasmuch as this relation is temporalized as a relation of praxis to its objects and its products of disassimilation: i.e. as the structuration of a society by the biological unity of a sovereign, and the socialization of a sovereign by the social retotalization of his orders. If failure or disintegration can be explained (wholly or in part) by inner determinations, this brutal end will dialectically help to clarify the undertaking – even as it used to be when marching to victory. But it may happen that the group's disappearance has no inner relationship with the development of its praxis. Although it does not involve a society with a sovereign-individual, I shall cite the [following] example, which clarifies the question quite well. Historians of Ancient Rome all agree upon the fact that social struggles of growing ferocity were taking place in Pompeii at the time of the eruption that destroyed the city and its inhabitants. The outcome of the same conflicts in the contemporary Roman world as a whole, moreover, certainly does make it possible to determine the maximum *possible* variation for a specific case. The annihilation of that town did not *punch a hole* in History. If we at least disposed of the necessary documents, however (which is not the case), it is not these abstract limits – things could proceed only *so far* – which ground the intelligibility of the antagonistic undertakings. It is in a very real sense – *from within* – their practical production of themselves towards objectives in the process of being more and more closely specified. In this case – precisely because the destruction of that society depended on socio-physical factors defining the technical relation of contemporaries to Nature, but not the singularized action of that particular social group, since there was a real exteriority of negation and it would have to be explained by a negation of exteriority (as when you read in Marx that the colonization of Asia Minor by the Greeks was due to the fact that the latter *did not know* how to apply the natural sciences to technology) – the Pompeiian adventure remains generally intelligible. Or rather – which amounts to saying the same thing in a more precise way – *its intelligibility depends only on itself*. If dialectical intelligibility must be able to be the characteristic of History *for itself*, this can *on no account* signify that History is simple and harmonious; that it develops without clashes, regression or deviations; *or even* – at the level of synchronic totalization* – that it has any meaning, or is 'going somewhere'. Moreover, it does not mean either that this intelligibility *imposes itself*, without previous research and as a contemplative intuition. The historian will find it if he has the means (which he does not always – or even usually – have) to reconstitute the movement of the enveloping totalization. All we were trying to say was that, in a practical system with unitary sovereignty, the intelligibility of the undertaking does not depend upon internal contradictions, or upon contingency as the inevitability of facticity (i.e. of the concrete as such), or again upon the final outcome.

So the totalization-of-envelopment is a material (i.e. human and practical) reality, which – turning upon itself – draws its unity from its transcendence towards a goal. This is true at all its levels of depth. Transmutations of energy, inasmuch as they would appear to positivist

---

* [Note missing in manuscript.]

Reason, would assuredly verify already established physico-chemical laws. But their irreversibility – i.e. their order of succession – would at this level remain as an unintelligible fact. Unintelligible *to the positivist*, since it is a matter not of physico-chemical irreversibility (which finds its explanation in the actual features of the 'reaction') but of an irreversibility whose principle is not given to analytic Reason. This signifies precisely that the materiality of such a real development is dialectical. It occurs through the total materiality of man – i.e. on the basis of the fact that physiological and practical interiority is the interiorization of the 'natural' exteriority; and that this interiorization is simultaneously the source of the problems (i.e. of the needs and the being-in-danger of interiority in exteriority) and the means of resolving them (at least provisionally), since it is itself, in itself, a mediation between the inert and praxis – and through this radical assertion of the unity of organic temporalization: need as the negation of a negation. Thus it is through need itself – seeking to be satisfied and producing, through labour and through unification of the practical field, a government of man by worked matter strictly proportionate to the government of inanimate matter by man (in short, the practico-inert) – that a practical configuration of exteriority (for example, a *geography of resources*: an illumination of the external possibilities by a synthetic regrouping of the 'natural' givens, in combination with tools and techniques and on the basis of the needs of an already structured social ensemble) and a practical configuration of society (a division of labour on the basis of techniques, serialization, etc.) are determined simultaneously and by one another. But both the need and the praxis attempting to satisfy it are themselves a mediation, and show us a rudimentary aspect of circularity. For it is the organism and its needs that define the resources (in their contingent distribution: contingent *for* these given organisms) which – determined by technology – recondition the latter, and pass with all their inertia (in the form of raw matter and worked matter) into the primary social structuration. In our chosen example, however – which, being already more complex, presupposes a previous history and a revolt of men against the practico-inert (in other words, through it, against other men) – the rigorous, biological unity of the sovereign was founded upon the urgent *need* to liquidate the practico-inert, as a legacy of the overthrown class. For its very being (if it did not change) would always condition the same social structures, whatever these might be called. That signified the obligation for praxis to transform equipment, resources, production and the producers – jointly and, of course, by one another. The radical signification of this praxis was thus unification as transcendence being temporalized towards a goal; and the sovereign was at once the organizer of the integrated society and its future objective. At this level – and by virtue of the very fact that society, despite the crazy swerves of the leadership and all the mistakes and conflicts, did *survive* – everything was reconditioned and totalized, at once by the labour of the apparatus with its coercive organs and by the practice of the rank and file. But this observation cannot lead to optimism. By dissolving the inherited practico-inert, the sovereign – and through it society – interiorized the social structures it had formerly conditioned. And the transcendence of this interiorization – i.e. its practical re-exteriorization – had the result, in a rather different technical context, of constituting another practico-inert* that reconditioned men, inter-human structures, institutions, and finally praxis itself. Inasmuch as the latter – deviated – constantly went back over the inert concretions and dissolved them, and inasmuch as it produced others by counter-finalities that re-exteriorized the former circumstances (i.e. the dissolved practico-inert), circularity manifested itself as an internal structure of the practical totality and became – in the form of spirals – the movement of its temporalization towards the objective. The axial direction represented the practical transcendence, inasmuch as – under the pressure of need, and in the emergency of the given situation – it had posited its own goals. It was in relation to this direction that the 'drift' of the action itself took place, in so far as the interiorization by circularity of its own results deprived it of the means to straighten the real direction and bring it closer to the virtual direction; or, more precisely, constituted it for itself – through new intellectual tools – as always transcending itself in the same direction.

This totalizing reality was thus characterized by the *immanence* of the bonds uniting the elements that made it up (synthetic structure of the field) and, at the same time, by the presence of practico-inert concretions producing collectives within it and tending to reify human relations. This contradiction, far from being in itself and formally the real destruction of the totalization, on the contrary constituted the motor of the temporalization. Without the internal existence of the practico-inert, the totalization would be a totality or it would not be at all. It *would not be*, since the practico-inert – founded upon needs, resources and techniques – is precisely the passive synthesis on the basis of which [the totalization] is engendered, and which the latter then envelops and dissolves. And if it were to be encountered (in inconceivable circumstances, formally possible *elsewhere*), then circularity would vanish, along with the spiral of

---

* For example, the 'necessity' of widening the salary range, or the 'necessity' of repression (to increase the means of production), are in part legacies of the abolished regime, inasmuch as *its own* practico-inert remains.

temporalized retotalizations. We should be faced with a whole: alive, assuredly, but without any temporal and practical determination, since the only mediation between the free organisms would be other equally free organisms. So the practico-inert appears in circularity as what has to be dissolved by praxis, and as the determination of praxis by itself in exteriority. It is what deviates praxis, but it is also what retains within it the deep layers of passive materiality; and it is through its inert synthesis that action can sovereignly regulate the order and proportions of trans-mutations of energy. In this sense, the inertia of exteriority rises up from the physico-chemical layers of the field to the sovereign organisms. To take just one example, it was 'natural' exteriority which – through the practico-inert – was to be found in the stratified hierarchy of the Stalinist bureaucracy. At the practical moment of circularity, however, praxis transcends its exteriority towards new objectives, thereby synthetically determining the opening of its practical field. It is within this interiority that relations of reciprocal immanence are established between all the elements of the field. The existence of series and collectives changes nothing of this. The serial impotence of this particular individual, and the reification of his relations with other persons within some serialized ensemble, do not imply that his other human relations are serial, nor (above all) that his behaviour patterns do not retotalize the totalization-of-envelopment – even, and above all, *with its structures of seriality*. Furthermore, in so far as seriality becomes a way of ruling, the relations between serial individuals – without losing their character of reified exteriority, or ceasing to unite those individuals *as Others* – by virtue of the sovereign practice take on a character of *quasi-interiority*.

What seems more important is not to misunderstand the meaning [of the term] 'circularity'. For if we look at a single practical decision, there is a moment of action in interiority – by internal rearrangement of the field – and a moment of determination in exteriority, in which the inert results of passive syntheses – through the agents themselves – infect with their inertia the structures of the praxis that has produced them. But this does not, therefore, mean that the sovereign *activity* has been interrupted, to make way for this skeletal image of itself. Quite the contrary; it carries on, and through it the inert strata of exteriority are maintained in unity and rendered effective. Moreover, other actions spring from the sovereign: united in their origin, and in their basic objective; diversified by their immediate objectives; connected by recip-rocal exigencies, which – by virtue of a slight lag, due to the pressures and order of the problems to be resolved – are produced in the moment of interiority, at the very time when the former praxis is already affected by the inertia it has created. So it is necessary to conceive the circularity of envelopment as actually constituted by *several circularities*, whose different lags make it impossible simply to find *one* circle and *two* complementary moments. Every element of exteriority, whatever the moment of its constitution, can directly or indirectly deviate any partial activity – even if this occurs much later. In the same way, every inert element is associated with other elements to make up the skeleton that the sociologist will study, whatever the period of its sedimentation. *But* if these passive interconditionings are possible – and if, through them, the ensemble of the skeleton influences the totalizing praxis – this is because the partial activities serve as a mediation between the various sediments. It is clear from this that a single totalizing praxis is reconditioned from within by deposits of differing ages. However, this makes no change to the law of circularity, since such deposits have been formed by the latter and recondition it through the current mediation of specific activities, inasmuch as these are integrated as its parts into the praxis of totalization. So the movement of circularity – far from preventing the most complex interplay of conditionings and reconditionings, with the temporal lags and delays characteristic of certain reactions – is their sole foundation. But precisely because it is produced as the intimate move-ment of temporalization, it is in depth that the historian must find it; and the totalization-of-envelopment (in the case of a sovereign-individual) first presents itself as an inextricable jumble of inert deposits and actions. If it remains at the level of such empirical knowledge, History will go astray. For it risks fading away before sociology, or juxtaposing institutions and practices, or deriving them from one another at random, so long as it has not understood the dialectical law of circularity and its epistemological corollary, the law of circular interpretation.

8

Meaning of the
Totalization-of-Envelopment

I F WE seek to grasp more clearly, on that basis, the *meaning* of the totality[75] of envelopment as praxis-process, we can advance the following remarks.

1. This reality is entirely a *human* realization of man. For it can be produced and develop only by positing objectives: i.e. by a negation of the past in terms of the future. In other words, the very structure of its development – the temporalization – is specifically human.* Even in the very heart of present reality, praxis-process is defined by the future that comes to negate the past in it. Furthermore, nothing occurs in it – whether in detail or in overall operations – that is not engendered by human effort, by labour. Even if it is carried out under coercion, this

---

* This does not mean there is no problem of temporalization. In fact, the praxis of the free organism is totalized and objectified in its result via what we shall call the constituent temporalization. Already in the case of the group, however, and especially in that of the totalization-of-envelopment, the question of the constituted temporalization is posed. The problem here is to know how the temporalization of envelopment can be produced, inasmuch as it is engendered by enveloped or constituent temporalizations *as such*, and how it can serve as a milieu for the latter. And also to know how constituent temporalizations are retemporalized in their turn, through interiorization of the temporalizing milieu that draws them towards the common objective. We have already seen how this essentially dialectical problem was radically distinct from another problem familiar to all: how is the unity of time-space in physics compatible with the multiplicity of constituent temporalizations? Or (if you prefer) through what mediations, and in what historical circumstances, did the practical temporalizations produce this abstract determination as their inert container, and how was the operation possible? The response to this second question is actually contained in these simple words: the time of clocks is a collective, hence – for everyone – *the time of the Other.* The totalizing and constituted temporalization, however, is a synthetic, dialectical development and would have to be followed dialectically to its genesis, in relation to every historical totalization.

75. See footnote 43 on p.187 above.

labour is agreed. Not – as has too often been claimed – because it is at all events preferred to death (I have explained how only specific circumstances were able to determine death as a possible term of an option[76]). But quite simply because its execution is an immediate reassumption of the goal. Or, if you prefer, because the agent is a man, and a man – even a slave – is sovereign in his labour, *even if* the practico-inert alienates its results as soon as the labourer objectifies himself in them, even if the labour is sold as a commodity, and even if it rises up as a hostile force and is realized as a 'loss of substance'. For he has to *perform* that labour – which means that he wants to do so. An integral praxis, suffered (interiorization) and repeated (exteriorization) by thousands or millions of agents, for whom it becomes at once the *being* (serial impotence, relapse into *hexis*, fate as a suffered future) and the *act*; the unity of a field to which *all the agents belong* (including the sovereign), where praxis itself defines what might be called the law of immanence (a bond of interiority between everything and everything) and the law of incarnation: all these features of praxis-process are *exclusively human* (in so far as we know no practical multiplicities other than human societies) and, from the viewpoint of knowledge, are intelligible *only for men* (and for practical multiplicities of an equal or greater mental development). Every attempt to reduce this totalizing progress to an ensemble of facts accessible to positive Reason alone would end up transforming the specific interiority of historialization into pure exteriority. The synthetic unification would thus be reduced to the statistical truths of positive Reason (incomplete and irrational truths, since they derive their coherence from synthetic structures that they negate).

2. However, the reality of the deviation (as it is produced in every spiral, and as it is encapsulated in the drift away from a given objective, fixed at the outset) comes to impose a term on pure and simple comprehension, precisely in so far as action, escaping, is exteriorized and comes – like a *vis a tergo* – to change from without those who produce it from within themselves as their transcendence. In so far as you then reach a result that had not been either projected or foreseen, or even discovered along the way – and in so far as you can say that things have produced men and given them a false consciousness of themselves, of the past and of their future objectives – the totalization seems *anti-human*. I say anti-human and not inhuman, for it is not a matter of a return to the natural world; and praxis-process, from this standpoint, does not reveal itself as a vague block of inanimate matter. Quite the contrary: like the Devil according to the Church Fathers, the exteriority

---

76. *Critique*, vol. 1, p.190.

of praxis is parasitic, borrowing its efficacy and its being – as we have seen – from interiority. It is through a wholly human field of immanence and teleological unification that sediments are formed, *via the mediation of all forms of activity*. Praxis, as it approaches its goal, in practice constitutes *an outside* for itself and, precisely in this, reveals itself as human praxis; for only a human society can establish synthetic relations of such a kind between inanimate objects, without present relations, that they wrest themselves out of their inertia and mutually manifest imperious exigencies, whose origin is a need for exteriority awoken, sustained and unified by the astringent milieu of practical syntheses. Praxis-process thus appears as a human process, without ceasing to be human action; and action is produced within it as burdening itself with the inertias freed by the dissolution or transformation of the inert structures of its field. Everything has its cost, and the totalization-of-envelopment shows us at once results and action paying its own expenses (for example, assuming the scarcity of resources or equipment, and reducing this gradually, at the price of being transformed itself by its own specific scarcity: the scarcity of men).

It is perfectly conceivable, to be sure, for the enveloping totalization to be produced *in itself* and *for itself*. In specific circumstances – ones, moreover, which would presuppose a less pronounced emergency, a more homogeneous culture of both leaders and masses, less scarcity of men, etc. – achieving awareness of deviation (at whatever level this might occur) would make it possible to control and reduce it. But of course, a very great fluidity and quasi-homogeneity of social milieux would be needed, and another relation *from the outset* between the sovereign and the ruled: i.e. a more advanced form of withering away of the State. Besides, even if one then succeeded in constantly rectifying the orientation of praxis, the practical results might be more favourable but the circularity as a formal structure would remain unchanged. And it would likewise remain unchanged in a more radical hypothesis, which would require a technology and economy entirely conscious of themselves, as well as the application of a transformed and developed cybernetics to the internal organization of an enterprise-society. For it is not inconceivable – at least for certain domains (particularly planning) – to condition circularity itself, and through it determine a kind of *feedback*. Indeed, since praxis-process is circular, it is itself a *feedback*: its consequences react upon its principles and its outcomes upon the forces that have produced them. This reconditioning in exteriority of the action by itself – via the agents – *is a feedback*. It will simply be called negative, since its effect is to warp praxis rather than to correct it. Hence, it might be imagined that a society in which science and technology were more advanced, far from claiming – like Stalinist society – to escape circularity, would submit to it in order to govern it and, by means of a system of compensating devices, automatically correct the deviation by its effects. But these two procedures interest us only from the formal viewpoint. For, in themselves, it can be said that they have always been used (even criticism used to exist in the Stalin period, while as for *feedback*, it is what democratic constitutions have often resorted to in order to guard the State against the danger of its own power) and, at the same time, that nothing guarantees that they ever will be (in the guise of systematic correctives of praxis). These remarks refer us back to the problem of the meaning of History, and to diachronic totalization. What I wanted to point out was just that – in both cases (the only conceivable remedies for deviation, in a period of scarcity) – the precondition for the procedures described above being applicable and effective is precisely the prior recognition that the historical process is that *feedback*: i.e. the disclosure of circularity. The practical progress would be immense, and the dialectical and formal transfiguration would be limited, if – *through the labour of men* – praxis-process controlled its deviations by a directed circularity. For with each new problem the wild circularity would reappear, and the need for new adaptations. Moreover – whatever the system employed, and because everything has its cost – awareness as much as *feedback*, while suppressing the primary deviation, would engender a reflexive circularity with second-level deviations.

3. From the viewpoint of historical knowledge, does circularity allow a total comprehension of praxis-process? For we know that the comprehension of constituted actions, although itself different from constituent comprehension, is nevertheless possible – and wholly appropriate – so long as an organized action is involved. For comprehension is *praxis* itself, nothing else. As constituted comprehension of a common praxis, it emanates simply from the historian, inasmuch as he can make himself into a common individual by virtue of a pledge. But the totalization-of-envelopment comprises a turning back of the inert upon the agent, to recondition him. Is it the task of comprehension to grasp this process of involution? We must frankly reply: yes. For such reconditioning at all events eludes positive Reason. It is true that it eventually constitutes the exteriority of the interior; but it does not itself operate in exteriority. The determinations of agents by the practico-inert they have themselves established are made through remote links, and by the enveloped incarnation constituted by each of their behaviour patterns. As we have seen, this is how, for example, the constitution and stratification of the Stalinist Bureaucracy can be interpreted. So it was a matter of dialectical intelligibility, at all events. There was intelligibility, since the process of stratification entailed its own obviousness; and this intelligibility was dialectical, since the practico-inert was refracted

through the dialectical medium of totalization and was effective by virtue of it alone, inasmuch as it borrowed from it its own synthetic activity. You will say it is still the case that *intelligible* and *dialectical* perhaps do not necessarily mean *comprehensible*. Is it not true that these remote determinations parasitic upon action are, in any case, not practical activities at all? No doubt. And this remark reveals to us one important aspect of that society closed upon itself, locked and bolted by its sovereign: it sought to integrate the field of the anti-dialectic into the totalization as a constituted dialectic. For us, as we ponder in the present chapter over the relationship between the dialectic and the anti-dialectic, here is a first example of their possible relations. One closed upon the other, in order to dissolve and assimilate it. It succeeded only by the realization of a generalized cancer. In so far as the practico-inert (i.e. the anti-dialectic) was used and suffused by the dialectic, praxis (as a constituted dialectic) was poisoned from within by the anti-dialectic. The deviation was the anti-dialectical reconditioning of the dialectic; it was the sovereign praxis, inasmuch as this was (partially) itself an anti-dialectic. For this very reason, however, those various transformations did not transcend the limits of constituted comprehension. For the latter does not confine itself – any more than constituent comprehension does – to grasping action in its purity. On the contrary, I have shown in *The Problem of Method* how the comprehension of an individual act (my interlocutor gets up to open the window) focuses at once upon the pure meaning of that act – i.e. upon the temporal relation of the need to the objective, via the mediation of the means – and upon its concrete reality, i.e. its incarnation and its deviation (there is too much in it, or not enough, or something else).[77] If my friend suddenly gets up, in the middle of an animated conversation, and rushes towards the window as though he were stifling, the particular features of his conduct are automatically revealed as not being required by the objective, or by the mere need for air such as I may imagine it abstractly. If he is suffocating, he should have thought *sooner* about opening the window. If it is very cold outside and the temperature is bearable inside, his haste cannot be explained by some dangerous emergency. If he knows that I always feel chilly, he could have asked my opinion at the beginning of our conversation or after an hour. But precisely these particularities – in so far as they distinguish the action from its 'normal', abstract model – refer me through a regressive act of comprehension to specific features of my interlocutor: i.e. to what he has himself made himself into, through the interiorization and transcendence of certain former conditionings.

---

77. *The Problem of Method*, pp.152–4.

Dialectical comprehension discloses the present via the future, and the past via the present: as soon as he gets up, suffocating, it passes from the open window to his red, sweating face and awaits him in the depths of the immediate future; at the same time, however, it plunges into the past in order to find, through various memories ('He is always like that'), the source of so many hasty, uncontrolled behaviour patterns, so much abruptness, and that odd unawareness of his body and its needs – which never manifest themselves other than at the last moment, when they have to be satisfied urgently. There is comprehension, for the simple reason that this slight maladjustment is realized in the form of behaviour patterns. The abruptnesses, the haste, etc., *are* actions: they transcend more basic conditions, defend themselves against them, negate them, preserve them, and try to adapt to them. So the circumstance itself is merely an abstraction for me – merely the back-meaning of a behaviour pattern – and I never encounter it except in this active form. It does not manifest itself – either to me or, above all, to itself – in the form of a *state*.

Well, the same is true for constituted comprehension and for reconditioned praxis. There is a Soviet *model-society* that the sociologist can reconstruct, if he has statistical information at his disposal, and that he will view as a prop for a process (grasped in exteriority) of planned industrialization. But the sociologist will throw light on this society by adopting a non-dialectical and non-comprehensive attitude – that is his right. The object described belongs to positive Reason: *it can be seen* with the eyes of a positivist. If we return to the concrete, however – i.e. to History – we grasp this social ensemble only through the deviations of common praxis and particular activities. To be sure, it is necessary first to question the sociologist and to consider with him his abstract model, the stratifications signalled by the difference in living standards, honours, powers, etc. But that is just in order to be able to reinteriorize [this model] at the heart of groups or common individuals, as the abstract meaning of the deviation that manifests itself *as a living feature of praxis*. In reality, the movement of circularity involves the establishment of exteriority only as an abstract, schematic geography of deposits, strata and sedimentations. If you like, it is the time of the anti-dialectic: the historian's comprehension has moved from former circumstances and the chosen objective to the bound, unified diversity of detailed actions (destined to produce the means for the means of attaining the objective); and he has grasped – in the very objectification of the agents through the results achieved – the ambiguity, or the uncertainty, or the contradictions, that characterize these first gropings. This is where a 'sociological' study can provide him with the systematic ensemble of the *gaps* between forecasts and achievements: such gaps – as an inert skeleton of abstract significations – will constitute the *model-society*. But this moment of the anti-dialectic is there only to guide research. Historical comprehension goes back to sovereign acts; it comprehends them in their particularity with respect to the new objectives and – as constituent comprehension docs for the individual – with respect to the past they illuminate. For the latter appears, in its transcended but preserved abstraction, through particularity and as its source. The past presents itself to comprehension as the new foundation which such acts have gained, on the basis of which they have produced themselves, and which they maintain in their very transcendence – without their author knowing it. And this abstract foundation of man, his praxis and the knowledge that can enlighten him, is precisely the *social model* established by the sociologist, but it acquires reality only as an abstract *reverse signification* illuminating the deviation of the sovereign's actions, those of the leading groups, and everyone's: what the historian will be able to grasp by moving down comprehensively from the sovereign praxis to the masses and the new modifications of the practico-inert, and then moving up again through new abstract, statistical determinations to the sovereign reconditioned by new results of its action. So circular intelligibility is always comprehensive, since the historian never has to deal with anything but praxis and discovers the inert like a residue at the bottom of the crucible of action. So the movement of his comprehension is regressive, then progressive; for he will discover the inert by the deviation, and interpret the latter by the former.

4. This comment on comprehension has brought us to a comparison between individual action and the sovereign totalization, which will enable us to clarify further the meaning of this totalization. For if it is true that the enveloping totalization confuses us by virtue of the element of inhumanity it secretes, it must be pointed out that the deviation of praxis is not something linked solely to common actions or collective ventures. The circular – and the exteriority of interiority – already reveal themselves even at the level of constituent praxis. We noted this in passing, when we returned to the example of *The Problem of Method*. In connection with that anyway very ambiguous example, however, it might be thought that the only alteration of individual praxis was its *alienation* in the practico-inert, and that its only source of deviation lay in the interiorization by the agent of former alienations. In reality, it is true that the most general foundation of individual deviations is the former or immediately future alienation, which – *in fact*, and by the introduction of transcendence (the realm of the practico-inert, and the third party) – obviously excludes the circular structure of the deviated praxis, even if methodologically the circularity of the inquiry is preserved by the historian. But circularity also characterizes certain aspects of individual praxis. From this viewpoint, the *universal* case of fatigue is characteristic. Here, of course, it is a question of considering abstractly the relationship between work and fatigue, without referring to any particular kind of society; or if it is a matter of our own, without knowing whether the worker is a smallholder, whether he owns the tools of his trade (as some taxi-drivers own their taxis), or whether he sells his labour-power as a commodity. What counts is that since *everything has its cost* (a synthetic principle defining praxis *in a field of scarcity*, and in terms of the principle of conservation of energy), any transformation of the individual practical field (e.g. any accumulation of initially dispersed energy resources: harvesting, gathering in, etc.) is effected as a transmutation of energy. Hence – if the worker is viewed *as a man*, rather than just a certain energy potential – it implies for the agent *an expenditure of energy* (oxidization and 'burning' of certain reserves; inevitable wastage of part of the energy in a degraded form, through raising of the outside temperature, transpiration, etc; production through combustion itself of waste-products, some of which are quickly eliminated while others remain for a greater or lesser time). On the most favourable assumption, this *expenditure* is the exact equivalent of the energy costs of the outcome that was proposed (it is the ideal case we shall consider: in reality, there are false costs which may be considerable). And if the outcome is despite everything a profit, this means that *from another standpoint* (that of need, or sales, or the protection of crops, etc.) and *upon another terrain* it appears as pure creation – as a sudden increase in the desirable potential. It also means that this increase – in the new field under consideration – finds itself constituted by circumstances *as transcending* the losses it has caused for the worker.

But need and danger create emergency conditions in any society. When famine threatens – or an enemy – work is harsh: one spade-stroke – or a hundred of them – to dig a ditch are not enough; ten thousand are needed to raise an earth rampart, and in the shortest time possible. So every individual repeats his action as often as circumstances require it; and each time he repeats it his fatigue grows (his reserves melt away, waste-products and toxins accumulate) and makes reproduction of the same action more difficult (precisely because of what every worker experiences as a 'loss of substance': 'I need to *restore* my strength', people often say).

In reality, things are not so simple. There is a psychophysiology of fatigue, and its *profile* in the course of a working day includes slack periods and others of sudden increase. What remains crucial is the fact that the accomplished action, through the inert modifications it provokes in the subject (a *negative* inertia – of *absence* of the resources consumed and *presence* of toxins and waste-products in the organism, as counter-finalities: *means* of no longer being able to work), makes the latter less and less capable of reproducing it. Since fatigue has qualitative effects, it is above all the fact that the action itself is modified (as in the case of the sovereign-individual) by the effect of its results upon the practical organism: once a certain threshold has been crossed, gestures become less precise and less effective, attention slackens, etc. If he is free, the worker stops, saying: 'I'm not doing anything useful any more.' If he is not free, or if he keeps working away but lacks self-control, the risk of mistakes grows, as does the number of 'botches' actually produced. Any one of these 'botched' objects can provide us with an objective example of the deviation. For a given worker, the goal was to increase his hourly production in order to obtain a productivity bonus, so it was a matter of producing x *perfect* items in the eight hours. The x items will have been produced, but the percentage n/x of 'botched' items denotes the deviation. Through fatigue, the objective is altered and becomes: not to let go, to hang on, to stick at all costs to the planned number of operations, etc. Blind exhaustion, wandering attention and above all contraction of his field are bound to create 'botches', since these are now the tools of his trade. Intent on transcending them, however (by keeping his eyes open, remembering all the instructions, etc.), he no longer maintains the necessary distance *to become aware of them* (i.e. to become aware of the fact that *an impoverished man* is working in his place). Objectively, as the supposed transcendence of his diminished functions is in reality only their pure and simple *exercise* (the only way for attention to realize its deficiency in a period of pressure is to struggle against this, mobilize itself totally, engross itself so intensely in taking account of everything and be so aware of its tasks that it realizes – in all his gestures and through the fight it puts up – the deficit for which it is seeking to compensate*), the 'botch' – as a deviation inscribed in worked matter (and as the synthetic unity of a counter-finality) – eludes the worker, precisely in so far as the worker has assumed himself such that his real acts and their objectification must elude him. Moreover, at the heart of this relationship between the man and his work represented by fatigue, we find the true problem of the practical totality as a responsibility. It is not just a matter of referring back to Kantism's positive intention (he has taken the risk of doing bad work). Fatigue *is* praxis at a certain moment, and the man is qualified at this moment by his way of living his fatigue: in relation to his physiological structures and the past these have

---

* I doubtless do not need to point out that I am not taking attention as a faculty – or even a function – but as the whole of praxis, inasmuch as it produces its own organs of control and conditions them by its total development.

interiorized (illnesses, injuries, work accidents), but at the same time also in relation to the internal fields that constitute him (interiorization of the social, transcendence, etc.) and to the multidimensionality of his personal significations through the forms of behaviour that actualize them. Everyone produces himself and re-produces himself wholly in his own resistance to fatigue; and it is at this practical level that he himself – *and without knowing it* – pronounces sentence upon his original intention (i.e. decides in practice whether he was wrong or right to set himself that increase in production as a goal*).

So circularity exists in individual praxis and, in a certain way, constitutes its basis inasmuch as it manifests itself as fatigue. So it is not something specific to constituted praxis, even though practical multiplicities in all their forms reproduce and amplify it as a fundamental structure of their totalizing temporalization. Rather, in a certain way it is the practical relation of the agent to worked matter. And its very principle is that, in the energy transmutation, there is and is not equivalence (independently of any 'dissipation') between the energy supplied and the energy received. For that which is supplied – as an expenditure made by an organism (or practical multiplicity) with a view to producing a result – is characterized for the organism (or multiplicity) and in the field of scarcity as an inert impossibility (temporary or definitive) of re-producing the result obtained, or of producing other transformations in other domains. Absorbed by worked matter, it becomes in itself the passive synthesis of exteriority. *Expended* by a whole or a totalization, its deficit is produced in the organism (or practical multiplicity) as the appearance of exteriority at the heart of a practical synthesis (not just as a lack, but also as a presence of waste-products). In other words, in these transformations there is an *expenditure* – which is a material and practical fact, since it presupposes a world of objectives, exigencies and risks compelling continual options and an economy of resources – and *an organic (or social) memory* of that expenditure, inasmuch as it is lived, for example, as an impossibility of carrying out a new piece of work, thus as an absence of practical connection with some particular new exigency of exterior objectivity. Circularity, for the organism, is rooted in what we may term the costs of action – and, for totalizations in progress, the costs of History.

This comparison had the aim of helping us to comprehend the relation-

---

* Taking the example abstractly, I am naturally not speaking about the individual's social responsibilities, in a society that seeks to push the growth of the general rate of production to the limit. Let us merely note that the practical sentence of which I am speaking, in a concrete society, is obviously conditioned by the worker's relation to his class and, through this, to the social ensemble.

ship between the human and the anti-human (praxis and anti-praxis, dialectic and anti-dialectic) at the heart of the totalization-of-envelopment. For in a certain way, and even outside of any alienation (although alienation inevitably captures it and is usually its source), the indissoluble unity of the human and the anti-human manifests itself at every moment of daily life, and in all the individuals we encounter. To tell the truth, it is this very unity that makes the man. This one laughs *too* much, that other one talks *too* loudly or *too* quietly, this third one is *too* clumsy. One takes such precautions in transporting a fragile object that he ends up breaking it, or else he files away a valuable document so carefully that he no longer knows where he has hidden it; the other organizes a reception but is *too* anxious for everyone to enjoy themselves – he spoils everything by his eagerness. Pointless to multiply examples: it is our very life. And these inadequacies or these excesses, this maladjustment at the heart of adjustment, is precisely in everyone what he does not know or what he learns from others: his exteriority, inasmuch as it reveals itself as an inner limit of his practical interiority. Perhaps an analyst, at the end of a therapy, might be able to reveal such secret inertias and deficits. But we do not see our own – since they are our spectacles, our very eyes – and we grasp those of others only through deviated praxis, as the abstract signification of that deviation. In other words, *the Other* offers himself up to my investigation as a practice, and only as such (even when he undergoes the coercion of oppressors or of the practico-inert); his exteriority *is merely the differential of his practice*. So the action itself of my friend – or of this passer-by – provides his objective and his drift away from it. Both – the signification and the anti-signification – are offered in the indissoluble unity of the investigation.

Accordingly, that signification overwhelmed by counter-finalities, albeit remaining practical, loses its logical rigour: active and passive present themelves to comprehension in the unity of *meaning*. This woman passing in front of me is certainly modest and decent; she works, and her serious face and unobtrusive manner show that she has little taste for scandal. Yet she is dressed in gaudy fabrics and wears a loud, vulgar hat. This apparel testifies to an action of which it is the result: she has purchased the dress and the headgear – she has chosen them. Through that action, however, something of its passive determinations – deviating the action that transcends them – has been incarnated in the violent clash between the bright red and the apple green, in the contrast between that 'loud' hat and that casual, unselfconscious head. The passivity of worked matter, and the inert synthesis of the 'cut', express pretty accurately the very inertia that the young woman interiorizes: in that sense, her clothes are *the exteriority* of her action. This exteriority can be grasped, moreover, inasmuch as the clashes noted above refer back immediately to the action (the choice, the purchase) and its drift, at the same time as to the transcended inertia that it contains and reactualizes as a deviation. It is because she is indifferent to her toilet and quite devoid of narcissism or coquetry, it is because she does not even imagine relating those fabrics to herself – in short, it is because of her inexperience and naivety (the counterpart to her true, practical seriousness as a mother or a worker) – that she has let herself be seduced by the crude flashiness of the fabrics and the 'amusing' shape of the hat, and has let the saleswoman palm them off on her. She was thinking about *owning* them – like a bit of that lively joy of which she knows nothing – rather than about *wearing* them. Yet this displacement of the immediate desire is like a distraction at the heart of the real action, since she did in fact – very rationally – go to acquire some clothes and so replace an outworn dress and headgear. Her action was premeditated – she had to save up for three months. Hence, in so far as the person is reactualized – inopportunely – in that distraction, her action undergoes a slight deviation while remaining largely unchanged. And although the *maxim* and the *objective* remain the same, the chosen object is altered by the way of choosing it: dark, plain dresses and neutral hues will be neglected in favour of that blaze of colour. In a sense, however, it can be said that she has performed the action she wanted to perform. She has spent her savings (amassed for that purpose) on buying a dress and hat. That dress and that hat have been chosen in her measurements – from this point of view they suit her. What is deviated is a more veiled, and vaguer, intention of her whole person in all circumstances. In her way of behaving, observing the rituals and customs of her milieu and speaking, a single concern always reveals itself: not to 'draw attention to herself'; 'to be just like everybody else'. And it is indeed true that she normally *goes unnoticed*. It is in so far as this aim remains implicit when she is choosing clothes that it may be unfulfilled. And it is in the clash between her unobtrusive behaviour and her shocking attire that the synthesis by praxis of two aspects of her *hexis* will manifest itself: through the practical option of the purchase, indifference to herself (and the very crude taste of her intuitive delight *in the object*) is combined with her wish to be unobtrusive, as what for the time being obscures her (whatever the other, deeper relations between these givens) and deviates her action towards an objective with unforeseen consequences. In fact, precisely because the woman is not rich, it will be necessary for her to wear the Shirt of Nessus – the scandal – until the material wears out. If the woman perceives that she is scandalous, she will strive to become more unobtrusive still. Rather than just modest, she will become hunted. But her unease – making visible to all the fact that she *is not cut out* to wear that outfit – will yield her up defencelessly to every eye. This signifying layer presents itself, of course, in unity with the rest in the field of our investigation. And this other too: those clothes have not been made by her and expressly for her; they are not unique items of finery, of the kind that expose the folly (the asocial nature) of those who rig themselves out in them. They are actually standardized products, and in making them the manufacturer has aimed at a certain social category. Which one? He is not quite sure himself: he just knows that in some shops, products of that kind always find takers. So the object designates its purchaser and classifies them socially: it will, for example, fit the youth, gaiety and exuberance of women of the town – very poor and very crude, with paint inches deep on their cheeks – for whom scandal is one means among others to attract clients. The exteriority of praxis is revealed by this last contrast, which is social. Through the deviation of praxis, the purchaser causes herself to be designated by her clothes as belonging to a social category of which it is obvious – from her behaviour and her expression – that she has never been a member. And what designates her as such is the judgement that other social strata deliver upon the borrowed category, which manifests itself in *the possible options* that society proposes to it (in this instance, through the clothes made for persons belonging to this category). Of course, the options retain – but recondition – the aspirations specific to consumers from the category in question. This complex signification – the demand, the reconditioning of the demand by a confection reflecting certain prejudices, the non-conscious acceptance of this reconditioning by those who express the demand – is sociality as a passive synthesis of worked matter, or (if you prefer) it is this materiality as a social idea. It goes without saying that it organizes itself independently in the situated investigation with the three other signifying layers. It then becomes a false designation – or rather false social identity – of the person, and also an overarching relationship between the woman and the social ensemble that must *situate* her. That is enough: the crucial thing is that all these significations – organized into the concrete unity of the person, her features, her gestures, her dress and her hat – constitute a very real obviousness, or even the person herself, inasmuch as she is produced in a practical field of social temporalization.

But this obviousness can no longer be termed a *signification*, in the sense in which the unity of such significations involves the deviation of each one by each and every other one. That is why we shall call this *situated* relation to the social future surrounding it, in the obviousness and intelligibility of its concrete presence, the *meaning* of the person rather than the signification of her behaviour. For it is enough to imagine the rationality of the options for a rich woman, a customer of the great couturiers, accustomed from childhood to reflect the taste of her class in her own taste, in order to understand the difference. In the latter case, everything is signifying; the meaning, if it exists, is elsewhere. In the former case, we do really see the exteriorization of interiority – but only inasmuch as this exteriorization is simultaneously recaptured by the interiorizing unity of individual praxis, and diluted in other layers of signification that drag it towards *socialization*. Here, the anti-human is the dress turning upon the woman and designating her (in vain) as a whore. The human is the woman mystified by her own modesty, loving the fabric and falling into the trap of objectivity, to end up wearing it as the uniform of a group that is not her own; and it is the woman reproducing herself – beyond that dress (but transformed by it despite everything), and against that choice now become a passive sentence – in her modesty and her discretion as an unobtrusive person, because she has neither the taste nor the time to think about herself. And it is also (human and anti-human simultaneously) the humble taste – profoundly legitimate, yet mystifying ... and mystified – for something that, in its objective, stands out against the greyness of life. For that *bad taste* – that *'vulgarity'* – is simply the vague presentiment of beauty.

It is at this level – i.e. at the level of *meaning* and no other – that the question is posed of the person with her objectives rationally defined, never wholly achieved or wholly unachieved; always overwhelmed by the transcendent meaning of what she realizes, and never being anything other than what she does, i.e. what she does with what has been done with her; human, precisely, as a suspended synthesis of the human and the anti-human – human, inasmuch as she eludes herself and is unaware of herself, inasmuch as she recovers, knows herself and controls herself, inasmuch as in that very control her praxis is deviated: in short, always reinteriorizing her exteriority and then re-exteriorizing it at a secondary level by becoming reflexively aware of herself. And it is, indeed, on the basis of this circularity that we *comprehend* a man: we grasp his action through him, we grasp him through his action. The *meaning* is the synthetic indication of the tasks to be accomplished – both regressive and progressive.

Taking the term in this sense, we can say – adopting this time the viewpoint of historical reconstruction – that praxis-process is disclosed as a temporalization that has taken the form of *realization of a meaning*. It is not yet, of course, a matter of the *diachronic* problem of the meaning of History, but quite simply of the synchronic meaning of a limited, elapsed temporalization. From this standpoint, although History manifests itself as praxis-process – i.e. (even in the case of *maximum* integration) as a *loss of control*; as an action that escapes itself and overflows and congeals its agent; as ignorance, non-consciousness or false consciousness, i.e. as praxis that does not recognize itself – and *for that very reason* is human, it is nevertheless dis-order in social ensembles, inasmuch as these pay the costs of the order provisionally established among things, and it is the alteration of this *real* order through the progressive intensification of social disorder (with or without a possibility of correction). Meaning, as an orientation of the temporal spiral, is itself a practical signification and can be comprehended only in and through temporalization. All those, for example, who present what they call 'Stalinism' as a strict mechanism that starts as soon as it is wound up, like a musical table-mat, are losing sight (because of the real sclerosis of the last years) of the fact that if Stalinism – as a theoretico-practical unity of *all* the results achieved (in the actual order that they were), the operations that enabled them to be achieved, the means used, the resources expended, the transformations of the agents by their action, and the theories engendered by and for the action itself – can be described in the form of a permanence (inert structures, repetitions, frequentatives), this mechanical inter-conditioning of the elements that make it up is just a purely theoretical view, or (if you prefer) a cross-section of praxis-process in the last moments of its temporalization. For – however, and via whatever mediation, I may combine the notions of planned growth in an underdeveloped country, bureaucracy, idealist voluntarism, cult of personality, etc. (I am choosing these determinations at random and simply as examples) – the constituted ensemble will present itself as a *prototype*. I shall thus be able to try and find it again – more or less deformed – in other historical cases (to the point where some observers think they can infer the following law from their comparisons: the dictatorship of the Communist Parties is the best or only way for underdeveloped countries to achieve their industrialization most rapidly). For this very reason, however, the prototype as an object of concepts (albeit synthetically linked) loses its temporal determinations and is universalized. It represents, in the last resort, the exteriority of the process inasmuch as it has been separated from practical interiority. It becomes a *signification* again, in the sense that the bound ensemble of verbal formulations relating to an inanimate and atemporal object (i.e. conceived in its relative permanence and by provisionally abstracting from the temporalization that produces it, wears it away and destroys it) – for example, to a tool or a physico-chemical fact – can be strictly defined as the *abstract signification* of that object. But meaning has disappeared with History. For what we shall call meaning is the indissoluble unity of Stalinism with the *unique* and *peerless* temporalization that constitutes it. If you like, it is the perfect reversibility – at the heart of that unity – of two movements: one regressive, moving back from the sclerotic practices of 1950 to the evolution that began in 1928 (or perhaps in 1917, or even earlier: it is historical comprehension that will determine the date), as if to illuminate every revolutionary action from the outset by the future Destiny of the Revolution; the other progressive, which in the circular comprehension of a unique adventure sees the gradual production – through toxic secretions and counter-finalities, at the same time as through the extraordinary victories of the struggle against scarcity – of deviations, always practical, always individual, always *invented as much as suffered*, whose ensemble will become *Stalinism* as a system when they are already part of the transcended past. In short, the *meaning* of planned growth as a venture of the USSR in its first phase is Stalinism, *inasmuch* as it is simultaneously today the future of a past temporalization and the past of the present temporalization; inasmuch as its genesis and its degeneration are integrated into this schematic system, in order to become its concrete (hence temporal) depth, its idiosyncrasy and its determination (as a negation and as a rejection of the universal). It is (to use a word that has just been of use to us) Stalinism-as-a-venture, containing within it its own temporalization, and not Stalinism-as-a-prototype (a schema whose elementary relations condition one another horizontally, without the sources of its being simultaneously being sought – and found – in the verticality of the temporalized past).

From this viewpoint, it can be said that *the meaning* of praxis-process is everywhere within it, in so far as a limited temporalization is incarnated in its interior. It is thus that the *meaning* of the *ancien régime* (to anticipate our further investigation[78]), of the minor German courts, of Protestantism in the early eighteenth century, of the clash between 'reason' and 'tradition', as well as of the social hierarchy and the status of the artist, etc., is *temporally reproduced* in our ears by the playing of a Bach fugue on the harpsichord. Through this *retemporalization* – an incarnation of Bach's life itself – the conceptual ensemble we have just described is reincarnated as an ongoing process-praxis *through our time*. And in so far as – without knowing the piece played, or even perhaps ever having heard many Bach compositions – we *recognize* that the work belongs to the baroque eighteenth century, this movement of the incipient century is 'presentified' as the transcendent *meaning* of the fugue: a *finite* synthesis of an *object* (*the* fugue, with its laws, its structures, etc.) and of a praxis (the performance – equivalent for the listener to creation) containing the totality of that historical movement between the two end limits of its actualization.

I have not scrupled to choose this example – although it in fact

---

78. Namely, of the diachronic. On meaning in history, see the fragment 'History *Appeals* to History' in the Appendix, p.453 below; also the notes on Progress, pp.402–24 below.

assumes that we have already reached a later, and more concrete, point in our critical investigation – because here it represents little more than an *image*. I wanted to give an intuitive idea of the real enjoyment of a historical *meaning*. However, returning to the case that concerns us – that of personal sovereignty – it will be noticed that the historian himself realizes the retemporalization of the entire praxis-process, when he temporalizes himself in the present by operating as a historian: for example, by producing the limited activity that consists in reading documents or eye-witness accounts and reconstituting a single event through the diversity of sources. In the act of reading, for example, the *meaning* is given in every paragraph, as a link between the future-as-destiny and the future-as-product: inasmuch as this paragraph can be comprehended only through the unity of the book, and the latter only through much vaster practical unities. The *meaning* is thus not the object of a concept, but an individual reality enclosing its own temporalization within the limits of its reactualization and through the re-production of certain enveloped totalities (in principle, *all* of them: but as we are here adopting the viewpoint of the situated historian, we take account of the resources he has at his disposal and the exigencies specific to his inquiry). The historian's explanation of that *meaning* will be dialectical, in that it will bring out its secondary structures as the different internal profiles of the temporalization, in the synthetic unity of the final outcome.

Will it be said that there are *several meanings* of the synchronic totalization rather than *just one*? That is as you like. Or, if you prefer, there are indeed *several* meanings – very different from each other, too – for the various levels and sectors; but in each, precisely (inasmuch as the part of a whole is that whole itself, if not in the determination that produces it at least in the substance that is determined), the unity of the total meaning is to be found as its foundation and its product. Conversely, that total meaning itself must be grasped as the mediation between all the partial meanings. It is often, moreover, the juxtaposition of these that will bring forth – first as an exigency, then as an invention – the totalizing meaning as first a mediation, then a substantial foundation of each.

The same reality will be a *totalization-of-envelopment*, inasmuch as it is produced by the temporalization of the historical agents, and a *meaning*, inasmuch as it is reactualized by the labour of the situated historian. But it should not be concluded that this *meaning* is relative to the knowledge the historian gains of it. It must first be noted that it exists implicitly in and through every particular action – and in the very interiority of praxis – inasmuch as every enveloped totalization incarnates also the relation of the latter to the future, as a product and as a destiny (a destiny that causes itself to be produced); inasmuch as every one is actualized through the rhythm of the temporalization, its slumps and its accelerations, etc. In short, every real stage in a historical venture has its *taste*, which is the objective presence of the whole in everyone. And that taste – explanation of which is prevented by the lack of a necessary distance – is the meaning's actuality. Hence, it is not that the historian *constitutes* it: he confines himself to explaining it. In relation to him, this practical determination has become an object. But it is not the historian who is responsible for this objectification: it is simply produced by the metamorphosis of praxis into a *past*. And, which comes to the same thing, by the – at least partial – realization of the objectives set. The historian uncovers, explains – that is all. He restores for everyone an objective mode of being of the historical totalization: its *being-already-past* (we shall return to this being in our study of diachronic totalization). And it can doubtless be said that the structures he uncovers are a function of his knowledge, the materials he has at his disposal, his intellectual tools, and – through all this – the social and practical ensemble to which he belongs. But this comment cannot *relativize* the 'meaning' of the reconstructed praxis-process. For if the historian circumscribes the *meaning* of the totalization by his assumptions and methods, this determination situates him in relation to the ensemble being studied as much – and more – than it situates this ensemble in relation to him. What is relative in the object, and provisional too, is the limitation of meaning (i.e. its determination as a negation). More appropriate procedures, unpublished documents, the liquidation of certain class prejudices (whose source is the very society that has produced him[79]), would make it possible to deepen and enlarge his results: integrating into them, for example, other facts that contradict them, but within the very unity of a synthesis founding and supporting its own contradictions. Furthermore, as we shall see later, the reactualization of *one* totalization can take on its true scope only if it is carried out against the background of human history as a whole. The broadest historical syntheses are still to come: they depend on future methods and the methods depend on them. In this *situated* inquiry, therefore, it is the object that situates the scholar in relation to the future. As a unique and concrete reality, and as a totalization totalized by Universal History, it prescribes an infinite task for him. This means that it refers – via the present generation – to the series of future generations, and defines the historian in relation to the historians of tomorrow and the day after as *being nothing except what he has discovered*. In this perspective, it can be said that it is Being that defines knowledge as relative (inasmuch as the latter is the objective bond joining the reality uncovered to the

---

79. That is to say, produced the historian.

historian who uncovers it). Knowledge – but not *the known*. What is in fact revealed through the situated reconstruction is that part of Being which the chosen perspective allows to be discovered. And this part of Being is totally and fully real. All that is relative is the limit which scparatcs within it thc known from the unknown, and reflects other limits: those of present-day historians. It is this limit which will give way, inasmuch as it is a determination of the known (hence a negation of all that remains to be known) – through a negation of a negation that the known being demands *right now* – in reference to a future where the present historian will no longer be.

Yet the historian, inasmuch as he belongs to a new undertaking, transforms the past event into its meaning. But this is inasmuch as that historian – as a participant in the present undertaking of all and, in this guise, *even as a historian* – contributes to the praxis-process, is temporalized in the temporalization of envelopment and towards its short-term and long-term aims, and – in himself and through all his activities – makes himself an enveloped totality. For through *History in progress*, the meaning of completed History is transformed.[80] I shall give just one example, but it is a striking one, which we shall examine in detail at the *diachronic* moment of our dialectical investigation. Let it serve here as a sign and as a schema. Past history is a *pluralist* history. Separated by obstacles that they do not have the means to overcome on a day-to-day basis, peoples – except in the case of great migrations and invasions – form relatively closed ensembles. And each is distinguished from the others by irreducible particularities: it is these, in fact, which first strike you and which foreign travellers report. This pluralism is tending to become reduced. However, up to (and including) the nineteenth century, reasons that we shall have to adduce kept the Asian continent – despite colonial and semi-colonial penetration – and the 'Western world' in a relative state of non-communication. The ensemble of present factors involved in the 'One World' (an industrial revolution requiring a global economy, through and by virtue of imperialism; regroupment and decol-onization of the colonial or semi-colonial peoples; industrialization of the underdeveloped countries under communist control) is for the first time leading the historical process to totalize the concrete, present humanity: i.e. the two thousand million men today working on Earth, whose needs, labours, the products of those labours, and the various social orders they generate, react upon one another, upon the condition of every individual, and – for the first time – within the unity of a mutual conditioning. Consequently, *the former pluralism is a unity*. First, because

---

80. See the fragment 'History *Appeals* to History' in the Appendix, p.453 below.

the unity in progress makes possible comparative sociology and comparative history (we shall see the sense in which the comparison is true
and concrete, and the sense in which it is abstract). Secondly, because
these separate ensembles are *constituted as convergent* by their future
unity. Precisely in so far as this 'One World' of our bloody struggles and
our alliances – of our indissoluble terrestrial unity – is constituted
through us as their Destiny, it creates them *in the past* as having that
Destiny as their *fatality* and as their *product*. A reclassification is carried
out, which – without neglecting the negative practices of separation,
ignorance and rejection – tends to place the accent on the positive
relations between groups, between tribes and between nations. The history
of trade, of communication routes (Silk Road, etc.), of the cultural links
established by wars, etc. – in short, of mutual interpenetrations and their
consequences for each ensemble, and ultimately for all – becomes the
crucial thing; not a priori, because it is the history of the positive, but
because the 'One World' of 1950 has made that positive into the truth of
History. We shall return to this, as I have already said. But what matters
here is the fact that one changes the *meaning* of a past totalization
(*indirectly*) by acting upon the present situation (and, through repercussion, upon the *past-being* in its meaning), but not by rounding *upon that
meaning* in order to know it. It is not *the historian* who imposes the
convergence of their practices upon the former ensembles. He *discloses*
it, on the abstract terrain of rigorous reconstruction of the past, because
he *constitutes* it through a temporalization that envelops him and totalizes
his partial action with those of all the others. This influence of the future
on the past, far from idealizing the *meaning* (as a present residue of a
totalization that was, and as a permanent possibility of its reactualization
in the form of a temporalization strictly confined within our temporalization), confirms the reality of its *being*. This *being*, in fact, *situates* those
who want to know it, through its passive resistances and through the
more or less superficial truths it yields to them. It is situated only *in
action* and *through it* (and we shall see that it changes the action
precisely in so far as the action can change it).

Being of the Totalization-of-Envelopment: Historical Idealisms and the Situated Method[81]

THESE *ontological* observations allow us to tackle the main question, the one that must precisely distinguish the situated dialectic from any idealism (be it a materialist dogmatism or a historical relativism). For we have to ask ourselves, on the basis of what we have established about *the being of meaning* – that form-in-the-past of the totalization-of-envelopment – what the *real-being* of that totalization is, as an ongoing praxis-process. I am not hereby intending to study ontologically the complex structures that constitute this *real-being*: i.e. the dialectical unity of the human and the anti-human in all their forms, inasmuch as this rests upon the practical unification of physico-chemical (and zoological) exteriority into a *milieu* (later into a field) by the organism, and upon the reconditioning of the organism by the physico-chemical through the indispensable synthetic unity of the *milieu* and the *field*. This difficult problem belongs to an ontology of History, not to the critique of dialectical Reason. What counts for us is simply to determine whether it is necessary to envisage the totalization-of-envelopment through a positivist nominalism, or in the perspective of a radicalizing realism. This moment of our critical investigation is crucial, since it determines the relations between Being and Knowledge, and since it calls into question again the very foundation of the situated dialectic. For the latter risks appearing as a phenomenological idealism, so long as the relation uniting situation and totalization has not been clarified.

---

81. This chapter appeared in Sartre's manuscript as section 5 of the foregoing numbered sequence. However, the argument became wider in scope as it went along, and changing the section into an independent chapter has allowed the various points treated to be thrown into sharper relief by giving them their own sub-divisions. It will be noted that the argument does not remain confined to the example of directorial societies.

The Being-in-itself of the Totalization-of-Envelopment
Can Only Be Vainly Aimed At

When we say that the dialectic is situated, what are we trying to convey? Just this: that historians cannot look at things *from the standpoint of the inhuman* in order to know and comprehend historical reality. There are two ways of *de-situating* yourself with respect to the object. One is to turn yourself into Nature and see yourself producing human history as one of your dialectical hypostases. The other – less easily detectable – is to reject the situation as a reciprocity: in other words, to situate the event or object being studied in relation to the researcher and his research, yet without situating the researcher and his discipline within historical development through the exigencies of that event or object and the way in which these are satisfied. The former type of de-situation leads to the dialectical dogmatism of the *outside*; the latter to the dogmatic and positivist idealism of conservative historians. At all events, the de-situation ends by positing objectivity – inasmuch as it is the actual object disclosing itself – as an *absolute reality*. If the researcher (or the ensemble of researchers who *make up* the current science) is de-situated in relation to the object under consideration – either because he considers praxis-process from the standpoint of 'natural' exteriority, or because he has a priori established himself in truth itself as an eternity contemplating the change from the viewpoint of what does not change – the object loses part of its qualification (its *human* meaning and its structure of practical interiority in the former case, its reality as a temporalization in the latter*), but wins (illusorily, of course) the absolute autonomy of its being. This passage to the absolute derives simultaneously from scientistic dogmatism and from the historian's negation of the relations of immanence binding him to his object. For the latter takes its being from Nature – an absolute being, and an absolute knowledge of the modes it [Nature] engenders – or from Truth, as absolute substance of the apparitions it produces and illuminates and as an eternization of their being as an eternal object of knowledge. But, in addition, the breaking of the bond of reciprocity confers in both cases a reciprocal independence upon the object and upon the researcher – an independence that is reciprocal in so far as it is reduced, basically, to the abstract negation of mutual dependency. This split, maintained within a reciprocity that is necessary to the situation, seems to realize the separation of Being and

---

* It should be added that, in so far as practical interiority is lost, temporalization is transformed into physico-chemical time; and conversely, the elimination of temporalization by the eternal must affect the agent's practical reality, to the very heart of his free dialectic.

Knowing, which develop in parallel but autonomously.

We discussed these views at the beginning of the present work,[82] and showed how the dialectic could not be the object of a critical investigation outside the practical milieu of which it is simultaneously the action (inasmuch as it gives itself its own laws), the knowledge (as dialectical control of action by itself) and the cognitive law (inasmuch as knowledge of the dialectic requires a dialectical temporalization of knowledge). The fundamental identity of *Doing* and *Knowing* thus presented the relationship between a praxis and the historian studying it as the bond of interiority linking *two actions* through a spatio-temporal gap; and this bond of interiority (which implied that the historian should be questioned about the praxis of his own society) was ultimately nothing but the *situation* of the two agents with respect to one another, inasmuch as this must be determined on the basis of the historical ensemble.

This bond of dependence, as we have seen, did not imply an ontological relativism. Precisely because *human actions* were involved, the *practical reality* of each eluded the other on principle. *Or rather*, we were able to assert that ontological autonomy – and consequently the irreducibility of Being to being-known – so long as the object of knowledge was being temporalized within a larger social ensemble, and so long as it was defined *solely* by *human* co-ordinates: i.e. as being *in its objective reality and in its autonomy* a mere determination and a singularizing incarnation of the temporalization in progress, i.e. of the totalization-of-envelopment.

It is at this level, however, that the question of idealism and realism will be posed. For as soon as we recognize the existence of a totality-of-envelopment,[83] considered as the temporalization of the praxis-process, we discover that our *analysis situs* [analysis of the situation] was incomplete, and that it can emerge from indetermination only by calling the ontological reality of the enveloping totalization into question.

An attempt has been made to avoid this problem by reducing the totalization-of-envelopment to being merely the ideal unity of enveloped totalizations: praxis-process would then be like a monadic universe reflecting itself differently in every monad and not existing outside its various reflections. At the same time, by a converse movement, every agent, every activity, every event and every product is here reduced to being just a determination of the human milieu. It is not produced in the void of universal exteriority but carved into the solidities of the practical temporalization, from which it receives its existence along with its its gradient, profile, speed, etc. The *human* (i.e. the historical

---

82. *Critique*, vol. 1, 'Introduction'.
83. See footnote 43 on p.187 above.

praxis-process) is here a finite but limitless solid (whose relations with the non-human no one can thus define, even as a problematic limit), producing its own specifications, incarnations, etc., in the way that the substance produces its modes for Spinoza. This way of suppressing difficulties by removing the means of unmasking them employs a conception of History that may seem close to our own, but is in fact radically opposed to it. This conception actually rests upon a system of metaphors, whose metaphorical character is concealed and which end up being taken literally. What such metaphors express is *true* if you bear in mind that they express it *metaphorically*.

To give an example of such terminology, the truth of its content and the deviation of the true by language, let us imagine we wanted to express *from this viewpoint* the differences separating the literary vocation in the USSR from its counterpart in the bourgeois democracies, during the second half of the first stage of socialism. We should show, among other things, how the singular objective of the Soviet writer is necessarily a specification of the common objective (via the mediation of socialist realism, etc.); how the orientation, speed, urgency and rhythm of the creative temporalization are determined by the sovereign and common temporalization (rhythm of planned growth) that nourishes and sustains it; and how *literature* (as a complex ensemble of social relations *situating* the writer under consideration with respect to his colleagues and the reading public) is at the same time metamorphosed into a necessarily *progressive* movement, i.e. contributes to the advances of socialist construction and progresses directly and indirectly through those very advances. So the temporal profile of his literary life merges with the rising curve of literature, inasmuch as this discipline is itself carried along by the rising industrial potential, standard of living and cultural level. The writer does not realize his full flowering – the great value of the works produced in his maturity, or the increase in his audience (numerically) and his influence over his readers – in the same way that his colleagues in the bourgeois democracies would: simply as the results of his personal labour, his experience and his age, and of some favourable conjuncture creating a temporary need on the public's part to receive the very 'message' he is able to deliver. To be sure, he does not discard any of these factors, in some of which he takes great pride; but he sees his merits and his successes above all as the products – and the incarnation – of the successes obtained in all domains by the sovereign planning. Moreover, as the writer – a member of the leading strata – has made his choice to write in his non-transcendable inertia as a common individual, and as this option has in the last resort determined only the particular way in which this common individual will serve the aim pursued by all, the movement of his life is realized as a singularizing incarnation of the movement of socialization, and his own success as the *incarnated* triumph of the praxis-process.

You will recognize this language. It is our own, it is that of all dialecticians, and indeed it presents no danger if you see it as merely an ensemble of swift, picturesque phrases, which save time and are annulled in the very act of comprehension. But if it is to be taken literally, it plunges us back into an idealist, unprincipled optimism. For if you take the words as they are – i.e. without correcting them – you are induced to identify *realism* with *humanism*. The internal limit of every situation is *actually* the relationship of men with one another, directly or via the intermediary of human things; or else the relationship between men and human things, directly or via the mediation of other men. This is what 'humanist realism' (that idealism of the human) expresses through images which make praxis-process – as a *human-reality* – into the substance of particular acts and local events.

Now it is quite true that – in a practical field unified by the sovereign-individual – every particular reality is conditioned from within by an essential structure of the field: the relations of immanence between everything and everything else. But it is also true that we should lapse back into the Gestaltist illusion if we forgot that a totalization in progress is not a totality, and that the elements of the field are discrete realities which produce their integration against the multiplicity that affects them, by transcending [the latter] without suppressing it. Above all, the totalizing temporalization is a result in progress – the result of particular activities, and of the sovereign praxis inasmuch as this reconditions them through the organs of propaganda or coercion with which it has provided itself – but it would be a terrible mistake to see it as the temporal evolution of some hyper-organism imposing itself on its social cells. Acts are autonomous and discontinuous. They arise everywhere at once. Each, to be sure, totalizes the others by incarnating them. Each modifies the milieu surrounding each of the others. But these incarnations have nothing to do with the production of finite modes by a substance. They are realized in discontinuity as autonomous transcendences, and most of the time what reconditions them is the ensemble of the material circumstances that they simultaneously transcend and preserve. From this viewpoint, on the contrary, it is necessary to return to the prime truth of Marxism that it is men who make History. And as it is History that produces men (inasmuch as they make it), we understand as self-evident that the 'substance' of the human act, if such a thing were to exist (if the biological organism could be designated by this name, without fear of misunderstanding), would *on the contrary* be the non-human (or, at a pinch, the pre-human), inasmuch as it is precisely the discrete materiality of everyone. Through the act, an organism *makes itself a man*, by interiorizing and re-exteriorizing the techniques and the culture which define man *in these historical circumstances* and within the (simultaneously human and non-human) perspective of reproducing his life (satisfying his needs). Precisely in so far as the individual is the product of his product (and in so far as the action of the productive process is inscribed in his very lungs or in his liver – occupational illnesses, etc.), he is the product of a certain man and a certain woman. If his parents are affected in their very bodies by the conditions imposed upon them by the exigencies of the sovereign (and, through these, of the practico-inert), moreover, he will integrate himself into the practical synthesis with a certain number of negative features, which he does get from the *social*, to be sure, but via the animal intermediary of an inherited constitution. If it is true that nature and culture are indissolubly linked in each and every person, this *also* means that culture *runs natural risks*: that it is in mortal danger in each and every biological individuality. We have already seen that this *facticity* of praxis is incarnated in the fragility of the sovereign-individual, i.e. in the dependency of the praxis-process in relation to *one* physiological organism. To be sure, *one* death has never sufficed to overturn praxis entirely. But it is still the case that the sovereign's is reinteriorized by everyone, then re-exteriorized as modifications – of varying importance, depending on the circumstances – of the totalizing activity and its objectives. So inasmuch as the individual integrates fundamentally non-human elements into the human synthesis, and inasmuch as his *specific* features represent his initial circumstances transcended and preserved – and the source of fundamental deviations, through which his *several* practices have been constituted (and which we inherit as incarnated culture and as accultured nature) – every social man must be defined as a certain reality of the material universe producing itself in and through its relation to all the others (from the same sovereign field) *as transcended nature*.

But through this irreducible materiality – which characterizes the agent and *realizes* the act that transcends it – the individual and the groups, through the practical field and beyond its limits, maintain an *ontological* relationship with exteriority: i.e. with the whole of the world. The being-in-the-world that defines the practical organism and circumscribes its field of action is coupled with a being-in-the-midst-of-the-world by virtue of which it receives the same status as all other realities. The mere possibility that a cooling of the sun might stop History – and leave its diachronic meaning for ever undecided – is enough to constitute him (even if it never happens) as an exteriority *in relation to his history*. For in this case he will not complete it, but neither will he be destroyed by it (as would happen if an atomic war were to cause the disappearance of humanity). So History becomes the undertaking you pursue *all other things being equal*, and whose chances of *succeeding* (assuming that a goal is proposed – we shall come back to this[84]) depend upon the maintenance of a status quo in at least this sector of the Universe: i.e. of an ensemble of energy transmutations operating *in exteriority** and without any teleological determination.**

So being-in-the-midst-of-the-world as an exterior limit upon being-in-the-world marks each and every one of us and constitutes the transcendent aspect of our materiality. This does not really involve anything fundamentally new. We have already seen the practical organism *in danger* in its practical field. In this field, moreover, which defines its powers, danger – even physical – is a human danger. The only difference is that being-in-the-midst-of-the-world as a limit upon being-in-the-world determines us *in relation to our impotence*. In that sense, the transcendent being of individuals and groups cannot be lived or known as such within the interiority of the field. Except in one specific circumstance in which it is incarnated as a negation, and to which I shall return shortly,[85] it is interiorized and re-exteriorized *practically* and

---

* If there were to be a 'dialectic of Nature', nothing would be altered in the conditions we have just described. Furthermore, scientific and technical advances indubitably have the effect of enlarging the practical field, and perhaps will in fact make it possible later on to avert some disasters. But this is not the real question. Even if, contained in germ in human knowledge, there were a practical possibility for man (once a certain scientific and technical level was reached) to survive any sidereal catastrophe, nothing would yet prove that such catastrophes would wait to occur until we had the means to avert them. Nothing would prove it, because nothing *can* prove it: two different series are involved. So if the ensemble of cosmic circumstances really allowed us to reach a certain threshold and pass beyond it, the conditions that gave us the opportunity of perpetuating ourselves would mark us in exteriority no more and no less than the cataclysm that destroyed our species.

** The modifications which experimental biology may introduce into the generation and development of the embryo are irrelevant here. To be sure, inasmuch as they derive from the application of technology and will be conditioned by social imperatives, they must be considered as *social*. However, even if people had succeeded in producing life and thereby creating 'synthetic men', these new individuals – as products of a society, i.e. of a concrete universality – would be determined, even in their very emergence, by sociality. But each of them, in his very weight and also in his fragility, through the laws that had directed his development – laws of inert matter and laws of life – would (even if as a man of anti-physis) remain bound in transcendence to the Universe, just like that Chinese vase or that block of steel. In other words, he would be produced – and be preserved in his reality – in relation to an infinity of exteriority whose characteristic feature (seen through our spy-glass) is to sustain or destroy practical individuals with equal indifference: i.e. to be all at once human, inhuman, pre-human, trans-human and non-human.

84. This topic, which belongs to the diachronic, was not in fact dealt with in the present work. Allusion is made to it on p.335 below: the essential aim of History-as-an-undertaking is linked to the existence and the perception of diachronic meaning, i.e. of 'the axial direction in relation to which every possible drift, today and in the infinite future of interiority, could be defined (and corrected)'.

85. See pp.309 ff. below: it is death which, lived as an absolute exteriority within interiority, gives the experience of the enveloping totalization's being-in-itself.

teleologically as a *de facto limit* to our power: i.e. as a human determination of technology by social history and the history of science, and *simultaneously* as a frontier to be *pushed back* – and which is indeed always *being pushed back*.

Moreover, we now understand that this transcendent limit does not confine itself to determining everyone (or the mere sum of all individuals) *from outside*, but is the being-in-the-midst-of-the-world of *praxis-process* itself. For the latter, when it succeeds, imposes itself in a restricted sector of Being; but its triumph over things, within this sector, presupposes that it is *tolerated* by the Universe. In other words, praxis-process is grasped, in its interiority, as making itself through its products. But its transcendent qualification constitutes it as a reality that is not the foundation of its own possibility. This real character of its being eludes it, as it eludes the individual. Praxis-process calculates and takes its risks in a given situation, e.g. by transcending a contradiction of the practico-inert or by giving itself the task of satisfying a need. Wholly defined *for itself* by this transcendence that brings a future objective into relation with a present danger or a need (and thus encounters the risk that the agent may no longer be able to act or even live – but an interiorized risk, i.e. one integrated into the field as a positive or negative exigency), it engenders its own knowledge to avoid the *interior* possibility of failure or disintegration, and has neither the need nor the leisure to grasp itself from outside as a dead-possibility defined in exteriority on the basis of undisclosed regions of the Universe. Yet – although this possibility remains a more or less formal determination so long as a circumstance has not *realized* as a threat-to-man some transformation of the sidereal field – being-in-transcendence imbues and qualifies praxis-process within its very interiority. For praxis-process produces itself in a world where the ensemble of celestial and cosmic revolutions, by virtue of the consequences they are in the process of entailing, pronounces sentence upon it, upon its possibles and upon its objectives.

So human idealism[86] is wrong twice over. The *practical* integration of individuals could not liquidate the multiplicity of exteriority that characterizes those same individuals as substances. The totalization-of-envelopment exists and is defined within the finitude of interiority of the undertaking (in short, it produces – through its objectives, the materiality of the field, etc. – its own limits). For that very reason, this finitude becomes a structure of exteriority in its being-in-transcendence. The feature specific to praxis-process is thus, from the ontological viewpoint,

---

86. Which is also a 'realism'. See above, p.305: this humanist realism is an idealism of the human.

the opposite of that which Hegel ascribes to the movement of consciousness in *The Phenomenology of Mind*. For idealism sees being-in-itself as
an abstract moment – that of essence – of the 'becoming-other' of the
living substance. It contrasts with the *for-itself* in dissociation, as the raw
given of objectification alienated to the negation which repeats and
posits itself in the unicity of the subject. Totalization will be carried out
at the moment when – with the in-itself transcended and preserved in the
for-itself – being is realized as in-itself and for-itself: i.e. as absolute-
subject containing its own determinations within itself, and defined by
the consciousness of being its own mediation in its *becoming-other*.
Roughly speaking, being-in-itself – as an essence – is that outer aspect of
Being that consciousness takes back into itself since it can exist only *for
consciousness*. In our dialectical investigation, however, we find the
being-in-itself of praxis-process as what might be termed its unassimilable and non-recuperable reality. And this being-in-itself, as an
exterior limit of totalization, realizes itself as an interior limit of
transcendent exteriority (it produces itself on the basis of the dispersion
of exteriority as a limitation of that dispersion *by a development in
interiority*). As a twofold limit, however, being-in-itself cannot present
itself to investigation, as we have seen. As a revelation immanent to the
practical field, the being-in-exteriority that defines its ontological status
eludes it by virtue of its very structure. It can at best be aimed at
abstractly (as is the case here), through verbal formulations. As an
interiority produced as a limit upon the infinite 'natural' dispersion, it
could be the object of a concrete knowledge only if this – as Naville
would like – came towards it from the infinite horizons of the Universe.
But this infinite thought would at once swallow it up as a moment of its
practical field. For the universe of dispersion, as object of a practical
thought, would become a field unified by praxis; and human history
would no longer contrast with this as the limitation of exteriority by
interiority, but as a local event contrasting with the total field. So what is
revealed to us is not *the anteriority* of being-in-itself in relation to being-
for-itself, but its autonomy. Not only does it not need to be known in
order to be, but it *on principle* eludes knowledge.

Death, Experience of Nothingness-in-itself as a
Window on to Being-in-itself: History Riddled with Holes

You will perhaps ask how it happens that we can so much as speak –
albeit formally and wide of the mark – about this ontological status, since
its very reality implies that it transcends knowledge. The answer to that
is, first, that this non-knowable is not an irrational: it merely signals the

impossibility for History to be at once, and *for itself*, immanence and transcendence. It is useless, of course, for the politician or technician to try and determine the limits of praxis-process: at least, it is useless in present circumstances – and all things being equal, moreover – since we have no knowledge of a sidereal catastrophe that might threaten our species (or slow evolutions certainly preparing our disappearance). But philosophical reflection (whose practical function we shall see more clearly in a forthcoming chapter[87]) is led to totalize the arguments against idealism by aiming wildly at this ontological transcendence: the being-in-itself of the enveloping totalization.

Above all, moreover, as I have already mentioned, there exists *at least one case* where we experience absolute exteriority within interiority: this specific case (but one which is reproduced everywhere, at every instant) is – to give it first in all its original complexity – violent death condemning an individual or group to utter failure. For such a death is realized as the incarnation of the enveloping totalization inasmuch as it *is in itself*, rather than as a determination for itself of intersubjectivity.

If, for example, you first take the simple case of an accidental death (whether it be that of a tiler having a fall or a motorist involved in a collision), the utensility and the counter-finalities that are the immediate source of this death (a brick came away under the worker's foot; the car was a standard model and all cars of that model had the same defect, etc.) do not manage to give the death a human character (nor – which comes to the same thing here – an anti-human, practico-inert one). Or rather, yes, such a death is wholly human: social ensembles choose their deaths (by applying different selective systems: the distribution of dispensaries, increased occupational risks – in a capitalist system thanks to competition and in a socialist one to exhaustion caused by the accelerated growth of industry – and so on) and certain men *chose this death* through their own battle against the inert exigencies of their task. The *practico-inert* goes further, it designates its victims: a supplementary determination will be enough for the choice to be realized by the event (the brakes drag to the left, so all purchasers are designated as belonging to a series of *possible deaths*; the determination *for this particular one* will come from additional circumstances, which for their part define possible but incompletely determined deaths: slippery road, rain, hairpin bends, lack of road signs, etc.). So it is perfectly legitimate to see every

---

87. The topic was not to be studied in the present work, but it was broached in a lecture that Sartre gave in 1959 (one year after the present text was written), entitled 'Why Philosophers?' and published in March 1984 in the journal *Le Débat*. See also the interview on anthropology in *Situations, IX*.

death as a social and human product taking place as a temporalized reality within the interiority of the enveloping temporalization. This will be the viewpoint of the legislator, magistrate or technician, for example. In a certain way it is also *partly* the viewpoint of parents and close relatives, who always (more or less vaguely) have it in for the collectivity that has allowed a particular individual to die (the car factory, which has abnormally increased the risks inherent in driving a motorcar; the whole society, which through its lack of organization has allowed him to run useless dangers or exhaust himself by toil; and so on); for the technicians who could have saved him but did not try (the doctor who treated him, the trade union which should long ago have insisted that the management should take safety measures, etc.); or directly for the roadhog 'who killed him' or the foreman whose idiotic order forced him to do a dangerous job that ended in the fatal accident. In this way, people make death into an event in human history – or rather an event in the individual life. And they are right. With the advances of medicine (which accompany the development of industry) a particular illness goes into decline or disappears, while another – occupationally based and thus directly connected with the use of certain machines to manufacture certain products – makes its appearance. The accumulation of capital makes it possible to increase the share of revenue distributed to unproductive people, so to increase the number of doctors, etc. From this viewpoint, we shall say that every violent death is the incarnation of the inner limit to the enveloping totalization. The boundaries of the practical field are touched, but from within – in immanence – and death presents itself as a destruction realized through the practical relations of men with one another.

At the same time, however, death is grasped by the survivors (sometimes even by the person who is about to die, if he becomes aware of his fate) as a *pure and simple deficit*: both in relation to the group which needs these men and can no longer use them (in history, it often happens that a revolutionary party is systematically deprived of its elites through decimation, continual death sentences, etc.) and also in relation to the actual agent (be it an individual or a sub-group) who is subtracted or stolen – as if by a trick – from his own future: i.e. from his destiny and his practical objectives, from his 'rendezvous with History', and from the life he had already traced for himself. From this new standpoint, comprehension in interiority finds its limit: *if* men are mortal, that death sentence and that execution – in other words, those two acts by living people exercised upon a living person – can and must be comprehended. Death is a means of History, or life and death occupy a specific (and always very complex) place in the system of values produced by praxis-process. But death itself is not a product of History: on the contrary (at least in the case of human history), it is what produces History. The struggle to govern things and enslave them to needs is produced as the labour of mortal organisms, for whom the non-satisfaction of certain needs entails death. And the struggle of men among themselves via the mediation of things and for the government of things draws its urgency from the danger of death. A transposition of emergencies, under pressure from the danger of dying, leads men to produce *for others* the death they wish to avoid themselves. And the revolts provoked by this oppression draw their climate of fraternity-terror from the twofold threat of death (dying of famine or poverty; dying through extermination). This interiorized threat is *itself* fraternity-terror, as a new displacement of mortal fragility: the interiorization of death becomes a *punishment by death* of secessions and betrayals within the combat group.

But however that may be, death as a determination of the human condition is a qualification of History *in transcendence*, since it is its (universal) presence which obliges us to make *a history of mortal organisms*: i.e. a history, every praxis-process of which is defined in terms of the necessity of dying. And the necessity of dying is itself defined as a necessity for every individual (and every group) to disappear in the course of its own action; to vacate the premises – the theatre – of its functions *before* it has completed its role (or sometimes *long after*: at all events the gap exists); which signifies – conversely – for every praxis the necessity of being deserted along the way by its agent and continuing as an inert praxis (of the same kind as counter-finalities), or of disappearing (leaving unresolved the practical question it sought to resolve), or of being taken up and deviated by others. From this standpoint death entails those faults in History (connected with new births) which people call 'generational conflicts' – and which are the source of the complexity of diachronic syntheses.[88] Through his death, the agent has this destiny: to begin or resume what he does not finish – and what no one will finish (since his replacement will deviate the praxis). This means that he must himself pursue his action, bearing in mind his ever possible death (i.e. make his will, or if he is a sovereign ensure his succession, etc.); hence, he must qualify it in its historicity on the basis of a trans-historical condition.* Through the very modalities of the transmission of powers

---

* That Science may one day be able to prolong life is a probability that in no way alters the fundamental question. For, so long as man is mortal in a field of scarcity, this question cannot find its answer in any variation of his life-span. Moreover, I refuse to envisage the hypothesis of an immortality technically acquired in the midst of abundance: this wholly indeterminate dream, if it were one day to be realized, would signal the end of *human history*, that is all. Furthermore, an immortality *become* in this way would necessarily retain its former mortality as the original source of its deviations.

88. *L'Idiot de la famille*, vol. 3, pp.436 ff.

– i.e. through the agent's anticipation of his own disappearance, and through his transcendence towards a modified, altered and continued praxis – the action *itself* receives its intra-historical description as non-historicity. Actually, it orientates itself in relation to a certain human fact – which in reality is the man's disappearance – and makes it into the agent's permanent possibility. Well, on the one hand this disappearance is a radical negation. As a contingent brutality – i.e. as a naked manifestation of facticity – it is unassimilable and non-transcendable, and at the very heart of History manifests itself as a rupture of the synthetic links of interiority.* From this point of view, it fundamentally eludes comprehension. On the other hand, it always manifests itself as a *cessation of History*, even – or above all – if it is the historical struggle that has provoked it. Not only has the individual been stripped away from History, but History required his death (inasmuch as he is the victim of a systematic repression) only in so far as it – and all human deaths – are at once transcendent conditions and transcendent aims in relation to History. Conditioned by death, History – through the praxis-process of the temporary victors – realizes itself by depriving the adversaries of any human possibility of making History. And this permanent deficit remains sustained by the subsequent development of the praxis-process, whatever it may be, as the inert unity of a lacuna in the historialization of that society (these men *were missed by* their practical group, their families, etc.). In the unthinkable moment when death reveals the conditioning in exteriority of all human action (it seems that his former actions were *tolerated* by circumstances, since they already contained the danger that came to an end through this death) – when, by a mystifying paradox, the mortal act (or the accident) occurs as a retotalization of a whole man and, by that very retotalization which attacks his innermost being, transforms him into nothingness: i.e. into an inert and non-totalizable lacuna, positing itself at the heart of immanence as a non-transcendable transcendence – History reveals itself to warring individuals and groups as *riddled with holes*. Its deaths are billions of holes piercing it. And each time, through that fundamental porosity, the fragility of the praxis-process presents itself experientially as the universal presence of its being-in-exteriority. Through the pitiless necessity of his death-agony, a traveller lost in the desert experiences the non-humanity of the Universe, and thereby the transcendent limit of the

---

* A *death*, as a negative and social event, becomes the term of an infinity of relations of immanence between agents. This particular death results in this particular promotion and the latter changes the lives of all the subordinates. In itself, however, the death of this or that person presents itself as the cessation *for him* (not for his work, whatever this may be) of all relations of immanence.

human adventure manifests itself to him in its full horror, as his impossibility of living and as the impossibility of being a man. But an insurgent – arrested by men, sentenced and kept in custody by men, and knowing that other men will put him to death – grasps no differently (through the failure of his attempt and the inevitable 'physical liquidation' that will follow it) the impossibility, for himself and those he was seeking to deliver, of living and of being a man. For what is lived and experienced here as the being-in-itself of History is not, of course, the ensemble of mistakes and bad luck that led the revolt to disaster. The fact is that – through this ensemble of errors and counter-finalities – the result comes inexorably to the agent as a definitive impossibility of acting historically, transcending his defeat or drawing the necessary experience from it to continue the struggle: in short (in so far as *the others* are 'anti-men' for him), as an impossibility for him and his allies to make human history. If the struggle continues without him, he may transcend this experience by *utilizing* his death – by making it into an exemplary *act*. But precisely in so far as he makes use of it and his comrades outside can exploit the popular indignation, this means that the *deep meaning of the event* is lived by the masses themselves as a non-transcendable, shocking inner fault of History; as an abrupt, terrifying apparition of the human adventure as conditioned in exteriority. Thus, through failure and death, the being-in-itself of History – as irremediable facticity of human organisms – reveals its omnipresence (*that* death poisons everything): it is the human adventure, inasmuch as its onto-logical status comes to it *also* from the outside world.

This experience, moreover (which may be more confused and, in the last resort, manifest itself in connection with anything, through the mere interplay of implications of synthetic reciprocity between deaths – as specific, dated events – and failures, etc., inasmuch as, even without costing human lives, these end up *incarnating* death), yields us no intuitive *knowledge*. For we know *nothing* of death: not in the sense that there is anything to know about it (leaving aside the biological knowledge that allows it to be defined), but precisely because it *is nothing*, or is the transformation of man's humanity – as practical existence in a field of interiority – into a mere inert lacuna. We do not *comprehend* it, not because it is some mystery surpassing human Reason, but merely because factors in exteriority realize in a certain case the rational (in the positivist sense) but non-comprehensible possibility that comprehension should be for ever impossible.

This experience terrifies, because it is that of Nothingness-in-itself as a window on to Being-in-itself. This signifies that in every case it disrupts and rends an optimistic relativism – which at once re-forms. This relativism is as characteristic of certain Marxists as it is of bourgeois historians. Materialist dialecticians are even especially liable to develop it. In vain do they define Being through praxis, or just through *efficacy*: the fact remains that they see the whole complex of processes as being within totalization (whether they call it that or something else); and that the formula 'being is acting or being-acted' is the principle of a pragmatic idealism, in the same way that the other formula, 'being is perceiving or being perceived', grounds intellectualistic idealism. At this level of optimism, there is a refusal to take account – for the ontological status of men – of their transcendent determinations of non-humanity. Or rather, everything is integrated. Of course, the action of previous circumstances is studied, and it is shown how the conditions of life and its reproduction, the contradictions between the productive forces and the relations of production, etc., are the very basis of History by virtue of the class struggles they engender. But the ensemble of these factors already belongs to the practical field: tools and machines undoubtedly determine phenomena as different as the *quantity* of production, the division of labour, the particular form of exploitation, etc. Doubtless, moreover, in a society that has not become aware of its contradictions and their true conditions, the conditioning of the political by the economic (for example) may more or less escape notice. Raymond Aron has spoken of societies that have an economy *in itself*, but which – because they do not *know* it (do not have the tools that would allow them to become aware of it) – will not transform it into an *economy for itself*.[89] Using this vocabulary, we could equally well speak of events *in themselves* (i.e. events whose meaning, and whose importance or efficacy, remained unnoticed at the actual moment when they were occurring) and events *for themselves* (wherein action produces its own knowledge not just in order to cast light outside, but in order to control itself). In a word, the theory of deviation that we have advanced (and, in a general way, our whole attempt to show History inasmuch as it overflows itself) could be expressed in terms of in-itself and for-itself. I have further described the practico-inert, and the drift that it continuously engenders in praxis itself, as 'exteriority'.

The Being-in-itself of Praxis-Process: an Exterior Limit of Interiority and an Interior Limit of Exteriority

However, this exteriority and this in-itself have only a relative meaning here. For let us remember that praxis-process resumes everything in

---

89. See editor's note on p.125 above.

interiority. Not only can the *in-itself* (in this sense close to Hegelianism) sometimes be dissolved – at least partly – into the *for-itself*, but even *in itself* it acts through its inert relations of exteriority only because it has been produced at the heart of a synthetic immanence that closes over it and serves it as a conducting medium. It is more or less *unified*, precisely in so far as it unifies (i.e. determines) – among the synthetically united terms of a multiplicity – the omnipresent unity of a reification. Thus, in *worked matter*, inert exteriority (under the pressure of the passive syntheses that give it form) acts upon man and the human via human mediation, inasmuch as needs – as historically conditioned – and praxis itself give it its efficacy. The error of naive materialism, as we have seen, is to believe that physico-chemical processes *as such* condition action and techniques, whereas – right from the univocal relation of the practical organism to its field of activity – inert materiality is already imbued with human significations: i.e. *already worked*. However, we should risk avoiding the pitfall of such an idealist materialism only to fall into that of an instrumentalist humanism if – because we never encounter material inertia except through the significations that unify it (which holds good, of course, through hodological[90] determinations of extension, for the environment whatever it may be: i.e. for any reality grasped in terms of the being-in-the-world of men of a given epoch) – we were to reduce that inertia to the pure and simple being of those significations, inasmuch as they posit themselves for themselves in the world of men.

For such is indeed the contradiction that pits historical realism – radically distinguishing being-in-itself from being-known or being-acted (or knowing and acting) – against the *situated* method, which brings to light significations, laws and objects in so far as it reveals them by modifying them and being modified by them. Each of the two positions is truth in itself, but each without the other slips into error and turns into one of the familiar forms of idealism. Our abstract investigation of *Being-in-itself* serves precisely to show the synthesis of the two truths in a totalizing ontological truth.

For the real mistake would be to believe that the being-in-itself of praxis-process, inasmuch as it arises within the exteriority of Nature, must be considered only as the absolute exteriority of the materiality of the practical field; or, if you prefer, considered only as if it were reduced to the ensemble of physico-chemical determinations, or – in a more exact

---

90. Kurt Lewin (1890–1947), founder of topological psychology, influenced by the Gestalt movement, distinguished a threefold series of concepts: topological (representing the structures of activity), vectorial (its causal determination) and hodological (representing the paths whereby tensions are resolved). [*Trans.*]

way – irreversible transformations of energy, which constitute history-as-a-process, through the labours and struggles of men and through the catastrophes (floods, fires, etc.) which destroy all or part of those labours (and whose negative efficacy in the practical field can be limited by human activity). In reality, in order to suppress the significations and practical orientations of such transformations, it is necessary to have chosen a perspective – a selective viewpoint. And this perspective is that of knowledge, for it is knowledge alone that can systematically set aside an ensemble of structures in the name of its right to select. In other words, it involves taking an overview of the whole universe *from the viewpoint* of a positive Reason that makes itself blind to signs, that takes – with respect to life and the human – the viewpoint of minerals or atoms, and that (as knowledge of the human by the physico-chemical) finds in man only that same physico-chemical. This attitude – entirely despite itself – has the result of treating the products of handicrafts and industry as the physiocrats once used to do. For, if the *being* of significations is negated – or at least reduced to what appears of them within the interiority of the field – then the specificity of the worked object *as such* (i.e. the gathering together of its dispersion through a passive synthesis, and the relative isolation that allows its elements to condition one another in a pre-established order) must be dissolved radically under the action of mineral Reason. For the ensemble of these modifications is reintegrated into the immense dispersion of exteriority, and its conditionings in exteriority are enough to explain the succession of these movements. To be sure, specific changes were necessary to produce this particular local vortex which exteriority will soon dissolve into its elements. But those very changes (which define themselves, within the interiority of the field, as action or labour) in the Daltonism of mineral Reason are reduced simply to their non-signifying exteriority: i.e. to transmutations that find their source in other, earlier transmutations. From this standpoint, History is only a local dream of matter: there remains the physical universe, *the sole reality*.

Precisely, however, the being-in-itself of the historical totalization cannot signify its non-being or its *being-known* through the anti-historical Reason of pure exteriority. The being-in-itself of praxis-process is precisely independent of *any* knowledge. It is the limitation of the interior by the exterior, to be sure, but it is also that of the exterior by interiority. This means that the conditioning of the totalization-of-envelopment in its being is produced in exteriority, as a determination by physical forces of a sector of the Universe on the basis of which it is necessary and possible; and that this totalization – engendered from top to bottom through the concatenation of these factors – will arise as the necessary mediation between themselves and their passive unity as a system. From the viewpoint of exteriority, the moment of signification is required as a necessary condition for the transformation of ore into an iron bar or, through alloys, into steel; for the liquefaction of air; or for the path of certain waves. If you like, physico-chemical conditions (for example) account for everything *except* for what – within the physico-chemical – is the negation of *natural* universality: for example, of the *unique* fact that, in a certain sector of the material dispersion, the ensemble of combined factors have produced the liquefaction of air, in conformity with the great laws of physics and chemistry – but *against all probability*. So being-in-itself itself produces the significations that engender its interiority – only it engenders them on the basis of the Universe. On the basis of the Universe, a certain sector is singularized by the apparition of life; and this life produces in this sector (on Earth, for example) – through a first interiorization – natural but improbable modifications of the milieu (e.g. of atmospheric pressure or the oxygen content of air), which condition *an* evolution in interiority whose profile is itself unique and, in its interior limit, *improbable*. It is on the basis of universal exteriority – in an ensemble of worlds in which all living kingdoms and histories are distributed in such and such a way, and which determines each of these adventures in relation to all the others (in its rhythm, its acceleration and its chances of succeeding) as a *production error*, or as the result of *exceptional chances*, at the same time as it realizes itself wholly as the destiny that can engulf them and against which they wage an uncertain battle – in short, it is on the basis of all these beings and of Being as a whole that human history produces itself, at the furthest point of the local movement of exteriority, as *determined in exteriority – to the very heart of its interiority – by the exterior* (from this standpoint, for example, it is the ensemble of the cosmic processes that is to be found in the very distribution of mineral resources, inasmuch as these govern History) *and in interiority – through infinite exteriority – by all the adventures of life on other planets* (if there is life *elsewhere*: but if, against all probability, the only place where the Universe has produced life as its own local interiority were to be the terrestrial Globe, even that would be a qualification interior to History by virtue of the absence of exterior interiority). At this level, interiority remains *a limit upon the exterior*, in the sense that goals are produced in the interior of History and without being able to transform the Universe into a practical field, or – at least for the time being – to have themselves acknowledged, shared or combated by other groups pursuing other histories elsewhere. So exteriority produces in exteriority a certain interiority that escapes it, and whose uniqueness is signalled in exteriority by the improbability of the concatenations that it in turn produces. On the basis of the finite and limitless dispersion of the cosmos, a being-in-itself is engendered whose relation-to-its-goals is *real but in itself* (inasmuch as its total being is not – as an interior limit to exteriority – a *being-comprehended*); whose *meanings*, as real mediations between exterior conditionings and their systematic reconditioning (*in its very improbability*), receive their ontological status – as a limit in interiority separating two processes of exteriority – from the cosmos; and whose *ensemble of immanent relations* is determined on the basis of the original sector as indissolubly linked to meanings and goals (as the generatrix of those transcendences of Being by itself, through the new structures determined by interiority: e.g. lack, all the categories of negation, and risk – as a calling into question of the unity of interiority by the universal bond of exteriority between all natural processes inside and outside it). The being-in-itself of praxis-process is the strict equivalence between the totalization-of-envelopment in the Universe and the Universe in the totalization-of-envelopment.

As deeply and traditionally idealist habits of thought risk obscuring this ontological investigation in the reader's eyes, I think it will be made clearer if it is transcribed for a moment – and in the guise rather of an image or metaphor – in terms of *transcendent* knowledge. Most readers of science fiction are, in fact, seeking to recover an awareness of the being-in-itself of our history. But their idealist habits oblige them to conceive this being-in-itself merely in so far as it appears to some Martian (a 1958 Micromegas) generally endowed with an intelligence and a scientific and technical level superior to our own, who thus reduces human history to its cosmic provincialism.*

---

* In reality, the idealist character of works of science fiction does not originate solely in bourgeois idealism – i.e. the ideology of the Western world. It springs directly from a relation between East and West. For, in a certain way, Westerners feel uneasily that the socialist world – even if it has so far used them very badly, and even if it does not have at its disposal the empirical knowledge Western researchers have accumulated over the past half-century – possesses cognitive tools that allow it to comprehend and situate both the ensemble and the details of capitalist evolution between 1917 and 1950. On the other hand, the empiricism of anti-Marxist intellectuals was originally a refusal to use the enemy's principles, which after a certain time became an incapacity to think the evolution of the world synthetically (that of the West and that of the East simultaneously: i.e. in the latter case an inability to *comprehend* – and consequently transcend – those who comprehended *that empiricism*, i.e. knew its origin and its role in the conflict rending the world and every Western society). That incapacity is felt as a malaise. One of the reasons for the American Great Fear was the confused feeling in everyone of being an *object* of History, of which the Soviets were the *subject*. For some months now, people have been discovering in the East too that History has been made in the darkness and that socialist man does not know himself: but this anxiety is of a very different order. For if he does not yet know himself, at least the man of the people's democracies has not lost the intellectual tool: he needs only to relearn how to use it. And so long as he has not done so, he will be able to say – and it will be true – that no human group *today* is any longer conscious of itself or other groups: in short, that History remains the same battle between black men in a pitch-dark tunnel that it has been for fifty years (it is *also* a vast progress in the

For this Martian, therefore, or this Venusian, who has long known the technique of inter-planetary navigation, we are – for example – an animal species whose scientific and intellectual development have been retarded by certain circumstances. He knows these circumstances, he has discovered our slow-wittedness and the factors conditioning it: factors, of course, that he sees as connected with the structure of our planet, and that he knows do not exist elsewhere – or at any rate not on the planet he inhabits. So he sees man, in the very comparison he immediately establishes between him and the inhabitants of other heavenly bodies, as a *cosmic product* retaining within him the particularities of his province – and, for example, the absence of certain substances highly necessary for cerebral and nervous activity. The differences in our respective physiological constitutions, histories, levels of development, etc., assuredly do not prevent him from comprehending us in our practical reality as individuals who are making a history in common. But the particular goals we pursue will, in a whole number of cases, remain alien to him: our aesthetic pleasures, for example, if he has different senses from ours. So he will define our goals in exteriority, without stripping them of their character as goals, but without being able to share them. He will merely note that the inhabitants of this underdeveloped planet have certain behavioural patterns orientated towards certain objectives; and that certain systems of social options or values condition the hierarchy of our preferences. Being unable to share some particular goal, he will grasp our *praxis* in a given case as *hexis*. He may say: 'men like alcoholic drinks'. The *characteristic* so etched no longer has anything to do with the evidence accompanying a man's comprehension of another man's goals; it refers to our *cosmic* facticity, i.e. to the fact that a certain cosmic scarcity (absence of certain substances, or presence of negative elements) has produced this half-failure: man.* In the same way, moreover, for this product of a high industrial civilization, our inter-minable history – endlessly dragging itself towards a level that Mars

---

achievement of consciousness: but this contradiction in any case operates to the advantage of the socialist forces). In a word, he will be able to recognize that present-day History is made *in non-knowledge*; but this observation – whatever disquiet and whatever rebellion it may entail – has nothing in common with the feeling that is so common in bourgeois societies: '*they can theorize us, for they have the tool and we do not*'. To a great extent, it is gloomy dreams about this strange situation (of groups whose objectivity is in the hands of their enemies) which have inflected novels of scientific prediction (whose origin has many other sources, though these are of no interest here) towards the idealism that characterizes most of them, and shows men seen by *anti-men* (i.e. by men constructed differently: more powerful, more lucid, but generally nasty).

* It goes without saying that I leave to the Martian the responsibility for this definition of man in interiority of exteriority.

surpassed three centuries ago – has the twin determination of a practice (it *is made*) and *a factual given* (his knowledge of historical conditionings allows him to grasp the fetters that prevent men from advancing more swiftly). In this way, our backward, provincial history seems to him also – in its cosmic conditioning of exteriority – to contain within it a *negative force* (that he discovers in interiority and through comparison, but that is only the pure *absence* of what, on Mars, is a favourable presence). In the same way, that which in the interiority of human history can in no case be taken as a *real* determination – for example, ignorance of exteriority – for him becomes a substantial qualification of praxis-process. By 'ignorance of exteriority' (which I mentioned earlier[91]) I mean, for example, the fact that in such and such a specific period – as a function of the positive development of technology and culture – such and such a society finds itself at one particular scientific level *and not at another*. As I have said, the italicized phrase '*and not at another*' can on no account be considered (in interiority) as relating to a real condition of backwardness: a negative and active impeding factor (it is not *for want of aeroplanes* that Napoleon lost the Battle of Waterloo). But this same ignorance, when it reveals itself to an exterior agent who *knows* what we do not know, becomes a deep opacity, shadows in our understanding, a negation of interiority in our hearts. The transformation is *real*. For if – as in the colonial wars of the nineteenth century – the natives *do not know* how to handle firearms and *are incapable* of manufacturing them, this ignorance is constituted by the colonial troops – in the relation of antagonistic reciprocity – as a *practical inferiority of the other*. For the Martian of science fiction (whether he wishes to conquer or to pacify Earth), our ignorance – whether it helps him to enslave men or prevents them from understanding him – will become *a determination of every one of us by the culture of Mars*: hence, a negative particularization. At the same time, this inter-planetary traveller (as numerous authors have described him to us), having made inter-stellar space into his practical field – with Earth inside it – is not unaware that we are threatened by a cosmic cataclysm (which the Martians have long been able to avoid). Precisely in so far as he sees our history emerging from the terrestrial silt and drawing its cosmic particularities and its negations from that mud, he grasps it as *anachronistic* in view of the danger that threatens it: the collision that may destroy it, and that it has not yet given itself the means to avoid. If the catastrophe is a long-term one, he sees us as involved in a race against the clock. Shall we win? Here prediction stops, even for a

---

91. In *Critique*, vol. 1, p.103. See also *Being and Nothingness*, pp.521 ff., and *Cahiers pour une morale*, pp.306 ff., 347 ff.

BOOK III

Martian, since the question is settled *also* in interiority. History is, in itself, its own acceleration. The fact remains that the witness can *particularize* the essential fragility that is proper to all histories. In *our* case, it is constituted as a still uncertain relationship with a risk of which we are unaware. It individualizes our adventure on the basis of the cosmos, and we shall for ever be those who will perish to the last man in that inter-planetary collision – or those who will manage to survive it. So through the myth of the Martian, a whole history in exteriority – made up of traps, ambushes, and possible or certain relations with other practical organisms inhabiting other planets, and revealing this character of *man* (which we are prone to take in interiority as the mark of the universal) to be an idiosyncrasy produced by the cosmos itself – a whole *exterior* history, unified by the reassumed consequences that it produces *in its interior*, is constituted and constitutes *us* as *cosmic individuals*.

If we leave the Martian for now in the property-room, this myth – for all its childishness – will at least have rendered us one service: we shall have understood that the being-in-itself of praxis-process is the foundation of any possible objectivity of our history for a witness external to the human species. It remains the case that man *cannot*, under any circumstances, make himself into that witness.[92] If he increases his technical and scientific knowledge, it is the scientific and technical knowledge of all that he will be developing – and we shall not leave the circle of interiority. The sputnik enlarges the practical field, but it does not leave it. And then, of course, the Martian's viewpoint – whatever his knowledge of the Universe – is a particularization and putting into perspective of certain relations. The disclosure effected is a *situation*: i.e. it reveals the Martian through men as much as the latter through the former. Being-in-itself overflows the knowledge he acquires of it, by virtue of his fundamental nature: he is the particular centre of infinitely infinite relations with the whole Universe. Thus, to take just one example, certain human goals are defined by the inhabitant of Mars as objective but alien goals: he does not share them. But the goals of the praxis-process, as considered in their being-in-itself, are neither *interior* nor *alien*; they do not take part only in *hexis*, or – in the guise of immanent objectives – in praxis alone. Or rather, precisely because our investigation bears on the conditions of Being and not on those of Knowing, they are at the same time immanent and transcendent, in the very indistinctness

92. On the impossibility for man to make himself into his own witness, it is interesting to read Frantz's dialogues with the Thirtieth Century in *The Condemned of Altona* (New York 1964), which Sartre was writing at the same time.

of their ontological status. Transcendent in their immanence, since the character of non-shared goals necessarily refers to the agent who *does not share*, so their being-in-itself – as grounding the permanent possibility of not being shared – is the mere ontological affirmation of themselves, inasmuch as (by virtue of the very fact of arising in the Universe) they overflow any immanent relation with the group or social ensemble that has posited them. Immanent in their transcendence, since – whether or not they are *known* by a witness, and whatever may be the reservation or rejection expressed by that witness if he exists – their inner relation to the agent remains etched in the ontological affirmation of tran-scendence, as the mediation required between a given series of physico-chemical transformations and a given system of energy transmutations flowing from it: this relation represents the irreducible structure of the act, the objective moment of praxis *as necessity of freedom*. We mean by this that the systematized – and temporarily isolated – results of mere *natural* transmutations could neither realize themselves (improb-ability) nor maintain themselves (pressure of universal forces) if praxis-*hexis* did not exist, at once as a being constituted on the basis of the Universe – qualified and limited by other histories – and as a creative and regulatory transcendence of exterior being towards itself.

Hence, our investigation of limits – through its failure to hit the mark – reveals the presence within being-in-itself of the infinite cosmic dispersion, as an absolute conditioning of human history by the universal forces of non-history (and the presence of the multiplicity of non-human histories as a limit in exteriority and as an external–internal relation: the possibility of one day being in the field of another species a priori modifying *the human object*). Conversely, however, it at the same time discloses the transcendent (and no longer for-itself, for-man) reality of the energy transmutation orientated by a future objective: i.e. the teleological structure of certain cosmic sectors. This means *neither* that these teleological sectors have themselves been prepared and defined a priori by agents (which would be absurd and return us to theology) *nor* that there is in 'Nature' – in the sense in which Engels understands it – a teleological principle, albeit embryonic (which – as I have already mentioned – as an inner, material content of our vain investigation of limits in exteriority can be neither asserted nor rejected). It simply means that – if we consider a sector whose main features allow life, and in which life through an embryonic circularity continually modifies these features (albeit in its most elementary forms, and by the sole action of choices of foodstuff, combustion, production of wastes, etc.) – it is necessary to view as an absolute reality the apparition of practical, tool-making organisms with their own temporalization, the trans-formation of the sector by their waste-products, and above all the *improbable** physico-chemical systems that these organisms engender and imbue more or less with their own circularity. The teleological structure (*hence, History*, at least in a field of scarcity) is not just an interior relation of the organism to its goals: in certain sectors, it is the inner limit of interiority of exterior being. Within the indistinctness of Being, the exteriority of dispersion produces this interiority (or at any rate makes it possible); plunges into it and transforms it into a world marketplace battered by every cosmic wind; constitutes its destiny by its permanently revocable *tolerance*; and makes itself into the universal factor of the historical idiosyncrasy's *outside*. Reciprocally, it is entirely *marked in interiority* by these circumstances of control, orientated conditioning, passive synthesis and 'feedback', as it is by interior limits of the exterior. It is untrue that the human adventure is, from this viewpoint, an adventure of Nature (or the Universe), as people too often tend to repeat. For that is to confuse the sector of our action and its interiorization (practical field) with the infinite dispersion in exteriority that we wrongly unify (in signification) by the word Universe.** We should limit ourselves to saying – as any realism requires – that the being-in-itself of human activity, even if replaced in the myriad of worlds, is an absolute *within its own sector and in its own place*. Whether or not there are other practical multiplicities, the history of man resists its determination in exteriority – and remains as the absolute centre of an infinity of new relations between things.

We can now understand that the movement of our investigation, although it has yielded us formal significations, contrasts with that of Hegelian idealism. The transcendent being of History is being-in-itself assimilating the being-for-itself of interiority without modifying its teleological structure, and becoming the being-in-itself of that being-for-itself precisely in so far as all human action (whether individual or common; whoever the participants may be, and whatever awareness they may have of their act and its signification within the interiority of the practical field: in short, whatever – within interiority – its structure of reflection upon itself may be) must eventually either be engulfed in ideality, dream and epiphenomenalism, or else produce itself in exteriority

---

* Improbable with respect to purely physico-chemical transformations. More or less probable – or absolutely certain – with respect to the ensemble of cosmic multiplicities of the galaxies, if such exist: a science that could extend to them might be able to determine what chance there is for practical ensembles to pass through the different moments of our history. And it might thereby increase the integration of the limits of interiority into exteriority, and vice versa.

** Not that there is a *pluralism* either, which would presuppose a plurality of incommunicable *unities*.

(and as a product of exteriority) in the absolute solitude of being-without-a-witness, *together with* its immanent and reflexive structures. For the in-itself here comes to the for-itself from its absolute reality. The reflection of praxis upon itself is human, practical and situated *in interiority*. Produced as it is, however, within the decompressed temporality of universal dispersion – and in relation to cosmic transformations that, through it, become transcendent factors of history – its reality eludes it, inasmuch as its knowledge comes from within and the limits that determine it come on principle from the *unknown and in practice unattainable* zone of exteriority; inasmuch too as its temporalization of interiority, by realizing itself in a sector of exteriority, constitutes from afar (and without even suspecting it) certain external circumstances as its destiny, and constitutes *itself* with its qualities and its destiny on the basis of these circumstances. This *freezing* of the living structures of interiority on the basis of external being, and as an affirmation of that external being, can be grasped from within – in relation to the experiences I have mentioned – as *our abandonment*. In exteriority, however, it presents itself only as being at once *the affirmation of these structures* and their limitation, on the basis of an external-being that supports them and reduces them to *being* what they are for themselves only through *what they do not know about themselves*. In other words, praxis-process has the ontological status of *absolute-being*, under its determinations in exteriority, in so far as its being fundamentally eludes man's practice and knowledge: i.e. in so far as it is fundamentally the outside of the inside. Of course, it will be clear that this elusive grasping of oneself has nothing mysterious or irrational about it. Practical knowledge can develop and extend to everything. But if it is to *be realized*, it must involve a fundamental ignorance: it cannot know the exteriority of its interiority.*

However, as long as it is not *objectified*, this ontological transcendence is not even an issue for agents, except as an abstract limit upon their possibility of action grasped in terms of death or circumstances linked to this. For *objectification* would be the practical localization of the human species, at such and such a level of development, in the practical field of Martians (or others) discovering our limits and conditionings as *a means to be set in operation* in order to enslave or destroy us. On this basis, man's praxis would involve – in the guise of a vital urgency and as his prime objective – the discovery of our cosmic conditionings in order to act upon these and shield them from hostile action. We encounter science

---

* Except, to a certain extent and in circumstances that we shall see, retrospectively: this is one of the abstract structures of what we have called *meaning*.[93]

93. See 'The Historical Event', in the Appendix, pp.397 ff. below.

fiction again here, but we encounter too a feature described in connection with antagonistic actions. As such objectivity – always partial, anyway – is not given, any more than the real or possible threats emanating from cosmic forces, the transcendence of being-in-itself reduces praxis-process to interiority as its *practical reality*. The absolute of exteriority refers back – as a necessary limit and a lack of knowledge – to the absolute of interiority: it is what a priori we cannot take into account. If we knew about some disaster that – in one thousand or one hundred years – was going to exterminate our species, the properly human and historical priorities of our present situation would not change in any way. For the men of today, it would be necessary to live, eat, work, and struggle against exploitation, oppression and colonialism. For the source of our present struggles lies not in *theoretical principles or values* (principles and values that the imminent death of humanity might call into question), but – directly or by way of mediations – in the absolute urgency of needs. This, moreover, is what makes the absurdity of the hypothesis all the more blatant. For the future catastrophe could be a *practical knowledge* (i.e. act upon men and transform their action) only if the ensemble of scientific and technical advances already made it possible to acquire this. But such advances would not take place without an enlargement of the practical field (inter-planetary journeys, etc.), and the new priorities could manifest themselves only within a totalization-of-envelopment modified by the development of our power, and by the consequent alteration of our objectives and the internal structures of our social ensembles. In reality, the present relation to our history of an unknown threat is exterior and univocal. It qualifies the totalization in progress *from outside*, it perhaps assigns it a destiny *from outside*, but the practical reality of our action cannot be determined as a function of that threat. Not just because we are ignorant of it (which would be a negative factor of exteriority), but above all because the positive fabric of our praxis-process has been woven in such a way that it leaves no place for it, as a condition of praxis in the interiority of the practical field.

These remarks, far from constituting praxis in interiority as an epipheno-menon, restore to it its absolute reality. And this reality is inscribed both in the immanence of the field and in being-in-itself. For in immanence – whatever its profile in exteriority – this action taken as a whole cannot be other than it is (which does not prejudge the question of interior possibles). The ensemble of previous circumstances – i.e. at once the original sector and the ensemble of deviated actions springing from it – in fact conditions the course of History, its speed, its rhythms, its orientation, and the regulated succession of its objectives. And it is praxis itself which, through the transcendence of these conditions, causes there to be *a* history in this sector. Without the reality of praxis-process, it would be impossible even to conceive the internal and external reality of inert and improbable material combinations (machines, etc.). Conversely, interiority is itself a limiting structure of being-in-itself, as we have seen. This means that finality – as an absolute structure of being-in-itself, and as a *reason* for the passive unity of improbable combinations – involves interiority as its immanent medium. For finality, even envisaged in its transcendent being, constitutes itself as revealing-transcendence of an ensemble of material circumstances on the basis of a need; and as the illumination of this ensemble and itself, on the basis of determination of a future objective. Thus, even in the in-itself, immanence is a mediation between two transcendent states. But just as the being-in-itself of praxis-process is an exterior limitation of the latter, it is produced as an interior limitation of exteriority. From the standpoint of knowledge this means that a Micromegas can grasp the interiority of the exterior as the meaning – and as a limit – of the process he is considering, but he can comprehend the movement of this history in interiority only by making himself (if he has the means) *interior to it.*

This observation can serve as an approach for grasping and fixing the *ontological* signification of the *interior* limit as a frontier of exteriority. In other words, this interiority is produced in the in-itself as a limit of dispersion, a passive synthesis, a unity produced and maintained by systems, and the relative isolation of a material ensemble. And these features of the in-itself are realized in it as alien, and as the results of a reflecting, conservative transcendence that – within the very fragility of its temporalization – affirms itself in its independence as *the indispensable autonomy of mediation.* In other words, interiority – as a mediation-cum-rupture between states and transmutations – is, in itself, the limit of its being-in-itself in so far as, within the framework of that being, it *is not* but *interiorizes itself.* Totalization is one moment of the process, but a heterogeneous moment in so far as – far from being (even a totality) – it *totalizes itself.* Being-in-itself is everywhere, transfixes everything, and in a certain way congeals everything; but it is its own limit, precisely in so far as – at the moment of mediation – the law of this being is to *make itself.* This distinction can be comprehended through an image: if, as I walk along the street, I see a certain employee sweeping the entrance of the same shop with the same gestures as she performs every morning at the same hour, her act becomes *hexis* and, through this *hexis,* I glimpse her class-being. Yet this *hexis* (however real it is) and this class-being can be realized in her, and for her, only through the reflecting transcendence of praxis. What holds good for these still human features of Being (praxis as interiority and meaning of *hexis*) we encounter again at the level of absolute Being: it is quite simply the in-itself closing again upon the for-itself and keeping it within itself as its inner limit, which can be lived only in the movement of a practical temporalization.

These comments are enough to show that being-in-exteriority, far from transforming interiority into a dream, guarantees it its absolute reality. For it produces – within the universal dispersion – the practical totalization as imposing the unity of its ends upon things (upon certain elements of the sector); as *an imparter of meaning*, by virtue of its very function; and as *having a meaning* (and signification) *only* in its interiority – for agents – although its structure of mediation, through a reflecting transcendence, is inscribed in being-in-itself as an abstract determination. As soon as there is a history, the practical multiplicity through which (and for which) this history exists finds itself defined and situated by the field that it determines. Each of the objectives it pursues finds itself, to be sure, defined in exteriority by the entire Universe. But for this transcendent definition to be able to occur, this same objective has to be produced in a relationship of absolute immanence, as the future determination of the need – its satisfaction – by the means at hand, via the *de facto* givens characterizing the situation. Similarly, from the ontological standpoint it is doubtless necessary to consider that every agent is the product, in his needs as in his practical structures, of an infinity of material circumstances which – overflowing History, pre-history, natural history and even geology – have produced him (in the real comparison that can always be instituted with other forms of life on other planets) as *being that* and *being only that*; and which, as a given material ensemble (on the basis of which it is possible to go back *ad infinitum* in physical time), have already constituted its organic features, means of action, etc., as a fundamental deviation of every possible praxis. But when you have gone back as far as possible – then when, through 'the history of Earth' and the history of all species, you have re-engendered the human species with its distinguishing marks (in relation not just to the lower animals but to other possible practical organisms) and with its practical lags and its drifts – nothing will prevent these features from being produced as *practical features*, through the action which instrumentalizes them by transcending them towards its objective and – in and through the use it makes of them – itself determines (on the basis of its goal, and in relation to this) the drift that they will cause it to undergo. The being of worked matter requires this leap outside Being, towards the Being that is praxis itself as interiority. And this praxis finds its limits (and the determined-being these confer upon it, on the basis of everything) from outside, only in so far as it is – in itself – its own internal limits, on the basis of the transcendence of former circumstances.

Such, therefore, is the being-in-itself of the totalization-of-envelopment, inasmuch as it is aimed at from within by the agents of History. It is everywhere. It is the infinitely infinite depth of this totalization, inasmuch as its depth is the Universe that conditions it from outside through an infinity of relations and – in this very way – pushes its idiosyncrasy to the utmost. It produces itself as the outer limit of the spiral, the deviation and the future illuminating it; and at the same time as the radical specification of this drift and its meaning, by virtue of its emergence in a definite sector of the world and – thereby – in the world as a whole, as being-in-the-midst-of-the-world. So it is at once deviation (in its relation to the History that produces it and that it produces) and abandonment (as the other-being of this absolute finality in a universe indifferent to its ends). All this, of course, refers the absolute of human history (or *any* history) back to interiority. In other words, abandonment creates the absolute of interiority: i.e. grounds the immanent-being of all historical ends. At the same time, it transfixes all interiority, it is everywhere: being-in-exteriority is the very being that makes the strength of our arms, our exhaustion, the continued inertia of passive syntheses, our multiplicity and, lastly, our waste-products and our drift. But we do not have any real experience of it, as an exterior limit of interiority any more than as an omnipresent inertia transfixing immanence. We disclose inanimate materiality by working it – in our practical field – as a mediation between man and the objects of his desire; and as a mediation between men, *already acted* by men whose inert materiality is already integrated by the organic synthesis, and transcended by the act or engendered by serial (but still human) impotence in the practico-inert.

Thus the reality of totalization stems from the presence of these two absolutes and their reciprocity of envelopment. If you now ask what is the being of a historical event like the insurrection of 19 August 1792, for example, we can answer that it is in fact reducible neither to the actions of the participants; nor to such awareness of it as the latter, or witnesses, acquired; nor, again, to the consequences it provoked (and which, ontologically, were homogeneous with it), i.e. its inner efficacy; nor to the energy transmutations that *produced* it, and that it produced on the terrain of pure exteriority. Rather, it was all at once a moment of the Revolution – as a totalization-of-envelopment grasped in interiority – and, in its absolute solitude as in its irreducible unity, the infinite determination by an infinity of exterior relations of that idiosyncrasy, inasmuch as its ends arise in the Universe as ends not shared and it constitutes itself as a unitary structure in the midst of a dispersed universe: i.e. as that line without thickness which is the interior limit of all exteriority. The totalization grasped in interiority is *praxis-process*; but when it is envisaged as a being-in-itself containing within it its being-for-itself, it becomes – as a vain object of our aim – what we shall call *process-praxis*. From the formal viewpoint which concerns us, at any rate – which is that of the dialectic – it goes without saying that the critical investigation has circumscribed the field of the constituted dialectic. For we do not know the true links between the cosmos and being-in-itself, except in their formal reality. The only domain in which the dialectic reveals itself as an absolute movement of temporalization is the field of practical interiority, so our investigation limits and establishes its scope.

We renounce the right to say anything about the type of relations uniting being-in-itself with cosmic forces and other practical multiplicities, if there are any. We know that some of these relations have to be grasped in pure exteriority, and this knowledge is founded on experience, since certain dangers which manifest themselves in the practical field (and consequently are already interiorized) present themselves to us immediately as *coming from pure exteriority*. Storms and hail may appear like this to farmers, so long as their society does not have the means to control climates and atmospheric precipitations. This particular storm formed *elsewhere*, outside History. If it never *really* belonged to the pure exteriority of the in-itself, this was because its *possibility* (as a common limit to our knowledge and our ignorance) was already given, in the society where it made its appearance. Similarly, as we have seen, defeat and death (and also, through the different structures of the event, all that directly or indirectly relates to these) make us realize the absolute but vain experience of transcendent-being as a limit of exteriority and a nullification of all comprehension. Whether there are – or can be – other relations of another kind, is something we can neither affirm nor deny a priori.*
What we can say at any rate – negatively and formally – is that these

---

* To give a purely imaginary example of these possible relations, it is what happens in science-fiction novels when men discover that they (they and Earth) are in the practical field of an organic multiplicity which is manoeuvring them by unknown means, and without their being able to discern it except through certain improbable events realized by it in the interiority of the human field. From the viewpoint of interiority, this exterior and exteriorizing interiority (its being-an-object for the alien multiplicity) presents itself as a reversed dialectic. In other words, it is necessary to grasp the interiorization of the exterior (integration of the human field into the 'Martian' field, or any other of the same dimensions) as a production of exteriority in the interior (an apparition of synthetic and dialectical events whose temporalization, inasmuch as it expresses that of the aliens penetrating our own, is a source *for us* – by virtue, indeed, of its very unity – of massification and reification of human relationships, to the point of complete atomization of individuals and disintegration of the practical field, or to the point of their total submission to the constituted practico-inert *of the exterior*: i.e. of the interior of the field enveloping our own). As can be seen, this reversed dialectic *can have its own intelligibility* (moreover, it merely radicalizes certain experiences of the struggle men wage among themselves – e.g. those of defeat). Whatever its *possible* intelligibility, however, we must recognize that it has nothing to do with the dialectic as an internal logic of action; and at the same time, that it has never (except in science-fiction novels) been the object of a *real* investigation that would make it possible to leave human interiority.

conditionings in exteriority (or even, as explained in the footnote, through interiorization of the exterior, a synthetic presence of total exteriority at the heart of the human field) have at all events no feature in common with the dialectic of practical interiority. For as the latter is all that it can be, it can be neither modified nor completed by the absolute transcendent, so the latter remains heterogeneous to it. For an outside witness, it would be the object of another knowledge; its relations with the limit of interiority it sustains would be of another intelligibility. We shall return to this problem, of fundamental importance for posing correctly the question of the diachronic meaning of History.[94] For the moment, it is enough to note that if temporalization involves deviations and instances of backwardness and ignorance, these are its own deviations and its own instances of ignorance and backwardness. It engenders them as a dialectical total-ization, and through the circularity which produces the interior unity of exteriority as a deviation of interiority. Of course, the exteriority present in the interior is the very in-itself and dispersive structure of the Universe. But, *precisely*, this in-itself appears only as a limit of exteriority vainly aimed at; and the exteriority of the interior appears and develops its efficacy within the framework of immanence. What we call process-praxis is the hidden card – the reverse side – of praxis-process. But despite everything, praxis-process – threatened, conditioned, determined from the exterior and as a being-in-itself – remains the formal foundation of its being-in-the-midst-of-the-world (if not of the latter's content), because it ensures that there is something in the Universe like the reverse side of cards.* So the ontological primacy of being-in-itself is transformed into a primacy of History. And the moment of praxis-process as an indispensable mediation of action is produced – as that of which being-in-itself is the infinite reverse side – in and through the medium of interiority. For it is necessary for everything to be *human* in the total-ization of human history – even anti-human forces, even man's counter-humanity (*except death*) – for man to be able, in his being-in-itself of exteriority, to produce himself as a limit of interiority of the inhuman

---

* I have already shown how the character of 'destructive force', in the practical field, came from human praxis to the catastrophes that overturned the latter's effects.[95] In absolute exteriority, there exists an analogous relation – but congealed in the in-itself – which determines the Universe as indifference, a milieu of abandonment, etc., *on the basis of* the limit of exterior interiority. In a certain way, this unification of the dispersed as such by the absolute but congealed unity of a solitary act may appear as the inert, negative synthesis of the Universe by the History it crushes.

94. See Preface above; also 'Totalization-of-Envelopment' in the Appendix, p.447 below.

95. *Critique*, vol. 1, pp.161 ff.

forces and, consequently, as an absolute equivalence between the humanization of the inhuman and the inhumanization of the human.

But *precisely* because the inhuman is everywhere in interiority, as the
resistance of History and its foundation, but *always transcended* –
disclosed or secretly conditioning the drifts of action, and in all cases
being effective through the latter and by virtue of it – the dialectic (rule
of being-in-interiority) presents itself to investigation as the absolute of
temporalizing transcendence. The transcendence of being-in-itself towards being-in-itself through interiority, proceeding from one absolute
determination to another, can be only an absolute efficacy. One would
have to go back here to the analyses of *existence* as nihilation which I
attempted elsewhere:[96] but that would be to move beyond our present
argument. It is enough to recall here that praxis *springs* from being-in-
itself as its negation. Hence it is not *relative* to the in-itself which it
negates, but *makes itself* its negation absolutely by temporalizing itself
towards its objective (which is that same negation, but etched into the in-
itself). The negation of a dispersion can be only the unity which preserves
this dispersion within itself at the same time as unifying it (transcendence
and integration into praxis), or else the passive synthesis which imposes
its sway over that very dispersion. *Need itself*, moreover, is *already* the
unity of what is missing – or the unity of what threatens – interiorized
and re-exteriorized in the field. Consequently, being-in-itself is
everywhere visible – through the transparency of praxis – as a condition,
a threat, an instrument, or a worked product. But that astringent transparency alone is enough to transform it: it is always discovered through
its future, i.e. inasmuch as its inert metamorphoses become *its human
future* through the praxis under way.

It is from this standpoint that the ontological status of the agents – and
through them of the totalization – is the fundamental unity of a
contradiction. The first synthetic transcendence of dispersion by praxis
(based upon an organic integration of the diverse) is the real production
of multiplicity. For the multiple is realized as exteriority only upon (and
by virtue of) the foundation of interiority. Every relation of one element
of this multiple with the rest presupposes a practical and formal synthesis,
and a dispersion (non-relationship of terms) accepted as the content of
this synthesis. The re-transcendence of the pure multiple by a fresh
project of integration produces the identity of the elements as content of
the formal unity, and realizes the quantitative status of the being-in-itself
on whose basis fresh determinations (particularly the passive syntheses
of work) will be obtained. But precisely in so far as praxis *produces*

---

96. *Being and Nothingness*, pp.21 ff.

quantitative multiplicities, the worked being-in-itself *modifies the agents* and transforms them into a multiplicity (the dispersion of organisms becomes a *numerable* multiplicity within the interiority of the field). The interiority of the in-itself as a quantity has the effect of affecting every practical organism with exteriority *in relation to the others*, and of introducing quantity as an element of separation *between agents*: i.e. *between actions*. This fundamental relationship between interiority and exteriority – realized in practice as a first circularity (unification of the diverse by the multiple and by quantity; actualization of the diversity of acts by the quantification of agents in terms of inert quantities) – is the ontological and practical foundation of the dialectic, as a totalization perpetually reconditioned by the dispersion that it totalizes and ceaselessly retotalizing the multiplicities that each of its practical syntheses produces within interiority.

From this viewpoint, *life* – as a fact of fundamental integration of the dispersed; as a harmonization of *guided* energy transformations – is the unitary process grounding the dialectic (relations between multiplicities through the mediation of unity; multiplication of unity through uni-fication). The future unity of projected objectives on the basis of need derives its reality from the ontological status of the living being, and from the perpetually maintained unity constituting the being-in-itself of the agent and the transcendent framework of every temporalization (for, once there is need, the relationship with the future as medium of the act is engendered). But these remarks, far from showing a *prime dialectic* in life, instead have the effect of asserting the autonomy of the constituent dialectic. The latter, as a mere internal alteration – linked to circumstances – of the shifting relationship between the biological organism and its milieu, is produced and sustained by the organism itself. But the transcendent unity of action comes and grafts itself on to the immanent unity of life, precisely in so far as temporalization (as a wrench away from the circular time of the biological) and transcendence (as a non-integral organization of the inorganic) represent a fresh solution – not contained in the very principle of life – to fresh problems (posed by scarcity). Through cyclical repetition – biological actions of lower life-forms and an archaic cycle of social labours – the organism rein-tegrates transcendence into immanence and vectorial temporalization into circular temporality. But already, through the praxis of *this* particular organism or *that one*, etc., there are *several* organisms. The practical unity of the field produces *as a multiplicity* (hence as separation, antagonistic reciprocity, etc.) the dispersion of agents (*scarcity* becomes an inter-human – and, in each person, anti-human – force). When, breaking the circle of the societies without history, a social ensemble is really overwhelmed by its own multiplicity, inasmuch as it is conditioned

by the real labour of its organisms and the real products of this labour –
and when the agents attempt to dissolve it (they and Others) by producing
themselves as the elements of their own practical field – at that instant
the stitch slips. The organic circularity is masked and deviated by the
spirals of reconditioned conditioning. And the movement of praxis,
whatever it may be, cannot turn back into the immediate unity of the
cyclical; for that unity has shattered, and its fragments will become the
object of a fresh attempt at unification, whose agents will in this very
way be diversified and come into conflict with one another – and attempt
to take themselves as the object to be unified – while, correlatively, the
type of passive synthesis determining the practical field is modified by
praxis, and imposes deviations and divisions on praxis which oblige it to
take itself as an object. Through its re-multiplication by the inert the
practical unity is once more called into question, and its objective
becomes its retotalization through a praxis that will reorganize it as a
function of its tasks and worked matter. But the interplay of the single
and the multiple, involving the permanent deviation of the former by the
latter (the unity of the multiple is a multiplication of the single), induces
the practical movement – inasmuch as it exerts its own control over it,
and has to control this control (as a new plurality), and so on and so forth
– never to close upon itself. From this standpoint, it can be said that
History appears as a brutal rupture of cyclical repetition: i.e. as transcendence and spirality. These two features represent the inevitable
recovery by praxis of its former conditioning. They are generators of
immanence and, at the same time, of the practical field: i.e. the sector of
the dialectic and the anti-dialectic as determinations of praxis. Making
oneself and overflowing oneself; gathering oneself only to flee oneself;
having oneself determined in the present by a future determination, and
thus producing oneself as a movement towards the infinite indetermination
of the future; realizing development in a spiral, as a compromise between
the axial line running from the need to the objective and the perpetually
recommenced failure of rewinding on to oneself (i.e. unifying the multiple
by a continuous displacement of quantity and scarcity); in short, at once
turning and simultaneously fleeing like a slipping stitch, engendering
not-knowing, the *not-known* and the *uncertain* (and, as we shall see, the
possible and the probable[97]) as determinations of being-in-interiority;
producing *within immanence* a reference back to limitless temporalization

---

97. Sartre was not to return to it in the present work (see pp. 41, 85, 183, 202, 208, and
219 ff.; also *The Problem of Method*, pp.93 ff.). In the margin of his notes on the
diachronic, four major problems to be dealt with are mentioned, as a reminder: Possible,
Chance, Progress, Violence. Consult also *L'Idiot de la famille*, vol. 2, p.1815, n.2.

(even if this would receive a limit in exteriority from movements of inert matter or the projects of other practical multiplicities) – it is precisely all this that our critical investigation reveals to us as an absolute event (or the advent of History): i.e. as the transformation of the free constituent praxis into praxis-process – in other words, into a *constituted dialectic*.

It remains to be signalled, of course, that the existence of a diachronic meaning of History is not even implied by the foregoing arguments, at this stage of our investigation. And by diachronic meaning we merely mean the axial direction in relation to which one might define (and correct) any possible drift, today and in the infinite future of interiority. We shall return to this problem, which requires intellectual tools that we have not yet forged for ourselves.[98] Let us recall, furthermore, that this wholly formal characterization of the totalizing movement has been made – as a pure, empty abstraction – from a standpoint of quasi-exteriority. In the immanent practical field, the goal is *under no circumstances* – in itself and absolutely – the reduction of multiplicity. Even when, as frequently occurs, unity posits itself for itself as an objective to be attained, or as a status to be maintained at all costs, it is always on the fundamental basis of a concrete objective: as a *means* of struggling against men or against scarcity, or as a *positive organization* of the productive forces around the means of production. Genuine practical problems (how to industrialize the USSR while safeguarding – in order to safeguard – its socialist basis; how to supply a growing working-class population by a dwindling peasant population whose productivity is not increasing; and so on and so forth) become genuine historical problems: was Stalinism a deviation? ... What did the cult of personality signify? ... What is the Soviet 'bureaucracy'? ... and so on. And the schematic circularity of the single and the multiple in the immanent field of scarcity is only the skeleton of the movement of enveloping temporalization. The concrete and absolute reality of History can be only in the singularity of the practical relations uniting singular men to the singular objectives they pursue, in the singularity of the conjuncture. The term *praxis-process* has no function other than to designate the totalization-of-envelopment, inasmuch as it forges its passive syntheses and these reintroduce multiplicity (and, in a more general way, extensive and intensive quantity) into it, as an internal risk of rupture (i.e. of multiplication and atomization).

From this viewpoint, it is also necessary to signal an ontological limit to totalization, such as this presents itself today to our investigation. Organisms, as active unities of the inert multiplicity of their elements,

---

98. See notes on 'Progress' in Appendix, pp.402 ff. below.

can produce only passive syntheses of physico-chemical substances. It is impossible to say today whether a temporary or a definitive inability is involved: the current state of the biochemical sciences does not allow this to be determined. But at all events – and even if it were to be assumed that, in a relatively distant future (for we are in any case very far away from the scientific level that would at least allow us to pose the question correctly), human societies inheriting our techniques will be able to accomplish the synthesis of life – it would still remain the case that humanity has historically defined itself as arriving at the reproduction of organisms (i.e. of unity maintaining itself autonomously within the framework of the limited variations of a given milieu) through the production of tools and machines (i.e. of inert unity sustained by the inertia of temporarily assembled materials). To be sure, life reproduces itself. Species – some at any rate – perpetuate themselves. And it is also true that we are able to act upon life *either through life* (grafts, hybrids, etc.) *or through inorganic substances* (medicine, surgery, biological experiments on chromosomes and the protoplasmic 'soup') *or through a complex praxis organizing both types of conditioning in conjunction*. But it remains the case that in all these activities life is a precondition which – in one form or another – must always be given. To sow, seed is needed. To fertilize a sea-urchin with sea-water, the urchin is needed. And whatever its goal and its technique, the praxis modifying life is similar – in its first moment – to that which is exerted upon inorganic matter. In its second moment, it entrusts the organic movement of life with the task of realizing the outcome of human action – ploughing and sowing, acts that are exerted or could be exerted upon the practico-inert – in accordance with its own laws of interiority. The gesture of the sower could be repeated identically if he were throwing lead shot. In reality, its breadth and rhythm are conditioned by the specific characteristics of grain (for example, its lightness), inasmuch as these make it more or less difficult to attain the objective aimed at. But these characteristics *are of a physical nature*. Physical too are the positive and negative determinations of the practical field (for example, direction and strength of the wind) to which the peasant has to adapt his behaviour. It is the seed itself that will see to the rest.

III

SINGULARITY OF PRAXIS: DISINTEGRATION OF THE ORGANIC CYCLE AND THE ADVENT OF HISTORY

1

Autonomy and Limits of
Praxis in Relation to Life

HISTORICAL praxis is thus characterized as a relation between the organism and the inorganic, or as its relation to other organisms via the common mediation of inorganic inertia (in *the agent* as in *the acted-upon* [*les agis*]). Praxis is in itself a degradation and a decompression of organic integration. A decompression, since it unifies as a function of perpetually future unities (the ends to be achieved); a degradation, since it does not integrate inorganic substances into a biological unity (i.e. does not produce a being whose ontological status is equal to its own), but confines itself to wresting them from the world of dispersed exteriority and marking them with the seal of life, without communicating this life itself to them. These passive syntheses have the object of maintaining the practical organism in life, and – depending on circumstances – they succeed in two ways. When the organism directly needs inorganic substances (water, air, etc.), or when it protects itself against over-abrupt variations in the surrounding milieu, worked matter directly conditions life (purification of an air laden with toxins, ventilation systems in mineshafts, etc., or heating appliances, etc.). When the organism nourishes its own life with living substances (which is a feature of historical facticity in man: he is the living being who feeds off plants and animals, but cannot by himself directly realize the living synthesis of inorganic substances), passive syntheses play the role of *practico-inert mediations* between life and life. If, as a purely logical hypothesis, we envisage a living species – on some other planet – already having the practical possibility of producing life from the inert, it will be easier to grasp the specificity of our historical praxis (considered up to the present conjuncture). For the agent who produces life by the integration of non-living materials thereby defines a praxis entirely different from our own.* In the first place, his action is *integrative*: i.e. it confers its own unity upon the physico-chemical substances it assembles (even if its aim was merely to use them for food). The action of life upon inorganic matter would here have the effect and aim of transforming the latter into life. The *objectification* of praxis would take on a quite different signification, since this praxis would be recovered and reassumed as an immanent free organization by its very product. The action of the living thing would become living, as the very being of another living thing; and it would be reflected back to the agent in its singularity: i.e. in its organic autonomy. *Doing* would here be the mediation between the living being (as a producer) and the living being (as a product, escaping the producer and realizing his objectives through its own autonomy). This *praxis* would as a rule suppress neither scarcity (everything would depend on the chances of producing life) nor the dialectic of the single and the multiple. But it would reduce (and could suppress) the practico-inert, since the origin of the latter is the worked inorganic as a mediation between men; and the creative praxis would produce organisms, as a mediation between other organisms (obviously this does not necessarily imply any massive reduction of the practico-inert, since production of the organic from the inorganic may necessitate the accumulation of tools and machines). Finally, in so far as this creation was total – i.e. the practical organism could produce its counterpart – the problem of scarcity of men as a condition of History would tend to disappear. In any case, the reciprocity of the producer and his product; the reversal of being-in-exteriority (the inert becoming the matter of life in its being-in-itself); the progressive dissolution of the practico-inert; and, above all, the subordination of action as a transitory mediation to integration, and to organic syntheses as a process of immanence – in short, all these features and many others that we cannot even conceive – would have as their inevitable consequence a profound transformation of History and the constituted dialectic.

But the sole aim of this science-fiction hypothesis will be to specify the singularity of *our* dialectic and *our* human history. Different from those fictive organisms in that we do not produce life, we differ too from plants – and perhaps from unknown organisms on other planets – in that we cannot realize in ourselves, and through the inner chemistry of the organism, the living synthesis of minerals. We really act only *upon the*

---

* It is necessary to imagine, of course, that the agent does not confine himself to realizing the elementary conditions for the living synthesis, but that he possesses the necessary techniques and instruments to guide – via a succession of already living reactions – the produced organism towards an idiosyncrasy defined in advance as the terminal objective.

inorganic (or through its mediation), yet we cannot directly assimilate minerals. We live by consuming other lives, but do not have the means to produce living syntheses. Our praxis is defined by this twofold negative relationship: we fashion only the inert, we assimilate only the organic. [Were we], like plants, directly linked to mineral substances, action would disappear or be reduced to a minimum. Scarcity could give way (under certain conditions) to abundance. If we were capable of producing life, however, life would become – as directed integration – the higher form of action; or, if you like, action would thicken into the immanent-being of the integrated organism. What (for us and in our history) ensures that action – whose original *raison d'être* is to reproduce life – is like a transcendence of the organism itself, and like the most complete and autonomous form of the living temporalization, is the fact that *through it* life does not move directly towards itself but, by virtue of the facticity of our organs and our condition, *escapes* and places its seal upon the inorganic. Praxis, as an intermediary between the synthesis in immanence of the living and the passive synthesis of the inert, receives from the former the very possibility of projecting living unity as its ultimate goal, and from the latter the *rigorous permanence* and the *exteriority* that allow the disclosure of objectives and means (for ex-teriority, as a synthetic negation at the heart of unity, allows the *distance* which engenders *objectivity*).

In itself, praxis is thus a synthetic mediation between interiority and exteriority: this is its autonomy in relation to life. It is itself, in itself, the unification of the unity of immanence with exteriority. That is what characterizes it in comparison with the organic function. For the *structures* of a praxis imply a reciprocal exteriority of its parts and – *at least as a moment positing itself for itself* – a kind of temporary stability in the orientated flow. A practical framework is established, as a structure of the practical temporalization at a particular moment of its development; and, within this framework, operations are governed and realized which eventually dissolve the framework into themselves, and posit themselves as *beyond* the dissolved framework while producing a new framed moment of action. The exteriority of the parts is precisely the exterioriza-tion (of the organic immanence of functions into organized action) required by the necessity for a praxis to be everywhere outside itself, in the inorganic dispersion that holds within it the interiority of its field. For the person who constructs and uses a tool, contradictory necessities must be united within the very structure of transcendence. No detailed operation can be attempted without a fundamental risk of failure, except on the basis of unity of the field, itself realized on the basis of the objective: i.e. of the maintenance or future restitution of organic integrity, despite the surrounding variations. The result is that everything in this field is a bond of synthetic immanence – even negations. But as the unified ensemble nevertheless remains subjected to its inorganic status (i.e. the dispersion of exteriority), the partial operation relates to *an exteriorized parcel of the field*: i.e. a unified, isolated parcel, whose unified solitude is itself the product of the two antagonistic, though solidary, statuses. It *isolates itself* in the infinite dispersion because of this dispersion itself, which precisely allows *this* to be exterior to *that*. It is still necessary that there should be *thises* and *thats*. And the dispersion of exteriority is produced as an exteriority of the parts of an ensemble only if *the ensemble is unified as dispersive*, and if dispersion is lived temporally in every singular operation as the unity of a local passivity, and as the halt provisionally imposed upon infinite dispersion – as an atomization of the interior by the exterior. However, the bonds of interiority are realities. Their synthetic power to unify is real, since in a Universe that had destroyed its men, as we have seen, fragments of physico-physiological unity would subsist in their absolute reality, even in the exterior transformations that would eventually dissolve them.

Precisely, however, the status of the bond of immanence is rigorously *practical*. In the social field, if some particular local transformation has the consequence of modifying *in its interiority* a certain ensemble – *from afar*, without touching it, through the mere reorganizing effect it entails – this is *obviously* because the modification has been constituted within a field of action. In other words, the distant modification modifies from afar the present object in its interiority, *through the mediation* of an already constituent action (i.e. one already being exercised on a field). If some death of an unknown person, which has taken place very far away from me in the Midi, has an influence on my career and thereby on my very reality, it is via a system of institutions (constituting, for example, the laws of recruitment and promotion in a particular branch of the civil service; or the more – or less – immediately established, more – or less – organized, customs corresponding to the same problems in private enterprises). But the Institution – as a reversal of worked materiality – gives human praxis its inert-being, for the simple reason that it imposes its indispensable practical synthesis on the multiplicity of agents. Through the mediation of inert permanence, it is practice that modifies my life. As a function of this practice – codified or traditional – the official's death is revealed as an exigency that provision should at once be made for his replacement (*his* action left in abeyance, for example, itself designates as incomplete and demanding to be completed at once – in the movement of common temporalization – the tasks with which he had recently been entrusted). In an organized and functioning system, moreover, this exigency itself becomes the reason why selective and restorative mechanisms swing abruptly into operation (replacements will be selected, in accordance with a certain practical schema, to put the system back in working order at minimum cost). So it is the practical tension that establishes the bond of immanence. In the example quoted, of course, a praxis highly conscious of its means and its ends may be involved: if, for instance, I had long been designated – in accordance with the very rules governing promotion in that branch of the civil service – to take the dead man's place (if I were *already* his deputy, privy to all his business, etc.). On the other hand, it may be a matter of a bond which – in the very interiority of the field – escapes action itself overwhelmed by its multi-plicity (by the multiplicity of objectives, dangers, means, agents, etc.). We have given some examples of this, which could be multiplied *ad infinitum*, since this immanence of everything in everything is the law of interiority. But when the bond is established via praxis without being foreseen or projected or perhaps ever known by it, praxis nevertheless remains the conducting medium of interiority, inasmuch as it draws everything in its temporalization towards an end. Thus the bond of immanence as a producer of events and objects is itself a primary product: the dispersive multiplicity at the heart of praxis is temporalized in the practical torrent as a multiplicity (otherwise the relation of immanence would become an interpenetration) and as material in fusion of the future unity. It is *as a multiplicity* (a dispersion already reunified by the practical synthesis) that it receives and transforms unification (as a *progress towards unity*) into a kind of *wandering unity of the diverse* – every element of the field being interior to everything, precisely in so far as each remains exterior to all.

In these few observations, I have been trying to stress the singularity of human praxis. For the inner cohesion of action is ensured by bonds of immanence. Now, we observe that these can present themselves as the pre-unification in progress of dispersion; but *equally well* as the relaxation of organic unity and its transformation into a practical unification, through its relation with the dispersive and via its first synthesis of exteriority (i.e. from the moment when, *through need*, the being-interior-to-itself of the living creature becomes its being-outside-itself in the field of scarcity, and when – in a form still more organic than practical – the restored organism, as an implicit objective and as the organism's future, finds itself separated from itself and reunited, in its first temporalization, by the milieu as inertia). To explain what I mean more clearly (and returning, just as an example, to the sphere of knowledge), we may note that praxis has forged *its idea of unity by unifying*; and that this very idea – as a schema regulating all human activity – is the equivalence between disintegration of the organic by the inorganic, and integration of the latter into a form engendered by the former. Nothing shows this better than the unity of Platonic 'forms', or that which philosophers still often

attribute to geometrical entities. For Liard (albeit a positivist), a geometrical figure – as a determination of pure space – keeps its parts
enlaced by a kind of cohesive force, which is its very being. However, it
goes without saying that its spatial essence makes it susceptible to
infinite division and, what is more, that this infinite division is an eternal
and eternally present feature of its essence. We find in this description
what so many other rationalists have said or implied (Spinoza, for
instance, speaking of affirmative particular essences). There is, as it
were, an aberrant mirror-effect here, wherein the figure is endowed with
a being *in actu* (as people also put it) and this act is endowed with two
simultaneous ontological statuses, whose incompatibility is concealed
from us by leaving them in shadow. The first is precisely the being of the
practical field during the action: in this case, however, the act emanates
not from the object itself but from the synthetic (and human) movement
that engenders it; it makes the geometrical object into a symbol of
worked matter; the human act here assembles and contains, in the unity
of a gesture, the dispersion of exteriority represented here by infinitely
divisible space. In this form, the conception is admissible. But the
rationalism of essences requires the act to be the unity that the object
imposes on itself of its own accord: the synthesis it realizes of its
multiplicities of inertia. Moreover, there is no man to *make* this act, and
thought is only the place where this form is actualized as unity of the
diverse (and without the effective presence of diversity). Seen in this
way (which is, indeed, how it is seen), this activity of the inert – this
unification by itself of dispersion, inasmuch as it remains wholly dispersion – *is not intelligible*. It is not a matter here of denying that unities
can be produced in the Universe (the living organism is one such); but of
stressing how this common conception attributes to the object, in the
form of a cohesive force, that which is the extended result of human
action. This conception thus conceals an underlying recourse to *the unity
that produces itself*: in other words, *organic unity*. Organicist thought is
everywhere, slipping in behind practical thought every time it is a
question of hypostatizing action by cutting it off from the agent. In the
example under consideration, however, the organic unity of envelopment
would not have been able to establish itself. For the organism, unity is
actually the perpetual restoration of unity. From this viewpoint, there is
no difference between its synthetic reality – as a consistency at the heart
of temporalizations of envelopment – and the accomplishment of its
functions: eating to live, and living to eat, are one and the same thing.

For unity manifests itself as the totalization of the functions that
preserve it. These functions, moreover, ceaselessly turn back upon themselves in a circularity that is only the first temporalization of permanence,
since their tasks are always similar and always conditioned by the same

'feedback'. For we find in organic unity neither the One-as-a-being nor the One-as-the-future-object-of-an-act, but instead the identity of Oneness [*Unité*] as an ontological status and Unity as a perpetual repairing of damage. It is *hexis* which realizes the living mediation between the two: Unity ceaselessly temporalizes itself by functions; but functions, through their infinite cyclical return, produce permanence as their *temporal being* (i.e. as the inert limitation of possible operations and of temporalization). *Hexis*, as an eternal return, is the permanent unity of the organism inasmuch as it is *living*; it is life itself, creating for itself its determinations of inertia.* But this *hexis* – even in the inertia that may affect it from outside (impossibility of adapting itself, when the variations of the milieu cross over a certain threshold) – rejects the dispersion of exteriority. It is neither a *whole* nor a *totalization*. The whole, if it is to have an ontological status, must produce itself – through a continued but purely *affirmative* creation – as the new being of diversity (with the diverse no longer being an obstacle, [any more than] an incitement, to unification, but – in an immobile transcendence of itself – becoming the means of which *totality* as a real being is *the end*, and finding in this totality as a realized end its meaning and its *raison d'être*: as though totality had retrospectively engendered diversity only to produce itself through the liquidation into it of the diverse as such, and through its preservation as a qualitative variety in unity). Totalization, for its part, is transcendence, always induced to retotalize itself and control its deviations. For, although the agent (simple or multiple) from which it emanates may himself be part of the practical field, totalization as a praxis effects the interiorizing synthesis of *extraneous* elements (i.e. of inorganic matter, and some-times – *through it* – of biological processes). In this sense, it is always *creative*. These remarks – a mere reminder of descriptions presented earlier[99] – allow us to comprehend that *hexis* is a whole only inasmuch as its totalization is effected upon itself and in its own interiority; and (do we even have to add?) inasmuch as the pure [cyclical character] without spirality of the totalizing operation determines it – on the basis of a future of inert exteriority (by virtue of their very identity, *the several* operations always repeated form a juxtaposition of destinies without inner relations) and a past ossified *ad infinitum* (as an infinite superposition of *the same* digestion, etc.) – as though stricken with immobility at the heart of its perpetual movement (thus people say '*my* liver', '*my* blood'

* Inasmuch as these disclose themselves as the reverse side of an adaptation to the specific milieu.

99. See, in particular, 'Introduction' to *Critique*, vol. 1, pp. 45–7.

and also '*my* digestion', to denote the kind of singular beings that can be called frequentatives, and that change only to remain the same in the midst of a changing environment).

2

Questioning the Category of Unity: Practical Organism or First of the Machines

S O THE organicist aspect of *unity*, as a synthetic category of praxis and knowledge, is at bottom only a determination of the inorganic by the organic *hexis*: inasmuch as it is contained in the objective that illuminates (while simultaneously delimiting) the field, as *what is to be restored*; and inasmuch as (like a quality of the objective's illumination and meaning) it reverts to the unified object. In fact, if we leave aside the sphere of arts whose objects are imaginary, human praxis – constituent and constituted – can *in any case* never produce a totality *in actu*. For every totality forces its diversity back into productive, unifying action. The *One* supports and produces the diverse. By contrast, in our inorganic products it is the diverse which pre-exists. Unity – as a passive synthesis – is etched into it with the help of certain temporary combinations (cohesion of a metal after casting) and is ultimately guaranteed by the inertia of the diverse. So long as external circumstances do not disperse these elements, they will remain bound together – for they are incapable of unbinding themselves. In a word, the terrestrial milieu – according to our investigation – produces *hexis*, that strange unity which takes itself as an end and automatically merges with the internal means of preserving it. And human *praxis*, as a transcendence (and preservation) of *hexis*, creates totalization as an ever open, never finished, spirality of temporalization. But the *whole* – as a hidden structure of the category of *synthetic unity* – is itself a schematic tool of thought and action, without any real correspondence in the practical field. It has been produced by the transcended organism, the transcending action and worked materiality all at once. When praxis discloses the produced object, its structure as a mediation (between two moments of the organic, via the inorganic) causes it to grasp the object *via life* and, at the same time, to qualify life by the object. It discovers the unity of the organism through the passive synthesis of the inorganic. For this unity – perpetually produced, reproduced and restored through cyclical changes – is not a *unity for itself*. Quite the contrary: within the interiority of the field it is the coherence of the tool, together with the link between its practical determinations and the goal being pursued, which appear to underpin the passive synthesis; while the latter, against the background of the practical field, yields its being-for-the-other (for the agent) *as unity* (which gives rise to a reversal and application of the unitary schema to the agent himself as an organism). Precisely, however, this unity would collapse into a pseudo-integration, should we see it as merely an inert synthesis of dispersion, the result of orientated transformations. In other words, the inertia sustaining the permanence of properties is disclosed *by action itself* as an act *producing* that permanence. What is involved here is both a projection of organic life at the basis of the synthesis as continued creation of a permanence; and, at the same time, an impregnation of worked matter by the act (labour), which is changed there into a passive structure precisely in so far as it surrenders its transcendence to it. For organic life is permanence *as hexis*: it is condensed into the renewed instant of passivity, and repetition of the *same* functional operations is transformed into a repetition of the creation of *the same object*. Here, the unity of the whole is the projective identification – *in the instant* – of inertia, as a pure negation of change, with the affirmative creation of the object by itself as a positive perseverance of Being in its being. It remains the case that the momentary unity of the implement (as passive flashes of Being), trapped by the infinitesimal moment, would run the risk of having suppressed the multiplicity of substances only to replace it by the infinite divisibility of time, and [causing us] to come up once more against the Cartesian problem (how to pass from one point in time to another), if praxis as a synthetic temporalization did not integrate into the practical field the inert dispersions of the time of things: enlacing instants by the movement that transcends them, and producing their succession (relations of strict exteriority between points in time) as a specific determination of unanimous interiority.

In the practical interiority of transcendence (i.e. inasmuch as the object remains in living history and is still active within it), organic life is transformed after that object into a totalitarian, continuous creation of its being by itself. In this sense, the inertia of Being is disclosed as identical to its affirmation.* At the same time, as we have seen, integration and

---

* That does not signify that this identification is *real*, in the sense in which we have said that teleological structures were absolutely real, right to the being-in-itself as a limit of interiority of the exterior.[100] Nor does it mean that it is *unreal* (as a dream or fiction may be). Simply, it draws its reality (*in the interiority* of the practical field) from the fundamental structures of praxis, and – in the practico-inert reversal – from its efficacy as a factor and qualification of the various species of alienation.

100. See pp.323–4 above.

transcendence of the implement reflect the action that produces it and the action that uses it – indissolubly linked – as *passive humanity of the tool* (and, as we have noted, as *human efficacy of the inert*: a magic power to cut and carve as the knife's *given* transcendence[101]). These different unificatory schemata (as produced and conditioned by the action of which they are the instruments of control and disclosure) constitute, in their turn, *an efficacy of worked matter* (inasmuch as it is defined as such, and from *these angles*, within the practical multiplicity: round the arrow poisoned with vegetable substances discovered and blended in a positivist tradition of empiricism and technicity, religious ceremonies are instituted to *reactualize* the ability to pierce living bodies and poison them, inasmuch as it becomes their practical reality as petrified action). Thus the practical unification and the functional unity (transcendence and organicism) in practice realize the being-one of inert matter as a deep truth of its inertia. Through it, in a reciprocity of perspectives, the organic becomes practical (*hexis* makes itself affirmation as the act) and the practical organic (the *function* of the tool, as congealed transcendence and signification, becomes a function of an organ, as mysterious and condensed life of a whole).

So the very category of *unity* – far from being a mere transparent principle – is characterized, like every human reality, as the twofold determination of worked matter by the organism (origin and final goal) and by action (as mediation), inasmuch as the law of interiority governing the practical field determines the two aspects of this determination by one another and in immanence. The unity of a tool is that: it is an action which becomes an organic *hexis* by defining the signification of the instrument; and it is an organic, diffuse life produced inside the object and within its very being, as an *ontological function* – i.e. as a continued creation and as a totalized totality.

To be sure, investigation will reveal other forms of practical synthesis: totalization-of-envelopment, incarnation, enveloped totalization, circular synthesis. Nevertheless, it must be noted that these different structures – which all relate to the dialectical development of praxis in the social and historical field – refer us to a *unification in progress* and *never* to the *accomplished* unification (except in certain relations to past-being that we shall find in problems of diachronic totalization).[102] The truth is that *unity*, as a practical category of labour and daily life, is only a deviant determination of the agent by the specific features of his praxis. Between

---

101. *Critique*, vol. 1, p.183, n.58, and p.515.
102. See Appendix, particularly the fragments 'History *Appeals* to History' and 'Is History Essential to Man?'

organic integration, maintained and restored by the *hexis-function*, and totalization, as a temporalizing unification of the inorganic, *unity* is required neither by analytic Reason (other than as a preliminary framework that analysis will dissolve) nor by dialectical Reason. Yet it characterizes the human act as such, since the practical organism, *objectifying itself in order to reproduce itself*, has man – as an agent whose task is to work upon the inorganic – announced to it through the inertia of passive syntheses. Therein lies the source of alienation, as we have mentioned. Anti-human matter – inasmuch as it is exiled from the pure realm of exteriority without ever attaining life – in the name of unity (and, in every instance, with the *content* of this unity) reflects man's anti-humanity back to all men as their true human reality. It is at this level that *essences* (pure practical ideas engendered by the worked object in its passive action, i.e. as a mediation between men) exist; and also contemplative thought, as a pure alienation of empirical intuition (and the action that produces it) to those abstract, inert unities and to the relations of interiorized exteriority they maintain (as the things which produce them through men) in the immanence of the practical field. This captive thought is also, quite simply, conceptual thought. Analysis dissolves it into external relations, the dialectic explodes it by virtue of its temporalizing power. But it is continually reborn as man's 'natural' thought, or rather as thoughts that things produce – in the totalizing circularity – by their reconditioning of men.

We have already said this,[103] and shall be returning to it. But what matters here is that conceptualist intellectualism – as determinations of the Logos by other passive syntheses through the agent – represents a particularity, i.e. a negative limit, of *human* praxis. It is because this praxis, a mediation between two heterogeneous terms neither of which it can *produce*, is in itself a passage from the organic to the inorganic – and on account of its twofold signification (the organism's becoming-inert producing itself with a view to organizing the inert) – that the dialectical ensemble of its structures exists and conditions the historical adventure in its specificity. Circularity, alienation, practico-inert, drift, etc. – all these features have their source (although, of course, a whole dialectical progression and the synthetic combination of other factors are necessary to produce them) in the following basic characteristic of human action: totalization and temporalization as transcendence spring from need, i.e. from an explosion of the organic cycle as *hexis*; and this explosion conditioned by scarcity manifests both the encompassing presence of inorganic exteriority and, at the same time, the impossibility for *these*

---

103. *Critique*, vol. 1, pp.170–71.

particular organisms directly to transform mineral substances into integral elements of the living substance. The organism's immanent, univocal relation to the inorganic milieu (with its uses and its adversity-coefficients) is already the action as a whole; and it is *our history* up until today, and very probably until tomorrow or the day after (we shall see what the *permanence* of a factor – throughout the totalizing trans-formation of the whole practical field[104] – signifies). But by governing its inertia to act upon the inert, the practical organism produces its action as a *non-organic* efficacy. Biological integration is projected as a totalizing temporalization; and its objectives, as future syntheses of present means, allow its organic cohesion and the deep solidarity of its organs to be *used*. However, by the very act which governs the organism *like an instrument*, the latter – as an agent – sustains a certain *non-organic* temporal reality. His own action is a production of himself as a passive synthesis, via the inert unification he imparts to the objects organized. To be sure, the action breaks the cycle of adaptation, in which it is the Universe which upsets the balance and the organism changes only to find itself in the same objective relationship with the environment. Whereas the act re-establishes the relationship by acting directly outside itself upon the Universe, and by restoring the former order or offsetting the changes that have occurred. It is this feature that makes the act into a transcendence of organic life, by giving it – as its fundamental structure of being – a synthetic and practical relation between the interior and the exterior. From the moment when the organism realizes modifications *outside* in the light of an objective, we can speak of an *act*. And this definition is enough to show that the first practices are far from beginning with the human species or even with mammals. If human acts alone concern us here, it is because – for reasons that it is pointless to go into – they are the only ones on Earth to be integrated into a history. But if we call the modification produced *an objectified act*, we show by this that – at a certain level of reality – the passive unity of the worked object is (grasped and contracted in the instant) the very unity of the act *'in person'*.

This is still clearer when *the tool* is considered as a materialized (inorganic) mediation between the agent and the inert thing. For the latter indicates *in its inertia* and by its structure (passively borne) the way in which the worker can use it. The act is an inorganic materiality, sealed in this momentary form. For the existence of the tool makes us see that action (whatever it may be), as imposing a unity upon the

---

104. This problem, linked to diachronic totalization, was not to be dealt with in the present work.

diverse, is itself fragmented (within unity) by the diverse to be unified. There are diverse *tasks*, whose origin is the quality of the diverse materials. The total operation is temporalized as unification, but installs exteriority within the temporalization itself. The necessity (deriving from objects) of *first* reducing some obstacle or other (by movements themselves separate or separable), then resolving some difficulty (preparatory activities) and tackling matter with some treatment or other (purification, for example), manifests itself as an exteriority (within the interiority of the temporalizing movement) of every action. Let us be clear: in a certain state of technology, means of production, etc., *this* or *that* operation is indispensable within the framework of the activity whose aim is to refine oil. It is *even* possible that *this* given action of a *political* nature (abandoning Venezuela, with all its unrest, and establishing refineries on the calmer island of Curaçao) was indispensable to Shell, as a huge capitalist enterprise. But it still remains the case that partial actions *reach completion* at the heart of the total action. Even if, for example, one were to reduce to an infinitesimal instant the moment separating construction of the oil city at Curaçao from the start-up of the machines, and even if (as often happens) one were to observe that construction of the buildings overlapped with their use in the first refining operations, the instant when some particular *segment* of the total action is suppressed (because it has reached its *terminus ad quem*) and some other is produced is in fact a *double negation*: *in it* the *terminus a quo* negates and rejects the *terminus ad quem*. The result of past action, as a *former circumstance*, participates in the inertia of the object and in the being of the transcended past.

This is well demonstrated by the historical fact of the division of labour and its temporary conclusion (prior to automation): i.e. the division of labour among men becoming a division *among machines*. A fundamental characteristic of the act is involved here: it can be reduced (depending on technology) to a multiplicity of tasks performed by a multiplicity of individuals. In other words, the inert multiplicity of the diverse, by requalifying the act that transforms it, designates itself through it as a possible multiplicity of agents (and one practically necessary in general circumstances). *Of course*, this new multiplicity refers to a new integration: in order to realize *this* particular passive synthesis (an alloy, a minting of coins, etc.), it is necessary to carry out *the synthesis* of the agents concerned. The objective has to be all the more clearly defined since it is that of a plurality, which could disperse if it were imprecise. The preparation of tasks and their distribution, the installation and use of mechanisms of control and constraint, etc. – all this shows that the practical unity has merely been displaced. It comes to the multiple from the manager or the management bodies. No matter. In the movement of the division of labour, the synthetic function of unity and control posits itself as exterior to the functions of production. And as for unity – considered inasmuch as it unites the workers in the factory, for example – it can be perfectly effective, in a given situation, when it is merely the passive synthesis of an atomized diversity. At this level – if, for example, labour is considered inasmuch as it produces unitarily a certain result in a certain factory at a certain moment and in a particular capitalist society – it can be observed (as we have already described at length) that the men are united by the machines[105] (*the assembly line* is the unity of those doing assembly work). Every human operation is isolated from the next by the material, inert separation of the two organisms. Every operation of *one* man is joined to every other by the operation of a machine (for example, the continuous movement of the assembly line) to which it is homogeneous. But precisely in so far as there is homogeneity between the specific operation of a compartmentalized machine and the action prescribed for an individual, this means that *praxis* itself is basically the directed action of inertia upon inertia. Or, if you like, in a field of interiority defined by need (hence, by the organism) – and on the basis of the objective, posited as meaning, orientation and unification – the inert acts upon itself. Eventually, the specialized machine replaces human specialization (as a qualification), and at a further level of technical improvement – with automation, 'electronic brains' and the control of *processes* by cybernetics – human labour consists in building the machine. But it is the machine itself which assumes the whole activity of production (under the control merely of small teams). The basic possibility of this transformation was given at any moment in History (as a *future* possibility, whose realization could remain uncertain or be interrupted through the agency of external factors), in the sense that in praxis – even individual praxis – the organism, by defining itself as directed inertia, constitutes itself *outside itself* and through the exteriority of its unity *as a machine*. The most backward peasant in the world, when he uses his weight to flatten freshly dug earth (or to tread grapes), is already behaving like a machine controlled by its operator. By jumping on the ground or dancing in the vat, he expends certain reserves of energy to produce a physico-chemical result (flattening or crushing, by weight). And when he uses his full weight to depress a lever, the machine is there in its entirety. Transmutations of energy, the action of his weight upon the lever and – through its technical use – the raising of some concrete object or other, all this has just one meaning: the use of inertia by organic inertia in the

---

105. *Critique*, vol. 1, pp.239 ff.

direction determined by 'the unity' of the organism, i.e. by the future restoration of its functions.

Action is disclosed to us, through a critical and regressive investigation (starting from robots as agents produced by action), as the inorganic transcendence of the organism inasmuch as it transfers the unity of immanence to exterior elements in the form of a passive synthesis, and inasmuch as it defines – by losing itself in this objectification – a spatio-temporal field of interiority as a medium for the relations between inert matter and men. The agent is not directly identifiable with the organism. Quite the contrary, he manifests himself in action as a practical exterior-ization of inertia: i.e. as a mechanical system, as an ensemble of weight and counterweight, and as a source of energy (through combustion of certain substances). And all the operations he carries out (all the treat-ments to which he subjects the raw material through the self-modifications he imposes on himself) are *on principle* reproducible by a machine (if not at the moment under consideration, at least as a basic possibility). From now on, moreover, *not only* is there no *action* for which a physico-chemical process is not – or could not be before long – a perfect equivalent, *but also* the perfecting of certain instruments makes it possible to exercise *through the intermediary of inert matter* forms of control or action of which the organism alone would be incapable. Finally, by reducing an ensemble of human operations (for example, an aerial duel) to *what they also are* – positions in a sector of practical extent – it is possible both to dissolve the human reality of the undertaking (for example, its antagonistic reciprocity) and, at the same time, to constitute through technique and calculation, on the basis of specific circumstances, instruments which modify their action depending on their positions or those of other material systems and which automatically take account of all the mechanical relations that are established in ensembles in movement (for example, in 'fighters', machine-guns which automatically correct their mistakes and rectify their aim *as a conse-quence* of these mistakes).

It is the paradox of *our* actions that they can all be – and most are in fact – reducible to a succession of inert processes. The great shock of the nineteenth century – which has been intensified in the twentieth, with specialized machines – was, through de-skilling of the worker, the more general de-skilling of *all human activity*: i.e. the discovery of the per-manent possibility of breaking down any praxis into elementary pro-cedures each of which could be carried out equally well by a practical organism or an inorganic system.

Unity as an Invention

B UT IF we were to leave it at that – if we were to break human conduct down in the way behaviourists do, or if we saw a human act as the mere assemblage (by bonds of exteriority) of simple or conditioned reflexes – we should see only the *negative* aspect of praxis. This aspect is the most important – as always when a dialectic is involved – because it manifests at once materiality, adversity and particularity (and thereby freedom as a practical perception of contradictions). But precisely because it is a *negative* determination, the critical investigation must grasp it in its relation with *that of which it is the negation*. Well, in so far as the organism can neither reproduce life within itself on the basis of the inorganic, nor create it outside as a transcendence of passive syntheses – in so far, too, as all life is in itself an integration and transcendence of non-life (not just because it has realized the organic synthesis within it, but because it is *also*, in relation to exteriority, an *exterior system*) – action is produced as the negation of the organic by the organism, inasmuch as the latter is attacked by the exterior and inasmuch as it seeks, by exteriorizing itself, to recover the functional interiority which determines it. So action is a succession of inert processes, in so far as the transcendence of the original situation towards the restoration of interiority *invents* the unity of these processes as the immanent meaning of temporalization. On this basis, it matters little whether unity lies in the *apparent* indissolubility of the moments of an action (as might be thought, watching the feint or dodge invented at the moment of danger by the boxer in the ring) or whether it resides in their recomposition after analysis has broken them down. Invention as synthetic unity – at whatever level it may be produced – is necessarily the projection of the living synthesis as an exigency *in the future*. The unification that causes a tool, a machine or an action to be invented is necessarily the intrusion of life, as an exigency of integration, into the world of exterior dispersion. At the

same time, however, *what is integrated* (at least until the synthesis of life
has been realized) is necessarily an ensemble of inert processes, whose
unity of temporalization – like its inert spatial gathering – cannot even
be conceived without the support of the practical project. The agent
relapses into the inorganic as a *performer* of his undertakings. He casts
himself *beyond* the organism, by *positing* biological integrity as an end
(instead of living it cyclically) and by producing – on the basis of this
living integrity – an absolute category (whose origin is neither the inert
nor life, but the shifting relations between these two statuses): the
passive synthesis, a petrification of the organic by the inert and a
subjection of the inert as such (and without modifying it) to organic
unity. This practical category – or rather, this synthetic schema – of all
objectivity is simultaneously: the production of a *distance* – a *perspective*
(or, originally, the possibility of a perspective) – whose origin is a
double negation (the impossibility of any distance-from-oneself in the
organism, and the non-organic-being of worked matter); the first illumination of the diverse from this perspective (unity, as an organic foundation
of the inorganic objective, everywhere realizes – on the basis of the
objective being pursued and within the practical field – provisional
passive syntheses, which liquidate themselves in the temporal development or are liquidated in favour of other equally provisional syntheses of
the same kind, and represent the first regroupments – quantities, unities
of multiplicities and of crowds grasped from afar, etc.: this is perception
itself); and the very framework of practical invention.

For there is no fundamental difference between knowledge and invention. Knowledge, such as we have just described it, is the unification of
the inert – as diversity of the practical field – on the basis of an aim to be
realized. This unity, however, is an invention. First of all, because it
comes to the diverse through human praxis. Before the latter, the diverse
is neither *multiple* nor *unified*, since these two practical notions come
from a qualification in interiority of exteriority. For this reason, to
perceive (for example) is to produce, in the simultaneity of praxis, a
series of *possible syntheses* of material pluralities; and these shifting
unities are completed, pitted against one another, and interpenetrated, at
the whim of *movements* of the body: i.e. of outlined synthetic realizations.
The specific character of perception – as a shifting unification of contrasting or interpenetrating unifications – is precisely that the disclosed
field is determined according to different directions and through various
interpretative possibilities. But such interpretations still represent the
outline of a praxis. Thus the mountains blocking the horizon reveal
themselves in and through the movement of my eyeballs. But this bodily
movement should not be confused with the one whereby – in Kant – the
mathematician *engenders the line*. First of all, because the opaque,

substantial unity of the mineral is given *before the movement*, as a synthetic and massive presence in the practical field and upon the foundation of the field's unity. In other words, the relationship between dispersion and the organism – in the practical field – manifests itself as an original presence in the field of dispersion, in the form of blocks of quasi-unities in permanent disintegration.* At once, the synthetic operation remains inessential. It does not really enlace the various elements or realize their quasi-unity – which comes from them. On the contrary, it merges into them and is entirely dissolved in them. For this movement of the eyes is not *in itself* constitutive and unifying, in the sense in which the realized praxis can be. It refers to the possibility of a true praxis, whose temporal orientation it realizes schematically. In the case under consideration, it is that of *struggling up* the slopes of the mountain, or that of coming back down again. An elementary form of thought is involved here, and the sign in its simplest function: the *meaning* of the block of compact presence is defined by the actions that unified it with the other elements of the field. But the solidarity of organic functions

---

* The quasi-unity of the block is a fundamental disclosure, not just because the totalizing unification constitutes the field of immanence in which it appears, but also because this indistinction is prior – all at once – to explicit syntheses, to realization of the One, and to syntheses of *detailed unities* allowing the disclosure of quantity as a sign of dispersion. In reality, the quantitative multiplicity is the result of a practical operation limiting unity by divisibility, as it does divisibility by the unity of indivisible elements; and in the form of summation (multiplication and division), providing the synthetic rule of its temporalization. But multiplicity, as a unity of the diverse *qua* disunited – and of its elements *qua* indivisible (more or less, relatively or absolutely) – constitutes for dispersion a *privileged* status: i.e. orders it *as an order* (relations between the multiple and the One). Plato saw this clearly: it is already a question of worked materiality. Take away the labour, the unity specific to the part disappears – and with it the divisibility of the ensemble under consideration. If *the parts* are lures, the ensemble is *without parts*. At once, its partless exteriority manifests itself as a quasi-unity. Of course, these quasi-unities reveal themselves *within the unity of the practical field* as a *real* and *pre-quantitative* relationship between an organism and blocks of exteriority. In this form – the most elementary – labour, properly speaking, has not transformed inert matter. But already the inert coherence of blocks is the grasping of their compact emergence within the interiority of the field. Already *Nature* is outside as our ignorance. Already the cliff, in the immanence of reciprocal relations, is *culture* – or (if you prefer) is *illuminated by culture*. In the being-in-itself of exteriority, in fact, the quasi-unity of the compact pudding formed by mineralities is indissolubly linked to quantity – as a complex relationship between multiple unity and multiple unities – as well as to the dispersed being's real pulverulence (depending on certain structures of Being) rather than its divisibility, which refers only to a certain human operation at once always possible and always limited by technology. Dispersion and opacity thus interpenetrate, as do other statutory qualities of Being. The practical operation seeks zones of cleavage, and chooses its operative perspectives as a function of these. In this sense – and by virtue of all the operational possibilities it harbours *for the practical organism* and in ontological indistinction – the quasi-unitary block of inert opacity is the practical status of inorganic matter (as present in the field, around the field, and in the organism) which comes closest to its ontological status of exteriority.

allows actions (as a synthetically bound ensemble of inorganic procedures of exteriority) to be performed in any way, by and in any part of the organic totality. If the eyes follow the sides of the mountain moving from the bottom upwards, it is the whole body which, through them, makes the climb. It is the body which comes down, if they come down. This is a matter not of a symbol, but of realizing an operation at the least possible cost. If the real ascent were to be attempted subsequently, one would have to see it as a *resumption* (rather than a first attempt) – which corresponds, moreover, to everyone's experience. The real undertaking (which brings the whole body into play) always appears in its relations (themselves variable, and sometimes founded upon the most violent contradictions) with *the same*, inasmuch as the body has realized it at lesser cost in different circumstances.

It is manifestly at this level that *thought*, as a relation of the organism to significations, is determined as action becoming its own knowledge. The ascending movement of the eye *is not* in itself a thought. It has not been produced *as a substitute* for an impossible operation. It is the operation itself, dictated by circumstances and reduced *to its simplest expression*. The movement is real and produces an objective determination of Being: the *objective* relationship between the mountain and the traveller (or the fugitive). At the same moment, however, through its functional unity, this schematic act is determined as a certain way of realizing the undertaking: a way at once total and abstract in relation to all others. So it refers back – in and through the unification it effects – to all the other ways of carrying out this operation: ways that have passed into it and are inscribed by it in the object as its destiny (to be accepted or rejected). Thought appears here as the relation between the real act of following the mountain slope with one's eyes, the constitution in this very way of the mountain as *ascending* in its very being, and the ascent as a concrete and totalizing practice of the whole organism, now become the *destiny* of this organism (the future *of this movement* of the eyes). The climbing movement of the eyes, as a schematic act of the whole organism, produces and discovers the mountain as a slope up which to struggle *by realizing there* – in the simple temporalization of this movement – *the whole organism* as disclosing the compact exteriority of that threatening block *by its abandonment on the mountain itself*, and the obligation of finding there its *de facto* contingency and its solitude in the indispensable and perilous undertaking of reaching the summit. Through the real and present (though schematic) act, two *objective realities* are disclosed, one as a *meaning* [*sens*, also = direction] *of Being*, the other as the orientation of a future (or merely possible) action. And the real invention of the present act (movement of the eyes) is expressed by a practical invention *in the field*: i.e. by a twofold reciprocal determination of matter by the total praxis, and of the latter by matter. The eye movement reveals that the mountain is a *rising up* of matter (this is the meaning of the myth of the Titans, and of Ossa on Pelion), in so far as this rising up is disclosed as an objective exigency through the future movement of the organism: of myself, *as far as my eyes can see*, and lost – tomorrow – in those snows. It is a future operation that I sense as my destiny (wresting of the practical organism away from itself, to await itself beyond the ordeal) in so far as the meaning of my effort – the orientation of my praxis – is defined by that *ascending structure* of the mountains. But the twofold determination is unified as a relation and in each of its terms, inasmuch as the perceptive interpretation invents its own practical meaning for itself, by inventing the unity to be produced (and disclosed) within the inert materiality.

It will be noted, however, that invention of the act of revealing and unifying transcendence is not necessarily realized under the pressure of acute dangers or immediate exigencies. There is no *need* whatsoever for me to struggle up the slopes of that mountain tomorrow, in order to be able to *realize* its 'steepness'. In this particular case, the practical relation is invented within a context, as a function of possibilities as yet ill defined, traditions and necessities regulating the relations between man and that massif with its peaks and its chasms, without determining them entirely and in detail. In this case, we observe: (1) that the unity of the material meaning has a tendency to dissolve along with the urgency of the operation. If I *must* go into exile tomorrow by crossing *that* particular pass, it is my sufferings, my exhaustion, and the dangers I shall be experiencing tomorrow that will disclose to me the terrible negative unity of the mountain. It is enough to struggle up it, to cross the pass, etc., in order to transform that block of opacity *into worked matter*. It is final success that will also disclose to me its *positive* unity: after all, there are routes in the mountains and the mountain itself is a route. But if I do not reckon to realize this undertaking by bringing my whole organism into play in every way *in its facticity*, the eye movement I make today is only the indication of a possible reading (by others, perhaps). Hence, this reading vanishes in the objective, but at the same time indicates a *practical direction* for grasping the vast objects rising before us. (2) On the other hand, the *descent* – on this basis – is a possibility likewise defined and corresponding to a reverse movement of the reading. It matters little that, from a logical viewpoint, you first have to go up before you can come down. Apart from the fact that there perhaps exist villages, meteorological stations, etc., whose inhabitants came up long ago and can now only remain at the top or go down – which tends to make those two contrary procedures wholly external to one another – there is above all the following consideration: since no *concrete* operation is required of the organism, reality does not impose any priority. The truth is, if I confine myself to grasping Being through the perceptual undertaking, I can equally well take a single leap to perch on the summit before coming down from it, or set off from the valleys and climb up. In reality, every onlooker does both: through the two movements discloses two opposite undertakings, and through these simultaneously produces two contradictory unities of the material block. Matter rises up proudly towards the sky (it is *upright*, like a man), and *at the same time* perpetually collapses: it is a frozen avalanche. Both meanings interpenetrate each other, in so far as our eye movements succeed one another contradictorily and without any logic (at least, without any logic determined in relation to the object). One is organic and characterized by interiority. The other is inorganic and characterized by dispersion in exteriority. The syncretism of these meanings (and twenty others linked to them) must make clear to us how the practical field – for any organism, as for any organized group – is an interpenetrating multiplicity of the possible unities of the diverse. Everything is always revealed as united to everything, precisely in so far as diverse and possible actions necessitate and reveal such unifications (and at the same time disappear, because the real undertaking sets them aside). Stable forms are isolated – as foundations and exigencies of the ongoing praxis – and it is *praxis* which determines, via the unity of the field, the relations of immanence (substance and form, whole and part, etc.) which people have sought to hypostatize and substantivize under the name of 'Gestaltist' laws. At the same time, it is the indeterminations and stases of this praxis which – by allowing other undertakings to be outlined (and roughly begun or at once abandoned) and by defining negatively the tolerated undertakings – allow the wandering and interpenetration of partial unities within the unification in progress (hence, within the immanence of the practical field).

The other essential feature identifying knowledge with invention (within praxis) is the fact that the organic unity of the aimed-at objective, by being produced as an inert synthesis of inorganic materials, gives an ontological status within the interiority of the practical field to these unified diversities, which is realized only through that unity and which – precisely because it is originally neither that of inert matter nor that of life – arises-in-the-world, in interiority *and in exteriority* (let us recall the absolute being of teleological determinations[106]), as a real and new determination, drawing its reality from its novelty and its novelty from its reality. Who then could deny this novelty of passive syntheses –

---

106. See pp.323 ff. above.

inasmuch as they reflect at once the organic, the inorganic, and the act as mediation? In the combination of words 'passive synthesis', an interior movement may be surmised: the synthesis makes itself inert – hence, loses its organic meaning and its content – so that inertia should make itself unity and present itself really as an improbable, systematic order of the combinations of matter. The object – a caricature of life by non-life, a wresting of inertia away from naturalness – by virtue of its status escapes any idealist reduction, in so far as it is *precisely not reducible to anything*: neither to the organ nor to pure dispersion. And it is this irreducibility that, in itself, constitutes the being-in-itself we were speaking of earlier. So any unity inside the practical field is already determined by this *new* production constituted by the field itself (or the organism negatively defined by need and making itself into knowledge in order to give the environment the unity of this negation). Furthermore, however, it produces itself in its most concrete determination, inasmuch as praxis is detailed and becomes ramified without dividing under the sway of objective exigencies (i.e. passive expressions of need by negations of inertia). On this basis, every object is at once *produced* (by labour) and a *reality* (inasmuch as it escapes labour by its very being and gives inorganic-being to the organic unity that is deposited in it). Well, every moment of praxis transcends and preserves former circumstances *inasmuch* as this moment assumes the organic unity of these inorganic beings: i.e. inasmuch as it rediscovers the unity deposited in them as a mark by past labour, and inasmuch as this rediscovery is effected in a new movement of temporalization towards an end – i.e. inasmuch as it produces a new unity on the basis of a recognition of past unities.

This operation is knowledge, precisely in so far as it discovers the real *such as it is* (and not such as it might manifest itself through categories and principles). It is an *invention*, in so far as the complex category of *unity* (as organic-inorganic, and as a mediation by the agent) is a category *of Doing* in the absolute sense of the term: i.e. in so far as it determines the orientation of an *absolute production* (or *creation*), i.e. the emergence – irreducible, overflowing and transcending at the heart of immanence – of those *beings* which impose themselves upon action and investigation, passive syntheses. To know is to create, since knowledge is a determination of Being based upon the practical category of unity. *De facto*, the unity of human experience is in fact a practical unification of the multiplicities interior to the field. Conversely, to create is to know, since it involves producing (through inert synthesis) beings wholly extraneous to man as a biological individual, whose exigencies – as a re-exteriorization of practical interiority – will have to be learned (i.e. *determined* by their negation, or in the practical transcendence that suppresses them by satisfying them) on the basis of a unification 'in progress': i.e. another synthetic, inert being in the process of being manufactured. The necessity of the laws of Knowing is simply the necessity of the laws of Being, inasmuch as they manifest themselves in the field created by the agent's free praxis and through the temporal-ization of this action. At the same time, however, they may be identified with the laws of *Doing*, inasmuch as practice is precisely the unification realized by the agent on the basis of the organism's future and past unity; and *above all* inasmuch as the knowable structures and processes of materiality are relations *condensed* and *actualized* by the unificatory integration of the diverse into the practical field, and by the specification of details.

The ensemble of scientific discoveries is so closely linked with the tools and techniques of the period that the system of knowledge con-stituted in the same period must be seen *simultaneously* as the techno-logical and anthropological expression of men's relations with the world and one another, via the mediation of their techniques *of construction* (i.e. via the techniques allowing these tools to be made, rather than those emanating from their use) *and also* as the *real-being* of the Universe: not as *relative* to science and technology, but – on the contrary – as the unification of an absolute reality by History, manifesting itself as an absolute reality by virtue of the History it produces for contemporaries and men of the future through the agents of its unification. Whatever illusions there may have been at the outset, the discovery of America was temporalized (as a diachronic process: exploration – conquest – exploitation of resources, etc.) as the discovery of a continent. And that vast continent itself crushed – and of itself annihilated – whatever might be left of medieval illusions concerning the Globe. It was its *being* which dissipated those outworn significations into *non-being*. But although its unity as a continent was one of the zones of cleavage constituting the directions of being-in-exteriority, for that zone to exist as such – and as a unitary determination – men had to exist in Europe: men who went to the Americas, through all the dangers of the sea, and constituted the perilous term of their voyage into the unity of an objective. And other men had to exist in America, for the limit in exteriority running round the continent to constitute it in interiority too, as a more or less specific practical field of the 'natives'. If practical agents on Earth were to live and move about solely *underwater*, the wheeling obstacle – closed upon itself (impene-trable) – that the two Americas would constitute to free movement throughout all seas could be only a *negativity* (the material combination of a type unsuitable for life with its adversity-coefficient). Perhaps the continents would then turn out to be those vast expanses of water (medium of all historical events for those sub-marine agents) the Atlantic Continent and the Pacific Continent. And History would change, to the very extent that the biological condition would have changed the geo-graphical *hexis*; for practical multiplicities would be able to communicate or fight only through the narrow polar straits, until such time as techno-logy allowed them to perfect machines enabling them to emerge, climb on to dry land and live there (and to cross the solid element, in order to go and attack their enemies in the liquid element). But that practical unity, belatedly discovered in its interiority, would always remain *second-ary* in relation to the unity of water. In other words, its interiority would be integrated into the practical field of agents as a *separation crossed* (a dangerous medium of non-life, whose perils appeared in and through the machines striving to avert them). To other organisms, differently constituted and possessing other techniques, the difference between the solid state, the liquid state and the gaseous state might well appear secondary. In that case, moreover, the precise limits *the continent* sets to our efforts to enter it (through the efforts of those who inhabit it) might well become blurred and be replaced by other groupings. It is true that continents acquire their historical being (and receive their modifica-tion *in itself* of gathered, configured inertia) on the basis of a complex and strictly human ensemble (navigational techniques; commercial geo-graphy linked to these techniques, and favouring one 'nation' or another on the basis of the technique in question; human conflicts arising between classes inside the country, and between governments representing the ruling classes of the various countries, creating *commercial exigencies* through the collected passivity of the sea, etc.). But it is equally true that the complex of anthropological determinations constituting the emergent land as a continent is the very same which – under the pressure of exteriority (*this* particular exteriority) suffered by organisms whose specificities come from it – has been constituted as the interiorization of a dispersion of men on Earth and will be re-exteriorized by the constituent discovery of the New Continent (as it already had been – in, and through, commercial voyages – from the days of Antiquity). If, as many historians believe today, the American Indians are Asians brought by some mysterious exodus to the territories now designated by the name *American*, and if geological upheavals subsequently cut them off from their region of birth by submerging all the solid land across which they had passed, it can just as well be said that *the continent* made them as it made itself. The extraordinary solitude of Maya history, for example, its almost total disappearance (other than as an *object of scholarship*, but without the reciprocity signalled above), and the extermination practices adopted by the Spaniards after Columbus's failure, etc. – all this accurately reflects the fact that the separation into continents, initially not known and ultimately transcended, was meanwhile constituted as *the destiny* of certain social groups and (for various material reasons that it would take too long to enumerate here) pronounced a death sentence upon them. *Colonization*, moreover, inasmuch as it negatively constituted routes and itineraries criss-crossing the World and was to become a factor of planetary unification against itself (through its total overthrow) – i.e. *modern* colonization, in the historical ensemble of its development – necessarily had to base itself initially upon the division of lands and continents, and upon its re-exteriorized interiorization.

This real, practical bond between the environment and the unificatory organism thus has nothing in common with those shown us by 'relativism'. In the reciprocity of conditionings, it can be seen that the surrounding produces the material content and that the surrounded organism gives *unity* to the forces conditioning it, through the biological structures and practical exigencies that these forces have themselves determined as the biological reality of its functional unity. The continent as a quasi-unity already has enough being to determine – in their 'nature' and in their 'history' – practical organisms, whose action will be unified within its practical field in the practico-human form of *a particular* continent. At all events, this final (though perhaps temporary, depending on trans-formations of techniques and historical objectives) integration is an invention of Being, as is clearly signalled by the labour carried out on language by earlier generations: *invenire* (to find) is the source of a French word meaning 'to create'. The ambiguity recurs even in the term 'inventor' which, in its relation to techniques, signifies the perfection of a *new* method, a *new* process for raw materials, etc., and also (as can be seen from the sign *'Inventeurs'* fixed over one of the counters in a French lost-property office) the discoverer of an object that exists, but is hidden or lost or forgotten. In the same way, to *discover* – which properly speaking means to reveal reality by removing its 'cover' – is a verb commonly applied to invention by a creator: gunpowder and the compass figure among Great Discoveries, as though they had been merely hidden in some basement where someone had found them. The fact is that unification of the means with a view to an objective is a real labour, which discovers actualized relations by integrating their terms into an inert synthesis.

The most elementary praxis of the organism is thus knowledge: unity of the field is the background against which the object's unification is produced (through a labour). Nothing would be more absurd than to separate action and knowledge at the level of manual labour (even the most primitive or fragmentary). Conversely, however, the most abstract knowledge is action. The geometrical figure whose being-in-act Liard used to describe is simply a passive synthesis *effected by a generating act*: i.e. by a construction unifying an ensemble of points or loci by means of a ruler. And it remains in its passivity, as a new determination and selective elucidation of an atemporal relation of exteriority, so long as it figures as an organized element in a vaster undertaking bringing other more complex figures into play (mathematical development). However, geometrical proof on the basis of a synthetic unification that is never considered dialectically (i.e. as such) rests solely upon relations of strict exteriority. So even in geometry we encounter the indispensable unification constituting human praxis, and the permanent possibility – precisely in the name of unity – of resolving the synthesis into an infinity of relations of exteriority. However, the needs of knowledge or practice deduct a specific number of determinations from the infinity – anyway indifferent – of these relations (every point of every figure has infinitely infinite relations with all the other points in space). So choice as a negative unity is invisible and present in exteriority itself, inasmuch as the latter suddenly reappears against the *masked* background of the unification of figures.

4

Essences as Labour and Alienation

THE FIRST aim of the foregoing comments is to make us understand that the Cartesians' problem (how to reconcile freedom of opinion with the eternal being of essences) is a false one. For every *essence* is constituted on the basis of objects as the passive synthesis of its abstract determinations, inasmuch as the combination of these qualities has to be produced by a practical, *autonomous* operation (for unity derives from the agent-organism, not from the unified reality). If the object in question is a man or a constituted group, it goes without saying that this object – bearing and creating its own unity – itself sustains its own determinations in the unification of the organism or of praxis. At this level, however, such a synthetic production is lived dialectically through the concrete. It is in no way comparable to the permanence of the inert synthesis. Production of the essence is, in this case, a specification of the relation of *alterity*. The *knower* situates himself as Other *vis-à-vis* the known being, in so far as he constitutes the latter as the Other. In the practical investigation, this Other (as transcended transcendence) produces himself (inasmuch as he is not *comprehended*, but *taken stock of*) through the reciprocal exteriority of his elementary behaviour patterns. From this standpoint – and *for the knower* – these various determinations lapse into the inert, inasmuch as they are exterior to one another and their sole unity is that of the agent (an abstract unity, grasped as a point of common reference rather than as a unifying activity). By reproducing this unity as a foundation for empirical determinations, the *knower* produces their inert synthesis. For it is on the basis of the unity of *his field* that he collects them, as disparate elements whose synthetic foundation is precisely his own praxis (on the basis of future unity as the organic destiny of *his own* organism). In this case, the particular essence of an individual – for example – is quite simply the passivization of his existence and its projection into the being of exteriority, simultaneously

366

with the unification of the diverse through the unifying praxis of the knowing organism. The operation is effected materially by the production of verbal formulations and their synthetic unification. Through the ensemble of these formulations – with the exteriority of sentences re-producing that of elementary behaviour patterns – an object is created which is neither the dialectical unity of a practical life, nor the re-grasping in exteriority of that life by being-in-itself. This object is the individual's *essence* (or, at a more advanced degree of degradation, his *character*). This inert synthesis – as a surrogate for the unifying praxis, such as it manifests itself in the Other (precisely in so far as the knowing witness refuses to share the other-ends of that Other) – possesses a practical efficacy that is the measure of its truth. On the basis of well-executed observations, I shall be able to define a *hexis*, or an inert system with cyclical repetitions. I shall say, for example: he *is* brave and intelligent, but scatterbrained, etc. And these characteristics will reassume a living unity of reciprocal conditioning *in and through* my action. I shall entrust him with my life, but not my secrets, if I am his hierarchical superior. This mistrustful trust as a quality of my relations with him is the reinteriorization of the dispersive unfolding of qualities. And it is incontestable that if the passive synthesis (as dialectical reality's surrogate for my action) has been properly effected, my behaviour – by virtue of its practical success – will discover (discovery-invention) its truth.

This does not stop the essence from being a *product*: the product of my labour. This labour has necessarily been carried out on the basis of my refusal to comprehend the personal aims of my subordinate, along with his origins, the circumstances that have qualified his project, and the dialectical development of his praxis. It has turned out, at the outset, that our common social situation (as much as the practico-inert condi-tioning our labours) has introduced a certain reification into our human relations. This reification is simply the reciprocal exteriority which manifests itself in rejection of the other's aims. It may have quite a number of sources, depending on how deep it goes, one of them (the most important) perhaps being the division of society into classes and exploitation. At all events, this reification is interiorized and re-exteriorized by practical knowledge. The resulting construction of the essence is, above all, the search for a *real means* of using the inferior as an instrument (or, negatively, the superior: he is angry, especially in the mornings; on Fridays – for reasons to do with his private life – 'he's like a bear with a sore head'; if you want to ask him for something, Tuesday afternoon is the best time, etc.). In conformity with this objective, moreover, it is the construction of a mechanical equivalent for his actions. As is well known, however, *the words are the thing*: in the absence of their object, they destroy it by passing themselves off as it; in its presence, they cluster round its physical being like real qualities (moreover, *they are* real qualities). In this sense the essence can be seen as the belonging, specific to a given organism, of the inertia (worked by Others) which constitutes its model in exteriority. It will be noted, of course, that this passive synthesis – as the *truth* of the actions of *both of them* (truth of the subordinate's actions, inasmuch as they justify the superior's predictions; truth of the superior's actions, inasmuch as these more complex activities involve an integration of the inferior as a subaltern agent into the global praxis, and inasmuch as this praxis has succeeded) – is linked to the real, dialectical praxis of the free organism through a relation of immanence. In so far as this relation ends up producing itself as *the essential* for the known too (through the actions of others, which constantly refer to it), the agent's relation to his particular essence must be seen as an important aspect of *alienation*.

To be sure, when the essence of inert objects (which *already* present themselves in the form of a passive synthesis) is involved, the integration of words into the real substance has the result of constituting a verbal body for that physico-chemical body. The agent makes himself a mediation between these two determinations in exteriority. It can legitimately be said that he determines verbal matter through the materiality of things. Passive syntheses, as a unification of the diverse (although resulting from different operations when they impose themselves upon physical bodies, for example, or upon the verbal body), nevertheless remain fundamentally identical, inasmuch as – in facts and in words – the organization of the inorganic is realized through the *passion* of organic unity. So the essence of inert bodies is most of the time produced directly – as a supplementary piece of work – by the labour that is carried out upon them (even if this crude essence [*essence*, also = fuel] later requires a special refining process, as a function of the evolution of techniques). On this plane, there are not *two* truths. A person thinks with his hands and with the tool they wield; and thought is forged by forging its object, which eventually closes on it and the words it expresses. But when it is a matter of practical organisms, there are two truths – both forged by action and with a view to action – one of which excludes the other. For the essence, as a thought of inertia, is an inertia of thought. It contrasts absolutely with what we have called *comprehension*. And it is here, in conclusion, that we shall discover the meaning of this contradiction: how can the dialectical unity of a praxis reconstitute itself in exteriority through the inert movements of a machine?

5

Dialectical Comprehension, Control of Positive Reason in the Name of the Totalizing Temporalization

COMPREHENSION is praxis itself as *accompanied* by the situated observer. Its structure is the very structure of direct action. It grasps the practical temporalization on the basis of its ultimate, future term: in other words, on the basis of its end. And although the teleological character of the act or its products can be observed from outside, without the witness taking up the ends being pursued, the only way of abandoning this schematic determination in favour of grasping the operation concretely (since plenary comprehension is comprehension of the concrete) remains to adopt – albeit temporarily – the objective, and then come back and illuminate by its light the moments of the totalization (in order to be able, conversely, to grasp the differentiation and growing enrichment of the end by the means). Hence, in comprehension – as the dialectical grasping of an orientated temporalization – the problem of the exteriority of actions is relegated to the background. For we understood by this exteriority (generating an inert succession) that every action was independent – as an isolated task to be performed at a certain moment and in a certain order – from every other previous or subsequent action. To be sure, it is necessary to have obtained result M before undertaking the construction of N which depends upon it. But provided that M is given in the agent's practical experience and accessible, it matters little to us – formally – whether it has been produced by the previous labour of the same practical organism or some other, or whether it is the result of an accident of nature.

But if we look more closely at this exteriority, we understand precisely that it is an exteriorization of the organism's mechanical (or physico-chemical) inertia, inasmuch as this inertia is closely applied to the inertia of exterior objects with a practical view to unifying them. So it is the means of unity, chosen on the basis of the future objective and in the light of this objective; and we must either see it, on the basis of the goal, as the progressive realization of the transcendent project, or else stop *comprehending* the action. And if we look more closely still, we observe that the inertia of the raw material defines the exteriorized inertia of the organism. It is the configuration of the worked object that governs bodily attitudes, *inasmuch* as the body's relation to the object is governed by an aim. The man who braces himself against that rock is a mechanical energy system acting upon it in exteriority, in conformity with the principle of inertia. But if this is the case, and he can actually be replaced advantageously by a bulldozer, this is because in the world of exteriority there is no way of acting on an inert body other than by communicating to it – as an inert body – an exterior movement, received from the exterior. By virtue of his reserves of fuel and his ability to expend these at the requisite moment, man is his own inertia and his own exteriority for himself. He communicates his own movement to himself *from outside*, by burning his essence. But this way – proper to the living being – of being his own exteriority can, in itself, be conceived only as an interiorization of the exterior by exteriorization of the interior. In short, on the basis of the objective we *comprehend* the exteriority of practical conduct: it is interiority producing itself in exteriority as a limit jointly defined by the living body and the worked object. And by this word *interiority* we do not mean to allude to some mysterious organic immanence or other, but simply to the fact that integration of the inert into the orientated temporalization can be conceived only as a structure of interiority.

In the same way, if it is true that the complex conditions of a craft worker can be broken down into elementary procedures, each of which can be reproduced separately (and by another), it must *first* be noted that the temporal exteriority of the successive procedures is conditioned by the exteriority of the tasks, and the latter by the inert dispersion of the raw material. It would be conceivable – logically, at least – for an operation directly performed upon living matter (which is a synthesis) itself to be synthetic, if it were directly to condition life. The fact that we act on life by the inorganic (medicaments, surgery, etc.) proves only, as I have already mentioned, that we set in train a transformation which we are neither able to produce in itself nor to control – and which is specifically organic. And if synthetic action (i.e. as a unity, impossible to break down, of unified procedures) is impossible *for us* in this domain, it is still the case that the procedures which take persons or groups for their object very often have to assume such a character. So this means that the practical movement is realized as a pure temporalization, and that the distinction into before and after is itself governed by the unity of the development and the reciprocity of immanence of its conditionings. We are here simply recalling the structure of any praxis – particularly social praxis – in which we have seen the future determining the past through temporalization of the present. So if the procedure which produces in exteriority the result M, as a first practical synthesis, is in itself separable from that which produces N, this is because the result M – albeit a condition of N – *in itself remains* exterior to the consequences produced. It is necessary to dig this ditch, if you want moist earth to construct a rampart or embankment. But the ditch is not *in* the embankment, nor is the embankment *in* the ditch. And if a truck bringing a load of earth in fact suffices to make digging pointless, this is precisely because the earth is in itself unaffected by the way in which we have obtained it. At most, it might be said that the act *is* the transformation of *this* particular matter inasmuch as it is produced by an exterior energy source; and for that very reason the avatars of the raw material *fall* outside one another. Exteriority here comes from the dispersion of inertia as a feature of passive temporality.* And if we were to imagine a fable in which an all-powerful demiurge produced modifications of matter by willed lightning flashes, these flashes would be successive (in the temporalizing unity of the terminal objective) because the succession of exteriority would be required by the material states to be produced. So action divides into exterior moments *inasmuch as it identifies with the movements of its object.*

For that very reason, however, comprehension restores to us the indissoluble unity in which an organism causes itself to be designated in its inertia by an exterior raw material, inasmuch as this organism itself, or its restoration (or preservation), defines the operation on the basis of the projected future (negation of the past). What is indissoluble is the invention of *this* particular group of procedures, inasmuch as this invention (continually corrected and enriched by the movement of its realization) defines in unity *an order* of their succession: i.e. determines, with a view to the goal, the necessary succession of passive states (inert syntheses) which will ultimately produce the required modification and its *organic* consequence (preservation of the living being). And it is actually precisely *this* which we comprehend: when we grasp a gesture of the worker and – by the modification this produces in exteriority – we suddenly comprehend its end and its beginning, we may possibly be incapable of predicting one by one the procedures that will ensue, and unable to recover those that went before. But what counts is the 'presence' of the future in that gesture: inasmuch as it illuminates the latter by subsequent gestures and the goal; and inasmuch as it makes the currently

---

* It is not part of the subject under discussion here to study passive temporality as a quasi-unity of dispersive succession with temporalization.

achieved result into *a means*, and thereby confers upon it its human signification – as transcendence (surpassal towards the future) and as exigency. In a word, if every operation is exterior to the rest, their ensemble is a *totalization*. Not in the sense that it would really be possible to unify them in their very multiplicity, but in the sense that each one, at the very moment when it is separated from the rest, can be comprehended only in terms of the result being aimed at, which – thanks to the organic end – presents itself as their totalizing summary. In this future objective, they are all folded back into a relative indistinctness. Not that there is no unity, or that this unity is not an order, but because every moment appears there as an abstract structure and, above all, as an option among various possibilities. For in that complex system it is above all the relations between relations that are elucidated in the order of a unifying temporalization. It is up to the realization and its concrete problems to determine the particular options and procedures. Praxis, through its finality, discloses the material characteristics of the object. It unfolds these one by one in the succession of exteriority characterizing the inert. But this succession is actually *integrated* into the interior temporalization, since the latter makes it into *the time for exploration* within the temporalizing invention. To give an example: the time of waiting – when an experimenter has realized the conditions for a chemical experiment and brought substances into contact, isolating them as he has decided – this waiting time, therefore, which measures in exteriority the speed of the chemical reaction, is like a rending of the practical temporalization (there is nothing more *to do*, it is necessary to *wait*) by the exteriority of successions. At the same time, however, recovered and engendered by the very synthesis that it rends, this exterior time – every inert instant of which is lived *actively* as separation, impatience, etc. – is merely the exterior limit of the interior temporalization; or, if you like, its way of integrating the time of things into itself as a direct contact with their inertia.

In this sense, inertia in human action is to be comprehended as itself being the fundamental act and the source of all acts. Through the metamorphosis that creates praxis before and beyond organic integrity, and in the latter's service, the temporalization arises as a synthetic and living inversion of the readings of succession; and the unity of invention consists in defining – on the basis of the present passivization, and in the light of the future – the general perspective of a *treatment* of that materiality. The determinations (first abstract, then gradually concrete) of the moments of this treatment are produced (in the temporalizing act of practical prediction – i.e. prediction-production – and then, later, in the course of particular options) as *neutral states*. This must be taken as meaning that praxis operates the rigorous unification of practical inertia (governing the agent) with the inertia of things (inertia of exterior processes). There is a prediction of *already united material states* (passive syntheses of the exterior multiple: i.e. passive syntheses of the body at work – including its tools – with worked matter), each of which, in its unity, is wholly unaffected by the following state, inasmuch as both are taken in absolute exteriority; but which, replaced in the movement of creation that is labour and in relation to the unity that gives them their meaning, are all indicated as a *precondition* and all realized as an inert designation-exigency of the following moment. Conversely, the latter – as a procedure-state – remains exterior to the previous one but, on the actual level of temporalization, conditions it in interiority (i.e. inasmuch as man as a historical agent is a mediation between these *neutrals*). The costs (i.e. in one way or another the expenditure of energy) have been so great that the action is produced and comprehended *in its irreversibility*. Either the agent gives up – but this means the ruin and disorganization of the temporalization (introduction of an inert *not*) – or his only way of recuperating his lost strength (and more than this, perhaps) is to push the act through to the end (between these two extreme terms of the option there are others; but they reflect one or other of them, to a greater or lesser extent). In both cases, going back is forbidden. In particular, the man who relinquishes an undertaking will for ever remain, *in the human milieu*, the person who began it.

So that is what characterizes *the comprehended action*. The organism invents for itself – in the unity of the project – the directions of its own exteriorization, inasmuch as it defines the perspectives of transforming passive materiality with a view to a goal. And this immediately practical invention is realized at once on all levels. The body becomes its own *exterior* source of energy, in order to communicate its movements from the exterior as received impulses. The concrete invention reproduces and sustains within itself the time of exteriority, as the sole milieu in which passive states can be foreseen and engendered on the basis of their abstract schemata; but this exterior time, within the temporalization, is merely the production through labour of a mediation between the unification in progress and the dispersion that it is to gather up. Technical thought, for example, after the syncretic movement of the project, *must* make itself in itself a succession of exteriority, since the thought of inertia is an inertia of thought. *For dialectical comprehension*, however, none of the moments of the metamorphosis, none of its states, none of its levels, is isolated. The organism attacked in its biological functions negates itself as an organism and – incapable (in the case of *our* History) of transforming the inert into organic – itself makes itself inert and commits its subsisting functions to producing and preserving this inertia, with an actual view to transforming exteriority through exteriority.

Through this negation of itself and the exterior milieu, it constitutes
exteriority within itself and outside as the *means* of restoring to itself the
integrity of its organic functions. The fundamental choice of this
passion, inasmuch as it is realized through labour, is simply *the action*.
But this new relationship at once produces the new existent who is to
realize it – *the agent* – who is neither the organism nor the confused
inertia of outside, but is actualized in the latter as a directed passion to
save the former (i.e. to destroy itself on behalf of biological functions)
and, through this passion, determined as mediation (between the organic
and the organic through the inorganic), transcendence, project and temporalization. None of these determinations can characterize the organism as
such, since each springs from its practical relation to exteriority. In that
sense, positivist Reason can ignore them. That *passion of thought* (for,
since the latter is the inertia of Reason, it must as such be the object of a
constant option) is merely *exteriority itself*, as a practical rule for
operations. It realizes the negation of the organism by itself, but at the
level of the inert. As such, it has no instrument for becoming aware of
the totalizing temporalization which governs and sustains it, although it
lives that unity as the very foundation of its reasons. It produces itself as
a *time of succession of exteriority* in the dialectical temporalization: i.e.
at the heart of a Reason that knows it and uses it, and that it does not
know. Through this passive synthesis of inert successions, the agent
knows himself and governs himself at the first level of action: i.e. in the
inertia of his procedures. The infinite divisibility of inert time constitutes
the infinite divisibility of behaviour, and – through the homogenization
of the latter with worked matter – the practical equivalence of energy
sources. It becomes immaterial whether a given result is produced by an
organism expending its reserves, or by any other energy source; immaterial, too, whether the passivized organism is a mediation between all
the successive states of the thing, or just the source of a physico-
chemical process.

De facto, the organism *is no longer*. Positive Reason does not know it.
There are only successive states of inert matter. Through this infinite
succession, dialectical Reason – by means of the forged tool that is
positivist Reason – will make its detailed options, illuminated by the
objective to be attained. In particular, dialectical unity – within the
perspective of the project being actualized – leads analytic Reason to
produce *orientated* physico-chemical processes, from which the factors
'organism' and 'human agent' are eliminated. Not because they do not
belong to them (although they might be only at their source), but because
they are anyway defined only in exteriority. Positive Reason – a passive
synthesis of inert successions – functions by its own laws of exteriority
within the unity of the dialectical temporalization, and provides its

results as a function of that unified exteriority: so it can be called our first machine. In reality, its historical development – as a Reason of exteriority (for it is *in the exterior*, rather than 'in us') – inasmuch as it is guided by creative invention (the unification of exteriority in passivity), necessarily leads it to produce machines. For machines are only itself as unified exteriority; and it is itself only a machine for producing machines. Between an electronic brain and positive Reason, there is equivalence. Or, if you prefer, one is the Reason of the other. And for these two equally inert and material Reasons, each of which produces the other, unity comes from the dialectical interiority surrounding and sustaining their exteriority. It is easy to understand, on this basis, that positive Reason – as an objective rule of interior exteriority – is at once the *passion* of the organism producing its own inertia as a contact with things and, at the same time, the grasping of every practical action as a pure inert process: i.e. an energy transformation. It can also be comprehended how the unity of its functioning comes to the machine (as a product of human labour) *via analytic Reason* (which is here simply labour, inasmuch as it makes itself exteriority and controls itself as such), but not *by virtue of it*; and how, ultimately, it remains unnoticed as long as the terrain of positivism is not abandoned. Or, if you prefer, positive Reason is the permanent means of praxis, but is not itself a practice.

A twin consequence flows from this observation, whose effect is to bring the inert and the organic agent closer. It is true that analytic Reason allows a rationalization of action, by virtue of its non-comprehension of the latter's synthetic character and by virtue of its molecular monism (which reduces *the element of action* – gesture, reflex, etc. – to a mere transmutation of energy). But *it is true also* that tools (and machines too) are no more accessible, in concrete reality, to that Reason of dispersed exteriority; and that – as tools and as machines – they require *comprehension* (the very same that uncovers the praxis of men) to come and disclose them in their truth.

For no one – whether an economist or a technician; and in any period whatsoever, at the time of 'universal' machines as much as at the time of automation – who is invited to visit a really modern factory, with the most up-to-date plant, can confine himself to studying the series of physico-chemical processes with their various conditionings. For his attitude (as a specialist who wants to *know* the most 'advanced' realization in his specialism) is *differential*. He reckons to assess (i.e. *measure*) the differences separating this establishment from those he already knows. *For him*, moreover, these differences must be *advances*. We know roughly what these *measurable* advances can be: lower costs, increased productivity of the workers, better safety and hygiene conditions, etc.

And these very general results can themselves be achieved only by detailed improvements, whose abstract features we roughly know. The new machine *consumes less*. This means that it does the same work for a lower expenditure of energy; or else that it involves some way of utilizing its waste-products; or that its exterior arrangements make it possible to organize the work (and the division of labour) in a more rational way that avoids time-wasting (and consequently to reduce 'extras', and payment for inefficient work, in favour of investment). *Safety is improved*. By reducing the risk of accidents at work, you necessarily reduce the expenses connected with them: i.e. there will be *less compensation* to be paid, and *fewer* of those ruinous strikes by which – when a man has died – the workforce seeks to protest at the risks it is forced to run. Of course, it must be clearly understood that the expenditure involved in improving safety at all events remains lower than – or at most equal to – the average costs entailed by accidents *before* the installation of the new machine. Most of the time, for this very reason, the problems of safety and productivity will be found synthetically linked in technological research: a combination will be sought that eliminates risks all the better in that it makes it possible to produce more, etc.

The ensemble of features that we have briefly enumerated remains inseparable from teleological structures. Every specific feature of the new machine manifests itself in its inertia as a response to an objective problem. The safety system has been produced *on the basis* of statistics for accidents at work, and *in order to respond* to the exigencies of production: how to devise and construct a new layout for the old machines, enabling the costs entailed by accidents to be reduced, without the expenditure needed for installation going beyond a specific threshold. In this case, as we saw in connection with the steam-engine, the inventor invents by making himself into the inert mechanism required by circum-stances.[107] And, for this very reason, the inert mechanism is an inert synthesis: i.e. the seal of finality marks it in its being (within the practical field and at the heart of dispersed exteriority). Through the inventor's mediation, the objective exigency is imprinted in matter as a negation of interiority, and as the condition for a transcendence of this matter by itself. And this transcendence towards the exigency is effected by inert materiality itself as a *passion* of the inventor, *inasmuch as* the lived unity of this passion determines it synthetically and orientates it irreversibly. From this standpoint, a change in the conditioning of the series brings a different (in exteriority) ensemble of changes into the

107. *Critique*, vol. 1, pp.191–3.

process. It is analytic Reason which determines this. But such changes are synthetically gathered up and grasped in interiority by the dialectical praxis, inasmuch as they directly find their signification – i.e. their unity – in *synthetic human facts*: such as the need for manufacturers, at a given stage of capitalism, to reduce costs by increasing production. Moreover, the inventor as a singular individual is further conditioned by his own needs and by his desire (for money, glory, honours, etc.): i.e. by the incarnation in his practical person of the objective exigencies of the ruling class. Invention is a mediation between this incarnation and the exigencies that it incarnates. It has to enrich the inventor in proportion to the advantages it brings to manufacturers (of course, it is *precisely not* what is produced; but the principle of the latter is posited by the creative praxis itself).

We have already shown how – when a 'primitive' gives information to an anthropologist and describes schematically the social structures that he realizes in practice with everybody – a broad, dialectical thought sustains and overflows a technical thought deriving its unity from it, which it handles like an inert object.[108] Here we encounter the same duality. The thought of inertia as an inertia of thought is at once the thought that thinks (it analyses the process, brings factors to light, determines all the consequences for such and such a variation of such and such an order) and, at the same time, the thought that is thought (its inertia would disperse it into *non-thought*, if the dialectical temporal-ization did not grasp it and produce it in its orientated unity – on the basis of passive or living syntheses, organizations and exigencies – by directing its inertia along teleological lines of force, albeit letting it string itself together alone in accordance with a *necessity* that the unifying synthesis has *created* in it, through a totalizing reconciliation of its terms). It is the thought of things and it is a thought-thing, an instrument perpetually *acted-upon* by the temporalization of free praxis. It is a technical invention – and, as such, could not be the true knowl-edge of molecularized exteriority. At the same time, however, it is wholly homogeneous with other technical inventions (as passive syn-theses) and reproduces their being in the form of signifying determina-tions of verbal matter. However, in so far as its forged (and inert) *unity* is what allows it to grasp [these passive syntheses] in *their* forged unity, this common unity is passed over in silence: it *does not belong to them*. It is they which belong to it, inasmuch as it can be produced – and, therefore, comprehended – only by a dialectical Reason, i.e. a totalizing practice.

108. *Critique*, vol. 1, pp.500 ff.

Hence, an expert studying the advantages of modern plant, in so far as he studies these within the teleological perspective of an *improvement*, has to *comprehend* the machines. His operations of positivist (and analytic) intellection are merely the means necessary for realizing the process in its *function*, and determining its *value* as a response to prior exigencies. He *comprehends* a machine (some of its features have initially disconcerted him, others may have escaped him, others have manifested themselves solely as processes conditioned by others) when he uncovers and unifies its structures and movements on the basis of the objectives pursued by its inventor, and when he can progressively enrich and concretize his knowledge of these objectives on the basis of a more thorough investigation of the machine. It is clear that the *comprehension* is not different in kind from that which uncovers, in their deep signification, the acts of practical organisms or organized groups. Let us add, moreover, that the technologist and the historian of techniques must also comprehend the *meaning* of such mechanisms, in the same way that we have shown the *meaning* of an action being grasped (its *hexis* disclosing the drift of praxis). To appreciate this, it is enough to visit a museum of industrial science or technology in any capital. You will see that the form of these inert syntheses is defined not just by their functions, but also by the options of the society they produced (we saw an example of this above: the first capitalists of the 'iron and coal complex' rejected the improvements to the steam-engine proposed by Franklin and Watt (the reburning of coal fumes; a device to reduce noise) because those violent bourgeois saw the chimneys, the black fumes and the din as signs of their power[109]).

If you ask, moreover, where the difference lies between the machine in operation and the man in action, we shall say that *from this particular viewpoint* there is none. To be sure, the man is a free practical organism – i.e. a living integration that makes itself into a passion in order to act – whereas the machine is not. And it is he alone who could attempt passive syntheses, since in him exteriority is interiorized and then re-exteriorized. But it is not that which counts, nor the infinite flexibility of his adaptations to the practical field (a machine too can be flexible; and when it involves 'feedback' it is *adaptable*). If the practical field is considered from the standpoint of positive Reason, human actions do not differ at all from the ways in which machines behave. It is true that *the man* is missing. However – and this is the essential point – if you consider the man or machine as a dialectical intelligibility, i.e. in *comprehension*, then what counts is the fact that the succession of inert determinations, processes and transmutations is rigorously and irreversibly orientated

---

109. *Critique*, vol. 1, pp.193–6.

towards an end, by the synthetic, creative movement of labour under the control of a positivist Reason always supervised by the totalizing praxis. And if it is precisely *this* which counts – if, *on the one hand*, the inertia-passion of the organism must use exterior mediations and construct tools as its preliminary syntheses; and if, *on the other hand*, the most *rational* machine (today, the electronic brain) exists only as a real product of human labour and can function only through the mediation of the labour impregnating it – then human action is effectively irreducible to any other process, inasmuch as it is defined as a practical organization of inert multiplicities (with a view to an end concerning the organism) by an inertia-passion and via an irresistible project to integrate all the elements of the practical field: i.e. inasmuch as it is transcendence, temporalization, unification, and totalization. But since that is its specific reality, and since it is inseparable from an organism producing its inertia and its own source of movement as exteriority, as well as from the inert elements of the practical field, it matters little ultimately – from the formal viewpoint we are adopting – that the elementary moments of action as inert processes should be directly engendered by *one* organism; that their exteriority should make it convenient or indispensable to redistribute them among various organized individuals, and thus reinforce their temporal exteriority by a spatial dispersion; or that – with the division of labour passing to the machines – the movements imposed by its structure as a passive synthesis upon an inert materiality should end up substituting themselves for the procedures directly followed by agents. All the more – as we have already pointed out – in that the agent belongs to the practical field and, within the indivisible unity of this field, suffers all the repercussions of his action.

So when he perfects that machine for making machines which we have termed inert Reason, it would be wrong to imagine that he has stuck a grid in his brain or distorting spectacles on his nose. It is an objective machine, which is coextensive with the whole practical field and conditions him like all the other elements of that field. This means he is himself situated inside all the practical syntheses of the inert and in its very inertia. Or, if you prefer, the advances of positive Reason (i.e. the accumulation of rational, reasoning machines) must be expressed for him by a constant deepening of his determinations in inertia. It is in the original fact of life itself that analytic Reason discovers exteriority and, ultimately, the inorganic. On the other hand, the very unity of human praxis – the totalization – is what defines action in its irreducibility; this praxis produces and supervises (we shall see in what sense) the development of its science and technology; and every supplementary determination in inertia of the organic body is produced as a new conditioning of the latter in exteriority, thus allowing the agent through a technical action to govern him better and more intimately. Consequently, the moment analytic Reason effected a radical decomposition of the organism into the inorganic, and of life into a physico-chemical process, would also be the moment when that same organism would be conditioned by its own praxis with the help of all the inert elements of the field, thus finding – in its total reduction to the inorganic through praxis – the power to transform inert substances into its own living substance. To be sure, this ideal goal of technical and scientific progress can be envisaged here only as a hypothesis. Yet it has a clear signification. The passion-inertia of the organism is produced within the framework of praxis as inert Reason or exterior power over exteriority. This Reason grasps it in the very field of its application as an ensemble of inert processes (inside, in the very metabolism of life; outside, in work procedures themselves). The inertia produced thus reacts upon it in the unified field (and through unification of the field) and is radicalized. Precisely, however, this return is the work of the practical totalization. It is in and through its irreducible praxis that the organism discloses itself to its means – inert thought – as an ensemble of passive syntheses. And the conditioning of the organism by the inert syntheses of materiality, effected under the control of action, must succeed in *freeing praxis* by affirming the commutativity of all elements of the practical field (i.e. the ever-growing possibility of replacing one by another in some praxis or other at some level or other of the *means* – inert syntheses – and according to specific rules). If the limiting-moment of omnipotence is envisaged, the striking thing is that the practical field is wholly subordinated to the organism, precisely in so far as the latter has been broken down into non-organic processes. For action presupposes the permanence of the practical organism, as an agent of transmutations and as an orientation of equivalences. It is itself permanent because of the permanence of the initial objectives (which are neither achieved nor greatly transformed, though they are constantly modified): i.e. because of the permanence of needs. The aim remains, roughly speaking, to ensure the possibility of life to human organisms in a universe that long ago disclosed its indifference to man's fate (roughly speaking, it is always in one way or another a matter of scarcity and its avatars, in a world governed by laws of exteriority). Despite the biological organism's dissolution into the inert, therefore, the practical organism remains, because the living organism with its functions and needs has not disappeared either. And finally, in this limiting case, the practical field – through a positivist dissolution of the organism-as-agent – has become a vast network of machines driven in sequence, whose aim (grasped in comprehension) is to satisfy the needs of the biological organism (which they negate) under the control of the practical organism, which they cannot even reproduce.

6

The Two Praxes

THIS example merely shows, by pushing equivalence to the limit, that praxis will develop the relation of inertia between the organ and the thing in two different directions. For on the one hand the organ becomes inertia, in order to modify the thing (as in original action). On the other hand, however, in this fundamental direction of the practical, a counter-shock (specific, moreover, to exteriority as a relation) is given: the conditioning of the organism in reaction, *via* its inert being, by the inertia that it works. This counter-shock – long maintained at the level of counter-finalities – appears at first only as the source of negative modifications (passivization of ever broader areas of the organism by work distortions and accidents, occupational illnesses, etc.), which praxis had only to seek to negate – and if possible destroy. Or else it is utilized, but against the enemy (a weapon is the adversity-coefficient of certain physico-chemical processes becoming a tool for annihilating the adversary: i.e. the anti-man). At the outset, medicine itself hesitates. Either it thinks to heal the organic by the organic, or else it seeks to eliminate the inert results of a process by mechanical means. Everything takes place in the shadow of fetishized praxis. Yet the new direction of action is already present everywhere – sometimes explicitly, on other occasions in an implicit state: guiding the *reactions* of the inert, predicting repercussions and using them to recondition the organism, directly or indirectly, through its inertia. The development of this form of action (positive transcendence of the negative of the previous praxis) must not be seen *first* as the possibility of causing inert materials to be assimilated by living organisms. And that would anyway not mean – in this perspective of negation of a negation – that the inert would be rendered assimilable; simply that one would act *by the inert* upon organic functions, in such a way as to give human organisms certain functions of plants. Whether this purely formal limit can be achieved or not, what counts today is the fact that, without *nourishing* the organism *by the inert*, one acts by the latter upon the former's functions, conditions them, regularizes them, slows down some of them and speeds up others, raises the individual's practical abilities and endurance for a specific time, even begins to replace certain organs by inorganic systems (which proves *not* that organic life and the machine are ontologically equivalent, but *on the contrary* that dialectical Reason, by directing the Reason of analysis, better knows the margin of the internal and external variations within which an organism can preserve itself as such).

It is remarkable, moreover, that the progressive replacement – in the exterior – of the practical organism by the specialized machine (which belongs to praxis type No. 1) should be contemporary with the first *serious* attempts to replace – in the interior – an organ *in its functions* by a machine that the whole organism controls and governs. Hitherto, replacement of the living by the inert would end in a net deficit (a war veteran's wooden leg; the hook fixed to an amputee's arm to replace his hand; the artificial anus of a cancer sufferer which, unlike the anal sphincter, allows all the matter excreted by the intestine to pass through it). Today, in a limited number of cases, the inert object – inasmuch as the organism survives as its support, its source of energy and its unity – can replace the organ by (more or less crudely) ensuring certain of its functions. In this case, action type No. 2 is necessarily grounded upon the advances of praxis No. 1. That is not all. The inert object introduced into the organism is the product of human labour. It has formed the object of research and discovery. It has been realized by machines, themselves constructed through labour. The circularity of the action manifests itself in the fact that this machine introduced into us is a product of human labour, and – within the perspective of absolute equivalence of means – carries out a labour under control (the organism exercises a first control, but it is medical praxis which – in reality – realizes this control, through the organism and for ends already defined in the future). In other words, this machine is an *action* of man at the heart of the organism. In certain conditions and for certain functions, the organ can be replaced by a product of action and the function by the action of this product. The action, as an exteriorization of the inert by the organism, completes the circle by reinteriorizing itself. In order to restore organic integrity, or in order to safeguard it, it decides – in certain specific sectors – to replace life by the act. It is in the perspective of this governed circularity (which, however, merely utilizes one of the forms of deviant circularity) that everything becomes an act in the practical field, precisely because this field is defined by the circular reconditionings of the inert by itself under the control of praxis, whose practical field ultimately becomes the *real body* (as facticity and as efficacy) and whose organic bodies remain the negative foundation as singularized facticity and *need requiring satisfaction*.

Such, therefore, is *our praxis*. On this basis, we have the necessary instruments to comprehend its structures, and in particular the moment of construction of the *means*. It is the restoration and preservation of the organism, as an aim projected into the future, which will determine the place of the means and its function in the milieu. In other words, the practical category of 'means' is grounded upon the heterogeneity of the milieu (as an inert environment), in relation to the two terms of the action: the organism, and its need for restoration of its functions and organs. To be sure, the means are not – in the course of the totalization – heterogeneous to such and such a result whose achievement they make possible. And these results – within the temporalization and before being achieved – have indeed received the structure of *objectives*. In reality, however, they are also means. Ends in relation to the present state of the practical field, they are means in relation to its future state – as is the latter in relation to some other state. But the whole series is suspended from an end which is not a means for anything, and refers to no state because it is not itself a state: i.e. the organism, demanding its restoration and preservation from the depths of the future. We in fact know perfectly well that in some societies the maintenance and reproduction of life may be reduced to the status of a means (as is the case when the wage allows the worker just barely to meet his elementary needs, *so that he can* carry on his labour: he eats to live and lives to work). But we are not placing ourselves here at the level at which technology brings about a reorgan-ization of social ensembles, and in the very course of this reorganization men are mediated by things. The direct movement of praxis remains that of an organism (or organized group) striving to make *its material milieu* into a combination of inert elements favourable to its life. So the practical field – as a fundamental, real but abstract unification of all the surrounding elements – is the totalization of possible means; or – which amounts to the same thing – the matrix of real means. Everything is a *possible means* (and simultaneously a possible risk) in this unity, *because it is itself a heterogeneous mediation between two moments of life*. So the four words 'mediation', 'milieu', 'intermediary' and 'means' designate one single reality: inert exteriority, in so far as this conditions organic immanence as a being-outside-oneself-in-the-world, and in so far as the transcendence of the project causes it first to be conditioned *by the passion* of the organism.

7

Conclusions: Safeguarding the Organism, an Irreducible Determination of Action

I T HAS doubtless already been noticed that I have not sought to plunge actions and machines back into the synthetic interiority of the historical field and the totalization-of-envelopment. We should then have observed that every process of exteriority, inasmuch as it is interior to the unitary field, is linked to all others and all agents by bonds of immanence. We have already spoken, moreover, of the *action from afar* that is typical in the common practical field. We have no intention of returning to that now, however, if only because the complex developments of action through the various dialectical fields do not constitute the present object of our study. What matters to us for the moment is to define human praxis – the only one we can *comprehend* – in the immediate and fundamental simplicity of its singularity. And by that I mean the following: since our intention is to provide the formal elements of a theory of practical multiplicities, we have encountered *one* praxis in our investigation – that of men.* The other possible types of praxis remain unknown, and can be abstractly addressed in their formal undifferentiation. If we wish – in a radical way and within human experience – to account for the formal possibility that different multiplicities may exist, differently conditioned and being transcended by different kinds of praxis, we have only one way of doing it: by positive comprehension of the relations of *our* praxis with our conditions of life, to stress what *today* makes our

---

* The whole complex of behaviour patterns of certain insects and mammals may be called action or activity. It can even be noted that activity on earth begins with single-celled creatures themselves. At all events, the questions posed by such activity have nothing in common with those that would be posed by the existence of practical multiplicities whose technological development was equal or superior to our own, albeit differently orientated by virtue of the difference in the organisms and the practical problems.

actions specific. Or, if you prefer, we shall have comprehended human praxis fully in its determination – i.e. *in its limits* – if we see it making itself by wresting itself away from a certain facticity: from the contingent (for us, today) form of our necessary contingency.

Now the foregoing comments have, on the one hand, revealed to us features characterizing *every* praxis: for example, transcendence (although this is not necessarily defined by the relationship of the organism to the inert), synthetic unity, temporalization, totalization, and finally – as the law of Doing, Being and Knowing – dialectical Reason. But these comments have also made it possible, through the specific determination of these schemata on the basis of facticity, to singularize our action as historical agents, inasmuch as these agents are men of the present or a knowable past. And it is precisely this overall determination that we can reproduce here, to conclude this brief study. To be sure, we shall not therefore know *in what* – and *by virtue of what* – other practical multiplicities (real or formally possible) differ from this one. But we shall know why this multiplicity produces its actions as a singularization of every possible praxis.

We already know that a practical organism, engaged in a field of scarcity in the midst of a universe of exteriority – if, furthermore, it can reproduce neither outside itself nor within itself the synthesis of life on the basis of mineral substances – makes itself into exteriority in order to condition the exterior and communicate to it, through passive syntheses, an inert finality: the inert concern to preserve life. We know too that action, as a mediation between the organic and the inorganic, is entirely both at once; that it is the inertia of the organism engendering the organization of the inert from the exterior; and that you can cut it at will into inert segments (Taylorization, etc.), or grasp it in the transcendent unity of invention – i.e. on the basis of its ultimate aim, the preservation of life.

But here precisely lies the fundamental character of human praxis and its singularity: in short, inasmuch as man makes History, the first determination of *our* historicity. As we have just said, human praxis has a non-transcendable aim: to preserve life.* In other words, praxis is originally a relation of the organism with itself, via the inorganic milieu; when the aim is achieved, this relation is suppressed. We shall return in a moment to objectification, so dear to Hegel and Marx. But we are obliged to

---

* Nothing warrants the assertion that this end would remain non-transcendable, even if humanity one day freed itself from the yoke of scarcity. On the other hand, it is clear that it is our own History – the history of need – which we are describing, and that the other, if it does exist one day as a transcendence of 'pre-history', is as unknown to us as that of another species living on another planet.

acknowledge that the organism which reproduces its life cannot be *objectified* anywhere except in the inert; at all events, it is certainly not objectified in its own restoration or health. For if by an act, whatever this may be, it succeeds in reproducing its life – i.e. in feeding itself, for example – it returns to the functional, cyclical unity from which need has wrested it; and this unity, precisely because it is living, preserves no trace of the inert syntheses that have made it possible. From this view-point, action is fundamentally the negation of a negation, and nullifies itself in its outcome. To the organism in the course of assimilating organic products, it remains a matter of indifference whether these lay directly within its reach, or whether it had to *change itself into an agent* in order to procure them. Yet it will be said that action modifies the organs. That is true, but we shall be coming to it. Let us for the moment simply note this primary characteristic of the act: it is relative, transitory, and governed by life; and it is abolished in life, which dissolves it into itself as it redissolves and reassimilates its inert-being. At all events, whatever we may be able to discover at present, this evanescent character of action – an inorganicity produced, sustained and dissolved in it by the organism – remains its original, fundamental determination: it can be disguised, but not suppressed.

However, this same action is a transcendence of former circumstances towards an objective only in so far as the transcendence is *real* and not ideal: meaning that it has to be realized through a rigorous orientation of physico-chemical processes and the determination of partial, inert unities (as particular *means*) within the unity of the practical field. The passive syntheses thus realized are not necessarily, or even frequently, dis-membered by satisfaction of the organic need. Very often, on the contrary, they remain – precisely because they can be used again. Now, we have already commented that the passive unity of the material combination was – right to its being-in-itself – the absolute hallmark of its teleological character. So action, which the organism reabsorbs, produces absolute realities in the field of the inorganic, and it is these inorganic realities which are its *objectification*. At the moment of success, the agent is dissolved by the organism and simultaneously preserved in the form of a passive synthesis by the inorganic. Or rather, action – inasmuch as its inert outcome prolongs it – becomes the mere relation of the 'mechanical slave' to the organism. It is *this heat*, inasmuch as it constitutes the organism's medium of life. But such a univocal and synthetic relation (the organism's functional development in a favourable milieu) no longer contains any trace of an act, but on the contrary is the reversal of one: inertia putting itself in the service of life.

In so far, however, as these 'realizations' are posited for themselves and – through a bond of immanence – entail modifications from afar of other objects and men within the practical field, the action of each and every person is reconditioned by his own products: *inert* exigencies develop, and it is necessary to readjust, correct, oversee, etc. This time, moreover, these actions are immediately governed by the inert. Of course, they have meaning only in relation to the non-transcendable aim. Why satisfy the passive exigencies of matter, unless by neglecting them you risked death in the shorter or longer run? Yet it is indubitable that an order of passive exigencies is constituted at the level of the practical field, via the determination of products by one another and of men by their products. This is the level at which we have seen the practico-inert appear; the level, too, at which groups will form to break its carapace. All this interests us here only in so far as the action, absorbed by its end, is nevertheless sustained, prolonged, posited for itself and developed by the very exigencies of its products. These products include the agent himself, whose inequality with the organism becomes more and more pronounced. His occupational deformations qualify him through his work, and his technical skills constitute a new *hexis* for him: practical and non-functional, although it can *act* upon his functions (night work alters the hours and the quality of sleep). So the agent has a twofold status *in the organism itself*: he is dissolved as acting; but he remains as *hexis*, and has himself supported as a passive synthesis by the living synthesis. Meanwhile, the progressive complication of the reasoning machine, and of inert Reason, tends increasingly to eliminate the organic as a support for the act, and thereby tends to qualify the agent by his practical transcendence of inert gatherings more than by his biological origin. So everything occurs, basically, as though a new existent – *the agent* – were tending to detach himself, with wholly original structures, from the organism whence he has emerged. The *de facto* effect of the division of social labour is that a given agent will be remunerated for an action which has no direct link with the reproduction of life (if, for example, he is a worker in a factory making candles and holy objects) and which, consequently, tends to present its own end as non-transcendable: its specific objectification as its actual reality. In exploitative societies, moreover (to consider only these two examples), it is the role of certain members of the ruling class to engage in activities posited in themselves in their absolute gratuitousness (arts, games, sports, the gratuitous acts of bourgeois moralists, etc.). At this level, action claims to be autonomous: it receives its laws from its end and from the determinations of the practical field. Acting seems the specific function of man, and practical idealism radically separates the action positing itself for itself from the organism that supports it.

On the contrary, however, it is necessary to point out the following.

1. The action positing itself for itself is reduced to producing a passive synthesis, for it is rigorously defined by the absolute end it has given itself.

2. The agent of the action is defined by this passive synthesis given as its objectification, and the latter becomes the signifier of which – through a counter-shock – his occupational deformations (along with illnesses and accidents due to his occupation) become the signified. This means that the passive synthesis is the robot engendering positive Reason, and reflecting to the person the inorganic image of his organism. In the last resort, indeed, the action – by positing itself for itself in exteriority as a relationship of exteriority – would lose its relation to its ends, since *nothing* in the world of exteriority (and ends not shared) can favour one material combination with respect to the others, or constitute some possible processes as *preferable* to others. For there are no longer any *standpoints* from which it is possible to *prefer* this to that.

3. So the world of ends-in-themselves (as inanimate syntheses) does not have enough being, and – although it forms constantly (at hierarchized, diverse levels of social praxis, moreover) – it could exist only in relation to a twofold foundation: perpetuation of the organism, as an end *transcendent to the action*; and the dialectic itself, as a law of creative transcendence of all means towards the end, and as dissolving within it all inert syntheses.

4. This is what is shown clearly by the observations which led us to discover the practico-inert. For at this level we see the action alienating itself into its products, and the latter – through the counter-finalities they develop as inert mediations between agents, and as an inert re-production of the agent who has produced them – manifesting anti-human exigencies: i.e. presenting the inert as the end to which organisms must sacrifice themselves. In industrial societies, the agent exists *for the machine*; and his very labour, as labour-power, is sold on the market as a *quantity of energy*.

Precisely, however, the practico-inert is possible – and the exigencies of the inert take on a meaning – because, *basically*, the ensemble made up of the economic process and the organization of labour *relates to preservation of the organism*. I do not mean by this that the laws governing the ensemble in question cannot, in specific circumstances, produce catastrophic 'crises', culminating in wastage of lives; nor that the ruling classes are *concerned* with preserving the lives *as such* of the manual workers; but simply that neither the practico-inert, nor oppression, nor exploitation, nor *this* given alienation, would be possible if the huge, ponderous socio-economic machine were not sustained, conditioned and set in motion *by needs*. Whatever theft may lie at the very foundation of the wage, it is *in order to live* (hence, in order to earn that wage and spend it on reproducing his own life) that the worker sells his labour-power. And if machines give him orders, and are constituted for him as imperious ends, it is in a milieu of scarcity where the reproduction of his life is at stake. Conversely, the most *gratuitous* labour – that which seems to set its aim autonomously and can wholly suffice the labourer, such as the labour of the artist – is fundamentally (and whatever the passion of the painter or sculptor may be) just a *means of existence*. What the painter may feel and think matters little here. Objectively, it is still the case that the artist sells his canvases to live, and that he makes them to sell. Let me be clearly understood. He can and must *through art* pursue certain cultural ends (we shall return to this) which are not directly linked to the satisfaction of his own needs. As we shall see, however, quite apart from the fact that the real aim of art is to recover the organic, and needs, and integrate these into the cultural field in new forms,[110] in a society conditioned by scarcity it remains a labour which takes the satisfaction of the artist's needs as a *means* to continue, precisely in so far as those needs have chosen art as the means of satisfying them – which appears immediately, in the signification of the painting or statue. In the same way, in the alienated world of exploitation, we have seen – when the satisfaction of needs is assured – practico-inert conditionings (e.g. interest or interests) replacing organic exigencies.[111] Well fed, well clothed, well housed, the manufacturer pursues *his interest*: in other words, he is alienated into his property (the factory with its machines) and obeys its exigencies. But apart from the fact that the wage he gives his workers is destined to maintain their existence (as a *means*, it is true, to continue the production of passive syntheses), it must be added that the very foundation of his interest remains the owner's own organic life, inasmuch as – in the world of scarcity and competition – this too gives its urgency to the exigency of the machine. The practico-inert, as a practical equivalence of the agent to his machine, can be constituted only on the basis of an action pursuing – with increasingly complicated means – an ever identical and non-transcendable goal: the perpetuation of life. And it is precisely when the *present* forms of the practico-inert tend, by virtue of their contradictions, to make this per-petuation impossible (or less and and less possible) for the majority: it is then, and *in the name of the need*, that groups organize to smash these forms or modify them in part. The bourgeois Revolution, at a certain level of historical significations, can be realized as the contradiction

---

110. The manuscript ends without this reflection on art having been initiated. It will be found in *L'Idiot de la famille*, vol. 3, an interpretation of Art-as-a-neurosis in Flaubert and some of his contemporaries, seen as an incarnation of the social antinomies of their period.

111. *Critique*, vol. 1, pp.197 ff.

between the relations of production specific to the *ancien régime* (landed aristocracy, feudal ownership, local particularisms, etc.) and development of the productive forces (industrial techniques, mercantilist universalism, economic powers of the bourgeoisie). This contradiction could not itself have been productive without the hunger of which it was both the source and the expression. Between June and October [1789], the bourgeoisie won the first round because the people lacked bread. In other words, just as according to Kant the dove thinks it would fly more easily without the air which supports it, so it is often thought that the act would be purer – and its end more rigorous – without its dependence, direct or indirect, [upon] the organism and its needs. But exactly the opposite is the case. There would be no acts without needs (at least in the present state of organisms and things) – not even any dream of acting. The most abstract, autonomous end ultimately derives its content and its urgency from needs. It would vanish along with them, and its autonomy would vanish with it.

So every study taking as its object a theoretically autonomous sector of human activity must obviously determine through experience the laws governing that sector. But nothing will have been achieved if this activity is not attached to the ensemble of organisms and needs in relation to which it has been produced, and if the autonomous laws governing it are not explained *simultaneously* – in their autonomous inter-conditioning within the practical unity and *in depth* – as the unfolding of a praxis born of a need, defined by it and receiving its first multiple determinations from inert exteriority. A relative autonomy of practical sectors, and at the same time a determination of the whole action by the need which it transcends to satisfy, and preserves within itself as its urgency and sole reality: such is the foundation of historical materialism. It is, of course, a matter of *human* action, since nothing justifies the claim that suppression of scarcity would have the effect of suppressing all praxis, in favour of a return to mere organic functions. But this twofold determination – inasmuch as we have grasped it in its origin, inasmuch as we have seen it spring from circumstances themselves, and inasmuch as we have been able to follow the movement of its genesis – is produced as the fundamental intelligibility of that materialism. The scarcity lived in interiority by the organ is the inorganic producing itself as a negative determination of the organism. And this *lacuna* – inasmuch as the whole organism is modified by it – *is the need*. But the need, in turn – [in] positing its suppression as an absolute end via the inorganic milieu – is *the materiality of the action*, its reality and its foundation, its substance, and its urgency. Through the need, the individual – whoever he may be, and however gratuitous his act may be – acts upon pain of death, directly or indirectly, for himself or for others.

5. But the real structure of the action cannot be grasped by positive (or combinatory) Reason. On the other hand, however, neither its objectification alienated in its product, nor its bond of dependence upon the organism (whether this grounds it at the start or reabsorbs it at the finish), will be what makes it possible to determine the action wholly and in its specific reality: i.e. to comprehend it. The action, as a mediation between the organic and the inorganic, can be neither one nor the other. Moreover, even if it were produced as the unity of these two statuses, such a unity would itself be an entirely new status, which would reveal itself only to dialectical investigation. For what appears striking is the fact that the action is transitive, whereas the inert is permanence (changes and wear come to it from outside) and the organism repetition. Unity springs, in fact, from the quartering of the cyclical [movement] by changes of exteriority (physico-chemical transmutations). The cycle is actually there, since the end as an ultimate term will be identified with the original term (the function before the need): in other words, since the organism must be at both extremities of the process. Only this projected restoration is *precisely not cyclical*, since it depends on a never previously encountered disposition of the field's inert elements; and since, moreover, this disposition – inasmuch as it must be produced by the agent – implies that the organism transforms itself in order to realize it, and is transformed by its realization. In the most favourable hypothesis, the restored organism is *other* in an *other* milieu. Only the relation of the former to the latter can remain identical. The irreversibility of processes of exteriority, inasmuch as it is produced and governed by a quartered and exploded cyclical [movement], is precisely that – in its transcendence of a given towards the deviated reproduction of the same, which is the practical unity (or, if you prefer, the ontological status) of the action. In this elementary moment, moreover, we grasp that the action as a process under way can never be a unity, only a *unification*: which means that every moment appears as a diversity that will find its integration in the previous diversity – total integration having to be the restoration of the organism. From this standpoint it will easily be understood that every stasis of praxis, defining the agent and his act by the object they have produced, gives the dead unity of a passive synthesis for the real movement of unification. In the course of the temporalization, in fact, it can be a matter only of a certain material combination that will be found at a higher degree of integration in the following movement, and that derives *its meaning* (as a passive transcendence) only from its relation to the subsequent moment. The alienating halt – the stasis – of the action can derive from the social order. At a certain moment of technology and social history, wage labour is defined by tasks that are shared among the labourers, none of which in itself constitutes

the totalization of the undertaking and most of which are reduced to elementary procedures. The man whom the regime determines *in his reality as an agent* by the number of needles he fixes hourly on to nautical instruments, and *in his organism* by the means it gives him to satisfy his needs, is alienated and reified: he is an inert synthesis. But, *precisely*, praxis refuses – in him and in all the others – to let itself be limited to *that*. The *action* struggles against its own alienation through matter (and through men, it goes without saying), inasmuch as it posits itself dialectically as the unifying temporalization transcending and preserving within it all forms of unity. So the dialectic appears as that which is truly irreducible in the action: between the inert synthesis and the functional integration, it asserts its ontological status as a temporalizing synthesis which unifies itself by unifying, and in order to unify itself; and never lets itself be defined by the result – whatever it may be – that it has just obtained.[112]

[The main (1958) manuscript breaks off at this point]

---

112. I have separated off the preceding fifty-odd pages and made them into an independent Section C, because they suddenly took on the aspect of an autonomous, partly recapitulatory, study of praxis, whereas what was initially involved was simply to indicate a limit to the ontology of totalization, linked to *one* feature of praxis: its inability to create life (see pp.35–6 above). This study could well have been envisaged as a transition to the projected second major part of the work, in which the question of diachronic totalization was to be posed; for we may note the stress on the temporal development of the constituent praxis, whose basic features condition the advent of History. However, the problem of synchronic totalization in non-directorial societies – announced on pp.121 and 183 as being planned to follow that of Soviet society – had not yet been broached.

APPENDIX
(1961–2)

The interest of the reflections contained in the following pages lies in the fact that they give the reader a glimpse of the route along which the author was intending to lead him to the book's end. Nevertheless, I hesitated before publishing them. Sartre was fond of saying that he thought as he wrote. *What does that mean? That he did not set down on paper just ideas already formed or in the process of germination. That instead it often happened that he would explore at length the possibilities of an argument, and simply break off if a difficulty arose (without seeking to correct his attempt), only to recommence his dialogue with himself from scratch on another sheet. Thus, more perhaps than for other philosophers, the status of his notes remains in doubt.*

A.E.-S.

The Historical Event[113]

Has the effect of transforming our own past ('39 war transforming our past into an easy prey): i.e. *its signification*. In short, of distinguishing the *lived*, which was nevertheless the absolute, from the reality which was lived. And of rejecting as an illusion what was grasped as an absolute. Whether one submits (as was the case with us in 1939); or whether one acts and fails (at bottom, failure necessarily condemns a conspiracy, and does so all the more, the fewer the chance elements to which it is due; it makes the person who fails into someone who has lived his life as a myth); or whether one succeeds (the triumphant victor is other, and sees his quest as other: secret failure of victory).

So the fact is that the historical event, whatever it may be, gives our past its transformation by virtue of the fact that it was not expected; or because – even if expected – it was the expected unexpected. Well, this past is the transcended; but it is also the essence created behind us, which helps us (a trampoline of transcendence). We modify it ourselves in our lives, but (apart from a crisis, an adventure or an accident) generally do so *continuously*. The historical fact: Charles Bovary discovering the letters.

So it is understood that the historical event rends the past. Well, *the past* is *being* (a social determination, a priori: the worker), *essence* (conditioning of oneself by the matter one has worked), and a *pledge* (membership of a group).

Well, *being* is transformed[114] (example: de-skilling of the craft worker,

---

113. In the main text of this second volume of the *Critique*, the titles and sub-titles have all been inserted by the editor. In the fragments which follow, however, Sartre has usually himself indicated the topic on which he is reflecting: only words between square brackets represent editorial additions.

114. In the margin of this sentence, Sartre noted: 'History = feedback. The effect transforms its cause.'

technological unemployment, etc., etc., through the transformation of worked matter). The *essence* is reversed: the matter worked by me assumes another meaning in the context. The anarcho-syndicalist trade unions, discovering the masses and their impotence in 1914, grasped themselves as not having been able to adjust, as having functioned ineffectually when they had thought they were functioning to full effect (bad faith: the truth was that in some way they had not been functioning all that well). In a word, changes to the world – exterior to me – transform me in my essence, which is an inner relationship (a negation retaining within itself in order to transcend). For example, it was the appearance of the masses singing the *Marseillaise* that stupefied the trade-union leaders and changed them. But they had not *made* those masses, and the masses did not act directly upon them. As for the *pledge*, they were not *released* from it, yet they were no longer obliged to fulfil it, since it was *impossible* to fulfil it. A choice: you will do what you swore to all the same (implicit pledge by Challe to the insurrectionists in January 1960:[115] 'Go home, Algeria will remain French'): you stick to it, in order to assert yourself. You may die (suicide): that means you affirm yourself by death as not changing. Suicide in this case = an aggressive act against History. You choose the absolute permanence of Being. Dupery: you have chosen non-being and *being-an-object-for* future History.

So the historical event appears as the exterior transforming interiority from the interior, but without any necessary action of the exterior upon exteriority (praxis-violence) and without an immediate act of interior-ization. The event comes *like a thief*. An ultimatum: either I must *be other* (and there is a good chance I will not be able to manage it), which means *make myself an other*, or I must kill myself, otherwise I shall remain in bad faith throughout my life ... The bad faith: History is absurd. An example: refusal to see decolonization (and permanent revolution) – a policy of betrayal is attributed to de Gaulle. A strange situation: one is *disqualified* and at the same time *free and powerful*. The Europeans of Algeria are *disqualified*, but they can revolt and kill. Can choose to die killing (which implies that they have lost and know it: interiorization as a negation – *in the name of being* – of the practical change). But you can also refuse to see your disqualification as *anything other than an accident* that you can change and so stand fast: betrayal, etc. You act with the feeling that you are *re-establishing the status quo* (13 May).

---

115. During the so-called 'Days of the Barricades' in Algiers – a reaction on the part of the European population to General de Gaulle's Algerian policy.

So the historical event modifies me *according to the past ek-stasis*: i.e. *in my being*.

But also in the ek-stasis of the future:

(a) The most important thing: it can destroy me or change me brutally in my inertia and my passivity. I am imprisoned. A war: I am killed. My interest: I am ruined.

(b) But also it makes me, in the praxis of the social individual, into *an other*. I become a warrior (1940), my concerns will be other: to kill, not to be killed, etc.

This may solely affect the individual in his individual life: the ruin of my parents (a social fact, but not necessarily historical in the active sense) cuts short my studies, obliges me to earn my living.

(c) But, above all, I am involved in a changed society and one that gives itself other aims. So I change.

Case of the man of the Left (an SFIO socialist) transformed by the general movement of History into a reactionary, albeit remaining what he is. Case of the Second International trade unionist (a craft worker). Case of the craft worker and his means of action: a limited strike, because he is needed; but – with specialized machines – a strike without power. While the masses find *their own* riposte, there is no longer any specific remedy for the craft worker. His strike becomes a trap, which hastens de-skilling and technological unemployment. So all that remains is to become like a new man. Try to get by, invent practices in a transformed practical field.

(d) But the free practical organism is himself affected. As a rule he has freedom to adapt, *on condition* that he systematically and dialectically carries out the liquidation *being, essence, pledge*. If he does not do so in time, he passes into another social category (example: reactionary, or *less* left-wing). In this position, however, his interests and needs lead him to perform acts and defend causes which can no longer be such: reason leads him to use arguments which are obsolete. A real transformation *through transformation of the practical field*. In other words: his obligations oblige him to seek arguments or practical defences which are no longer there. He has become *stupid*. And yet he may remain brilliant, impressive: people do not see his objective stupidity (which is interiorized – he does not see it either).

This radical transformation is *real* (decline in purchasing power, mobilization, etc.) and *material*: for its source is always, more or less directly, transformations of worked matter. An example: German industrial expansion before 1914 leads to the imperialist struggle for markets. Hence, war. Problem posed anew after defeat – leads to World War II. With a second solution – still capitalist. Ruin of social democracy.

Inasmuch as this transformation is material, it is incomprehensible at first for individuals and ensembles: *comprehension* is praxis. But we are at the level of the practico-inert, and it is the practico-inert which transforms itself in the individual (lesser evil), and transforms the social individual and even the free practical organism. But the practico-inert is anti-dialectical and not comprehensible: it is reversal of praxis, and counter-finality. So the non-comprehensible enters into the comprehensible and the modification is an unintelligible *theft*.

At the same time, it is an *apparition of the Other* (for example: advancement of the Arabs) as an other: i.e. the Other I become for myself springs from the revealed existence *of others*. Of course, alienation is daily (example: a worker). But the change of alienation comes from others (a mobilized worker).

Lastly, I am myself responsible and I feel it (the settlers in bad faith). In a certain way, I produce the exterior object which comes upon me like a thief and I grasp myself as producing it (even on the Left: the generals' revolt[116] was a reaction to an action that had comprehended the virtual certainty of that revolt).[117]

---

116. In Algiers, in April 1961.

117. Compare this with what Sartre says about the historical event in *L'Idiot de la famille*, vol. 3, p.434. The three volumes of that work are interesting to read as a complement to the *Critique of Dialectical Reason*. In them, Sartre went more deeply into numerous themes dealt with here, especially in volume 3, where he interpreted the *objective* side of Flaubert's neurosis: i.e. what it owed to the social environment and historical events.

Time

There are several kinds in history.
1. Time of the system: capitalism.
2. Time of secondary systems: colonialism.
   If capitalism can sustain the cost of decolonization (even temporarily –
   in the long run it cannot), the secondary system is overthrown inside
   capitalism.
3. Time of general and partial *events*: Algerian War – seven years *were
   necessary*.
4. Very swift time of the April military insurrection (won or lost in three
   days), time of particular men.

Progress

I SIGNIFICATION AND MEANING IN HISTORY

(a) First resolve this question. The signification of a history is not its *meaning*. An arrested history (that of Pompeii or the Incas) has no *meaning* for us. It had one for those who lived it in interiority. It may have a *signification*: if we find the ensemble of factors that helped to arrest it. At the same time, the factors that developed it. An example: agrarian society, its ceiling reached, demographic growth (or a catastrophe, a famine), system no longer functioning (institutions no longer allowing counter-measures: stockpiling, etc.) = *signification*. Meaning = what is lived in interiority. The meaning of an agrarian society may be its *everlasting nature*. Let us be clear: an archetype, etc. (an ideology) and a practice of preservation. In other words, *meaning* is a practice setting its goal via an ideology.

Nevertheless, *meaning* may be partial (never false) or total, depending on whether it is set on the basis of a total or a partial conception of man (for example, the *meaning* of conservative histories – negating History – is partial: in them, History is made by negating itself and consequently escapes the practical and becomes part of process). Moreover, as we shall see, the total meaning is grounded upon need and the human relation. (Another example: end of the ancient world. No meaning. Or a Spenglerian meaning. Or a meaning of universal history.)

(b) Progress cannot be a *signification*: it is *lived* in interiority, a practical organization of the totalization. It is an *act*. For it includes the future (in the form of belief-will). And, at the same time, a totalizing knowledge: society *is in progress* and I continue its progress.

Whether History has a meaning: a dialectical problem.[118] To be

---

118. In order to follow the evolution of Sartre's thought regarding the relationship between dialectic and History, and regarding progress, see the 1947 *Cahiers pour une morale*, especially pp.54–71.

considered inside History, as a conception of totalization. Basically, a totalization under way = a meaning. But this is not enough: the totalization must be given as being *this particular* totalization. (Destiny. Permanence. Decadence and involution. Progress.) At the same time as being a practice, however, meaning overflows the agent: there is a dialectical rigour that escapes. I make History, like everybody, but I *am* not it: if it has a meaning, this is inasmuch as it is.[119]

II   PROGRESS IN THE USUAL PRACTICAL SENSE

De facto, whether progress exists in History or not, the fact of giving a name to the total meaning of History is an *extrapolation* of its *primary meaning*.

So what is progress (non-relative: an artist's progress is absolute, for example) but inside History?

This basic *notion* is also a knowable, comprehensible and lived reality: on the basis of the practical free organism.

In so far as the organism reproduces his life and on completing his effort finds himself *the same*, it is possible at a pinch to speak of a progress on the basis of a deterioration. But this is in order to re-establish what is. The interest of this progress (progress of digestion: people hardly speak of it in those terms) is that it shows the necessity, in order to define progress, of an original term restored in the future. The progress after deterioration of an organic ensemble is a movement towards its restoration. But the limit imposed here by restoration of the identical (in theory) causes progress to be given as *limited*. It is a passage from the identical to the identical. Hence, a means and not an end. Extrapolation, if the end is infinitely distant, makes the latter into a directing idea (in the Kantian sense) and progress into an end in itself.

Characteristics of progress:

1. A phenomenon of *direction*. Goes from x to y. Hence, observable: an organism.

(a) Nutrition and assimilation.

(b) Reproduction.

Note, however: a *recurrent* phenomenon. Hence, one *already observed on numerous occasions*. Even for reproduction: recurrence and preservation

---

119. Insertion on the back (normally left blank) of the preceding MS page:
'Does History *have* a meaning? But "having" is absurd. In reality:
  (a) History, if it exists, is the permanent possibility of a meaning for human life.
  (b) Meaning is the permanent possibility, for the man of the present, that a History exists.'

of an order; the directing elements protect the specific features. Originally: karyokinesis = *reconstitution*. Whence the idea of immortality. In case No.1 (nutrition), the aim is the *preservation of order* through an exterior change. The result, in spite of everything, is an interior change: (i) food: may be inadequate, adequate, poor or too abundant → causes disassimilation, and if it is too rich → karyokinesis; (ii) *karyokinesis*: maintenance of order, immortality, but identity becomes dual. Order is not preserved, but *recommenced*. In short, a complex fact: identity is aimed at, as against change, but achieved by change – and at once changed in its very reality. Changing to remain the same. At once, it remains the same and changes. It is *other* and the *same*. Changing to remain the same means remaining the same and changing. It is opting for change (rather than for death). The wealth of the organism comes from the fact that it is a nihilation of identity, i.e. of *inert-being*. It is inertia that is lacking, and wishes to reconstitute itself, and – instead of *being* – becomes the possible of an organism that is simultaneously all inertia and, at the same time, an absence of being: i.e. an absence of inertia.

But the *orientated process* is not of itself a progress, although it shows us the dialectic of change and the identical, at the level of the single direction.

Why? Because there is no *finality*. Even though, dialectically, we did see the end emerge at this level. For there is no perseverance of the organism in its being, since the organism *has no being*, merely a tendency to acquire its being – to be that being which it is not. So we do not have the immanent end that people suppose, but already – in part – a transcendent end. The organism in the circularity of its functions, for example, is perpetually itself (it is itself: breathing, even when it breathes out or breathes in) at whatever moment it is viewed. Yet practically it never stops changing. This means that the end is not in it, but haunts it.

2. But the *term* must really be posed *as an end*. It is not necessary to adopt this end, it is enough to *recognize* it, i.e. *comprehend* it. Analytic Reason cannot comprehend progress: it is an object of comprehension – which, of course, first means that only a *praxis* can recognize progress. In other words, progress is a *practical structure* in its dialectical completion. The progress of culture. But you can also worry about the progress of illiteracy. An end is ascribed to a serial consequence of some given policy. Actually, that is not so wrong: a counter-finality and sometimes (no elite) a finality. Enemy forces are progressing (at the cost of heavy losses) inside the country, towards the capital. In this case, an orientated process in space-time is involved (advancing at such and such a speed), but one where space is given as the dominant. (Time is crucial, and can lose or win everything for that process. But the aim is to occupy space, as quickly as possible. In the case of digestive processes, time is

crucial – restoration as fast as possible – space is the means.) Assimilation to an end: the illness is progressing (counter-finality: the illness holds its totalitary unity from the retotalizing movement of the organism).

In short, at the point we have reached:
– progress implies a practical comprehension;
– progress = comprehensive study of a praxis in development;
– progress implies a transcendent goal first set;
– progress = constituent dialectic;
– progress = contradiction between change and permanence. In fact, in this contradiction a term always escapes man *as an agent. Both* the permanence of relations must adapt to the change (but is always affected) *and* the change has to break permanent structures. Hence, at the very source (constituent dialectic) of the notion, there is in the very notion of progress the idea of something escaping action – being exteriority with respect to action and yet a result of it. We can count upon man to accomplish his aim, but something outside of him and us must (if you like) be a *favourable counter-finality.*

From this viewpoint, the tendency to isolate progress from the goal is very significant: you make progress; there is progress. In the child's upbringing, it is ultimately (given these aims) the current *praxis* which serves as a means (apprenticeship: you do the work in order to do other work). Progress is grasped not solely in some success (a problem resolved) but in its speed, decisiveness, elegance, etc. The assumption is thus: *making teaches you to make.* The tool is forged as it forges. But this signifies a certain inertia at the basis of activity (motor habits, mental schemata, etc.); and this inertia itself (inasmuch as it will be something *to be transcended*: both in order, via it, to manage the next exercise, and in order to transcend yourself via the exercise towards a new complex of schemata and set-ups) becomes a *moment* of progress. Similarly, progress will manifest itself inside the practical field through every moment of the reorganization. A tool is made at every moment of the operation; a certain state (recorded labour) of the inert, bringing the tool closer to its end, represents a moment of progress.

3. Progress is originally the *fact of direction*, the orientated process called *labour*, grasped in its development. But this implies, at the very level of the free practical organism, that progress is *dialectical*: i.e. that the only technique of progress is *contradiction*.

(a) Direct meaning of praxis:
practical field,
contradictions through determination, etc.

(b) Temporally:
if there is progress, there is an irreducibility of change, i.e. of one moment to the preceding moment: not an irreversibility (for you can

undo what you have done) but an inability to assert the identity of M_1 with M. No causality. A dialectic. And non-retrogradability: you can return to 0, but you are no longer the same. In every sense. Hence, ontological non-retrogradability and irreducibility, in the sense of *knowledge* and *reality*.[120]

So progress cannot – except in very particular instances, and above all as a momentary determination – present itself as continuous growth. The fact of moving from one point to another (a simple growth-curve) cannot characterize a progressive process: that would be to forget counterfinality. Practical field. Worked matter. Counter-finality (expenses; or else, by acting upon a given element, you make some other element more fragile, etc.). Reduction of counter-finality. Return to the task, but obligation to *compensate*. In short, constant control, constant *correction*. Even if you know in advance the moments of labour, the counterfinalities that will develop, and the means to reduce them, it will nevertheless be necessary to carry out the operation anew, dialectically. Even if the circumstances are still the same. (But that is an abstract: in fact, they are always new in some way.) But how to know that a new (and perhaps stronger) contradiction will bring you closer to your goal? You know it if the operation has already been carried out. Or if you can *see ahead*.

Regarding dialectical predictability: it is not, like analytic predictability, the projection into the future of the present invariant system. The latter is necessary (with its mathematical apparatus), but true prediction retains it within itself: it is a reasoned invention of the future. On the basis of relatively fixed structures, and of invariant and combined elements. But, above all, on the basis of an 'idle' *practical* movement, by an *abstract* operation producing an abstract future.

In other words, the dialectical future is alone capable of justifying prediction: in order to be other and the same, I cast myself towards a future that already reveals itself as the same and other. The irreducibility of the new would make prediction impossible, if my relation to the coming new were not already an irreducibility. In short, if the practical organism were not its own future. Or, if you like, if the dialectical

---

120. See, in vol. 1, a critique of the Cartesian notion of time as a *homogeneous continuum* – such as is still accepted, according to the author, by contemporary Marxism – and of the conception of progress which such a notion determines: 'Dialectic as a movement of reality collapses if time is not dialectical ... Marxism caught a glimpse of true temporality when it criticized and destroyed the bourgeois notion of "progress" – which necessarily implies a homogeneous milieu and co-ordinates which would allow us to situate the point of departure and the point of arrival. But – without ever having said so – Marxism has renounced these studies and preferred to make use of "progress" again for its own benefit.' (*The Problem of Method*, pp.91–2.)

movement were not originally the lived relationship of the irreducible, predicted future (i.e. made present to me, without leaving the future and abstraction), inasmuch as it creates the present through determination of the past. X is going to leave Y. He *foresees* his regret. But to foresee, here, is not to know: it is already to experience, as an emotional abstract, the irreducible novelty of his solitude. I have taken a negative example as being simpler, but positive ones abound. In other words: *in interiority*, quantity is transformed into quality. Simply because it is interiorized. The increased quantity is thus predictable by analytic Reason, on the basis of precise data. But through it (because dialectical Reason maintains unity) the qualitative transformation must itself be *foreseen*: i.e. *experienced*.

The time of History is a *dialectic*. But it is a *constituted dialectic*.

To foresee the present = to comprehend the present as it will appear in the future. To effect the reclassification of forces that will be implemented in itself (by placing oneself inside).[121]

4. Internal contradiction of progress.

Progress is necessarily a *totalization*. For it is pursuit of the restoration or establishment of a totality (the organism restores itself, in order to remain whole). A student advances towards interiorization of a knowledge that is a totality.

Let us take this example. We know:

(a) that he will never succeed, should that totality exist;

(b) that this totality does not exist outside the permanent totalization of totalizations;

(c) that during his study, achieved science (assumed to be total) is transcended by developing science (which is not taught);

(d) that the student wants the science only in order to transcend it (for example, as a scientist, he wants to go further) and not merely in order to apply it.

For this *very reason*, however, every new degree of progress represents the totalization of acquired knowledge by that which has just been acquired. The new knowledge includes within it all the old forms of knowledge that illuminate the new. The new knowledge is a totalization of all the old forms set in motion by the resolution of the new problem, which assumes something more in addition. Conversely, the novelty illuminates the old forms of knowledge: the fundamental is in the future, because it is the total. The original foundations are abstract. In reality, there is always a *circularity*: the new turns back upon the old, which conditions it. 'Feedback.' But circularity = totalization; praxis = totalization. The enemy Army's progress towards the capital implies

---

121. This paragraph is on the back of the preceding MS page.

organization of the conquered provinces. The fall of the capital is aimed at as a negative totalization (disappearance of the means of defence); and also – positively – as a total occupation, or (Paris 1940) the equivalent of a total occupation (with the industrial and developed zone in Army hands).

This totalization is at once a totalizing reorganization of the practical field, and a totalization of the time of the practical operation. The operation as such has always *become*: i.e. the present praxis, as a temporal development, envelops the past praxis within it. But immediately – in human progress, i.e. progress *towards an end* – the end achieved (*Madame Bovary* written) is in no way the realization pure and simple of the pro-jected end. It is its totalization *with* all the totalizations of totalizations which have been its moments. In such a way that

the contradiction of progress

is that

prediction is necessary: the end is pro-jected in order to be achieved, and, in a certain manner, something is known, something is pro-jected; from another angle, however, the prediction – the original pro-ject or end – is itself retotalized by the end achieved and thus can in no way predict its concrete retotalization. It predicts that it will be retotalized, but not how.

So *in progress* we go towards what we want (goal) and what we could neither want nor predict (totalizing end).

Furthermore, labour transforms us and we arrive other at the pursued end.

But how to judge, in such conditions, whether there is progress, since we know schematically in the abstract – but do not know in its total concrete reality – the end which turns back upon the project, in order to absorb it and illuminate it otherwise? In order to give ourselves – become other – another illumination of ourselves having an abstract project at the outset?

Here we find all the difference that separates the process of *direction* (going from the organism to the organism – where all this exists, but enveloped) from *progress* (as a passage by human praxis from its abstract goal to its realization). Progress does not *restore*, it *institutes*.

So we arrive at the following first conclusion.

Progress *is never a restoration*. If it exists, it is as orientated change. And this *real* change (constant irreducibility, irreversibility) takes place towards a term that the free practical organism can know only in part. This term, at the same time as it realizes the original prediction-intention, envelops and transcends it by *totalizing* it – with all the subsequent moments that are irreducible to it (temporality) and with all its results (inscribed in matter) – and by *incarnating it* (contact with the world, unforeseen results). It is already not entirely [a restoration] for the organism itself. For the restored term, despite everything, implies a change (as we have seen), and besides, there is a practical action in the fact (for example) of eating. You transform the field: e.g. you cancel the surrounding food, and compel yourself – as a pure organism – to abandon the place or die (animal migrations).

In this case, however, how do you determine whether you are going towards realization, or towards (for example) death or a lesser being? Who says that what you *want* – no longer existing, other than as a partial structure, in what you will have done – will not be a change such that: (a) in the simplest case, it contradicts the schematic beginning; (b) in the more complex case, it creates a practical individual radically different from the one existing at the beginning? In other words, what element of comparison will ensure that you decide you are getting closer to a goal, such as it was originally given?

If there is *repetition*, progress may be noted: *I foresee the past.* Hunting or gathering: repetition of the act. Known consequences. If there is innovation (the hunter moves territory): impossible to be entirely sure of the result. Change of hunting grounds, change of weapons: unforeseen consequences *to be totalized* (I am not even thinking about incarnation – action of the world – but about elements of the circuit: appearance of some different mode or other). Introduction of the slave (for a family) = progress, but transforms its internal structure. Appearance of trade and trading posts for the Eskimos = progress and also destruction. The Danish economy is introduced into the circuit. The reproduction of life (a direct relationship between you, your labour in the environment, and your self) gives way to the indirect relationship: I produce for the other (division of labour), who – in exchange – conditions me (rudimentary colonization). I change my hunting (walrus, seal, bear $\rightarrow$ fox, formerly despised because its meat is poor). I enter the circuit of *profit*; i.e. these *pelts* are sold not for the needs of others, which would still have been direct, but for the profit of some people in a developed society where the satisfaction of needs is always *indirect*, as a (hidden) economic motor, and where accumulation allows luxury (i.e. symbolic, rather than productive or reproductive) expenditure. Who shall say if this is progress? And from what point of view? However, it might be said that *if need is satisfied more easily, and if this is the aim*, studying the standard of living allows one to pronounce. *Cf.* Eskimos: standard of living higher than an unskilled worker's? But are such comparisons really possible? Do they have any meaning? Furthermore, is this change that will liquidate the superstructures (Christianity, money) an advance in this domain (pauperization)? Lastly, does the change of diet (albeit limited) not destroy the organism?

The example must be taken up individually. On the basis of trading posts being set up, let us imagine a family head tempted to exploit their advantages: the idea of *improvement*.

In this sense, for the person who has historical awareness at the outset, progress becomes no longer maintenance by the act but a positive transformation of the practical field by me, of me by my totalizing effort, and of me by the practical field, leading to transformation of myself and the field in such a way that, between this new being and this new field, the relations will be better than between me and my field.

But this presupposes a hazard – an element continually eluding me – given that, even thus, positive (purely positive) improvement is a gamble. Also, a calculation of the new counter-finalities.

No matter. What may it be, this relationship with *something other* than me and my field, which is none the less *me and my field*?

Two aspects:

1. the most common: changing to stay the same. Here again, two aspects:

(a) the field's resources increase, but also its counter-finalities – or its resources change. I preserve the relationship: changing to stay the same. The image of change may be supplied to me by others, without my appreciating the consequences (1830: purchase of machines).

Enlargement of the field   situation I   situation II

Narrowing of the field

(b) The field's resources diminish. [Conditions] tougher. So I invent a tool; or I make (marginal) sacrifices to remain alive – or what I was. It may move towards *regression*: I change by diminishing, in order to keep the minimum of what I call *me* (perhaps the simple life).

2. Changing to improve yourself: in power, in efficacy, or in interiorized qualities (knowledge, etc.).

(a) Negative:

This is still simple. The situation is unacceptable. An unacceptable practical field, because – for example – food is inadequate (I emigrate, I ruin my neighbour, I invent a tool). Comprehensible, because I move from the non-human to the human. An out-of-work Italian from the South, I leave Italy or go up to the North, because I am *other* than an enforced idler; because – as a man – I consider myself a *worker*. Because I want to realize my possible, which is to work and reproduce my life. So I go to Milan. But in Milan I am proletarianized (if I used to be a peasant) and northernized. *Rocco and his Brothers*:[122] *uprooting*. An

---

122. Film by Visconti (1960).

unpredictable transformation. The person who ends up there *will make me into an other*, at the same time as realizing the possible that I am.

(b) Positive:

This is the hardest to grasp. Basically: I take advantage of favourable circumstances to increase my potency, my efficacy, my assets, beyond what (see *1.* (a) above) would be necessary – in a milieu in growth – to maintain me such as I am (changing to be the same). *Changing to become other.*

Reasons:

1. It is perhaps circumstances themselves which oblige me to do it. *The new incarnation* in the practical field does not allow me to remain the same any longer. It is necessary to disappear, or else to become much more effective – much more powerful – in the new society than you were in the previous one. The process embarked upon implies abandoning, one by one, all the set-ups and all the structures that made me what I was; and furthermore acceding, *in* the society itself, to a *new* level of power, wealth, etc. I buy a machine, but competition operates in such a way that this is not enough. If I buy several, I beat my competitors but find myself at the head of a large enterprise. To protect my interests I become quite other, with other interests and an other fragility.

2. The main [reason]:

Contradiction in us between repetition and change. Our person is sanctioned at the outset by recurring feasts – repetition. For example: I am my birthday, or my name day. I am French and 14 July. It is sanctioned at the same time by rites of passage, which integrate development as being my essence. Initiation. Marriage, etc. In firms, promotion. The source is the biological movement of the organism; and integration into a society for which my education is a *cost*, and which consequently wants the expenditure to have a return and pushes for more and more integration. I must move from one (maintained) state to the other (as a producer, or at any rate a worker – liberal if not manual). Even this is a *repetition*: the common ensemble, today as yesterday, needs manual workers with the same technical ability (assuming that, over a short cycle, techniques do not change – or barely so). And the child already knows he is going to *repeat* (his father, or the people of his father's generation). At the same time, however, he has to *change himself in order to repeat* (apprenticeship, etc.) and the change brings him into a certain ambiguous position. It makes him become what he is: i.e. gives him the (past) essence of his predecessors as a future. At the same time (diachronic element) it posits in the form of an essence (a transcended past) a less determined future, whose origin comes from the (interiorized) contradictions between the teaching of science and technical innovations. So he will be beyond his past essence: he will transcend it towards

himself (actualization). This *himself* is an essence, but constituted contradictorily by a past being (that of fathers) and a possible. The possible is
beyond the transcended being; but although rigorously given as a *transcendence towards*, it does not have the precision of being. It envelops that
precision, transcends it and keeps it, and moves towards a state of greater
precision: well defined *inasmuch as it will be greater precision*, but in
reality indeterminate (precision of instruments: but *which ones?*, etc.).

In short, in so far as the child changes to be the same (as his father) he
will affirm his possibility *of being other*, inasmuch as he is beyond his
father to the extent that the emergent techniques are beyond the old ones.

It goes without saying that this incipient movement can be carried out
only in certain classes and at certain moments. The young worker, before
being a revolutionary and in a period of technical stagnation, sees before
him his father's destiny recommenced. That can happen in the bourgeois
class (see Nizan). In short, his destiny is his father's past (combination
of the two ek-stases: future and past). This may bring about a *rupture*,
through a rejection of Destiny. But then, a rejection of oneself: oneself –
that was the possible beyond being; by breaking one's being, however,
one finds oneself on the naked path of one's own relation with the
indetermination of a possible. What to become?

So we have:

1. continuously appearing progress (transcendence without contradiction). In reality, contradiction is instantly given in the negation of the
already given being. In a word, the *self* of a child is the negation through
transcendence of the roles that constitute the essence he is given (his
father's being);

2. catastrophic progress: the negation of Destiny drives you to break
the essence rather than transcend it (you do both: you break, but you
preserve). Nizan retaining to the end a relationship with his father that
ultimately manifested itself in his break with the Party (1939): rediscovers
his alienation. However, the broken essence ceases to be an element of
direction; between the past alienation and the new alienation, there is a
transcendence without any clear determination.

In other words, continuity is never really continuous – discontinuity
presupposes continuous transcendence or, if you like, presupposes references of continuity.[123]

But above all, from the outset, there is an ontological interiorization of
the organic development, through *negation* and preservation in tran-

---

123. In *L'Idiot de la famille*, vol. 3, pp.434–43, Sartre carries on his meditation on the
interplay of the continuous and the discontinuous in history – no longer simply at the level
of the child and the previous generation, but now considering the succession of generations.

scendence: of itself, the organism is a system in progressive, then regressive, development. The regression is grasped only dimly at the outset: the child fears death but not old age. Even the adult finds it hard to imagine. Trotsky: old age is the most unpredictable event that can happen to man. He meant that forces in mid development cannot transcend themselves towards the prediction of their regression (it is on the basis of an incipient regression that it becomes possible for downcast spirits to foresee their decrepitude). So the child conceives change towards the plenitude of his being (when I'm grown up, etc.). At that moment he is going (see *Being and Nothingness*[124]) towards his being (already alienated: 'What will you be when you grow up?' 'I'm going to be an admiral, a boxer, a pilot', etc.), or perhaps: 'I want to *be* Chateaubriand and nothing else.' Role of identification with the father, or of *models*. At this level, being (in itself and for itself) becomes the regulating idea of change. It orientates transcendence. It alienates. At the same time: violent negativity (contradictions, etc.). Impossibility for Flaubert to identify with his father as his elder brother does. These two aspects are linked: profound negativity of socialized facticity. *Socialized facticity*: not only am I not the foundation of my own existence, I am not even that of its social predeterminations. Example: for young Algerians since the Constantine massacre,[125] impossibility of demanding integration (not just out of resentment, but through disintegration of the concept); instead, they were (and other generations still more so) conditioned to demand independence and the nation by their fathers' defeat. However, at the same time they have been formed by previous circumstances and assimilation. Hence, catastrophic progress induced by consequences. What is left? Ambivalence towards France. With every Frenchman who sees them as brothers, they have a feeling of brotherhood. And at the same time *socialized facticity* = future. Their future: a future of change and repetition. And within, novel transformations of the situation (technology, Constantine massacre, etc.).

It is the ensemble of this catastrophic side (a negation of socialized facticity) and of this repetitive but actually changing side (a realization of socialized facticity by apprenticeship, and disparity between the situation foreseen by the fathers and that lived by their children) which constitutes *progress*, as a march towards everyone's *being* (at once determined and indeterminate).

Synthetic organization of the whole:

---

124. *Being and Nothingness*, pp.124 ff. and 566 ff.
125. The reference is to the harsh repression of the riots which occurred in the Constantinois in May 1945.

(a) Biological change gives (maturation) identity as a *reason* for change (a rule). It is the structure itself of progress. *Nature*.

(b) Upon this fundamental structure, every *culture* is built. *Apprenticeship*, exercise, rite of passage. Along with the myth that man is the *adult* (an equilibrium until the beginning of old age).[126] Hence, social life and technical life upon the biological temporal structure. But entirely socialized (hence, transformed). Result: progress = *movement towards oneself*, but a self in perpetual retreat. An attempt, in reality, at realizing *socialized facticity*. Roles, attitudes, set-ups, knowledge. Aim: I'm going to be a doctor, etc. Essence of the *past* adult to be realized in the future.

(c) Within the a priori givens (essence of the adult, set-ups, etc. + a priori determinations of the child by family and social structures), the true *negation*. Negation of the given as self-assertion. Hence, identification with the father, and rejection of the identification; apprenticeship, and escape from apprenticeship towards the assertion of a self who is other.

(d) Technical inequalities (differences between the transcended world taught to him and the present and evolving world), grasped as means to transcend socialized facticity towards his own being (accepts socialized facticity: I'm going to be a doctor, but this doctor is going to be better).

The ensemble – through actions and reactions, all comprehensible – thus constituting the singular progress of everyone towards himself.

Of course, this must be in a class and at a historical moment in which the advances of technology and science are directly utilizable. Whence *a circularity*: the origin of social progress must be sought in *individuals in progress*. And, conversely, the very idea of *personal* progress – its original impetus – must be sustained by social progress (a society of repetition without technological progress = suppression of progress. Progress = passage from potentiality to the act. Nothing more).

So the fact that *some* people can be defined as progress towards themselves depends upon social progress, and refers us to it. Conversely, however, social progress must be to individual progress as the organization (with its dialectical reason and its practico-inert) is to the practical organism.

Example of progress: Verdi.

(a) Free progress in the sense of *development* of the system up to about 1870.

(b) From *Don Carlos* onwards:

---

126. See *L'Idiot de la famille*, vol. 3, p.12.

Threats to him $\left\{\begin{array}{l}\text{Wagner}\\\text{Chamber music}\\\text{Musical internationalism}\end{array}\right.$

Response:

He is, for himself, assimilable to the Nation (Risorgimento. *Viva Verdi* = Long live King Victor Emmanuel).

And since politics is linked to music (a basic element): musical nationalism. Theatre and *bel canto*.

His ideological interest: to be the national representative of Italy, seen as *bel canto* and theatre. Minimal role of the orchestra. His interest (himself as an inert reality in danger: his *œuvre*) is musical nationalism: no foreigners, secondary role for the orchestra. Hence, in the first place negative: a sharp check. A marked contradiction: Wagner the symphonic and Gounod the intimist.

But, precisely, *to save* his interest is to integrate the contradiction into the work: *Don Carlos*. Hence, *progress*. What does this mean? He wants to keep lyricism and singing. That is the vital thing. But it is necessary to integrate harmony (ponderousness of *Don Carlos*) and develop the role of the orchestra. If he were to subordinate the voice to the instrument, he would simply change and become a Wagnerian. But wanting to subordinate the instrument to the line in order to enrich it, he creates a new tension (*Otello*) and thus *progresses*: for the preserved unity is enriched (increased complexity in the tension and order). Thence, a new meaning sought: 'total opera', which is modern but *Italian* (i.e. voices predominate).

In sum: a spontaneous progress, which could in itself have led him (though less profoundly) to break the barrier between aria and recitative (as early as *Il Trovatore* and *La Traviata*), but in addition *forced* progress: changing and enlarging himself in order to remain the same while developing the orchestra. On that basis, a synthesis (*Falstaff*): the role of the orchestra, its dialogue with the characters, is more effective still at allowing the integration and disappearance of the recitative.

Interest (my inert reality, my seal) is in danger. Progress consists in preserving it as a regulatory ideal (it is my *project*), by introducing into it external modifications that risk destroying it. Progress: interiorizing the adversary in an undertaking which transforms interest (work *done*) into an end (asserting it again by integrating the remainder without causing it to explode).

An example to be given – for changing to stay the same.

III SOCIAL PROGRESS

Societies without progress: they need to be taken into account first. They are:

societies without history (repetition)

societies which deny their history (a past superior to the present): agrarian societies, for example.

These societies are *either* without real progress (the first kind) *or* have not reached any awareness regarding progress.

But *in addition*

these societies *as such* are not necessarily constituted so that progress would affect them.

Societies investing 5 per cent in the production of industrial goods,

societies *having reached a ceiling* (with agricultural production having reached a ceiling, *given existing techniques*),

societies in regression (production having reached a ceiling → demographic growth).

These societies cannot progress. Progress can be established only on *their ruins*. This means that another society with other structures (and sometimes, in part, with the same men) is established on the ruins of the former. And that it is *better*. Or (more accurately) *more advanced* in the direction of the final term.

In the light of this, two questions are posed:

1. Who originally fixed the term?

2. Who benefits from progress?

3. Progress over a short cycle – long-term progress.

Problems:

1. Comparison [between] continuous growth curve and real curve (Vilar). Progress over short cycles not admissible. In fact, *contradictions*. Passing from one contradiction to another: what is progress, if the next one is more catastrophic (where is the progress in the passage from slaves to capitalism?) Economic, yes. But human (for those people)? Progress over long cycles, very well. But:

2. In that case, what is *the subject* of the progress? Who are the people making progress? Or who benefit from the progress?

3. In the short cycle, counter-finalities do not allow us to *calculate* progress. [The problem] has to be envisaged from the standpoint of the long cycle. In that case, however, progress eludes man: (i) because it cannot be foreseen over a long range. We can say today that the appearance of mechanization was a progress. But contemporaries? We can conceive of a fact of contemporary progress today, but that is because we have discovered progress. Progress is our myth.[127] (ii) Because it is constituted, at least partly, by the interplay of counter-finalities that are not our own: in other words, inasmuch as matter serves as a mediation between men. (iii) Because the men who will benefit from progress will be other than those who are victims of a catastrophe: the increase in wages caused by the Plague certainly constitutes a progress (from the very general standpoint of humanism) – but not for the workers whom the Plague killed. Does progress = a natural dialectical necessity, or an action of praxis?

4. What is the aim of the orientated movement? Who can decide that it is this or that? And how?

Social problem of progress. Conclusion: the answer is in the question – which makes it hard to grasp progress; which masks it, or constantly brings it into question, or deprives it of all possibility? The organization of need → labour → practico-inert → counter-finalities/alienations. Which makes progress genuine: the same organization of factors, but seen differently.

Science and Progress

Reason for the progress of science: it has to do with pure exteriority grasped as pure exteriority. Hence, quantity. But also the possibility of accumulating (which presupposes dialectical unity: you do not accumulate without a tension of the field). In a word, progress comes from a relationship in exteriority within a relation. Transition from the ancient world (which is already imbued with it) to the modern world: a reversal of dialectical interiority into exteriority. (The phenomenon of the *natural bond*: interiority. The phenomenon of exteriority: if it goes up, that is because it is pushed). Analytic Reason, etc. Will science always remain like that (problem of the dialectic of Nature)? Impossible to know. Mathematics deals with everything, you will say. Yes, but in exteriority: provided you exteriorize. In short, science is exteriority itself disclosing itself everywhere.

Science: a dialectical invention of exteriority. How?

It is contained in the moment of inertia of the organism, subsequently

---

127. With respect to the myth of Progress as alienation, linked to the industrial revolution, consult *L'Idiot de la famille*, vol. 3, pp.272–84: 'Interest thus manifests itself to the owner as a twofold alienation: to others, through manufacture; to manufacture, through all the others. It is profit, as man's objective truth and an inhuman necessity; it is the inexorable obligation to advance ... '

transposed by the tool: an exteriorization of inertia which is transformed into an inertia of exteriority (homogeneity: the tool can be wielded only by an organism *making itself passive*). Science (anthropology itself) is the exploration in exteriority of exteriority. Why *in exteriority*? It is necessary from the start to act from the exterior upon the exterior to interiorize it. A moment of pure exteriority: the organism making itself inert in the face of the inert, in order to seek the inert means to wield through its inertia. This practical moment is precisely also the moment of nascent analytic Reason: a totalizing organism, whose aim is to reinteriorize its totalization, makes itself exterior in order to interiorize the exterior. And, at that moment, the totalizing unity of interiority seemingly gives way to exteriority, but remains as the directing schema of the transformation. So dialectical Reason directs the scientific operation, but gives way to *analysis*. Science is given at the outset: a practical investigation of exteriority, inasmuch as I am exterior to it. The fact that in micro-physics one discovers an interiority of the experimenter to the experiment is certainly striking, but does not modify the general idea. The fact is, if you like, that at a certain level praxis is discovered (the luminous ray changes the movement of the atom), but only in its results of exteriority. It merely reveals that our exteriority is a moment of the interiorization of the practical field. Hence, (i) a tendency to interiorization: an immediately dialectical tendency (anthropomorphism), called observation; (ii) this tendency is always combated by the need and search for tools (higher apes): the former, in fact, comes from a kind of perceptive interiorization of the field. We grasp it as an organism through our own. Hence, modifications appear *organic*. But decomposition by praxis: need is already a conditioning by the outside, and negation is to condition the outside by need. All this refers back to the very level of the organism that is constituted by the inert and the exterior (chemical products) and is of itself a totalization of this exterior (an orientated maintenance of relationships, exchanges, the metabolism, etc.). So the child grasps dialectical Reason and analytic Reason *at their source*. Examples of scientific exteriority: they are nothing but *practical* elements – a transformation into something else. This means a constant struggle against the tendency to give a synthetic and interior coherence (a circle) to the exterior. For the aim is: how *in inertia* to act *upon inertia*: hence, to cut up inertia, to see it as exterior to itself, to eat into it. Hence, to show it as other than itself. A circle cannot have the coherence of a circle unless it is practical (inasmuch as it is traced). But this movement in space explodes into points in the very movement which follows the line. And thereafter an explanation has to be given for those points, suppressing the earlier movement and considering them as outside one another.

So the movement of science, as soon as exteriority becomes aware of itself, is in continuous progress (not necessarily the total *practical* movement, which for its part is the dialectical ensemble of this movement and its exploitation with the result: a practico-inert). Science is the permanent dissolution of the practico-inert into its element of pure inertia. In that sense, it is the non-dialectical remedy for the anti-dialectic (hence, a liberation of the dialectical movement). In the practico-inert, it sees only the inert. The inert is a pure quantity. [Science] is inertia seen by itself (in reality, by a *made* inertia: real but disengaged).

In other words,

as soon as I transform the inert by the seal of praxis, it becomes practico-inert: ranged against me by the inert's turning back of praxis into a negative. But if I maintain it in its inertia, while preserving the simple unity of the research, it is given as inert and the new elements discovered are given only as inert – and in exteriority with respect to it. This means that they collapse into inertia, and consequently divide up (analysis) once I am pure inertia of exteriority in relation to them. On this basis, there is accumulation. At once by new domains (in the practical field) being conquered for the inert, and by division of the conquered inert (division by itself). However, permanently practico-inert character of scientific conquest: numbers are qualitative, inasmuch as they are totalized in the practical field. [The figure] 3 is a magical singularity (as a consequence of praxis); but remove the latter, be exterior, and the singularity collapses. Thus, in the practical field, Engels is right and quantity becomes quality. Conversely, however, it must be said (this is dialectical too) that every quality can be resolved into a quantity. In other words, the qualitative moment (unification of the purely quantitative into the practico-inert: machines, etc.) is a practical product of accumulation, and immediately disassimilable by a return to the quantitative. This is what explains the paradox of quality: measurable or non-measurable? Answer: never measurable *as quality*, but measurable the moment before and after. Necessarily linked to the measurable, but on the basis of a decision of exteriority.

Science and praxis: science is the moment when the residue of praxis is no longer considered as practico-inert, but as pure inertia of exteriority. In that sense, the vicissitudes of praxis creating the practico-inert can condition science: it creates new objects (with counter-finality), but for science these are objects that it gives to be dissolved. First numbers – then measurements and mathematics – then measuring instruments.

Science progresses by contradictions. But it remains inert in relation to these contradictions: the irrational number. It is not changed (praxis), it is christened, thereby breaking a mythical pseudo-unity of numbers. In such a way that contradictions are resolved in favour of the greatest exteriority, the greatest inertia.

The irrational number does not become *a thing* because it has been named: it remains the mere passive negation pitted by inertia against a human totalization. Of course, it can be unified as a counter-totalization (made *by man*), like the *fiendish* chords people speak about in music. But [this counter-totalization] will also be broken. Not in favour of a wider totalization that would be *number* (imaginary *and* real, finite *and* transfinite, rational *and* irrational, etc.) but in favour of a constant maintenance of non-human inertia as apprehended by human inertia.[128]

In science, man makes himself into pure matter in order to be a non-*practical* mediation (non-intentional, non-totalizing) between two states of matter.

Science is always *open*, since it does not totalize in its current state. The scientist totalizes in spite of himself (praxis), but not science, which explodes his totalization. And this *openness* results in its permanent progress. Accumulation – no scientific counter-finality.

Progress in science is straight – axial – certain, because the inertia of the known is communicated to knowledge (under dialectical control) and this exteriority, maintained at the heart of the practical field by a fictive and totalizing destruction of the practical field itself (one of its avatars given from the practical beginning: the organism making itself into inertia envisages the elements of the field that will assist its inertia – as an inert), engenders organization in exteriority – i.e. accumulation – as an ensemble of knowledge. At least for a long while: grand hypotheses are the organization in exteriority of the exterior, but they arise after millennia. The original system is an inert system: the law = an outline of inertia as a practical element to be found. $Y = f(x)$ originally means: upon what inertia should I act, in order to accomplish my aim? The inert in exteriority sought by praxis is precisely the independent variable. This is on all levels. Gandhi looks in inertia at the caste system and seeks the independent variable: it is the caste of Untouchables. Not that this is not a result of the whole system; but, for that very reason, if you act upon it – which though created by the system supports and maintains its frame-work – the lot comes down. At all events, $y = f(x)$ is exteriority. If x changes to a specific extent, y changes to an equally specific extent.

The contradiction of science (a *propulsive* contradiction) is precisely between its dialectical unity and its analytic accumulation. A twofold contradiction. On the one hand, to be sure, all scientific progress destroys a partial totalizing unity – hence, avoids *the practico-inert*: i.e. the anti-dialectic. On the other hand, however, the unity of scientific praxis (i.e. praxis reduced to unity) is that of the practical field, and imposes

---

128. Paragraph added subsequently on the back of the preceding MS page.

accumulation (i.e. the quality of quantity) within the interior of this field (accumulation of known zones – accumulation of knowledge).

Science appears, from the first human action, as the theoretical moment of practical action. But this theoretical moment has the same structure as the practical moment as a whole: inertia seeking the inert. At this level, however, the totalizing element (the drive, the end) masks the aspect of inertia, just as – in the act as a whole – praxis masks *pathos* (a finger pressing a button is a button which presses the finger). The moment of science is praxis going back over its theoretical moment to suppress the false totality, and to specify the moment of inertias by this rejection of totalization. Science is praxis asserting itself through the search for conditionings in exteriority; $y = f(x)$: if I do this, that happens.

[*Abundance, Progress, Violence*]

The man of scarcity, seeking his abundance, seeks it as a determination of scarcity. Not abundance for all, but his own, hence the deprivation of all. The initial aspect −n individuals; enough food for $n - 2$; hence, possible exclusion of the 2, or constitution of a group sharing $m - 2$ food out among m members (undernourishment) – is only a theoretical aspect. The man of scarcity does not remain in the category that would be $n - m$ (this category being $n - m$ people eating $n - m$ foodstuffs, or disposing of $n - m$ tools or means of protection). In reality, the new principle given is that certain people eat their fill, the others do not. And, of course, the minority $(n - m)$ disposes of goods, to the exclusion of the majority. So it constitutes itself of its own accord as *scarce*. Scarcity moves from this moment of satisfaction of needs to the man who satisfies them. The interiorization of scarcity in the first place gives the scarce object its *precious* character. First, really: air is not scarce, food or tools are. The tool is valorized by scarcity before being an object of exchange. Simply because it is worth stealing, winning, obtaining at the price of hardships (cost). This relationship precedes trade: a battle between tribes – the victory may *cost dear*. In short, scarce as a first value = object determining an action: i.e. a labour, whatever its modalities may be (war, or abduction, is labour). Precious = scarce object generating a praxis (it is perhaps *a means* of satisfying need: i.e. perhaps *the end*). But the minority owner of this ensemble himself thereupon becomes *scarce*. First, for the majority he is the image of the man they would like to be – the man they cannot be, without becoming a minority. In the second place, he is assimilated to the scarcity of the objects he owns. The scarce man is the one for whom socially scarce objects are abundant: he is classified as scarce from outside, by the majority. In the third place, however – here comes the mystification – this scarce man is accepted as such (whether he rules by force or is publicly invested with an office which gives him the right to own the scarce abundantly). On this basis, he interiorizes scarcity by becoming *the precious man* – and this is ambivalent: it means the man whose power is accepted, and of whom all the others are secret but sworn enemies (without necessarily admitting it). In a period of famine, the scarce man who does not have the right to be scarce (the merchant, the Jew) is massacred; the man who does have that right is not – or more rarely. The scarcity of the scarce man itself becomes a *value*, in the sense that it presents itself as worthy of an action. It is an end: it presents itself as demanding an action which will, at once, win scarce abundance and acquire that social scarcity as a right (due to merits, social role, etc.): i.e. as an exigency of being accepted by those who lack the necessary. It cannot be denied that the division of labour intervenes here. The scarce man is he who administers, while the others work (for example). He is the leader who guides the expedition (and who has more than the others: *cf*. Lévi-Strauss). Thus the interiorized scarce man feels that his scarcity is due to his wealth. He is *exceptional*, because he owns the scarce. And that exceptional value is recognized by society. Within himself the man feels like a jewel, for example – and what is more, he is called one. There is a dialectic of scarcity, which moves from the recognized ownership of goods to the recognized ownership of abilities (accumulation of cultural advantages, etc.). But at once the scarce man is shown as the exception who must live in abundance: even if he does not have abundance, he has the right to it by virtue of his scarcity. And people give themselves scarce abilities, in order to obtain scarce provisions (ambition, choice of the warrior profession: you accept what others reject – death – in order to have everything).

At once, costs go up in the owning class: everyone wants to be *scarcer*, and becomes it *in the social order*. (The oppressed class cannot *have* the scarce man; it wants to *be* him, or be blessed by his scarcity until emancipation. *To show the serfs*.)

A reversal: scarcity (modern society – saints) will consist in being worthy of everything and accepting nothing.

Thus scarcity = an *active* element of history.

Scarcity is not just *the milieu*. Becoming interiorized in the man of scarcity, it first constitutes an initial antagonistic relation between every individual and each and every other. In addition, however, it constitutes in the dominant group ambition, violence, and a determination to go to the extreme limits of the scarce. It does so, moreover, through this dialectical transposition: the man of the scarce becomes the scarce man, and is interiorized as precious.

Of course, this in no way means *individualism*. Individualism is a form of interiorized scarcity belonging to bourgeois times. It can equally well mean family scarcity or class scarcity. You are what you have. Since the family's (or individual's) being is its possessions, to possess the scarce is to be scarce. At once, the scarce group's being is in danger in the world of the inert – for it is its goods, its property. At once, the scarce property becomes the *interest* of the group in question: i.e. its being, inasmuch as this is defined in exteriority by the inertia of its possessions. But it must be understood that the original force here is *need*. Need is the primary drive. It feeds ambition. Why? Not because there is a *need* for the rich man. But underpinning his being as a rich man there is his need which can be satisfied only because he is *among the scarce people* who have rare products in their possession. Because they live *in abundance of scarcity*. In other words, in order to have sufficiency they already have to *be scarce*. A system of constraints and myths is already needed, to deter the majority (the *non-scarce*) from demanding sufficiency: in short, exploitation, oppression and mystification are needed. In a word, violence. And from this violence – which they do not remain an instant without objectively exercising (whether they are aware of this or no matters little) – springs scarcity-as-an-aim. When they want to be *scarcer*, this is *on the basis of* the original scarcity of their being, which is undernourishment of the majority. It is the violence of the majority's need that is the rich man's necessity for counter-violence. Equal counter-violence. This, moreover, simply so that he has his sufficiency. The rich man's scarcity is a violence *in actu* (even when it is exercised by others – militiamen, centurions, etc.). It is the essential nature of his satis-faction. Moreover, it represents the rich man's foundation: i.e. need satisfied by the permanence of violence, which without violence would no longer be satisfied (take away his weapons or his troops, the rich man is impotent; a stratification of violence – in exteriority and in interiority – this is the institution of his oppression and the deepest layer of his being). This exasperation of need (the majority's), which is the indispen-sable nucleus of the satisfaction of his own need – and is this as violence to be exercised without flinching – is the very force that causes a person to climb all the rungs of scarcity. On the one hand, in the very struggle to be scarcer (within the group) there is an 'all or nothing' which comes into play. It is necessary to climb (by violence) or risk returning to the level of need. Not because this happens constantly, or perhaps in the majority of cases (it is possible to stop without tumbling all the way down, to regress without leaving the rich group, or to be helped by allies – family, interested persons); but because it is the disclosed truth of the thing: the fundamental possibility that the latter implies. In the case of a struggle to be leader, no place is left for the defeated man (execution, enslavement, etc.).

Of course, this would be simply a psychological rather than a historical description, if we were not to add that the model of the scarce man is defined within the socio-economic system that has been constituted. It is the model of scarcity in the system (from scarcity of food to scarcity of time) which constitutes the interiorization of scarcity. But the problem lies elsewhere: it lies in the fact that the system would not survive without the men it constitutes, who – so far as the rich are concerned – are the system stratified and its transcendence (towards another echelon of the system). A fall in the rate of commercial profit can lead to a shift elsewhere only if the men involved are already profit-men. But this must be taken as meaning the free and permanent transcendence of interest (profit). And in order to understand that *profit* is directly linked to violence, these paradoxes must be recalled: progress towards abundance is fettered (buying oil in order to sell it at a high price, or in order not to sell it) because profit springs from the non-sufficiency of satisfaction (worker and wage) and from non-abundance. The man of profit (the capitalist and his customers, in a given period) is not feudal man (the man of land revenue); but in both cases he aspires to super-abundance, because he cannot have satisfaction *alone* without carrying on to the end of the system of scarcity.

Here, introduce everything that, in the system itself, drives him to raise himself.

The Idea
and its Historical Action

There is a history of ideas. They are not mere reflections, but action. See the meeting of the Jesuit idea (good savage) – already praxis (Council of Trent) – with the still passive idea of Nature in the bourgeoisie seeking a means to present itself as a universal class (reversal of pessimism: very important), and with the analytic notion of Reason $\rightarrow$ inertia and natural exteriority.

The representation that Christians harbour of the Jew becomes constituent of the Jew. See Poliakov: racism. Semitism (p.56, note on Massignon[129]).

The idea and the word (word: inert and material condensation of the idea; likewise syntax, language).

There is a *practico-inert of the idea*.

So the idea becomes a historical moment *of action*, as worked matter.

The word retaining the idea: a material synthesis of various (different) meanings. Poetry and materiality: poetical praxis utilizes the inert synthesis (or rather the inert contiguity of various seals imposed upon verbal matter) and makes it into a poetical synthesis – mixing historical meanings (general history, individual history) and *practical* signification.

---

129. In his *Histoire de l'antisémitisme*, vol. 2 (Paris 1961), Poliakov, ruminating on a possible 'kinship' between Jews and Arabs as a historical factor, disputes that this is of a biological nature and speaks of the linguistic kinship between the two peoples. In this connection he quotes a text by L. Massignon, a comparative analysis of the Semitic and Indo-European languages (in *Essai sur les origines du lexique technique de la mystique musulmane*).

[*The Word*][130]

The word is perpetually serializing and institutional. It is the term of the series. Its reason. And I give it *its* meaning, because others as Others give it that meaning. If the word 'flower' does not signify 'rain' for me, it is not *first* because I would not be understood, but first because the others in the series give it this meaning, which thereby escapes from me. At the same time, however, using a word is a praxis, since it tends to create a group. For the word tends simultaneously to mediate and create reciprocities. At the same time, it functions as a third party. Thus communication is effected not through the word, but by reference to the word: at once as an institution, as a direct relation to the context, and as a serialized third party. The verbal institution is the serialized third party. Which, no doubt, is what every tool in the workshop is. But the tool has a more immediately obvious practical function (because of its tangible results and its visible inertia). By means of the tool, I make myself inert to act upon the inert. By means of the word, this is less obvious. Yet, of itself, it is an institution, inertia. And the first aim is to awaken it as inertia in the other; or rather to affect the other by this word *transcending* inertia. The written word would never have been invented (a material object, a depiction on clay or stone) if the spoken word had not *already been written* (potentially). The same thing is involved: determination of a breath through structures and *hexes* (phonetics) or determination of a stone, etc. In the former case, however, the materiality is more tenuous (in the sense in which a gas can be tenuous): not visible.

Hence, a transcendent, practico-inert word is designated and designates. Inert, it marks my inertia to recall inertia in the other: I make myself inert by speaking, but in order to awaken inertia in the other. It is precisely a matter of practical activity *utilizing* inertia to transform the practical field dialectically. However: (1) the word is thus utilized *in a praxis* (even if the latter's aim is to preserve seriality and the inert); (2) it awakens the inert in the other, inasmuch as this inert may be the beginning of a praxis: *order*; (3) it suppresses reciprocity through apparition of the serialized third party. Preservative character of the word: it recalls institutions and society as a whole.

Modern poetry: an attempt to play on the materiality of the word.[131]

---

130. See also *Critique*, vol. 1, pp.98 ff.

131. In *L'Idiot de la famille*, pp. 929–34, Sartre carries out an analysis of this game, into which he integrates the imaginary: 'For me and for many other people, the Château d'Amboise is linked with words like *framboise* [raspberry], *boisé* [wooded], *boiserie* [panelling], *ambroisie* [ambrosia], and Ambroise [Ambrose]. It is not a matter here of the idiosyncratic relations which may have been forged in the course of my personal history,

Let meanings interpenetrate via the practico-inert (half inertia, half unitary seal) with the evil spell of materiality. Meanings at once united and interpenetrating, without modifying each other (instead of being pure exteriority). Kindling words by one another. In short, using the relationship between words so that each – as inert – seems to make the negative synthesis of its meanings.

---

but of objective, material relationships, accessible to any reading. As these have not been established by an act of the mind, yet they impose themselves in an indissoluble unity, they may be termed *passive syntheses*. In fact, the more you abandon yourself to dreaming, the more they emerge ... '

Totalization in Non-Dictatorial Societies

A. Synchronic

1. Each person (privileged classes) is a human pyramid.

2. Each person (exploited classes) is the base of that pyramid and constitutes it.

B. Each class constitutes the other. Error of Marxism: always to consider the exploiting class [as being] on the defensive: this is correct, but it must also be seen *as an agent.* As such, it determines *the product* (technical revolution) and, at once, its product's product. But immediately the exploited (the product's product) *make* the product and determine class: (i) inasmuch as accumulation of the product pursues the economic movement (transition from family capitalism to monopoly capitalism); (ii) inasmuch as the exploited, in that he is a certain product of the product, constitutes the exploiter as his product (defines his struggles, his relations, etc.).

C. The diachronic (we shall put it last). It is the interiorization of the practico-inert. What does being French mean? It is *History* (monumental past) as a dimension in depth, against the historical process.

D. [... [132]] as an interiorization of the viewpoints of others.

E. [...] as benefiting in common from a situation (colonies). Yes. And if they do not benefit from them – then 'proletarian nations': they make

---

132. Implied here: 'Each class constitutes the other'.

428

use of this ensemble as a myth.

In that case,

totalization-of-envelopment: wholly given everywhere that the incarnation has a relationship in exteriority with a larger incarnation. For example: incarnation as an unskilled worker and relationship with the whole working class (?).[133]

---

133. The question mark figures in the manuscript.

Plan

1. Retotalization in a dictatorial society. (Stalin.)
2. Retotalization in a non-dictatorial society. Unity and class struggle. Already, problems.
3. Retotalization of several linked histories. (History of Europe, etc. – its proletariats and its proletariat): a pure query, so long as we do not know what History is.

History, on the contrary, appeals to itself: everlastingness of History (as consciousness negating death), temporal infinity. No end. And, on the other hand: History = rigorous objectives (achieved or not) and death fought against but determining.

The constants of History: example, *death*. Without death, *another* History (or no History).

A formal problem: is the historical fact qualitatively different today and yesterday? Or the same? Problem, for example, of greater consciousness (Marx): does that change praxis? The class acts, enlightened by scientific and practical knowledge. Whereas a century ago myths, etc., obnubilated what was only intuitive prediction.

Totalization
[in a Capitalist System]

Totalization here does not mean suppression of conflicts, a mediation; it means that every conflict is the incarnation of the most general conflicts, and of unity.

What is totalization in a capitalist system? Erroneously: individuals. An individual *produces totality*.

Individuals: describe the *forces of massification* in a democracy. Work contract, etc.

In *Reply to Lefort*.[134]

Stress the existence of the interiorized *Other* in everyone.

Impossible to comprehend the status of the practical organism – as social (a common individual) – without starting from totalization. Here a *system* (capital, for example).

There is no atomic solitude.

There are only ways of being together. Solitude appears within ways of being together.

The ensemble has ways of being together [*ensemble*] at its disposal: groups – serialities (with the familiar differences internal to groups and series).

So the series, in its ensemble, is an incarnation of the system. Naturally, this occurs *on the basis of* the relationship between the ensemble and its individual members.

Circularity: the series reconditions the ensemble, as it does the existence of the reified man within it. The series is inert man: hence, man-as-worked-matter. It has a type of action inasmuch as it is inert, since the series is *qualified*; and this type of action – which is wielded like a tool – is defined by society, but defines society itself and acts upon its history.

---

134. In *Situations VII*, Paris 1965.

Hysteresis: [for example] musical instruments. Their reality *retards* the evolution of music, because they are made. They exist as such (inert). They have to be changed. But they are institutions (a collective: seriality produced among the players of these instruments).

The problem of non-totalitarian societies is, *inter alia*:
– the relationship between series and groups,
– the retotalizing factor of series,
– the historical role of the series.

There is a historical life of the series (it changes – a chain of modifications). So there is a serial transformation of institutions. Example: linguistics. As such, [the series] acts serially upon the totality in interiority. But it is itself, in its life, provoked to its serial action by the action of groups or series. So the ensemble of the system, manifesting itself as an action upon the series, results in a serial response which deforms it (even if it is *confirming*: there is always a deviation).

Example: colonies. Native serialization – demographic (agricultural) movement. The population increase is *serial*, and quantity comes from quality (a type of maintained, proletarianized society and an improvement [with respect to] mortality, lack of hygiene, etc.: represents the colonized society; an incarnation). But quantity becomes quality: lowering of everyone's standard of living. Poverty. New serial facts: emigration to France. A fact of pure quantity, but [which becomes] quality: growing difference between the colonizing group and the colonized group. More blatant injustice. Retotalized into a *group* (constituted praxis) by the native, and into a counter-group by the settler (the seriality of the settlers dissolves: a common threat, a common relationship with the metropolis). The group dissolves peasant seriality through people's war.

1. The system is invented, conceived and put in place by *persons*: Leroy-Beaulieu, Jules Ferry.[135] Retotalization of the *difficulties of capitalism* (protected markets, protected investments).

2. It is realized by men: praxis of a group (a society constituting itself), *individual praxis*.

3. Theory and practical ideology. Imperialism = nationalism.

4. The system as
– praxis (an ensemble of groups that condition one another and know one another),
– praxis-process (techniques, migrations {serialization}),
– practico-inert (an ensemble of investments – materiel; men as serialized worked matter).

---

135. The system in question is colonialism. See *Critique*, vol. 1, p.714.

The praxis of atomization of the native (battles, civil law, tribes suppressed).

Atomization of the settlers.

Impossible to act other than serially (demography, European serial solidarity).

5. Reversal (new revolutionary praxis. Groups. Anti-groups).

Contrast: *A*. Men are seeking to take responsibility for the economy. So the system is interiorized and re-exteriorized. This is Stalinism or collective leadership.[136] *B*. They are seeking to set the system on its feet. In this case, the system incorporates the men and works through them. The totalization is a process-praxis. In this case: take up incarnation, circularity and retotalization again; but show that the system is incarnated by men, and that the drift is realized by men, against the system.

A. Stalinism: men take over *everything* as their own. So they have *projects* on the basis of the given practico-inert. These projects constitute a new system, inasmuch as the new practico-inert is a link. But this system (totalization-of-envelopment) is at once the inner framework of the undertaking and its *drift*. It supports the undertaking, expresses it and deviates it. But the undertaking closes over the system, because – to the end – men are held responsible for the drift. Praxis-process.

B. Men pursue various undertakings within the same practical field.

First unity: a practical field.

But this is not a true unity. Merely a common determination. *Received from outside*. The field makes itself *inhabited* for everyone.

Next: the unity of the practical field ensures that elements interior to the field are – as worked matter – elements of unity (each is defined by the already populated field, and works as a man who has only these techniques and who, in a certain order, is redundant). At this level, everyone is already an *incarnation*. Collectives emerge *spontaneously* inasmuch as matter serializes. Institutions of stone. Everyone retotalizes in his own way (by labour – he produces – or by technical improvement). And this retotality implies: (a) that he projects himself as a seal on to matter, which turns him back into a negation of man; (b) at the same time, as such, he is in danger (interest) in the field; (c) that these counter-men are susceptible to accumulation. Quantity and inertia ensure that nothing opposes anything. So an ensemble is constituted, mediating between men and totalizing (machines, as a product of the practical, turn back to men and totalize them). The practical field – as bestrewn and

---

136. See pp.187 ff. above.

worked by such tools producing *everything* – turns back to men and qualifies them from the interior in exteriority.

At this level, we have seriality and the institution. And every serial and institutional ensemble does not *entirely* hang together because of scarcity. Hence, the group and the invention (which is simultaneously a technique, an organization, and a decision on those sacrificed). For example: the invention of plough-shared implements creates a first scarcity of men. Not enough men in relation to the plough: men are simultaneously scarce and redundant. Invention of slavery. At this level, every group modifying the institution works on the series. And transformation of the series and the institution by a group produces the *system*.

The system is defined as a process of unintentional circularity, inasmuch as it is on a large scale (putting a slave to work is not inventing slavery), but intentional on a small scale (heterogeneous: quality depends on quantity). Why a *system*? Because the unity of the practical field comes back to the invention and qualifies it in the name of all. The practical field comes back – as mine, and as *other* via the Others – to me and qualifies me as my-Other: i.e. qualifies me externally but in immanence as the man (among others) of this field, and my practices as *practices in this field*. In short, unity is the return of the practical field – through the mediation of Others – to its inhabitant, in order to qualify him in exteriority of immanence as an *inhabitant*. In this way we shall all be *inhabitants* and the series is constituted. I see myself as *other* in the Other's home. And the external threat may lead the practical field to create the group, but as *other* in interiority (a nation).

From the moment when, in a field, money (for example) is invented, it becomes an institution. Either it disintegrates the group (if it comes from elsewhere) or it adopts its circularity. This means that monetary effects modify causes. Circularity (as complex as you like) coming to objects (imposing their practices) from the existence of these objects in a dialectical field: that is the system.

Themes[137]

Incarnation
Totalization-of-envelopment

---

137. Recapitulation of the themes deployed notably in the study of directorial societies (see pp.118 ff. above), which Sartre intended to reutilize in his study of bourgeois democracies.

Totalization of exteriority
Totalization of interiority
Anti-labour
Immanence
Transcendence
Exteriority of immanence (*cf.* totalization of exteriority)
Transcendent exteriority (an unthinkable limit)
Transcendence and internal limit of practical freedom
Unity – Unification
Conflict – Contradiction
Totalization and retotalization
Retotalized totalization
Alteration and Alienation
Drift – Deviation

In bourgeois democratic societies, unification requires non-unity (as massification).

Regarding the vote, as a unitary decision to choose the sovereignty of series (i.e. non-sovereignty).

The serial man as a retotalization of serialization:

A.   A man of the masses.
      (Interchangeability in work. A mass consumer.)
B.   A voter.
C.   Propaganda: he is treated as an *Other* by advertising.
      Do as others do: become *other*.
D.   Identity against unity.
      This man is a *product*.
      Of what?
      Of the mode of production.
      So there is unity of the mode of production. How?
      Because it is:
          (a) Conceived as a mediating relationship between men. I produce
               for others in exchange for what they give me.
          (b) Because its dispersive force has to be retotalized by man.
               Organization.

1. Every man in the group is retotalized as an Other by the practical field: i.e. inasmuch as I grasp him as an object in my totalization.

2. Every man retotalizes the practical field in retotalizing me.

Ensembles of wheeling totalizations which involve an agreement: the practical field as totalizing. Example: Eskimos. The Other is the Same, in the sense that he is subjected to the same dangers. In the Other who dies, I read my own death. In the Other who works, my work. Man arrives *constituted*. Interiorization of the practical field.

3. On this basis, conflicts or mutual aid merely express the transcendent unity of the practical field. If the man of scarcity is *redundant*, it is within this practical ensemble. If he threatens me, it is inasmuch as worked matter (the first synthetic union of the field) designates him as redundant for me, and me as redundant for him. Interiorization of scarcity (in its concrete forms: scarcity of fuel, food, women, etc.) affects the counter-man of a wheeling unity. The fight, as a contradiction-conflict, is capable of being totalized *on the basis of* the practical field: hence, as common inertia interiorized. 1st common inertia, *negative*: I can go no further, I'm staying here, etc. 2nd inertia, *positive*: there are foodstuffs or elements capable of assuaging our needs; this conditions everyone, since it is why they enter into conflict. And 3rd inertia, *negated* positive: there are not enough of them for coexistence.

Very well. But coexistence = an indifferent contiguity: animals cropping or grazing. Non-coexistence = a rejected duality. Hence, in a certain way, unity is posited as to be made (by suppression or hierarchization). Unity – re-exteriorized reinteriorization of the retotalization of men by the practical field. Privative unity: reconstitution (or constitution) of a community through suppression of disruptive elements. The Chinese killing girl children: reconstitute the family as a practical unity. In addition, every conflict causes the totality – as affected by this conflict, existing within the conflict – to appear negatively. For if X and Y fight because both groups are redundant, they are redundant for each other inasmuch as all others are redundant for them. (The conflict takes place for specific reasons between X and Y, but it could just as well have been between Y and Z.) Furthermore, they are redundant in relation to all others and show it (they *disclose* superabundance as being in them), so that the conflict interests everybody and retotalizes the whole as hoping for a liquidation of certain elements. At this moment, the whole becomes an arbiter or is dragged into the conflict.

So scarcity is a retotalizing element, as a reciprocal condition lived in the midst of third parties. As for the conflict, it is the bringing to light of the fundamental contradiction: i.e. the impossibility for X and Y to live together. But this contradiction precisely presupposes the impossibility of not living together (separation into two groups, scissiparity), because of the practical field (it matters little whether separation is due to the virgin forest, the snows, powerful neighbours, etc.). In other words, the conflict expresses a retotalization by the field, which acts like the enemy wanting to massacre the lot. But: (1) it is a retotalization in the inert; (2) all are concerned, apart from X – who are left undetermined. This brings about not *unity of the group*, but *immanence*. We call immanence the relationship of a practical ensemble, inasmuch as the impossibility of living together in the field is itself defined through the impossibility of not living together. Immanence is not *unification*, but a dead-possibility of unification. It is the sealed inertia of the practical field (its common *unity*), returning to everyone to create a milieu of interiority for all inter-individual relations, and obliging every group to present its conflict with every other as a movement towards unity. Or, if you prefer, the common unity of the field returns to propose unification as a struggle: i.e. retotalizes itself as something to be transcended by the unifying praxis. It is what is to be transcended towards unity. The latter is always given in the group, at once as already existing (it is the inner inertia of praxis) and as to be re-established: a struggle against the Counter-man.

But the practical field is not homogeneous: it is diverse, favouring some groups at the expense of others (nature – culture). As a consequence, there is a quasi-hierarchy in immanence, to be destroyed or consolidated. Every new reality appearing within the field modifies (tools, slaves, etc.) all the sub-groups which occupy it. Immanence is a tension that creates a dialectical reality. There is a totalization, in the sense that every reality transforms all others from afar.

An example: in a given practical field, with given provisions, the increased birth rate affects my life and that of my children (whether directly – growing scarcity of provisions – or indirectly: standard of living). I am *altered* by an event interior to the field, just as by an event (an eruption) reaching the field from the exterior. Altered by: (1) everything that brings about the increase or decrease in provisions: (a) transcendence but interiorized, (b) increase or decrease in the population – minimum number for a given field; (2) every transformation of relations between people (a tool, a machine, a differential in the mode of production) that creates groups and serialities in immanence. In other words, in the field of scarcity an increase in the number or power of my neighbours has the result of increasing the precariousness of my exist-ence. For that power seeks both to produce more (a *ceiling*, though) and to eliminate me. My alteration is suffered, and is what incarnates the transformation in me.

[An Example of Alteration and Unification by the Machine: the Appearance of Radio and Television]

1. Technological unemployment: [for example] for music-hall troupes in the Nord.

2. Intensified serialization of the listener (radio + TV).

3. Constitution of restricted groups – serialization of groups (group–series dialectic): (i) serialization of the instrument; (ii) economic neces-sity: people form groups which are (a) true: friends buy a set in common and entrust it to one of them, (b) false: cafés project the showing to ensembles without unity – but still capable of fusing; (iii) serialization of groups (side by side in bourgeois democracy); (iv) possible regroupment (at the level of a policy: de Gaulle accentuates serialization, Castro does the opposite,[138] etc.). But at this level there is a concerted praxis *dissolving* serialization. For example: [groups] are summoned to unity. But the dissolving praxis basically confines itself to serializing the group in so far as it groups the series: *this* given small group is integrated into the nation by Castro's voice; but it is integrated as a serial group (thousands of other groups). So you need a carnival, or the apocalypse, or some upheaval, in order to make a comparison (one million people assembled, etc.).

4. In a bourgeois democratic society, the existence of a group or ensemble of individuals owning a TV is a cultural enrichment which, if I do not have one, causes me an impoverishment. In a retotalizing (in immanence) practical field, it will thus be said that every increase in the possibilities of one ensemble is constitutive of an impoverishment of other ensembles included in the field. That comes down to saying that in the totalization perpetually in progress, the isolation of one part creates a contradiction in the field. If the tiniest number owns a TV, it appears both as positing itself for itself within the totality (hence, a closed element of contradiction) which, for its part, remains deprived of TV, and at the same time – inasmuch as *it precisely is* the totality – as representing the condition to which the totality must accede. If no practical frontier divides the field, the solution is without real violence: the field *organizes itself* to be totally supplied with TV sets (this does not mean that everybody buys one, but people regroup to constitute buying groups, club together, etc.[139]). In relation to the owner, equality replaces inequality, in the sense that *everyone* will see TV. Differences persist (it is sometimes more convenient to have one's own set; on the other hand, it will be adjusted and serviced better if it is collective). But these inequalities are secondary and negligible in relation to the aim achieved: watching the programme. However, they may bring structural problems to light (without these necessarily being placed in the foreground): collective appropriation – individual appropriation. In this case, the poorest are referred to their destiny: socialism, which is announced here (all the more so, in that it is induced by another route). So inequality is found on another level. If the ensemble is relatively homogeneous, the mode of appropriation will be the same (e.g. collective); and though

---

138. Sartre had been to Cuba in 1960.
139. We may recall that this text was written at the beginning of the sixties.

initiative may come from one corner or another of the field, it will later be forgotten by those who have drawn their inspiration from it: it is inessential. The restoration of totality (i.e. the new totalization) annihilates the original initiative – which is forgotten. If the ensemble is heterogeneous with an impassable threshold (the wealthy owners – the poor) the fact of totalization remains, but now the contradiction is impassable (temporarily, but perhaps in the long run too) and *incarnates* class differences, for example, or different levels within a class (well-paid aristocracy of labour, unskilled workers) which are incarnated in many other ways. In other words, the incarnation is that of a contradiction. The disadvantaged are *impoverished* with respect to the advantaged. And this impoverishment

1. comes to them from outside and qualifies them from outside;

2. incarnates in its singularity a contradiction extending to many other sectors;

3. but increases the *tension* of the contradiction;

4. provides the material and visible signs of it (aerials on some roofs but not others).

Practical field as spatio-temporal. Time, a limit on space. Space, a limit on time. Scarcity of time: you do not have time to do everything. Wealth: time-saving (gadgets). For a given extension, time is scarce. Too scarce to be crossed (unity of a life). For a given time, space is its limit: this time depends in its temporalizing efficacy on the space envisaged (Brazil/USA) and the labour supplied by this space.[140]

5. [Television] lowers elites and raises popular culture. For the television programme is constituted at the level of the most numerous (hence, least cultured) viewer. But *for him* it is culture (initiation into life in common, the *right note*, pretty women, smart clothes, etc.). For the bourgeois elite: mindlessness. But we meet again the movement which, in revolutionary and underdeveloped countries, lowers the intellectuals and raises mass culture.

6. At the same time, however, another contradiction: mass culture will be bourgeois. That means the dominant class finds a new means of diffusing its own ideology (i.e. the practical justification of its praxis) ... The part provokes the contradiction by posing as the whole (universal culture). This is called 'integrating one's working class'. But this integration is false, because it gives a culture of the advantaged to men who remain disadvantaged. It gives the enjoyment of luxury *by sight*,

---

140. This paragraph, which in the MS begins with a parenthesis and has no logical connection with what precedes it, seems to be the result of an association of ideas, jotted down there as a reminder.

rather than by lived reality. There is a working-class and peasant culture that is prevented from emerging or developing. Hence, a contradiction between the universal and the class divide. The latter being deeper and more definitive. However, even as the universal veils the struggle, this is a superficial unification which brings out more clearly the reality of the contradiction (bourgeois culture is exposed, as soon as the workers go back to work). In short, a false totalization (a totalization-manoeuvre); vacuity of a bourgeois culture adapted for the people, and true contradiction incarnated by a culture not concerned with truth.

Process:

1. Praxis: mass production. The cheapest possible, so already: the popularized cultural instrument. There are two logical ways of conceiving television: either total distribution and popular culture (Castro) or – in a capitalist society – an organ of restricted distribution of non-vulgarized bourgeois culture. But the second way is impossible, by virtue of the very fact of the necessary distribution of sets. So industry imposes its culture. Capitalist mass production = massified bourgeois culture. Mediation: Poujadist petty bourgeoisie. It is the latter, ultimately, which receives *its own* culture (an impoverished, massified bourgeois culture). In a word, the practico-inert of production (machines demanding their market) leads to the cultural practico-inert. It is the necessity of producing a million sets that produces that of producing a culture. With Castro, it is the opposite: production is intensified *for* culture. An interior practico-inert. It may deviate, but not initially govern, the process.

2. But mass production creates the mass media. So class and government propaganda cannot ignore these. Production thus creates a practico-inert: TV as a talking machine, and this talking machine demands its own *voice* in the present situation of capital. And its voice is governmental, and a class ideology. It demands its own voice, and its institutionalization. It is the machine that demands its own unity. On this basis: either the State directly, or interchangeable private sets (competition barely differentiates them). There are accidents, of course: most of the directors harassed by McCarthyism worked in TV. So rather more radical. But only *barely*, of course.

Conversely, the public is conditioned into exigencies. Serial exigencies: outrage. TV's precautions. New exigencies: appearance of the spectacle *in one's home*. Idea of propriety (an interior practico-inert): someone comes into my home to insult me. And: I have paid. But exigencies are varied: confessional (Catholics, Jews, Protestants), religious in general, classes, opinions. In short, it is a matter of unifying. Unifying policy: ideological propaganda, *but without saying anything*; unity is negative, and consequently serial. Saying what pleases everybody. But nothing pleases *everybody*. So you have to say *nothing*.

On this basis, there is TV thought, TV behaviour, etc., which belong to the practico-inert. It is simultaneously other-direction and senseless discourse.

Unification by the machine:

1. The machine is *unity*.

2. The machine is *synthetic*: it puts into itself various interpenetrating practical significations (government, mass media, etc.)

3. There is *only one*.

It is the same everywhere. You go and watch TV *as such* (competition, difference between sets, etc.: practically negligible from the angle that concerns us).

4. Being inert, however, it unifies via the serial.

5. Nevertheless, *in immanence*, relations between series are not serial and modifications are received in reciprocity. And this is due to the fact that everyone's praxis interiorizes the practical field. On this basis, the series is a synthetic and dialectical determination of the field, at the same time as being sealed inertia. In other words, the *series* has a twofold constitution: inert as a multiplicity sealed by identity, it is active from afar as a part of the whole. In that sense, it is neither a totality nor a totalization. The whole series, considered as a transfinite ensemble, is a determination of the practical field; as such it is a part of the whole, an incarnation of the whole, and a retotalization of the whole. In immanence, and considered by the third party on the basis of the common field, the man of the series is integrated into the unity of the field as the third party.

An Example of Unification

the bourgeois class threatens the nobility,

the latter transforms its *de facto* state into a *de jure* state,

the serfs and peasants are promptly constituted as a class.

Everything is done from afar. Especially for the serfs, however, there has been the disintegration of a servile but human bond, and the constitution of a still serial unity.

The whole issue is that totalization is always indirect: it is effected by worked matter, and with the mediation of men. It is because the practical field is a sealed unity that man turns this sealed unity back upon other men. In short, matter unites through the intermediary of man.

Totalization: [the History of] Venice

Problem: totality-totalization.

1. Numerous islands inhabited early on by a population of fishermen-sailors.

Unity of the practical field: islands and raw material (sea). Sea = fish – saltworks.

Sparse crops (vines, vegetables, fruit).

2. Unity of the practical field tightened by transcendent totalizations:

(a) Major centres on the mainland: Aquileia, Ravenna. Shortest route: by the lagoon. Hence, coastal trade.

(b) Saltworks.

Exchange salt for manufactured objects. Equip fishing and cargo boats.

Practical field *determined* by the exterior. At once traversed and squeezed.

Traversed: a route. Retotalization by travellers. Reason: production/communication: long, uncertain roads. Coastal trade.

Interiorization of the retotalization: ensuring coastal trade by their boats.

Saltworks: likewise traversed; already *exchange*, money, etc. So people do not reproduce their lives. An *already indirect* system.

But *internal retotalization by praxis*. A SYSTEM.

$$\text{Saltworks} \rightarrow \text{salt} \rightarrow \text{exchanged} - \text{finished products} - \text{boats} \begin{cases} \text{coastal trade} \\ \\ \text{fishing} \end{cases}$$

Fishing as a reproduction of life depends on the saltworks as merchandise. But the saltworks also make it possible to monopolize the coastal trade, thus to subtract the practical field of the *lagoon* from the mainlanders (otherwise Aquileia and Ravenna would have built boats). *Salt*: the field is traversed by the exterior and conditioned by it. Precisely as a result of this, it is squeezed: conditioned, it seeks to escape its conditioning through coastal trade. For salt introduces transcendence into immanence: dependence on a market. But the traditional market (before the invasions) is relatively stable. And poor. What is involved is an arduous extractive industry. It extracts in order to give abroad. It enters into a system of division of labour and commerce. On the other hand, by transporting travellers and goods, it recuperates the field: by ploughing foreign waters on *its own* boats, it turns them into *the means* of earning its living. It transports the inert (travellers = an inert) over *its* lagoon (an enlarged field): the inert traverses without marking. But this passage into a sector of practical tension which passivizes it *yields a return* to the field. The salt (sold) gives the boats (their own), but the reproduction of life (fishing) is at once dependent upon the external market. Fragility. The economy is open, but the field is totalized: *islands* (as a habitat), *lagoon* (as a conquest: knowledge of the lagoon necessary for the coastal trade – a channel, etc.).

How is the totalization effected?

I

Quasi-perceptional totalization by every third party of every other, on the basis of the field. Community of the field through diversities: rough life, hence few differences in fortune. Do they form a group? A historian: 'They are not jealous of each other.' Rather, they form series of families with similar work, but are neighbours. Perhaps the saltworks are more or less common.

Retotalization on the basis of the field is thus effected by the praxis of everyone who grasps his life as contained in community with others on *the island* or *the islands*. Relations between islands. The practical totalization is farming and fishing at this level. With boats, totalization is extended to the archipelago. A totalizing factor: marriages (between islands, etc.).

Totalization of exteriority:

they are utilized practically by wider organizations, as producing salt and coastal trade. These are two operations which place them in the broad circuit of the ancient economy, but specialize them. So they grasp themselves in practice as totalized people retotalizing.

Interiorization, through practice, of the external or transcendent totalization. The transcendent totalization is a direct unification (as much if it dreams of massacre as if it says *the producers of salt*, or *coastal trade*).

In proceeding to his labours, the producer of salt or the sailor reinteriorizes the transcendent unity into an insular practical unity, *at the same time* as he places this unity in danger because of the whole economic circuit. The lagoon is defined as a lagoon through the intermediary of the mainland. Villages with local headmen: hence, integrated communities. Seriality of villages, of families, of headmen and groups. Relations between serialities and groups defined by interiorization: (1) of the geographical totality; (2) of the geographical totality unveiled abroad by a more considerable praxis.

Fifth-century invasions: integration by the Goths into the Italian kingdom. Little change (no cruelties on land, no importance of the lagoon). The big changes have little effect on this small totality, and its economic activities – because they are minimal – survive. Restoration by Justinian (555). The Veneto-Istrian region re-enters Roman unity.

II

The migrations. Lombard kingdom (568) on the mainland. Aquileia and Padua in the hands of the Lombards.

Transformation of the exterior:

1. the lagoon becomes a *refuge*, a *sanctuary*;

2. it remains in Byzantine hands, and finds itself a neighbour to the Lombard kingdom.

A. Refuge, sanctuary: it receives exiles (a massive exodus). But these are assimilated. Or rather, they are integrated and they assimilate at the same time. Relations between rich but unorganized individuals and organized ensembles. At the same time, this increases the real size of the inhabited regions, but within the tension of the totality. Nothing is *destroyed*: the activity of the saltworks remains preponderant. Moreover, there is homogeneity: the exiles disclose from outside (a transcendent totalization) the lagoon's character as a *shelter*. But they disclose it to people who at once interiorize it: *they too*, though non-refugees, are living there *sheltered*. And the refugees, in passing from a transcendent state to an interior state, interiorize a totalization of exteriority which itself becomes interiority. On this basis, the economic, demographic, etc., transformations – upheavals introduced by the exiles – are always in immanence and totalized from within. The conflicts (fear that exile may lead to reprisals, greed, jealousy) are contradictions moving towards unity.

B. New relationship disclosed internally, in immanence.

A *political* relationship (both interior and exterior). The political relationship: a dual totalization.

The lagoon remains under Byzantium (Ravenna exarchate). It now has a neighbour (the Lombard kingdom).

These two relationships are *novel*. Before, as we saw, the Veneto belonged wholly to the Goths or wholly to the Latin Empire (Justinian). So that its external unity was essentially economic and social (whence its totalization in immanence by a system). Furthermore, its unification was monovalent. Here, an ambivalent unification: the Lombards and Byzantium. Two transcendent totalizations. For the Lombards, the Veneto is a poor region which they leave to Byzantium; it is too difficult to capture for what it is worth. For Byzantium, on the other hand, permanent contact with the enemy (a frontier zone). This dual totalization is necessarily interiorized as a tension by Venetian society. An autonomy threatened above all by the nearby Lombards, albeit under the protectorate of Byzantium (too far away to inspire fear). First, *a regional unity* (the *magister militum* is at Cittanova). The tribunes administer and deliver justice under the authority of the Byzantine representative. Then they elect a leader. Hence, *factions already*: terrestrial interests (in Charlemagne's day: Doge Obelerio) – maritime interests (for Byzantium: the population). The dual totalization of transcendence is thus interiorized as ambivalence (it is *politics*: the great leaders at this time pursue a cautious policy – treaty with Liutprand, the Lombard king) *or as conflict*. But the conflict precisely represents, for everyone, the ambivalence in immanence of a twofold transcendent determination. And this conflict causes the struggle between the two transcendent forces to explode into a contradiction. The contradiction itself (see MS above[141]) is a dissociation *in unity*. Each faction's interest is to rend the other and liquidate it *on behalf of* a common constituted praxis. At the same time, however, what is involved is no abstract, but a realistic determination. Yet undoubtedly the population has interiorized fidelity to Byzantium, precisely in so far as it orientates itself towards maritime operations and the Byzantine fleets can protect it. It is basically the economic situation that is decisive. At the same time, the geopolitical situation (remoteness of Byzantium, and difficulty for the Lombards to attack the villages – fortified camps) is lived in interiority as independence, *autonomy*. And politics becomes: exigency of a mediation between the factions (realization of unity) which, through an ambivalent policy (i.e. through a policy *tout court*), realizes autonomy under the protectorate.

All this, of course, occurs in the interior of interiorized upheavals (iconoclasm, the controversy over Images). Internal revolt and submission of Doge Orso.

---

141. See pp.63 ff. above.

An Order

Move on to totalizations:
    1. dictatorial
    2. disunited societies
    3. generations (diachronic)
But precisely it is History, so:
    1. Historical elements
        elements of History:
            (a) what History and the historical are:
                societies without history, etc.;
            (b) the possible, etc., etc.;
            (c) historical links:
                infrastructures and superstructures.
    2. Problem of totalization:
        totalization-of-envelopment,
        incarnation,
        Stalin,
        class struggle, etc.
    3. The meaning of History.

Totalization-of-Envelopment

Is never graspable in transcendence. Other than for a partial totality (Venice at the outset), by the greater powers (Ravenna exarchate – Lombard kingdom).

Moreover, does not exist in transcendence.

A. For the transcendent totalization of all History, who will do it? See description of transcendence of exteriority.[142]

B. For a partial transcendent totalization. Interiority does not resemble exteriority.

Venice seen by Liutprand is an exterior object, with numerous aspects either not elucidated or merely not known, and characterized in relation to the Lombard kingdom (frontier zone of influences – defended by Ravenna – vain expedition – nevertheless anxiety, possible surprise attack – lagoon ≠ dry land, etc.). Of course, transcendence = a bond of interiority (relationship of negation of interiority. Coexistence is not contiguity). Of course, too, the transcendent bond of interiority – reinteriorized in immanence – is one of the interior bonds of the totality in the process of totalization (geopolitical structure, internal disputes, possibility or impossibility of an alternative policy, etc.). In this sense, it extends everywhere if it is a *threat* (everyone is a traitor, for example, in a revolutionary moment: opposition is treason, everyone can be the interiorization of the enemy; moreover, everyone *is that*, as an Other – i.e. inasmuch as he is determined like me, by the enemy and *non-brother*). Totalization of immanence can be reduced to being simply the retotalization in interiority of totalizations of transcendence. But it reconditions them by a fresh confrontation (Byzantium and Lombardy confront each other in every group and every praxis, but with different features).

---

142. See pp.307 ff. above.

In short, the totalization-of-envelopment is the interior limit of immanence.

For us, what does this mean?

That it is impassable.

A Venetian ambassador incarnates his country abroad; he is retotalized as such at home. A merchant too.

It is possible to pass (exile – flight) the real limits, but: either a person remains conditioned in interiority (the exile who is merely Venice abroad), or else – integrated into another totalization – he becomes a non-Venetian (exteriority of transcendence – bitterness, treason, naturalization).

Totalization of immanence (and of envelopment) – what is it? It is the fact (from the standpoint of knowledge) that we can interpret as its incarnation – on the basis of the totalization in progress – any praxis (incarnation) and any relation (including that which is institutional or serial). But it must be understood that what is involved is a temporalization: i.e. an interior passage from minus to plus, from plus to minus, from a quantity to a quality, and vice versa. In short, this presupposes a detotalization in act – or threatening – against which the totalization is perpetually effected. Otherwise, there would be merely a *totality*. A priori we do not decide that there should be a totalizing *praxis*: i.e. one giving itself the aim of totalizing. We say that a totalization would be either useless (a totality) or pure repetition (societies of repetition) if – precisely – detotalization did not appear at every moment. So totalization is the way in which detotality is totalized; or again, in which detotalization is retotalized.

This means:

1. that totalization is never completed (otherwise: totality). Let us clearly understand, moreover, that abundance or the end of pre-history change nothing here: a dialectical relationship is involved;

2. that detotalization never happens to the detotality;

3. that detotalization is a product of totalization, which makes it always precarious (in the sense that totalization is a practice: it produces, so detotalizes – through the increase of its product, for example);

4. that totalization is itself a product of detotalization, in so far as the latter is an ever-reducible deviation or cancer.

So totalization resembles unification. But it is not comparable to the rigorous unification of a body (an army, for example) attempted by groups in the government. Unification posits (partial) totalization. This means that so far as the decrees are concerned, the practical moment conditioning the reorganization implies totalization: i.e. a synthetic grasping of the whole *in its disorder*, as well as the comprehension of disorder by its reasons. Hence, a totalization of detotalization. Disorganization of the Army (lack of means of communication; anarchy – through a revolt of subordinates, or the leaders' indifference; interests of the Army, etc.) is the object of a theoretical totalization: organization as an ensemble (bound by links of immanence) of disorganization [...] This presupposes that they are themselves an organization on the way to disappearing. Or, if you prefer: their exteriority is itself a fact of immanence. It is an internal relationship inasmuch as they secrete it as an internal negation of exteriority. In other words, the fact of anarchy is simultaneously the negation of the parts–whole relationship and the retotalization – as existing throughout the Army – of factors of anarchy (malaise).

Is History Essential to Man?

No.

It is the outside lived as the inside, the inside lived as an outside.

It is man's own exteriority (his being-an-object for cosmic forces, for example) lived as his interiority.

It makes him,[143] however (by intervening), but precisely as a being existing his own outside in the form of interiorization: in short, as the being who cannot have an essence (for it is really *something else* that he recuperates into himself as his being – and not as his essence). It makes him, as conceptually unable to think himself (since his being – Pascal – is always characterized by something fundamentally other than himself). The free practical organism, abstractly considered (outside of his conditioning by the exterior), has a formal singularity. But this singularity remains universal and abstract, so long as its content – which is singular, because irreducible to an essence – is not seen. (A chance) i.e. heterogeneous. For example: no link between the human condition and its singular transcendence and the fact of belonging to such and such a society or race.

Yet History – which makes man *non-conceptual – comprehends* him; or, if you prefer, the man made by History makes himself by making it through transcendence. And transcendence totalizes the practical field and totalizes *itself* as an interiorized exteriority. This totalization makes the synthesis of the heterogeneous. For example, every man is *accidental for himself*. He *is born*. Here rather than there. And he is, for himself, the person who is born. And that is how he is born a Jew. But he *can no longer* consider his being-a-Jew as a chance; for he exists only in order to be a Jew (birth is not the apparition of a soul waiting in limbo). As

---

143. History makes man.

soon as the chance is posited, it is negated. It is no longer to be found. In a certain sense, it is an imaginary backward extension of birth. But this chance – unthinkable *in isolation* – becomes a determination demanded (in order to affirm or destroy it) from the moment of the project. 'A Jew by chance': practically no Jew says this, and those who do say it out of weariness do not think it. It is the recuperation of 'former circumstances'. So History appears as the outside constitutive of the inside, in the capacity of an undetectable, yet assumed, chance. For in the transformation of my being-a-Jew into a status, by assuming it I cause this chance to sparkle. Assuming it, it is what I give myself as being able not to assume it and (at once) what would then become a chance. For, in birth, it is only an imaginary chance. In reality, a rigorous necessity (objectively: a son of Jewish parents, he is a Jew). But by the fact of *reassuming* it, I give it – i.e. to this characteristic – that of 'being able not to be assumed': hence, a determination as chance. At the same time, however, the chance is what makes me comprehensible (my relations with Israel, if I am Jewish, etc., will be understood: Aha! he's a Jew). But precisely 'Aha! he's a Jew' means not: on the basis of an initial given, I understand the consequences (an accident of birth from which everything will flow), but: he makes himself a Jew, and his relations with Israel are comprehensible on that basis. He makes himself one, because he is one; he is one, because he makes himself one. Chance is non-conceptual and it makes man non-conceptual; conversely, however, man making himself discloses chance in its dialectical intelligibility.

The same will be the case in all events: there is always (even wholly suffered – apart from death) an *appropriation*.

History is essential to man in so far as it makes him into the non-essential intelligible. Man is never essential (other than in the past). He is, in himself, a *being-other* (because he makes himself an interiorization of the world); but that *being-other* does not presuppose that there is a *being-yourself* blocked from underneath. Being-yourself is precisely the recuperation of being-other. It is the dialectical movement of comprehension.

The inner contradiction between the universal and the singular is realized in interiority in everyone, by the appearance of the new within repetition (which remains a repetition). For example: undernourishment appearing (as a slow but novel circumstance) in a cycle of labours makes the labourers concerned into contradictory, singular beings (*vis-à-vis* the ensemble), through the lowering of their productivity, etc. The contradiction is basically between what comes from outside into the interior (contingent with respect to a *relative* universal – for ultimately these labourers are singularized at least by their labour) and the 'primary custom' repetition that comes from the inside. Or, if you prefer, between what is *instituted* (cyclical labour and and its repetitions) and what, as yet, is not.

Study the passage of the event (meaningless) to the institution (signifying), which is effected through man and presupposes a group and a series.

1. The event is meaningless (change of climate, etc.).

2. Lived, [it] transforms men who *adapt to it* (reorganize to negate it) and negate it through a praxis (migration) that is a decree. Instituting group.

3. Series → institution. Refracted praxis becomes an institution through the separation of everyone.

History *Appeals* to History

It can exist as history (even dead) only in the interior of another history (today dead or living) which serves as a mediation for our own: Mayas – Spaniards – contemporaries. As a consequence, the mode of relation which perpetuates *a particular* history in History is itself historical (that means it evolves). That also means that every history, as soon as relationships in the present or past are established with other histories, is the incarnation of History. There are histories, but each of these histories (even dead and reabsorbed into the past) is History. (Temporal) History appeals to temporality as consciousness to consciousness: it can be comprehended and revived (by its practical exploitation) only through a historical praxis defining itself by its temporal development. An absolute mind without *development* (intuition) could not *comprehend* History. It has to be historical itself. Furthermore, a free practical organism will be able (in monuments, etc.) to rediscover the former presence of other free organisms, but not History itself. This free organism must himself be historical: i.e. himself conditioned by the interiorization of his bond in exteriority with the totalization; himself an *incarnation*; himself *History*. Conversely, he discovers himself as historical in his own movement of *restoration* of made history.

Translator's Note

In translating this second volume of Sartre's *Critique*, I have been helped enormously by being able to consult the Alan Sheridan-Smith/Jonathan Rée version of Volume One, and Ronald Aronson's perceptive *Sartre's Second Critique* (Chicago 1987). It seemed obviously best where possible to make the terminology consistent between the two volumes, but in a small number of cases readers will find a discrepancy. Like Aronson, and for the same reasons, I have preferred 'group-in-fusion' as a rendering of *groupe en fusion*, and in general have sought to retain the *active* dimension Sartre so often strives to impart to his vocabulary (sometimes at the cost of linguistic orthodoxy or stylistic elegance) – hence, 'indetermination' (rather than 'indeterminacy'), 'to deviate' in its transitive sense, and so on. I have also preferred 'singularization' for *singularisation*, rather than 'individualization' which breaks the linguistic link with 'single' and 'singularity'. I have hyphenated Sartre's *totalisation d'enveloppement* as 'totalization-of-envelopment', by analogy with 'group-in-fusion'. Although an attempt has been made to find a single English rendering for each French concept, there are certain words (*conduite*, for example: rendered variously as 'behaviour', 'behaviour pattern', 'action', 'procedure') where I felt that any attempt to do so would be self-defeating. I have not followed Smith/Rée in indicating (by giving the original term in brackets) whether 'transcendence' translates *transcendance* or *dépassement*. Square brackets indicate interpolations by the editor or the translator.

The glossary which follows is basically a combination of Arlette Elkaïm-Sartre's glossary to the French edition of Volume Two with that appended to the English edition of Volume One. Since most readers of Volume Two are likely also to have Volume One, in cases of overlap I have usually preferred to give A. E-S's definition, which is often in fact extracted from Sartre's own text (in which case it is enclosed in quotation marks).

Glossary

active passivity   activity of the common individual, who freely consents to a certain inertia (discipline, differentiation through his function within the group) in order better to serve the common praxis

adversity-coefficient   term coined by Gaston Bachelard, referring to the amount of resistance offered by external objects to the projects of the For-itself

alienation   'the theft of the act by the outside: I act *here*, and the action of an other – or a group – *over there* modifies the meaning of my act from without'

alterity   a relation of separation, opposed to reciprocity

analytic Reason   the form of reason appropriate to the external relations which are the object of the natural sciences

anti-dialectic   intelligible moment of transcendence by materiality of individual free praxes, inasmuch as these are multiple

anti-labour   twofold (or plural) antagonistic activity, which produces objects to be considered as the results of a negative collaboration that none of the adversaries recognizes as his own

Apocalypse   the violent process of dissolution of seriality, under the pressure of an opposing praxis (see: group-in-fusion)

class   the developing totalization of three kinds of ensemble: institutionalized groups, pledged groups and series

collective   'the two-way relation between a material, inorganic, worked object and a multiplicity which finds its unity of exteriority in it'

common individual   individual whose praxis is common, and who is created by a pledge

comprehension   the understanding of a praxis in terms of the purposes of its agent or agents (see: intellection)

constituent dialectical Reason   translucid but abstract praxis of the individual considered in isolation (or practical organism)

constituted dialectical Reason   intelligibility, based on constituent dialectical Reason, of every common praxis

critical investigation   study (itself dialectical) of the foundations, field of application and limits of dialectical Reason

destiny   man's future, inasmuch as it is inscribed in worked matter

diachronic meaning of History   'the axial direction in relation to which one might define (and correct) any possible drift, today and in the infinite future of interiority'

diachronic totalization   intelligible development of a praxis-process across vast temporal ensembles in which account is taken of the discontinuities produced by generational shifts

dialectic (or dialectical Reason)   'the living logic of action'

ekstasis   Greek: 'standing out from'

ensemble   a collection of individuals, however related

exigency   a necessity imposed by the practico-inert

exteriority/interiority   terms not to be understood in a purely spatial sense: in an ensemble, there is a relation of interiority between all the elements as defined and modified by their membership of that ensemble, and a relation of exteriority between elements coexisting inertly

facticity   the For-itself's necessary connection with the In-itself

fraternity-terror   statutory relation between the members of a pledged group inasmuch as their new birth as common individuals gives each the right of violence over the freedom of all the others against the dissolution of the group

gathering   a series capable of constituting a group

group   an ensemble each of whose members is determined by the others in reciprocity (in contrast to a series)

group-in-fusion   group in the process of being constituted by the dissolution of seriality, under the pressure of an opposing praxis (see: Apocalypse)

hexis   inert, stable condition opposed to praxis

incarnation   process whereby a practical reality envelops in its own singularity the ensemble of totalizations in progress

institution   group which develops from a pledged group through the ossification of its structures and the emergence of sovereignty and seriality within it

intellection   the explanation of a praxis, not necessarily in terms of the purposes of its agent or agents (see: comprehension)

interest   in a social field conditioned by scarcity and need, a relation of man to things such that he sees in them his being and his truth and, seeking to preserve and develop the material ensemble which is himself, finds he is wholly subordinate to the exigencies of the practico-inert

interiority   see: exteriority

investigation (*expérience*)   the process of understanding History, as corresponding to the historical process itself

mediated reciprocity (in a group)   human relation between third parties, passing via all the members of the group forming the 'milieu' of this relation

multiplicity   a collection of individuals, however related

négatité   characteristic of types of human activity which, while not obviously involving any negative judgement, nevertheless contain negativity as an integral part of their structure: e.g. experiences involving absence, change, interrogation, destruction

nihilation   process whereby consciousness exists, through making a nothingness arise between it and the object of which it is consciousness

organized group   group based on a pledge

Other   capitalized as a pronoun representing a *person* or an adjective qualifying one, stressing the latter's radical alterity: the other, inasmuch as he governs or is capable of governing laterally (or being governed by) everyone's activity

other-direction   operation of a sovereign group upon serial ensembles, which consists in conditioning each by acting upon the others, thus falsely producing the series as a whole for each Other composing it

passive activity   activity of the practico-inert (of worked matter inasmuch as it dominates man and of man inasmuch as he is governed by it)

pledged group   a group which develops from a group-in-fusion through an organized distribution of rights and duties enforced by a pledge

possible   a concrete action to be performed in a concrete world, as opposed to the abstract idea of possibility in general

practico-inert   'a government of man by worked matter strictly proportionate to the government of inanimate matter by man'

praxis   'an organizing project which transcends material conditions towards an end and inscribes itself, through labour, in inorganic matter as a rearrangement of the practical field and a reunification of means in the light of the end'

praxis-process   praxis of an organized social ensemble, which recuperates within itself – and transcends – the conditionings and counter-finalities which it necessarily engenders in being temporalized, and which deviate it

process-praxis   praxis-process no longer viewed in interiority as a totalization, but in exteriority (inasmuch as it arises in the dispersion of the Universe); as such, it can only be aimed at

project   a chosen way of being, expressed in praxis

scarcity   contingent impossibility of satisfying all the needs of an ensemble

seriality   mode of coexistence, in the practico-inert milieu, of a human multiplicity each of whose members is at once interchangeable and other by Others and for himself

sovereign   individual (or group) who (or which) manipulates series within an institutional group

statute   condition of an individual (or ensemble) in so far as it is prescribed by the kind of ensemble to which he (or it) belongs

structure   adopted inertia, characteristic of organized groups and open to investigation by analytic Reason

synchronic totalization   development of praxis-process inasmuch as its temporalization is one and it continuously reunifies its means in the light of a common objective, on the basis of a *defined* ensemble of former circumstances

temporalization   'the plurality of temporalizations together with temporal unification (a synthetic unification of the antecedent by the consequent, a present unification of the new multiplicity through old frameworks) actually constitute the evolution of humanity as the praxis of a diachronic group, that is to say, as the temporal aspect of the constituted dialectic'

third party   each of the members of a multiplicity inasmuch as it totalizes the reciprocities of others

totalization   labour of synthesis and integration on the basis of determined circumstances and in relation to an objective; totalization defines praxis itself (for the distinction between totality and totalization, see: *Critique*, vol.1, pp.45 ff.)

totalization-of-envelopment   It would be rash to seek here to fix the meaning of this concept. Throughout this unfinished second volume of Sartre's *Critique*, it remains the animating intuition which the author attempts to define and deepen: at stake is the intelligibility and meaning of History. Moreover, its sense varies depending on the reality under consideration. Thus, in the case of an organized group, the totalization-of-envelopment is simply 'the integration of all concrete individuals by praxis' (p.86). In the chapter on directorial societies, it is defined as '*autonomous* praxis asserting itself as such, *inasmuch* as it produces, undergoes, harbours and conceals its own heteronomy as the passive and reactualized unity of its own by-products', or again as 'the interior exteriority of a vast common undertaking' (p.242). But these formulations do not hold for a 'disunited' society, in which there is not *one* common undertaking, but a mere unity of immanence. And what would be the case with a larger-scale (diachronic) historical process? These questions are touched on, but certainly not resolved, in the notes included in the Appendix above.

At various junctures, the author introduces the idea of corporeity to help us grasp what the totalization-of-envelopment might mean: common praxis, *overflowed by the depth of the world*, produces its exteriority as its own body. This metaphor gives a glimpse of two essential features of the totalization-of-envelopment: its practical unity and its materiality, and also the spiral movement (circularity and deviation) whereby it might be apprehended (p.244).

It should be pointed out that in the notes included in the Appendix above, the author identifies totalization-of-envelopment with system, which – like the notions of overflowed action and heteronomy – returns us to the 'totalization without a totalizer' whose possibility is announced at the end of Volume One. Readers will also find in the Appendix the more general statement: the totalization-of-envelopment exists if any praxis or any relation whatsoever can be interpreted 'as an incarnation of the totalization in progress' (p.448). Readers may also refer to the chapter on the being of the totalization-of-envelopment (p.301), which explains what this incarnation certainly *is not* for the author (a critique of the Marxist dialectic).

Index